SUSTAINABLE BANKING

THE GREENING OF FINANCE

Edited by Jan Jaap Bouma, Marcel Jeucken and Leon Klinkers

Sustainable Banking

THE GREENING OF FINANCE

EDITED BY JAN JAAP BOUMA,
MARCEL JEUCKEN
AND LEON KLINKERS

Published in association with **Deloitte & Touche**

Greenleaf
PUBLISHING
2001

© 2001 Greenleaf Publishing Limited unless otherwise stated

Published by Greenleaf Publishing Limited
Aizlewood's Mill
Nursery Street
Sheffield S3 8GG
UK,
in association with Deloitte & Touche

Typeset by Greenleaf Publishing.
Printed and bound, using acid-free paper from managed forests, by
Creative Print & Design (Wales), Ebbw Vale.

British Library Cataloguing in Publication Data:
    A Catalogue record of this book is available from the British Library.

ISBN 1874719381

CONTENTS

3. A green package to promote environmental management systems among SMEs 56

Davide Dal Maso, Avanzi, Italy, and
Carlo Marini and Paola Perin, Unicredito Italiano

4. Sustainable banking and the ASN bank 66

Michel Negenman, ASN Bank, Netherlands

5. Assessing the sustainability of bank service channels: the case of The Co-operative Bank 72

Penny Street and Philip E. Monaghan,
National Centre for Business and Sustainability, Manchester, UK

14. The corporate environmental performance–financial performance link: implications for ethical investments 187
Céline Louche, Erasmus University, Netherlands

15. Sustainable development funds: progress since the 1970s 203
Stefan Schaltegger, University of Lüneburg, Germany, and
Frank Figge, University of Lüneburg, Germany/Pictet & Cie., Switzerland

16. The transition from environmental funds to sustainable investment: the practical application of sustainability criteria in investment products 211
Andreas Knörzer, Bank Sarasin & Co., Switzerland

17. The Dow Jones Sustainability Group Index: the first worldwide sustainability index 222
Alois Flatz, Lena Serck-Hanssen and Erica Tucker-Bassin,
SAM Sustainability Group, Switzerland

25. International financial institutions and the Three Gorges hydroelectric power scheme 348

Kate Kearins and Greg O'Malley, University of Waikato, New Zealand

26. The Hungarian Environmental Credit Line 360

Zsolt Pásztor, Deloitte & Touche, Hungary, and
Dénes Bulkai, European Bank for Reconstruction and Development

27. The Growth and Environment Scheme: the EU, the financial sector and small and medium-sized enterprises as partners in promoting sustainability 372

Marc Leistner, European Investment Fund, Luxembourg

FOREWORD

Hans N.J. Smits
Chairman of the Executive Board,
Rabobank Nederland

Much of the 20th century's focus has been on economic progress, in which humankind has made giant steps. Increasingly, side-effects such as loss of biodiversity, climate change and various forms of environmental pollution are becoming more manifest and demand attention. The same is true for social issues such as poverty alleviation and equal development opportunities for all. Therefore, the issue of sustainability has become increasingly important; in my opinion it will be one of the key issues for the 21st century. As such, sustainable development is about the welfare of human beings and a natural environment that does not reduce the possibilities of future generations, without losing sight of economic continuity of the current generation.

The path towards sustainability will involve governments, NGOs, citizens, companies and, obviously, the financial sector as well. In addition to The Rabobank Group's historical socioeconomic objectives, our mission statement also expresses the ecological dimension: 'The Rabobank Group believes sustainable growth in prosperity and well-being requires the careful nurturing of natural resources and the living environment. Our activities will contribute to this development.' These activities are numerous and include standardised environmental risk assessments and products such as our RG Sustainable Equity Fund, our RG Green Interest Fund and our environmental loans, leases, mortgages and insurance products. Obviously, we also continuously try to improve our internal environmental efforts as well and report on all sustainability issues in a transparent manner. Moreover, The Rabobank Group is a signatory of the 'UNEP Statement by Financial Institutions on the Environment and Sustainable Development'.

As a large multinational, All Finance and co-operative bank, and globally a major player in agri-business finance, we are quite naturally involved in the concept of sustainable development. In our policies we focus on the sustainability leaders (best-in-class) of today and also help those companies that are having difficulties in integrating sustainability into their activities. In my opinion, sustainable banking is about both these approaches: supporting the innovative and proactive companies; and stimulating the lagging and reactive ones. Alliances and co-operation between NGOs, governments, companies, consumers and the financial sector are natural outcomes of this 'double strategy' and will pave the way towards sustainability. As the major financial player in the Netherlands with a large local network, our bank is well placed to do so and is involved in various examples of such alliances. In my opinion, this joining of forces is the best strategy towards sustainable development.

This book is a good example of joining forces and I think the editors have done a great job. The scope of *Sustainable Banking* is impressive, with insights from various fields—science, advisory, banks, NGOs and governments—and various geographic regions from around the world. I hope this book can improve the dialogue within the financial sector and with their stakeholders and encourage many to envision a sustainable future.

FOREWORD

Preben Sørensen
Global Director, Environment and Sustainability,
Deloitte & Touche

Today the market for sustainable investment is rapidly growing. Environmental and ethical issues, as well as sustainable development, are becoming more significant among an increasing number of institutional and private investors. This trend is emphasised by the number of investment institutions using sustainability aspects in their investment criteria. By June 2000 the asset volume managed on the basis of Dow Jones Sustainability Group Index (DJSGI) had reached €1 billion. DJSGI maintains that the index is based on a demonstrated positive relationship between a company's sustainability performance and the performance of its stock prices.

Corporations are increasingly expected by shareholders, business partners and other stakeholders to improve their competitive advantage by demonstrating economic progress while maintaining environmental care and social responsibility. Corporate front-runners have realised the value potential of meeting and shaping these expectations proactively and by creating innovative and sustainable solutions in their marketplace.

This leads to a very different and new positioning of environmental issues. In combination with social and economic issues, environmental responsibility is becoming an intrinsic part of a corporate strategy towards sustainability. Environmental and social issues are transformed from a matter of risk and additional cost into opportunities and the creation of value for the company and its stakeholders.

Deloitte Global Environment & Sustainability help identify value drivers and demonstrate the relationship with shareholder value. To give an illustrative example: climate change is an emerging value driver accentuated by the Kyoto Protocol. Though this protocol is directed at national governments and may never be ratified and implemented as originally intended, the stipulated emission targets, or rather stretch targets, may provide useful benchmarks in long-term corporate planning. We are already seeing a number of emissions trading deals. There are buyers and sellers on the unregulated market although the price of a ton of CO_2 is still very much an unknown quantity given the large number of uncertainties.

We are pleased to contribute to this book on Sustainable Banking. For years the 'environmental community' has cried out for the banking sector and financial institutions to partake in sustainability to help advance the sustainability agenda. This book testifies to the increasing response of the financial services sector to this call and provides an excellent overview of the achievements in recent years.

The way ahead is clear: While the mainstream financial services sector has largely ignored sustainability issues up until now, it can no longer afford to do so. The idea is outdated that sustainability relates to emotional and ethical issues only with little, if any, relevance to the bottom line and that it cannot, therefore, be factored into a share price or risk premium because it is not quantifiable. Sustainability has a direct impact on a company's financial performance, and businesses will be prudent to take these issues and concerns into account if they want to thrive in the business world of tomorrow.

INTRODUCTION

Jan Jaap Bouma
Erasmus University,
Netherlands

Marcel Jeucken
Rabobank, Netherlands

Leon Klinkers
Deloitte & Touche,
Netherlands

Banking is often associated with formal and rigid approaches; however, the context in which banking operates is constantly changing. In recent decades changes in organisational structures have been witnessed as well as new attitudes to environmental issues. The activities of the financial sector are, of course, of great importance to business generally, and the relationship between the financial sector and firms has been experiencing changes that to some extent are explained by social pressure to manage environmental problems. It is even suggested that the financial sector will have an important role to play in progress toward sustainable development in general, and, for example, in the allocation process of emissions rights in particular.

Although organisational changes within firms are regarded as quite substantial, and terms such as 'environmental management' have become established within the overall management structure, this seems less apparent within the financial sector. Increasingly, however, the process of financing business activities is being regarded as a vehicle with which financial institutions can stimulate firms to control their environmental impacts.

In this book the international financial sector (and, more specifically, banks) and its stakeholders present their viewpoints and share experiences on this sector's role in sustainable development. This Introduction provides a map on how the book is structured, outlining the framework of changes within the financial sector that are transforming banks in the direction of sustainability. Chapter 1 further elaborates on the framework and explains the development of environmental concern in banks, their environmental impacts, their role in economies and their drivers to action. It is shown that banks can be categorised into four different types depending on the stage they have reached—from a defensive approach to environmental policy, up to preventative, then offensive and, ultimately, sustainable.

◢ The structure of the book

The book is divided into five parts. While reviewing the contributions, it became clear that 'sustainable banking' is by no means a rigid term. The term is *dynamic* because its definition changes over time; also, it has *no clear borders*—the relationships of banks with their stakeholders makes the concept relevant to actors other than just the banks themselves. Therefore, the topics presented here are diverse. Nevertheless, it seems that some themes are regarded as fairly central; these are:

- Policies of banks
- Transparency and communication
- Environmental investment funds
- Environmental risks and their repercussions for banks' products
- The role of governments, NGOs and multilateral banks

These themes are very much interrelated, and the interrelations are crucial in understanding the changes that the financial sector is undergoing. This is reflected in the book's contributions—in several instances, a chapter could easily be placed under more than one heading.

The framework presented in Chapter 1 attempts to acknowledge the characteristics of sustainable banking. The background for this framework is established by having insight into the central themes of sustainable banking. Below, these themes are briefly discussed; some chapters are used as examples, but not all chapters are covered. However, all the chapters will be introduced in greater detail in the introductions to each of the sections.

Part 1: The environmental policies of banks

Policies regarding the role of banks in sustainable development vary significantly from bank to bank. In this section a number of policies are described. The results of a pan-European survey of 68 commercial banks shows, for example, that a majority of banks wish to avoid the role of moral arbiter and do not consider themselves to be regulators (Chapter 7). Also, on a global level, changes in the financial sector have occurred that are precipitated by environmental concerns. The study by Zimmermann and Mayer (Chapter 10) shows how, in Thailand, banks are aware that the importance of environmental issues is constantly growing. However, they have not developed an environmental framework within which to work because environmental risks are not an immediate issue. In the Barta and Éri contribution (Chapter 9), the results of a survey of selected Hungarian financial institutions show that the environmental commitment of Hungarian banks was at a rather low level in 1997–98. The policy of Austrian banks is assessed by Jasch (Chapter 8), and it is found that certain unique legal drivers triggered banks to integrate environmental concerns into their internal procedures. The description of ASN Bank (Chapter 4) by Negenman shows how one of the first ethical banks in Europe has the practice of ethical banking concretised in its mission statement.

In short, Part 1 illustrates banks' environmental policy-making using practical examples. Some of these policies are designed with close consideration of external factors, the existence of which may depend on the country in which a bank is situated—too close a link between national specifics (culture, legislation, etc.) may hinder the broader applicability to other countries. However, cases are presented here that can have an international application, an example being The Co-operative Bank (Chapter 5), which is highly innovative with respect to external reporting.

Part 2: Transparency and communication

The studies in Part 1 suggest the importance of transparency in bank policies on environmental issues; and in Part 2 transparency and the role of communication for banks is explored further. Tarna (Chapter 11) describes current practice in the financial services sector. Environmental reporting is an established method for stakeholder communication, but is still rare in the financial sector. Signs are noted that the situation is changing and that some banks are producing environmental reports of a high standard. It appears that the trend in the financial sector is to show an increasing interest in the social component of sustainability. Nevertheless, environmental issues themselves remain important, and this may have a far-reaching effect on other business sectors that are put under pressure to communicate their environmental performance with financiers and investors. The chapter by Kahlenborn (Chapter 13) illustrates the need to increase market transparency and the visibility of green investment from the perspective of the green investment market. Also, the contribution by Louche (Chapter 14) stresses, from the perspective of ethical investment, the crucial role of reporting on environmental and social performance by the business sector. These two chapters are closely linked to the third part of the book.

Part 3: Environmental investment funds

In describing the issues of transparency and communication, the development of the green investment market and ethical investment is addressed. The significance of these innovations in the financial products offered by banks leads us on to Part 3, where cases on sustainable investment funds are presented.

Mainstream commercial banks are offering new investment products that incorporate environmental and sometimes broader sustainability criteria. Knörzer (Chapter 16) analyses the transition from environmental funds to sustainable investment and concludes that both new products and new concepts will ensure that this niche market will enjoy dynamic growth over the coming years. The role of government policy in creating tax incentives for private investors may prove important for such growth. The Dutch example presented by van Bellegem (Chapter 18) shows how a Green Fund System was introduced in a co-operative effort of both government and the financial sector. Whether new products, new concepts and an active role by government will actually result in higher investment volumes depends, according to Knörzer, on the ability of providers to cater for customer needs with individually tailored investment concepts. Criteria such as financial indexes play an important part because insight into the risk–return performance over time achieved by 'sustainable funds', when compared with traditional investment funds, allows optimisation of the risk–return profile of the overall portfolio. In this respect the Dow Jones Sustainability Group Index, described by Flatz *et al.*, can play an important role (Chapter 17). The new Dow Jones Sustainability Group Indexes provide a bridge between companies implementing sustainability principles and investors wishing to profit from their superior performance and favourable risk–return profiles.

Part 4: Environmental risks and banks' products

The impact of environmental performance on the financial performance of banks' products are, in addition to investments, relevant for other activities undertaken by the financial sector (see Chapter 21). This broader perspective on product innovation and risk in banking is dealt with in Part 4. Barannik (Chapter 19) provides insight into current experience on environmental risk management and providers of financial services. The relevance of environmental risks to lending practice is focused on by Coulson (Chapter 23), an evaluation based on a detailed case study of corporate environmental assessment by lending officers within Lloyds TSB. There seems to be an ongoing development of tools to integrate environmental aspects in credit evaluation; the chapter by Atkins and Pedersen presents such a tool (Chapter 22). Such tools also seem to be relevant for investment decisions, and are backed up by the theoretical perspective of environmentally induced systematisation of economic risks (Chapter 20).

Part 5: The role of government, NGOs and multilateral banks

The preceding parts show how banks' policies and financial products are shaped in their own contexts. The attitudes and actions of banks' stakeholders are crucial in the change process towards sustainable banking (see e.g. Chapter 28). Some major stakeholders and their active role in achieving sustainable banking are discussed in this final part, which does not attempt to present the complete picture but zooms in on special cases on the role of governments, NGOs and multilateral banks.

◢ Understanding the changes towards sustainable banking

A move towards sustainable banking can be described as a development process that begins with banks being defensive, then acting more proactively and ultimately moving towards becoming a 'sustainable bank'. Banks' policies are reflected in their communication (e.g. external reporting) and the products they offer. In particular, investment funds and other financial products, such as lending using environmental assessment criteria, are those areas where change is most apparent. This is reflected in volume (increase in the volumes of sustainable funds) and in the tools used to integrate environmental criteria. The case studies in this book provide insight into the role governments, NGOs and multilateral banks can play in moving towards sustainable development.

1

THE CHANGING
ENVIRONMENT OF BANKS*

Marcel Jeucken   *Jan Jaap Bouma*
Rabobank, Netherlands   Erasmus University, Netherlands

Sustainable companies will need to consider their long-term strategies more seriously in business decisions. In fact, the very existence of many companies will depend either on the continued availability of certain natural resources or their ability to adapt and reinvent themselves.

So how is the banking sector responding to the new challenges that sustainability presents? Basically, it has responded far more slowly than other sectors. Bankers generally consider themselves to be in a relatively environmentally friendly industry (in terms of emissions and pollution). However, given their potential exposure to risk, they have been surprisingly slow to examine the environmental performance of their clients. A stated reason for this is still that such an examination would 'require interference' with a client's activities. Empirical research from 1990 concluded that (European) banks were not interested in their own environmental situation nor that of their clients (*Tomorrow* 1993).

This situation is now changing. There is growing awareness in the financial sector that environment brings risks (such as a customer's soil degradation) and opportunities (such as environmental investment funds). On the risk side, there has been an enormous raising of concern in the United States since the late 1980s. Banks could, under CERCLA,[1] be held directly responsible for the environmental pollution of clients and obliged to pay remediation costs. Some banks even went bankrupt under this scheme. Due to these developments, American banks became the first to consider their environmental poli-

---

*   This chapter represents the personal views of the authors.
1   To cover the costs of Superfund (especially soil contamination), the US government initiated the 'Comprehensive Environmental Response, Compensation and Liability Act' (CERCLA) in 1980. In the 'US versus Fleet Factors Corporation' case, a bank was held responsible for the environmental pollution of its client. The outcome of this trial sent an immense shockwave through the US (and international) banking community. For details of this trial, see Bryce 1992.

cies, particularly with regard to credit risks. European banks were not exposed to these liabilities and only began to develop policies toward environmental issues during the mid-1990s. The focus here was less on risk assessment and more on the development of new products such as environmentally friendly investment funds.

Both risk and opportunity are now becoming established elements in banking policies towards the environment. Empirical research on the environmental activities of banks by the United Nations Environment Programme (UNEP) in 1995 stated that 80% of the respondents made some kind of assessment of environmental risks (UNEP 1995). An investigation from 1997 concluded that many banks have set up environmental departments and are developing environmentally friendly products (Ganzi and Tanner 1997). In Asia, South America and Eastern Europe, change is also under way, mostly through the influence of environmental standards from multilateral development banks, such as the World Bank, the International Finance Corporation (IFC), the Andean Development Corporation (ADC) and the European Bank for Reconstruction and Development (EBRD).[2] Strong evidence that sustainability has reached the mainstream financial community was provided by the launch of the 'Dow Jones Sustainability Group Index' in September 1999 (DJSGI 1999). For the first time, a mainstream global index is tracking the performance of the leading sustainability-driven companies worldwide.[3]

The role of banks in contributing toward sustainable development is potentially enormous, because of their intermediary role in an economy. It is exactly this intermediary role that has attracted the interest of governments and institutions such as the EU and UNEP in their environmental activities (UNEP 1997; European Commission DG XI 1998). Banks transform money in terms of duration, scale, spatial location and risk and have an important impact on the economic development of nations. This influence is of a quantitative, but also of a qualitative, nature, because banks can influence the pace and direction of economic growth.

At the Earth Summit in 1992, the 'UNEP Financial Initiative on the Environment and Sustainable Development' was established in order to initiate a constructive dialogue between UNEP and financial institutions. The financial sector incorporates a broad set of institutions, which includes commercial banks, investment banks, venture capitalists, asset managers, multilateral development banks and rating agencies. The mission statement of this initiative declares:

> This initiative, which operates under the auspices of the United Nations Environment Programme, promotes the integration of environmental considerations into all aspects of the financial sectors' operation and services. A secondary objective of the initiative is to foster private sector investment in environmentally sound technologies and services (UNEP 1999).

The initiative ultimately resulted in a statement by banks (the 'UNEP Statement by Financial Institutions on the Environment and Sustainable Development' in 1992) and

---

2 For the World Bank, see www.worldbank.org; for the IFC, see www.ifc.org/enviro. See also ADC 1998 and EBRD 1995.
3 See *International Herald Tribune* 1999 or www.sustainability-index.com.

by insurance companies ('Insurance Industry Initiative for the Environment, in association with UNEP' in 1995). At the beginning of November 1999, approximately 160 banks and approximately 85 insurance companies had signed the respective statements.

This chapter explores the role of banks in the progress toward sustainable development. First, we map out the role of banks in a macroeconomic system by looking at their products in general. We then analyse the environmental impacts of banking, before describing the driving forces on banks to take environmental action. In the subsequent section we present a typology of the actions that banks are taking. We then examine the role of governments in establishing a role for banks in achieving sustainable development, with particular regard to the experience of the Netherlands. Finally, we provide some conclusions about the current dynamic and likely changing role of banks in the future.

1.1 The role of banks

Banks have an important role in an economy: they are intermediaries between people with shortages and surpluses of capital. Their products include savings, lending, investment, mediation and advice, payments, guarantees, and ownership and trust of real estate. These core activities generate two principal sources of income: interest earnings and provision earnings. In the first case, a bank is working on its own behalf and risk; and in the second case on behalf of and at the risk of its clients. It is usual to distinguish between different banking departments such as investment banking, commercial banking, corporate banking, private banking, trade finance, electronic banking, securities, financing and loans, savings and so on. Some banks specialise in one or more of these areas. Universal banks usually cover all activities.

Figure 1.1 represents the typical cyclical process of a macroeconomic system. In this simplistic model one can clearly see at which points in an economy banks are present and have influence (represented by the shaded areas). The arrows represent money flows. Households pay taxes, consume and import goods and save money. Companies produce, invest and export goods and receive investments. Governments receive taxes, pay subsidies and invest. Through the international markets, goods (imports and exports) are traded. Surpluses and shortages of the government, the international markets, companies and households are dealt with by financial transactions through the financial markets. The importance of the financial markets is evident. In many countries, banks are the most important financial intermediaries in an economy.[4] The traditional intermediary role has consisted mainly of bridging savings and investments. Today, it more usually consists of bringing together people with shortages and people with

---

4 This is true for continental Europe, Japan and most of the developing countries. In countries such as the US and the UK, the importance of banks is much smaller. The share of banks in the financing of the American economy consisted of 80% in 1970. By 1990 this had gone down to only 20% (Albert 1991).

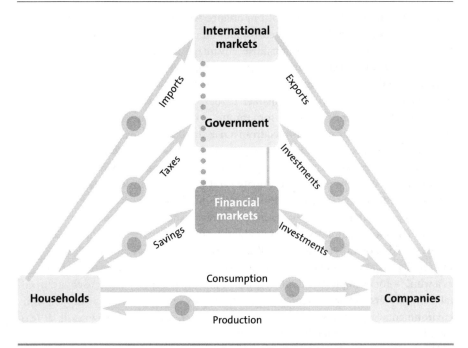

Figure 1.1 **The role of the financial markets in an economic system**

Source: Jeucken 1998

surpluses of capital. The traditional profits of banks have largely consisted of interest earnings. Today, and due to this shift, more than half the profits of banks are often generated through provision earnings. Securitisation and investment banking are important examples of this shift, which is of some importance with regard to sustainability because it involves the increasingly direct influence of clients on the investments that banks make.

As a financial intermediary between market players, a bank has four important functions:

- First, it transforms money by scale. The money surpluses of one person are mostly not the same as the shortages of another person.

- Second, banks transform money by duration. Creditors may have short-term surpluses of money, while debtors mostly have a long-term need for money.

- Third, banks transform money by spatial location (place). For example, a bank brings money from a creditor in New York to a debtor in London.

- Finally, banks act as assessors of risk. As a rule, banks are better equipped to value the risks of various investments than individual investors who have surpluses available. In addition, through their larger scale, banks are more able to spread the risks.

This last function in particular is of importance with regard to the achievement of a sustainable society. Banks have extensive and efficient credit assessment systems and because of this they have a comparative advantage in knowledge (regarding sector-specific information, legislation and market developments). Through this knowledge of environmental and financial risks, banks fulfil an important role in reducing the information asymmetry between market parties. A bank will attach a price to this reduction of uncertainty (through, for example, its interest rates). So tariff differentiation for sustainability can be justified from a risk standpoint: clients with high environmental risks will pay a higher interest rate. The possibilities for tariff differentiation will be even larger if banks can attract cheaper money—by paying less interest for their own funding because of the relatively high quality and lower risk of their credit portfolio. This tariff differentiation by banks will stimulate the internalisation of environmental costs in market prices. In this sense, banks are a natural partner of governments.

A sustainable bank may well go a qualitative step further and contribute to sustainability on ideological grounds as well as on risk assessment grounds. Through their intermediary role, banks may be able to support progress toward sustainability by society as a whole—for example, by adopting a 'carrot-and-stick' approach, where environmental front-runners will pay less interest than the market price for borrowing capital, while environmental laggards will pay a much higher interest rate. This may result, at least initially, in a loss of profitability, but certainly doesn't require a loss of continuity.

The question is if, or to what degree, banks are willing to take such steps. Schmidheiny and Zorraquín's book, *Financing Change* (1996), asks the fundamental question whether banks are a driving force or a hindering force for sustainability:

> Do the financial markets encourage a short-termist, profits-only mentality that ignores much human and environmental reality? Or are they simply tools that reflect human concerns, and so will eventually reflect disquiet over poverty and the degradation of nature by rewarding companies that treat people and the environment in a responsible manner? (Schmidheiny and Zorraquín 1996: xxi).

Schmidheiny and Zorraquín conclude (based on interviews throughout the financial sector) that banks are not hindering the achievement of sustainability. We believe that this conclusion may be flawed. Intuitively, banks have a hindering role in the achievement of sustainable development. First, they prefer short-term payback periods, while many investments necessary for achieving sustainability must be long-term. Second, investments that take account of environmental side-effects usually have a lower rate of return, while financial markets usually look for investments with the highest rate of return. It is therefore the case that sustainable investments are unlikely to find sufficient funding within the current financial markets.

In an economic paradigm of profit and benefit maximisation, companies and households will not take account of the environmental side-effects of their economic decisions as long as the environment is not represented in the prices on which they base these decisions. There will always exist an alternative investment that will yield a higher profit or benefit than an investment that takes into account all environmental side-effects. For example, an investment in a factory that legally pollutes heavily (and passes the cost burden onto society at large) will—*ceteris paribus*—have a higher rate of return than a factory that has invested in expensive technologies to combat that pollution. Banks will often reward the first company with a lower cost of capital or request for collateral. In the long run, an investment in the second factory would have been a better investment for the bank (and society at large), but, by the time the first factory is confronted by tougher legislation, greatly increased costs and even threats to its licence to operate, the bank has made its profit and pulled its money out of the factory (*ceteris paribus*).

If Schmidheiny and Zorraquín are right after all, then the 'highest return effect', as outlined above, has to be overcome by far stricter environmental legislation and enforcement or dynamic environment-related market developments. An alternative reason for banks not to hinder progress toward sustainable development is stakeholder pressure—such as NGOs, shareholders and employees—to act 'sustainably' (see Section 1.3).

1.2 The environmental impacts of banking

To understand the environmental impacts of banks, one has to make a distinction between internal and external issues.[5] Internal issues are related to the business processes within banks, while external issues are connected to the bank's products.

1.2.1 Internal

Internally, banks are a relatively clean sector. The environmental burden of their energy, water and paper use is not comparable to many other sectors of the economy. However, the size of the banking sector overall is large enough to make the environmental impact significant. A research study among Dutch banks in 1995 reported that waste was perceived as the biggest single environmental issue faced by banks (SME Milieuadviseurs 1995). In addition, three-quarters of the banks interviewed claimed to be working on energy efficiency. In the Netherlands, banks used approximately 550 million kWh of electricity and 72 million m^3 of natural gas in 1996. The financial sector has also made a voluntary agreement with the Dutch government to cut its energy use by 25% from a 1995 baseline by 2006 (Jeucken 1998).

The potential energy savings of banks are huge, as can be seen by the achievements of the more proactive companies. Between 1990 and 1993, UBS reduced its energy use by 25% (UBS 1999). Between 1991 and 1995, NatWest saved approximately US$50 million in energy costs (NatWest Group 1998). The measures were taken not because of legislative pressure but because they were cost-effective. Some banks are also now using renewables, particularly solar energy (for example, some of the branches of the Rabobank Group). Other initiatives include the more efficient use of water and transport policies and the

---

5 Labelled 'operating' and 'product' ecology by the VfU (1998) and the Schweizerische Bankier-vereinigung (1997). See also e.g. the environmental report of UBS (1999) or Credit Suisse (CSG 1998).

development of more environmentally benign credit cards. One of the leaders in such practices is The Co-operative Bank in the UK, who introduced the first biodegradable credit card in 1997—an affinity card that supports Greenpeace.[6]

Credit Suisse has developed an instrument to measure the environmental impacts of its bank which concluded that energy use is by far its most serious impact, accounting for 90% of all cumulative pollution within the organisation.[7] UBS came to a similar conclusion on the basis of its so-called 'Environmental Performance Evaluation'.[8] Other environmental reports from banks also concur that energy is the most significant aspect.[9]

However, the measurement of environmental performance and comparison of that performance between banks remains difficult. To address this, VfU (1998) has developed a methodology to standardise the measurement of environmental pollution within banks. Table 1.1 presents the environmental impact of six German/Swiss-based financial institutions who have reported (partly) using this VfU methodology: three German banks (Landesbank Berlin [LBB], Landesgirokasse [LG], Bayerische Landesbank [BLB]); a major insurance company (Allianz); and two Swiss banks (the Credit Suisse Group [CSG] and UBS).[10] The relative figures make it possible to compare the eco-efficiency of these institutions. Unfortunately, the tool does not take into account the size or specific operations of organisations, which leads to some anomalies. For example, smaller banks are obviously likely to use less paper, while multinational banks will incur a much larger score for (transcontinental) business travel. The VfU methodology certainly needs to be improved, but is a positive development towards standardised measurement of internal environmental performance in the banking community.

1.2.2 External

Here we consider the environmental impact of banks' products. The problem with this is that, contrary to other sectors in the economy, the products of the banks themselves do not pollute. Rather, it is the users of these products who impact on the environment. This makes it very hard to estimate the environmental impact of banks' external activities. In addition, to date, banks feel that external environmental care would require inter-ference in their clients' activities. This is one reason why banks have been reluctant to promote environmental care on the external side of their business (even when they are likely to be exposed to risk). However, in recent years, by developing a selection of products from which a client can choose, banks have tried to cope with this dilemma.

One could take one of two extreme standpoints on the environmental impact of banks' products. On the one hand, all pollution caused by companies who are financed by banks

---

6   www.co-operativebank.co.uk/greenpeace.html

7   The so-called 'Environmental Performance Indicators'. See www.csg.ch.

8   See UBS 1999. The methodology identifies business travel and paper consumption together as the second most relevant environmental issues.

9   See e.g. www.natwest.com; www.ing.com; www.bankamerica.com.

10   CSG has followed the lines of VfU in its environmental report 1997/98. UBS also published aggregate figures according to the VfU guidelines. It does not follow the guidelines, but publishes the figures to make comparison between banks possible. For other banks, it is not possible to extract the figures to the standardised VfU form.

Parameter	LLB	LG	BLB	Allianz	CSG	UBS
Electricity consumption (kWh/employee/year)	2,886	4,627	4,816	4,110	7,500	7,300
Heat consumption (kWh/m²)	n.a.	n.a.	n.a.	n.a.	98	104
Water consumption (m³/employee/year)	145	98	100	76	119	94
Total paper consumption (kg/employee/year)	120	113	120	258	240	252
Copier paper consumption (pages/employee/year)	3,997	3,895	5,200	7,200	8,850	10,600
Computer hardware (numbers/employee/year)	0.5	0.2	0.3	1.03	n.a.	n.a.
Business travel (km/employee/year)	321	1,040	1,500	3,700	1,700	3,000
CO₂ emissions (kg/employee)	n.a.	n.a.	n.a.	n.a.	2,850	2,800

Table 1.1 **Internal environmental burden of German/Swiss banks**

Source: European Commission DG XI (for LBB, LG, BLB and Allianz; 1996 figures); CSG 1998 (1996 figures); UBS 1999 (1998 figures)

is the responsibility of banks. It is easy to make an estimate of the environmental impact in this sense: it would equate to almost the aggregate pollution of the whole economy in many countries. On the other hand, as the products of banks do not pollute, the users of those products—the clients—should take sole responsibility for the pollution they create. Of course, both standpoints are absurd. The truth lies somewhere in the middle— as CERCLA has demonstrated in the US—but still remains almost impossible to quantify.

1.3 Driving forces to take action

There are both internal and external driving forces for banks to integrate sustainability within their day-to-day business and corporate policies. Internal driving forces are likely to emanate from employees, shareholders and the board of directors. External driving forces result from pressures from governments, customers, competitors, NGOs and society at large (the public). Whether banks are made liable for the environmental pollution of their clients or not, the risks of customers are also the banks' risks. If the continuity of a customer is threatened by new environmental legislation, the continuity of the bank will also be affected.[11]

11 Of course, a distinction has to be made between the environmental risks of private and business clients. Furthermore, clients may have conflicting interests; large banks in particular will need to pick the best of both sides—for example, support organic farmers while still financing more intensive agriculture: a problem that faces the Rabobank Group in the Netherlands.

However, driving forces derive not only from the need to minimise exposure to risk. There are also opportunities to be gained from moves towards sustainability—particularly with regard to new business. For example, ABN AMRO and UBS have a growing interest in market developments for wind energy. Traditional forms of finance may be sufficient, but banks are also being challenged to develop new products that fulfil the specific needs of customers. The growing market for sustainable investment funds, such as the Storebrand Scudder Environmental Value Fund (WBCSD 1997a) or the UBS Eco Performance portfolios (UBS 1999), is a good example of this trend. The growing importance and number of such funds illustrates that competitive pressures are driving more banks to diversify their product range in response to market demand.

Governmental policy is another major driving force for banks, particularly with regard to internal aspects. To date, banks have reacted cautiously to government attempts to legislate on their external side and are unwilling to become the enforcers of government policies (see Section 1.5). Other driving forces include the changing expectations of society, media, suppliers, other financial institutions (such as rating agencies and the World Bank), employees, boards of directors, shareholders and various kinds of NGO such as Greenpeace and the World Business Council for Sustainable Development (WBCSD). Figure 1.2 presents an overview of the internal (the middle circle) and external (the outer circle) stakeholders of banks.

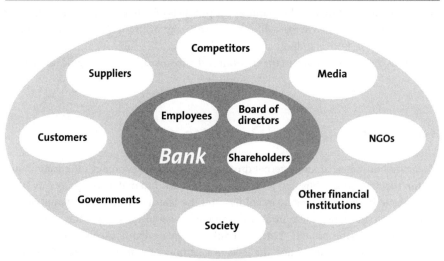

The inner circle represents the bank and its internal stakeholders;
the outer circle contains the external stakeholders.

Figure 1.2   **A bank's internal and external stakeholders**

Source: Based on Jeucken 1998

1.4 Actions taken by banks

To understand the actions that banks are taking towards sustainability, we have identified four stages or attitudes. Although each bank will normally go through all of these stages, some banks will probably never reach the holistic final stage which will continue to evolve as stakeholder expectations change. Also, some banks, mostly niche players, will skip the first and second stage. This model is depicted in Figure 1.3. Each outer layer contains the previous layer (with the exception of the first layer, 'defensive banking'). In other words, sustainable banking will contain the characteristics of both preventative and offensive banking.[12] In principle, banks develop from the inner layer (defensive) to the outer layer (ultimately sustainable). Although the model will be used in relation to banks as a whole, it can also be used with regard to the differing stage developments of departments within banks. Because the general aim is to determine at which stage one can classify a bank as a whole entity, this differentiation between departments does not invalidate the model. This differentiation will be of use from a standpoint of strategic management within companies or banks.

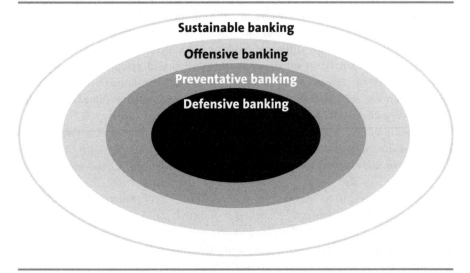

Sustainable banking

Offensive banking

Preventative banking

Defensive banking

Figure 1.3 **A typology of banking and sustainable development**

Source: Jeucken 1998

The first stage is **defensive banking**. In this stage, a bank is non-active and may even try to delay or oppose new environmental legislation, because it may damage the interests of the bank directly or indirectly (through damage to the profitability of customers). Opportunities from cost savings through initiatives such as energy efficiency are not taken up. Environmental management is seen as an avoidable cost. Very few

12 Note that the terms 'defensive', 'preventative' and 'offensive' are defined in relation to environmental issues.

banks in the North can said to be at this stage today, but certainly some departments of banks or niche players—particularly within investment banking—still show symptoms of this attitude.

The second stage is **preventative banking**. This stage diverges from the previous stage, because potential environmental cost savings and eco-efficiencies are actively taken up. Preventative banking is in some ways inevitable because government and NGOs will directly or indirectly put constraints on the activities of banks, through legislation, social pressure or jurisprudence. Preventative banks will integrate the potential revenues, costs and risks into their day-to-day business. However, banks at this stage will only consider their internal processes such as environmental management and credit risk assessment. The National Westminster Bank has, for instance, cut back drastically on energy costs through energy efficiency. Another example is the reduction of credit risk by integrating environmental issues in the credit risk assessment processes (for example, UBS, Bank of America, Deutsche Bank and ING Group). UBS is also integrating environmental issues into its investment banking branch (Warburg Dillon Read). This so-called 'Global Environmental Risk Policy' for investment banking activities was implemented in February 1999 (UBS 1999) and is the first such initiative by a major bank. Although the nature of this initiative is preventative, it will only be found in banks who are also offensively oriented (as shown below, UBS is also very active in the offensive stage).

Banks in the third stage, **offensive banking**, consider their external activities in addition to the internal. In other words, they are also developing and marketing environmentally friendly products. Examples include the development of environmental investment funds (such as the Storebrand Scudder Environmental Value Fund and the Eco Performance portfolios of UBS), the financing of sustainable energy (such as the so-called Solaris Project, a collaboration between Greenpeace and the Rabobank Group [Rabobank International 1998]) and the signing of the UNEP Banking Charter (by organisations such as Bank Austria, UBS, Kenya Commercial Bank Group and Salomon Inc.[13]). Banks will also report on their environmental activities (see, for example, the environmental reports of the Bank of America, UBS, Credit Suisse, ABN AMRO and Barclays Bank). The attitude can be labelled as proactive, creative and innovative. Offensive banks are continuously looking for win–win solutions. The problem is that, as long as negative environmental costs are not completely integrated into the price system, win–win solutions will not lead to sustainability.

In the fourth stage of **sustainable banking**, while win–win solutions are embraced, the corporate philosophy also fosters projects at a higher risk, lower rate of return and longer payback periods. The bank does not look for the highest financial rate of return, but for the highest *sustainable* rate of return, while being profitable in the long run. Such banks require that their shareholders have the same vision and ambition. Unfortunately, the current status and demand for sustainability in society is not sufficiently developed to make the goal of sustainable banking possible for large banks. Such policies would result in a loss of profit, as the bulk of their current activities simply could not be financed. At this time, the goal of sustainable banking appears to be feasible only for

13   See www.unep.ch/eteu/envr-fin.htm.

niche players such as the Triodos Bank in the Netherlands or The Co-operative Bank in the UK.[14]

On an even smaller scale, debt-for-nature swaps (DNSs) and micro-credit are interesting examples of elements of sustainable banking (see e.g. *Latin America Weekly Report* 1994; World Bank 1996d; OECD 1997a). DNS involves exchanging a part of the huge outstanding debt of developing nations for an obligation by that country to put measurably more effort into nature conservation. Another example that contains characteristics of sustainable banking is the initiative of various Swiss banks; and also Den Nordske Bank's directed tariff differentiation (the above-mentioned 'carrot-and-stick' approach).[15] In these cases, banks look not only at environmental risks (a negative driving force) but also at stimulating certain developments in society towards sustainability (a positive driving force). It may mean that a bank will not invest in a financially sound business if it is ecologically unsound. Again, this may mean a loss of profitability (business) or even continuity for the bank—unless all banks were to act on a similar basis. The Swiss initiative is interesting for exactly this reason, as a majority of Swiss banks are involved (but not all—leaving opportunities for 'free-riders'). Another example is The Co-operative Bank in the UK, which has made a pledge to its customers not to invest in socially or environmentally damaging sectors such as tobacco production. Companies who are deemed acceptable are eligible for favourable interest rates, with higher interest rates on savings and lower interest rates on loans. The net earnings/savings for a company can be as high as 30% when compared with standard interest rates.[16] A final example is ASN Bank in the Netherlands which has launched an interest-free fund: investors who want to foster sustainability but do not require any financial return are in this way funding the activities of some (selected by ASN) front-runners in the environmental, social or equity (North–South) field.[17]

1.5 The role of governments in sustainable banking

As discussed above, the major environmental impacts of banks are not physically related to their production processes and products, but to those of their customers. This has historically created difficulties for policy-makers. However, some governments are now becoming increasingly concerned about the intermediary role banks play, particularly in the achievement of environmental policies.

In the Netherlands, environmental policy has taken a unique course with the establishment of national environmental targets as stipulated originally in the National Environmental Policy Plan (NEPP) (VROM 1989) and the National Environmental Policy

---

14 See www.triodos.nl *or* www.co-operativebank.co.uk.
15 See van der Woerd and Vellinga 1997 or www.unep.ch/eco.
16 See *Green Futures* 1998 or www.co-operativebank.co.uk/ecology.html.
17 This initiative is of particular interest to those who do not wish simply to donate money for certain projects, but want some kind of market control on how their money is being spent and controlled. See www.asnbank.nl.

Plan Plus (NEPP+) (VROM 1990). These policy plans provide environmental targets for several sectors of the Dutch economy: agriculture, industry, transportation and consumers. By examining the progress of Dutch national environmental policy over the last ten years, it is possible to identify different stages in the development of such proactive environmental policies.

In the NEPP, the banks were not direct players in the design of environmental policy but were confronted with the clean-up costs of their customers. However, these financial burdens did not significantly affect the banking sector as they did not generally result in bankruptcies. As a consequence of compliance with environmental standards, new industrial sectors quickly evolved that specialised in environmental technologies. Banks began to develop special funds that invested in this sector—a side-effect of the environmental policy. Clearly, banks started to become more offensive through the identification of environmental challenges that were accelerated by the governmental policies that promoted environmental technologies.

The following stage, the NEPP+, featured the growing importance of voluntary agreements between industry and governments. Environmental objectives and plans to reach these objectives were formulated in dialogues between large industry groups and government. Once again, banks were not directly involved in this process.

However, in the third and current stage, as laid out in the so-called 'Policy Document on Environment and Economy', the environment is no longer the exclusive concern of government and the direct polluter, but also of other business partners and intermediaries such as the financial services sector (VROM 1998). In this stage, the life-cycle approach became integrated into environmental policy. The continuous improvement of products, the use of environmental management systems, and instruments such as environmental reporting were widely implemented by industry. Government strategy was to decrease direct involvement and increase the responsibility of the polluting target groups in reaching objectives. Moreover, financial institutions were directly addressed by Dutch environmental policy for the first time as part of this process. In contrast to the first and second stages, where the environmental policy of the government set the environmental context in which banks operate, this third stage involved the banks as players in designing environmental policy.

As a consequence, the role of the government in the Netherlands is now to stimulate, facilitate, monitor and actively co-ordinate. To this end, a variety of tools are used: the financial support of environmental sound product development; the development of an environmental information exchange system; financial instruments such as green investment; eco-labelling; exploration of life-cycle methodologies and eco-indicators; green procurement; the stimulation of sustainable consumption; and the introduction of a product-oriented environmental management system.

Because mandatory regulation of extended or shared responsibility on the total environmental impact of products is almost impossible to impose on all market actors, other means have been sought to implement this voluntarily. Banks have been at the heart of this process. For this purpose, the 'Environmental Dialogue between Banks and Governments' was established in April 1999 in the Netherlands in an attempt to stimulate environmental improvements through the development of new financial products and services and through an optimal match between the environmental and fiscal policy of the government. The policy goal is to further explore ways in which banks can stimulate sustainable development. Standardisation of the environmental information provided by companies (indicators), benchmarking between banks, and developing fiscal and financial instruments are cited as main underlying aims. At the first meeting of the 'Environmental Dialogue between Banks and Governments' five observations were made as starting points (VROM 1999):

1. Banks have already taken a number of steps in assuming responsibility with regard to the environment; it is unclear to what extent these activities are to be regarded as niche or mainstream activities.

2. The Dutch government has made a formal request in its Policy Document on Environment and Economy (VROM 1998) to banks to play a role in achieving sustainable development.

3. The stage of policy development regarding the role of banks in the European Commission is at the same level as that of the Dutch environmental policy.

4. At a global level, the financial sector is encouraged to take a role in sustainable development through the UNEP initiative.

5. There have been specific developments related to the introduction of policy instruments such as tradable permits, joint implementation and the clean development mechanisms of the Kyoto Protocol.

It would appear that, even in an environmentally advanced country such as the Netherlands, constructive dialogue between banks and governments has only just begun. However, it is clear that there is considerable scope for the process to advance.

1.6 The dynamic and changing role of banks

The banking sector has taken some steps to stimulate sustainable development. How-ever, because of the critical role that finance plays, much more needs to be done. International institutions such as UNEP must continue to increase the awareness of banks and hence stimulate new product development. The World Bank must draw attention to the relationship between the environmental impacts of investments and financing decisions. And banks themselves must engage further with their customers, rating agencies, insurance companies, competitors and governmental policy-makers in order to establish:

- The role of different actors in achieving sustainable development

- The motives of actors for incorporating environmental awareness into their decision-making

- The rules of the game for banks (e.g. transparency issues, codes of conduct and legislation)

- The products and services banks offer to their customers

- The products and services that are offered to banks by the other actors

- The stimuli and impediments for the further development and success of the products and services offered by the banks

Ecologic and Delphi International state in their recent report to the European Commission that, if financial institutions are to integrate environmental considerations into their decision-making, they need to be convinced that not only are they profitable in the narrow sense, but they are also sufficiently important to merit their attention (European Commission DG XI 1997). This may be a serious obstacle in the real world, despite the fact that good environmental performance is often linked to good financial performance (WBCSD 1997a). For many banks, it is questionable whether this link is strong enough to make the environment a critical feature of investments. It is likely that this link needs to be strengthened by addressing:

- The significance of environmental performance to financial risks and returns on investments

- Taxation schemes (e.g. tax credits for good environmental performance)

- The quality of communications by firms to financial institutions about their environmental performance

Currently, there are wide geographic and organisational differences in how banks relate to their stakeholders' concerns about sustainability issues. This is true even within the EU. To gain further insight into the possibilities of the financial sector playing a constructive role in sustainable development, multinational studies need to be performed that adapt the framework according to the specific circumstances in a country. However, focusing only on the financial products and services that financial institutions offer in a country is not sufficient. The interplay between the actors will determine the success of the financial products and services. By comparing the behaviour of financial institutions (the financial products and services they offer and the internal processes of the banks) in conjunction with the context as shaped by the other actors, proposals for all actors can be formulated that contribute to a more constructive role for the financial sector in progressing toward sustainable development.

Part 1
THE ENVIRONMENTAL
POLICIES OF BANKS

IN THIS PART OF THE BOOK THE CHAPTERS DEAL WITH THE ACTUAL POLICIES OF banks. The section explores the environmental impacts, driving forces and concrete activities of banks to foster sustainable development. For example, regarding *impacts*, the chapter by Street and Monaghan illustrates this issue for the service channel of The Co-operative Bank (Chapter 5). Most papers tend to discuss the environmental aspects of sustainable development, with traditional financial issues and social issues (such as human rights) only partially addressed. However, social issues increasingly seem to be rising on the management agenda of banks as well as other sectors. Regarding *driving forces*, the chapter by Hugenschmidt *et al.* explores the motivations for UBS to integrate environmental issues into asset management and investment banking (and also presents examples of action by the bank in this area). Regarding *concrete activities*, the chapters show that some banks are active in micro-credit schemes in developing countries, some are pioneers in the sustainable banking field, some are innovative on the product side (e.g. investment banking and CO_2 emission credit schemes) or process side (the sustainability of the service channels of banks), and some are actively progressing sustainability within SMEs (small and medium-sized enterprises). As well as studies of individual banks, some chapters present an overview of the activities of banks in various geographic regions—for example, a comparison is made between the activities of international and domestic banks in Thailand (Chapter 10). Other examples are developments towards sustainable banking in Hungary (Chapter 9) and Austria (Chapter 8).

Heinrich Hugenschmidt *et al.* in their discussion of UBS in Switzerland (Chapter 2), show how environmental aspects are integrated into various banking activities (commercial banking, asset management and investment banking) and it is seen why this bank was awarded ISO 14001 certification for its worldwide banking activities. The chapter provides examples in the areas of asset management and investment banking, as well as predicting future trends.

Davide Dal Maso *et al.* (Chapter 3) describe an innovative initiative launched by Unicredito Italiano (UCI), one of the largest Italian financial groups, to promote the diffusion of environmental management systems among SMEs. This initiative is the first of its kind in Italy, and presumably also in Europe. The results—and, moreover, the means of obtaining them—show that banks can play an important role in promoting sustainable development and that environmentally sound operations can make business sense as well.

The chapter by Michel Negenman of ASN Bank in the Netherlands (Chapter 4) explores the developments and products of one of the first ethical banks in Europe. The chapter begins with a brief description of the history of ASN Bank, followed by a more specific look at how it tries to achieve its 'sustainability' goals. ASN Bank has developed an ethical assessment process on which all its products (saving accounts, investment funds, micro-credit schemes, insurance products) are based, which are briefly discussed.

The chapter ends with a discussion of the role that ASN Bank has played and still plays in stimulating the development towards sustainable banking among the (Dutch) banking sector and presents the outlook of the ASN Bank in particular and its vision of the future of sustainable banking in general.

The chapter by Penny Street and Philip Monaghan of the National Centre for Business and Ecology (NCBE) at the University of Salford in the UK (Chapter 5) demonstrates a highly innovative approach to assessing the sustainability impact of all The Co-operative Bank's service channels. Using indicators, The Co-operative Bank can evaluate all its strategic decisions regarding its service channels (for example, the adoption of an Internet banking strategy or the closure of some small bankpoints) in relation to the consequences for the environmental and social dimensions of sustainability.

Firoze Siddiqui and Peter Newman (Chapter 6) provide a unique overview of how the Grameen Bank in Bangladesh has developed an international reputation for assisting small rural enterprises in a manner not normally seen in conventional banking practices. The chapter illustrates this bank's activities with the 'Grameen Shakti' that has been established under the Grameen Bank umbrella with the purpose of supplying renewable energy to villages without electricity in Bangladesh.

The aim of James Giuseppi's study (Chapter 7) is to identify investment opportunities for SRI (socially responsible investment) funds. The chapter identifies a number of banks that have made considerable efforts towards sustainable development. In this respect, the important role of banks is highlighted. Also, some guidance is given to those banks that want to develop ethical criteria regarding their loan or investment policies.

Christine Jasch (Chapter 8) describes the trends of sustainable banking in Austria, highlighting achievements and barriers. Internal aspects (environmental management systems) and external aspects (green funds, direct investments) and verification experiences are dealt with.

Judit Barta of the GKI Economic Research Co. and Vilma Éri of the Centre for Environmental Studies in Hungary present some results of a survey of selected Hungarian financial institutions (Chapter 9). In a market situation where official financial assistance is associated with credits, and where a new, fiercely competitive, market segment is opening up for banks, environment-related credit assessment and the environment business in general have achieved greater importance. It is indicated that this process could lead to heightened awareness of sustainability issues by Hungarian commercial banks.

Willi Zimmermann and Beatriz Mayer (Chapter 10) discuss an analysis of 30 domestic and foreign-owned banks in Thailand regarding the level of awareness of and current responses to environmental issues and environmental risks. Results indicate that banks are slow to follow the trend towards sustainability begun in the West and that foreign-owned (i.e. Western) banks in general do not perform any better towards sustainability than local banks.

From this selection, it seems that banks are active in a broad range of fields. This variety shows that sustainable banking involves more than just reduction in energy use or sustainable investment funds. Although many banks of various sizes are active, it still seems to be a niche market—that is, most banks are only active in one or two fields of sustainable banking, rather than integrating sustainability into all their activities or corporate philosophies. Exceptions are the smaller banks such as ASN and The Co-operative Bank. Also, some large international banks, such as Unicredito Italiano, are, very progressively, aiming at integrating sustainability into all their activities. However, it must be remembered that the banks that responded to our call for papers are probably the most active banks in the sustainability field. Moreover, it seems that the same names continually appear whenever sustainable banking is discussed: the Dow Jones initiative (see Part 3), for example, was mentioned in most of the papers we received; and UBS is a well-known example of environmental reporting (see Part 2), sustainable investment funds (see Part 3) and interaction with NGOs such as the United Nations Environment Programme (UNEP). Although not mentioned here, assessing credit risks has been one of the most important driving forces for most banks active in the sustainability field (see Part 4). By demonstrating good financial performance, these pioneers can show the way for other financial institutions worldwide, which are in general still very slow to address the sustainability issue. Linking outstanding financial performance, customer satisfaction, increasing market shares and shareholder value to sustainability may be the most important driving force for 'changing finance'. This part of the book presents an impressive overview of the kinds of activity that banks are undertaking in the sustainability arena, most of them demonstrating just such a link.

SUSTAINABLE BANKING AT UBS*

Heinrich Hugenschmidt,
Yann Kermode and Inge Schumacher
UBS AG, Switzerland

Josef Janssen
Institute for Economy and
the Environment, University
of St Gallen, Switzerland

In 15 July 1998, shortly after the merger between UBS and SBC, the group executive board of UBS AG passed a new environmental policy which symbolised the high priority it assigns to environmental issues. For UBS, environmental sustainability plays a considerable part in robust and responsible management practices. In May 1999 UBS AG received certification according to the ISO 14001 environmental standard, making it the first bank worldwide to have its environmental management system in banking operations certified according to ISO 14001 on a global basis. The bank's in-house operations in Switzerland were also recognised as being in accordance with ISO 14001.

UBS, like any other business, has a direct impact on the environment through its in-house operations. However, as for any service provider, the most relevant environmental impacts will often be indirect; such impacts may be influenced, but are hard to control. Indeed, for many of UBS's clients, environmental considerations not only represent financial risks, they can also mean new business opportunities. This chapter sets forth examples in the areas of investment banking and asset management, as well as examining possible future trends resulting from the Kyoto Protocol.

2.1 Investment banking: environment demands a long-term perspective

Warburg Dillon Read (WDR), the Investment Banking Division of UBS AG, is one of the world's leading investment banks. The business area of investment banking covers issues

---

* Opinions expressed herein are the authors' and do not necessarily reflect the opinions of UBS.

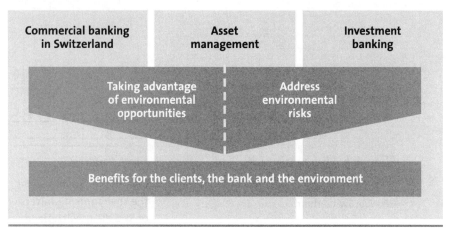

Figure 2.1 **Banking and the environment**

of securities, trading and corporate finance. Corporate finance itself provides financial advice on mergers, acquisitions, bid defences, restructurings and disposals, as well as capital-raising services, to major companies, sovereign governments and other global institutions.

UBS has recently begun to implement an environmental management system within WDR. In November 1998, WDR approved the new Global Environmental Risk Policy, which came into force in February 1999. WDR is, to our knowledge, one of the first investment banks to adopt such an environmental policy.

The rationale for implementing such an environmental management system is that environmental problems can become financial risks for the bank; the viability of UBS's clients' businesses may be affected by poor environmental performance. Moreover, the necessity to comply with new environmental regulations, or the obligation to clean up contaminated sites, may result in high costs and may diminish future cash flows. With regard to Initial Public Offerings (IPO) and Equity Underwriting, UBS endeavours, where appropriate, to take environmental risks into consideration when pricing and placing with potential investors. The bank may also have to take into consideration investors' requirements such as compliance with World Bank standards. Finally, environmentally controversial transactions are increasingly being targeted by pressure groups. UBS is sensitive to public opinion and aware of the efforts being made by pressure groups to raise the profile of these issues.

2.1.1 *Environmental risk management processes in investment banking*

UBS's environmental goals for investment banking are based on its environmental policy, the objective being to incorporate due consideration of environmental risks into risk management processes, especially in lending and in investment banking. The WDR Global Environmental Risk Policy provides an outline of environmental risks and sets out principles to be considered, where appropriate, in the business commitment and credit processes at WDR.

In order to properly identify and manage environmental risks, consideration must be given at an early stage to whether there is environmental risk in relation to a transaction as this will allow the bank to make cost-effective decisions. Due consideration of environmental risks will be incorporated, where appropriate, into the business commitment decision, the credit analysis, and the due diligence and credit decision processes.

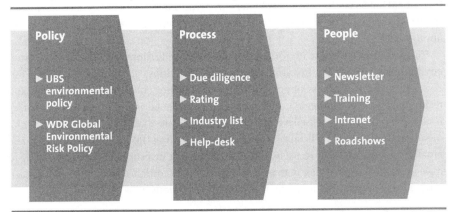

Figure 2.2 **Comprehensive strategy in investment banking**

The environmental services at corporate headquarters, known as Environmental Risk Management Services (ERMS), has established a help-desk to assist business and credit officers in the assessment and management of environmental risks associated with financial transactions. Typical services of the help-desk include the identification of external experts, the establishment of a due diligence strategy, the evaluation of environmental assessment reports, training, summaries of environmental risks, and the handling of enquiries relating to the environment from environmental groups or investors. Tools available from the help-desk are World Bank standards and guidelines, which include, for example, sectoral emission standards as well as terms of reference for environmental assessments. A list of consultants for due diligence investigations is also available.

ERMS and its help-desk is launching a large-scale information and training campaign to publicise the policy and processes across WDR. It is also running an intranet website, which offers tools and information on environmental risk management at WDR, and an online help-desk request facility. A monthly newsletter covering sector, policy and regulatory trends relating to the environment is also published and is available on the same site.

2.1.2 *What are the benefits?*

UBS's clients can benefit from its own professional risk management. Financial risks linked to environmental issues always affect the client before they become a risk for the bank and, by asking questions, UBS can raise awareness that may lead its clients to reduce their own risks.

From the point of view of the environment, benefits are sometimes obvious: by financing clean technologies and environmentally sound products, UBS can help reduce emissions and waste. But in traditional investments as well, environmental risk management can have positive effects when potentially harmful emissions and risks are identified. Another indirect effect results from the fact that WDR is, we believe, one of the first investment banks worldwide to implement an environmental risk policy: as a first mover, it may influence other financial institutions and governments to value these issues appropriately.

For the bank, the most important benefit is the reduction of financial risks, from environmental aspects, in investment banking transactions. UBS also ensures that it can take advantage of business opportunities in the fields of environmental products and technologies. Furthermore, as controversial environmental issues can harm the bank's image and reputation, we believe that leading a proactive dialogue with environmental organisations is also beneficial as a means of safeguarding UBS's reputation in this area. Finally, the fact that WDR is, we believe, one of the first investment banks worldwide to have an environmental risk management system in accordance with ISO 14001 contributes to UBS's reputation as an environmentally conscious bank.

2.2 Environmental opportunities in asset management

Motivated by increasing customer demand and supported by its own environmental commitment, UBS launched two 'Eco Performance' portfolios in June 1997. This investment strategy is based on the assumption that ecologically efficient companies can cut costs and environmental impacts by using resources efficiently, and create growth opportunities and new markets for innovative products.

About 20 years ago, the first of a whole range of socially and ethically responsible funds began to attract investors in the USA and UK. A second generation of ecological funds with a main focus on environmental technology emerged some ten years ago in the German-speaking part of the world. Due to the limited investment universe, and to industries' tendency to integrate environmental factors into product and process design instead of adding end-of-pipe technologies, this concept met with little success.

2.2.1 Efficient use of resources leads to economic and environmental benefits

The UBS Eco Performance portfolios are based on the much broader concept of 'creating more wealth by using our natural resources more efficiently'. In the area of resource efficiency, the concepts of 'Factor Four' and, latterly, 'Factor Ten' have been proposed as necessary targets for improvement. There is fast-growing evidence that, in certain areas, improvements of factor four or even ten can be achieved even with existing technologies. In order to realise these business opportunities, the Eco Performance portfolios apply a twofold strategy: the funds consider companies that display an above-average commitment to environmental protection (the so-called 'eco-leaders'), as well as companies whose products embody a high degree of resource efficiency (the so-called 'eco-innovators').

In each important sector of the market, the UBS research team identifies the best large blue-chip companies with the most convincing proactive environmental strategy in place. Through continuous improvement of their ecological efficiency, we expect these eco-leaders to achieve substantial savings and, at the same time, significantly reduce their environmental impacts.

2.2.2 *The screening and evaluation process*

In order to analyse companies' environmental performance, UBS developed a criteria system that systematically screens company activities. The system makes use of a number of qualitative aspects (Table 2.1) to obtain a better picture of a company's strategic approach. The UBS research team tries to identify how environmental activities have been integrated into the corporate strategy, and if the company also seeks to enhance its shareholder value by taking advantage of environmental issues.

I	**Environmental policy and strategy**
II	**Environmental management**
III	**Ecology-related costs and savings**
IV	**Environmental communications**
V	**Process strategies**
VI	**Environmental data (input–output)**
VII	**Environmental product strategies**

Table 2.1 **The companies are analysed using a detailed, sector-specific criteria system.**

Implementation into the organisational structure is the next step. Although certified environmental management systems may demonstrate that a system is in place to ensure continuous improvement, they do not provide any guarantee concerning environmental performance. For this reason an analysis of the concrete process and product strategies is conducted. The process part includes measures to increase energy efficiency, the support of renewable energies or the waste management systems. The product strategies include the integration of environmental criteria into the product design, the development of life-cycle analysis, and relations with suppliers. The current outsourcing trend is increasingly important: the UBS research team discovered that only a few companies offer customer services such as leasing or rental of products. As responsibility and motivation lie with the producer, there is a potential here for significantly reducing environmental impacts. There is also room for improvement regarding contracting or consulting models.

As well as qualitative analysis, the environmental performance evaluation also includes quantitative criteria, which are designed to analyse results of environmental programmes and measures. Only a few companies are able to provide data relating to their energy use, waste generation or greenhouse gas emissions at corporate level. The UBS research team tries to encourage companies and their sector associations to develop sector-specific environmental performance indicators for benchmarking purposes. Data concerning financial consequences is also often missing. The UBS research team focuses on operational costs that can also reflect efficiency in financial terms. Environmental managers have yet to focus on this area and convey financially relevant success stories to convince, internally, their financial control or investor relations colleagues and, externally, the financial community as a whole.

As each sector faces different challenges, the criteria system was deemed most appropriate. As an example, the focus within the electronic industry lies in the energy efficiency of products and on product design. If take-back and recycling requirements are already taken into account in the design phase, electronic companies have a competitive advantage regarding new regulation. For utilities, emphasis is also on financial benefits: if utilities can improve efficiency by constructing cogeneration facilities and reduce losses within their distribution network, this will result both in lower greenhouse gas emissions and cost savings.

Some company examples illustrate this point. The Eco Performance portfolios chose to invest in Bristol Myers Squibb (BMS), as it is among the sector leaders in environmental and health and safety protection. Successful environmental management is seen as a competitive advantage, so BMS analyses the life-cycle of all important product lines in order to identify any serious environmental implications of production, packing, sales and disposal. This procedure also results in cost savings by converting to less toxic materials and processes. BMS has also realised that increases in turnover can also be achieved by supporting the environmental management of its clients. It therefore advises hospitals and pharmacies on environmental issues and provides information and training. Canon was chosen because the company has implemented a convincing recycling strategy and has achieved impressive efficiency improvements in production and product design. Canon's eco-conscious product design combined with its 'Copier Remanufacturing Programme' opens up the opportunity to bring recycled machines of high quality to the market.

Smaller companies with products and services to satisfy specific needs with a high degree of resource efficiency comprise the most innovative and future-oriented potential of the fund. Good examples are investments in the renewable energy sector: Vestas (wind energy), Spire (photovoltaics) and Ballard Power (fuel cells). Other successful investments are Whole Foods Market and Shimano. Whole Foods Market shows impressive growth rates with its natural food supermarkets and Shimano is the world market leader in bicycle components (80% of market share) which make cycling—a healthy and environmentally friendly activity in itself—easier and much more attractive.

2.2.3 The plausibility check: external analysis adds social corporate responsibility criteria

However, before the fund invests in a company, UBS's ecological analysis must be confirmed by a 'plausibility check' provided by an external consultant. This complementary analysis concentrates on important social and ethical factors and uses public information to verify what UBS obtained directly from the company. This is important as a quality check and provides a more comprehensive picture, so that all three elements of sustainability are integrated (see Fig. 2.3).

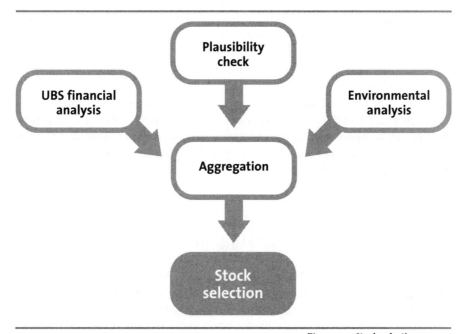

Figure 2.3 **Stock selection process**

2.2.4 Broad diversification by sector and country generates attractive results

This 'best-in-class' approach leads to a broadly diversified portfolio of highly profitable companies covering all the important sectors and markets. The innovators additionally provide a high growth potential in attractive markets.

The fund's orientation to the MSCI (Morgan Stanley Capital International) World Index allows for risk and performance comparison with the whole universe of globally investing equity funds. The first results are encouraging: the increase in value of more than 80% since inception outperforms the MSCI, and supports UBS's view that companies committed to proactive environmental strategies are also successful in economic terms.

2.2.5 Eco Performance portfolios are attracting increasing attention

UBS's concept has attracted a great deal of media attention and customer interest. The fact that, within the last two years, six other ecologically oriented funds have been launched in Switzerland alone shows that there is serious growth potential in this market segment. The increasing awareness that proactive environmental activities are an indication of good management and financial success will slowly change the old prejudice that has hitherto equated environmental issues with costs and legislative burdens. An increasing number of the companies selected for our fund are beginning to understand environmental issues as an important challenge for the coming century and are therefore expressing interest in UBS's screening and evaluation process and in constructive dialogue with its research team to explore the potential for further improvements. Some of the companies are proud to be selected for the fund and use this positive message in communications with their employees, clients and the media.

A recent development on the Japanese market demonstrates an overwhelming interest in environmental funds from the media and investors. UBS has initiated a co-operative project with Sumitomo Bank and launched a Japanese environmental equity fund in October 1999. The research was conducted by the Japan Research Institute, supported by the knowledge of the Swiss eco-team.

2.3 Future trends in banking: the Kyoto Protocol

But what does the future hold? No measures have been implemented to date, but UBS is currently looking at the increasingly significant impact of global climate policies on its banking business. The basis for an emerging market was created in late 1997 when more than 150 governments adopted the market-based mechanisms of the Kyoto Protocol, a political response to the threat of anthropogenic climate change. In other words, the Kyoto Protocol might convert a global environmental threat into new global market opportunities.

As the Kyoto Protocol is an agreement between nations, the question might be raised how companies will be affected. The answer is simple: governments will most likely pass on their Kyoto commitments to greenhouse gas-emitting companies. There are several possible ways they may do this: some countries may follow a highly market-oriented approach (e.g. energy or CO_2 taxes, or national emission trading schemes), while others may focus more on direct regulations (e.g. energy efficiency standards). From the perspective of a private-sector company, all alternatives share one common feature: greenhouse gas emissions will affect the cash flow negatively while emission reductions may create extra revenue. In other words, there will be a strong incentive to reduce net greenhouse gas emissions (see Fig. 2.4).

Companies can respond to these requirements not only by directly reducing their emissions but also by taking advantage of the so-called Kyoto Mechanisms. From a

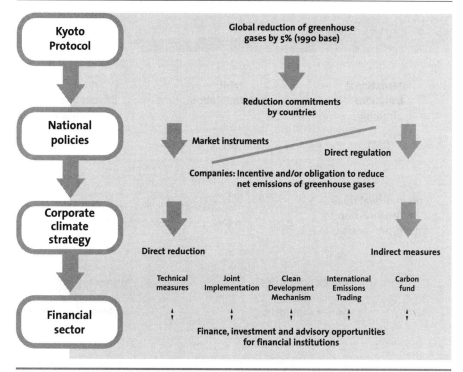

Figure 2.4 **The Kyoto Protocol and its business implications for financial institutions**

company perspective, it is very likely that efficient use of these mechanisms is as important a cost driver as the actual amount of greenhouse gas emissions.

2.3.1 The Kyoto Mechanisms

The Kyoto Protocol allows the use of the following three market instruments at international level (Fig. 2.5):

- Joint Implementation (JI)
- Clean Development Mechanism (CDM)
- International Emissions Trading (IET)

The basic idea of these instruments refers to the possibility of achieving emission reductions abroad via JI or CDM and/or importing them via IET. These emission reductions are called emission credits, since they can be credited towards the domestic emission reduction obligations of individual countries, sectors and companies. Due to the fact that emission abatement costs differ significantly across countries, sectors, firms and plants, the use of the Kyoto Mechanisms may lead to huge cost savings or profit opportunities at firm level, and corresponding societal gains at the aggregate national and international level.

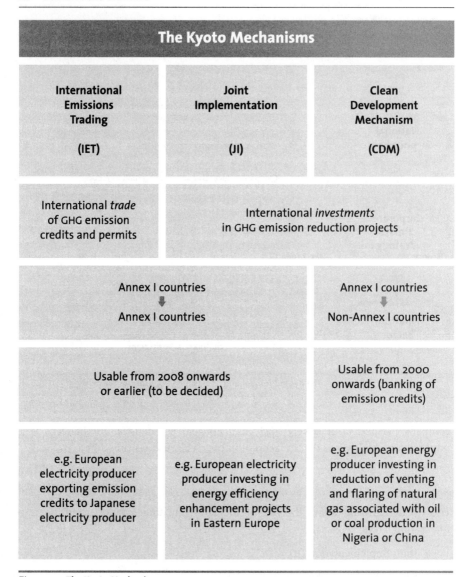

Figure 2.5 **The Kyoto Mechanisms**

2.3.2 How will this affect the financial sector?

Before analysing the business consequences for financial institutions, it is necessary to take a closer look at the cash flow implications of the Kyoto Protocol on companies and corporations. Basically, cash flow can be affected in two ways:

- **Cost side of cash flow.** Companies may be regulated by future climate policy inducing additional costs of emission abatement. The cost burden will vary according to the country, the sector and the company's specific capability to reduce its emission of greenhouse gases.

▨ **Revenue side of cash flow.** Companies may generate extra returns if they produce emission credits that could be sold to other companies. A company is very likely to generate extra emission credits if its marginal reduction costs are lower than the expected market price of emission credits.

Banks that are able to provide sound services to these companies will gain from a new, emerging market for financial services in the context of the Kyoto Protocol. The following main business areas will be affected by the Kyoto Protocol.

2.3.2.1 Corporate banking

Technical measures to reduce greenhouse gas emissions usually require investments. This can lead to an increasing demand for loans by companies and subsequently to new business opportunities for banks.

2.3.2.2 Project finance

If a project is likely to be exposed to future climate policy regulations, costs of compliance could be reduced by appropriate use of the Kyoto Mechanisms. This would be economically viable if local compliance costs exceed the costs of producing abroad via JI or CDM or importing via IET the emission credits required for achieving compliance. This strategy could be more important for enhancing the cash flow of existing projects because planned projects usually employ the most advanced technologies, which are more likely to be in accordance with climate policy regulations. On the revenue side, it may also be economically viable to upgrade existing or planned projects in such a way that actual emissions of greenhouse gases of the project are below respective baseline emissions. Rules and guidelines for determining these baseline emissions should be finalised by 2000. The difference between baseline emissions and actual emission levels constitute marketable emission credits. The extra revenues obtained by selling these credits will improve the project-related cash flow.

2.3.2.3 Equity analysis and investment banking

To a large extent, the assessment of equities is based on the expected cash flow of the company considered. Since climate policy is very much about energy production and consumption, future climate policy regulations will especially affect companies operating in energy markets. For this reason, cash flow analysis of energy companies should take into account the company's future exposure to climate policy regulations and its ability to adopt cost-efficient or value-creating response strategies. These strategies include effective and efficient capturing of the opportunities provided by the Kyoto Mechanisms as well as intra-firm trading schemes for greenhouse gas emissions undertaken, for example, by European oil companies.

2.3.2.4 Emissions trading and brokerage

The market for emission credits will be organised as over-the-counter trading and/or trading on regulated exchanges. Although some companies requiring or supplying emission credits will establish internal brokerage services within their own group, there are market opportunities for financial institutions. Investment banks already active in commodities and securities trading could expand their services towards trading and brokerage of emission credits and emissions permits.

2.3.2.5 Carbon reduction investment funds

More than other investments, JI/CDM investments are associated with various risks, including technological, economic and political risks. One strategy to mitigate such risks is diversification, which may be achieved by investing in JI/CDM investment funds. In addition, the transaction costs can be lower compared to stand-alone JI/CDM investments—especially for investors seeking smaller investments. Banks would set up and manage the investment fund and invest globally into several different JI/CDM projects. One of the main challenges in managing such funds is the selection of efficient JI/CDM portfolios, which is based on the analysis of risk correlation between different projects. Investors are invited to put their capital into a fund while the bank designs the fund according to the needs of its clients. Subsequently, investors share—according to their individual investment quota—the total amount of emission credits generated by the portfolio of different JI/CDM projects. Instead of distributing the emission credits among the investors, the fund could also sell the emission credits on national or international markets and distribute the cash returns to the investors.

2.3.3 Remaining challenges

Although some principles of the Kyoto Mechanisms are defined in the Kyoto Protocol, the operational procedures and guidelines are still under development. From a business perspective, the most important challenges in this context are:

- **Transaction costs.** It is crucial to keep the transaction costs of the Kyoto Mechanisms low, otherwise the economic attractiveness of these instruments will be very limited. Therefore the operational rules and procedures should be as simple as possible.

- **Wide price range.** Currently, estimates on future world market prices for a ton of CO_2 equivalents varies very widely. Companies that enter the market today should therefore assess the economic feasibility of transactions very carefully.

2.4 Conclusion

To sum up, we regard sustainable development as a fundamental aspect of sound business management, and we believe that UBS's environmental commitment strengthens its competitive edge: by identifying environmentally related risks in investment banking, UBS is able to take systematic steps to consider these risks. At the same time, UBS also takes advantage of environmental opportunities in asset management. But the integration of environmental aspects is an ongoing learning process; in the future, the

Kyoto Protocol may change existing businesses and may lead to new business opportunities. Financial institutions entering this emerging market early may be able to create new competitive advantages. UBS is therefore currently working on establishing these factors in a more concrete form within its normal banking activities.

A GREEN PACKAGE TO PROMOTE ENVIRONMENTAL MANAGEMENT SYSTEMS AMONG SMEs

Davide Dal Maso
Avanzi, Italy

Carlo Marini and Paola Perin
UniCredito Italiano

UniCredito Italiano (UCI) is the name of the financial group formed in 1998 by the merger of five Italian banks (Credito Italiano, Rolo Banca 1473, CariVerona Banca, Cassa di Risparmio di Torino and Cassamarca), which took over CariTRo and CRTrieste in 1999. UCI operates throughout Italy via a network of 3,600 branches with a total of 60,000 employees. According to available estimates, in 1999 UCI showed the highest commercial profits in Italy of all financial groups and the fourth highest in Europe. It is one of the 15 largest European banks. UCI's market share in Italy is around 12%.

The environment as an issue became prominent in UCI due to an internal study on the potential market for green financial products. The work was subsequently delivered to some of UCI's managers, who found in it valuable elements and this prompted internal discussions. Some two years later UCI invited Avanzi, a Milan-based institute that had run theoretical studies on the same subject, to devise a research project with the aim of constructing a comprehensive framework of the environmental aspects of banking according to an Italian perspective. UCI contacted UNEP (United Nations Environment Programme) Financial Services Initiatives and was asked to join the group of signatories of the UNEP statement on banks and sustainable development; it was signed by chairman Lucio Rondelli in May 1998. UCI subsequently initiated a number of valuable contacts with foreign colleagues.

Some weeks later, an international conference was held in Milan, in co-operation with UNEP and Avanzi and under the auspices of the Italian Minister of the Environment and the EC. The conference updated the Italian financial community on the risks and opportunities linked to environmental variables, highlighting out both the direct and the indirect liabilities of banks. UCI and the Italian Minister of the Environment signed a Memorandum of Understanding in March 2000.

3.1 The launch of 'Project Environment'

After this first, theoretical, phase, Alessandro Profumo, UniCredito Italiano's CEO, instructed the Corporate Division to develop the research further through more focused studies, also oriented towards the commercial development of the environmental angle, especially in relation to the SME (small and medium-sized enterprise) market.

3.1.1 The analysis phase

The first step was dubbed the 'analysis phase', the aim of which was to define an action framework with relevance to the Italian context. The initial undertaking was to identify the factors that had determined the evolution of foreign banks' policies and strategies, emphasising what had succeeded and what had not. Surprisingly, a wide range of different approaches is in evidence (bottom-up versus top-down; an emphasis on external or internal dimensions; a focus on the lender's liability; green products; 'good housekeeping'). These elements were considered in relation to the Italian context and UCI's culture and strategies. This benchmarking project was completed with two case studies on banks which, according to size and certain other characteristics, such as markets and organisational structure, bear comparison to UCI.

As a consequence, efforts to translate the bank's environmental policy into practical objectives concentrated on the business sector that has always been a strong point for UCI: SMEs. A sample of five industrial sectors[1] was selected, in an attempt to cover all the different variables that characterise the Italian SMEs market. The following criteria were considered for each sector:

- Macroeconomic features
- Market trends
- Environmental aspects linked to sector-specific legislation and specific processes
- Potential business areas for the bank

The research was based on a review of current literature and direct interviews with stakeholders.[2] This process led to the first set of results, which was to form the basis for UCI's commercial strategy:

- Certification of environmental management systems (EMSs) for SMEs is an objective that the bank wishes to support, although it is likely to remain a niche phenomenon in the near term. In fact, certified companies represent an attractive market, since certification is indicative of a proactive approach and a long-term view. These companies are better equipped to cope with environmental risks and opportunities and therefore are more likely to prevail over competitors.

1 The sectors studied were: chemicals, textiles, tanneries, ceramics and downstream petrochemicals.
2 More specifically, for each sector those interviewed consisted of a representative of the organisation (usually the officer in charge of environmental affairs) and a neutral expert.

- On the other hand, the cost of the certification procedure is not especially high and, also, these environmentally proactive companies are usually financially quite strong. Hence, the interest rate is not enough, alone, to make a green loan attractive and to differentiate UCI. Rather, companies seem to be more interested in a range of services—including those not normally associated with banks—which might offer a consistent answer to a number of interconnected problems.

- Finally, and this is probably the area of largest potential interest for the bank, the research indicated that the certification process often generates a need for further investment (e.g. technology upgrading to improve environmental performance).

In the meantime, UCI was invited by the Polytechnic University of Milan to join the 'Eco-efficiency Club', a group of large industrial companies whose aim is to promote the diffusion of modern techniques for proactive management of environmental issues. This offer was taken up immediately, as it provided an opportunity to get in touch with key actors and therefore to better understand the dynamics of the market as regards environmental issues. Besides, UCI was aware that large companies can play a critical role in the diffusion of a green culture. In fact, as was the case with the certification of quality assurance systems, large companies that operate at the top of a value chain can push their suppliers to adopt policies and strategies consistent with their own. In other words, what large companies want becomes a selection criterion. On the other hand, client companies tend to be more in favour of an incremental approach rather than imposing rigorous conditions.

Studies of SMEs showed that one of the reasons why they are hesitant about environmental certification is the lack of market stimulus. In simple terms, SMEs do not certify their management systems (which, in some cases, are already in place without being formalised) because nobody asks them to. At this point, UCI made closer contact with some of the members of the Eco-efficiency Club, with the aim of:

- Improving its knowledge of environmental problems along the value chain

- Understanding the decision-making process that favoured the adoption of proactive environmental policies

- Identifying to what extent the diffusion of certified EMSs among the supplier system was important for large companies

In this regard, direct interviews with environmental managers were undertaken and information was systemised into a consistent framework. In particular, four areas were investigated:

- Environmental policy

- Impacts along the product chain

- Environmental certification

- Relationships with suppliers

The focus of the survey was concentrated particularly on this last issue. Almost all of the respondent companies[3] showed a willingness to see a sound environmental approach extended to their suppliers. Most are not prepared to impose EMS certification as a condition of contract, but rather favour a smooth path towards eco-efficiency with eventual certification under ISO 14001 or EMAS (EU Eco-management and Audit Scheme) once the organisation is ready. The most widely held reason for this is the opinion that environmental culture should be disseminated by making SMEs understand the related advantages and opportunities—which of course takes time. The sudden introduction of a new model, it is generally agreed, might cause organisational and potentially also financial shock.

A further element highlighted by the interviews is that corporations are not interested in promoting the introduction of certified EMSs among *all* of their suppliers, but will focus on companies that are large enough to be able to offer a product/service mix that represents not only supply, but an integration with their clients' processes. In this perspective, some suppliers—the strategic ones—can be considered more as partners. The integration between client and supplier often also involves design and production phases, so that environmental responsibility is clearly broadened.

A final aspect that has been emphasised is the concern for possible consequences in cases where a supplier has been prosecuted for violation of environmental regulations: certified businesses, such as large client companies, can be considered responsible for the environmental integrity of their suppliers and can therefore suffer reputation damage if they are linked to them; in fact, EMS standards require sound environmental criteria in selecting suppliers. On the other hand, the damage could also be financial if heavy fines or closure forced a supplier to cease operating.

All in all, the outcome of the research was quite encouraging, in that, although levels of emphasis varied, a significant share of large companies are in favour of the progressive introduction of EMS certification as a criterion for selecting suppliers—at least the larger, strategic ones.

3.1.1.1 Some conclusions

The conclusion of the analysis on SMEs was that the factors that determine the importance of the environment among the priorities of companies' strategies can be grouped into three categories:

- **Cultural.** This aspect has to do with the general attitude of the organisation towards environmental issues and, more specifically, with the sensitivity of individuals working in it. Many examples of environmental proactivity are linked to the personal values of managers or owners and their capabilities of disseminating them. The social context is very important (whether operating in a geographic region where environmental values are considered important or not), as are commercial relationships (for instance, contacts with clients or suppliers that operate in countries where the level of environmental responsibility is higher). In general, cultural aspects are the most difficult to quantify.

3 The panel included some of the major Italian multinational corporations such as Fiat Auto, ABB, Ciba, IBM and Telecom Italia.

- **Administrative.** Environmental risks and opportunities are often overlooked by companies because accountability is not transparent regarding these variables. SMEs' management systems are not sophisticated enough to enable their users to identify how much the company is losing or earning as a result of its approach to environmental matters. The environment will not be an issue for a company as long as there is no reliable translation into financial terms.

- **Financial.** Contrary to expectations, financial considerations are not viewed as a major barrier to the implementation of environmental strategies: managers generally feel that, as long as the investment is likely to pay back within a reasonable time-frame, it is worth undertaking, even if extra borrowing is required. On the other hand, the possibility of having access to a specifically designed financial product may be the factor that starts the decision-making process.

In addition, a more proactive environmental policy helps small companies to anticipate legislation that is becoming increasingly strict; to gain from the opportunities of a market that is increasingly environmentally aware and selective; and to reduce diseconomies related to environmental operating costs and investments.

In sum, the diffusion of EMSs can be considered a difficult but nonetheless achievable target. To succeed, there is a definite requirement for training—for owners, managers, employees, public authorities and the financial community. Companies will start to realise that costs linked to improved environmental management will lead to an economic return that is in the long run higher than the investment. Banks and insurance companies are slowly introducing the environmental variable into their assessment procedures, rewarding eco-efficiency and risk reduction.

From the bank's point of view, the objective is to introduce eco-efficiency into the criteria it uses:

- To assess credit risk
- To define the spread to be applied on loan rates
- To orient the strategies of portfolio mix in investment products

In other words, EMSs may become indicators of the extent to which companies have achieved a real improvement in environmental performance and reduced their risk. Unfortunately, incentives from public authorities are still quite weak and companies cannot gain any real advantage as regards permits, controls or other forms of regulatory incentive.

3.2 Operation 'EMS Certification'

At the end of analysis phase, the various information that had been collected began to form a complete picture: on the one hand, large companies showed interest in grading their strategic suppliers according to environmental performance; on the other hand, SMEs made requests (not always clearly expressed) for capital to support the investment necessary to reach EMS certification or to improve environmental performance. The elements of this relationship can be seen in Figure 3.1, where each step is numbered in order. A breakdown of the process according to the various actors is shown in Table 3.1.

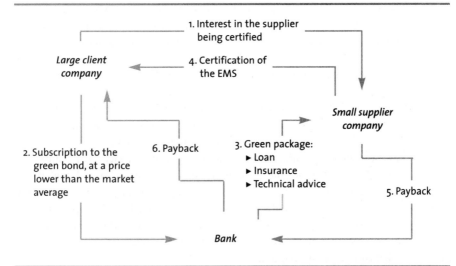

Figure 3.1 **The relationship between SME suppliers, large clients and the bank in 'Operation EMS Certification'**

Actors	Interests	'Price'	Expected advantages
Large companies	Qualify the strategic suppliers	Financial investment pays a little lower than usual	More reliable supplier system
Small companies	Consistent organisation of the EMS	Organisational and financial effort	Closer relationships with their business clients
Bank	Facilitate financial flow of finance	Lower spread on transaction	Satisfy large and small clients; acquire new clients; improve image

Table 3.1 **Actors and interests in 'Operation EMS Certification'**

Based on these findings, UCI Corporate Division undertook to design a specific product targeted at SMEs, called 'Formula A'.[3] It is primarily a 'green package' composed of three elements. The first is a specific loan, used to pay for the certification process, with a special rate (Euribor + 0.50), lower than the market average. As previous research demonstrated that the financial aspect alone was not the core of the problem, UCI attempted to augment the product with related services that could make it more attractive. The bank thus oriented itself as a 'solutions' provider. The second element comprises technical advice on the practical implementation of an EMS. In fact, for this, external contributions may be necessary in order to draw together the requisite expertise in the specific industrial process related to the company in question, along with experience in both organisational and environmental matters. UCI agreed a contract with a large qualified consulting firm with a double aim: first, to lower the price of consultancy (in fact, the prospect of a sizeable new market—acquired at next to no cost—was enough to convince the consultancy to reduce its fees); second, since choosing the right consultancy firm is not always easy, by selecting an appropriate professional partner in advance UCI was assisting its clients with an often fraught problem.

The third element is the offer of an insurance package. In fact, civil liability for environmental damage is among the most serious threats to companies. Although Italian legislation on liability is not fully consistent or stringent, managers are nonetheless beginning to show concern about the possibilities of large penalties. The opportunity to cover this risk is therefore perceived as an important plus within the green package. A further incentive is that those companies that achieve certification are granted a significant discount on their premiums.

In order to raise the money needed to kick-start the operation, UCI plans to issue a bond targeted at large companies or institutional investors. The goal is to create a 'virtuous circle', in which subscribers are the driving force in pushing their suppliers toward environmental certification. This bond pays an interest rate slightly below the Euribor (Euribor − 0.375). Money earned through subscription to this green bond will form a fund that is at the disposal of eligible SMEs—i.e. those that are suppliers of multinationals (the subscribers)—at a particularly favourable rate (Euribor + 0.125) and granted solely on the basis of an intention to initiate a certification process.

3.3 Future developments

UCI believes that the grant awarded for EMS implementation can be an effective commercial lever. Because of this, UCI advisers (who are in all the bank's branches) have been informed and trained both on the technical characteristics of the Formula A package and on the background environmental issues. In other words, the EMS is expected to lead to improved environmental awareness and therefore to push SMEs to undertake further action which will in turn generate further financial requirements: for instance, improv-

---

4 'A' for *ambiente*, Italian for 'environment'.

ing the technology in plants, equipment and machinery, or increasing research, training and other organisational aspects.

In this respect, Formula A is expected to become a sort of trademark that will characterise a line of financial services, each of which addresses a specific demand. The areas in which UCI intends to invest primarily are:

- **Extending the scope of the green package to cover all environmental investments, not just EMS certification.** More specifically, UCI is willing to rapidly adapt the characteristics of the product to the needs that often arise suddenly when new legislation is introduced. (An example is the recent implementation of the Seveso 2 directive, which will require SMEs to undertake significant investments, and the Integrated Pollution Prevention and Control [IPPC] Directive.)

- **Creating a customised solution for specific sectors.** The design of Formula A is based on the results of the study of different industrial sectors. The product is intended to be applicable across a wide spectrum, and a balance has been struck between the specific needs of certain sectors and the danger of expending too much time and energy in diversifying the product. In the future, as long as Formula A's continued success justifies it, a higher level of customisation will be pursued in order to meet the requirements of specific targets.

- **Advising customers on public funds.** UCI has established a specialised office which regularly monitors the most important sources of public aid funding environmental expenditure—Europe-wide, national and regional.

- **Promoting the project finance mechanism** for environmental investment, undertaken both by private companies and government.

- **EMAS.** UCI has started the procedure to join EMAS, and is confident of receiving certification, by the middle of 2001, for its own site in Milan. It would be the first Italian bank to achieve this.

- **Issuing a comprehensive environmental and social balance sheet**, which will be presented to the General Annual Assembly in May 2001.

However, the most challenging objective for UCI Corporate Division is to develop a business area linked to environmental drivers based on an innovative marketing tool, i.e. the Internet; to this end a website ('Greenlab')[5] has been running since February 2000. Initially, it contained only a description of UCI's environmental policy and of the Formula A mechanism, but the target was to enlarge the site and to make it a gateway to a number of services provided by UCI itself or by its partners. Now this gateway covers a wide range of subjects, addressing both environmental and health and safety issues. Through a dynamic and interactive approach, it offers updated information and innovative services about policies and strategies, certification procedures, clean technologies, ecodesign, etc. There will be various types of service available to Greenlab's users: a

5 www.greenlab.it

database of legislation and technology, expert advice, distance training, market information, etc. The gateway, which is still work-in-progress, is intended to grow to become a standard reference source for SMEs.

3.4 Conclusions: a new role for the bank

The mechanism described in Figure 1 highlights an interesting pattern, the elements of which are:

- The environmental impact of an industrial sector has to be seen no longer as a problem of a *single* company, but more and more as a problem of the *system*.

- If, as in the recent past, a company might be considered proactive as long as it took care of its own impact, now proactivity means taking care of the impact of the system in which it operates; large companies are becoming aware that their environmental responsibility does not end at the factory gates, but extends along the supply chain.

- If a single company is *a part* of the problem, then site-related environmental management tools, such as EMAS or the ISO 14000 series, have to be considered as *a part* of the solution, in the sense that they are effective as long as they are applied as part of a logical systemic approach.

- This new approach entails the involvement of a larger number of stakeholders—such as financial institutions—which used to consider themselves as neutral. The consequence is that environmental awareness and responsibility is devolved throughout society as a whole.

In other words, the economic system and, more generally, society as a whole, may begin to be perceived more as a wide net, within which all actors are linked to each other and share—along stronger or weaker lines—various interests. Although some of the connections are more important than others, the stimulus that kick-starts a change process will not necessarily always be from these areas. In the context of the subject of this chapter, for example, the bank is not the leading actor: in fact, the environmental issue under review is the concern particularly of industrial companies (since they are the source of the most significant direct impact) and governments (as regulators). Nevertheless, banks, although more marginally involved, have an interest in seeing the market develop harmoniously and therefore may wish to play a promotion and innovation role. The green SMEs package is an example of how a third party can initiate a virtuous circle that has positive effects for the whole system: companies improve their environmental performance; society benefits from this; and the bank creates added value.

This experiment, the results of which are yet to be the subject of comprehensive assessment, afforded UCI the opportunity of doing business in a new way: the view of the bank as a 'neutral' actor has now been superseded. The growth of the industrial system is a condition for the survival of the bank itself and hence it has a strong interest in this occurring in an optimum manner, according to socially shared values and according to a sustainability perspective. Continuity, an essential element of every sound business, cannot be pursued without a long-term view, which must take the environment into consideration.

In addition, UCI believes that the whole financial community should be aware of its role and looks forward to seeing other institutions follow suit. Of course, the first mover gains a competitive advantage, but in this particular field it is not necessarily so beneficial to move alone. The industrial sector must be aware that the attention paid to its environmental performance is not motivated by the unilateral policy of one bank, but is the answer to a real need for financial operators to limit the risk of their business.

UCI, along with other Italian banks, is studying the possibility of introducing the assessment of some environmental aspects into its mainstream credit procedures. If it were to do this alone, its client base would simply switch banks; but, if a critical number of major banks were to realise that it is in their own interests to select clients according to an environmental quality ranking, the whole industrial system would probably be stimulated to move a significant step forward.

SUSTAINABLE BANKING AND THE ASN BANK

Michel Negenman
ASN Bank, Netherlands

The Algemene Spaarbank voor Nederland NV (ASN Bank) is one of the first 'ethical' banks in Europe. It is a company that has charged itself with a mission, and that mission is 'a better world'. We believe this calls for a society in which sustainability is the key objective. For ASN Bank, the label 'ethical banking' is visualised in our mission statement, from which the following is an excerpt:

> Enhancing the sustainability of society is ASN Bank's key objective and leading principle in all its economic activities. Enhancing the sustainability of society means contributing to changes that aim at ending processes in which the adverse effects are pushed to the future, or passed on to the environment, nature or poorer sections of the community. Economic activity means recognising that a return has to be made in order to secure a healthy future for ASN Bank over the long term and also recognising the necessity of managing the funds entrusted to ASN Bank in a manner that justifies our clients' expectations in this respect.

As an autonomous subsidiary of the Dutch SNS Reaal Group, our business approach is what we call 'community banking', by which we mean that not only society in general but also the local communities in which SNS Reaal Group has its branches should benefit from our presence. In our day-to-day business, 'ethical banking' has been translated into a clear set of guidelines, in which sustainability is the key issue. With reference to these guidelines, we consider ourselves to be a specialised 'ethical' bank and a niche player. As a fully licensed savings bank, our balance sheet total equals about €1 billion and we have funds under management of about €300 million (at the end of 1999). ASN Bank has 50 employees and one office, situated in The Hague, Netherlands. In our view, ethical banking is the practical translation of caring for our environment.

In this chapter I begin with a brief description of the history of the ASN Bank, followed by a more specific look on how we try to achieve our goals, starting with the ethical assessment process we have developed. In the subsequent section I describe some of our specific products and I conclude the chapter by considering the role that ASN Bank has played and still plays in stimulating the development of sustainable banking among the (Dutch) banking sector.

4.1 A brief history of ASN Bank

ASN Bank was founded in 1960 by the Nederlands Verbond van Vakverenigingen (trade unions) and the Centrale Levensverzekeringsbank (insurance company for labourers). Both invested a mere 1,000 guilders (approximately €450) at the time. Their aim was to draw together a significant portion of the cash flow of the labourers, their organisations and related groups in their own financial institution in order to earn money that would benefit them directly. The labour movement already had its own insurance company at this time (de Centrale), but no bank. One of the arguments in establishing the ASN Bank was that one cannot reform society without sufficient influence in the world of finance.

ASN Bank began in 1960 with 5,312 accounts with savings totalling 2.4 million guilders (approximately €1.2 million). In 25 years the number of accounts grew to 75,472 with savings totalling 419 million guilders (€190 million); in 1992 it reached one billion guilders (€453 million). At the end of 1999, the number of accounts totals 150,000 with savings totalling €1 billion and €300 million in funds under management.

4.2 Ethical assessment

In our investment portfolio we look for projects and companies that either reduce the negative effects of economic activities or, better still, contribute actively to a more sustainable economy. When assessing new projects either for ASN's portfolio or for those funds under our management, our most important asset is a clear set of criteria that we have developed to determine whether a project fits. The most relevant of these are:

- Companies should have an active and comprehensive environmental policy. This policy is measured by our analysts, on the basis of concrete environmental aspects such as energy use and the nature of raw materials and end products.

- Companies should implement concrete measures to ensure humanitarian working conditions. These measures should include an equal opportunities policy and, if applicable, a contribution to improved human rights in those countries where human rights are most under threat.

- Some sectors are explicitly excluded from our portfolio— specifically: the arms industry, the nuclear energy generation and distribution industry, and companies involved in genetic modification. Companies that produce exclusively tobacco products or alcoholic drinks are also generally discriminated against; the same applies to companies that operate exclusively in the gambling industry, those that make large-scale use of animal testing in developing their products, those that are active in factory farming, and those that do not operate an equal opportunities policy, discriminating against women and minority groups, or denying employment opportunities or training for disabled people, or allowing unacceptable working conditions.

ASN Bank puts significant emphasis on the assessment of a company's track record and its policies on the above criteria. This assessment remains an ongoing activity for as long as a company is in our investment portfolio. Our ethical researchers visit companies on-site, and a company's management is required to answer a questionnaire regarding our criteria. This research forms the basis for the investment portfolio both for the bank and for its funds under management. When we began these ethical research activities in 1993, we were one of the worldwide pioneers of this approach. Today we still are among the leading financial institutions in this field.

The bank is now gradually expanding its traditional portfolio based on its ethical research guidelines. Green investments and other projects have thus been added to our traditional portfolio. The portfolio now consists not only of loans for public housing and to cultural institutions and development banks, but also includes, for example, wind turbines, and a company that has developed low-energy cooling technology, based on the Stirling motor—in this company the investment consisted of a mix from ASN Bank and ASN Aandelenfonds.

4.3 Our (speciality) products

ASN Sparen and ASN Milieusparen both offer savings accounts without any restrictions: savers can withdraw money at any time. These accounts are invested—especially in the case of the latter, environmentally friendly, option—according to ASN Bank's sustainability investment criteria. ASN Werknemerssparen (company saving regulation accounts) offer employers and employees the chance of investing money in accordance with the Dutch company saving regulation in a sustainable portfolio. ASN Depositosparen (deposit accounts) allow savers to deposit an amount for a specified number of years for a specified rate. These funds are also invested in accordance with the ASN Bank's sustainability investment criteria.

The ASN Aandelenfonds is an open-ended investment institution for publicly listed and private companies. Our ethical criteria have been implemented successfully with regard to this fund, which was launched alongside the introduction of the ethical assessment criteria. At the end of 1999, the ASN Aandelenfonds holds investments worth €200 million for 60 companies, spread all over the world.

Stimulated by the success of the ASN Aandelenfonds, ASN developed a unique and innovative index for publicly listed companies, based on its ethical criteria. This index, the ASN–Trouw Index, compares the performance of a traditional investment portfolio with a portfolio that meets our ethical criteria. With this, we expect to show that the companies in that index will perform better than those in the traditional index. The main reason is that, if sustainability is part of corporate policy, it avoids major and inefficient investments in the future. In addition, we believe that these companies create extra earning capacity by being better tuned to society's future requirements. The ASN–Trouw Index is weekly published in *Trouw*, one of the Netherlands' largest newspapers.

Another example of our investment strategy is the *ASN–Novib Fund*, which was developed in co-operation with the Dutch developmental organisation, Novib. The aim of this fund is to finance small-scale enterprises and projects in developing countries. In the assessment of projects for this fund, our ethical criteria are also applicable, although the criteria have been adapted to the particular context of the fund.

ASN Bank was one of the pioneers and designers of the current tax exemption rule for green investments in the Netherlands (the Green Fund System). Most of our efforts in green financing focus on our own green fund, the *ASN Groenprojectenfonds*. This fund (€80 million at the end of 1999) has financed a number of pilot projects, including a substantial number of wind turbines and a project for recycling grit that has been used on roofs or for railways. More recently, a biogas project was financed that recovers natural gas from the recycling of sludge from paper mills.

As a joint venture between ASN Bank and the ASN green fund, we have developed the 'Green Mortgage', which offers private home-owners a substantial discount on their interest rate, which enables buyers to overcome the price difference between traditional housing and housing built according to sustainability principles. Also, the first sustainable building project to be undertaken by a housing corporation was facilitated by ASN Bank. By introducing the Green Mortgage with widespread publicity, we have increased public awareness of sustainable building and energy efficiency.

The *Wereldpartnerpolis* (insurance policy) offers an opportunity to invest in a sustainable portfolio, combined with donations to projects in third-world countries, via Novib. Of the savings, 50% is invested in companies with a proactive environmental and human rights record, and who have a strong social policy; the other 50% is invested in bonds such as loans to the health sector, the education sector, etc. The *Wereldpartnerpolis* is aimed particularly at improving conditions in developing countries. The *Spaarbewustpolis* (also insurance) offers a similar 50:50 split, but the motive behind this fund is primarily environmental.

ASN offers savers an interest rate based on the market average, which means they can contribute to a more sustainable society without paying a premium for that support. Savers have a number of options on where their money is invested: it can go exclusively to environmental projects, which is a popular option; to a selected group of non-profit organisations such as Pax Christi and Greenpeace; or to organisations that are active in the field of sustainability, especially those that promote and implement the concept on a day-to-day basis.

4.4 The role of ASN Bank in a sustainable banking sector

The reason for citing examples of ASN products is to emphasise the basis of successful green financing: creative product development at a practical level, and persistent government lobbying, a substantial part of which, in the Netherlands, has been by ASN. Our role in this field is based on three key premises:

- Demonstrating the commercial viability of a banking institution governed by ethical investment principles

- Setting examples of innovative financing of sustainable projects and companies

- Generating the support of an growing number of clients

Our role in the financing of environmental projects, or 'green financing', is of course directly related to our ethical investment principles. 'Green financing' has become a recognised concept in the Netherlands; it attracts state-of-the-art scientific research and development, as well as government subsidies and specialised investment funds. Financial institutions play an important role in this infrastructure. Within this framework, the role of a specialised and dedicated bank such as ASN has proven to be crucial.

ASN has put substantial efforts into removing formal and practical obstacles and bringing these projects onto the market. The green tax exemption in the Netherlands has been particularly successful. Currently, almost €1.5 billion has been invested in green projects in the Netherlands and all major Dutch financial institutions now have their own dedicated instruments for green financing. As it stands, financiers are proactively seeking green projects that meet the criteria of their funds.

4.5 The role of ASN Bank in the future

A significant problem is that there are currently not enough suitable environmental projects in the Netherlands. Part of the issue is that, due to formal regulation, green money can only be used in projects with very low investment risk, which means that a vast number of interesting and innovative projects are simply not eligible. It is my view that green funds should be combined with other finance instruments, which could range from regular business financing and project financing to more investment-like instruments such as venture capital. In doing this, the financial sector could encourage new green technologies and products, and also provide a workable outlet for the growing supply of green capital. Some of the major Dutch financial institutions and energy utilities have suggested loosening the eligibility criteria for green projects. This would certainly allow a greater flow of finance, but it would also mean that green funds would invest in projects that do not really qualify for the interest discount from the green tax exemption. In my view this option primarily serves commercial objectives and does not stimulate the innovative green projects that we need to create a more sustainable economy. Combining green funds with other financial instruments, on the other hand, will definitely create new opportunities for innovative sustainable projects.

Our business has been primarily in the Netherlands, with the exception of the ASN–Novib Fund. However, I can see two ways of ASN contributing to international developments. First, we will be glad to share our knowledge and experience in ethical banking and green financing with financial institutions abroad. National differences notwithstanding, it is my opinion that our experience would be beneficial in developing and implementing green financing strategies. Second, and more importantly, we could act as a catalyst for other organisations. It is my belief that organisations should include the sustainability principle in their mission statements, in their strategies and in their day-to-day operations. Only then will they truly contribute to a more sustainable economy.

ASSESSING THE SUSTAINABILITY OF BANK SERVICE CHANNELS
The case of The Co-operative Bank

Penny Street and Philip E. Monaghan*

National Centre for Business and Sustainability, Manchester, UK

As in many business sectors, the more forward-thinking banks and financial service providers are currently looking at the need for, and possible ways of addressing, sustainable development. In some cases, the attempt to deal with sustainability has been little more than a bolt-on to normal operations. However, there have been some clear attempts to address the environmental and social agenda in a more integrated and holistic way. The National Centre for Business and Sustainability (NCBS) has been working with The Co-operative Bank (henceforth referred to as the Bank) on an innovative project to assess the ecological and social impacts of the way in which the Bank delivers its services, and to develop indicators to monitor those impacts. The Bank is recognised as a trailblazer in corporate reporting of ecological and social responsibility. The NCBS project makes a major contribution to the way in which ecological and social sustainability is assessed and reported, and plays a key role in assisting the Bank in its move towards sustainability.

This chapter starts with a brief outline of the Bank's 'partnership' approach, as a way of setting the context for the NCBS project. It goes on to look at the way in which the Bank delivers its products and services (its 'service channels'). The potential ecological and social impacts of those service channels, and the development by the NCBS of a set of indicators that can be used to inform Bank decision-makers and improve sustainability, are then presented. The chapter ends with some general comments on the implications of this project for sustainable banking.

5.1 The Co-operative Bank partnership approach

The Co-operative Bank was founded in 1872 to serve the UK co-operative movement. The Bank now enjoys a 3% share of the UK banking market, is the largest Gold Card issuer in

---

*   Philip Monaghan is now with WSP Environmental Ltd.

Europe with the biggest stand-alone Internet banking service in the UK, and employs over 4,000 people.

Founded on co-operative principles, the Bank's approach to business is reflected in its Mission Statement, drawn up in 1988. But it was really in the 1990s that the Bank started to take on board the key challenges of sustainability, and put in motion a series of initiatives that have served to bring it to the forefront of best practice in ecological and social performance. 1992 saw the launch of the Bank's Ethical Policy, followed in 1996 by its Ecological Mission Statement. In 1997 the Bank consolidated its approach to social and environmental issues through the launch of its partnership approach. The basis of this approach is a commitment to serving the interests not just of shareholders or customers, but of everyone involved in the Bank's activities. Having identified seven partner groups—shareholders, customers, staff and their families, suppliers, local communities, national and international society, and past and future generations of co-operators—the Bank went on to find ways of measuring performance in delivering value to each group, and to assess whether such value was being delivered in a socially responsible and ecologically sustainable manner (Co-operative Bank 1998).[1]

The Bank's independently verified *Partnership Report 1997* (Co-operative Bank 1998) identified key indicators for assessing delivery of value and social and ecological performance, and set 68 targets for improving the way the Bank's operations are carried out. The partnership approach and report has put the Bank at the forefront of sustainable banking, both in terms of assessing bank activities and operations in an ecological and social context, and in subsequently reporting and using that information.

The partnership approach continues to form the basis of the Bank's unique approach to sustainability. Having assessed the direct environmental and social impacts of its operations (NCBE 1999), the Bank is now committed to looking at the 'secondary impacts' of its activities—that is, the way in which its activities influence its partners' behaviour, and the social and environmental impacts that arise from that. There are two components of those secondary impacts: the social and environmental impacts arising from the way in which the Bank delivers its products and services; and the impacts arising from the Bank's products and services themselves.

This chapter focuses on the first of these—the work undertaken by the NCBS to assess the environmental and social impacts of the Bank's service channels.

5.2 Background to the service channel project

There was a time when the only way to deal with a bank was through a local branch. However, as in many sectors of society, the financial services sector has embraced the opportunities provided by developments in information technology. This has allowed customers to access bank products and services in a variety of new ways, and has opened up new service channels such as automated teller machines (ATMs), telephone banking

---

1 'Value' is defined by the partner, not the Bank. More details of the Bank's partners and the partnership approach can be found in Co-operative Bank 1997.

and, most recently, Internet banking. But have these new service channels benefited customers? And what are the wider impacts of these changes in terms of their effect on ecological sustainability and corporate social responsibility?

In early 1999, the UK National Centre for Business and Sustainability (NCBS) carried out a project to look at these issues (NCBS 1999). The project was designed to show how each of the 'channels' the Bank uses to deliver its services could affect its partners. Specifically, the project aimed to assess the ecological and social impacts of the service channels, and to develop a set of indicators that would help the Bank optimise their development and operation and increase their sustainability.

5.3 The Bank's service channels

The Co-operative Bank offers its services through a number of different channels. Customers can choose from a number of channels when carrying out a transaction or communicating with the Bank on a particular issue, although not all services or transactions are available through all channels.

Broadly speaking, there are three main types of channel:

- **Physical channels**—where services are delivered at or through a particular physical location. These may be staffed (such as bank branches or Bankpoint shops, Financial Service Centres, Handybanks or post offices), or unstaffed (e.g. kiosks and ATMs or cashpoints).

- **Remote channels**—where the Bank's services are offered at a distance, such as telephone banking, use of the postal system to make deposits or issue instructions, or PC banking. A transaction using a remote channel ultimately requires a member of Bank staff to take action, although the customer may not actually deal with a person.

- **Virtual channels**—where a customer can access a service directly, at a distance, without input from bank staff. Virtual channels include Internet banking and TV banking.

In order to assess the ecological and social impacts of different service channels, it was necessary to define clearly the activities and infrastructure associated with each individual channel. This was not straightforward, as there is a certain amount of overlap and interaction between the service channels. Despite this, for the purposes of the project a limited set of activities was defined for each channel. For example, the ecological impact associated with using the post office as a service channel were restricted to the way in which the customer uses that channel and the way the Bank receives information about the transaction, and did not include the impacts associated with the actual building.

Obviously, all the service channels are serviced to some extent by staff at regional and head offices, and supported by core infrastructure such as premises and information and communication technologies (ICT). As these are common to all channels, they were not included under the definition and assessment of the key features and impact of each channel. The key characteristics of each of the service channels are listed below. Unless otherwise stated, the figures refer to early 1999 when the project was carried out.

5.3.1 Characteristics of service channels

Bankpoints. This category of service channel covers both traditional bank branches and the newer Bankpoint shops. Bankpoints offer customers the opportunity to go to a physical building, with a staff presence, to carry out face-to-face transactions or to use other channels within the building. In this project, impacts of this channel are confined to the activities directly associated with using that building: the customer and staff travel, the running and maintenance of the building, and the use of paper in the Bankpoint.

The Bank currently has 65 branches and 45 Bankpoint shops. There are approximately 750 Bank employees working across the branch network. It is estimated that there were over 8 million customer visits to branches/Bankpoints (excluding ATM and depository users) in 1998.

Post Office Counters Ltd (POCL), Financial Service Centres (FSCs), Handybanks. Co-operative Bank customers can make deposits and withdrawals across post office counters, FSCs (outlets located within Co-op Retail Society stores) or Handybanks located within Co-op stores. For the purpose of this project, it is considered that transactions carried out at any of these locations comprise: a customer travelling to the PO/FSC/ Handybank for counter service, and using paper to carry out that transaction. Use of plastic cards over the counter is not included here, nor are the impacts associated with the building itself and staff travel.

Bank customers can use 15,500 post office counters in England and Wales, and around 1.5 million transactions were made through this channel in 1998. There are 240 Handybanks, which accounted for over 1 million transactions in 1998, and 10 FSCs which accounted for almost 0.5 million more transactions.

Kiosks. The Co-op Bank kiosks are stand-alone, 24-hour self-service banking outlets. Larger kiosks have an ATM, depository and telephone connection, whereas small kiosks only contain an ATM. The activities associated with using a kiosk depend on the service channels it contains. For the purposes of this study, the very limited set of activities associated with a kiosk was defined as the customer travel to that kiosk, and the use of a physical structure/small building which has a power supply and lighting. Other activities and their impacts are associated directly with the specific channel being used in the kiosk. The Bank has 38 kiosks which, in 1998, accounted for around 0.75 million transactions.

ATMs. These provide customers with the opportunity to carry out transactions automatically, without the presence of Bank staff. The Bank's ATMs are located in Bankpoint shops (59), kiosks (45), branches (43), or in a remote location (116). For the purposes of this project, a transaction associated with using an ATM does not include the customer travelling to that ATM, except in the case of remote ATMs. Travel associated with ATMs in Bankpoints or kiosks is considered in connection with the Bankpoint or kiosk.

The use of ATMs has shown strong growth in recent years, with over 80% of personal cash withdrawals now being made through ATMs. A 1996 survey by the Bank of personal customers indicated that younger, upmarket customers tend to make greater use of ATMs.

Post. A traditional but declining way in which the Bank delivers its service is by post. Activities associated with the use of this channel basically comprise the customer using and sending paper, the transport of that post, and staff at a central location processing that transaction.

Service centres. Service centres (call centres) provide a service channel through which customers can access the bank remotely, yet still have contact with staff at the other end of the telephone. For the purposes of this project, these activities mainly comprise: staff travel to the service centre, the running and maintenance of the building and equipment, the use of paper systems, and use of the telephone by the customer. (Travel to one of the Bank's phones—if that takes place—is included in consideration of the kiosk, Bankpoint, etc.)

There has been a significant growth in telephone banking, and The Co-operative Bank has the second-largest market share in this area, with five Service Centres employing approximately 2,000 staff. In 1997, Personal Customer Services (PCS) dealt with over 8 million calls and processed almost 2.5 million pieces of incoming paper, while Business Customer Services (BCS) handled around 800,000 calls and 400,000 pieces of paper in 1998.

IVR. The Interactive Voice Response (IVR) system is closely related to service centres. Customers can use this channel to carry out their transactions automatically over the telephone. In the context of this project, use of this channel involves very few activities—the customer has to use the telephone, but the transaction is then dealt with automatically.

PC banking. this is currently targeted at corporate and commercial customers, providing them with details of their account through a modem link to their PC. Activities associated with this channel focus on the downloading of information to the customer's PC by Bank staff, and use of that information by customers in their own offices or homes. Over 750 corporate customers currently use this channel.

Mobile phone banking, TV banking and Internet banking. These three service channels all operate as 'virtual' channels. For the purposes of this study, the same activities are involved in the use of any of the three: customer use of the appropriate ICT (phone, TV or PC plus network connections). No travel is involved (or, if it is, this is accounted for under the activities associated with the Bankpoint, the kiosk, or wherever Internet access is obtained). The Bank currently has about 23,000 Internet customers.

Plastic cards. Plastic cards are the 'critical enabler' for many of the above service channels. This project focuses on the use of Visa debit and credit cards, as these are used in ATMs and to support transactions over the counter. Activities associated with the use of the card basically involve the manufacture and use of that card, and the ICT network to process it. There are currently around 2.5 million Co-operative Bank Visa credit and debit cards in circulation.

5.4 Ecological and social impacts of service channels

There are a wide range of ecological and social impacts associated with the Bank's service channels. Ecological impacts can be attributed to different activities associated with the channels, such as the running and maintenance of a physical building, the IT infrastructure required to support transactions using a channel, or the activities of staff and customers. The social impacts derived from the Bank's service channels are in some ways more difficult to define. This is partly because, unlike the basic laws of nature which go some way to attracting consensus around issues of ecological sustainability, the array of issues relating to social responsibility shift in time and are not open to consensus.

The assessment of ecological and social impacts was carried out by way of:

- A detailed literature review

- Assessment against the Bank's Mission Statement and Ethical Policy

- Assessment against the Bank's Ecological Mission Statement (which is based on 'The Natural Step' (see Robèrt *et al.* 1997)[2]

- Consultation with relevant individuals

The NCBS's review identified 15 key areas of potential ecological and social impacts of the service channels. These are summarised in Table 5.1 and discussed below.

---

2 The Natural Step (TNS) is a tool to help organisations assess and improve the sustainability of their operations. The approach is based on the application of four principles or 'systems conditions' (SCs). TNS has become the foundation of The Co-operative Bank's Ecological Mission Statement, which commits the Bank to assessing its activities against the following four principles: (1) Nature cannot withstand a progressive build-up of waste derived from the Earth's crust; (2) Nature cannot withstand a progressive build-up of society's waste; (3) the productive area of Nature must not be diminished in quality (diversity) or quantity (volume) and must be enabled to grow; (4) society must utilise energy and resources in a sustainable, equitable and efficient manner. The principles correspond to those of the four system conditions, which are used as a way of assessing the ecological impact of the service channels.

Category of ecological or social impact	Description of key issues	Main impact against: Ecological Mission Statement (TNS System Conditions),* Mission Statement or Ethical Policy	Main service channels to which this applies (in terms of core activities)
The building/location	Building construction		▸ Bank branches ▸ Call centres ▸ Post office/kiosks/ATM
	▸ Use of stone, bricks, wood, building materials	SC 1, 3	
	▸ Use of PVC (windows), certain preservatives, chemicals/paints	SC 2 (1)	
	▸ Greenfield/brownfield site	SC 3	
	▸ Energy (during construction)	SC 1	
	▸ Waste (during construction)	SC 4	
	Building use		▸ Bank branches ▸ Call centres ▸ PO
	▸ Energy/energy efficiency	SC 1, 4	
	▸ Water	SC 4	
Electronics (computers/ telephones)	Manufacture/disposal		▸ Bank branches ▸ Call centres ▸ Kiosks/ATMs ▸ PC ▸ Internet/phone/TV
	▸ Raw materials and metal use in wires/components	SC 1 (3, 4)	
	▸ PVC cabling/plastic housing, chemicals for PC boards	SC 1, 2 (3, 4)	
	Energy in manufacture	SC 1	
	▸ Waste—in manufacture, and disposal/upgrading of equipment	SC 4, 2	
	Use		
	Energy/energy efficiency	SC 1, 4	
Paper use	▸ Use of wood pulp ▸ Clay minerals ▸ Energy in manufacture ▸ Chemicals/chlorine	SC 3 (1, 2)	▸ Bank branches ▸ Call centres ▸ Postal ▸ Kiosk/ATM ▸ Post office

* TNS: The Natural Step; SC: system condition; impacts were assessed against SCs 1–4 (see footnote 2, page 77)

Table 5.1 **Ecological and social impacts of The Co-operative Bank's service channels** (continued opposite)

Category of ecological or social impact	Description of key issues	Main impact against: Ecological Mission Statement (TNS System Conditions),* Mission Statement or Ethical Policy	Main service channels to which this applies (in terms of core activities)
Plastic cards	▸ Manufacture, use and disposal of PVC	SC 2 (1)	▸ Smart cards—kiosks, ATMs, bankpoints, etc.
Transport	*Vehicle and road construction*		▸ Bank branches ▸ Kiosk/ATM ▸ Call centre ▸ Post office
	▸ Minerals and metals for manufacture ▸ Loss of green space	SC 1, 3	
	Staff transport		
	▸ Energy use	SC 1, 2	
	Customer transport		
	▸ Energy use	SC 1, 2	
Financial inclusion		▸ Participation ▸ Trade and social investment	All
Convenience		▸ Quality and excellence ▸ Retentions (loyalty of customers)	All
Personal contact		▸ Participation	All
Security and rights of privacy		▸ Quality and excellence ▸ Integrity	All
Quality of service		▸ Quality and excellence	All
Job security		▸ Quality of life; Education and training	▸ All, but particularly bank branch
Working conditions		▸ Quality of life	All
Local economic development		▸ Quality of life ▸ Trade and social investment	▸ Bank branch ▸ Post office ▸ Call centre
Sound sourcing		▸ Freedom of association ▸ Human rights	▸ Business and customer service centres ▸ PC ▸ Internet
Joint business ventures		▸ Co-operation	▸ Financial service centre ▸ ATM

*TNS: The Natural Step; SC: system condition; impacts were assessed against SCs 1–4 (see footnote 2, page 77)

Table 5.1 (continued)

5.5 Selection of ecological and social indicators

Once the range of ecological and social impacts that could be associated with the Bank's service channels had been identified, the next stage of the NCBS project was to select a limited number of key indicators to reflect those potential impacts. According to the British government's Interdepartmental Working Group on Sustainable Development, indicators should 'simplify, quantify and communicate information' (DoE 1996). The working group noted some of the limitations of indicators, such as the facts that they rarely measure every impact, may not measure total impact, and tend to focus on issues that are readily quantifiable. However, provided these limitations are understood, indicators can be invaluable in helping understand impacts and trends over time.

After much research and deliberation, the NCBS proposed a set of 19 indicators which reflected the key ecological and social impacts of the service channels, and also covered aspects of delivering value to the Bank's partner groups. The indicators were selected to be easy and simple to use and interpret, to provide opinion-formers with a way of assessing past trends and possible future developments, and to enable comparison between service channels.

The 19 indicators were then put before a panel of independent advisors for comment. The advisors were drawn from a variety of backgrounds and included either recognised representatives of partners, or experts in the field of ecological sustainability and social responsibility more generally. The panel was asked to consider and comment on the NCBS's review of key ecological and social impacts of the Bank's service channels, and on the selection and justification of a set of indicators. The panel was not asked to comment on the Bank's actual performance, as this is yet to be determined.

On the basis of the panel's comments, the NCBS amended the selection and formulation of some of the indicators. A final set of 25 indicators was put forward, of which 19 were considered by the Bank to be high-priority; these form the basis of the project summary published in the Bank's *Partnership Report 1998* (Co-operative Bank 1999).

5.6 Summary of impacts and final set of indicators

The range of potential ecological and social impacts of the Bank's service channels is summarised below. Indicators are proposed for the majority of impacts although, in the context of the selection criteria (above), indicators were not selected to reflect all impacts identified.

5.6.1 Construction, maintenance and location of premises

The construction and maintenance of a building or smaller physical structure can have significant ecological impacts through, for example, the use of: natural and man-made building materials; preservatives, paints and chemicals; land; and energy for heating and lighting. Impacts from buildings and lesser structures are significant for those channels requiring a physical location. The indicator selected reflects materials used and also gives an indication of the area of land occupied by Bank premises that is no longer available to natural systems.

Indicator 1: Building floorspace and land occupied by premises (square metres)

5.6.2 Information and communication technologies (ICT)

The use of ICT (including telephones, computers, modems and the associated wiring) is an underlying feature of all the service channels. The ecological impacts of ICT are varied, but include those associated with the use of metals, PVC, chemicals and energy, and the generation and disposal of waste. The move away from personal face-to-face banking towards more electronic delivery channels would necessarily mean an increase in the volume of ICT. The indicator chosen accounts for both the volume of electronic equipment in use and the manner in which it is disposed of.

Indicator 2: Proportion of electronic equipment leaving the Bank to be re-used, repaired and recycled

5.6.3 Energy

All the Bank's service channels need energy to operate. Energy is used in the construction and maintenance of buildings, heating and lighting, manufacture and use of ICT, transport, etc. The major part of the UK energy supply comes from fossil fuels, the consumption of which contributes to global warming and acid rain. The indicators chosen measure both energy use and the proportion of that energy derived from renewable sources. Factors such as energy consumed by partners in their travel to use a particular channel will be added to the energy consumed directly by a given channel.

Indicator 3: Energy consumed (kilowatt-hours)

Indicator 4: Percentage of energy derived from renewable resources

5.6.4 Transport

Transport is used by the Bank's staff and customers to reach premises housing those service channels that require a physical presence, and in the movement of Bank paperwork between different locations. It is also an integral part of the Bank's postal service channel. The ecological impacts associated with transport—including at the very least the impacts of road construction, the manufacture and disposal of vehicles, and the use of energy to power them—are the focus of much public and political concern around the world. The indicators chosen to reflect these impacts relate to customer travel and the transport of paperwork.

Indicator 5: Emissions as a result of customers' travel (CO_2 and particulates)

Indicator 6: Emissions as a result of transport of bank paperwork (CO_2 and particulates)

5.6.5 Paper use

Although some of the newer service channels do not depend on paper, paper is used in significant amounts across many channels (e.g. for cheques, transaction notices and general office purposes). Paper manufacture frequently involves the use of non-sustainable sources of virgin paper fibre, minerals and energy use, and the use of chlorine for bleaching. In the context of this project, however, a key factor is the difference in paper usage between the different service channels. It was therefore decided to monitor the total amount of paper used, as well as its 'eco-friendliness'.

Indicator 7: Amount (kg) and type of paper used

5.6.6 Use of plastic cards

The vast majority of Bank credit and debit cards are made from PVC, although the Bank has stated its intention to develop a PVC-free card and to introduce a phased plan its withdrawal from plastic cards.[3] Until then, however, the manufacture and disposal of plastic cards has a range of ecological impacts.

5.6.7 Financial inclusion

Social exclusion is a shorthand label for what can happen when individuals experience a combination of linked problems such as unemployment, poor skills, low incomes, poor housing, bad health and family breakdown, which can act together so as to exclude them from a minimally acceptable way of life (see SEU 1998). Financial exclusion is one of the many strands of social exclusion, although unemployment and low income rank highest among its underlying causes (Sen 1997). Financial exclusion is particularly important to this project because the different service channels that the Bank (like other retail banks) uses to deliver its services are more accessible to some groups of customers than others. Access to the Bank's services can be considered from the perspective of three potentially vulnerable groups of customers: individuals, small businesses, and organisations in the 'social economy'.

A detailed examination of the nature of financial exclusion is beyond the scope of this paper (see NEF 1997; NCC 1997; Kempson *et al.* 1994). However, a number of elements contribute to the accessibility of bank services, and are thus key factors in financial exclusion. Four of these are of particular relevance in the discussion of service channels:

- **Geography** is an important factor in access to banking services, particularly for low-income customers. The widespread policy of bank closures has led to claims of financial exclusion and implicit red-lining in poorer areas of the UK.[4]

---

3 Investment in 'Biopol' formed part of that long-term strategy. Biopol is a plastic derived from the fermentation of sugar rather than fossil fuels, and has been used by the Bank in its Greenpeace affinity card.
4 Red-lining is defined as a conscious or unconscious policy of discrimination against areas on grounds of deprivation.

- **Technology** developments in general may not improve access to basic banking services by a low-income customer, unless steps are taken to include those without access to a telephone line or a personal computer.

- In respect of **cost**, personal bank accounts run in credit are generally free to customers in the UK. This means that costs are borne to some extent by those who fall into difficulties. Strong customer resistance to paying for a bank account means that the banks would rather encourage customers to pay additional fees for additional levels of service. To persuade customers to change to the cheaper service channels (such as Internet, PC or telephone banking), banks will pass on to the customer the financial benefit of operating a lower-cost product.

- **Competition** may lead sectors of the banking community towards a 'flight to quality', seeking higher returns and lower costs. There is a compelling argument that this may lead to discrimination against low-income and disadvantaged groups, since it is increasingly difficult for certain people to gain access to the mainstream financial system.

Indicators chosen to represent financial inclusion could cover a range of areas. After much deliberation, and for the sake of clarity, the NCBS selected two which represent inclusion of two of the most vulnerable consumer groups: low-income households and small businesses.

Indicator 8: Number of accounts provided to low-income households

Indicator 9: Number of accounts provided to small businesses with a turnover of less than £500,000

5.6.8 Convenience and quality of service

Different service channels will offer varying levels of convenience to different bank customers, depending on their wants and needs. Key factors include location, business hours, speed and efficiency, and usability. Another impact of service channels is their effect on the quality of service, such as handling errors or bank charges. Findings from the Bank's 'Partnership Ballot'[5] and focus groups revealed that quality of service is one of the most important issues for both personal and corporate customers.

Customer satisfaction is a key factor when comparing the performance of different service channels. The Partnership Ballot found that convenience and quality of service were rated by customers as being the two most important things to them, and so the indicators chosen reflect these two concerns.

Indicator 10: Personal and corporate customer satisfaction with convenience

Indicator 11: Personal and corporate customer satisfaction with quality of service

---

5   Conducted in May 1997, the Partnership Ballot involved sending every one of the Bank's customers a copy of the *Partnership Report* and a feedback form.

5.6.9 Personal contact

Opportunities for human contact are restricted by some service channels. This may have social as well as financial consequences (with personal contact possibly facilitating a more flexible decision-making process on a case-by-case basis).

5.6.10 Security and rights of privacy

Different service channels afford customers different levels of security. One of the biggest concerns that users have about banking by virtual channels (e.g. PC or Internet) is security. Privacy is another key concern for users of electronic banking. The same technological advances that can bring benefits to customers (e.g. profiling to create tailor-made products and services) can be misused to infringe individual privacy. However, on the basis that the Bank's systems are fully secure (through the use of cutting-edge technology) and that the data held on individuals is already regulated, this impact is considered to be of low significance.

5.6.11 Job security

Each service channel requires staff with varying levels of expertise. The market shift from staffed physical channels to unstaffed remote channels raises concerns over job security in the retail bank sector. The banking sector in general has seen recent job losses, associated with the closure of bank branches. Although new jobs may be created in telephone banking, these may be in a different geographic location, require different skills, etc. It should be noted that The Co-operative Bank has a policy of no compulsory redundancies for full-time staff. Given the high number of jobs lost in the banking industry since the end of the 1980s, staff perception of job security is a major issue, particularly when comparing the Bank's different service channels.

Indicator 12: Staff perception of job security

5.6.12 Working conditions

Working conditions for staff vary considerably between different service channels (BIFU 1998). Redeployment of staff from branches to telephone banking centres has implications for job specifications, such as the working environment, business hours, personal contact and gender roles. For example, bank branch work is conducted during the hours of nine to five, Monday to Friday, and involves a variable workload. By contrast, telephone service centre work is 24 hours, seven days a week, centralised and automated. Three-quarters of service centre employees in the banking sector are women; members of ethnic minority groups are under-represented; and new technology can also strip out many higher-paid jobs.

Differences in the way in which the Bank's service channels are operated have implications for the staff involved. The indicators chosen to reflect these focus on the quality

of working life (which encompasses a range of issues, measured here at a generic level) and working hours (specifically the opinion of families of staff members).
Indicator 13: Staff satisfaction with the quality of their working life
Indicator 14: Level of satisfaction, by families of staff, about staff working hours

5.6.13 Local economic development

Banks contribute to local economic development primarily by providing employment opportunities, but also by offering financial services to local businesses. The community involvement of banks also extends to the way in which it redistributes monies that have been deposited on a geographical basis (UKSIF 1998). The closure of branches impacts more heavily on some geographic areas than others, with the last bank to close in an area typically having the greatest effect. In many remote or rural communities the Bank provides services via approximately 15,000 post offices, thus providing an additional or alternative focus for towns. In December 1998, 60% of the Bank's staff were located in the north-west of the UK, including all customer service and telephone banking centres.

One indicator that can be used to measure the impact on local economic development, and which is representative of all service channels, is the relationship between the number of jobs provided by the Bank and the level of local deprivation.
Indicator 15: Number of Co-operative Bank employees working in areas of local deprivation

5.6.14 Sound sourcing

The problems associated with ethical trading are complex, sensitive and vary throughout the world according to the type of employment (ETI 1998; CEPAA 1997). The two main ways of tackling the issues are 'Fair trade' and 'sound sourcing'.[6] The use of ICT and other equipment for banking service channels raises issues of sound sourcing. This is particularly the case for remote and virtual channels. There is increasing reliance on suppliers of ICT with manufacturing bases in South-East Asia, and concern that some ICT factories may not reach Western standards of pay and conditions for employees.

The selection of an indicator for the sound sourcing of products and services is difficult due to the range of concerns over fair dealing and human rights, and the length of supply chains. Two indicators have been developed to reflect these concerns: one examines how responsibly the Bank deals with its suppliers, and one examines how these suppliers deal with their own suppliers. In terms of capturing the issue of fair dealing down the supply chain (indicator 17), attention is initially focused on areas of supply related to IT, as this is something that underlies all the service channels to a greater or lesser degree.
Indicator 16: Supplier satisfaction with fair handling of prices and contracts
Indicator 17: Payment of a 'living wage' to workers involved in assembly of IT systems

---

6 Fair trade aims to enable small-scale farmers and other community enterprises to get a fair price for their product. Sound sourcing aims to improve the conditions of employees, rather than independent or marginalised growers.

5.6.15 Co-operative movement inclusion

Given the diverse nature of co-operative enterprises and various impacts of service channels already identified, there are opportunities for collaboration across the co-operative sector (comprising agricultural, banking, community, credit unions, housing insurance, retail and workers' co-operatives). The potential for collaboration to tackle issues such as financial exclusion varies between service channels.

One indicator is proposed to measure satisfaction with the supply of Bank products and services to the co-operative membership base. A further indicator assessing whether the Bank acts as a good role model for co-operation is proposed in view of the pressure on the co-operative and mutual movement to convert to shareholder-focused corporations.

Indicator 18: Satisfaction with The Co-operative Bank as a fully participating member of the co-operative business community by members of the co-operative movement

Indicator 19: Satisfaction with The Co-operative Bank as a good example of co-operation by members of the co-operative movement

5.7 Next steps

As explained above, the development of indicators to measure impacts of the service channels took into account a range of views and expertise, including those of an independent advisory panel. However, the complexity of the issues and incomplete data available meant that the process did not involve direct engagement of all partner groups, and this is something that will be addressed in the coming months. As part of this process, the Bank invited feedback on the proposed indicators, providing pre-paid cards for this purpose in each of the *Partnership Reports*.

The indicators will be reviewed and refined in the light of any feedback, and the NCBS will be closely involved in the process of finalising and testing the indicators. This phase of work will involve the development of appropriate systems for monitoring and measuring the indicators, including agreeing appropriate accounting units, and is key to ensuring the usefulness of the indicators. So, for example, the Bank is considering ways in which the issue of fair dealing along the supply chain can be managed, and how the 'living wage' indicator can be effectively measured and monitored. Once finalised, the indicators will be reported in the Bank's annual *Partnership Report* and subject to external audit and verification.

Different partner groups may have conflicting needs and demands. Once the indicator system has been set up, the Bank's management will be able to use this new methodology to assess the impacts of its different service channels and will be better placed to reconcile these differences and act in accordance with each partner's expectations.

5.8 Conclusion

The development of indicators is a complex process. It involves a comprehensive review of all potential ecological and social impacts that might occur through use of the different channels, plus a process to ensure that these views are shared by partners or stakeholders. It also involves identifying an optimum number of indicators to reflect those key impacts.

If carried out correctly, the development of a set of indicators such as those shown here can serve to highlight key environmental and social impacts of particular activities. Measuring and monitoring those indicators can further serve as an invaluable tool for decision-makers, by providing a clear demonstration of the consequences of decisions or actions. They can also provide a concise way of reporting publicly on activities and on progress towards stated goals and objectives. Independent verification by a professional auditor should be used to demonstrate the credibility of both the selection of indicators and their measurement and reporting.

This project shows just how much further banks and financial service providers can take their responsibilities to act in an environmentally sustainable and socially responsible way. It is no longer sufficient to focus on the direct environmental impacts of operational activities. There is a compelling case to scrutinise any secondary impacts that might arise, for example, through the way in which banks deliver their services or through the types of product they make available. The development of indicators to assess the impacts of The Co-operative Bank's service channels demonstrates how and why this might be done.

GRAMEEN SHAKTI
Financing renewable energy in Bangladesh

Firoze A. Siddiqui and Peter Newman
Murdoch University, Australia

The Grameen Bank (GB) is one of the great stories of hope to have emerged in the last years of the millennium. Poverty is entrenched in groups, regions and nations for a range of reasons and to burst out of it usually requires the breaking of some entrenched cycle. The genius of Grameen's founder, Mohammad Yunus, was to believe in the credit risk of the poorest in a community.[1] For those who have absolutely nothing, the offer of a loan, even if it is tiny by most standards, is the opportunity of a lifetime and they will return the trust with extraordinary fastidiousness. This is especially true when the loan is made to individuals in a peer community group that has a responsibility to ensure the person granted the loan does indeed repay it, or else their own turn will not come.

The success of the GB is evident in its performance, with 2.34 million borrowers, 94% of whom are poor women, located in 38,957 of Bangladesh's 85,650 villages. By June 1997 total lending grossed US$2 billion and the repayment rate was an astonishing 95% (Grameen Bank 1998). This growth has occurred in just 20 years and has been a substantial boost to development in rural Bangladesh (BBS 1998). It is also the basis for many similar banks across the developing world (HABITAT 1996). A total of 223 'Grameen'-type financial programmes have so far been established in 58 countries. Thus this micro-financing approach is expanding rapidly.

Most of the GB's lending has been for housing and small rural enterprises such as for livestock. In June 1996 the Bank decided it was time to make a special foray into renewable energy and founded Grameen Shakti (literally 'rural energy'). This chapter examines why this has occurred, how it is being done, and how well it is doing as a model for sustainable banking.

---

1 See GB website: www.grameen-info.org.

6.1 Why does Grameen Shakti focus on renewables?

The GB has so far provided a mechanism for two of the three key factors in sustainability: economic development and community development. This is no mean feat in a period where the two appeared to be separating as goals into a trade-off of one for the other (Korten 1996). However the great challenge of sustainability is to attempt to support the third factor—environmental development—along with the other two (Newman and Kenworthy 1999).

Grameen Shakti has this third factor firmly in its focus, as it only works on renewable energy. This is unusual internationally as most financial institutions invest in a portfolio of traditional fossil fuel systems while attempting to bring in renewables whenever possible. However, it is a little less remarkable in the light of the fact that the vast majority of rural villages in Bangladesh are without any form of electricity.

Bangladesh's electricity grid reaches only 15% of the population, mostly in cities (80% of the people live in rural villages) (BBS 1998). Thus, as the GB is a rural bank, the natural focus was to find energy projects that are not grid-based. New fossil fuel resources have recently been discovered in Bangladesh, especially natural gas in the eastern part of the country. Nevertheless, Grameen Shakti has been firmly focused on renewables and thus is an important contributor to the international notion of 'sustainable banking'.

Of course some form of electricity, and a more advanced form of cooking fuel than firewood or dung, are basic to rural development. In Bangladesh, the World Bank suggests that 36% of the population are 'very poor' and 53% are 'poor'—most of these being in rural areas (World Bank 1998a). With lighting and access to communication technologies the potential for education improves significantly. Electricity can enable cottage industries to become far more efficient and can help many rural industries to develop beyond subsistence. Health can be greatly improved as the simple provision of a fridge in a community health centre enables vaccines and antibiotics to be kept at hand. Health is also improved if gas or a similar clean fuel replaces smoky wood and dung in cooking.

The renewable resources of Bangladesh are adequate for wind and sunlight-based technologies as well as having significant untapped opportunities for providing biogas (from digesting animal manure). There are also some hydro opportunities in the hills and some potential for tidal power in the delta islands of the south (BCAS 1998; BCSIR 1998; Newman *et al.* 1999). They offer the opportunity for the country to 'leapfrog' to 21st-century renewable technologies rather than keeping to traditional development pathways (Goldemburg 1998). The application of this approach to the developing world in general is well recognised by UN agencies and other development organisations (World Bank 1999c).

Thus Grameen Shakti's focus on renewables makes sense both at a global level, where it recognises the importance of the sustainability agenda, and also at the local level, where energy for rural villages offers an important step to break the poverty cycle using these innovative technologies.

6.2 How does Grameen Shakti achieve its goals?

6.2.1 Programmes

Grameen Shakti has established a number of specific programmes to implement its goals in renewable energy. These consist of:

- **Solar home systems (SHS) programme**. Homes are provided with photovoltaic (PV) roof collectors that provide a small amount of electricity, mostly for lighting.

- **Wind power programme**. Larger-scale systems are being trialled in some coastal locations.

- **Hydro programme**. Mini and micro hydro systems are being investigated in some hilly areas.

- **Biodigester programme**. Households are financed to build small digesters to produce gas for cooking as well as a fertiliser by product.

- **R&D and technology transfer programme**. Innovation is being assisted to ensure that Bangladesh gets the most out of its energy transition.

- **Training programme**. To improve the technical and managerial skills of Grameen Shakti's staff and to educate and popularise renewables among rural people in general.

Each of these will be expanded on below, but first the 'how' of Grameen Shakti's approach to any project, including energy projects, is outlined.

6.2.2 Financial credit policies

The bank establishes its branches, under a branch manager and a number of bank workers, usually with a catchment of between 15 and 22 villages. Grameen Shakti has established 17 branches so far with a further 3 in 1999.[2] The manager and the workers start by visiting villages and familiarising themselves with the local environment in which they will be operating. They explain to the local community the Bank's purpose, functions and operational system and identify the prospective clientele.

The borrowers are organised into small homogeneous 'Groups' organised into 'Centres'. The Centres are functionally linked to the local branch of the GB. The Groups and Centres are the primary building blocks of GB's loan receiving system and, as outlined above, provide the peer pressure so critical to the bank's success at achieving repayment. GB's field workers attend Centre meetings every week. One of their main aims is to strengthen the organisational capacity of Grameen clients to enable them to acquire the capacity for planning and implementing micro-level development decisions by themselves. In the first stage, five prospective borrowers form a Group but only two of them will be eligible

---

2   See Grameen Shakti website: www.grameen-info.org/grameen/gshakti.

for a loan at the first stage. The loans are repayable in weekly instalments spread over a year. The Group is observed for several weeks, to see if the members are conforming to the rules of the Bank. The other members become eligible for a loan only when the first two members have begun to repay the principal plus the interest for a particular period (normally six weeks or so). The collective responsibility of the Group (and the broader Centre) serves as the group pressure to keep the individual repayments on schedule.

Loans are small, and there is no lower limit as such. They may amount to as little as US$10. About 95% of loans amount to US$160, but even this modest sum is sufficient to finance the micro-enterprises undertaken by the borrowers for household-based rice husking, rural machine repairing workshops, purchase of rickshaws for transportation of goods or passengers, equipment for blacksmithing, pottery, handicrafts or energy systems.

GB's credit delivery system has some unique features apart from its focus on the poorest in the community, its emphasis on women and its group pressure approach to repayments. It also has the following characteristics:

- Loans are given without any collateral.

- Loans are repayable in weekly instalments spread over the year.

- Eligibility for a subsequent loan depends on full repayment of the first one.

- Transparency in bank transactions is much higher than in normal banks to enable group pressure to work on individuals and to enable the bank staff to maintain easy and close supervision.

In the vast majority of credit delivery financial systems collateral is a prerequisite irrespective of the size and category of the loans. The Grameen system is the exception in this respect. For Grameen, credit is not a privilege; it is a right of the poorest of society to have access to credit.

Overall, GB is much more community-oriented than individual-oriented. Individuals do have responsibility but only within the context of a community. This is the spirit of communitarian movements, social capital and civil society ethics as developed by Western authors such as Bellah (1991), MacIntyre (1981) and Sennett (1974). The links between this social capital and economic processes are increasingly being observed (Newman and Kenworthy 1999) in developed-country markets, but were intuitively recognised by Professor Yunus in establishing the GB *modus operandi*. The question now is whether this philosophy and approach has been found to work on renewable energy projects.

One immediate difference has emerged. GB's niche of lending to the poorest is not as applicable in rural energy systems as there are very few other financial institutions willing to get involved in this field, even with more wealthy clients. The problem is that any energy system (especially for electricity) is generally far more expensive than other rural products. The capital required is vastly more than normal Grameen loans.

Hence, Grameen Shakti offers special credit policies to those other than normal GB borrowers, who want to buy an energy system on credit. They are offered a 15% downpayment, and the remaining 85% of the cost is to be repaid over the next three years in equal monthly instalments (instead of weekly repayments), with a 12% service charge on any outstanding amount. Such a system is not likely to be accessible to the poorest in the community though its focus is still on helping poor rural people. Thus Grameen Shakti is more like normal banks (as it requires some upfront capital) but still does not have a collateral requirement.

6.3 The programmes: progress to date

6.3.1 Solar home systems programme

Individual homes are given PV collectors for their roof and from these batteries can be charged to run simple lights or appliances such as small black and white TV sets. These systems are expensive so Grameen Shakti has (a) introduced the soft financing scheme outlined above to lessen the load; and (b) developed small systems for just one or two lamps.

Thus low-income people are able to access the technology. In the first year of operation 1,033 solar home systems (SHS) were installed, providing 38 kW installed capacity.

The programme aims to provide an expanding number of these systems as set out in Table 6.1.

Year	1	2	3	4	5	6	7	8	9	10
Number of systems	1,200	1,800	2,400	3,000	4,000	4,000	4,000	4,000	4,000	4,000

Table 6.1 **SHS programme goals for ten years**

Source: Grameen Shakti 1999

Over ten years this represents 32,400 homes provided with some electricity.

The low power of such systems is seen when the first year is analysed: the average is a mere 37 W of installed capacity per household. This is only able to provide simple lighting in most cases. Although most of this power is being used for lighting, some income-generating enterprises are apparently developing from the programme (Grameen Shakti 1999):

- Some customers are using PV systems for heating soldering irons for repairing radios, TVs or other household appliances used by more wealthy people who have electricity.

- Rural carpenters and other craftsmen are extending their working hours after sunset.

- Some buyers have installed PV systems to sell battery-based power in rural market places, especially to shop owners to help light their shops. This micro utility service concept will be expanded below.

Obviously the big problem with this programme is that it is too small—both in what it can give to each household (there are already problems with the expectations raised by having electricity and the little that can be achieved with it) and also the number of households being assisted. The major reason for this is that household PV systems are still much too expensive, though their price does continue to fall (Flavin and O'Meara 1998). The best way to overcome this problem is for the programme concept to be broadened in some way to enable other renewable sources such as wind power, hydro power or tidal power to be linked to PV systems. This raises questions about whether household-based power options are inherently flawed and it may be more socially and economically appropriate to utilise Grameen's community-scaled social processes for power options. This will be pursued in the final evaluation section of this chapter.

6.3.2 Wind power programme

Demonstration wind power projects are being established, especially in the coastal areas of Bangladesh, and data is being collected to better evaluate the wind resource. The demonstration projects are:

- Two small wind turbines (300 W and 1 kW) at Sitakunda and Chokoria in Chittagong district to provide power for fish farms established by the GB.

- Four hybrid power stations (combination of wind, diesel and PV) which have been installed in four cyclone shelters (set up by GB) to provide power for Bank members to start micro enterprises in and around the shelters.

The financing of these systems has not yet been thoroughly researched; they are being evaluated technically first to see how they could be extended or applied elsewhere.

6.3.3 Hydro power programme

This programme is still in the preparatory phase, with sites being evaluated. It is not likely to be very large as few people live in the hilly districts being examined. This programme could be diverted into a tidal evaluation as a concept has been developed for small-scale tidal systems using flood control barrages and sluice gates (see Newman *et al.* 1999). This is highly appropriate to Bangladesh as it builds on water (and mud) management systems already well developed in coastal communities. They are also likely to be cheaper and fit into the community scale of power production outlined below.

6.3.4 Biodigester programme

Biodigesters are not as well used in Bangladesh as they are in India, Vietnam and China, probably because there is no shortage of wood for domestic cooking as Bangladesh villages all grow trees (very rapidly) for fuel. However, gas is cleaner burning and so has some appeal. Demonstration biodigesters are being developed to ensure the best model for Bangladesh is available before it is put into mass production for villages. There is considerable potential here as long as villagers keep a minimum of five cows and can obtain financing (Grameen Shakti 1999).

An example of an innovative and relevant technology being examined is biomass gasification. A biomass gasifier (10 kW generating capacity) in the northern part of the country has supplied 45 connections with a total of 1,125 W load. It is planned to extend this to supply 100 consumers. Grameen Shakti is now conducting a study on technological performance as well as the economic aspects of the technology in existing rural socioeconomic conditions. This technology has many advantages as it can use as its feedstock weed species such as water hyacinth and convert them into a gas that feeds into a diesel generator. Its scale is again more appropriate to be applied at the village or community scale rather than household scale.

6.3.5 R&D and technology transfer programme

The Grameen Shakti R&D programme is researching technology suitable for Bangladesh, as well as financing such technology through its innovative style. Its stated goals are:

- The exploration of ways to develop appropriate renewable energy technologies and their uses

- The development of possible ways to popularise renewable energy systems that will be easily accessible to a large number of rural communities and institutions

- Introduction of innovative financial service systems for customers to facilitate rapid expansion of renewable energy use

6.3.6 Training programme

Special training is being instigated to enable Grameen Shakti professionals to become technically literate as well as to ensure there is good backup for the renewables systems when they are installed. Community-based education is also developing in an attempt to popularise renewables.

6.4 Conclusion

The Grameen Shakti approach to financing development among the very poor is well under way in the area of renewable energy. Most programmes are in the very early stages, but the two most significant programmes warrant some further comments.

The **solar housing scheme** was the way chosen to begin the Grameen Shakti process, mainly because an international loan was provided to finance solar housing. The very small-scale PV systems fit into Grameen's social model based on individuals in a transparent and supportive community context: i.e. individual households can receive loans to purchase PV systems as long as they are part of a Group and a Centre. However, the systems are too expensive to be very useful in themselves as a model for any extensive application of sustainable development. And if they were adopted by a whole Group (and then a whole Centre) economies of scale would still not be enjoyed as each household remains unconnected to each other in terms of the power system.

The other major activity undertaken by Grameen Shakti is the testing of larger-scale renewable systems. In particular, the valuable demonstrations of **hybrid power stations** (at the cyclone shelters); the **biomass gasification system** and, more recently, the opportunity of small-scale tidal power are all community-scale power systems. As such they offer a model for how Grameen Shakti may have to shift its focus and its financing approach. These systems can provide much more substantial amounts of power at a considerably reduced price. The question remains how these systems could be grafted on to Grameen Shakti's social process. The model being suggested by our research group (Ellery 1999) for a demonstration project in rural areas of Bangladesh is:

- To incorporate a hybrid power plant into a village as a community facility (using wind, PV and diesel backup that uses biomass gasification), together with other opportunities such as tidal or microhydro power.

- To provide power to individual households and small enterprises in the initial stages through a battery charging and distribution system (rather than a small grid as it saves considerably on costs and keeps the system all DC [direct current], avoiding the need for costly inverters); as needs grow a grid can be built and even connected to the main grid in a distributed power system (Flavin and Dunn 1997).

- To finance the system through the establishment of Groups and Centres (as in all Grameen projects); the Centre then acts as a 'mini utility' for the village or part of the village. The particular clients chosen to be funded as participants would need to demonstrate they could make payments for their electricity to the Centre, which would run the power plant. When households show they can pay, then other participants could be invited in; the hybrid power plant could be extended through extra PV, wind and biomass gasification modules when necessary, or be supplemented by innovations such as tidal power generators.

This model would enable Grameen to exploit the scale advantages available in the renewable energy systems identified so far in their research and could at the same time make the most of Grameen's unique social model, which appears to work so well in Bangladesh. The scale of the technology fits the scale of Groups and Centres in the GB model, so tying together energy technology with an already well-developed finance system. The model is thus attempting to facilitate village community development, improve rural and regional economic development and assist global and local environmental development, i.e. sustainability. Its application to other parts of the developing world becomes obvious.

Such matching of appropriate technologies and financing via the development of packages that build on community values is the kind of challenge that faces all who seek to pursue new models for sustainable banking.

ASSESSING THE 'TRIPLE BOTTOM LINE'

Social and environmental practices in the European banking sector

James Giuseppi
Henderson Global Investors, UK

Socially responsible investment (SRI) funds aim to provide good financial returns for investors, while promoting sustainable development, i.e. the ability of current generations to provide for their needs in a way that is not detrimental to future generations. By taking a more holistic view of companies' behaviour and contribution to society, SRI funds intend not only to provide good investment opportunities, but also to encourage companies to address their 'triple bottom line'. The triple bottom line includes the **social** and **environmental** performance of a company in addition to the **financial** results.

The Henderson SRI team uses both negative and positive screening to find companies suitable for investment. Negative screens are used to exclude companies that are involved with certain specified 'negative' industries, e.g. tobacco, gambling, pornography, nuclear and military. Positive screening is employed to find companies that employ best practice within their relative sectors, i.e. 'best in class'. Such screening is also used to identify companies that provide a social or environmental benefit: companies that are considered by the SRI team to be 'industries of the future', e.g. healthcare, education, information technology, renewable energy, water and mass transportation companies.

This pan-European survey sought to identify which banks are best in class in terms of their social and environmental performance and business practices in order to identify investment opportunities for SRI funds. It is also hoped that, by drawing attention to the key issues below, change and progress will be further stimulated in the banking sector. The report has the following additional aims:

- To recognise those banks making efforts to improve their social and environmental performance

⬛ To highlight the important position of banks in society and business and their role in helping to develop sustainable business

⬛ To provide a stimulus for those banks that are doing little in this area

The financial institutions included in this survey are publicly listed, commercial banks. A total of 68 banks were surveyed, with a response rate of exactly 50%. The research investigated the following issues, as these are seen as the areas of highest potential social and environmental impact:

⬛ **The environment and sustainable banking.** The direct and indirect impact of banking operations was investigated, as were the measures being taken by banks to encourage sustainable business.

⬛ **Overseas operations: third world debt and human rights.** European banks continue to have considerable influence on how the South develops, and responses to the questions in this section reveal how the banks perceive themselves. Steps to alleviate the debt burden are discussed.

⬛ **Community involvement.** Access to banking and the problems of social exclusion were assessed. The banks were also asked what community initiatives and charitable giving programmes they conduct.

⬛ **Business practices.** The survey sought to determine whether banks have ethical criteria regarding their loan or investment policies. Specifically, the survey aimed to identify the banks' policies regarding their loan portfolios. Responses received also highlighted the issue of their attitude towards disclosure. A case study of retrospective liabilities is examined in relation to disclosure.

A model bank is illustrated, operating in line with best practice in the above areas.

7.1 'Best-in-class' banks

The following banks have been identified as the most progressive in their sector, i.e. 'best in class'. This classification was made by considering whether a bank was applying best practice in the majority of areas relevant to its business operations.

The list is alphabetical by country. It is not a table of ranking.

Dexia (Crédit Local de France) was found to be a bank that has a comprehensive environmental policy, which is applied to its operations, and progressive workplace practices. Dexia has a reputation of good disclosure to shareholders, and was forthcoming in disclosing details of its operations and policies for our survey.

Commerzbank is recognised in Germany as a family-friendly employer, with progressive environmental policies, good housekeeping and responsible lending practices.

Through the Commerzbank Foundation, local community and social initiatives are undertaken. The bank's disclosure should be commended. It was one of only two respondents who named companies in the military, tobacco or nuclear industries to whom investments or loans were made.

DG Bank (Deutsche Genossenschaftsbank) replied with a good level of disclosure and explained the extent of its operations, and those of its subsidiaries. Environmental screens are used to judge loan decisions and the bank has good housekeeping practices. DG Bank is a signatory of UNEP,[1] 'which demonstrates the awareness of the existing problems', as it stated in its response. The bank disclosed that it earned revenues from military, tobacco or nuclear industries, but reported that DG earned less than 0.01% of its total loan portfolio from them.

HypoVereinsbank, Europe's leading real-estate financier, has progressive policies in terms of community initiatives, environmental matters and overseas operations. In the response to the questionnaire, the bank stated that 'loans strictly follow the UNEP guidelines'.

AIB (Allied Irish Banks) responded fully to the survey. The bank has progressive community initiatives to avoid social exclusion, such as working with the Irish government to automate state benefit payments. As part of its progressive environmental stance, AIB is part of the European Commission-sponsored working group, which is developing a standard 'Eco-management and Audit Scheme for Banks'.

Argentaria has an active role in supporting community initiatives, such as subsidised housing and social exclusion avoidance, as was evident from their reply. Argentaria is a leading lender to local municipalities, generally avoided by other Spanish banks. Argentaria has a code of conduct that is widely regarded as exemplary in Spain. Following recent downscaling, the bank conducted a responsible redundancy programme. The bank stated that it will adhere to widely supported international initiatives to alleviate debt burden on a case-by-case basis. Argentaria obtained the top score in a survey of the IBEX35 Stocks for best corporate governance in 1998.[2]

BCH (Banco Central Hispanoamericano) acted as a creditor to third world countries in the past, but now participates in measures to alleviate the debt burden. As the name suggests, BCH has operations in Central and South America and operates to the same standards in these markets as in their domestic market. BCH stated that it does not earn revenue from the military, tobacco or nuclear industries. The bank takes a proactive stance regarding the environment, including good housekeeping, with measures such as a credit card linked to Adena, a Spanish nature protection organisation, and sponsoring campaigns with FAPAS, an animal protection association. BCH's community activities also

---

1   The United Nations Environment Programme's 'Statement by Financial Institutions on the Environment and Sustainable Development' (see pages 397-400).
2   According to a survey by *Actualidad Economica*, a Spanish economic weekly.

deserve praise, especially the steps to avoid social exclusion. An example is its co-operation with local governments to help those people in deprived areas, offering preferential financial conditions for small and low-income businesses and financing social housing. BCH was classed as **Best Overall in Sector**. BCH recently merged with Banco Santander, and the new bank is called BSCH.

Lloyds TSB adopts an innovative approach towards the environmental screening of its lending portfolio, supported by a comprehensive employee training programme. The bank has the largest corporate community investment programme in the UK. Lloyds TSB is considering publishing a social report and is proceeding on the basis of obtaining independent verification of stakeholder dialogue,[3] a fundamental part of the process. Of note is the bank's attitude towards overseas lending, where it chose not to dispose of its Latin American debt during the debt crisis. However, it was found that Lloyds TSB has board representation at a UK military equipment supplier. Although the revenue earned is negligible in relation to the bank's total income, the fact that the bank has board representation, and therefore a degree of executive control, excludes Lloyds TSB as an investment potential for our SRI funds.

National Westminster Bank (NatWest)—the first major publicly listed UK bank to address environmental issues and produce an environmental report on a regular basis. The bank has experienced considerable savings from the pioneering policies of its EMS (environmental management system). NatWest conducts environmental screening of customers' credit applications. The bank's 1999 *Social Impact Review* shows that it is keen to continue developing its progressive record on addressing stakeholder issues, with a strong commitment to staff communication and training. It also helps to illustrate the bank's proactive stance on community issues and addressing social exclusion.

Royal Bank of Scotland has addressed issues of environmental and social concern with policies of incremental improvement, and by adopting an attitude of enlightened self-interest. The bank has a progressive attitude towards communication with an emphasis on using suitable language, illustrated by its disclosure during the survey, its policy of employee training and feedback, and by its community involvement.

A list of the best-in-class banks, and their key strengths, is given in Table 7.1.

7.2 The model bank

A hypothetical model bank exhibiting the best practices that already exist in this sector, together with proposals for improvements, is described below. Such a bank would include within its operations the following:

---

3   Lloyds is currently discussing the process of social reporting with the Institute of Social and Ethical Accountability.

Company name	Country	Strengths (see below)
Dexia (Crédit Local de France)	France	2. 3. 5. 6. 7. 8.
Commerzbank AG	Germany	1. 2. 3. 5. 7. 8.
DG Bank	Germany	1. 3. 7. 8.
HypoVereinsbank	Germany	1. 5. 6. 7. 8.
Allied Irish Banks	Ireland	1. 3. 5. 7. 8. 9.
Argentaria	Spain	1. 2. 3. 5. 6.
Banco Central Hispanoamericano	Spain	1. 2. 3. 4. 7. 6.
Lloyds TSB	UK	1. 2. 3. 5. 6. 7. 9.
National Westminster	UK	1. 3. 5. 7. 8.
Royal Bank of Scotland	UK	1. 2. 3. 4. 5. 6. 7. 8.

Key to 'strengths'

1. Responsible lending
2. Progressive workplace practices
3. Good housekeeping
4. Ethical business policy
5. Supporting community initiatives

6. Progressive workplace practices in overseas operations
7. Proactive environmental stance
8. Good disclosure
9. Responsible financing of trade to developing countries and/or debt relief

Table 7.1 **'Best-in-class banks' according to the Henderson SRI survey**

- Application of the guidelines of the UNEP Statement, as practised by Hypo-Vereinsbank.

- Addressing the issue of accountability through independently verified social reporting on a regular basis, along the lines of The Co-operative Bank in the UK. Such reporting requires communication with all stakeholder groups and transparency of all actions. As a step towards that goal, banks can encourage and support customers to conduct better environmental practices and regular environmental reporting.

- Environmental screening of customers' operations, including measurement of customers' environmental performance. The latter area is one that banks are generally avoiding, claiming that they should not act as the environmental policemen. However, unless performance is measured, companies tend to operate only to minimum compliance. Larger business customers should be implementing an independently verified environmental management system (EMS), to ensure that resource usage is monitored and can therefore be targeted for efficiency savings.

- Supporting community finance initiatives, adapted to local requirements, as well as innovative lending and knowledge of the market and borrowers, as practised by Triodos Bank. Support may also include premises use, staff secondment, knowledge transfer, training and mentoring, which is currently conducted by a number of the surveyed banks.

▧ Implementing fully transparent overseas lending policies, which use lessons from previous debt crises to reduce risk to the bank and the debtors. Transparency, as recommended by the Jubilee 2000 coalition and similar organisations, is a fundamental criterion to ensure that sustainable lending terms may be agreed by all stakeholders.

▧ Publishing an ethical policy that clearly states any areas to which the bank would refuse to lend, and that also highlights the standards by which customers and suppliers would be required to operate. The ethical policy of The Co-operative Bank in the UK was ground-breaking and provides an admirable template for others.

▧ Adapting social inclusion policies to improve access to banking services for those sections of society that are being increasingly excluded. This would include, for example, providing simple, easy-to-use accounts, access to branches or at least the placement of ATMs, which also accept deposits, in convenient locations.

Such features in a bank do not preclude making a profit, as has been proven by those companies incorporating some of the above practices. But in addition to providing a financial return, such a bank would provide social and environmental benefits. Self-regulation of the European banking sector, or EU regulation, may be required to create minimum standards for banks to apply. Alternatively an extension of the UNEP Initiative guidelines could provide global standards, incorporating the above benchmarks.

7.3 Environment

7.3.1 Sustainable banking

By definition the term **sustainable development** means meeting the needs of today's generation without compromising the ability of future generations to meet theirs. **Sustainable banking**, therefore, should be interpreted as the decision by banks to provide products and services only to customers who take into consideration the environmental and social impact of their actions.

Although banks themselves are not the worst offenders in terms of direct environmental pollution, they have significant indirect impacts, because of where and to whom they loan money. Public opinion will not judge banks purely on a business efficiency criterion, but will accord an equal level of importance to social and, increasingly, environmental responsibility. Such obligations include the challenge of incorporating and applying environmental criteria to loan policies and company evaluations.

One part of sustainable banking is **responsible lending**. The standards that were used to judge this criterion are whether or not the banks have environmental screens included in their lending policies and whether they conduct environmental checks of their customers' businesses or projects.

Twenty of the 34 responding banks are signatories to the UNEP Statement. This statement commits signatories to support sustainable development and environmental protection, and to effectively communicate their policies in these areas. This document of best-practice guidelines unfortunately does not enjoy widespread support or application in the banking sector. It does, however, draw benchmarks of expectations. DG Bank stated that signing up to the Statement 'demonstrates its awareness of the existing problems'. Only HypoVereinsbank stated categorically that 'loans strictly follow the UNEP guidelines'.

Only ten respondents stated that they carry out some level of environmental screening. The majority of banks refuse to accept responsibility for their clients' actions, by claiming that they are not the environmental regulators or enforcers and that their financial services are merely products. This means that banks are not measuring their customers' environmental performance, and, until this happens, the customers will not feel obliged to implement any measures beyond legislative compliance. Access to financial services leads to empowerment, without which the customers' operations would be severely curtailed.

An example of where implementation of social and environmental policies raises questions is the role of UBS in funding the Ilisu Dam project in Turkey, which violates World Bank standards on 18 accounts.[4] When lending to customers in its home territory, UBS checks the environmental impacts of its customers' operations. UBS also has a strict environmental policy to control its own direct impacts, and it is noteworthy that UBS was one of the first banks to sign the UNEP Statement. However, Friends of the Earth have stated that they believe that construction of the Ilisu Dam will cause major environmental damage, further increase tensions with Kurdish communities and may trigger conflict with neighbouring countries due to the disruption of water supplies from the Tigris. The companies involved in the Ilisu Dam project should report to shareholders on the political, social and environmental risks associated with the project. Reputational risk is obvious and future civil claims by those made homeless and losing income may not be out of the question.

By comparison, The Co-operative Bank in the UK would be an example of best practice. It has a policy of refusing loans to companies that operate without consideration for their environmental impact, and will conduct checks to verify risk.

The European Commission has provided, through the European Investment Fund, guarantees for banks to offer loans on preferential terms to EU-based SMEs (small and medium-sized enterprises) that are either operating on an environmentally beneficial basis or providing products or services that are environmentally beneficial. European banks were offered the opportunity to act as the local intermediaries and adjudicators for such loans. BCP in Portugal highlighted in the survey response that it has made use of this opportunity and now positions itself as the 'Environmental Bank' in Portugal.

---

4   Peter Bosshard, Berne Declaration. The Berne Declaration is a Swiss public-interest group with 16,000 members. Through research, popular education and advocacy work, it has promoted more equitable and sustainable North–South relations since 1968.

7.3.2 *Good housekeeping*

Although banks are not obvious environmental polluters, they do tend to be large consumers of energy and resources, e.g. paper, and they can also be major property holders. The term 'good housekeeping' refers to the steps that the banks take to reduce their own direct negative impact upon the environment: for example, through management of their facilities and properties. Such measures would include practices such as recycling waste, reducing CO_2 emissions and using renewable energy. To effectively implement such practices, the norm within the sector is for the bank to issue a formal corporate environmental policy or an environmental report so that such practices could be communicated not only to customers and outside observers, but also to their own staff. The survey investigated whether employees receive environmental training and whether part of managers' responsibilities would include the implementation of the bank's environmental policies.

7.4 Overseas operations

Banks with overseas operations have the opportunity, and indeed the responsibility, according to the Rio Resolution Statement, to integrate environmental and social criteria into their lending and investment policies when financing trade or development projects.

7.4.1 *Human rights*

As banks become multinational organs, they often face criticism for operating in countries with oppressive governments. If the banks issue and apply a code of conduct for their operations in countries with oppressive regimes, investors may then be able to judge on their corporate social responsibility.

As part of such a code of conduct the banks should also address the issue of the arms trade. The World Development Movement publication, *Gunrunners' Gold*, recommends that

> . . . irrespective of government licensing, banks should themselves agree not to finance or in any way support arms sales to countries that:
>
> - Abuse human rights,
> - Are in regions of conflict or tension,
> - Have excessive military spending in relation to economic and social needs.
>
> Those banks which have agreed, fully or in part, to do this, should ensure they have systems of independent verification and audit to ensure that customers have confidence that they are implementing their policy (World Development Movement 1995).

The rights of individuals also need to be upheld in such countries, if banks wish to avoid being seen in a negative light. A template for such codes is Amnesty International's publication, *Human Rights Principles for Companies*, published in January 1998. Encouragingly, HypoVereinsbank and Anglo Irish Bank support the proposals 'in principle' but 'not formally', and Bank of Ireland, Erste Bank, Banco Central Hispanoamericano, Christiania and Banco Comercial Português also confirmed support for the document. Credit Suisse claimed they were 'not actually supporting Amnesty's principles; however, we have taken due notice of the document'.

7.4.2 Burma

The US Federal Government has issued a law banning new investment in Burma. In the state of Massachusetts, and many US cities including New York, Los Angeles and San Francisco, there are 'selective purchasing laws'. Such laws effectively create a boycott of companies that have business interests in Burma. Although there is no specific legislation in Europe that forbids companies to operate in Burma, the EU has revoked tariff privileges for Burmese imports due to Burma's record on forced labour.[5]

Despite the above measures and calls for divestment by the democratically elected leader, Aung San Suu Kyi, some European banks still have interests in Burma. BNP has a representative office in Burma, which it states has contact with local banks 'sporadically' for documentary credits. However, such credits may be used by the Burmese authorities to purchase products or services. BNP stated that they have 'very limited business to date'. BNP prefers to 'consider our representative office as an observer in the hope of better days'. HSBC has a single staff representative office, which it states is to internally monitor developments within the country. Deutsche Bank also admitted having interests in Burma, but failed to specify details.

7.4.3 Third world debt

During the 1970s, European banks were encouraged by their governments to lend money to developing countries. However, the loans were often granted on unsustainable terms. For example, sovereign debts had unrealistic terms of hard currency repayment based on commodity export prices, which fluctuate. When such prices dropped too low, the debtors defaulted on their repayments.

The levels of debt were so high that defaults caused **debt crises**, creating hardships for the debtor countries and financial risk for the lenders.

Lenders faced reputation risk. NGOs, such as the Lloyds and Midland Boycott (LAMB) in the UK, were established to draw public attention to the irresponsible lending that had occurred and the subsequent problems it caused for debtor countries and their populations. **Boycotts** may lead to a detrimental financial impact on the lenders because they aim to encourage existing customers to close their accounts and deter potential customers from opening one.

The IMF and the World Bank issued further loans to indebted countries to repay the original debts. European governments took over portions of the debt, and banks sold

---

5   Personal communication with Simon Billenness, Franklin Research & Development, 16 May 1999.

some of the debt on the secondary markets. These measures saved the relevant banks and had the effect of **transferring the responsibility** of the loans from the private to public sector, but created no relief from the debt burden for the indebted countries.

The **lack of transparency** of the relationships between the banks, central banks and governments, means that it is extremely difficult to establish on what basis the bail-outs were arranged. It is not legally required for banks to disclose the basis on which such arrangements are made; nor is it necessary by law to report to whom money is lent. This means that most debts are virtually untraceable. European banks are therefore able to avoid disclosing who they have lent money to. By comparison, in the US all companies, including subsidiaries of foreign-based companies, are obliged to declare where they are lending or investing money abroad on the form '20F'. In Europe, only limited information is available concerning which countries, but not which individual companies, are creditors (Eurodad 1998).

The nature of third world debt has changed during the 1990s. Of the world's poorest nations, the amount of total debt to private banks is now down to around 10%–12% (Eurodad 1998), whereas previously they held the majority portion.

Concerns raised by pressure groups such as LAMB remain relevant, as can be seen from the recent Asia–Pacific and Russian debt crises. Will public money continue to be used to bail out the banks when they make irresponsible lending decisions which later backfire? On what terms did the European governments agree to save those banks at risk of collapse? Such questions remain unanswered.

The essence of **Jubilee 2000**, the international campaign to reduce the developing world's debt burden, is to motivate the general public across Europe to put pressure on their governments to work with the banks to write off such debts, as banks are opposed to acting unilaterally.

The Initiative for **Heavily Indebted Poor Countries** (HIPC) is targeted at relieving the world's poorest countries of their debt burden. However, it is unlikely to achieve its aim, due to the widely unachievable conditions (Hersel 1998), and because 'creditors remain all powerful, judge, jury, bailiff, interested party and witness, all in one'.[6]

Eurodad 1998 states that, while Germany, Japan and Italy formally support the initiative, they practically block its implementation by insisting on the strictest compliance with the rules. Their stance appears due to their own current domestic economic difficulties. However, as noted by Jubilee 2000, Germany is forgetting that, without the massive cancellation and restructuring of her debts to sustainable levels after the Second World War, the country would never have achieved its 'miraculous' economic and social recovery. However, certain German banks stated that they are involved in programmes to alleviate the debt burdens. Such action primarily takes the form of debt rescheduling, e.g. by Commerzbank, Deutsche and DG Banks.

The lack of an **international insolvency law** needs to be addressed in order to overcome the problems arising from earlier irresponsible lending and prevent future similar mistakes. 'Commercial banks have quite often, though not always without

---

6   K. Raffer, Introductory Statement, Panel Discussion, 'Insolvency and Arbitration within a New
      International Financial Architecture' Seminar, London, 18 March 1999.

"persuasion", granted debt reductions in various forms, [but] if international insolvency allowing countries to go bankrupt had existed in the 1970s, loans would certainly have been given more cautiously' (Raffer 1998).

At a meeting in Tegucigalpa, Honduras, in January 1999, representatives from 16 Latin American countries gathered to formulate a continent-wide agreement, and to co-ordinate campaigning across the continent. The Tegucigalpa Declaration called for:

- Transparency in the lending/borrowing process and inclusion of all parties involved

- Integration and co-ordination of all parties involved, applying an insolvency procedure to indebted countries along the lines of bankruptcy laws existing in countries such as the United States

- Indebted countries to be given the right to declare themselves insolvent[7]

The establishment of an **independent debt review body** (DRB) is required, set up by the UN or international court of justice, to act as an arbitrator, to defend the sovereignty of a debtor nation, while being fair to creditors.

Poorer countries do require finance in order to develop. Best practice would be for lenders to provide finance for socially responsible projects, with sustainable lending terms.

7.5 Community involvement

7.5.1 Access to banking

Access to banking services has become an indispensable necessity for people of all classes, in order to receive payments, to finance consumption and to provide for retirement. The 'strategic economic position [of banks] coupled with their State charters and guaranteed deposit insurance renders them *quasi*-public institutions or at least positioned to be more socially responsible than ordinary private undertakings' (Granger *et al.* 1997). The commercial banking sector has a key role and responsibility in overcoming the problems arising from social exclusion, as recently stated by the UK government.

Although in some EU states there is legislation to ensure access to banking for all individuals, the actual services offered by banks are often inappropriately priced for lower-income sections of society. 'Less financially sophisticated and low-income consumers may be generally time-consuming for banks' (Granger *et al.* 1997). In the present era of high competition and 'lean banking', devoting resources to this area of business can be overlooked due to the overriding concern to achieve profit.

The banks' products are often priced out of proportion to the service offered. For example, very high penalty charges are incurred for going overdrawn without prior

---

7   Ann Pettifor, Director, Jubilee 2000 Coalition UK, 'Concordats for Debt Cancellation', 18 March 1999.

permission from the bank. In France such action can lead to the exclusion of that individual from the right to hold a bank account and therefore become an *interdit bancaire,* which can further lead to exclusion from the workforce because salaries are paid directly into bank accounts.

The banks responding to the survey were aware of the issue of access to banking. However, only a few of the retail banks had formalised specific policies and products to address this issue, and, of those, their efforts were more directed towards supporting small and low-income businesses, rather than individuals. For example, banks such as Deutsche, Den Danske, Banco Popular Español and Banco Central Hispanoamericano stated that small and low-income businesses are part of their retail banking focus. An active stance to address the problem is taken by Allied Irish Banks, which is working with the Irish government to automate state benefit payments through the electronic banking infrastructure. Another Irish respondent, Anglo Irish Bank, although not a retail bank, has extensive relationships with the Credit Union movement, which often provides financial services to individuals otherwise excluded from using banks.

Social inclusion has become a specific focus of attention for the major UK banks, who are all, to varying degrees, now investigating or introducing services in the areas of community banking and micro-credits. Such projects have previously been addressed by the smaller banks in the non-listed sector, such as the pioneering Triodos Bank. This bank lends only to 'value-led projects' with social and environmental objectives. It operates in the Netherlands, Belgium and the UK and has a combined balance sheet of £250 million across the three countries. Although this figure is relatively small, Triodos Bank has a very low loss rate because it insists on being knowledgeable about its markets (Mayo *et al.* 1998).

Also in the UK, NatWest stated that social exclusion is in the bank's top five priorities to address; it has established a Social Exclusion Unit to explore how the bank can improve access to banking for disadvantaged individuals and communities. Lloyds TSB is supporting initiatives to provide community-based financial services to deprived areas.

In Germany, Commerzbank states in its environmental policy that, through the 'Commerzbank Foundation', cultural and social issues are addressed because 'the quality of a society can also be gauged by how it treats its disadvantaged members'. It is evident, however, that throughout Europe if banks are really to address the issue of access to banking then more attention needs to be spent on developing appropriately priced services for the lower-income sections of society.

In the United States, the Community Reinvestment Act (CRA) places an affirmative obligation on banks and thrifts to meet the credit needs of their communities. 'Historically, CRA has been a critical tool in improving access to credit and promoting development in lower-income communities' (Immergluck 1998).

As banks come under increasing pressure from shareholders and the threat of corporate take-overs, more branches are being closed. In order not to provoke political and public reaction, banks need to compensate by increasing access through partnerships with other banks, e.g. the UK 'Link' ATM system, and through the use of technologies such as telephone and Internet banking

7.5.2 *Charitable giving and community involvement programmes*

The CRA also ensures that financial institutions whose annual turnover is above a certain level reinvest into registered community programmes. CRA has been a key tool in the redevelopment of lower-income and minority communities since its passage in 1977. In recent years, the regulations that implement CRA have undergone substantial revisions, in part, so that the law would reward institutions based more on performance and outcomes (loans to lower-income communities, bank branch locations) rather than on promise and process (e.g. marketing, documenting contacts).

Such 'compulsory community giving' does not exist in Europe and it is the prerogative of each bank to decide how, or indeed if, it wishes to address the issue of community reinvestment and charitable giving.

Jyske Bank in Denmark considered that payment of the high level of Danish corporation tax was equivalent to community reinvestment, as the government decides where the money is spent. Bankinter in Spain appears to hold a similar view. Meanwhile, Banco Pastor concentrates all its operations in the area of Galicia, where the bank was founded and a local charitable foundation, 'Foundation Barrie de la Maza', owns a 42% share of the bank, due to the generosity and lack of heirs of the bank's founder. Argentaria supports community initiatives through Fundación Argentaria.

Some 32% of the responding banks chose to disclose the amount reinvested back into the community. The remaining respondents did not wish to disclose how much was spent or donated to the community, or stated that their programmes were either ad hoc or changed annually.

An example of best practice again seems to be the approach of Allied Irish Banks, which has a strong programme of charitable giving and community initiatives. Each year approximately 2% of pre-tax profits is allocated for community-based initiatives. In 1997, £5 million was donated in Ireland and the UK through its 'Corporate Giving Programme', addressing issues ranging from poverty and business start-up support to youth, environmental and arts projects. Anglo Irish Bank also annually allocates a similar percentage of pre-tax profits.

In the UK in 1998, Lloyds TSB donated £30 million, over 1% of its pre-tax profits, NatWest £14.3 million and Barclays £13.5 million. These companies are among the top ten corporate donors in the UK.[8] Such donations are primarily focused on education, the arts and sport, as well as varying degrees of community support. Lloyds TSB invested £9 million in community programmes in 1998, mainly to support regeneration in socially deprived areas. Barclays highlighted the fact that it offers secondment placing for staff, mainly in the charitable organisation or social banking sectors. Such advice and mentoring can be of immense value to the recipient organisations and individuals. A lack of knowledge of financial processes and management is often the biggest barrier to accessing financial services

Commerzbank, through its Foundation, is another leader in this sector, allocating 3% of pre-tax profits. The Foundation is primarily focused on improving both the living and working conditions of people in the vicinity of Commerzbank's head office, while also taking into account environmental considerations.

---

8   Figures taken from Smyth and Cassan 1999.

7.6 Business practices

This section in the survey referred to how the banks treat suspicious deposits and whether they invested or lent money to 'negative criteria' types of business, i.e. military, tobacco or nuclear industries. These issues gave information about the level of disclosure by the banks. A lack of disclosure can ultimately prove to be financially damaging, as discussed below in the case study.

7.6.1 Disclosure in general

As mentioned above, the lack of transparency and disclosure is one of our major concerns with the European banking sector. Of the banks that did reply to the questionnaire, the majority declined to provide any details of their interests in military suppliers, tobacco companies and the nuclear industry.

There was a poor reply rate from Italian banks, with only one reply—from Banca Fideuram. The language barrier may be a partial cause for the low level of replies. However, the Spanish banks responded well. They appear in a favourable light due to their generally good levels of disclosure and the fact that most appear to be making some efforts to improve their environmental stance in a country that is not traditionally a leader in this field.

The results of the survey for the Danish banks were surprising for a country that is generally considered to be proactive in the area of environmental protection. Both BG Bank and Jyske Bank would only respond to the questionnaire over the telephone. Disappointingly, Den Danske Bank did not return the questionnaire, but instead chose to send a standard reply letter. Although this indicated a willingness to disclose and publicise Den Danske's positive environmental and social practices, the bank thereby avoided replying to some of the more difficult questions.

German DG Bank and Commerzbank did disclose that they have business interests in the listed negative industries. Such openness can be seen as a positive aspect, especially as DG stated that the negative industries amount to only a minute portion of its loan portfolio and Commerzbank named those to whom they make such loans. Such disclosure may encourage investors to believe that the bank is less likely to be hiding potentially damaging information.

Credit Suisse and UBS both showed willingness to respond to aspects of the survey, but the restrictions placed on the banks by Switzerland's privacy laws were evident (see below).

The example set by The Co-operative Bank in the UK of providing an independently verified Social Report can be regarded as best practice within the sector. The bank's *Partnership Report* includes the views of seven interdependent stakeholder groups: shareholders, customers, staff and their families, suppliers, local communities, national and international society, past and future generations of co-operators. Such a balanced approach to reporting provides clear information as to the operations and attitudes of the bank, and gives the potential investor the confidence that there is less likelihood of any damaging information appearing in the future.

7.6.2 *Money laundering versus secrecy laws*

The European banks that are based within the EU are obliged by directives to prevent money laundering (The Implementation of the Money Laundering Directive 91/308). However, non-EU European banks—for example, the Swiss banks—are not obliged to comply.

The principle of the Swiss Banking Secrecy Law protects the financial privacy of clients to the degree that bank employees are criminally liable if such confidentiality is broken. Similar laws exist in Austria and Luxembourg. Approximately 99% of all Swiss banks are members of the Swiss Bankers' Association and the sector is strongly self-regulated. The self-regulatory Swiss banking sector and its supervisory body only recently bowed to US financial and political pressure to allow details of pre-1945 dormant accounts to be made public. Federal regulation concerning all dormant accounts is currently being considered, and the banking sector is urging that the time lapse for release of details to the state authorities is 20–30 years. This comparatively long period, compared to five years in the US, is due to the banks' wish to maintain the traditionally long relationships between the banks and clients and their families.[9]

Exceptions to the Swiss Banking Secrecy Law do exist in other regulations, such as in the case where the client is under criminal investigation in Switzerland, or in case of bankruptcy. The Swiss banks are not obliged to report any suspicious deposits in accordance with the EU Money Laundering directive, because Switzerland is, of course, not a member of the EU. Since 1990, in Switzerland there have been regulations stating that deposits that are suspected of being connected to money-laundering activities, must be reported to the authorities. However, primarily due to the Secrecy Law, Swiss bank accounts have a reputation for being the preferred destination for money transferred from dubious sources. Allegations of deposits, such as 'Marcos's Millions', continue to abound. The two Swiss banks responding to the survey, Credit Suisse and UBS, refused to disclose any details of the banks' investments or lending, stating that those details were 'proprietary business information'.

7.7 Disclosure case study: retrospective liabilities

7.7.1 *The role of European banks in their dealings with the Nazis*

Although this subject was not part of the survey, it is relevant, as a case study, to the issue of business practices and disclosure because this is a social issue that gives rise to financial liability.

It has taken more than half a century for dealings with the Nazis to be acknowledged by German, Swiss, Austrian and other European banks. The findings of the Independent Committee of Eminent Persons (ICEP, or Volcker Committee), published in 1999, and the results of the Bergier Commission, are likely to create further claims. The French

---

9 Personal communication with Silvia Matile, Swiss Bankers' Association, March 1999.

banks, SocGen and Paribas, and the British bank, Barclays, have also been in negotiations relating to settlement of claims against them concerning their actions during the war.

7.7.1.1 The Swiss banks

It was the need for US regulators' approval for the UBS merger with SBC that finally forced the Swiss banks to address the issue of dormant accounts. This coincided with the decisive class action taken by the New York State Pension Fund, a socially responsible investment fund. It was not from a moral desire to make amends for the banks' actions during the war, otherwise the banks could have acted much earlier.

The Swiss banks, acting in concert, were far more biased towards the Nazis and, indeed, assisted in the financing of the Nazi military effort, than the Swiss had previously admitted.

Nevertheless, the Swiss are now acting positively, with the establishment of the Holocaust Fund by the major Swiss banks, the Swiss National Bank and private Swiss enterprises. In 1998, UBS and Credit Suisse reached agreement with lawyers and representatives of the class action plaintiffs and certain Jewish organisations to settle claims of Holocaust victims and survivors. The two Swiss banks agreed to pay US$1.25 billion, with UBS responsible for two-thirds of this amount.

7.7.1.2 The German banks

It has been revealed only recently that both Deutsche and Dresdner Banks bought gold from the Nazi-controlled Reichsbank, while being aware that such gold had been stolen from Jewish companies, homes and individuals. Dresdner Bank was known as the SS Bank, while Deutsche Bank helped to finance the construction of concentration camps. Such revelations appeared in the wake of the US class actions by potential investors against the Swiss banks. Deutsche Bank's planned merger with America Bankers Trust has also forced such issues into the open as the US regulators probe Deutsche's past.

German companies originally stated that they are not liable for any claims because these were dealt with by the terms of settlements after the end of the war. However, Deutsche and Dresdner have now agreed, together with other German corporations, to contribute to an umbrella fund to make reparations.[10]

7.7.1.3 The Austrian banks

Like some of their other European counterparts, the Austrian banks have so far avoided addressing the issue of compensation to the depositors, or their relatives, whose accounts were seized under the instruction of the Nazis. However, Bank Austria has been more forthcoming than PSK, the Post Office Savings Bank. PSK does not wish to admit its active role during the period of Nazi 'occupation' and therefore does not acknowledge the claims for repayment.

---

10 *International Monitor*, March 1999, produced by the office of New York City Comptroller Alan G. Hevesi: www.financenet.gov/nycnet.htm.

7.7.2 *Summary of case study*

The process of settlement is likely to drag on for several years, with the banks facing embarrassing and damaging claims for some time to come because of their lack of disclosure in the past. However, there is no likelihood that this episode will stimulate any change in the Swiss Banking Secrecy Laws. Improved disclosure will only be possible through action by the banks themselves. By highlighting the potential financial losses caused by their lack of disclosure, it is hoped the banks will learn from their mistakes to avoid such scandals in the future.

7.8 Conclusion

Although certain banks are taking steps to become more progressive in their attitudes towards sustainable development, the sector as a whole is only slowly beginning to address the issues involved.

The prime areas of concern are the banks' attitude towards transparency and accountability with regard to their lending policies. Transparency of the banks' operations at every level is necessary to instil confidence among shareholders, employees, customers and other stakeholders that the banks are addressing sustainable development. European banks generally remain conservative in their attitude towards transparency, but accountability and liability will ultimately decide how they progress in the future.

Banks are taking steps to improve their own operational housekeeping. However, the incorporation of environmental aspects into the banks' products and services is currently made to reduce their financial risk. In order to promote best practice, the banks need to start measuring their customers' environmental performance. Until this occurs on a widespread basis, the majority of commercial customers will do nothing more than adopt minimum compliance to existing regulations.

As knowledge of sustainable development improves, governments, companies and individuals pay more attention to this matter. Companies, by necessity, are becoming more accountable to a broader range of stakeholders.

If small banks, such as those in the co-operative, mutual and social sectors, are able to impose environmental and ethical conditions in their loan portfolio and not only survive, but also make a profit, then surely the bigger commercial banks could be more proactive in this area?

We commend all respondents for their disclosure, and encourage commitment to regular social and environmental reporting, which necessarily indicates social responsibility. Europe can learn from the implementation in the US of steps to address social exclusion. As branch closures increase, demands may grow for US-style CRA statutory legislation. It is therefore important that banks, should they wish to maintain their self-regulatory status in this area, do not exacerbate social exclusion through panic 'restructuring'. Progressive banks will assess the social impact of branch closures and provide accessible alternatives.

Banks have always been keen to promote themselves as cornerstones of society. However, the majority of the banks wish to avoid the role of moral arbiters and do not regard themselves as regulators. They do play a key role in society, but generally seem unwilling to accept and adopt the linked responsibility. Too many banks still consider that what they provide is merely a retail product, with responsibility ending at point of sale. By adopting a more progressive attitude towards sustainable development, the banks can maintain such a position in our society of rapidly evolving expectations. A change of attitude by the banks has been shown over the last few years, reflected by the increase of environmental reporting within the sector. The banks now have the opportunity to anticipate further change, develop progressive policies and adapt their operations accordingly.

SUSTAINABLE BANKING IN AUSTRIA

Christine Jasch

Institute for Environmental Management
and Economics (IÖW), Austria

8.1 Austria's route to sustainable banking

Austria was the first country in the European Union (EU) whose banking industry was allowed to participate in the European Eco-management and Audit Scheme (EMAS). The draft ordinance to this effect had been circulated for inspection and comment as early as February 1996. At the time, a number of Austrian banks had already begun to establish internal environmental management systems.

Österreichische Kommunalkredit AG, which presented its first environmental report in summer 1996, was EMAS-certified in April 1997. Raiffeisen Landesbank AG (RLB) was certified to ISO 14001 in February 1996 and to EMAS in April 1997.

No other banks achieved certification, even though several of them had very committed environmental managers. As early as 1993, for example, Bank Austria and Creditanstalt had issued checklists for the inspection of contaminated sites before a loan could be granted, and had organised training schemes in order to increase environmental awareness. In the case of such banks, management declined to give the final go-ahead for EMAS participation. This is partly due to the Austrian law for EMAS participation for this sector, which required the inclusion of one-third of all branch offices, together with the head office, at first verification, two-thirds at the second verification (after one to three years) and five-sixths of all sites in the next round in order to fulfil the legal authorities' interpretation of the site approach of the EMAS Regulation. This law has recently been withdrawn, and it is unlikely that the EC will come up with similar interpretation guidelines once EMAS is open for all sectors everywhere.

In August 1999, the Österreichische Nationalbank (OeNB), whose printing facilities for paper money had been certified to ISO 14001 in December 1997, had parts of its administration certified to EMAS.

The sudden international interest in sustainability will hopefully provide new stimulus for national activities in the future.

8.1.1 Kommunalkredit AG

Kommunalkredit is the investment bank for Austria's municipalities and handles all environmental support programmes of the Austrian Ministry of the Environment, especially those concerned with municipal water supply and waste-water treatment, remediation of contaminated sites, energy supply using renewable resources and cleaner production projects. Kommunalkredit signed the UNEP Declaration in 1994, and in the following year it initiated the Austrian funding system for SME participation in EMAS on behalf of the Ministry of the Environment. In 1996 the bank presented its first environmental report, but it was only able to sign up for EMAS in April 1997 when the possibility of EMAS participation for this sector was raised. Over the past few years, Kommunalkredit bonds (rated Aa3 by Moody's) have become increasingly appealing to investors focusing on sustainable development.

The bank has no branches and operates from just one site. Because the employees deal with requests for the funding of environmental projects on a daily basis , environmental awareness is exceptionally high. In terms of the bank's environmental management system, checklists are provided for the following aspects: green purchase of office supplies; environmentally sound office furniture; environmental aspects of telecommunication; transport; room climate, heating and fresh air; risk assessment when awarding loans; waste prevention and separate waste collection.

In addition to recording its input–output material balance, the company publishes absolute and relative environmental performance indicators in relation to number of employees and operating earnings. The performance indicators for 1998 are shown in Table 8.1.

As mentioned above, the bank's core activity is the handling of subsidies and funding for pollution prevention projects on behalf of the Austrian Ministry of the Environment. Another strong market is the financing of energy contracting for municipalities. There are no other business activities, and the bank does not have branch offices. It is therefore comparatively easy for Kommunalkredit to comply with environmental product policy. The bank also recently issued internal guidance for environmentally sound investments, and all its public bonds (which means 70% of all company bonds) are issued as environmental bonds.

8.1.2 Raiffeisen Landesbank Wien (RLB)

The Raiffeisen banking group was originally formed from agricultural lending co-operatives and has very strong roots in natural resource-related industries. Environmental awareness has been on its agenda for many years and is completely consistent with the overall management policy. Thus, its positioning as 'the green bank' comes naturally, even though it makes life rather hard for the other banks by leaving them little room to position themselves in the 'green' niche.

Office space (m² per employee)	42.7
Energy input	
Electricity (kWh per employee)	3,736
Electricity (kWh per €1,000)	14.91
Heating energy (kWh per m²)	165.8
Water	
Water input (litres per employee per day)	45
Paper	
Paper (sheets of paper per employee)	13,637
Paper (sheets of paper per thousand euro)	54.43
Percentage of recycling paper	99
Traffic	
Business travel (km per employee)	4,999
Business travel (per €1,000)*	19.95
Percentage car-kilometres to total traffic	56.68
Percentage train-kilometres to total traffic	5.83
Percentage air-kilometres to total traffic	37.5
Waste	
Waste paper (percentage of total waste)	64
Percentage municipal waste of total waste	29

* Related to operational earnings

Table 8.1 **Kommunalkredit AG's environmental performance indicators for 1998**

RLB's environmental strategy is based on the following principles, to be applied internally and externally:

- Raising awareness on environmental issues

- Supplying information and solutions

- Providing a good example itself

Its goals focus on:

- Signalling environmental competence by regularly performing workshops and seminars on critical and/or currently strongly debated environmental issues

- Providing special services, sponsoring and funding for environmental NGOs

- Reducing potential risks when granting loans by contaminated site inspections

- Active awareness raising in politics and industry

■ Supply assistance on integration of environmental aspects to the numerous branches in the villages

■ Mobility and logistic issues

■ Optimisation of site management with regard to water and energy saving, green purchase and minimisation of material input

The RLB also publishes detailed environmental data and indicators. The indicators for 1998 are shown in Table 8.2.

As previously mentioned, raising environmental awareness through various information and sponsoring activities is one of the core elements of RLB's environmental strategy. In the past the bank also tried to place a green product on the market, but with little success. In autumn 1989 there was a tight race between Raiffeisen and another Viennese capital investment company, Zentralsparkasse (now part of Bank Austria AG), to become the first to offer Austria's first environmentally oriented investment fund. Zentralsparkasse's 'z-Umweltfonds' was wound up at the end of March 1994, however, because,

Office space (m² per employee)	30.63
Material input	
Paper (kg per employee)	95.78
Office material (kg per employee)	15.43
Cleaning material (litres/m²)	0.157
Water (m³ per employee)	43.45
Energy input	
Electricity (kWh per employee)	3,999
Petrol (litres per employee)	122.82
Business travel (km per employee)	1,176
Municipal steam (kWh/m²)	141.76
Waste (kg per employee)	
Non-hazardous waste	
Municipal waste	121.66
Office material	1.79
Electronic material	0.93
Workshop waste	81.10
Recycling materials	
Paper	102.67
Plastic	0.27
Glass	2.85
Hazardous waste	
Batteries	0.37
Glass tubes	0.65

Table 8.2 **RLB environmental performance indicators, 1998**

according to Bank Austria AG, volumes did not warrant its continuation. Sales had amounted to about Sch2 million (€872.068). RLB also had to withdraw its 'green fund' in January 1997; it seems the Austrian market is simply too small for such an instrument.

Currently, it is only possible to participate in foreign 'green' funds, or else to make direct investments, mostly in Austrian and German projects for energy supply based on renewable resources, which often also have a tax incentive. In a country with only 7 million inhabitants, the market for purely national activities is limited.

8.1.3 Österreichische Nationalbank (OeNB)

OeNB's banknote printing facilities were certified to ISO 14001 in December 1997. In January 2000, the bank registered some of its banking activities to EMAS. The daily banking operations, apart from the printing facility, have two significant environmental aspects, one being the energy consumption of the storehouse and computer areas' air-conditioning system, and the other being the scrapping of paper money, which requires special precautions to be taken. OeNB's product policy is regulated by law and therefore provides little opportunity for initiatives on the part of the bank; this topic is not even mentioned in its environmental statement.

8.2 Conclusion

In 1996, the Austrian Ministry of the Environment initiated a number of pilot projects related to the planned extension of sectors eligible for participation in EMAS. This was followed by sector-specific manuals for EMAS implementation. The Austrian IÖW (Institute for Environmental Management and Economics), together with the IMU (Institute for Management and Environment), Augsburg, provided a manual for the implementation of the EMAS Regulation in the banking and insurance industries (see Jasch et al. 1997). The guidelines gave sector-specific recommendations, with a special focus on benchmarking indicators. The manual was discussed in workshops attended by the environmental managers of banking institutions, and subsequently distributed widely. But, apart from the institutions already preparing for EMAS, the response was disappointing.

It seems that, even in a country with outstanding environmental awareness such as Austria, it is difficult for organisations to pursue environmental management once the forerunners have gained public attention and the spotlight is off the subject. For institutions that have specifically included environmental aspects in their management policy, it was easy to achieve extra credits by pursuing the road towards sustainability. Kommunalkredit's core business is financing environmental protection. RLB, with its agricultural background, can easily use the corporate identity of 'the green bank' to shift the emphasis from agriculture to ecology. Even OeNB profits from its very limited scope, as the bank simply cannot carry out product management beyond the environmentally friendly design of packaging materials.

But for all other institutions covering the normal range of banking services, the decision to enter the field of sustainable banking is far from easy, and obviously interferes with strategic business practices. Apart from the verification costs, the internal handling of several hundred sites seems to present a frightening challenge.

At the initial review of environmental aspects, all banks found significant improvement options within the operational system, but also often limited implementation choices. This is the case with business travel and buildings: the location of clients with regard to their connection to public transport is difficult to influence, and so is the decision whether to abandon the 1970s skyscraper with its inefficient heating and air-conditioning system. The initial review often revealed some room for improvement in the area of legal compliance, as the application of some of the environmental regulations is not immediately obvious for the service sector as a whole.

Now that the European market is opening up and there is growing European interest in green investments, sustainability reporting and disclosure of environmental issues in annual reports, environmental management is again rising to the top of the agenda. I believe this is more pronounced outside Austria than inside the country, however. Austria is saturated with environmental projects and initiatives, and local consumer awareness and pressure have declined. It may be that Austria was simply too quick in implementing sustainable banking and will only now be rewarded internationally for its pioneering role.

ENVIRONMENTAL ATTITUDES OF BANKS AND FINANCIAL INSTITUTIONS*

Judit Barta
GKI Economic Research Co.,
Hungary

Vilma Éri
Centre for Environmental Studies,
Hungary

9.1 Financial institutions and the environment

Between 1995 and 1997, Hungary spent 0.6%–0.7% of its GDP on environmental investments—a rather low share compared with that of OECD countries. Of this amount, just 3% was financed from loans while more than 70% was financed from governmental resources. Hence, the direct impact of financial institutions on the environmental performance of companies through their financing of environmental investments was not significant.

Until 1997, in Hungary the indirect influence of the banks and financial institutions on the environmental policies of businesses, i.e. through their loan-making practices for general company investments, was also limited as the share of loans to the business sector in general was low. In 1996 it hardly exceeded 30% of balance sheets, while the share of state bonds on balance sheets was rather high. In addition many companies, among them environmentally sensitive ones, became loss-makers after the country's economic transition had begun, so they were not attractive business partners for the financial institutions anyway. These companies did not get loans, no matter how significant or insignificant the environmental risk posed by their activities. This situation started to change in 1997, after economic reforms had brought about an upward trend of economic growth.

The influence of financial institutions on the environmental performance of companies may grow, too, if these institutions pursue environmentally conscious lending and

* Originally prepared as a part of the project 'Strengthening Business Contributions to Sustainable Development in Central and Eastern Europe', led by Dr Zbigniew Bochniarz and supported by the Charles Stewart Mott Foundation and the Rockefeller Family Associates.

investment policies. The most significant driving force for increasing environmental awareness on the part of banks comes from outside, namely from Hungary's proposed future integration into the European Union. As integration proceeds, environmental legislation and enforcement is becoming increasingly strict. Sooner or later, Hungary will have to comply fully with EU environmental regulations. Practices that were tolerable years ago will have to be phased out, which implies increasing environmental expenditures. This means that the environmental risks of banks will increase substantially in a relatively short period.

A recent survey investigated the extent to which Hungarian financial institutions are aware of environmental risks related to their activities, and how successfully they integrate environmental considerations into loan-making and investment decisions. The survey used the questionnaire of the 1995 'UNEP Global Survey on Environmental Policies and Practices of the Financial Services Sector', prepared by Environment and Finance Research Enterprise (UNEP 1995).

The sample consisted of 11 financial institutions: eight commercial banks, the Hungarian division of an international financial institution and two investment fund management companies. Among the eight commercial banks there were three significant (in Hungarian terms) commercial banks, two smaller commercial banks, and three specialised development banks (Fig. 9.1).

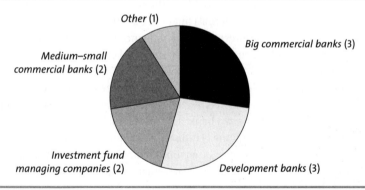

Figure 9.1 **Breakdown of the sample**

The eight commercial banks represent 20% of all Hungarian commercial banks in terms of numbers. However, they represent 49% of the banking sector's total assets and roughly 40% of business sector commercial bank credits.

One of the two investment fund managing companies in the sample is significant on the Hungarian scene, while the other is a rather small and new one, representing a foreign investor.

The sample did not include Hungary's National Environmental Fund because the Fund operates as a government agency rather than a financial institution.

The environmental awareness and environmental 'friendliness' of financial institutions was investigated in two aspects.

On the one hand, questions probed perceptions and intentions in order to learn whether financial institutions view themselves as important stakeholders in environmental protection. They were asked how they perceive their role and understand their opportunities, and if they operate accordingly, i.e. if they incorporate environmental issues into various fields of their operations such as financial services, human resource management, corporate organisational structure, public relations, etc. The other group of questions investigated to what extent banks pursue environmental protection-related activities and how these activities influence the environmental behaviour of their business partners.

Questions relating to the integration of environmental protection into managerial issues, as well as to actual financial services, could also provide a control for responses given to questions related to perceptions and intentions by revealing potential inconsistencies between actual banking practices and declarations on environmental commitment made because of perceived public pressure for environmental friendliness.

Declarations on environmental perceptions and commitment, however, proved to be modest and realistic. Responding financial institutions did not feign a stronger environmental commitment than they actually have. This is not surprising because public environmental pressure, though growing, is still concentrated on local and national governments and some polluting businesses and has not yet reached the banks.

Only one of the institutions surveyed said that it was greatly affected by environmental issues (Fig. 9.2). This is understandable as the respondent was an environmentally committed international (supranational) financial institution. Hungarian banks, on the other hand, stated that environmental issues influenced their activities 'somewhat' or 'slightly'. The investment fund managing companies said that these issues influence their decisions only slightly, if at all. The answers showed another interesting tendency. Bigger commercial banks and the bigger investment banks answered with 'somewhat' and the smaller ones with 'slightly'. The answers also reflect the extent of the banks' credit practice. The only exception is a middle-sized bank, a relatively small one in this category, which formerly had many dealings with the National Environmental Fund.

In the opinion of the respondents, the environmental involvement of banks is affected mostly by external factors. It is a result of legal regulations and the requirements of major

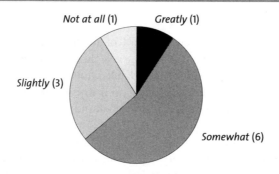

Figure 9.2 **To what extent do you believe that environmental issues affect your institution?**

business partners rather than an internal effort of financial institutions themselves. Most financial institutions interviewed are aware of legal environmental regulations affecting them, though not all of these respondents know the specifics.

Eight organisations out of 11 stated that they have to comply with governmental legal regulations. Six out of 11 also felt obliged by international development banks, private banking partners, private multinational corporations, trade associations and industry groups to follow environmentally conscious banking practices. Most organisations mentioned international development banks as sources of these obligations. The most frequently mentioned partner requiring environmentally sound banking practices was EBRD (European Bank for Reconstruction and Development). The significant role of international development banks in the environmental education of Hungarian banks is reflected by the fact that, for one big commercial bank, pressure from international banks was more important than legal regulations.

Respondents were clearly well aware that co-financing with the World Bank, EBRD or EIB (European Investment Bank) means a thorough analysis of environmental aspects. There are some credit lines in Hungary where the applicants have to demonstrate their environmental responsibility: for instance, in the case of the special energy conservation fund set up with the financial help of Germany, or the fund offered by the Japanese Exim Bank which finances non-polluting activities only. Environmental aspects are also very important for the JOP programme, a sub-programme of the Phare assistance which supports the co-operation of EU and Phare-country firms in the form of joint ventures. Among other goals, the programme seeks to help with the preparation of environmental projects, and promote co-operation in quality control and standards.

Non-governmental organisations, private business partners, private multinational corporations and industrial groups, on the other hand, seem to have very little impact on environmentally conscious banking practices.

Only four financial institutions out of the 11 interviewed have documented environmental policies: three of the bigger commercial banks and the international financial institution interviewed (Fig. 9.3). This latter organisation and one of the big Hungarian commercial banks were found to have formulated environmental policies both for internal housekeeping operations (i.e. use of environmentally friendly office supplies,

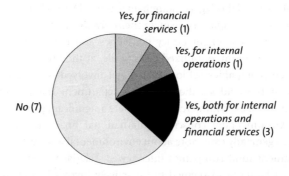

Yes, for financial services (1)

Yes, for internal operations (1)

No (7)

Yes, both for internal operations and financial services (3)

Figure 9.3 **Does your firm have a documented environmental policy?**

energy conservation, applying environmental criteria in procurement, etc.) and for their financial services. The other two policies are less comprehensive. One of them relates to internal activities, the other to external financial services.

Those institutions that had internal environmental policies adopted them between three and five years ago. The low level of company lending at the time, however, restricted the actual impacts and significance of these policies in most cases. Consequently, even institutions that have internal environmental policies may operate without internal environmental experts. Nine of the 11 financial institutions interviewed had no employees with environmentally related responsibilities as a major component of their jobs, let alone environmental departments. The only exception was the above-mentioned middle-sized bank, which has no policy declaration and no environmental department as such, but employs two people for environment-related jobs. (This is the bank with former experience and practice in evaluating environmental programmes.) The international financial institution, on the other hand, maintains its sizeable environmental department at its headquarters abroad, not in Budapest.

Though, as mentioned earlier, most financial institutions interviewed do not have staff members who devote more than 50% of their time to environmental issues, in their occasional involvement in environmental tasks banks either rely on their own staff members to perform the work or the job is done by the partner organisations that require the environmental assessment. It is probable that environmental investigations (if any) are carried out by consultants or by professional organisations, as only one bank reported having employed environmental experts. Only one bank reported the involvement of a third party, i.e. an environmental business selected by a business partner to make the analysis. Even where environmental tasks are performed by internal staff members, these staff do not spend more than half of their time on such tasks—another sign that financial institutions are not significantly involved in environmental issues.

There is a close correlation between the lack of environmental staff and policy and the lack of practice (Fig. 9.4). Most responding banks are rarely involved even in environmental credit risk analysis or audits. They also seldom seek information on environmental regulations. They rarely extend loans to, or invest in, environmental businesses or engage in environmental impact assessment. This latter fact is understandable as it is the investor that has to provide the assessment and obtain environmental licences. Banks would only check if this legal requirement was met by the claimant. They would carry out the environmental impact assessment themselves only if they were the direct investors.

Banks with environment policy guidelines and environmental staff engage more frequently in environment-linked tasks while, at the other end of the spectrum, fund management companies seldom if ever get involved in such tasks. The most active institution in this field was the Hungarian department of a large international financial institution, and a big commercial bank where a significant proportion of equity is owned by an environmentally conscious international financial institution. Again, bigger institutions generally care more about environmental aspects than smaller ones. One of the investment fund companies interviewed, relatively small compared with the big commercial banks, also seemed to be actively involved in environmental credit risk analysis.

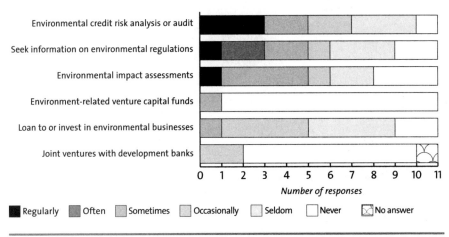

Figure 9.4 **How often is your organisation engaged in the stated activities which address environmental issues?**

The infrequency of some environment-related transactions, however, is due rather to general circumstances than to the limited environmental awareness of financial institutions. For instance, joint ventures with development banks are not common in Hungary. Also, according to Hungarian banking regulations, venture capital investments are regarded as too risky for banks, so this type of financing is provided mostly by specialised financial institutions—venture capital companies that were not represented in the sample. Strict banking regulations restrict the financial activity of commercial banks to the traditional lending and deposit collecting. Whatever the reason, financial institutions' involvement in these environmental issues is also low and does not necessitate the employment of extensive environmental staff and the operation of environmental departments.

Again, it is probably the limited number of environmental issues that explains why banks have not found it difficult to meet the environmental requirements of the law or their business partners. Financial institutions reported that it was easy to comply with these requirements. The only institution that replied that it was 'slightly difficult to comply with' was the previously mentioned medium-sized bank with its relatively long record of environmental transactions.

The UNEP Statement by Financial Institutions on the Environment and Sustainable Development is not well known among Hungarian financial institutions. It is likely that it was poorly advertised in Hungary; only the international financial institution and one big commercial bank interviewed had signed up to it (Fig. 9.5). Respondents had to express their familiarity and agreement with the statement on a sliding six-point scale (Figs. 9.6 and 9.7).[1] In most cases, the respondents did not even know whether their

1   Familiarity had to be graded on the following scale: 'very familiar', 'somewhat familiar', 'slightly familiar', 'slightly unfamiliar', 'somewhat unfamiliar', 'not familiar at all'. Agreement could be scaled as 'agree completely', 'agree somewhat', 'agree slightly', 'disagree slightly', 'disagree somewhat', 'disagree completely'. The labelling of the six points may be not very precise, but it is the positioning of the answers on the scale rather than the term used for the degree of agreement or familiarity that is important.

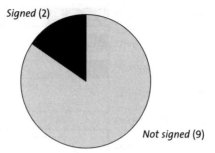

Figure 9.5 **Has your organisation signed the UNEP statement?**

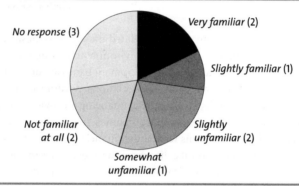

Figure 9.6 **How familiar is your organisation with the UNEP statement?**

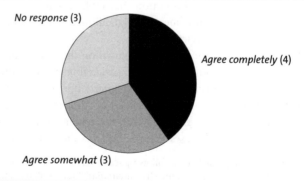

Figure 9.7 **Rate your organisation's level of agreement with the UNEP statement.**

institution was a signatory to the statement or not, and they were forced to carry out some inquiries before answering this question.

From those that had signed the statement, only the Hungarian signatory stated that this decision had resulted in an increase in environmental activity on the part of the bank.

After having read the statement, six out of the nine respondents that have not yet signed the statement declared that they agreed (more or less) with the statement. Their statements about their potential signing were somewhat less positive (Fig. 9.8), but two-thirds of the banks would probably sign the statement if there were a new initiative. On the other hand, it is also likely that some responding Hungarian financial institutions have already become signatories of the statement through their mother banks, without being aware of this fact.

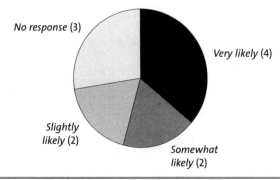

Figure 9.8 **Rate your organisation's likelihood of signing the UNEP statement.**

9.2 The banks' impact on environmental performance of businesses

Due to the vague perception of the environmental responsibilities of financial institutions and the lack of environmental commitment, as well as the limited experience with environmentally risky financial transactions, Hungarian financial institutions are still rather passive with respect to environmental challenges (Fig. 9.9). Instead of integrating environmental considerations in their financing practices, actively looking for risks stemming from environmental problems in order to abate them or looking for opportunities related to the rational use of natural resources and successful environmental management, they deal with environmental issues only when they cannot avoid doing so.

Unsurprisingly, in view of their general ignorance of environment-related issues, the institutions seem to care rather more about activities that may affect the business risk of transactions than about financing environmentally friendly activities. For instance, they care more about adding environmental criteria to the credit review process or educating internal staff about environmental issues than about energy conservation, resource

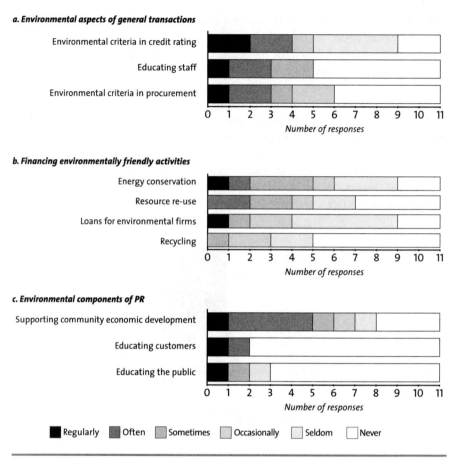

Figure 9.9   **How often is your organisation involved in the above environmental efforts?**

reduction and re-use. In fact, recycling is the least important environment-related activity for them, which might indicate that recycling is not safe and profitable enough for banks.

The public relations activities of financial institutions do not frequently include environmental components, either. Supporting economic development in the communities where the banks operate is definitely a more popular PR tool for the banks than educating customers or the general public about environmental issues. In general, however, banks do not often support the development of their communities either. Here again, larger commercial banks with longer environmental records seem to be more active. The commitment of smaller institutions, including the investment fund management companies, seems to be less significant.

Despite their lack of practice in evaluating environmental liabilities or risks, eight banks answered that they took into account these risks—when assessing large loans or investments, at least (Fig. 9.10). All of these institutions have rejected loans or refused investments on account of environmental liabilities, exposure or risk. The proportion of

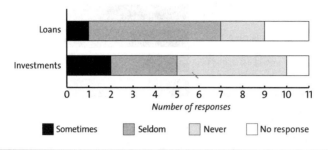

Figure 9.10 **How often has your organisation rejected loans or refused investments owing to environmental considerations?**

financing proposals declined on these grounds was in most cases 1% or less, however, and it never exceeded 4%. The low level of rejections does not necessarily indicate environmental negligence. Financial institutions that have not declined financing proposals for environmental considerations may not have been confronted with such investment decisions due to the characteristics of their business portfolio.

It is important, and encouraging, that most banks attach environmental conditions to loan agreements. All the bigger commercial banks reported doing so; only small banks and investment fund companies do not attach environmental provisos.

Despite these conditions and provisos, the majority of responding banks do not require regular control of environmental issues. Only the international financial institution and one large Hungarian bank required regular yearly environmental updates, assessments or audits; two other organisations requested less frequent updates, while six institutions did not ask for special environmental information at all (Fig. 9.11). In the case of investment contracts, monitoring is generally even less frequent (with the exception of the international financial institution) than in the case of loans.

In general, the information package that claimants have to provide for financial institutions does include some environmental information. This includes the obligatory appendices to the company annual report required by the Accountancy Act. Figures relating to tangible assets directly serving environmental protection purposes, for instance, must be included in these appendices. Since 1994 the Accountancy Act has provided an opportunity for companies to make provisions to cover the expected amount of environmental damages and liabilities. The amount allocated to this type of provision shows the extent of environmental risk of a firm, but it also shows that firm's level of environmental awareness. Another opportunity to investigate environmental liabilities of the firms is the profit and loss statement which in the line of extraordinary expenditures may include information on various fines, penalties and indemnifications. Though the appendix includes only one total for extraordinary expenditures without a breakdown, a thorough investigation may reveal the individual components of that amount. All this information, however, is not sufficient for a strict environmental credit risk analysis and cannot replace regular updates of environmental information.

Despite the lack of regular control, the surveyed financial institutions had experienced no financial liabilities and had not been held responsible for any remediation. These

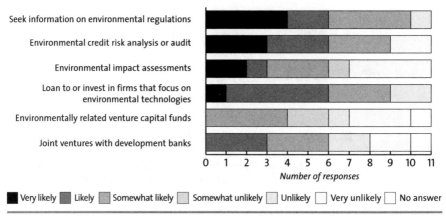

Seek information on environmental regulations

Environmental credit risk analysis or audit

Environmental impact assessments

Loan to or invest in firms that focus on environmental technologies

Environmentally related venture capital funds

Joint ventures with development banks

0   1   2   3   4   5   6   7   8   9   10   11

Number of responses

■ Very likely ■ Likely ▨ Somewhat likely ☐ Somewhat unlikely ☐ Unlikely ☐ Very unlikely ☐ No answer

Figure 9.11 **How likely is your organisation to participate regularly in the stated environmental activities?**

answers may refer to the fact that environmental regulations do not affect banks directly and/or the loan agreements are constructed so that no responsibility is put on the lender.

Banks also reported a minimal number of loan failures. Those banks of the sample that regularly controlled the environmental components related to their services had no problems with environmental issues, except for one commercial bank. This bank reported two to five cases, which is insignificant in comparison to the number of loans it issues.

Financial institutions expect that their environment-related activities will probably be expanded in three to five years' time. Besides carrying out more intensive environmental credit risk analyses and seeking more information on environmental regulations, financial institutions foresee that they will increase their loans to or investments in environmental businesses.

9.3 Conclusion

The survey (started in 1997 and finished in 1998) showed that the environmental commitment on the part of Hungarian banks was not very great. Although no new surveys have been carried out since this one, and only two interviews have been repeated, we think that the basic situation has changed somewhat. The main reason for this is that the financial resources that became available from 1997–99 provided the banks with new credit resources and clients. The resources opened up by Phare, the EU and the World Bank were available only to banks that could fulfil special requirements on the part of the lenders. It meant that the selected banks were forced to educate their staff, introduce guidebooks for managing this type of credit and include different aspect of environmental risk to the process of credit rating. The other effect was caused by EBRD, IBRD and EIB. These international banks forced their client/correspondent/partner or daughter banks to introduce environmental aspects to the process of credit rating.

Currently these provisions have little impact in banking, as the 'old' resources (i.e. credit lines provided by international organisations or foreign governments) have been used up while new resources have not opened. The already-mentioned special energy conservation revolving fund set up with German financial help or the environmental credit line offered by the Japanese Exim Bank have not been refilled as repayment of loans began only recently. At the same time, the use of financial resources from Phare and SAPARD (Special Accession Programme for Agriculture and Rural Development) are delayed because of the tardiness of the Hungarian authorities in administering and managing these funds (e.g. the Phare criticism of Hungary).

It is probable that the general environmental risks of credit increased as the major borrowers were the utilities (especially electricity and gas) and heavy industry. On the other hand, the majority of new investor companies were/are under foreign ownership, i.e. their commitment to environmental regulations is significantly stronger. So, as a whole, new investments require a significantly higher environmental protection level than that formerly demanded in Hungary.

Environmental regulation developed at a slow pace here. This is reflected in two statements of the EU Commission. Both the 1997 Commission's opinions on the progress of the candidate countries[2] and the subsequent regular reports on progress towards accession by each candidate country recommended that the environmental situation and environmental regulation in Hungary should receive urgent reform. To this end the Hungarian parliament approved the guidelines of the National Environment Programme for 2000–2002. Its main aims are:

- To increase competitiveness with the help of environmentally friendly methods

- To draw up regional development programmes

- Water savings and the development of sewerage systems

- Local and industrial waste management

- Energy and raw material saving; the development of renewable energy resources; recycling of waste

- The development of environmentally friendly transport systems

- The protection of nature and the development of sustainable agricultural production

- The promotion of environmental safety

By the time the 2000 budget was announced, financing possibilities had increased somewhat. New resources were established with the help of state funds for regional development (including the Phare Interreg Programme and Phare Regional Development Programme), and for the development of local authorities/municipalities, especially in the areas of infrastructure/water and sewer systems. The financing possibilities of agriculture have also increased significantly. The tenders for financial assistance mainly

2   http://europa.eu.int/comm/enlargement

support production or market entry, but there are some topics related to environmental protection in a broader sense. One of the biggest Hungarian banks has been tasked with choosing candidates and financing this agricultural project.

The National Environmental Fund was incorporated to the central budget in 1999 and a special dedicated resource was formed within the budget for environmental development, mainly continuing the former goals. In 2000 the resources were increased with the financial help of the Danish government. This special credit programme focuses on environmental projects that are not financially viable or competitive.

With the new financing facilities in place and considering the determination of the government to improve Hungary's position in negotiations with the EU, an increase in environment-related credits is foreseeable. From 2000 on tenders will use up the frozen international financial help of Phare, etc, and the new credit facilities. As competition between Hungarian banks is rather keen regarding the enterprise sector, all new market niches are of great value. This will mean that more commercial banks will be willing to participate in paying out the resources of the separate fund and Phare contribution. This process will strengthen the expertise of banks in establishing credit ratings in this very specialised area. The other effect of this process will be a gradual one: namely, that banks will apply their knowledge of environment protection to other, more general, credit rating activity; for example, they will use the risk-management methods, guidebooks and elaborated environmental risk data in their daily credit decisions. Gradually environmental impact assessment of credit applications will become commonplace. This practice will influence the investors' way of thinking.

On the other hand the environmental situation in Hungary and the relatively high requirements of EU membership have created another market niche: namely, environmental businesses. Firms that are helping Hungarian companies to catch up with European environmental standards or to achieve ISO certification need investment, and companies need financial assistance to carry out the programmes they recommend. Taking into account all these opportunities, we foresee relatively rapid development in the environmental attitudes/commitments of Hungarian commercial banks.

BANKS AND ENVIRONMENTAL PRACTICES IN BANGKOK METROPOLITAN REGION
The need for change

Willi Zimmermann and Beatriz Mayer
Asian Institute of Technology, Thailand

Banks' involvement with environmental issues was first formalised a decade ago when a number of financial institutions backed the United Nations Environment Programme (UNEP)'s initiative, 'Statement by Financial Institutions on the Environment and Sustainable Development'. Since then the list of signatories has grown to over 155 banks worldwide; however, most of these institutions are from developed countries (UNEP 1998a). The minimal participation in this initiative by financial institutions from developing countries is reflected also in the lack of research on environmental management issues within the banks themselves.

As every region experiences its own specific environmental risks determined by its unique economic, social and historical factors, a developing country such as Thailand needs to generate and analyse its own data on the relationship between banks and environment. In order to understand this relationship in the Thai context, the research presented in this chapter attempted to analyse the links between environmental awareness and lending practices in Bangkok, where the headquarters of the country's principal national and international banks are located.

In Thailand, industrialisation has overwhelmed the country's environmental capacity. This is particularly true for Bangkok Metropolitan Region (BMR),[1] the centre of government and of industrial growth, and which accounts for 75% of total Thai manufacturing output. As a consequence, it also experiences the largest pollution concentrations in the country. A very high percentage of all industrial enterprises in the area are sources of water pollution, air pollution and hazardous waste generation—for example, 77% (1,258

---

1 Bangkok Metropolitan Region includes Bangkok and five surrounding provinces: Pathumthani, Nakhon Pathom, Nonthaburi, Samut Prakan and Samut Sakhon.

factories) of all the industrial enterprises in Samut Sakhon and 57.6% (11,585 factories) of all the industrial enterprises in Bangkok (20,119 factories) cause water pollution (levels of output not specified by the Pollution Control Department). Factories here also produced 71% of the hazardous waste generated in the area, including oils, halogenated organic sludge, etc. (Bello *et al.* 1998: 118-19). There is no doubt that banks in Thailand have participated in this industrial development, but the question remains whether their operations have taken environmental issues into account or whether they have been guided by environmental legislation. These and related questions were addressed by a survey carried out in spring 1999.

10.1 The survey

Currently, there are 33 commercial banks in Thailand: 13 domestic and 20 foreign fully licensed banks. Domestic Thai banks account for about 80% of banking assets, while foreign banks control the remaining 20% (US State Department 1999). To assess the banks' environmentally relevant activities, attitudes and practices, exploratory research was carried out among the headquarters of these Banks in April–May 1999. All 33 banks were approached and interviews requested of senior managers of the lending departments (see Table 10.1). A questionnaire was also distributed. The response rate was just below 66% (21 banks); the response rate among the domestic banks was relatively high: 85% (11 banks), whereas foreign banks' participation amounted to just 50% (see Fig. 1). It is worth noting before more detailed data is presented that the overall impression gained from respondents was one of a general lack of awareness of significant environmental issues (see Box 10.1).

10.1.1 Environmental management in Thai banks

Do banks in Thailand think that environmental issues exert any influence over their operations? In general, the answers were affirmative: the majority said they were either very much (18%) or somewhat (41%) affected by these issues, while 32% said they were slightly affected and the rest (9%) not at all affected. Domestic banks taken on their own seemed to show a higher concern regarding these issues: 22% said they were very much affected by environmental issues and 56% said they were somewhat affected. A low percentage (22%) thought they were just slightly affected, while none believed that they were not affected at all (see Fig. 10.2).

Does this relatively high show of concern translate into action? It is reasonable to assume that the existence of an environmental policy within an organisation is an indication of that organisation's commitment towards the environment. Such a policy serves as a foundation for planning and action and provides a unifying vision of the environmental concerns of the organisation. It also sets the major objectives and targets. In an ideal situation, the key policy commitments will include pollution abatement and

Thai banks	Foreign banks
▶ Bangkok Bank	▶ ABN AMRO Bank NV
▶ Krung Thai Bank	▶ Standard Chartered Bank
▶ Thai Farmers' Bank	▶ The Chase Manhattan Bank, NA
▶ Siam Commercial Bank	▶ Overseas Chinese Banking Corp. Ltd
▶ Thai Military Bank	▶ The Bank of Tokyo–Mitsubishi Ltd
▶ Bank of Ayudhya	▶ Citibank NA
▶ Siam City Bank	▶ The Sakura Bank Ltd
▶ Bangkok Metropolitan Bank	▶ The Bank of Nova Scotia
▶ Bank of Asia	▶ Bank of America NT&SA
▶ Thai Danu Bank	▶ Credit Agricole IndoSuez Bank Ltd
▶ Nakornthon Bank	▶ Bharat Overseas Bank Ltd
▶ Radhanasin Bank	▶ Deutsche Bank AG
▶ BankThai	▶ The Dai-Ichi Kangyo Bank Ltd
	▶ Dresdner Bank AG
	▶ Banque National de Paris
	▶ The Sumitomo Bank Ltd
	▶ The Industrial Bank of Japan Ltd
	▶ The International Commercial Bank of China
	▶ The Bank of China
	▶ The Hong Kong and Shanghai Banking Corp. Ltd

Table 10.1 **Banks contacted in the survey**

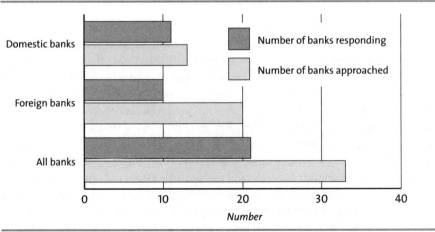

Figure 10.1 **Survey response rate**

IN SOME CASES THE INTERVIEWEES WERE NOT ESPECIALLY AWARE OF THE relationship between banks and the environment and were unable to answer some of the questions. Although 'complex' notions such as the Global Reporting Initiative (GRI), the 'triple bottom line', and issues relating to the Kyoto Protocol (emissions trading, joint implementation, clean development mechanisms) were assumed not to be known and therefore avoided during the survey, the authors were still struck by a general lack of awareness regarding the links that exist between the financial sector and the environment. For example, some of the respondents had not heard of lenders' liabilities at all. In addition, concepts such as environmental auditing, environmental reporting and environmental impact assessment were often confused.

Box 10.1 **General awareness deficit in survey respondents**

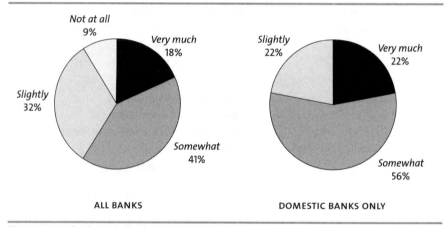

ALL BANKS   DOMESTIC BANKS ONLY

Figure 10.2 **Do banks in thailand think that environmental issues exert any influence over their operations?**

prevention, compliance with relevant laws and regulations and commitment to continuous improvement. In ten cases the representatives of the banks answered that they had an environmental policy. Of these ten, six are Thai banks (more than 50% of all Thai respondents). However, positive answers were supplied when, in many cases, no formal written environmental policy existed. These may be construed as examples of the respondents broadening the interpretation of 'environmental policy' to show their organisations in a favourable light. In reality, only three of the ten banks that answered affirmatively have a formal written policy; and all these are foreign banks whose environmental policies were developed in their countries of origin. Four banks stated that their policy was an implicit one only, and the remaining three did not know for certain whether a policy existed or how it was framed. The six Thai banks that claimed to have an environmental policy either said it was in an implicit form (three banks), or were unable to say whether it was in a written or implicit form (see Figs. 10.3 and 10.4).

Many bank headquarters in Western countries have organisational units and personnel that deal with environmental issues such as environmental risk assessments,

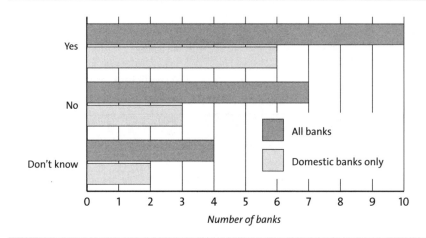

Figure 10.3 **Does your bank have an environmental policy?**

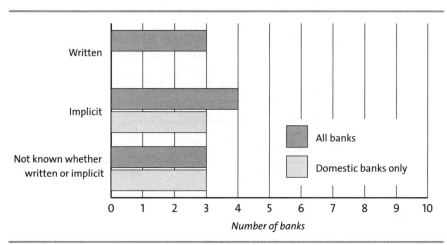

Figure 10.4 **If your bank has an environmental policy, what form does it take?**

environmental reports, etc. Most of the banks surveyed in BMR have no organisational unit or human resources responsible for environmental matters; only three foreign banks, and no Thai banks, have such a department (see Fig. 10.5). Where they exist, these departments are not consulted regularly.

In terms of their internal operations, nearly all the banks said they had taken measures to reduce paper and energy consumption, while almost 80% were doing the same for water. They are less proactive in reducing transportation and there is relatively little activity regarding environmental training programmes for employees (see Fig. 10.6). How effectively these activities are carried out remains a matter of discussion. Box 10.2 describes the kinds of activity performed.

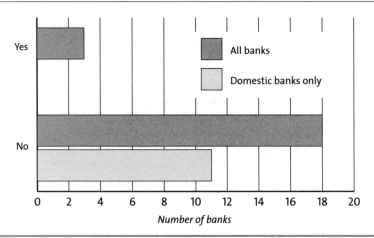

Figure 10.5 **Does your bank have an environmental department?**

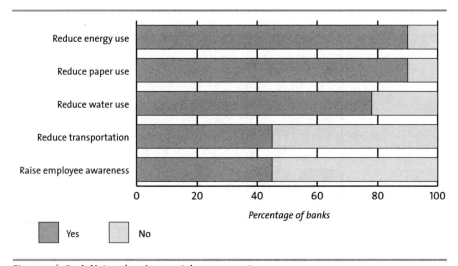

Figure 10.6 **Banks' internal environmental management**

IN THE INTERVIEWS SOME RESPONDENTS EXPLAINED THE WAY IN WHICH activities are carried out to reduce natural resources consumption and waste generation within their banks. It was apparent that none of these was a systematic operation. Answers included explanations that employees save energy by trying to turn off the lights during lunch break or turning off air conditioning after working hours, or that they use both sides of draft paper. One respondent also explained that signs were posted in offices encouraging employees to save electricity and water. One bank was slightly more systematic in that it had exchanged conventional light bulbs for more energy-efficient ones, and conventional taps for those with automatic cut-off.

Box 10.2 **Examples of banks' internal environmental activities**

The existence of measures to conserve resources is the most encouraging sign from this survey. However, the banks do not generally see their activities as polluting or resource-consuming. Most of the banks (72%) refuted this statement (see Fig. 10.7), while 23% said that it was only somewhat true. Only 5% thought that it was true. Thai banks taken alone were more emphatic, with 92% of respondents refuting the statement. Economising on resource use is motivated by an attempt to reduce operating costs rather than environmental principles, a fact that also helps to explain the lack of a systematic approach.

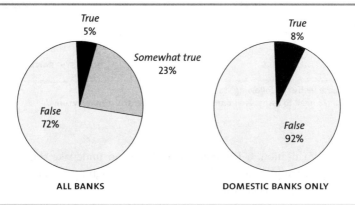

Figure 10.7 **Please verify the following statement: 'The bank is a polluter, i.e. the bank uses up natural resources.'**

10.1.2 Environmental credit risk assessments

Worldwide, bankers, investors, insurers and analysts are slowly discovering that 'going green' is financially rewarding; that environmental management and eco-efficiency can be competitively advantageous, enhance performance, improve financial prospects, and reduce risks.

In BMR. the 'greening of the market' is somewhat slow: 15% of the banks consulted said that they do not need to assess environmental risks in order to estimate returns, while 45% thought it merely somewhat necessary and 40% said it was necessary. Thai banks offered slightly stronger affirmations: 58% said that the statement is somewhat true and 42% thought it true. None of them thought it unnecessary to perform an environmental risk assessment (see Fig. 10.8).

However encouraging these figures might be, they are somewhat misleading, as banks in Thailand perform only very rudimentary environmental controls in the case of credit risk assessments: most of the banks consulted (seven) require only the factory licence issued by the Department of Industrial Works. Even though a few foreign banks do have regular and systematic procedures to assess a company's environmental risks, foreign banks account for only 20% of the total financial market in Thailand.[2] However, despite

2 It can be argued that these practices have effects beyond this 20% figure, due to the importance of spillover effects that international banks might have within the Thai banking sector. However, there is no empirical data to support this.

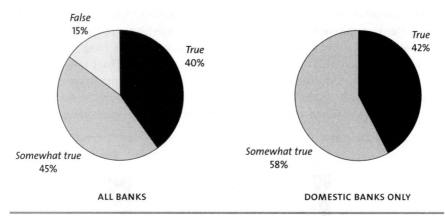

Figure 10.8 **Please verify the following statement:**
'Banks need to assess environmental risks in order to estimate returns.'

the lack of systematisation, a few banks have begun to undertake some superficial environmental screenings, especially in the case of some high-profile, environmentally risky sectors, such as petrochemicals.

The reason that environmental assessments in Thailand have not become more developed is that the environmental legal system is based on a command-and-control approach without strict enforcement. In other words, environmental risk is not a very pressing issue. Similarly, there has never been a case in which a company has been found liable for the costs of a site clean-up, for example. And, although the sizes of fines have increased significantly, since there is no litigation culture in Thailand, banks or enterprises do not perceive themselves to be at risk.

Banks were also asked to rank the importance of different factors when assessing customers. Financial performance was accorded the highest importance, followed by economic performance, reputation and management performance. Environmental, social and ethical performances are perceived to be of secondary importance (see Fig 10.9).[3]

This ranking order implies that the banks do not reject loans because of applicants' poor environmental performance. In fact, none of them has ever done this, as common practice has it that several factors have to be combined in order to refuse a loan. Only two banks stated that, in very rare cases, a loan might be rejected based on a single reason (which has, so far, never been heavy pollution). However, companies that are struggling from an economic point of view will be the same ones that are reducing environmental expenditure (so some interviewees argued). The majority of the banks agreed with the idea that there is a strong relationship between a company's management quality and its environmental performance: 63% of the banks said this was very true or true (18% and 45% respectively), 32% thought it just somewhat true, and only 5% said the statement

3 Although the level of importance that environmental, social and ethical performance have for banks is surprisingly high, the questions were in the form of a matrix and the authors have no further evidence to support or refute these answers.

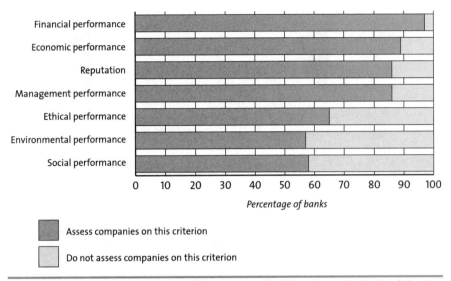

Figure 10.9 **Banks' assessment criteria for customers in the Bangkok region**

was false (see Fig. 10.10). However, Thai banks taken on their own have a slightly more moderate view: they do not see a very strong link (none responded 'very true')—42% thought it is true and 58% thought it is somewhat true. Similarly, banks confirmed that the converse also holds true: usually, heavily polluting companies do not have good management.

Regarding the role of banks and the influence they might have on customers, in general the respondents did not find these particularly important: 24% said that they did not have any influence, and 42% said the statement was only somewhat true (see Fig. 10.11).

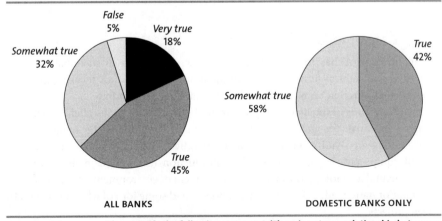

Figure 10.10 **Please verify the following statement: 'There is a strong relationship between a company's management quality and its environmental performance, so that environmentally clean companies generally perform better than dirty ones.'**

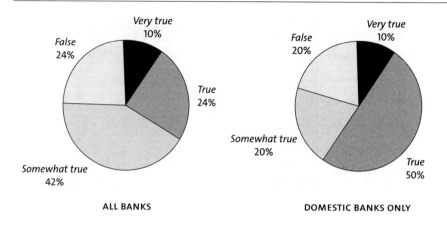

Figure 10.11   **Please verify the following statement: 'The bank is a lender that can influence the management of companies to improve environmental performance.'**

Only 24% said that banks exert an influence and the rest (10%) found the assertion to be 'very true'. Thai banks taken on their own have a more positive outlook: 10% believed they could play a significant part in influencing companies' management to improve environmental performance, 50% thought this assertion true and 20% somewhat true, while 20% did not believe they could exert any influence.

10.1.2.1 Monitoring loans

Once loans have been provided, hardly any of the banks undertake any follow-up of environmental issues. During regular site inspections, some might ask to see environmental performance data and pollution control equipment, but effective interpretation and assessment of these is questionable, as bank employees and managers have no technical or environmental background.

10.1.3   *Green products and services*

'Green investment' has moved forward in Western countries in identifiable stages, beginning with ethical funds in the early 1980s, followed by funds focusing on green technologies. In recent years, green stock funds have been expanding.

One of the aims of the BMR survey was to find out whether banks offer any kinds of financial incentive for 'green projects'. This term is intended to be broad-ranging, incorporating any kind of environmentally friendly project: investment in pollution control equipment, introduction of clean production technology, manufacturing of environmental technology, research and development of environmental technology, etc. The questionnaire made this clear, so respondents had some idea of what was meant by 'green projects'.

In general, the banks have a reasonable awareness of their role as promoters of environmental sustainability. Most of them thought that they are suppliers of the financial means required to achieve sustainable development. About two-thirds (68%) thought that this statement is somewhat true or true, while 18% thought this to be very true and just 14% considered this statement to be wrong. Thai banks taken on their own were slightly more positive: 33% said this is very true, and 45% that it is true. Only 22% thought it somewhat true, while none thought it wrong (see Fig. 10.12).

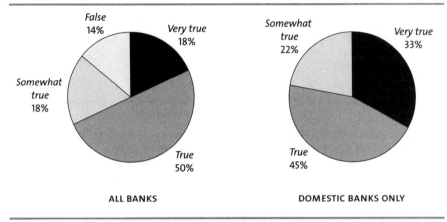

False 14%
Very true 18%
Somewhat true 18%
True 50%

ALL BANKS

Somewhat true 22%
Very true 33%
True 45%

DOMESTIC BANKS ONLY

Figure 10.12 **Please verify the following statement: 'The bank is a supplier of the financial means required to achieve sustainable development.'**

When it comes to practicalities, however, the banks are much less sustainability-oriented. Only one bank offers the 'soft loans' provided by the Bank of Thailand. And these loans are said to be far from being popular, as they are earmarked particularly for investment in pollution control equipment rather than clean production equipment. Enterprises are reluctant to invest in pollution control equipment—according to some interviewees—since this type of expenditure does not lead directly to cost reduction and increased profits (however low the interest rates); and, because pollution regulations are not strictly enforced, there is little fear of penalties.

Banks are not very enthusiastic or positive about the market for green investment funds or soft loans for environmentally friendly projects. Nearly one-third of the respondents do not consider this to be an interesting market for their bank; the rest are merely 'lukewarm' (see Fig. 10.13). Thai banks taken on their own, however, do show an interest in this type of market: 67% said they were interested or very interested in this kind of scheme (45% and 22% respectively), the remainder being somewhat interested. However, declaring interest is not the same as putting such policies into action and, as stated above, only one of the Thai banks consulted actually offers the Bank of Thailand's 'soft loans'. This contrasts with experiences in other countries. The Storebrand Scudder Environmental Value Fund (a US–Norwegian joint venture) has matched and sometimes even surpassed the growth of Morgan Stanley's non-environmental index.[4]

4   *International Herald Tribune,* 22 September 1999: 25.

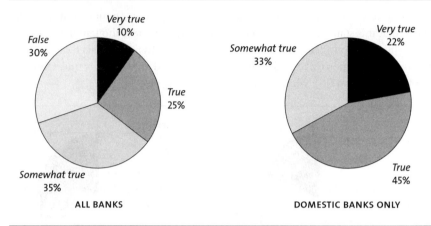

Figure 10.13 **Please verify the following statement:'Investment funds or soft loans for environmentally friendly projects constitute an interesting market for your bank.'**

10.2 A lack of environmental drivers

The range of areas in which banks can introduce environmentally oriented practice is broad: internal operations, credit risk assessments, preparation of environmental products, multi-sectoral work, support of environmental projects, green funding, etc. However, the survey shows that banks, even if they are aware of the importance of the environment, are yet to introduce it in a meaningful way into their practices. A main reason is that environmental risks, which are a key driver in promoting banks' involvement with environmental issues, are perceived to be generally low by bankers in Thailand.

At the same time, there has been a historical lack of 'formal' banking management. The Thai economy, in the decade from the mid-1980s to the mid-1990s, was led by a tightly knit business élite who owned many Thai banks. They were often entrepreneurs first, and bankers second. The banks they owned generally served as funding tools to advance their own businesses and strengthen ties with their key business counterparts. As such, loans were often granted within an informal framework that did not necessarily measure the specific economic or financial risks associated with the intended use of funds (Casserley and Gibb 1999), let alone environmental risks.

Currently, banks in Thailand are still emerging from a very serious economic and financial crisis that began in 1997. As in many other countries, in times of economic difficulties the environment does not figure particularly high on the agenda. In the case of the foreign banks operating in Thailand, their general attitudes towards the environment do not differ from the domestic banks as much as the authors anticipated. It is true that, in some cases, the foreign banks display more advanced attitudes regarding environmental issues (for example, some have an environmental policy). However, either because they are not engaged in environmental practices in their countries of origin, or because they still do not have the means or the incentives to apply their home practices in Thailand, they do not show high levels of concern.

10.3 The changing scenario

If the authors of the wide range of articles compiled in *Contemporary Capitalism* (Hollingsworth and Boyer 1999) have addressed their subject comprehensively, then we can infer that capitalist economies have not yet succeeded in valuing sustainability,[5] as none of the enlightening chapters deals with ecological issues let alone sustainability. Nevertheless, on a global scale, the environment is becoming an increasingly important issue in politics, society and economies. In Thailand, specifically, there is a number of issues that require attention.

The weak public administrative performance that has been a key obstacle to Thailand's environmental improvement (Bello *et al.* 1998) is causing the World Bank as well as other international organisations to exert pressure and also provide financial assistance for capacity-building in Thailand in order to achieve institutional effectiveness. At the same time, local public opinion is becoming a key factor in Thailand. The increasing number of formal complaints and public demonstrations is urging authorities to enforce environmental regulations and make them stricter.

International pressure for industries to introduce environmental management systems will continue to grow. The intensification of economic globalisation is leading to more efficient global economic surveillance, enhanced supervisory activities and deepening international regulatory activities—with interest in environmental standards growing significantly—for instance, through the World Trade Organisation (Held *et al.* 1999). Improved international competitiveness for Thai exporters and ultimately their domestic suppliers is linked to pressure for higher environmental performance in order to avoid production cost dumping, etc.

The increasing trend towards producer responsibility—for the environmental performance of a product along its entire life-cycle (Smith 1994)—is also being extended to include service providers such as banks. There are moves to expand the concept of environmental liability from a strictly causal one to 'collective attribution' (Teubner 1994: 17): if there are financial penalties exacted for ecological damage, then it should no longer be a single actor, but the collective that is responsible for them. Several liability techniques are available based on new forms of (risk) liability: reversing the burden of proof, probabilistic causation, joint liability in multiple causation, enterprise liability, market share liability, Superfund liability and pro capita liability. The last one, a US initiative, will draw banks into the 'membership' of those who are responsible for environmental protection and sustainability in the US and eventually beyond.

---

5 Sustainability goes well beyond environmental and economic issues—social responsibility in this case becomes an essential aspect of eco-efficiency. In the wake of globalisation, liberalisation and the rise of market instruments, multinational and global companies and banks are now also seen to be responsible for social change. The first social accountability standards have now been developed (e.g. SA 8000).

10.4 Conclusion

Banks in Thailand are aware that the importance of environmental issues is constantly growing. However, because environmental risks are not an immediate issue, they have yet to develop an environmental framework to work in. The lack of know-how is a problem, and the fact that banks do not share information does not help the situation either. However, banks, as key players in the economy, should be able to anticipate changes—changes in customers' needs, in the market, and in social and political spheres. This would ensure their business activities and mean that they can aim for sustainability *within a context of self-regulation*. That is the real challenge.

Part 2
TRANSPARENCY AND COMMUNICATION

THIS SECTION OF THE BOOK FOCUSES ON BANKS' COMMUNICATION WITH VARIOUS stakeholders. The way in which banks describe and expose their internal operations (transparency) with regard to the environment is reflected in their external communications. This can be through corporate environmental reports where they report on their environmental policy, management system and products and funds. However, a system of metrics and reporting with comparable indicators is still not in place—a management tool that could allow banks and the interested public to compare reports and identify a link between environmental performance and shareholder value.

More fundamental questions are addressed, too, such as: How to increase market transparency and visibility of green investment? How to evaluate the quality of green investment? How best to promote green investment? What role will governments, financial service providers and investors play in future development regarding sustainable investments?

The four chapters in this section begin with an investigation by Kaisa Tarna (Chapter 11) of environmental reporting in financial institutions. In a comparative study she gives a clear answer to the following questions: Why do financial services institutions publish environmental reports? To whom are these reports targeted? and What are the issues reported and the forms of reporting?

Björn Stigson (Chapter 12) discusses a framework, developed by the World Business Council for Sustainable development (WBCSD), to bridge the gap between environmental and financial performance, which helps to measure progress toward economic and environmental sustainability in business. The concept, in the form of metrics, could help the financial sector in delivering shareholder value by providing a new (sustainable) basis on which they decide whether to invest in, lend to and/or insure companies.

Walter Kahlenborn (Chapter 13) describes the growth of the green investment market and the increasing range of related products, describes the current conditions in the green investment market and discusses the issue of market transparency and consumer information. He also discusses some barriers and introduces a number of instruments that could improve transparency.

Céline Louche (Chapter 14) investigates the relationship between corporate financial and environmental performance and the problems for ethical fund management in dealing with this relationship in their investment behaviour. Financial institutions are showing increased interest in corporate environmental performance, and an indicator of this is so-called ethical investment, which claims that corporate environmental performance and corporate financial performance are positively related. However, as Chapter 14 shows, there are several impediments in integrating this assumption into the management of an ethical fund. The chapter explores the relationship between the financial performance and environmental performance of companies using a statistical analysis of 40 European companies. The problems in obtaining reliable information and in managing an ethical fund are illustrated by the case study of the Added Value Investment Fund offered by the Triodos Bank.

REPORTING ON THE ENVIRONMENT
Current practice in the financial services sector

Kaisa Tarna
KPMG, Finland

11.1 Introduction

To date, more than 150 financial institutions worldwide have signed the amended UNEP (United Nations Environment Programme) Statement by Financial Institutions and, in doing so, have made a public commitment to sustainable development.[1] According to the statement, it is recommended that financial institutions periodically report on the steps they have taken to promote integration of environmental considerations into their operations. So far, environmental reporting in the financial services sector has been rare, but the situation has started to change. Today, 15% of the *Fortune* 250 largest financial institutions produce an environmental report, even though this sector is traditionally viewed as being non-polluting (KPMG and WIMM 1999). Indeed, the direct environmental or social effects of financial institutions are minor in comparison to manufacturing industries, but the indirect effects through lending, insurance and investment decisions can be substantial. As a consequence, financial institutions are now coming under increasing pressure to develop sound environmental policies and practices and to report publicly on these.[2]

---

1   The UNEP Financial Institutions Initiative on the Environment was founded in 1992. A core part of the initiative is to foster endorsement of the UNEP 'Statement by Financial Institutions on the Environment and Sustainable Development', which commits signatories to incorporating environmentally sound practices into their operations (see pages 397-400). The corresponding initiative for the insurance industry, 'Statement of Environmental Commitment by the Insurance Industry', has been endorsed by over 80 insurers.
2   There are also other examples indicating growing interest in environmental reporting in the financial sector. For example, of the nine largest banks in the world (according to balance total), a majority has already either published a report or was going to publish one for 1998 (KPMG

11.1.1 Reporting guidelines

In the field of corporate environmental reporting, several reporting guidelines have already emerged.[3] VfU (the German Association for Environmental Management in Banks, Savings Banks and Insurance Companies) has published an initiative specifically directed at financial institutions. 'Environmental Reporting of Financial Service Providers' includes guidelines for report content, structure and performance indicators. According to VfU's initiative, a good environmental report includes the following features: general information and environmental policy; environmental management system; operating ecology; product ecology; communication and dialogue with stakeholders; and a summary. In VfU's terminology, 'operating ecology' means environmental aspects caused directly by the operating business in the main administrative buildings and branches, such as the consumption of energy or resources, or the creation of emissions and waste. Product ecology includes aspects of the financial products: lending; capital investment; insurance; and environmental information and advice (VfU 1997).

11.1.2 Scope and method of the study

This study aims to find answers to the following questions:

- Why do financial services institutions publish environmental reports?

- To whom are the reports targeted?

- What are the issues reported and the forms of reporting?

To explore these issues further, 12 environmental reports from the financial sector were selected for analysis. The reports were selected from different countries and both from banks and insurers. The main reason for selecting a specific report was the reporter's public commitment to environmental reporting. The data was gathered during spring 1999, consisting mainly of reports covering the year 1997. The reporters included in this study are presented in Table 11.1.

Content analysis of the reports was made with a help of a checklist that covered six main areas divided into more detailed questions (see Table 11.2). The categories and their contents are based mainly on VfU's template for a good environmental report (VfU 1997), which was supplemented by additional recommendations from the Global Reporting Initiative's (GRI 1999) 'Sustainability Reporting Guidelines', a checklist used in a study

> 1999). Also, according to a survey distributed to UNEP Statement signatories, of which 55% responded, 46% of the respondents were producing some form of external environmental report (UNEP 1999).
>
> 3 Examples of international reporting guidelines include UNEP's 'Company Environmental Reporting: A Measure of Progress of Business and Industry towards Sustainable Development' (1994); the CERES (Coalition for Environmentally Responsible Economies) Principles; PERI (Public Environmental Reporting Initiative) Guidelines (1993); WICE (World Industry Council for the Environment)'s 'Proposal for the Contents of Environmental Reports' (1994); as well as the ongoing GRI (Global Reporting Initiative)'s 'Sustainability Reporting Guidelines' (draft report March 1999).

Name	Year of the report	Country	Banking	Insurance
1 *ING Groep* (www.inggroup.com)	1997	Netherlands	●	●
2 *Credit Suisse* (www.csg.ch)	1997/98	Switzerland	●	●
3 *Swedbank* (www.foreningssparbanken.se)	1997	Sweden	●	●
4 *Storebrand* (www.storebrand.no)	1998	Norway	●	●
5 *NatWest Group* (www.natwest.com)	1996/97	UK	●	●
6 *BankAmerica* (www.bankamerica.com)	1997	USA	●	
7 *Deutsche Bank* (www.deutschebank.com)	1998	Germany	●	
8 *The Co-operative Bank* (www.co-operativebank.co.uk)	1997	UK	●	●
9 *Kreditanstalt für Wiederaufbau (KfW)* (www.kfw.de)	1997	Germany	●	
10 *Swiss Re* (www.swissre.ch)	1996	Switzerland		●
11 *Allianz SGD* (www.allianz-versicherung.de)	1996/97	Germany		●
12 *Tokio Marine* (www.tokiomarine.co.jp)	1997	Japan		●

Table 11.1 **Reports included in the study**

Category	Examples of aspects belonging to the category
General information (see Section 11.3.1)	General overview of the reporting entity, scope, information on reporting and accounting policy, CEO statement, verification
Environmental management (see Section 11.3.2)	Strategy, environmental management tools and organisation, training of employees
Operating ecology (see Section 11.3.3)	Energy, paper, water, waste, emissions, transport
Product ecology (see Section 11.3.4)	Product-related risk management, environmental products
Financial management (see Section 11.3.5)	Savings, revenues, costs, investments, financial risks, liabilities, donations, asset impairments
Stakeholder management (see Section 11.3.6)	Target groups, communication methods, rewards

Table 11.2 **Checklist for environmental reporting**

by KPMG Netherlands on environmental reporting in the financial sector (KPMG 1999) and the benchmarking tool of KPMG Finland (KPMG 1998).

Not only the content, but also the forms of reporting were examined: whether the information reported was qualitative, quantitative or financial. Of interest also was the reporting of goals and targets and specific performance indicators related to different categories. Furthermore, some additional questions related, for example, to reasons for publishing an environmental report and target groups of the report were asked directly of the contact persons for environmental issues in the companies. Further information of this nature was received from eight of the selected financial institutions.

11.2 Why report and to whom?

11.2.1 Communicating with stakeholders

According to Gray *et al.* (1996), corporate social reporting is the process of communicating the social and environmental effects of an organisation's economic actions to particular interest groups within society and to society at large. As such, it involves extending the accountability of organisations beyond the traditional role of providing a financial account to the owners of capital—in particular, shareholders. Such an extension is predicated on the assumption that companies have wider responsibilities than simply to make money for their shareholders. This also implies to need to broaden the concept of good corporate governance from a supervision of shareholder interests to the interests of a wider range of stakeholders (see e.g. McIntosh *et al.* 1998).

Another way of examining the issue is based more on a self-interest perspective, which relates to the possible benefits to be derived from environmental reporting. Brophy and Starkey (1996) divide the benefits into two categories: financial and strategic. If a company can demonstrate good environmental performance to its stakeholders, it may benefit financially, in that the value of its share price increases. Strategic benefits include improved corporate image, better relations with the relevant stakeholder groups as well as keeping ahead of regulations and competitors.

Some further motivations include mandatory reporting and the company's commitment to a voluntary code of conduct or management scheme, which requires or recommends external reporting.

Generally, environmental reporting is a means of stakeholder communication. Table 11.3 presents more specific reasons given for reporting by the selected companies. Main reasons given directly by companies are related to transparency and accountability. The majority had endorsed the UNEP Statement, which has most likely also been one reason for going public. Lack of direct references to strategic and financial motivations is a bit surprising, but this doesn't necessarily mean that financial institutions neglect these considerations. For example, 'to give an overview of the company's efforts in the field of environmental management' might also include aspects leading to possible strategic and financial benefits.

General motivation	Specific motivation	Amount of reporters
Transparency	▶ To give an overview of the company's efforts in the field of environmental management	75% (9)
	▶ To increase credibility	17% (2)
	▶ Response to increased information requirements of stakeholders; openness	8% (1)
Accountability	▶ Responsibility towards the environment	33% (4)
	▶ To increase environmental awareness (internal and external)	25% (3)
Strategic	▶ Competitive advantage	17% (2)
Financial	▶ To identify savings potentials	8% (1)
Voluntary code of conduct	▶ UNEP statement	75% (9)
	▶ ICC charter (mentioned in the report)	25% (3)
	▶ CERES principles (mentioned in the report)	8% (1)

Table 11.3 **Reasons for going public**

11.2.2 *Target groups*

As environmental reporting is a form of stakeholder communication, there will be target groups to which a company wishes to direct its report. It is evident that the potential audiences for an enterprise's environmental report are extremely diverse, from shareholders to non-governmental organisations. Different stakeholders have different information needs and this will naturally have an effect on a report's contents. For example, shareholders and investors are interested in financial information, whereas employees, neighbours and customers are more interested in qualitative, societal aspects. Environmental organisations possess ideological interests and authorities require information on regulatory compliance (KPMG 1997).

Among the reports analysed, by far the most typical target groups were shareholders, customers and employees. In Figure 11.1, all target groups mentioned by the reporters are presented. Usually, reported target groups belonged to primary stakeholders, who are closely related to the reporting entity's operations (such as employees, customers and shareholders).[4] Secondary stakeholders were cited more randomly but, on the other hand, over half also targeted their report to the general public, which relates more to secondary than primary stakeholders.

4 'Primary stakeholders' are those that have a formal or contractual relationship with the firm; remaining interest groups are 'secondary stakeholders' (Näsi 1995).

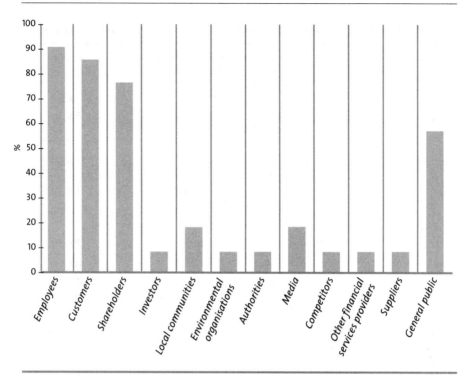

Figure 11.1 **Target groups of the reports (%)**

11.3 Reporting practices: issues reported and forms of reporting

11.3.1 General information

General information is often provided in environmental reports to increase the comprehensibility, relevance and credibility of the other information provided. Such information might include an overview of the reporting entity's operations, the scope of the report, a CEO statement communicating top-management commitment, information on accounting policy, as well as verification.

According to the GRI (1999), an overview of the reporting entity and scope of the report provide a context for understanding and evaluating information provided in other sections of the report. Information on reporting and accounting policy improve the transparency and credibility of the disclosed data. Some companies also choose to have their environmental reports verified by an independent third party, which is also a way of increasing the report's credibility.

Results concerning the reporting of these issues are presented in Table 11.4. There are some issues calling for further improvement, one of which is how to expand the reporting

Issue reported
General overview of the reporting entity (e.g. financial key figures, major products and services) (75%)
Scope of the report ▶ Not defined (8%) ▶ The whole group (33%) ▶ Part of the group (58%)*
Top management commitment: foreword signed by the CEO or another member of the board (87%)
Information on reporting and accounting policies (25%) ▶ Followed reporting guidelines (VfU) mentioned (8%)†
Report verified (17%)

* *When the report covered only a part of the group, the limitations were as follows: exclusion of group companies outside the country of origin (50%); only one company of the group included (12%); geographical limitation (country of origin) in the operating ecology part, other parts of the report referring to the whole group (38%).*

† *Despite the lack of information on guidelines followed, 33% of the reports used VfU's division of product and operating ecology in the structure.*

Table 11.4 **General information**

to cover the whole group. The transparency of the data disclosed could also be improved further. At the very least, more information on accounting policies and methods would be a useful addition. Verification seems still to be rare in the financial services sector, which might be due to the fact that verification of environmental reports is also a relatively new phenomenon in other industries.[5] Nevertheless, verification could bring benefits to financial institutions in the form of improved credibility and thus an enhanced and more progressive corporate image regarding environmental issues.

11.3.2 *Environmental management*

The term 'environmental management' usually relates to a systematic approach, the purpose of which is to integrate environmental issues into an organisation's day-to-day operations. To examine how financial institutions conduct environmental practices, a number of issues were selected for analysis. These include environmental strategy, management tools and organisation, as well as training and rewarding of personnel.

11.3.2.1 Environmental strategy

Environmental strategy is an organisation's comprehensive approach to environmental issues (Mätäsaho *et al.* 1998). It defines how the environment is considered within an organisation: whether it is a matter of legal compliance; risk management; an opportu-

5 According to KPMG's survey (KPMG and WIMM 1999), 18% of the studied reports were externally verified (sample consisted of 1,100 companies from 11 different countries).

nity; or whether the organisation wishes to be a truly sustainable company by balancing all three dimensions of sustainability—economic, social and environmental—in its operations (see Fig. 11.2).

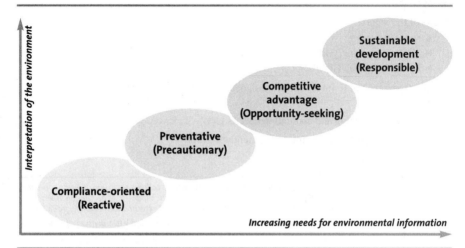

Figure 11.2 **Environmental strategy**

Source: Niskala and Mätäsaho 1996

A company's strategy is not usually easily interpreted from an environmental report. In this study, the issue was examined by placing emphasis on the role the organisation wished to play. In general, two roles were cited: the majority of the companies saw themselves as intermediaries and facilitators, but also many (42%) stressed that they wanted to be industry leaders and were thus clearly seeking competitive advantage. Elements of an opportunity-seeking strategy were discovered in all the reports: all institutions were improving their energy and resource efficiency, which will eventually lead to cost reductions, and the majority had developed environmental products. One of the companies, The Co-operative Bank, was moving strongly towards a comprehensive sustainability strategy.

Schmidheiny and Zorraquín (1996) describe the commercial success of The Co-operative Bank's strategy in the following way:

> The Co-operative Bank turned its previous losses into profits in 1992/1993 by publicising its ethical stance [see Box 11.1] in an advertising campaign using graphic images of industrial pollution. As a direct result of the campaign the Co-op's retail deposits increased by 13 percent, with half the new customers mentioning the bank's ethical stance as reason for joining. It has to be said though, that such a strategy is not open to many banks. A similar campaign by a bigger bank would have affronted some of its most valuable customers.

11.3.2.2 Tools and organisation of environmental management

Environmental policies and management systems are tools for putting the strategy into practice. According to Brophy (1996), an environmental policy serves a dual purpose in

Following extensive consultation with customers, the Bank's position is that:

► **It will not invest** or supply financial services to oppressive regimes or organisations, torture instrument manufacturers, the manufacturers of weapons selling them to any country having an oppressive regime, tobacco product manufacturers, businesses involved in animal experimentation for cosmetic purposes, factory farming, production of fur or blood sports (e.g. fox hunting and hare coursing).

► **It will not speculate** against the pound and tries to ensure that its financial services are not exploited for the purposes of money laundering, drug trafficking or tax evasion.

► **It will support** organisations promoting fair trade, avoiding repeated damage of the environment and having a complementary ethical stance.

Box 11.1 **The Co-operative Bank's ethical policy (modified)**

any organisation. First, there is the purely functional role, which means that the policy acts as a guide for future action. Second, the policy has an informative role in communicating the level of commitment an organisation has towards the environment. An environmental management system is defined in the ISO 14001 environmental management standard as 'the part of the overall management system that includes organisational structure, planning activities, responsibilities, practices, procedures, processes and resources for developing, implementing, achieving, reviewing and maintaining the environmental policy' (ISO 1996a).

The majority (75%) of the financial institutions reported their environmental policies. The policy aspects covered most frequently included a commitment to continuous improvement, compliance with legislation and targets being aimed for. Two-thirds of the companies analysed reported having a formal environmental management system either under development or in place. One of the corporations, Credit Suisse, was ISO 14001-certified, and it cited the motivation for a financial services provider to seek certification as the following:

▨ The company can be evaluated more simply and effectively by environmentally-oriented investors.

▨ In terms of environmental management the company may position itself as a progressive provider of financial services.

▨ The company may gain credibility in the eyes of the public and the personnel.

▨ The company gains more detailed first-hand knowledge of the facts when performing credit analysis of certified corporate customers.

The structure of environmental administration was mentioned in most of the reports (75%). A typical body with such responsibilities within a company was an environmental committee including a member of the board; this structure was reported by half of the companies. Environmental co-ordinators (central: 33%; decentralised: 25%) were also cited frequently.

Having a formal organisation in place is not sufficient in itself; it is also important to motivate all employees to take environmental issues into consideration in their daily work. In the reports analysed, training or awareness-raising of personnel was mentioned in all cases. For example, Credit Suisse reports on its training activities in the following way:

> The personnel concerned are provided with training in general environmental matters by means of blocks of lectures. Personnel with specialist responsibilities are offered practical ongoing training (e.g. energy management and building ecology). In the field of product ecology, the environmental risk unit provides credit specialists with special training in identifying environmental opportunities and risks.

BankAmerica also reported that it uses environmental performance as a factor in bonuses and awards for individuals responsible for the management of the bank's premises.

Even though there was plenty of information concerning training activities, related performance indicators (e.g. number of hours of training received per employee) were hard to find. In addition, information related to management training activities or specific information on key environmental personnel was unavailable.

11.3.3 Operating ecology

Operating ecology refers to material and energy flows caused directly by corporate operations. VfU has defined a set of core internal environmental performance indicators (EPIs) for financial institutions (VfU 1998). EPIs can either be absolute, providing total consumption of resources and emissions or waste per reporting period, or relative. Relative performance indicators, meaning the absolute consumption or emissions related to an appropriate denominator—such as per employee or per square metre of office— are especially useful when comparing branches or institutions. Information concerning operating ecology can be used in external communications and reporting to demonstrate the environmental performance and commitment of an organisation. Measuring operating ecology also assists internally in identifying savings potentials through more effective resource and energy use.

All the reports studied included information on operating ecology. Qualitative information as well as absolute performance indicators were common. Relative performance indicators were disclosed systematically by two companies, Allianz and Credit Suisse, which reported in line with VfU recommendations. Allianz was also the only company in the sample to present a complete eco-balance. Targets were frequently reported, but not systematically. Most companies (67%) disclosed the negative results of the indicators (e.g. increased energy use) and shortfalls in target achievement. Benchmarking information (comparisons with other organisations) was found in two reports.

Figure 11.3 presents reported information relating to different aspects of operating ecology—quantitative targets as well as absolute and relative performance indicators. The high coverage of operating ecology might be partly due to the fact that improving operational performance has often been the starting point for environmental work in financial institutions (VfU 1998). Comparing organisations remains difficult, however, as relative performance indicators are generally missing.

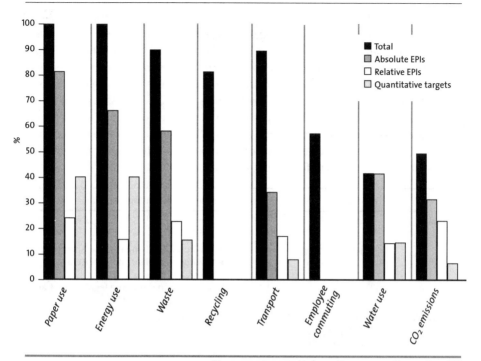

Figure 11.3 **Reported information on operating ecology (%)**

11.3.4 *Product ecology*

From an environmental perspective, product ecology is the major issue for financial services providers. Through credit and investment choices, and insurance policies, financial institutions play an important indirect role in the negative and positive environmental activities of their clients (KPMG and WIMM 1999). Concentrating on product ecology is also good business for financial institutions, as it is likely to bring direct financial benefits. Product ecology can be divided into two categories: environmental risk management related to financial products; and specific environmental products.

11.3.4.1 Risk management

A primary concern related to product ecology in banks and insurance companies is usually *risk management*. UNEP has listed various types of environment-related risk that lenders may face (Vaughan 1994). For example, the collateral for real estate or property to be acquired may be drastically reduced in value if contamination is discovered. Or borrowers may not be able to repay loans if they have to pay environment-related fines, penalties or clean-up costs. In some countries, lenders may also be held liable for their customers' actions, so that they might end up themselves paying remediation costs for contaminated soil. Insurers have an important self-interest at stake as well, as they are the ones bearing the costs of realised risks. They might also be directly affected by global environmental problems such as global warming (Schmidheiny and Zorraquín 1996).

In Table 11.5 different financial products and related risk management tools are presented as observed in the reports analysed.[6] Integration of environmental considerations into normal banking products seems to be common, but this is likely still to be somewhat unsystematic. For example, Credit Suisse reports, as a weakness, a 'so far not adequately systematised review of environmental risks and opportunities in project financing'. Regarding banking products, it is usually also unclear what happens if an environmental risk is perceived. Does it lead to refusal of the financing application, higher tariffs, or requirement for insurance cover, etc.?

Area	Product	Risk management tool
Banking	Lending	▶ Environmental checklist/risk rating (88%)
	Project financing	▶ Environmental impact assessment (50%) ▶ Environmental due diligence checks (12.5%) ▶ Enquiries to clarify the legal context and insurance cover (12.5%)
Insurance	Insurances (e.g. motor vehicle, building or property, marine and agricultural insurance)	▶ Environmental risk rating (57%) ▶ Premium diversification (43%)

Table 11.5 **Examples of financial products and related risk management tools**

11.3.4.2 Environmental products and services

Financial organisations may also develop completely new environment-related products and services. These include green or ethical investment products, environmental insurance, financing of environmentally favourable projects and investments and environmental advisory services (Schmidheiny and Zorraquín 1996).

In Table 11.6 examples of environmental products and services provided by reporters are presented. Three institutions reported having an environmental or ethical investment fund: Storebrand Scudder Environmental Value Fund; Swedbank's Miljöfond; and Credit Suisse's Eco Efficiency and Fellowship Trust funds. Information of funds' yield was reported by all, and two companies compared the performance of their funds to average funds. All funds employed environmental criteria, such as eco-efficiency, in stock selection. One bank also employed social and ethical considerations and screened its investments with negative criteria (see Table 11.7). New products in development were rarely discussed, possibly for competitive reasons. Future market opportunities for banks from trading of emission rights were mentioned in two reports, and financing opportunities

---

6 Of the reports analysed, 67% reported on banking activities and 58% on insurance activities. In Tables 11.5 and 11.6, percentages for adoption of risk management tools and new financial products are calculated for each industry accordingly: e.g. adoption of an environmental checklist for lending is compared to the total figure of institutions reporting on banking services.

Area	Product/service	Details
Banking	Financing 'green products or investments' (75%)	Providing financing with lower interest rates and/or longer payback periods for environmentally favourable investments or projects (e.g. environmental technology, energy-efficiency investments, environmental management systems, soil remediation, cycling infrastructure)
	Special products:	
	▶ 'Green' credit cards (25%)	Part of the turnover generated donated to an environmental NGO
	▶ Environmental mortgage (12.5%)	Lower interest rate for buyers of houses built according to sustainable requirements
	▶ Preferential banking package (12.5%)	Available to organisations fulfilling certain ecological criteria: includes lower interest rates on loans, reduced banking charges and special rates on funds deposited
Insurance	Environmental liability or damage insurance (57%)	Provides insurance cover for (certain) environmental liabilities or damages; includes risk rating and premium diversification
	Environmental research (71%)	Related e.g. to causes of accidents, environmentally friendly car repair methods, climate change and natural disasters
	Special products:	
	▶ Recycling of car components (14%)	Recycling of car components from vehicles written off as a result of an accident
	▶ Catastrophe bond (14%)	A bond, annual coupon payments of which are tied to occurrence of hail and storm damage
Banking and insurance	Advisory services (50%)	Environment-related counselling
	Real estate (42%)	Environmental rating and improvement of owned buildings, due diligence checks in acquisitions
	'Green' contracting (25%)	Energy or waste management services contracting
	'Green' investment funds (25%)	A fund investing according to environmental or ethical criteria; see text for more details

Table 11.6 **Environmental products and services**

Positive criteria	*Exclusion criteria*
▶ Companies with a good environmental track record	▶ Companies involved in the sale or manufacture of goods or services for military use
▶ Companies that make a positive social contribution (mainly in relation to their employees and their local area)	▶ Companies that have attracted adverse attention as a result of environmental pollution in the past
	▶ Companies known to be distributing pesticides in the UK that contain substances banned in other countries
▶ Companies that engage in energy conservation, waste reduction through recycling and efficient waste management	▶ Tobacco producers or companies that derive over 10% of their reported annual turnover from the sale of tobacco products
	▶ Companies that make profits from gambling
	▶ Companies that print, publish or distribute pornography
▶ Companies that offer alternatives to products tested on animals	▶ Manufacturers of alcoholic beverages or companies that derive over 10% of their reported annual turnover from the sale of such beverages

Table 11.7   **Investment criteria of Credit Suisse's (UK) Fellowship Trust Fund**

related to international environmental agreements, such as the Biodiversity Convention, were mentioned once.

Information on product ecology was found in all of the reports studied. However, compared to operating ecology, product ecology is a more difficult reporting area, especially in terms of comparability between different companies. The information presented was mainly in a qualitative format. Only a few reports (25%) included absolute performance indicators, e.g. volume of financing for environmentally favourable projects or investments. One interesting feature was an environmental dividend reported by Storebrand for its Environmental Value Fund: an environmental dividend is measured as the difference between the average eco-efficiency of the fund and that of the market as a whole. Targets, mainly qualitative in nature, were reported by half of the companies. A clear challenge for the future is to provide more systematic and comparable information in this area.

11.3.5 *Financial management*

Financial management reflects the economic component of corporate sustainability and shareholder interests. Financial aspects related to the environment are, for example, environmental costs and investments, risks and liabilities, asset impairments caused by environmental aspects, revenues related to environmental products or services, and savings through eco-efficiency.

Among the reports studied, disclosure of financial information is an area still in need of improvement. Most of the companies (75%) presented some financial information, but still in a very disorganised and fragmented manner. The relevance of the information given was usually difficult to relate, for example, to the overall financial situation of the company. Commonly reported areas were donations and sponsoring (50%) as well as financial benefits in terms of new products (33%) and eco-efficiency savings (58%). For example, Credit Suisse reported on savings of one million air-kilometres as well as cost savings totalling CHF750,000 through use of video-conferencing facilities. Environmental costs (25%) and investments (17%) were reported more rarely, and none of the companies reported on future investments, financial risks, liabilities or asset impairments.

The lack of financial information is rather surprising, considering that the majority of the reports were also targeted at shareholders. One explanation for this might be the fact that, as in other sectors, environment-related financial reporting is still an evolving practice. Another reason might be that VfU's environmental reporting initiative fails to include any detailed recommendations for provision of financial information.

11.3.6 Stakeholder management

Stakeholder management means managing and balancing expectations deriving from the different values of a company's stakeholders. Questions related to stakeholders are, for example (Mätäsaho *et al.* 1998):

- Who are the company's stakeholders?
- What is the relevance and influence of different stakeholders?
- What are stakeholders' interests and values related to the ecological and social environment?
- What are stakeholders' information needs?
- What are stakeholders' opinions of the company's environmental management and reporting?

The benefits a company might expect to gain from stakeholder management include: increased employee support; greater public acceptance of corporate activity; and reduced risk and liability as stakeholders provide early warning and better insight to the future in general (see e.g. Schmidheiny and Zorraquín 1996).

All reports describe some activities aimed at reaching stakeholders. Common methods used concern one-way communication: providing information on the reporting entity's environmental performance or awareness-raising about global environmental problems. Many institutions (58%) also provide information on external recognition (environment- or community-related awards) they have received.

In addition, many financial institutions are already taking steps towards a more active dialogue with their stakeholders. A majority of the reports (83%) include information on community involvement or co-operative engagement with environment-related organisations and authorities (83%). Environmental reports can also be used to promote dialogue through feedback systems. A majority of the companies (92%) took advantage of this: a contact address appears in 75% of the reports; a contact person in 33%; and an evaluation form in one report. An Internet report was provided by 75% of the institutions.

The Co-operative Bank has taken a step further to move from dialogue to true co-operation with its stakeholders. In its report, it interestingly describes its attempts and achievements in delivering value in a socially and ecologically responsible manner to all its key stakeholders.

A typical breakdown of stakeholders consisted of employees, customers and local communities (mentioned by 58%), which was also complemented by certain others (see Fig. 11.4). The interesting feature is that shareholders, one of the major target groups of the reports, are rarely mentioned in relation to the reported information on stakeholder activities. The most common communication methods used to reach stakeholders are shown in Figure 11.5.

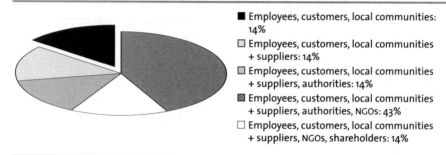

- ■ Employees, customers, local communities: 14%
- ☐ Employees, customers, local communities + suppliers: 14%
- ☐ Employees, customers, local communities + suppliers, authorities: 14%
- ■ Employees, customers, local communities + suppliers, authorities, NGOs: 43%
- ☐ Employees, customers, local communities + suppliers, NGOs, shareholders: 14%

Figure 11.4 **Target group compositions of reported stakeholder activities (%)**

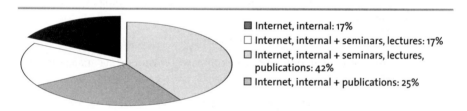

- ■ Internet, internal: 17%
- ☐ Internet, internal + seminars, lectures: 17%
- ☐ Internet, internal + seminars, lectures, publications: 42%
- ■ Internet, internal + publications: 25%

Figure 11.5 **Composition of communications methods used (%)**

11.4 Conclusions and future trends

Environmental reporting in financial institutions is still rare, but there are signs that the situation is changing. Leaders in environmental reporting in the sector are already producing reports of high quality, with good examples in a number of different reporting areas: for example, Credit Suisse (environmental management, product ecology), Allianz (operating ecology) and The Co-operative Bank (stakeholder management). One area urgently in need of further improvement is financial management: if the reporters wish to reach their shareholders, they should certainly also disclose information on those environmental aspects related to financial performance and the company's value. Reporting on product ecology also demands further attention, as it is, after all, the major issue, from an environmental perspective, for financial institutions.

The relevant new trend in the sector seems to be an increasing interest in the social component of sustainability. As early as 1997, The Co-operative Bank had published a report that included social issues (*The Partnership Report: Seven Partners, A Balanced View*), and, recently, NatWest has issued a *Social Impact Review* for 1998. In addition, ING Group, Storebrand and Credit Suisse have expressed an interest in integrating social issues into their non-financial reporting. Another interesting trend is the launch of the Dow Jones Sustainability Group Index, highlighting the growing importance of environmental and social factors not only in financing but also in investment decisions.

The most exciting aspect of the growing environmental awareness of financial institutions is the fact that it is likely to lead to much wider effects than just the greening of the financial sector. Financiers' and investors' interest in environmental issues also puts pressure on other business sectors, and this could have some interesting consequences:

- Environmental management and socially responsible corporate behaviour could increasingly become strategic issues, to be integrated into normal business management.

- The integration of financial and non-financial reporting will be encouraged, as the main users of financial information begin to require non-financial information as well. However, the complete merger of these two areas in the near future still seems unlikely. Financial reporting is mandatory and strictly regulated; as long as corporations are not required to disclose non-financial information in the same way, it is more probable that separate financial statements will continue to exist.

Of course, these developments are not only significant from a business point of view: the greening of the financial sector has a huge potential to contribute indirectly to a development of a more sustainable world.

MAKING THE LINK BETWEEN ENVIRONMENTAL PERFORMANCE AND SHAREHOLDER VALUE
The metrics of eco-efficiency

Björn Stigson
President, World Business Council for
Sustainable Development, Switzerland

Until recently, the financial markets' recognition of environmental performance was restricted to legal liabilities and to negative risk factors. Today, a growing number of players within the financial markets are starting to factor environmental considerations into their thinking—albeit not all at the same pace. Insurers and bankers are naturally concerned about the financial risks posed by specific environmental issues, such as climate change. But some are also recognising that good environmental performance can translate into shareholder value. What's been missing, however, are metrics that would allow financial markets to measure eco-efficiency so that it makes sense on the balance sheet.

The World Business Council for Sustainable Development (WBCSD) has devised a framework to do just that: bridge the gap between environmental and financial performance, and help measure progress towards economic and environmental sustainability in business. The concept, in the form of metrics, recommends a two-level approach with commonly used generic core indicators and business-specific supplemental indicators. While 'core' indicators are internationally agreed and valid for virtually all businesses, they may not be of equal value or importance for a given company; nor are they necessarily comparable between different businesses. All other indicators have been called 'supplemental' as their relevance and pertinence varies from one business to another.

It is clear that the transition toward a 'positive' integration of environmental benchmarks into financial valuations and investment decisions will take time. Businesses that use and sell natural resources and cause pollution have grappled with environmental and sustainable development issues longer than have companies dealing in shares, banking and insurance. These businesses have adopted eco-efficiency, increasing value while decreasing pollution and resource use. They have also been responding to changes in the marketplace, such as the 'polluter pays' principle, which will force the cost of a company's environmental damage on to the company's books; greater use of economic instruments, which reward the eco-efficient and punish their lagging competitors; and possible changes in tax structures and national accounting systems. It is our belief that, as these trends change the bottom lines of companies, financial markets will change the ways in which they value companies. The financial community will start to reward eco-efficiency for purely financial reasons.

We are much closer to achieving that recognition today than we were some years ago. At the end of 1995, the WBCSD carried out a survey (WBCSD 1997a) among financial analysts and investment managers about what they thought were the most important drivers of shareholder value. Environmental drivers were mentioned only when there was an evident downside risk on business results. This was not surprising, considering that financial markets traditionally encourage short-term goals, undervalue environmental resources, heavily discount long-term future values, and work with accounting and reporting systems that do not reflect environmental risk and opportunities. This has been further hindered by the absence of a financially relevant framework—in effect, a generally accepted reporting language—for assessing companies' environmental performance.

But market forces will soon begin to alter tradition. The new millennium has brought a series of far-reaching trends that will radically change how companies and banks, insurers, analyst and others in the financial market respond to sustainable development (see Schmidheiny and Zorraquín 1996). Governments will make greater use of economic instruments to reward companies that become more eco-efficient, while punishing those that do not. National accounting systems will be revised to reflect environmental damage and resource depletion accurately. Banks, concerned about their own legal liabilities and borrowers' possible difficulties in repaying loans if they face large pollution clean-up bills or fines, will take an even closer look at borrowing companies' eco-efficiency records. Insurers, themselves faced with making huge pay-outs for past pollution damage by companies they have insured, will also take closer looks at the eco-efficiency performance of companies seeking insurance (see WBCSD 1997b). In addition, the public will use its buying power to discriminate between products based on environmental factors. Finally, tax shifts that discourage pollution and resource over-use are being contemplated, and the majority of environmental costs largely deemed to be external (such as the cost of pollution to a nation) will be paid for by the polluter (or 'internalised'), which includes the consumer. This trend could strengthen, especially with increasing pressure from the investment community to identify environmentally determined business risks.

In such a scenario, the balance sheets of companies would change dramatically. Entire business sectors would change the way they do business. Financial markets would change the basis on which they decide whether to invest in, lend to and insure companies. The financial community could assume that, if a company was financially successful in a world of internalised environmental costs and taxes on pollution, it must also be eco-efficient. For banks specifically, this scenario would mean that they move from perceiving the environment as a 'risk' to an 'opportunity' to improve both short- and long-term profitability. Just as analysts look at factors such as product launches, market trends and research expenditure to predict the share price, environmental factors would be included in the equation as well.

12.1 Banks look beyond liability to opportunity

We are still far from achieving the situation described above, but there are a growing number of signs that tell us we are well on our way. Many banks are looking beyond the liability issue and instead finding opportunities to make new business and even to create new markets. Commercial banks, in particular, are starting to respond to the sustainable development agenda. Their attention was first caught by court cases in the United States in which a few banks that had loaned money to companies were held liable for those companies' clean-up costs.

In 1992, about 30 leading banks signed a 'Statement by Financial Institutions on the Environment and Sustainable Development'. By signing on, the banks asserted that they 'regard sustainable development as a fundamental aspect of sound business management' and noted that 'environmental risks should be part of the normal checklist of risk assessment and management'. Today, the number of signatories totals 160 and continues to grow.

Some banks have shown that they can save money, and attract new, young customers, by being eco-efficient in their internal operations, saving energy, paper and transport costs. But the question remains: can banks encourage customers toward eco-efficiency? Should they? The benefits are many; not the least of which is that customers with few environmental liabilities will be in a better position to repay loans. The stumbling block is the difficulty on the part of banks to be cost-effective in encouraging eco-efficiency in small borrowers; and it is small enterprises that cause much of the world's environmental degradation, simply because there are so many of them, particularly in the developing world.

One important way in which banks are playing a role in helping companies improve their bottom line through environmental drivers is by reducing the cost of credit. Kvaerner, a leading international engineering company, secured funding for a revolving credit facility of several hundred million US dollars in 1995 at a rate that was a few points cheaper than the standard rate, in part because of its environmental performance. The facility was arranged by Swiss Bank Corporation, Dresdner Bank, Enskilda and Chemical Bank. While the parties involved in arranging the facility did not divulge the details, no party denied that the credit was granted on preferential terms partially because of Kvaerner's good environmental record.

Banks nowadays routinely look at the environmental performance of a borrower. While it is still more usual to be penalised for having a shaky environmental performance than to be rewarded for having a good one, all financial institutions are working very hard at pricing risk, and that includes environmental risk, more accurately.

12.1.1 *Growing economies sustainably*

A major step in the right direction is the introduction of metrics for eco-efficiency and reporting. Eco-efficiency, a management approach developed by the WBCSD, can help companies to improve their environmental performance while meeting the demands of the market and improving the bottom line. It allows companies to make production processes more efficient and create new and better products and services with fewer resources and less pollution along the entire value chain. The ultimate goal of eco-efficiency is to grow economies qualitatively—in other words, to provide more value rather than to transform materials and energy into more waste.

A business concept can be said to have 'come of age' when the top management in leading companies want it quantified and reported upon. The OECD has also enrolled its own programme on eco-efficiency, and launched several cross-cutting projects on sustainable development. Also, when investment analysts start using the concept to aid their investment decisions and start wanting quantifiable and comparable data from companies, then you know the concept is definitely headed for the mainstream.

This is clearly evident in the recent formation of the European Eco-Efficiency Initiative (EEEI), one of the first regional efforts to solve environmental and social problems through an alliance of multiple players. Jointly launched by the European Partners for the Environment (EPE) and WBCSD, in partnership with the European Commission's Enterprise Directorate General, governments of EU member states and several European partners, the EEEI has two objectives:

- To install eco-efficiency as a leading business concept throughout Europe

- To integrate eco-efficiency into EU industrial and economic policies

With the world's population set to reach ten billion by the year 2050, the challenge is to ensure that people have equal opportunity for economic and social development. But creating a sustainable society demands a fundamental change of direction, not only in patterns of production and consumption but also in terms of social and cultural aspects.

Eco-efficiency is a key critical component on the road to sustainable development, and a powerful driver for widespread, root-and-branch change if properly implemented on a large scale. It impacts the entire product chain, by addressing the whole life-cycle, promoting a shift from products to services, encouraging green purchasing and enabling sustainable consumption patterns.

12.1.2 *Measuring eco-efficiency*

So far, individual companies have tended to develop their own measurements of their eco-efficiency performance; these differ greatly between companies and even more so between sectors. This is not surprising, considering the complexity and specificity of the various key aspects of eco-efficiency. We believe that the time is now ripe for some standardisation to be brought to this area of eco-efficiency. So, in late 1997, the WBCSD formed a Working Group on Eco-Efficiency Metrics and Reporting.

We recognised several principles that we considered to be of paramount importance. In our view, eco-efficient metrics should:

- Be relevant and meaningful with respect to protecting the environment and human health

- Inform organisational decision-making to improve the eco-efficiency of the organisation

- Recognise the inherent diversity of business

- Be conducive to benchmarking and monitoring over time

- Be clearly defined, measurable and verifiable

- Be meaningful to stakeholders

- Be timely

- Be based on an overall (holistic) evaluation of the organisation. Starting from the boundary of direct management control, life-cycle issues should be considered when relevant

- Be appropriate for the decision being made

We certainly do not believe we can develop a one-size-fits-all metric. The accountancy profession has struggled for years to try to come up with one set of simple accounts that meets everybody's needs, even though accountants, unlike environmentalists, have the enormous advantage that everything they deal with can be converted into pounds, shillings and pence, or into dollars and cents. Despite this, the accounts that company managers find most useful are very different from those that the shareholders need. Government tax authorities insist on yet another approach, while the financial analysts look at companies' accounts from a completely different viewpoint. The accountants have not come up with a single set of comprehensive universal accounts after many decades of concentrated effort. It would be arrogant to believe that we can rapidly develop a few all-encompassing measures and ratios with regard to eco-efficiency.

What is important is to concentrate on key aspects and make the information available in a form that enables both companies and the financial community to use it, work with it, and build on it. Banks, insurers, and financial analysts have the incentive to be particularly ingenious at taking the underlying data within corporate reports and devising ways to compare different companies' relative performance within a particular sector and even in comparison with other sectors. Our philosophy is to seek a standardised methodology and to encourage companies to publish their resulting performance data in such a form that analysts and others can make such comparisons.

12.1.3 Pilot programme

We have compiled an initial set of indicators and are now piloting these among 25 companies. Participation is not limited to members of the WBCSD but represent a cross-section of business types, sizes and industry sectors as well as departments and functions. Along the way, participant companies will benefit from a series of experience-sharing meetings.[1] The programme was completed in March 2000, and the results are available in two reports (see WBCSD 2000a, 2000b).[2]

The WBCSD's ultimate aim is to establish a voluntary framework that is flexible enough to be widely used and that will be broadly accepted and easily interpreted throughout the business community and, indeed, throughout the world.

Five elements are envisaged in the framework:

- Agreed definitions and terminology for environmental and value-related indicators and indicators' principles

- A recommended set of 'core' indicators that follow a widely agreed measurement methodology, and that are relevant to virtually all businesses

- A process for developing 'supplemental' indicators relevant to specific businesses

- A means by which the relationship between economic/value performance and environmental performance, using the eco-efficiency indicators, can be quantified

- Recommended ways for companies to communicate eco-efficient measurements to top management for better decision-making and to external stakeholders

12.1.4 Cross-comparable indicators

Monitoring performance and setting targets is an effective management tool, but is most valuable when it allows cross-comparison of data. Cross-comparable indicators are parameters that are universally measurable and valid for business, even though they will not be of equal relevance to all sectors. For some businesses, additional information might be necessary to explain how certain indicators apply to a specific industry. Other indicators may be desirable in areas beyond those covered by the cross-comparable classification.

Future challenges to designing indicators lie particularly in the area of identifying indicators of product/service use. Additional work also needs to be done in the area of understanding data collection, the consequences and limitations of weighting and normalisation, and indicators regarding the description of environmental management systems performance. In these areas, and in the selection of company-specific indicators, the WBCSD believes that the draft ISO 14031 'Environmental Performance Evaluation' provides important guidance for companies.

---

1 Companies wishing to adapt measurement and reporting of eco-efficiency are encouraged to consult the guidelines (see WBCSD 2000a) or see the WBCSD website (www.wbcsd.org) for eco-efficiency case studies to benefit from the learning process so far.
2 All WBCSD eco-efficiency reports are available at www.wbcsd.org.

12.1.5 Sustainability as an 'investable' concept

As institutional investors, banks need to know to what extent the environmental performance of a company impacts on its shareholder value. A system of metrics and reporting with cross-comparable indicators is precisely the management tool that will allow banks to measure the link between environmental performance and shareholder value. Some progressive banks have already begun to devise their own set of indicators for assessing environmental performance.

What banks now need are international standards for corporate environmental costs/ savings accounting, auditing, and reporting procedures, in order to provide investors with a clearer and more transparent picture of the financial implications of companies' environmental performance.

The recent launch of the Dow Jones Sustainability Index is a testimony to the fact that the concept of corporate sustainability is gaining ground among investors. For the first time, a mainstream global index is tracking the performance of the leading sustainability-driven companies worldwide (of which seven WBCSD members were selected out of an élite group of 18). As it states: 'Sustainability companies not only manage the standard economic factors affecting their business but the environmental and social factors as well. There is mounting evidence that their financial performance is superior to companies that do not adequately, correctly and optimally manage these important factors.' The conclusion is that corporate sustainability has become an investable concept that increases long-term shareholder value.

Therefore, although the rationale for the existence of business is to generate returns for its shareholders and investors, mere short-term profitability is no longer sufficient. Eco-Efficiency Metrics and Reporting, as it continues to evolve, will go a long way toward fulfilling the needs of financial markets. Our ambition is that, further down the road, this framework will provide a scorecard for them to recognise and reward eco-efficiency in business. Sustainable banking will thus be one step closer to reality.

TRANSPARENCY AND THE GREEN INVESTMENT MARKET*

Walter Kahlenborn
Ecologic, Germany

The importance of the interface between financial services and the environment is increasing steadily, both in economic and in environmental terms. In particular, an increasingly important role is being played by green investment[1] as a unique opportunity to integrate environmental concerns into the core business of the financial services sector.

With the green investment market growing steadily, the issue of market transparency is becoming a more important factor. Not only might the number of environment-related investment opportunities rise substantially, but also the number of—at least with respect to the green investment market—inexperienced investors. Low market transparency could become a serious obstacle to further market growth. On the other hand, high transparency could even provide a boost to the market.

This chapter aims to assess current conditions in the green investment market, analyse its potential, and discuss the issue of market transparency and consumer information. The area of environmental investment funds as part of green investment is receiving particular attention. The elevated position of these funds is motivated by their special function as a 'door' or 'public magnet' to the green investment market (Kahlenborn 1998).

The chapter is structured as follows. After a short discussion of what green investment actually entails or how it can be defined, there is a section on the ecological usefulness of green investment. Then the past and future development of this segment of the

---

* This chapter represents the outcome of an international workshop on 'Green Investment: Market Transparency and Consumer Information', held in Berlin, 7 October 1998. The workshop was organised by Ecologic on behalf of the German Federal Ministry for the Environment and the German Federal Environment Agency.

1 In discussing 'green investment', this chapter refers only to financial products, e.g. green savings accounts, green saving certificates, environmental direct investment and environmental investment funds.

financial market will be explained, before specific problems relating to 'market transparency' and 'market visibility' are addressed. The subsequent section is devoted to already-existing mechanisms that promote market transparency and visibility, with the last section proposing some improvements to the current situation.

13.1 A definition of 'green investment'

There is no general definition of 'green investment' at present; nor is it the intention of this chapter to predetermine what makes an investment 'green'. There are in principle two different approaches to the definition of the concept. On the one hand, 'green investment' can be understood as any form of financial investment whereby the investor pays attention to ecological goals[2] as well as the traditional aims of investment.[3] On the other hand, 'green investment' can be understood as an investment that successfully counteracts negative influences on the environment, or serves to produce goods or offer services that have positive effects on the environment.[4]

The problem with the first type of definition is obvious: it is the (subjective) opinion of the actual investor that determines whether an investment project can be categorised as green or not and not the objective properties of the investment itself. This hinders the academic and political treatment of the topic. Despite this disadvantage, the first type of definition is often preferred. The decisive justification for this choice is usually that the dynamic nature of the green investment market does not allow for the distinction between the possible products that would be necessary for the second definition. The green investment market has been under development for some time and is still under development. New products are continually appearing that work according to different criteria from an environmental perspective. Establishing clearly defined parameters for green investment involves the risk of limiting further market development by blocking new initiatives—both on the side of the producers of new products and on the side of the consumers in the development of new demands.

One of the advantages of the first definition over the second is also that it has a better chance of integrating the various perceptions of green investment in the different

2 Obviously, this is meant in a positive sense, i.e. the attention paid to ecological criteria is with reference to an improvement in the environment and not with reference to a deterioration, as would be the case in, for example, certain investments in industrial ventures that are major polluters.

3 One example of such an approach is the following definition: 'Green investment shall be defined as a form of investment where in addition to the traditional targets of an investor—liquidity, safety and performance—ecological criteria are also considered, when making an investment decision' (Christian Armbruster in Ecologic 1998: 99).

4 For example: '[Green investment is] investment in environmentally sound companies/projects such as: companies that systematically, comprehensively and successfully minimise their environmental impact by reducing the consumption of natural resources, substituting harmful substances with less damaging ones and lowering emissions to air, water and soil; companies/projects that try to maximise their environmental benefit by environmentally intelligent and innovative products and services' (Robert Haßler in Ecologic 1998: 100).

countries in which such a market can be found. Differing opinions on whether a particular investment opportunity is 'green' or not are inevitable, given the different views held internationally on the environment and its protection.

In addition, modes of thinking in the USA and UK have for some time focused on a broader, ethical approach, in which the ecological aspect is just one—possibly small—part of the question. Investors in these countries who are interested in green investment are mostly also interested in other ethical goals so that a division between the two is barely possible. Within German-speaking areas, there is a stronger division between 'social' and 'ecological', but even here the boundaries are not always clear.[5] However, the more the hitherto largely national markets of green investment come into closer contact with each other and increase in volume, the more a harmonisation of views of the market participants will be possible—as far as the content of the concept 'green investment' is concerned.

13.2 The ecological usefulness of green investment

Traditional investment opportunities are mainly selected on the basis of three criteria: risk, liquidity and return on investment. However, other factors, especially cultural and social,[6] also play a role. In some cases, the relatively new phenomenon of selecting investment opportunities on the basis of environmental considerations can be regarded as an outflow of the traditional set of criteria: for instance, if investors believe in a higher financial return of green investment. In other cases, the phenomenon of selecting investment opportunities on the basis of environmental considerations genuinely adds a new dimension to the previously existing dimensions of investment decisions.[7]

At least in the case of many private investors, the reason for taking into account the environmental dimension is the wish to apply ethical values to financial decisions. Hence, green investment opportunities offer first of all the (subjective) advantage to express and implement personal values in one particular area of private activities. Even though this might be of high importance to private investors, from a policy perspective it is more important to determine the positive effects of green investment on the environment. While the substantial amounts of green investment (see Section 13.3.1) certainly do have a major impact on the quality of the environment, up until now it has been difficult to quantify the actual effect.[8]

This holds true especially for environmental investment funds. Here not only the quantity but also the very existence of positive impacts on the environment is disputed.

---

5 Recently, the discussion on sustainability has had considerable influence in slowly bringing together the two dimensions—social and ecological.
6 For example, the prestige connected with a particular investment opportunity.
7 Depending on the cultural and social background of the investors, the content of this dimension certainly differs widely.
8 In stating this, however, distinction has to be made between the different kinds of green investment. Thus, in some areas, such as direct investment in wind energy systems, it might well be possible to determine how much harmful emission has been prevented.

Even supporters of green investment often remark that environmental investment funds have no effect, since these funds normally trade in existing securities which in consequence of investment decisions by the fund managers are merely transferred from one owner to another. However, there are a range of counter-arguments to this position, which will be summarised here briefly.

First, regarding the core investments of environmental investment funds, which constitute a certain number of shares that are bought and sold on the stock exchange, there is initially merely a change in ownership when an environmental investment fund invests in such shares. However, the increased demand for the shares tends to lead to a rise in share prices. In this way, obtaining new capital becomes cheaper for the company whose shares are held by environmental investment funds; it thus can save costs if it requires new capital. This results in a support for environmentally benign economic activities.

Second, because interest from an environmental investment fund in a company has positive effects on the share prices, the management of such an environmentally friendly company also receives the message that it is performing well. It is thus encouraged to continue its existing policies.

Third, the positive publicity that a company achieves from being selected by an environmental investment fund is a further advantage for the company. It can take effect through both improved motivation on the part of the company employees as well as increased interest from clients. It can also motivate other investors to seek these particular shares.

Fourth, some environmental investment funds include unlisted companies (depending on the legal requirements under which they operate). In this way they support environmentally friendly projects that would otherwise not obtain financial support.

Fifth, another direct positive effect of environmental investment funds results from the possibility of shareholder activism: that is, the direct communication between shareholders (environmental investment funds) and the management of the companies regarding company questions. By discussing environmental issues such as, for example, waste-water discharges, managers of an environmental investment fund might convince the management of a company to tackle the environmental problems caused by its activities.

Finally, one should mention the considerable contribution made by environmental investment funds to the development of information services related to environmental issues. In the past, the analysis of companies applying environmental criteria, either by the environmental investment funds or by external institutes acting on the mandate of the environmental investment funds, has made an important contribution to raising the quality and quantity of the information we have about companies. This, too, ultimately benefits the environment.

Despite these positive environmental effects[9] resulting from environmental investment funds and other areas of green investment, there has been little interest even among experts on the actual as well as potential contribution of green investments to achieving

---

9 There are still further positive effects not mentioned here: e.g. increased environmental consciousness of the 'traditional' financial services providers.

environmental goals, and few attempts have been made to assess the environmental impact of green investment.[10]

13.3 Green investment: the size and development of the market

13.3.1 Market development up to the present

Estimates of the total volume of the green investment market in various European countries are relatively difficult to make. Not only is there no generally accepted definition of 'green investment', but also there are no official statistics, and parts of the market in some European countries are handled by very small players (e.g. direct investment in limited companies). Most reliable are the statistics concerning environmental investment funds.

In September 1997, about US$250 billion had been put into investment funds in the German-speaking countries (Germany, Austria, Switzerland and Luxembourg). Environmental or ethical[11] funds, which have been of importance since the beginning of the 1990s, at this stage amounted to US$0.6 billion—approximately 0.2% of the market (Deml and Baumgarten 1998: 192; Armbruster 1998).

In the UK, where environmental/ethical investment funds have been on the market for almost twice as long, the volume of such investments at the same time (September 1997) was about US$1.7 billion, which corresponds to almost 0.5% of the market. In most other European countries, the volume of such investments is far lower than in either the UK or the German-speaking region. In France, for example, these funds amounted to about US$60 million in 1998 (Deml and Baumgarten 1998: 193; Armbruster 1998). However, the volume of environmental/ethical investment funds in the Netherlands amounted to approximately US$1 billion (Jeucken 1998).

In the US, where there is a long tradition of green investment and particularly ethical investment, much higher figures have been reached. In September 1997, the volume of ethical investment funds almost topped US$16 billion (Deml and Baumgarten 1998: 195). However, more than two-thirds of this amount are invested in funds that do not apply environmental criteria.

The total volume of finance put into 'green investment' (green savings accounts, green saving certificates, environmental direct investment, environmental investment funds) is much higher than the volume invested purely in environmental investment funds. In Germany, the total volume of the green investment market is at least ten times higher

10 One study on this issue has now been commissioned by the German Federal Environment Ministry and will be carried out by Ecologic.
11 Ethical investment funds include not only environmental but also social and cultural criteria in the process of selecting assets. For example, such funds might avoid investing in corporate activities relating to alcohol, tobacco, gambling, pornography, etc., or they might seek to support corporate activities relating to community involvement or equal opportunities (EIRIS 1998).

than the total volume of investments in environmental investment funds. In the US, the total amount of investments that are made on the basis of ethical criteria is estimated to be 50 times larger than the amount invested in ethical investment funds (Deml and Baumgarten 1998: 154).

If we consider the development of green investment, particularly that of environmental investment funds, through its history, we can see an almost constant increase in invested amounts in all countries in Europe (see UK example in Fig. 13.1). It is particularly important that the traditional market is growing more slowly than the green (niche) market, as is shown clearly in the area of ethical/environmental investment funds. In this way the percentage of environmental ethical investment funds in the market as a whole rises consistently.

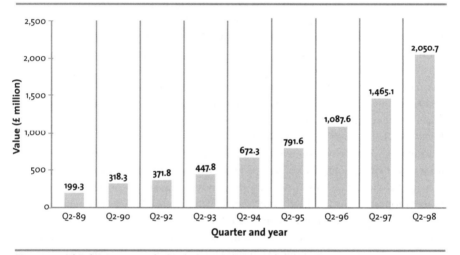

Figure 13.1   **Ethical unit trusts and ethical investment trusts 1989–98 in the UK**

Source: Belsom 1998: 23

It is not just the volume of the market that increases daily, but also the multiplicity of products. This is true of the green investment market as a whole, where, with a few exceptions (such as share warrants), almost all traditional products can also be found in a green form. This diversification is not merely a result of the fact that 'green' products are entering the market in an increasing number of categories; the diversification also takes place within the various product categories. Once again, environmental investment funds are a good example.

Initially, environmental technology funds came onto the market as a natural extension of the traditional investment market (specialised funds). These were followed by environmental investment funds which worked on a very simple system of negative criteria. Over time, positive criteria were used more frequently. The next step was the development of eco-efficiency funds, which worked less with positive or negative criteria but instead systematically looked for the ecological leaders in the various industrial branches ('environmental pioneers'). The most recent extension of the environmental investment fund market is to be found in the attempt by some investment fund corporations to make the broad concept of sustainability the fundamental philosophy for the choice of investments.

This roughly outlined sequence—there are obviously some exceptions to it—of the different phases of development of environmental investment funds occurred only occasionally within individual funds. In practice, we can observe the arrival of new investment funds rather than the modification of existing ones, so that today there is a wide palette of environmental investment funds with very different investment philosophies and methods (Hyde 1998: 22). The precise number of environmental investment funds is not known, but incomplete listings suggest about 70 such funds existed in Europe in 1998 (Deml and Baumgarten 1998; Mansley *et al.* 1997).

The increase in the number of environmental investment funds is accompanied by a shift in the spectrum of fund corporations. Initially, it was mainly the idealists who, rather as outsiders, pushed for the establishment of environmental investment funds. In recent years there has been a slow but clear growth in the interest of traditional financial services providers. In the meantime, the first major international banks have begun to set up environmental investment funds and an increasing number of new channels are being opened for green investment, including some from providers of traditional financial services. These are, naturally, less interested in the formation of new ethical options and more interested in the financial opportunities that are available in the green investment market segment. Now that this market segment has been able to show steady growth and financial analyses have, moreover, demonstrated that intensive efforts to protect the environment do not necessarily result in a loss of profit to a corporation— indeed, that they tend to have a positive correlation with profits (see e.g. Butz and Plattner 1999)—the earlier resistance to dealing with this issue has disappeared.

The increasing willingness of people in the financial services sector and also in other industrial sectors to deal with ecological questions has also had a positive effect on the market of environmental investment funds in another way. Nowadays it is, for example, much easier to obtain information on the environmental impact of individual corporations.[12] This has enabled the development of more differentiated methods of analysis and more complicated criteria in the selection of investment opportunities, such as can be found in the investment strategies related to ecological efficiency.

In addition, the overall increase in willingness on the part of corporations in many countries in Europe to co-operate in this area has improved the chances for shareholder activism or engagement. This is significant particularly with regard to the changed investment strategies of the new generation of environmental investment funds. When corporations are selected from the viewpoint of eco-efficiency or sustainability, there is an extension of the spectrum of investment opportunities beyond environmental technology and 'green' corporations (i.e. producers of environmentally friendly products and services) to almost all areas of the economy. The attempt to influence the management of corporations, selected on the basis of these investment strategies, is much more important than the involvement with the management of 'green' corporations. Whereas

12   However, many problems still exist in this area.

'green' corporations are initially built on the notion of environmental protection and cause negligible amounts of environmental damage by nature of their products and production processes, the companies selected on the basis of eco-efficiency or sustainability might still have considerable potential for improvement.

The increasing interest that has in recent years been demonstrated by investment trust corporations in shareholder activism should be seen against this background. A strategy of shareholder activism is important as a justification towards its own investors, particularly in the case of environmental investment funds, which, while investing in 'environmental pioneers', often invest in environmentally unfriendly branches as well. Hence, environmental investment funds are seeking closer contact with the management of the corporations in which they invest, which transforms them into a new and important ecological pressure group.

13.3.2 Future development in the market

There are currently no estimates of further development in the area of green investment— that is, no speculations on whether the current rise in interest will continue or whether there will be a stagnation or even a deterioration in investments. However, there is a range of arguments in favour of the notion that the green investment market will grow considerably in the years to come.

First, in several European countries, particularly Germany, investors are becoming increasingly more prepared to take risks. The savings account is losing its significance and other forms of investment—not least of which are shares—are gaining. This tends to favour the area of green investment. Not only are there many more green investment opportunities in environmental investment funds and shares than there are in saving accounts, the rejection of the traditional, very uncomplicated alternative to shares investment means that potential investors will engage actively with their investment decisions and weigh up the various alternatives.

Second, the generation that is now inheriting large amounts of money approaches investing with a set of values different to the previous generation. It is more common for this generation, especially in many northern European countries, to consider the environmental aspects of consumer decisions. Thus this motivation will also play a role in investment decisions.

Third, a further argument for the continuing expansion of the green investment market is the fact that only a small portion of the population is informed of the opportunities of green investment and that far more people express an interest in green investment than are currently actually investors in the area (see below).

Fourth, in almost all European countries the growth of the green investment market is being obstructed at the moment by the lack of involvement in this area by major banks. However, as soon as there is a swing towards this area, possibly resulting from the pressure exerted by more intensified competition, the green investment market will attain a great deal of significance relatively quickly. The vicious circle of insufficient familiarity and demand can then be broken. Such developments are already evident in the UK, the Netherlands and Switzerland.

Finally, the extension of EMAS[13] to the financial services sector will probably also have a positive effect on the further development of green investment. The implementation of EMAS will remind banks and insurance companies more strongly of their duties to the ecological development of their products, because EMAS will oblige them to at least think of the product side as well.

The development that has been evident over the past few years in green investment will probably not relate just to the quantitative aspect of the market. Also from the qualitative perspective, many of the already-mentioned basic trends are likely to continue. It is therefore probable that there will be a further expansion of the spectrum of green financial products. This is the case not only because the new providers of financial services must make their mark against the old providers on the market, but also because the formation of new client groups will also lead to new demands in green investment, which can be met only through specially tailored products.

The opening of the financial markets in the EU will also lead to a wider palette of opportunities, because green investment offers from other member states of the EU will enter national markets.

13.4 Transparency and visibility

13.4.1 Market visibility

Up to now, only a few surveys have been conducted on the public's interest in green investment. The results of those that are available[14] agree substantially. On the one hand, they show that green investment is known to only a minority of potential investors. On the other hand, they make clear that many more people are interested in green investment than are currently making use of such investment opportunities. This is further demonstrated by the fact that, when the subjects of the questionnaires are given further details about green investment, their interest improves visibly (see Fig. 13.2).[15]

The low level of knowledge about green investment is found not only with regard to demand, but also concerning the providers of financial services. Only a few providers of such services are currently aware of the various financial products within green investment, and even fewer are in a position to inform investors about the details and relevant characteristics of these products. This relates especially to those characteristics that are decisive from an ecological viewpoint—those that go beyond the daily business issues of the investment advisors in the traditional investment market (Hyde 1998).

---

13   The Eco-management and Audit Scheme (Council Regulation 1836/93/EEC).

14   There are a number of studies that have been conducted by individual financial services providers for their own marketing or product development purposes. However, these studies are not usually made public.

15   The interviews were conducted with consumers in the UK (NOP) and Germany (*Finanztest*, imug). NOP is a British polling institute; *Finanztest* is a journal of Stiftung Warentest, a German foundation for consumer protection. Emnid is a German polling institute.

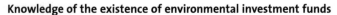

Knowledge of the existence of environmental investment funds

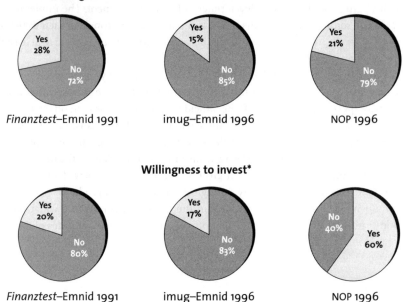

* *NOP explained the idea of ethical investment to the interview partners before questioning them in the second step on their interest in green investment. This probably explains the difference between its results and those of imug and Emnid.*

Figure 13.2   **Selected results of questionnaires on environmental investment funds**

Source: Armbruster 1998 with references to *Finanztest* 1991 and Devries 1997

As mentioned above, the negligible knowledge of the green investment market is also connected to the small size of this market. As only a few clients have used these opportunities up to now, in most European countries the market is not yet respected by the big providers of financial products. There has been correspondingly little invested in advertising for green investment. In this opening phase of the market, every form of information on green investment is of particular importance.

13.4.2 *Market transparency and the 'claim' of being green*

As already explained above, the market on green investment has shown considerable growth since its inception. This has in turn led to an ever-increasing number of green investment products, particularly noticeable in the area of environmental investment funds, where the client can now choose between several dozen products. In such a situation it is difficult for the average investor to obtain an overview of the market. At the same time, the multiplicity of available financial services makes it possible for products to be brought onto the market that do not live up to their claim of being environmentally friendly.

The danger of deliberate misinformation on the ecological qualities of an investment product is particularly high for environmental investment funds, because the actual investment of the funds is less apparent to the client than it would be in the case of, for example, direct investments. At the same time, investment trusts also function as easy entry points to investors who are only beginning to deal with their investments and are easier to deceive. There have actually been cases in the past where investment funds invested in contravention of the criteria set by the funds themselves (Sandoval 1995; Deml and Baumgarten 1998: 185) and money was invested in assets that were not compatible with the requirements of an environmental investment fund.

It is even more difficult for both the private investor and the professional financial advice corporations to determine to what extent the environmental investment funds already on the market live up to their implicit claim to manage their investments beyond the selection process in a particularly environmentally way. For example, the ecological effectiveness of environmental investment funds depends partly on how much of the investment capital is actually invested in medium- and long-term projects and how much is simply assigned to (very) short-term bonds. Other factors, such as shareholder activism, the portion of 'seed capital', etc. (see Section 13.2), also play a role. Whether a particular environmental investment fund actually satisfies its own claims is not ascertainable for the average private investor.

With the liberalisation and Europeanisation of the (hitherto national) financial markets within Europe, the problem of insufficient transparency in green investments and particularly in environmental investment funds increases even further. In particular, for Euro-based securities, trade across national boundaries will probably grow. In this way, already-existing, but also possibly the future national regulations for the protection of the shareholders and the environment, will be dodged more often.

13.5 Instruments to convey information on investments

As an answer to the current problems regarding market transparency and visibility, but also as a reaction to many other demands, a network of different consumer information instruments has been set up in recent years. This guarantees more and more that potential investors can receive the information they need.

Important instruments are, for example:

- 'Eco-rating'
- EMAS environmental statements
- Corporate environmental reports
- Magazines and books on green investment
- Consumer protection magazines
- Product tests
- Environmental accounting

A range of institutions has been set up to support these functions. Apart from financial advice specialising in green investment, there are also rating agencies, research institutes and special departments in financial corporations.

Experience with these instruments is substantially positive. Admittedly, many of them are still in their initial phases and are consistently being adapted, but they have undoubtedly contributed to the development of the green investment market, in that they have created more certainty on this market and increased its credibility.

At the same time, it is undeniable that there are many problems connected with the available instruments. A first and important problem is simply the level of familiarity with the instruments themselves. Many of the specialised magazines, as well as 'Eco-rating' and the existence of environmental reports, are not known to most private and institutional investors and therefore cannot be fully effective.

A further problem with many instruments for environmental information is that the institutions that support them are yet to develop. Hence there is often no way of realising the capacity of those instruments already developed or to transfer them to the traditional financial market.

A final, important problem is insufficient co-ordination within the instruments themselves. Because they have been developed from different perspectives, are supported by different organisations and partly meet different needs, the co-ordination of these instruments between one another follows only after a fairly long phase in which they learn to work together on the market. The potential synergy that would result from a more co-ordinated approach is still some way off.

The problems described above are present to a greater or lesser degree in various instruments. However, even today, they affect only a proportion of those available. It is to be expected that, with the growth of the green investment market, the information instruments will develop as well. It is still an open question whether the network of information instruments on investment will actually become more efficient, widen its reach and simultaneously tighten its control, or whether the qualitative and quantitative growth of the green investment market will not perhaps partially overshadow the progress of the information instruments. This would ultimately be a disadvantage for the green investment market, since its development also depends on the development of the information instruments relating to the market. While an insufficient level of information would hinder the development of a green investment market in the long term, a considerably improved level of information for potential investors could add fresh impetus to the market.

13.6 Labelling

A debate has arisen in recent years on the introduction of one very specific new instrument to overcome existing obfuscation in the environmental investment funds market: eco-labelling (Kahlenborn and Kraemer 1997). Until now, ecological labels have been used only for products. In recent years, the idea has gained approval that ecological labels should also be used for services. Since then, suggestions have been considered both at national (e.g. the 'Nordic Swan' eco-label in Scandinavia) and EU level to introduce eco-labels into particular services, such as tourism. As soon as this fundamental step is taken, eco-labels will spread to other services as well, at which point financial services might also be taken into account.[16]

The fact that labels have already been set up by private organisations (e.g. Ethibel in Belgium) and the existence of systems similar to labelling (such as the evaluation of environmental investment funds by the London-based Ethical Investment Research Service [EIRIS]) show that there is a need for such an instrument. The advantage of such a labelling system is found not only in increased market transparency but also in the simultaneous visibility of the market: that is, in the advertising that it provides for green investment in general.

At the same time it can be observed that the dynamic nature of the environmental investment fund market currently opposes labelling. The rapid changes that are evident with regard to the investment criteria and the methodology of the funds obstruct the establishment of standards for a labelling system. At the moment, the rapid changes in the market would produce almost insurmountable problems for the awarding of labels, even in the case of labels not based on the investment assets themselves (such as a label for funds with investments in assets to be found exclusively in the NAX[17]). In the long term, however, it should be practicable to establish minimum standards regarding the procedural, informative and organisational dimension of fund management for a possible labelling system. Evaluation criteria could, for example, include:

- Information for the investors
- Regular reporting on the success of the fund from an environmental perspective
- The existence of an independent investment committee
- The existence of an internal research team
- Rules for handling the investment criteria
- Carrying out research on-site
- The organisational separation of the financial evaluation of assets from the environmental evaluation
- Investment management/shareholder activism

Because of the problems that would arise in practice if national or European-wide labelling systems were introduced, it appears necessary to raise market transparency by the introduction of other measures—those that are better suited to the current market situation than labels (e.g. independent guides on environmental funds). These measures can, however, also create a set of criteria against which labels can be awarded at a later date.

16 The Dutch government has been considering the idea of an eco-label for financial products since 1995. However, no further steps have been taken so far.
17 Natur–Aktien–Index, an environmental share index including companies that are highly eco-efficient and regarded as ecological pioneers.

13.7 **Conclusion**

Despite certain problems in the definition of green investment, this part of the investment market is gaining in importance from both an economical and an ecological perspective. Many examples of the effectiveness of green investment in the promotion of environmental goals or in achieving concrete environmental improvements do exist.[18] Furthermore, the green investment market has achieved a constant, indeed even rapid, upswing and could be expected to show further growth in the future—particularly when this is seen in relation to the investment market as a whole.

In the light of the ecological usefulness already shown by green investment, and in the light of the expansion of this market segment and thereby its increasing relevance to the solution of environmental problems, it appears necessary to deal with this topic more intensively from an environmental policy perspective. However, there are many open questions, which call for further clarification before concrete environmental measures can be taken. The fundamental questions raised in this chapter are:

- How to increase the market transparency and the visibility of green investment

- How to evaluate the quality of green investment

- How best to promote green investment

- What role governments, financial service providers and investors will play

These must be answered step by step in the coming years in further discussion and investigation, both at a national and international level.

---

18 For example, the introduction or improvement of environmental reports by some British companies in response to the activities of environmental investment fund managers. Another quite visible example is the large number of wind stations in Germany financed through green investment.

THE CORPORATE ENVIRONMENTAL PERFORMANCE–FINANCIAL PERFORMANCE LINK
Implications for ethical investments

Céline Louche
Erasmus University, Netherlands

Increased concern within the financial community about environmental matters has implications for the way in which financial analysts assess corporate performance. Non-financial criteria are now being introduced along with purely financial criteria. From a strategic perspective, environmental concerns are emerging as factors influencing decision-making. Hamel and Prahalad (1994) indicate that the industry-based competitive forces identified by Porter (1980) are no longer the only issues that drive strategic decisions; other variables such as environmental issues are also taken into account.

Triodos Bank is one of the financial institutions that has integrated environmental concerns within its core business. The bank is well known for its innovative and transparent approach to banking. Triodos Bank NV was founded in the Netherlands in 1980 and is a fully licensed independent bank, owned by public shareholders. The bank has offices in Belgium, the Netherlands and the United Kingdom, with a total staff of about 78 people. It belongs to a widespread network of national and international financial institutions active in the social economy. Triodos Bank is a founding member of INAISE (the International Association of Investors in the Social Economy) and of the Social Venture Network Europe (SVNE).

The bank strongly believes that financial institutions can play a vital role in making positive changes in society. Triodos Bank deals solely with the financing of projects involving renewable energy sources (solar and wind), organic agriculture, art and culture, protection of the environment and conservation of nature. It also plays an active role in the developing world (micro-credit). In May 1997 the bank teamed up with Delta Lloyd to launch a so-called 'ethical fund', the Added Value Investment Fund. With a profit of €1.24 million in 1998, Triodos Bank showed that a combination of social, environmental and financial criteria are possible for successful operation.

To illustrate the growing concern about environmental matters within financial institutions, one can look at the ethical investment movement. In the UK, ethical investments have been multiplied by 7.14 times in eight years (from £280 million in 1990 to £2 billion in 1998); in the same period the number of funds has risen from 18 to 24. Ethical fund analysts are required to screen potential investments carefully both on financial and ethical (social and environmental) performance criteria. Parallel to that, independent services have sprung up that specialise in evaluating companies on their environmental performance. Organisations such as the Council on Economic Priorities, EIRIS in the UK and Kinder, Lydenberg and Domini (KLD) in the US have long evaluated companies on a range of social dimensions, including specific criteria for the environment. As a result, environmental ratings are now available to the investment community as an input to investor decisions (Waddock and Graves 1997).

14.1 The environmental–financial link: the theory

The notion that environmental performance is an important component of competitive advantage is becoming more and more acceptable to corporate leaders and financial institutions. According to Azzone and Manzini (1994), environmental issues can influence both revenues and costs. They can influence revenues when a firm follows a 'green strategy', and they can influence costs by diminishing spoilage and waste. Little academic research has been carried out on the link between environmental and financial performance, and results indicate an ambiguous relationship. Most of the research in this area has focused either on the performance of socially screened portfolios relative to broader market indices (White 1991; Preston and O'Bannon 1997; Griffin and Mahon 1997), or on corporate environmental responsibility and stock market performance. Furthermore, the question of causality has not yet been explored; in other words: **'Does environmental performance influence business financial performance, or does financial performance influence environmental performance, or is there a synergistic relationship between the two?'**

Results from earlier studies are inconclusive on this issue. Bragdon and Marlin (1972) found a significant correlation between environmental performance and financial performance in firms in the pulp and paper industry. Using the same original data, Chen and Metcalf (1980) argued that performance was not related to financial performance once differences in firm size had been taken into account. More recently Bloom and Scott Morton (1991) and Cohen *et al.* (1997) have suggested that environmental issues do affect the performance of firms in Western countries. Johnson (1995) found that superior environmental performance is related to superior economic performance only for certain types of environmental performance, and, more particularly, certain types of environmental performance within certain industry sectors. On the other hand, in some cases, poorer environmental performance can be economically rewarded. Hart and Ahuja (1996) examined the relationship between emissions reduction and company performance for a sample of S&P 500 firms using data drawn from the IRRC Corporate

Environmental Profile and from Compustat. Results indicated that efforts to prevent pollution and reduce emissions dropped to the 'bottom line' within 1–2 years of initiation and that those firms with the highest emission levels appeared to gain the most financially. Pava and Krausz (1996) reviewed 21 empirical studies on the association between corporate social responsibility (environment being one of the criteria) and financial performance. Of these studies, 12 showed a positive association, one showed a negative relation, and eight showed no association at all.

The linkage between environmental and financial performance is still unclear. Furthermore, even when a positive link is established, it is unclear whether financially successful companies simply have more resources to spend on environmental issues and therefore attain higher standards and performance, or whether better environmental performance itself results in better financial outcomes.

Nevertheless, the relationship between environmental performance and financial performance is a key concern for the financial sector. The application of environmental criteria by investors and financial analysts amounts to sensitive asset management; it is not merely carried out to meet the demands of ethically motivated clients. It is fully in tune with the current interest in performance measurement and argues that, although the ultimate objective of private sector companies may be to seek a profit, the most effective way to achieve this is to concentrate not on pure financial ratios but on the non-financial aspects of business performance that drive subsequent financial performance (Kaplan and Norton 1996). Environmental information is a consistent indicator for estimating future financial results of a company. It is also of great importance for promoting ethical/green investments. Surveys (Ullman 1985; Mathews 1987) point out that investors are likely to be almost entirely uninterested in corporate social and environmental reporting except insofar as it influences their financial position. Proving a positive link would be a key argument in favour of ethical investment funds (Delphi 1997). Regarding the performance of ethical/green portfolios, opinions and studies are contradictory. Snyder and Collins (1993), the Social Investment Forum (1998) and many ethical fund managers argue that portfolios with social/environmental screening outperformed regular portfolios, while Alexander and Buchholz (1978), Klassen and McLaughlin 1996, Hamilton *et al.* (1993), Diltz (1995) and van der Meulen (1997) found no significant connection.

14.2 The environmental–financial link: empirical analysis

A study was carried out in 1998 on the relationship between corporate environmental performance and financial performance in Europe (Louche 1998). The hypothesis tested in this study was whether or not firms that perform well in the environmental arena also perform well financially. The correlation between these two areas was also looked at. According to the literature review and previous studies conducted on the relationship, a positive relationship was argued: that is, caring about the environment leads to good financial performance and, conversely, bad environmental performance leads to bad financial performance. The original reason for testing the correlation was to find out whether an investor could benefit from choosing firms with high environmental performance relative to other firms. But the research process highlighted the difficulties associated with assessing corporate environmental performance. These difficulties have direct impacts for ethical fund managers, as outlined later in this chapter.

14.2.1 Data and methodology

The study gathered data on seven parameters encompassing financial and environmental aspects of corporate performance: CO_2 emissions, energy consumption, water consumption and waste disposal for the environmental dimension; earnings per share, ROA (return on assets) and ROE (return on equity) for the financial dimension. The environmental parameters were based on the eco-efficiency approach within an eco-balance model (see Fig. 14.1). Eco-efficiency is the positive combination of economic and ecological excellence. In other words, it means adding more value for money while creating less environmental impact and consuming fewer resources (WBCSD 1998; Ayres *et al.* 1995; Schmidheiny and Zorraquín 1996). The eco-balance approach to environmental indicators is an analytical model, involving the identification and measurement of all company or entity inputs (materials, water, air, capital assets, etc.), and the similar identification

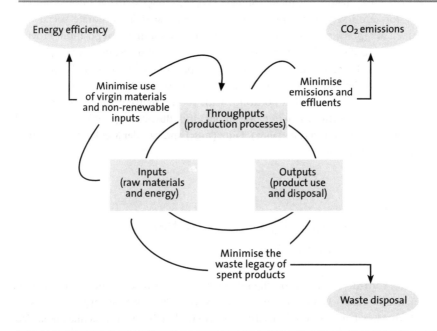

Figure 14.1 **Eco-balance consideration**

Source: Shrivastava and Hart 1994

of the firm's operations (throughput) and process outputs (goods produced, waste and emissions, changes in land or capital assets) (Newson and Deegan 1996).

The financial parameters chosen are the most important ratios for evaluating a firm's profitability, management performance and future prospects (Woelfel 1994; Gibson 1995). Ullman (1985) analysed numerous studies on the relationship between corporate social performance and corporate financial performance. Hart and Ahuja (1996) used ROE and ROA in order to analyse the relationship between emission reduction and company performance.

Corporate environmental reports were used as sources for data on environmental performance. For the Louche 1998 study, the availability of data was an important determinant of the constitution of the sample. At the beginning, there were 80 potential European firms for the database, but after collection of the data the sample had dropped to 40. There were two criteria for selecting companies for the sample: first, the biggest European companies; second, companies that had published environmental reports. Out of the 80 potential firms, only 50% had data available for at least two years and fulfilled the necessary criteria in terms of quantity and quality of information. When three years' data was required, the sample dropped to 25 companies. The population of the sample incorporated companies from all economic sectors (see Annexe 1, page 199). The need to collect data for at least two consecutive years was due to methodological problems. Companies report differently on environmental issues in terms of measurement, the unit used and the type of figure reported, absolute or relative. There is no standard method of collecting environmental data, which makes analysis very difficult. In order to overcome these problems and to enable comparison, the statistical analysis was carried out on indexes of environmental as well as financial data. The index represents the rate of change between two consecutive years, that is:

$$\frac{\text{Year 2} - \text{Year 1}}{\text{Year 1}}$$

14.2.2 Findings

To test whether there is a positive relationship between the two variables, environment and finance, regression analysis was used. The two variables were the outcomes of factor analyses on first environmental parameters and then financial parameters. The regression analysis was carried out twice: first based on data from a two-year period (S1) and, second, on data from a three-year period (S2). Table 14.1 shows the results of the correlation analysis between financial and environmental variables.

The most striking result of these computations is that out of the correlation computed among the environmental and financial parameters, there is not a single positive result. On the contrary, a slight trend suggests a negative association between CO_2 emissions and ROA and ROE (respectively −0.365, −0.461) when tests were carried out on sample 2. No other significant results were found. The results show any significant correlation. The hypothesis of a positive association has been rejected. Out of this study, no relationship,

	Earnings		ROA		ROE	
	S1	S2	S1	S2	S1	S2
CO_2	0.151	−0.118	0.001	−0.365*	0.096	−0.461**
Energy	0.137	0.176	0.115	0.18	0.233	0.218
Water	0.076	0.073	−0.057	−0.131	0.055	−0.102
Waste	0.033	−0.017	0.097	0.045	0.091	−0.001

*   Correlation is significant at the 0.05 level (2-tailed)   ROA   return on assets
**   Correlation is significant at the 0.01 level (2-tailed)   ROE   return on equity

Table 14.1 **Correlation between financial and environmental parameters**

positive or negative, between environment and financial performance has been found. Preston and O'Bannon (1997) defined this kind of relation as 'synergetic'.

14.2.3 *Pitfalls in assessing corporate environmental performance*

Beyond statistical results, the study points out a number of factors that hinder any exploration of the relationship between corporate environmental and financial performance, and create methodological problems. First, there is a lack of consensus when it comes to defining environmental performance, and, second, data available on environmental matters are not reliable enough to allow steady analysis.

Many indicators are available to assess a company's financial performance, but assessing environmental performance is not as straightforward. Environmental performance is a measurable result of the environmental management system, related to an organisation's control of its environmental policy, objectives and targets (ISO 14001, 1996). Its evaluation is a process to measure, analyse, assess, report and communicate an organisation's environmental performance against criteria set by management (Working Draft standard ISO/WD 14031.4). Difficulties arise when specifying indicators to assess environmental performance, considering that each user has its own need, knowledge and philosophy. Ultimately there are as many definitions as there are users. If they are to be usable and useful, indicators need to have policy relevance and utility for users, analytical soundness and measurability. Apart from the difficulties in reaching sound definitions, environmental data tends to show weaknesses in terms of quality and quantity. Three major problems were raised during the study: availability, reliability and comparability. Comparability expresses the relationship between two pieces of information. As a qualitative characteristic, it enables report users to identify similarities and differences in the disclosed information. Reliability is a qualitative issue. Users must have faith in the information presented. This includes the assumption that the information is free from error or bias, that the accuracy of measurements is guaranteed and that a neutral form of presentation has been chosen. Without these prerequisites, analysis of the relationship is likely to be unsuccessful.

The study relied on external voluntary information (environmental reports). This caused numerous problems. Although there have been real improvements in environmental reporting since the late 1980s, the quality and quantity of information displayed does not fulfil the minimum requirement, i.e. that it should be reliable and comparable. This generates difficulties and uncertainty (Newson and Deegan 1996; Rossignol 1997; UNEP 1995; SustainAbility/UNEP 1997; Bennett and James 1998; PIRC 1998):

- The quantity and quality of the information vary widely from sector to sector as well as between companies from a same sector (to a slightly lesser degree).

- In the case of companies that have been reporting for several years, there is no consistency in information given over the years.

- It is difficult to understand the data as it is sometimes vague and the boundaries of firms are not clear.

- Indexes are difficult to understand, very diverse and therefore hardly usable. References are often missing.

- The link between a firm's activity and environmental data is missing in most cases.

Such problems directly affect the methods used to assess businesses' environmental performance. The relationship between environmental and financial performance criteria has to be revised taking into account the available data. That means the number of criteria has to be reduced to accommodate the amount of available information. The initial study included 24 parameters of theoretical environmental performance, but this was later reduced to four. The shortcomings in the data also meant that a number of assumptions had to be made. This in turn raised the possibility that the accuracy of the analysis would suffer. As explained below, these factors have direct repercussions not only for researchers but also for ethical investments.

14.2.4 *Case study: Triodos Added Value Investment Fund*

We have seen how crucial the relationship between environmental and financial performance is for the ethical investor. We have also seen just how unclear this relationship is. The case study of the Triodos Added Value Investment Fund (Triodos MeerWaarde Fonds) places these issues in a practical context.

The Added Value Investment Fund is an ethical investment fund managed jointly by Triodos Bank and Delta Lloyd Asset Management. They have been working together since 1990 in investments based on social and environmental criteria. Their starting point was the conviction that it is possible to combine good returns on investment with a responsible use of natural resources by enterprises and institutions (Triodos Bank 1998). The idea was clearly based on the recognition of non-financial, i.e. social and environmental, factors. These factors have an effect on both the financial performance of the company and on society as a whole.

Triodos Bank has distinguished itself since 1980 by specialising in financing innovative environmental and social enterprises and initiatives. The bank strongly believes that social and environmental interest should be taken into account in economic decisions.

The Delta Lloyd Asset Management NV (Delta Lloyd Group of Insurance Companies) is one of the largest insurance companies in the Netherlands and a fully owned subsidiary of Commercial Union Assurance in London. With invested capital of approximately 35 billion Dutch guilders, Delta Lloyd is one of the most significant investors in the Netherlands. Delta Lloyd has broad experience in managing investment funds.

The Added Value Investment Fund was launched on the AEX (Amsterdam Stock Exchange) in May 1997. The fund invests in companies that are able to demonstrate a higher-than-average level of business ethics combined with a good financial performance. They tend to be companies whose activities have positive social effects and a minimal impact on the environment. This may be either through their products or services, or a well-considered social and environmental policy.

From May 1997 to the end of that year, the Added Value Investment Fund achieved a return of 2.8% compared to a return of 9.8% for the benchmark. The main reason for this result was the predominance of fixed-interest securities over stocks during the first months of the fund's existence. This predominance was reduced considerably during the first quarter of 1998, resulting in a performance that was essentially equal to that of the benchmark (7.6% compared to 7.7% for the benchmark). In 1998, the return on investment was 10.9% and for the first half of 1999 13% (Triodos Bank 1999). The composition of the fund is shown in Table 14.2.

Invested capital	NLG 42.6 million (€ 19.33 million)
Fixed interest securities	68%
Dutch stocks	19%
Foreign stocks	13% (of which 80% are American)

Table 14.2 **Added Value Investment Fund composition (31 December 1998)**

Source: Triodos Bank 1999

14.2.4.1 The environmental–financial performance link

The belief that environmental/social and financial performances are related was one of the grounds for launching the Added Value Investment Fund. Delta Lloyd reckons that the ethical investment movement might register a boom in the near future. Therefore it is strategically crucial to be one of the front-runners of the ethical investment movement. Social and environmental issues are deeply grounded in the *raison d'être* of Triodos Bank. The case study focuses on the environmental–financial performance link in two ways: first in terms of performance and second in terms of fund management, i.e. how environmental/social and financial performance respectively are managed in day-to-day fund management.

Two groups of companies were compared. One, MWBF IN, consists of companies selected for the portfolio of the Added Value Investment Fund. The second group, MWBF OUT, consists of companies that are not included in the portfolio for the Added Value

Investment Fund. The third group, UNIVERSUM MWBF, includes all companies, selected and non-selected. The period analysed was 10 January 1996 to 13 January 1999. The graphs in Figure 14.2 and Figure 14.3 compare the return of investments of the three portfolios.

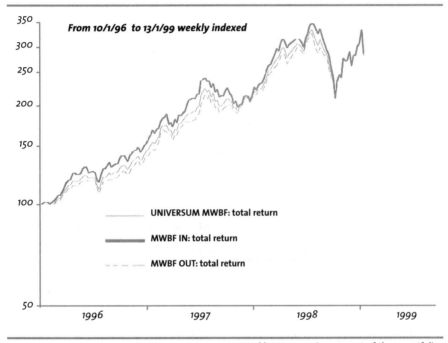

Figure 14.2 **Weekly return on investment of three portfolios**

Source: Delta Lloyd

The graph in Figure 14.2 is based on a weekly return on investment. It shows the performance of the three portfolios from 1996 to 1999. In the long run MWBF IN seems to have performed better than MWBF OUT. From the end of 1998 on, we can notice an overlapping of the curves. The graph in Figure 14.3 shows the daily return on investment from January 1998 to January 1999. Until the autumn of September–October 1999, MWBF IN outperforms MWBF OUT. The ranking of the two portfolios shifts at the beginning of the dramatic fall of the markets. From mid-September, curves tend to overlap and from October MWBF OUT outperforms MWBF IN. January seems to record a reverse of tendency, and the curves overlap again.

The most significant factor contributing to the shift in the ranking between MWBF IN and MWBF OUT during the autumn of September–October 1998 is the small-company bias of the portfolio and the fact that small companies in general performed badly over the analysis period and are in general more sensitive. MWBF IN consists of smaller companies than MWBF OUT; this result is therefore due to the screening process. It is noticeable that MWBF IN shows the same behaviour as MWBF.

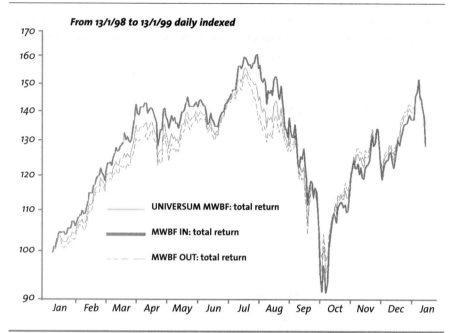

Figure 14.3 **Daily return on investment of three portfolios**

Source: Delta Lloyd

From this analysis, it is hardly possible to draw any conclusions about the influence of social/environmental performance on financial performance. It seems that in the long run the portfolio consisting of the top 50% of companies in terms of environmental/ social performance performs better than the portfolio with the bottom 50%. The MWBF IN also seems more sensitive to market disturbances.

14.2.4.2 Fund management

Two different organisations, Triodos Bank and Delta Lloyd, jointly manage the fund. The management benefits from the expertise of the two organisations: Delta Lloyd for the portfolio management and Triodos Bank for social and environmental matters (Fig. 14.4 shows the fund's management system). Triodos Bank deals with social and environmental screening and monitoring. Delta Lloyd is in charge of the financial screening and monitoring. In other words, Triodos Bank defines the investment parameters and Delta Lloyd takes investment decisions within those parameters (selling or buying shares). Triodos Bank can at any moment ask Delta Lloyd to remove companies from the portfolio for social and/or environmental reasons. In turn Delta Lloyd may suggest to Triodos Bank the inclusion of new types of company in the fund's orbit, because of financial opportunities that may arise. Theoretically, Delta Lloyd's fund managers do not invest in companies without the agreement of Triodos Bank. The two organisations meet every two months and communicate regularly.

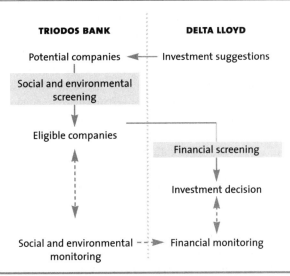

Figure 14.4 **Fund management system**

Because of the way the fund management system is structured, financial and social/environmental matters are processed independently. For Delta Lloyd, the management of the Added Value Investment Fund is no different from that of other funds except that the pool of companies from which the portfolio is drawn is smaller and the investment strategy is oriented over a longer term than for most funds. Note also that Triodos Bank requests the immediate sale of shares on ethical grounds, without taking into consideration the financial performance of the shares.

14.2.4.3 Environmental and social screening of companies

All companies that might be eligible for inclusion the Added Value Investment Fund portfolio are investigated to determine whether they fulfil the exclusionary criteria (of which there are 21) related to social and environmental aspects. Companies that do not fulfil the exclusionary criteria are excluded from investment. Companies are eligible for investment if they fulfil the exclusionary criteria and if they belong to the top 50% of the eligible companies in a given sector ('best-in-class' approach). To identify the best 50% within a sector with regard to environmental and social performance, a sector investigation is carried out through the collection of publicly available company information (mainly environmental and annual reports), consultation of independent experts and third parties (NGOs), and interviews with companies. Companies are assessed on a series of criteria related to social and environmental strategy, organisation, performance and measures.

14.2.4.4 Analysis

The case study reveals several important points. The most striking of these is the **assumption of a positive link between environmental/social and financial performance**. From the description of the Added Value Investment Fund, one can see that the fund is based on the assumption that companies that rate better on environmental/social performance will rate well on financial performance. In other words, it is based on a positive correlation between environmental/social and financial performance, although, as we have seen, in theory no evidence of a positive link has been found.

The second important factor to emerge from the case study relates to the **direction of causation**. Companies are first screened and ranked on environmental/social criteria and then on financial ones. According to the previous assumption of a positive relationship, the management system indicates implicitly that financial performance reflects environmental performance, or more specifically that improved environmental performance leads to better financial performance.

Another interesting finding is that **social and environmental screening is conducted separately from financial screening**. Environmental/social criteria are not integrated with the investment decision but added to it. Environmental/social performance and financial performance are not interconnected; in the fund definition social/environmental performance is used in the pre-selection of companies.

The impediments that are encountered when assessing the environmental performance of a company have been dealt with above. As the investment decisions for the Added Value Investment Fund are made on the basis of the environmental reports, the fund managers encounter the same difficulties and uncertainties in reaching their decisions.

14.3 Conclusion

This chapter has attempted to address a question that has become crucial for the financial sector in general and for ethical investments in particular: is the financial performance of a company influenced by its environmental performance?

In undertaking the empirical analysis, we explored whether or not linkages exist between corporate environmental behaviour and financial performance. Using four environmental and three financial parameters, we did not find any conclusive results invalidating or confirming the assumptions that environmental responsiveness is positively and significantly related to economic performance. We have pointed out the difficulties inherent in the assessment of corporate environmental performance, which have biased the statistical analysis. These difficulties directly affect the screening process of ethical investments. Ethical fund analysts face similar difficulties that might corrupt the ranking system. Although they are the most commonly used sources among financial institutions, environmental reports show some limitations if used to make realistic assessments and comparisons. In Europe there are no absolute standards or mandatory requirements for environmental indicators in environmental reporting and therefore there is no obligation to report on quantifiable targets or to disclose performance. As a result, the quality of information can vary a great deal.

The relationship between environmental/social and financial performance is a crucial issue for the Triodos Added Value Investment Fund, as well as for all ethical funds. Studies have shown that ethical investors are not prepared to sacrifice their essential financial requirement (Lewis and Mackenzie 2000; Lewis *et al.* 1995; Lewis and Cullis 1990). Any ambiguity about this relationship would scare off investors, or at least make them cautious in investing. A positive link would definitely boost interest in such investment from private investors and financial institutions alike. A rise in uptake of ethical investments would help the sector reach the necessary critical mass to enable ethical investment fulfil its main aim, i.e. stimulating change towards sustainable development.

Numerous initiatives[1] show the increasing involvement of the financial sector in sustainable development. The UNEP Financial Institutions Initiative identifies ethical investment as one of the key areas leading financial institutions to sustainability. Nevertheless, some experts question whether ethical investment really favours the 'greening' of the financial sector. In the case study, we have seen that social and environmental screening and financial screening are done by two different organisations. This is true for many, if not most, financial institutions managing ethical investment funds. Very often, financial organisations ask independent rating organisations to provide them with a list of companies suitable for 'ethical' investment. Thus environmental and social issues are not integrated within financial institutions but remain external to them. Under these circumstances, it is debatable to what extent ethical investment can influence financial institutions to invest more heavily in sustainable development in the future.

◢ Annexe 1: Empirical analysis

Tables 14.3 and 14.4 give a listing of the companies according to the sector and the country. Table 14.5 gives descriptive statistic for all variables used in the study. Regression analyses were used to test our hypothesis.

Sector	Number	%
Chemistry	14	35
Car	5	13
Airline	5	13
Paper and pulp	3	8
Pharmaceuticals	3	8
Metals	3	8
Electronic	3	8
Food	2	5
Water supply	2	5
Total	**40**	**100%**

Table 14.3 **Distribution by industry sector**

---

1   UNEP Financial Institutions Initiative, 1991; The fifth EC Environment Action Programme, 1993; WBCSD 1997a; among others.

Country	Number	%
Germany	11	28
Switzerland	7	18
Sweden	6	15
UK	3	8
Finland	3	8
Netherlands	3	8
France	3	8
Denmark	2	5
Norway	1	3
Italy	1	3
Total	**40**	**100%**

Table 14.4 **Distribution by country**

	N	Minimum	Maximum	Mean	Standard deviation	Skewness
ROA	51	−4.803	1.522	0.71594	0.98861	−4.152
ROE	51	−2.116	6.617	0.97073	1.19007	1.854
Earnings	51	−2.444	3.085	0.99590	0.72835	−1.938
Energy	51	0.782	1.332	1.05612	0.11488	0.027
Water	40	0.311	1.320	1.06890	0.1699	−2.501
Waste	51	0.763	1.693	1.13608	0.16594	0.882
CO_2	51	0.803	2.000	1.08039	0.16149	3.787

ROA return on assets   ROE return on equity

Table 15.5 **Descriptive statistics**

◢ **Annexe 2: Triodos Added Value Investment Fund portfolio**

Dutch enterprises

Accel Group NV
Airspray NV
Arcadis NV
Bam Groep NV, Koninklijke
CVG
Delft Instruments NV
Elsevier NV
Grontmij NV
Heijmans NV
Hoek's Machine- en Zuurstoffabr.
Holland Colours NV
ING Groep NV

NBM-Amstelland NV
Nedlloyd NV, Koninklijke
Numeco NV, Koninklijke
Oce NV
Sarnus Groep NV
Van Leer, Koninklijke
Wegener Arcade NV

American enterprises

Apple Orthodontix Inc.
Boston Scientific Corp.
Compaq Computer Corp.
Compdent Corp.

Gap Inc.
Heartport Inc.
Ionics Inc.
Symphonix Devices Inc.
United States Filter Corp.
Whole Foods Market Inc.

Other enterprises

Fresenius AG (Germany)
Teldafax (Germany)
Vestas (Denmark)

Triodos MeerWaarde Fonds Portfolio (31 December 1998)

Part 3
SUSTAINABLE
INVESTMENT FUNDS

ENVIRONMENTAL OR SUSTAINABLE FUNDS ARE STILL A NICHE MARKET—ALTHOUGH it is rapidly growing—and this section deals with the historical development of these funds. The transformation from 'environmental funds' to 'sustainable funds' is also discussed. The role of criteria such as financial indexes that link sustainable performance to financial performance are important for the growth of these funds. Furthermore, governments can induce growth using tax incentives.

The four chapters in this section begin with Stefan Schaltegger and Frank Figge of the University of Lüneburg in Germany (Chapter 15), who present a historical perspective on how sustainability issues have entered the investment business and offer an outlook of future developments.

Andreas Knörzer of Bank Sarasin in Switzerland examines trends in environmental funds in Continental Europe (Chapter 16), both in terms of volume and share price, in light of the latest market developments. The chapter then goes on to discuss the innovative application of comprehensive sustainability criteria, using the example of two Sarasin funds, OekoSar and ValueSar, the maxim of which is 'investment with a sustainable future'. The chapter concludes by providing an outlook of market expectations and new product offerings.

Alois Flatz, Lena Serck-Hanssen and Erica Tucker-Bassin of SAM Sustainability Group in Switzerland present a description of the Dow Jones Sustainability Group Indexes (Chapter 17). In this chapter they describe a systematic methodology for identifying leading sustainability-driven companies.

Theo van Bellegem of the Dutch Ministry of Environment offers a description of the origin and the background of the Green Fund System (GFS) in the Netherlands (Chapter 18). In 1992, a Green Fund System was introduced: a co-operative venture between the government and the financial sector. This combination of a tax incentive, a specially designed framework to designate green projects and an active involvement of the financial sector is described and assessed.

SUSTAINABLE DEVELOPMENT FUNDS
Progress since the 1970s

Stefan Schaltegger
University of Lüneburg, Germany

Frank Figge
University of Lüneburg, Germany/ Pictet & Cie., Switzerland

In the discussion about the relevance of eco-investments two seemingly contrary, and extreme, positions emerge. On one side 'hard financiers' insist that investors should concentrate solely on shareholder value. The goal of sustainable development is seen as an ideological menace. Many 'greens', on the other hand, refute this view completely and regard the stakeholder approach as the only valid way to provide space for environmental concerns. Financial markets are regarded by this faction as a menace to sustainable development.

Both of these positions take a simplistic view of what 'shareholder value', the 'stakeholder approach' and 'sustainable development' really mean. In this context three points should not be overlooked. First, the group defending the shareholder value approach forgets that stakeholders are groups that have an influence on how the management of a company meets its goals—in other words, 'green' stakeholder concerns have an impact on shareholder value. Second, the group promoting the stakeholder approach often forgets that the owners of a company, i.e. the shareholders of a quoted company, pursue a legitimate goal in their self-interest, just as stakeholders do. In short: shareholders are stakeholders and have an influence on the success of companies.

The concept of sustainable development highlights the links between economic, ecological and social aspects. This is why suppliers of sustainable fund products would be wise not to regard these factors as three separate issues, but rather to consider the links between them. By adopting this 'three-dimensional' thinking, innovative banks and other suppliers of financial products are building on the bridge of sustainable investment.

15.1 Why are investors relevant for sustainable development?

Entrepreneurial decisions are made by weighing benefits and costs. In many capital-intensive companies the costs of financing are among the most relevant costs. Capital costs are influenced by financial markets, and these markets are in principle future-oriented. The return on capital required by investors depends on how they judge the future prospects of a company.

As environmental factors have an influence on the future business prospects of a company they can be expected to influence the price of capital for this company. These links are not limited to specially 'green' companies or investments, but can result in either lower or higher costs of borrowing capital. The potential influence of investors and financial institutions on the piloting of sustainable development is often disregarded. Investors not only finance environmental technologies; they also influence whether and to what extent sustainability criteria are considered in the strategic management and all capital investment decisions of the company.

If investors and asset managers considered sustainability issues more thoroughly in their allocation of funds, they could exert a far greater influence on corporate environmental management and contribute to the structural change of the economy.

The economic relevance of sustainable development for investors, and the relevance of investors' behaviour for sustainable development, are of course interlinked. The more environmental and social aspects influence the economic success of companies, the more the profitability of investments depends on sustainability aspects. As a consequence financial institutions will give more weight to sustainability issues in their financial analysis and thus exert more influence on the socially and environmentally relevant activities of companies.

15.2 Sustainable investment: the banks' perspective

More and more banks have realised that the relevance of sustainability issues is not limited to financial risks of environmental catastrophes, wars or other upheavals. Sustainability issues have entered the investment business in four steps:

1. Supply of ethical funds

2. Supply of environmental technology funds

3. Development of eco-efficiency funds

4. Extension to sustainable development funds by including social issues

More financial institutions are entering this business field all the time, and those already established in the market have started to develop a wide range of special customer-oriented 'eco-financial' and 'socio-financial' products. In future it can be expected that sustainability criteria will be increasingly included in financial institutions' general financial investment research and asset management policy.

15.2.1 *Investment procedures and products in an opportunity–threat scenario*

One way of looking at sustainable products and investments is by weighing up the 'opportunities' as against the 'threats' they contain. Figures 15.1 and 15.2 show such opportunities and threats from an investor's perspective. Not shown in the diagrams are other financial risks, as well as possible trade-offs, which may occur, for example, when the

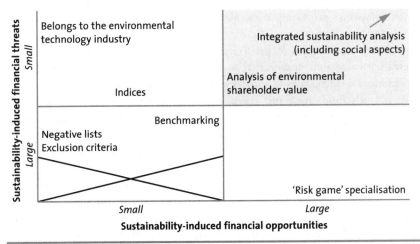

Figure 15.1 **Approaches of sustainability investment processes**

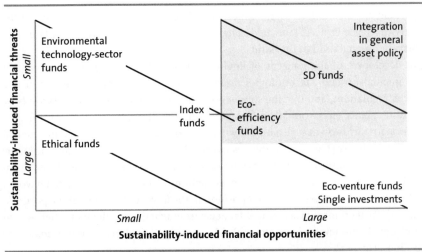

Figure 15.2 **Sustainability investment products**

reduction of sustainability risks leads to a limitation of the portfolio and thus a higher risk of smaller diversification. Figure 15.1 shows the most important factors to be considered in the sustainability investment process as a whole, whereas the position of different investment products is illustrated in Figure 15.2.

15.2.2 Historical development of sustainable investment products

15.2.2.1 Ethical funds

In the 1970s social, and sometimes also environmental, issues were addressed for the first time by US investors. From a methodological perspective, ethical funds work with **negative lists and exclusion criteria** based on ethical values (Fig. 15.1). In terms of this approach companies producing arms, alcohol, tobacco, pornographic products, etc., were excluded from the fund.

Ethical funds can be seen as predecessors or early forms of sustainability funds. Through their evaluation approach they can partially exclude environmentally and socially induced financial risks (e.g. socially induced financial risks of alcohol).

However, such funds have not taken into consideration any possible economic opportunities of ethical behaviour. Furthermore, the environmentally and socially induced financial risks of ethical funds are fairly high, as the social and environmental risks of industries and companies that are not excluded are not taken into account (e.g. environmental liabilities or the risk associated with the production of contaminated baby food). In addition, the general financial risks of ethical funds are increased because they are limited in terms of diversification possibilities. It is clear from the above limitations that the mere use of negative lists and exclusion criteria as an investment evaluation approach is ethically and economically insufficient. It is perhaps not surprising that in continental Europe ethical funds have remained fairly small for the last three decades.

15.2.2.2 Environmental technology funds

The first environmental technology funds were developed in Europe at the end of the 1980s. With its 'Eco Protect', launched in 1992, Credit Suisse is believed to have launched the first continental fund of this kind.

The developers of the concept of environmental technology funds assumed that environmentally friendly technologies would become more common in the future due to stricter regulations, and that the suppliers of environmental technologies (scrubbers, waste-water plants, etc.) would therefore grow substantially and become very profitable. A criterion for inclusion in such a fund is whether a company is part of the environmental technology industry (Fig. 15.1). In this respect this kind of fund is no different from any traditional-sector fund. The fund concept was nourished by the hope that the environmental technology industry could solve most environmental problems and that it would therefore grow substantially (expected position in the lower right corner of the portfolio in Fig. 15.1). Furthermore, it was assumed that environmental technology suppliers would be confronted with fewer environmental risks (position left above ethical funds in the portfolio in Fig. 15.2).

What this assessment concept did not anticipate was that integrated environmental technologies would become more and more important in the design of production systems and facilities generally. Instead of applying individual solutions for existing production facilities, integrated solutions are now designed in advance. As a consequence, the growing environmental awareness and stricter regulations are increasingly less reflected in market and profit growth of specialised suppliers of environmental technologies (actual position in the upper left corner in the portfolio). Analysts have also realised that this industry may even be exposed to more environmentally induced financial risks than the market average of companies. In addition, these funds are exposed to the additional general financial risks of lower diversification.

The misjudgement of the growth of the environmental technology industry was reflected in the moderate success of these funds. They were not able to accumulate enough assets to be profitable for the banks, and they did not offer a particularly attractive investment opportunity for the investors. This is why most of them have been terminated.

15.2.2.3 Eco-efficiency funds

The buzzword 'eco-efficiency' was coined in the late 1980s and promoted at the 1992 Rio UNCTAD conference in particular. New fund products based on this new concept were introduced. 'EcoSar', the world's first eco-efficiency fund, was launched in 1994 by the Swiss Bank Sarasin & Co. As the concept caught on, various other financial institutions followed, either by changing their old investment strategy (e.g. Credit Suisse's Eco Protect) or by founding specialised investment companies (e.g. Sustainable Performance Group).

The process of assessing companies suitable for eco-efficient investment is more extended than in the case of normal funds. It starts with a financial analysis, and those investments that are found economically interesting, i.e. with expected high profitability, are then analysed with regard to their environmental impacts. Only companies that are superior in both the environmental and economic dimensions qualify as investment candidates for eco-efficiency funds. Unlike the process followed with environmental technology funds, this approach aims at reducing environmentally induced financial risks and increasing environmentally induced returns.

15.2.2.4 Sustainable development (SD) funds

In the past few years the relevance of social aspects as one dimension of sustainable development has been increasingly recognised by the analysts and fund managers of environmental funds. It is thus not surprising that social aspects are being included in the assessment analysis more and more frequently. For the first time the evaluation approach is conceptually tackling all three dimensions of sustainable development.

However, most financial institutions apply a fairly superficial assessment approach, which in many instances is based on case studies of specific industries or of high-profile companies. None of the assessment approaches used to date has established a conceptual link between the social and the economic performance of the companies. Nevertheless, many suppliers are working on more sophisticated assessment approaches, especially concerning the social impacts of business. This development should provide the tools to realise additional financial opportunities and to uncover so-far undetected risks.

15.2.3 *Product differentiation and integration into general policy*

Despite their tremendous growth in recent years, sustainability funds account for only a tiny fraction of the assets managed by banks. There are, however, two developments that indicate that the market will continue to expand rapidly. First, we continue to observe a further differentiation of funds and some new and innovative fund concepts (e.g. sustainability bond funds, eco-venture funds and index funds). **Eco-venture funds** represent 'risk games' and are of interest to investors who accept high risks when striving for extraordinary high yields (Fig. 15.2). **Index funds**, in contrast, help investors to follow a specific benchmark and banks to supply more standardised financial products for the mass market. The continuing **specialisation** is illustrated by some new concepts that are beginning to focus directly on the preferences of each investor (e.g. 'Pictet Sustainable Equities', offered by the Geneva-based private bank Pictet & Cie.), which leads to an even higher degree of differentiation. **Differentiation** is a typical sign that the market is maturing. Some banks have begun to integrate environmental aspects into their investment strategies on a broad basis: a decisive step for eco-efficiency. Environmental aspects are becoming part of daily investment research and asset management. The objective is to shift the focus from a separate consideration of environmental aspects to a full-scale integration in the financial decision-making processes. This is essential for the greening of the financial markets. It can be compared to the move from end-of-pipe to integrated environmental protection measures in industry during the 1980s.

One of the reasons for this development is that the increasing standardisation of the instruments used by the actors of the financial markets today makes it more difficult to differentiate the financial institutions on the various markets (Schaltegger and Burritt 2000). Environmental and social assessment has up to now seen very little standardisation. Traditional financial information, on the other hand, is highly standardised both by its content (e.g. accounting standards) and by the information sources used (e.g. information sources such as Bloomberg).

The recent performance of most eco-funds has, however, been disappointing. The main reason for this under-performance is that most funds fail to exploit the full potential of eco-efficiency. A concept that contributes to shareholder value must explicitly assess the impact of environmental aspects on the earning capacity of a company. This is the main characteristic of the 'environmental shareholder value' concept. This concept assesses whether and how the environmental management of a company contributes to its value, either by a reduction in (systematic) risks and/or an increase in expected return (Schaltegger and Figge 1997, 1999). A financial analyst must appraise the 'environmental' impact on the value drivers of shareholder value (Schaltegger and Figge 1997):

- Fixed and working capital investments

- Sales growth, operating profit margin and income tax rate

- Value growth duration

- Cost of capital

It is therefore the main task of a financial analyst to uncover **what kind of environmental protection** a company has practised and what the impact has been on the value of the company. This differs substantially from the assessment methods used by most green funds today, which examine **how much environmental protection** has been put in place by a company.

Environmental protection measures that are value-creating can be characterised as follows (Schaltegger and Figge 1997):

- **Capital-extensive**: software rather than hardware ('smarter', smaller, cheaper installations)

- **Low-material-consuming**: reduced throughput (lower purchase, storage and depreciation costs)

- **Sales-boosting**: increasing the benefit and attraction to customers (more desirable products and services for more customers)

- **Margin-widening**: increasing the benefit to customers and reducing the costs of producing the products and services (higher prices due to greater benefit and lower operating costs through improved operating efficiency)

- **Safeguarding the flow of finance**: confidence of the capital market (lower and less systematic risks, and [if applicable] 'green bonus')

- **Long-term value-enhancing**: anticipation of future costs and earnings potential

It should not be forgotten, however, that the success of a company does not depend only on its success on the sales market. It depends also on its ability to anticipate and manage the relationship with its non-market stakeholders. A popular example is the (potential) impact of environmental groups such as Greenpeace. Their actions can be seen as both threats and opportunities for companies. Any action on the part of a stakeholder that can have an impact on the expected return and risk of an investment is relevant for financial markets. It must therefore be taken into account, even if it is very difficult to quantify.

15.3 Outlook

Ethical or altruistic considerations are becoming increasingly less necessary to justify the consideration of environmental and social aspects in asset management. The faster environmental issues turn into business issues the more obvious becomes the rationale of integrating them into financial decision-making. As their financial impact is anticipated by the financial markets, the environmental incentives become stronger.

The greening of financial markets poses a threat as well as an opportunity to asset managers. First of all, passive asset managers will attract bad risks. Risks that have been turned down by proactive asset managers will end up with those asset managers that do not yet have the appropriate screening and assessment methods in place. What has been distributed among many market participants becomes concentrated in the passive few.

On the other hand, the greening of the financial markets offers opportunities for proactive banks. It gives banks the chance to differentiate themselves from other banks. This is of vital importance as products become increasingly homogeneous.

Banks should, however, in the future refrain from creating separate 'environmental' or 'sustainable asset' managers. As environmental considerations increasingly enter the mainstream of banks' decision-making, it is important to ensure that all employees are trained and qualified to deal with them. To integrate environmental aspects into asset management, analysts and portfolio managers must be able to appraise their economic impact. New information and communication instruments and new analytical tools must be developed to meet this challenge. One important topic in this respect is the development and wide application of standards for the reporting of environmental impacts of companies.

THE TRANSITION FROM ENVIRONMENTAL FUNDS TO SUSTAINABLE INVESTMENT
The practical application of sustainability criteria in investment products

Andreas Knörzer
Bank Sarasin & Co., Switzerland

The new insights brought about by recognised management concepts such as shareholder value or the stakeholder philosophy—often juxtaposed in public discussion as implacable opposites of one another—have encouraged a degree of reorientation in the content of new 'green' investment products in recent years.

16.1 Development of environmental funds

This chapter examines the continental European market, concentrating specifically on investment funds authorised for sale in German-speaking countries. Trends in ecological funds in France, Scandinavia and the Benelux countries (especially the Netherlands) display a similar pattern.[1]

16.1.1 Volume trends

Table 16.1 provides an overview of the number of products in this area and their volume growth over the last five years.

One thing is clear from the figures: although funds invested according to environmental—and in some cases also social—criteria have grown by 25% p.a. over the past five

---

1 Sources: Sarasin's own research and Standard & Poor's Micropal investment funds database.

Fund name	Investment category	Market share 31/3/99 (%)	Volume of funds (€)					Growth p.a. 31/3/94–99 (%)
			31/3/99	31/3/98	31/3/97	31/3/96	31/3/94	
Credit Suisse Eco-Efficiency	Equities world	3.2	16	15	11	11	14	2.3
Focus GT Umwelt-technologie	Equities world	0.6	3	4	3	4	8	−18.2
Hypo Eco-Tech	Equities world	4.8	24	33	33	46	65	−18.0
KD Fonds Oeko-Invest	Equities world	6.1	31	13	16	18	18	11.0
Luxinvest Oekolux	Equities world	7.9	40	36	20	17	18	17.3
OekoVision	Equities world	7.5	38	27	11	–	–	–
Sun Life GP Ecological	Equities world	0.6	3	5	5	4	4	−3.6
Storebrand Scudder Environmental Value	Equities world	26.3	133	155	87	–	–	–
UBS Eco Performance	Equities world	13.3	67	62	–	–	–	–
Swissca Green Invest	Equities world	5.9	30	–	–	–	–	–
Luxinvest SecuraRent	Bonds	5.1	26	28	23	22	24	1.6
OekoSar Portfolio	Balanced world	16.8	85	58	26	13	2	111.7
Prime Value	Balanced world	1.8	9	7	5	2	–	–
Others	–	–	–	–	6	6	10	–
Total		100.0	505	442	245	142	163	25.3

Equities world is a 100% based equities fund with worldwide stock selection.
Balanced world is a mixed fund based on worldwide equities and bond selection.

Table 16.1 **Volume trends for 'green' funds in German-speaking markets**

years, this has mainly been the result of the 'mini-boom' over the past two years, after years of stagnation and even decline. The main driving factor has been the launch of innovative products. Only a handful of funds (OekoSar Portfolio, OekoVision, Luxinvest Oekolux and to a limited extent KD Fonds Oeko-Invest as well) have achieved steady volume growth since their inception. It is interesting to note that these funds are not offered by big banks, but by medium- to small-scale financial service providers. The Storebrand Scudder Environmental Value Fund is a special case. Underpinned mainly by investments from a number of large insurance companies, it is authorised for sale in German-speaking countries but does not appear to be actively marketed. A clear categorisation is also possible in terms of content. All new product offerings, plus the few funds with a consistent growth record, have shifted away from environmental technology and an exclusive concentration on environmental factors towards the broader concept of sustainability, with environmental aspects being interpreted more widely (e.g. through the inclusion of eco-efficiency criteria), and at least some social criteria also being taken into account.

It is very interesting to note that funds marketed and/or managed by Swiss financial service providers (Credit Suisse, OekoVision, UBS, Swissca, OekoSar Portfolio, Prime Value) command a combined market share of 48.5%. This can be attributed to the generally quite proactive approach of Swiss banks towards environmental issues. These institutions are, for example, key participants in international environmental committees (e.g. UNEP Statement by Financial Institutions on the Environment and Sustainable Development), they pursue excellent environmental management practices (increasingly certified to the ISO 14001 standard) and increasingly take environmental criteria into account when granting credit. So far, however, the environmental ratings of borrowers have not generally resulted in a differentiated pricing policy.

Similar observations can be made in other European countries. In Scandinavia, new products, such as KPA Etisk funds, have also only entered the market in recent months. Furthermore, these product offerings differ substantially in terms of content from the large number of funds that still operate with just a few exclusion criteria or invest in environmental technology companies. The social feature of these products lies chiefly in the contributions they make towards a wide range of charitable organisations, which are deducted from the fund management charge. The same applies in France. Here, too, the market is dominated in volume terms by funds characterised by social (solidarity) attributes. Actual environmental funds, as currently offered in German-speaking countries, are clearly in the minority. The situation is quite different in the Netherlands, where the range of environmental funds is much wider both in terms of content and number, encouraged by tax incentives for investments in renewable forms of energy.

16.1.2 Performance trends

Table 16.2 shows the performance of funds over time-periods that are relevant for a meaningful comparison of prices.

In terms of price, the funds with a higher than average performance are those that apply wide-ranging criteria rather than pursuing a one-sided investment approach, and those that have steadily grown in volume terms. If a fund's assets are consistently small, or even start to shrink, it becomes very difficult to implement an investment policy with risk diversification. Another interesting point is that only the two funds managed on global balanced guidelines (Prime Value and OekoSar Portfolio, with equity quotas generally less than 50%), and with an investment policy most geared towards all-round sustainability, have in the past two years managed to keep up with pure equity funds over a longer period, and have actually done better after adjustment for risk.

Fund name	Investment category	Performance (€) as per 31/3/1999				Yield p.a. 5 years	Risk (%) 5 years
		1 year	2 years	3 years	5 years		
Credit Suisse Eco-Efficiency	Equities world	−3.2%	Due to relaunch 1997 no data available				
Focus GT Umwelt-technologie	Equities world	−14.7%	9.2%	31.7%	36.8%	6.5%	14.3%
Hypo Eco-Tech	Equities world	−16.1%	12.3%	32.6%	34.0%	6.0%	14.0%
KD Fonds Oeko-Invest	Equities world	5.0%	40.0%	57.8%	53.2%	8.9%	12.3%
Luxinvest Oekolux	Equities world	−17.5%	13.1%	26.2%	21.8%	4.0%	14.7%
OekoVision	Equities world	−16.2%	14.0%	–	–	–	–
Sun Life GP Ecological	Equities world	−10.1%	3.7%	27.5%	8.6%	1.7%	13.6%
Storebrand Scudder Environmental Value	Equities world	6.8%	54.0%	–	–	–	–
UBS Eco Performance	Equities world	−1.1%	–	–	–	–	–
Swissca Green Invest	Equities world	Start October 1998	–	–	–	–	–
Luxinvest SecuraRent	Bonds	3.8%	18.7%	31.4%	37.0%	6.5%	4.7%
OekoSar Portfolio	Balanced world	−3.3%	16.7%	27.8%	38.0%	6.7%	7.8%
Prime Value	Balanced world	6.5%	22.8%	36.1%	–	–	–
Average		−5.0%	22.7%	38.7%	32.8%	5.8%	11.6%

Table 16.2 **Performance of funds over time-periods that are relevant for a meaningful comparison of prices**

However, a comparison shows that the available funds have on the whole failed (albeit to a differing degree) to keep pace with the relevant stock market indices over the past five years.[2] The main reason for this is the environmental funds' high allocation to small and medium-sized company stocks, a market segment that has not matched the price performance of large cap stocks.[3] This phenomenon had a particularly negative impact in the second half of 1998, making 1998 as a whole a bad year for ecological funds and

2 Stock market indices: Morgan Stanley Capital market Index (MSCI World), MSCI Europe, Swiss Performance Index (SPI), Deutscher Aktienindex (DAX), J.P. Morgan Bond Index.
3 Large cap stocks are stocks of corporations with a multi-billion-dollar market capitalisation, i.e. number of free-float shares × share price.

halting the improved price performance relative to the index that had started in 1997. In addition, the stock selection adopted by environmental funds led in some cases to a heavy underweighting in sectors that were well represented in the index and performed strongly, such as pharmaceuticals, and also meant that Asian stocks were under-represented in portfolios because there was insufficient information available for a sustainability analysis. Considering that the lion's share of such fund assets comes from private investors, it is especially important that investors see themselves as being compensated for the risk they assume when investing in equities rather than savings deposits (still the most popular investment category for private investors).

16.1.3 Summary

The widest range of green investment products, both in terms of content and investment category (pure equities, balanced, pure bonds), is available to investors in German-speaking countries. These funds apply the most comprehensive environmental criteria, as do those marketed in the Netherlands. However, their market share is still small—as in the rest of Europe—although they have managed to achieve higher-than-average growth in the past two years. The leaders in the field, both in terms of volume growth and performance, are usually the products that adopt more comprehensive sustainability criteria. The optimisation of wide-ranging sustainability criteria with acceptable (if not maximum) returns and relatively low risk has proven to be the most successful concept to date. Another finding has been that providers must offer good support for successful products, not just in terms of the necessary research and portfolio management resources, but also in terms of marketing.

16.2 Transition from environmental to sustainable investments

One interesting development is that the investment content of ecological funds has become more complex as new economic players (state, private individuals, companies) have entered the environmental debate. Initially funds investing in environmental technology were launched in response to new legislation and conditions imposed by the authorities, as well as greater environmental awareness on the part of consumers. Eco-efficiency funds were only launched as companies began to show an interest in environmental management and the associated environmental reporting, and capital market players became more interested as well. More recently, the debate on globalisation has made it clear that only comprehensive sustainable investment strategies are sufficiently forward-looking.

Bank Sarasin's concept of sustainable asset management is based on the systematic analysis of the three key dimensions of sustainability: the economic, environmental and social criteria.

Potential investment candidates are tested against all three criteria, as well as the interplay between them. The goal of this sustainability-oriented financial analysis is to identify what we call 'value stars': in other words, companies that can be described as sustainable and forward-looking when all relevant aspects are taken into account. This approach is comparable to the style known in the UK as socially responsible investment (SRI). These companies provide the investment pool for all the bank's mandates for assets that have to be managed on the basis of ecological and social criteria. Interestingly enough, this all-round approach does not impose a further restriction in investment opportunities, but rather enhances them. The integration of clearly defined social criteria allows the bank to select investment sectors and industries that almost all ecological funds have traditionally viewed as inappropriate. The sectors of education, health, technology or even publishing may, for example, offer attractive sustainable investments, particularly when social criteria are taken into consideration.

16.2.1 The underlying concept

The Sarasin approach is based on the realisation that sustainable business objectives must be compatible with the company's competitive strategy (cost leadership, quality leadership or niche provider). Depending on the strategy selected, environmental and social criteria have a different impact on a company's value drivers (e.g. sales, margins, capital costs). Here there are many examples with a valid financial rationale. A company that strives for quality leadership with a highly qualified, well-paid workforce can have problems achieving this goal with a fluctuation rate of 20% or more. Or a company that competes on a cost leadership basis might incur problems in negotiating prices with suppliers if it is known as a structural late payer.

Another principle of the Sarasin approach is that qualitative analysis of the company's ecological and social standing continues to be essential for forward-looking investment decisions, and should remain a central element, especially since quantitative environmental data are geared to the past and are still a long way from being compiled according to standardised reporting guidelines. Nonetheless, both the quality and volume of quantitative data have improved, and can support qualitative analysis in a much more systematic way.

The Sarasin approach also relies heavily on recognised management standards such as EMAS or ISO and international agreements (such as the Montreal Protocol, the Rio/Kyoto Protocol, the Basel Convention) and organisations (e.g. the World Business Council for Sustainable Development [WBCSD] and the International Labour Organisation [ILO]). We check how companies put these standards into practice and at the same time we 'reward' companies with a track record of proactive management.

Another speciality of the Sarasin approach is to consistently clarify for each criterion what implementation stage the relevant measure is currently at (not yet implemented, only partly implemented, or fully implemented) and which business units, production plants or products are affected. In other words, each question assesses the implementation 'depth' and 'breadth' of every measure. A corporation that has only implemented an environmental management system in production facilities in two countries of ten countries it operates in would thus not receive full points on this issue, but merely 20% of total points achievable.

16.2.2 Sarasin environmental assessment

As Figure 16.1 shows, the focus of our environmental assessment is on the analysis of the life-cycle of a company's products and services, starting with pre-production and moving on through actual production to consumption and eventually disposal. After all, the company's responsibilities do not stop at the factory gates: it is also responsible for ensuring that its products are used, maintained and recycled in an environmentally considerate way. Of course, all its efforts in this field must be incorporated into suitable environmental strategies and supported by environmental management systems.

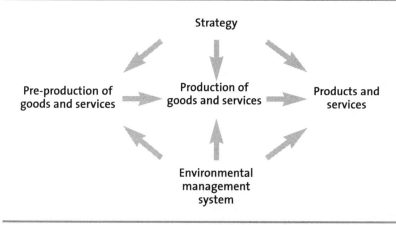

Figure 16.1 **Schematic view of environmental assessment**

The main thread of our environmental analysis is the understanding that the successful investments of today must take into account the shortages of tomorrow. This means that eco-efficiency is a key component in Sarasin's environmental assessment, based on the WBCSD declaration.[4] We therefore examine the three phases of the life-cycle against the following eco-efficiency criteria: reduction of material and energy intensity, reduction of toxicity, increased revalorisation, greater use of renewable resources, increased durability and higher service content. The key figures measure the success (or failure) of environmental measures to date and must be included as complementary information in the analysis. They allow eco-efficiency values to be computed for comparison purposes within a sector, but still require interpretation in the absence of uniform standards.

4 'Eco-efficiency is achieved through competitive goods and services that satisfy human needs and assure our quality of life, while at the same time reducing environmental pollution and the intensity of resource consumption over the entire life cycle until it reaches a level that is in harmony with the sustainability of our planet.'

Environmentally induced financial figures (costs, reserves, investments) are also relevant for the analysis.

16.2.3 Sarasin social assessment

As Figure 16.2 shows, the stakeholder approach, which is key to the social assessment, can rely conceptually on much the same procedure used in the environmental assessment. The company's various stakeholder groups can also be classed into pre-production providers, production/service providers and sales/marketing. No provision of business services is possible without suppliers or capital providers, or the public that provides the infrastructure. Each company obviously has a special responsibility to its employees, and in the marketplace the interests of the client have top priority, but fair behaviour towards competitors can also enhance a company's reputation.

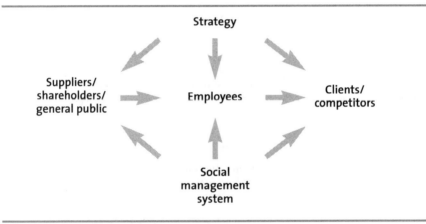

Figure 16.2 **Schematic view of social assessment**

The aim of our social analysis is to examine how systematically a company develops its relations with stakeholders. The analysis of social criteria is not a 'snapshot' but a study of stakeholder relations over time: even stakeholders have a life-cycle as far as the company is concerned. These cycles can be described as building up, cultivating and ending stakeholder relations.

Distinctly economic arguments are possible here. It is widely recognised, for example, that fostering relations with employees and customers is considerably cheaper than trying to rebuild them if the relationship has been broken off by a disgruntled party.

In this context it is particularly important that consideration is given to increasing globalisation. Most companies listed on stock markets have cross-border or global activities, and therefore have to come to terms with very different cultures, religions, expectations, client needs, traditions and laws, etc. Here it is important that standards applicable in the home country are sensibly adapted to local circumstances and the company does not practise 'social dumping'. Other points include local management responsibility, technology transfer, relations with undemocratic regimes, state organisations, etc. Here, too, the Sarasin approach relies on the agreements and standards of international organisations.

16.2.4 Analysis steps

The analysis involves six transparent and plausible steps, as shown in Figure 16.3.

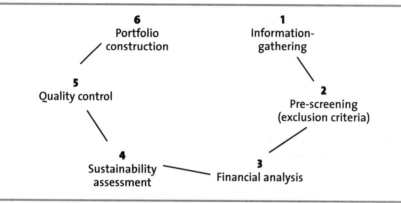

Figure 16.3 **The six analysis steps for stock selection**

Information-gathering (1) plays a more important role in sustainability assessment than in traditional financial analysis, since the spectrum being studied is substantially broader. At the heart of the process lies the industry-specific questionnaire that we developed in-house, which after preliminary processing by the analysts responsible (pre-entry of information already known) has to be completed by different specialists within the company in question. Good communication is achieved with the company if the procedure contains a feedback component.

Depending on the mandate, different exclusion criteria may be applied as a form of pre-screening (2). After financial analysis (3) has been performed, the sustainability assessment (4) will be performed, including comparison of the results against predefined environmental and social benchmarks. These benchmarks take into account the environmental and social exposure of a sector or company.

Consideration is also given to sector-specific circumstances, by giving a different weighting to the criteria groupings examined, depending on their relevance. For all companies the following rule applies: its 'stated intentions' are only given a weighting of 20% both in the social and environmental domain (strategy and management systems), while the firm's actual behaviour has a weighting of 80%. This avoids a situation in which companies that are merely skilful at PR do unjustifiably well.

Another rule that applies for almost all industries is that a strong weighting is given to the direct area of responsibility for the life-cycle of products and services (own production and workforce). This procedure produces comparable results despite heterogeneous sectors, which is essential for investment diversification across different industries. Quality control (5), with the inclusion of additional information, company visits, etc., is an important instrument for verifying the findings of our own research. Portfolio construction (6) means the combination of financial, environmental and social ratings and the portfolio composition derived from this. In the knowledge that being 'best in class' is important, but does not unconditionally result in a truly sustainable investment, Sarasin also includes the sustainability rating of actual industries when putting together the portfolio.

Through the Sarasin sustainability research process, companies within various industry sectors are analysed and only corporations that perform above our internal benchmark are selected for the investment universe of OekoSar Portfolio and ValueSar Equity. Based on a financial analysis, a stock selection from the universe is made for inclusion in the investment funds.

16.2.5 Conclusion

The innovative approach described above offers substantial advantages over methods used to date. It is a genuine sustainable analysis and investment process in the wider sense. If specific social and communal criteria are included, the focus of sectors worthy of investment can be extended, thereby allowing a more optimised portfolio composition. This procedure combines existing knowledge with more recent findings. Through the combination of relative ratings (eco-efficiency within an industry) with absolute criteria (intrasector comparisons), the sustainability of an investment portfolio can be increased. Despite the greater complexity, the schematic process described produces transparent, meaningful results.

16.3 Outlook

Both new products and new concepts will ensure that this niche market will enjoy dynamic growth over the next few years. Whether this will actually result in higher volumes depends on the ability of providers to cater for customer needs with individually tailored investment concepts.

It is crucial that the many products now being offered to private investors are followed by practical and subsequently more attractive concepts for big institutional investors. Criteria such as market liquidity, risk control, performance measurement versus the index, etc. are important here. Institutional investors must be made aware of the importance of sustainable investment as a diversification of investment styles. This is relevant because the varying risk–return performance over time achieved by sustainably managed investments (caused by quite substantial differences in sector weightings compared with the relevant benchmark indices) when compared with traditionally managed funds allows optimisation of the risk–return profile of the overall portfolio.

Another way to expand the product range is to offer genuine venture capital investment funds.[5] Here again, the target audience is institutional and wealthy private investors. This caters for a growing interest from customers and is also a trend that benefits the general economy as well, as it allows the financing of young, mostly small companies in leading-edge industries that have the potential to create new jobs to compensate for those lost in the restructuring process.

A bigger selection of high-quality products offered by a larger number of financial service providers will help this niche market, which is still very small, achieve greater acceptance and attract more demand from customers.[6]

5 Venture capital investment funds mainly invest money directly into promising unlisted companies that need cash to develop the business. From a sustainability investment point of view, money might be invested e.g. in companies developing new technologies with clear environmental benefits, such as fuel-cell technology.

6 Since gathering the basic data for this chapter, the market has developed positively both in terms of number of products available, variety of concepts and performance.

THE DOW JONES SUSTAINABILITY GROUP INDEX
The first worldwide sustainability index

Alois Flatz, Lena Serck-Hanssen and Erica Tucker-Bassin
SAM Sustainability Group, Switzerland

Increasingly, investors are diversifying their portfolios by investing in companies committed to corporate sustainability. Investors are attracted to corporate sustainability because, as a business approach, it creates long-term shareholder value.

Corporate sustainability recognises that corporations exist primarily to increase shareholder value. The primary purpose of companies—to create wealth—is built into the investment concept.

The desirability of an investable benchmark index of such well-managed companies, region by region, covering the whole world, is obvious. The problem for an index provider has been breaking down the concept of superior long-term-oriented management into objective, measurable, quantifiable facts that can be translated into a transparent benchmark that really does measure what it is supposed to measure.

The recently reviewed Dow Jones Sustainability Group Indexes (DJSGIs) provide a bridge between companies implementing corporate sustainability and investors wishing to profit from their superior performance and favourable risk–return profiles. For the first time, corporate sustainability performance is assessed, scored, ranked and quantified through the DJSGIs and the SAM Corporate Sustainability Assessment. Investors are now able to track the corporate sustainability performance of companies. The DJSGI family consists of one global index, three regional (North America, Europe and Asia–Pacific) indexes, and a United States index. Each of these five broad indexes has four narrower, specialised indexes that exclude: (i) alcohol; (ii) gambling; (iii) tobacco; and (iv) all three. All 25 DJSGI indexes are calculated in price return and total return forms in both US dollars and euros, making a total of 100 indexes.

The DJSGI addresses increasing investor interest in companies committed to the elements of corporate sustainability. Corporate sustainability has long been very attractive to investors because of its aim of increasing long-term shareholder value. Corporate

- Dow Jones Sustainability Group Index (DJSGI) is the world's first global sustainability index tracking the performance of the leading sustainability-driven companies.
- The DJSGI is a partnership of Dow Jones Indexes, a leading index provider, and SAM Sustainability Group, a renowned pioneer in sustainability investing. The selection process is based on SAM's Sustainability Rating, Zurich, and the calculation and dissemination of the data is generated by Dow Jones Indexes, New York.
- The DJSGI family is derived from and fully integrated with the Dow Jones Global Indexes. They share the same methodology for calculating, reviewing and publishing the indexes.
- The DJSGIs consist of more than 200 companies that represent the top 10% of the leading sustainability companies in 61 industry groups in the 27 countries covered by the DJGI.
- All the DJSGI indexes will be free-float market capitalisation-weighted—i.e. based on the number of free-float shares outstanding for each of the component stocks—effective 6 October 2000.
- At the end of August 2000, the market capitalisation of the Dow Jones Sustainability Group World Index exceeded US$5 trillion.
- The DJSGI family includes one global index, three regional indexes—covering North America, Europe and the Asia–Pacific—and one country index covering the United States.
- Each of the above five broad regional indexes has four narrower, specialised sustainability indexes that exclude alcohol, gambling, tobacco, and all three together.
- Each of the above 25 DJSGI indexes is calculated as price and total return indexes in both US dollars and euros, giving a total of 100 indexes. All sustainability indexes can be converted into any other currency on request.
- The base value for all DJSGIs is 1,000 on 31 December 1998.
- The DJSGIs are calculated by the widely used Laspeyres's formula.
- The DJSGIs are reviewed annually with the component changes implemented on the first Friday in October and effective on the next trading day.
- The Index Design Committee consists of at least two representatives of each of the two partners and is responsible for all decisions affecting the DJSGIs, including changes to the composition and methodology.
- The real-time calculation of the price indexes are published by Bloomberg (W1SGI), Reuters (W1SGI/A1SGI), the most important media and on www.sustainability-index.com.
- Corporate sustainability is a business approach, which creates long-term shareholder value by embracing opportunities and managing risks deriving from economic, environmental and social developments.

Box 17.1 **Key facts about the Dow Jones Sustainability Group Indexes**

sustainability, as defined by the SAM Sustainability Group, is a business approach to achieving long-term shareholder value by embracing opportunities and managing risk deriving from economic, environmental and social developments. This definition is based on the Brundtland definition of sustainable development, i.e. 'development that meets the needs of the present without compromising the ability of future generations to meet their own needs' (WCED 1987: 43).

Leaders in corporate sustainability can be identified and ranked for investment purposes according to their management of sustainability opportunities and risks deriving from economic, environmental and social developments. These opportunities and risks are directly related to a company's commitment to the five corporate sustainability princi-ples: innovation, governance, shareholders, leadership and society.

A key principle of corporate sustainability is product and service innovation. Corpo-rate sustainability leaders are committed to investing in product and service innovation that focus on technologies and systems, which use financial, natural and social resources in an efficient, effective and economic manner over the long term. Changes in the ecological, social and technological environment mean that companies are being forced to take increasing responsibility for the entire life-cycle of their products. Managing the life-cycle of a car, an oil platform or genetically engineered foods places completely new demands on the design of products and services. Depending on the industry in question, the economic fundamentals and the factors determining future success can change radically. Businesses that manage to incorporate sustainability into their strategy can generate substantial competitive advantages.

Leadership and governance are two more principles to which corporate sustainability leaders are highly committed. Companies pursuing corporate sustainability lead their industry in that direction by setting standards for best practice and maintaining superior performance. They aim to set highest standards of corporate governance.

Last, corporate sustainability leaders are committed to their shareholders and society. By interacting with different stakeholders (e.g. clients, suppliers, employees, government, local communities and NGOs) they encourage long-lasting social wellbeing in commu-nities in which they co-operate and interact. As a result, corporate sustainability leaders secure a long-term 'licence to operate' by responding to stakeholders' changing needs and, thus, fostering superior customer and employee loyalty.

The above-mentioned principles of corporate sustainability are also the criteria by which sustainable companies can be identified and ranked for investment purposes. They facilitate a financial quantification of sustainability performance by focusing on a company's pursuit of sustainability opportunities—e.g. meeting market demand for sustainable products and services—and reduction (ideally, avoidance) of sustainability risks and costs.

Sustainable investing revolves around integrating long-term potential for adding value into professional investment strategies. It entails broadening the scope of traditional financially oriented analysis to include sustainability-related factors. As a result, corpo-rate sustainability is an investable concept. This relationship is crucial in driving interest and investments in sustainability to the mutual benefit of companies and investors. As this benefit circle strengthens, it will have a positive effect on the societies and economies of both the developed and developing world.

17.1 What is different about sustainability investment?

Sustainability, as we have suggested, differs fundamentally from socially responsible or eco-efficient investing (see Table 17.1). The corporate sustainability approach involves substantially broadening the scope of traditional analysis to include sustainability-

Criterion	Socially responsible investment	Eco-efficiency investment	Sustainability investments
Focus of investment	Companies and industries are excluded from investments that fulfil certain negative social criteria (e.g. armaments production, activities in South Africa—apartheid, discrimination of gender or race)	Companies with high eco-efficient production in almost all industries	Companies that profit most from the sustainability trends in almost all industries
Driving forces	Public awareness of social issues and rights	Rising costs due to tighter environmental controls (legal limits, fiscal measures, resource prices, waste disposal, etc.)	Business opportunities arising from political, social, environmental, technological and economic trends
Criteria	Social criteria focused on the elimination of the investable universe	Ecological criteria focused on the production site (corporate environmental management systems, audits and reporting)	Multi-factor criteria (social, ecological, technological, economic) Product portfolio
Risk/ opportunities to traditional investment	Lower risk due to the elimination of industries with high public awareness Higher risk due to a reduction of the investable universe	One additional analytical criterion No significant reduction of the investable universe	Greater opportunities thanks to a broader analytical concept (multidimensional criteria) No reduction of the investable universe per se

Table 17.1 **Differences between socially responsible, eco-efficient and sustainability-oriented investing**

related factors. In contrast, socially responsible investment reduces the investable universe in industries, companies or countries by applying negative social criteria (e.g. nuclear energy, discrimination by gender or race) to eliminate a company.

Socially responsible investing—at least, as it has been understood in the United States—grew out of the protests against South Africa's apartheid government and policies 25 years ago. Part of these protests took the form of boycotting companies that did business in or with South Africa, both refusing to buy their products and also pressuring pension plans and other investors to sell their stocks. These were fairly typical tactics for activists, but they left an essentially negative legacy in terms of an investing style.

Socially responsible investors from this school still exclude stocks of companies from their portfolios that offer certain products and services or whose activities result in undesirable side-effects. These companies are, by their definition, socially irresponsible. But many 'traditional' investors have problems judging which companies act responsibly and which do not, especially since the definitions can be arbitrary.

When we developed a systematic 'Socially Responsible Approach' for SAM Sustainability Group a few years ago, we discovered that the exclusionary socially responsible investment (SRI) approach is rather backward-looking, while investing is all about focusing on the future.

Research at SAM Sustainability Group begins with the creation of industry-specific sustainability scenarios. The use of scenarios means that sustainability is not assessed only in terms of past performance, but that the focus is on assessing the future sustainability potential of industries and individual companies. Realising that the concept of corporate sustainability and what it actually implies for companies varies widely from industry to industry, we include industry-specific criteria in addition to the general criteria used in assessing all industries.

Investment vehicles, which invest on the basis of eco-efficiency, concentrate primarily on reducing the investment risk by selecting the most eco-efficient companies in the industry. Criteria for eco-efficiency include environmental management systems, as well as measures to reduce emissions (waste, and air and water emissions). Eco-efficiency takes only minimal account of new market opportunities that arise from dynamic trends towards sustainability—opportunities that are not ignored by a sustainability-driven approach. In the corporate sustainability approach, the focus is much broader: not only are social or eco-efficient criteria applied, but also technological and economic criteria, e.g. corporate governance or instruments for strategic planning.

When describing sustainability to investors, we position the concept as a unique investment style. Companies pursuing growth in the triple bottom line tend to display superior stock market performances with favourable risk–return profiles. Thus, sustainability becomes a proxy for enlightened and disciplined management—which just happens to be the most important factor that investors do and should consider in deciding whether to buy a stock.

Successful investments assuring both long-term success and sustainable investments need to:

- Be capable of adding value to existing valuation methods (for the relevant industry group)

- Be forward-looking and performance-oriented

- Be based on industry-specific value drivers (including relevant trends and technological developments as opposed to generic data)

- Allow for optimal risk management within the eligible investment universe (this means portfolio diversification and therefore a wide investment universe without too much limitation)

- Be transparent, replicable and easily understood

Sustainability investing strives to combine these criteria in its investment approach. Analysing a company's ability to manage its opportunities and risks deriving from economic, environmental and social developments involves measuring its business approach to create long-term shareholder value. This means managing innovation and turning it into intelligent sustainable products and services, aiming for industry leadership, balancing shareholder needs and stakeholder requirements, taking care of the environment as well as employees' skills and intellectual assets, and finally contributing to society as a good corporate citizen. And, ultimately, it is about good-quality management that understands sustainability and its future orientation.

We believe investments focusing on eco-efficiency (common in Europe) and socially responsible investment (common in North America) are increasingly being replaced by a much broader concept of sustainability. Investments in the sustainability concept are growing rapidly: at least 20 investment products based on the DJSGIs have been launched. Financial institutions such as Nikko Asset Management Co. Ltd (Japan), Bear Sterns (UK), Deutsche Bank (Germany), ING Fund Management BV (Netherlands), Baloise Insurance Company (Switzerland), Rothschild & Cie. Gestion (France), Kepler Fonds (Austria), Banque Générale de Luxembourg (Luxembourg) and others are using the index as a benchmark or as a basis for index-based financial products.

17.2 The stock selection process: building a quantifiable concept

The DJSGIs are reviewed annually in September to ensure that the index composition accurately represents the top 10% of the leading sustainability companies in each of the DJSGI industry groups. The reassessment consists of two parts: an annual review and an ongoing review. The annual review consists of an industry group classification, corporate sustainability assessment, corporate sustainability monitoring, ranking within the industry groups and component selection. Once the components are selected, they are continuously reviewed and monitored throughout the year.

17.2.1 *Corporate Sustainability Assessment methodology*

The DJSGI Corporate Sustainability Assessment methodology identifies the leading sustainability companies from the DJSGI investable stocks universe for each industry group. The methodology is based on the application of specific criteria to assess the opportunities and risks deriving from economic, environmental and social dimensions of each of the eligible companies in the DJSGI investable stocks universe. These criteria consist of both general criteria applicable to all industries and criteria applicable to companies in a specific industry group.

The criteria are built into the corporate sustainability assessment, which quantifies the sustainability performance of a company by assigning a corporate sustainability performance score. The sustainability score is used to identify the leading sustainability companies in each industry group. For each company, the input sources of information for the corporate sustainability assessment consist of the responses to the corporate sustainability assessment questionnaire, submitted documentation, policies and reports, publicly available information and personal contact with companies.

Monitoring media and stakeholder information assesses a company's ongoing involvement in critical social, economic and environmental issues and its management of these situations. Companies that score poorly in the ongoing Corporate Sustainability Monitoring are excluded from the annual Corporate Sustainability Assessment. Companies that successfully pass the ongoing monitoring process and annual assessment process qualify for the DJSGI component selection.

To ensure quality and objectivity, an external audit and internal quality assurance procedures, such as cross-checking of information sources, are used to monitor and maintain the accuracy of the input data, assessment procedures and results. PricewaterhouseCoopers annually reviews the index methodology; in other words, they verified the application of the methodologies described in the *Guide to the Dow Jones Sustainability Group Indexes*, which is the basis for the assessment process.[1] The review by PricewaterhouseCoopers showed no aberration of the methodology described.

17.2.2 *Corporate Sustainability Assessment criteria*

Through the assessment of economic, environmental and societal driving forces and trends, general corporate sustainability criteria are identified. Criteria are identified for each dimension and are applied to all industries, identically and without exception. These general criteria are based on widely accepted standards, best practices and audit procedures.

In addition, industry-specific related criteria covering each dimension are identified for each industry group. The industry group-specific criteria reflect the economic, environmental and social, political and technological forces driving the sustainability performance of a particular industry group. They are based on extensive input from industry specialists and consultants. As a result, at the industry-specific level, the criteria differ between industry groups, whereas the general criteria are the same for each industry group.

In a second step, both the general and industry-specific criteria are then equally defined in terms of sustainability opportunities and risks. These opportunities and risks are divided into classes. The overall rating of opportunities and risks can be subdivided into strategy, management and industry-specific criteria or classes (see Table 17.2). Based on these classes, the Corporate Sustainability Assessment scores a company's strategy, management and industry-specific opportunities and risks deriving from economic, environmental and social driving forces, trends and developments.

Classifying criteria either as an opportunity or risk is the basis for the SAM Sustainability Rating. The criteria can be identified and ranked for investment purposes. The SAM Sustainability Rating provides a rating both for sustainability opportunities and risks and is an invaluable tool for investors as well as for companies, since it can be used as both a corporate sustainability indicator and an incentive.[2]

---

1   This guide can be downloaded from www.sustainability-index.com/news/guidebook.html.
2   For more information on the SAM Sustainability Rating, see www.sam-group.com.

CORPORATE SUSTAINABILITY ASSESSMENT CRITERIA

	Opportunities	*Risks*
Economic	**Strategic** ▶ Strategic planning ▶ Organisational development **Management** ▶ Intellectual capital management ▶ IT management and IT integration ▶ Quality management **Industry-specific (e.g.)** ▶ R&D spending	**Strategic** ▶ Corporate governance **Management** ▶ Risk and crisis management ▶ Corporate codes of conduct **Industry-specific (e.g.)** ▶ Product recall
Environmental	**Strategic** ▶ Environmental charters **Management** ▶ Environmental, health and safety reporting ▶ Environmental profit and loss accounting **Industry-specific (e.g.)** ▶ Eco-design ▶ Eco-efficient products	**Strategic** ▶ Environmental policy ▶ Responsible person for environmental issues **Management** ▶ Environmental management system ▶ Environmental performance **Industry-specific (e.g.)** ▶ Hazardous substances ▶ Environmental liabilities
Social	**Strategic** ▶ Stakeholder involvement **Management** ▶ Social reporting ▶ Employee benefits ▶ Employee satisfaction ▶ Remuneration **Industry-specific (e.g.)** ▶ Community programmes	**Strategic** ▶ Social policy ▶ Responsible person for social issues **Management** ▶ Child labour ▶ Conflict resolution ▶ Equal rights and non-discrimination ▶ Occupational health and safety standards ▶ Lay-offs/freedom of association ▶ Standards for suppliers **Industry-specific (e.g.)** ▶ Personnel training in developing countries

Table 17.2 **Sustainability-related opportunities and risks**

Both the general and industry-specific criteria used in the Corporate Sustainability Assessment are addressed in the SAM Sustainability Questionnaire. The questionnaire is divided into three separate and distinct sections, covering the economic, environmental and social dimensions. Companies witness that each dimension—economic, environmental and social—is equally developed and assessed. The SAM Sustainability Questionnaire supported by company documentation is the most important source of information for the assessment.

17.2.3 Corporate sustainability evaluation

Each company's sustainability performance is given a score. Reviewing, assessing and scoring all available information in line with the corporate sustainability criteria determine the overall sustainability score for each eligible company in the DJSGI investable universe.

The Corporate Sustainability Assessment enables a score to be calculated for each dimension, sustainability opportunity, sustainability risk and class. To calculate the total sustainability score, the different opportunity and risk classes are weighted according to the scheme in Table 17.3. The two management classes are assigned higher scores because of their broader coverage. On an overall level, the economic, environmental and social dimensions are equally weighted with one-third of the total weight each. Slight deviations to this rule are possible in industries with a higher exposure to either the economic, environmental or social dimensions in the industry-specific classes.

17.2.4 Corporate Sustainability Monitoring

Corporate Sustainability Monitoring is based on media reviews using full text database services (e.g. Dow Jones Interactive Publishing) and analysis of stakeholder information and publicly available information. The objective of Corporate Sustainability Monitor-

	Overall weighting (%)
Opportunities	
Strategy opportunities	15
Management opportunities	20
Industry-specific opportunities	15
Risks	
Strategy risks	15
Management risks	20
Industry-specific risks	15
Total maximum score	**100%**

Table 17.3 **Weighting of opportunity and risk classes**

ing is to verify a company's involvement and management of critical environmental, economic and social issues or crisis situations that can have a highly damaging effect on its reputation. In addition, the consistency of a company's behaviour and management of crisis situations is reviewed in line with its stated principles and policies. Corporate Sustainability Monitoring can lead to a company's exclusion from the index, regardless of how well the company performed in the Corporate Sustainability Assessment. The following issues are identified and reviewed in the monitoring process:

- Illegal commercial practices: e.g. tax fraud, money laundering, anti-trust, balance sheet fraud and corruption cases

- Human rights abuses: e.g. cases involving discrimination, forced resettlements, child labour and discrimination of indigenous people

- Lay-offs or workforce conflicts: e.g. extensive lay-offs and strikes

- Large disasters or accidents: e.g. fatalities, accidents, workplace safety, technical failures, ecological disasters and product recall

Corporate Sustainability Monitoring begins with an impact evaluation. If a crisis occurs, then the extent of the crisis within the company, geographically and in the media, is monitored. More importantly, the impact of the crisis on the reputation of the company and its core business is assessed. If the impact of the crisis is far-reaching, is covered worldwide in the media, or is an important concern for the company, then the company is considered for exclusion from the Corporate Sustainability Assessment.

In a second step, the quality of a company's crisis management is verified. In a crisis situation, how well the company informs the public, acknowledges responsibility, provides relief measures and develops solutions is monitored. The DJSGI Index Design Committee further reviews the companies scoring poorly for their quality of crisis management.

The final step in Corporate Sustainability Monitoring enables the Index Design Committee to review the Corporate Sustainability Monitoring results in line with the company's track record, political and cultural setting. If the crisis management of an important sustainability and stakeholder issue is considered poor, the DJSGI Index Design Committee decides whether to exclude the company from the DJSGI investable universe.

17.3 The index characteristics: a favourable risk–return profile

Companies that integrate corporate sustainability into all aspects of their business strategy benefit from long-term shareholder value and superior performance. This is evidenced by some key financial parameters. In the first half of 2000, the average return on equity (ROE) of companies in the DJSGI World Index averaged 14.89% against 8.43% for those in the DJGI World Index. Other key parameters, such as the average return on investment (ROI) (DJSGI, 11.09%; versus DJGI, 7.37%) and the average return on assets (ROA) (DJSGI, 5.81%; versus DJGI, 3.63%) for the first half of 2000 also positively show that corporate sustainability is a successful business approach.

The performance in 2000 is in line with the trend over the last five years, when the average DJSGI World Index's ROE was 14.73% against 9.87% for the DJGI World Index. During the same period, the average ROI (DJSGI, 8.86%; versus DJGI, 6.97%) and the average ROA (DJSGI, 5.49%; versus DJGI, 4.77%) were also superior for sustainability-driven companies (see Figs. 17.1 and 17.2). At the same time, the member companies of the DJSGI showed higher—one-year projected—price–earnings ratios (DJSGI, 24.0; versus DJGI, 20.6) as well as a higher dividend yield (DJSGI, 1.27%; versus DJGI, 1.25%). Long-term earnings growth is also higher for sustainability-driven companies (DJSGI, 10.0%; versus DJGI, 9.1%).

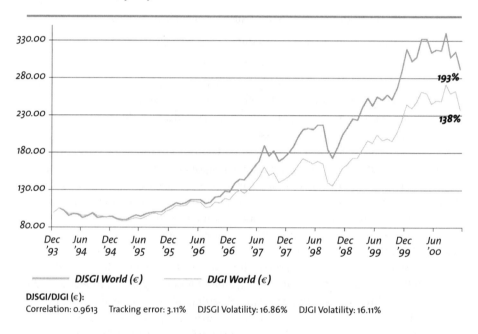

Figure 17.1 **Dow Jones Sustainability Group Index World and Dow Jones Group Index World, price index, December 1993–November 2000**

The performance figures speak for themselves. Companies pursuing corporate sustainability tend to display superior stock market performances with favourable risk–return profiles; leaders in corporate sustainability deliver more predictable results, which means fewer negative surprises; and corporate sustainability provides information on the quality of management—a basic consideration for an investor taking long-term decisions. Investors will seek out leading sustainability companies not for their outsized performance, which is always temporary, but for above-average growth, on which they can rely. Corporate sustainability provides value to investors. It not only improves long-term shareholder value, it is an investment in the future.

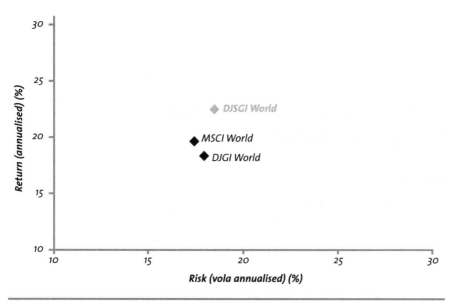

Figure 17.2 **Risk–return profiles (five years: November 1995–November 2000)**

17.4 Conclusion

The DJSGI provides a bridge between companies implementing sustainability principles and investors wishing to profit from their superior performance and favourable risk–return profiles. For investors, the DJSGI provides global, rational, consistent and flexible performance tracking of the leading sustainability companies worldwide. The integrity of the sustainability assessment and the index calculation provides an investable sustainability concept. For companies, the DJSGI provides a financial quantification of their sustainability policy and strategy and their management of sustainability opportunities, risks and costs. Because 'what gets measured gets done', companies will be driven to increase long-term shareholder value by integrating economic, environmental and social factors into their business strategies. The DJSGI 'sustainability principles-to-performance bridge' will provide companies and investors with insight into the trends and events that are driving global supply and demand of sustainable products and services. With this will come a greater appreciation of the importance of integrating sustainability principles into both corporate and investment strategies.

THE GREEN FUND SYSTEM IN THE NETHERLANDS

Theo van Bellegem
Ministry of Housing, Spatial Planning and the Environment, Netherlands

The Green Fund System (GFS) was introduced in 1992 as a joint operation between the Dutch government and the financial sector. Although each of these parties had different objectives, they produced a successful system that differs radically from any other similar system known. The combination of a tax incentive, a specially designed framework to designate green projects and the active involvement of the financial sector have contributed to its power and its public support.

Private savings invested in Green Funds (GFs) are available in a soft loan system with low risks for the saver. Total investment in the system now amounts to between €2 billion and €3 billion.

18.1 The GFS mechanism

The system as operated in the Netherlands is quite different from any other known ethical fund system. The major differences are:

- The strong role of the government. The GFS was initiated by the Dutch government and it continues to play an important role in the system. The GFS is incorporated into the income tax system so that if private individuals participate in a GF they receive a tax exemption. This is one of the driving forces behind the GFS.

- The GFS is restricted to green (environmental) projects (e.g. forestry, wind energy, organic agriculture, nature conservation, etc).

- The GFS operates on a projects basis and not on a corporate basis (e.g. by participation or by buying shares).

The GFS offers financial advantages for entrepreneurs who initiate or own green projects. This has boosted the number of environmental projects being undertaken.

In the Netherlands the income of a private person is subject to income tax. Dividends or interest obtained from savings or investments only escape income tax when they amount to less than about €800 a year. Higher income is subject to the top rate of income tax payable. The top rate payable depends on the individual's total income level in any given fiscal year. For private savers participating in the GFS, the top tax rate is estimated to be about 50%, but income derived from capital invested in a GF is not subjected to income tax. This tax advantage is one of the major incentives for a private person to participate in the GFS. However, in practice, the tax advantages of the GFS are not fully enjoyed by the private saver, if at all. The major tax advantage is enjoyed by the entrepreneur who invests in a green project, in the form of a lower interest rate.

Table 18.1 gives an example of the working mechanism of the GFS. In practice, the interest rate for the saver and the interest rate of the green loan depend on the specific circumstances; this example is intended only as a general guide. In this example, the difference in interest between a GFS loan and one obtained from a normal commercial bank amounts to 2.3%, but the net rate obtained by the green saver may be influenced by the term of the loan. Bank charges generally may depend on the size of the loan and the risk level. The saver investing money in a GF is exposed to a low risk level, as the bank guarantees both repayment and the payment of interest.

	Normal commercial loan (%)	Green Fund loan (%)
Net Interest Saver	2.5	2.5
Tax	2.5	0
Gross Interest Saver	5	2.5
Bank interest costs	5	2.5
Bank costs, profits, risk	1	1.2
Interest level, loan entrepreneur	6	3.7

Table 18.1 **The working mechanism of the GFS system**

The interest levels of green loans and those issued by commercial institutions are linked to some extent. A rise in the commercial rate will lead to a rise in the green loan rate, but it will probably be lower. The relationship between interest rates is shown in Table 18.2. As can be seen, the GFS results in a soft loan system with low interest rates for loans for green projects. In this way the GFS promotes investment in projects with low returns. This low interest rate is a major factor in projects with high capital costs, a long technical lifetime and low operating costs, such as wind energy, district heating and sustainable housing projects. For this type of enterprise the GFS system could result in an important reduction of annual costs.

Interest rate: commercial loans (%)	Interest rate: Green Fund loan (%)	Difference between interest rates (%)
2	1.7	0.3
4	2.7	1.3
6	3.7	2.3
8	4.7	3.3
10	5.7	4.3

Table 18.2 **The relationship between the interest rates of green loans and commercial loans**

18.2 Finance company involvement in the environment

In the Netherlands the financial sector is actively involved in implementing the government's environment policy, and it plays an important role in mechanisms to promote investments in clean technology and energy-saving equipment. The most important governmental incentives to speed up these types of investment are shaped to be attractive for the financial sector. The greatest of these incentives in the Netherlands is the mechanism of **accelerated depreciation** (see VROM 1996). The accelerated depreciation of environmental investments offers entrepreneurs an immediate financial advantage when investing in designated environmental equipment, in the form of more cash in hand and a more favourable interest rate.

Accelerated depreciation is a fiscal scheme and consequently of interest to taxable companies only. Moreover, only companies that owe tax or have made a profit for fiscal purposes are in a position to benefit directly from the arrangement. Nevertheless, non-tax-paying organisations can obtain the benefits of the scheme by applying an operational lease. The lessor (a financial company) invests in the equipment and claims the fiscal early depreciation. The benefit can be passed on to the lessee in the form of lower lease instalments.

The use of operational leases is even more widespread in tax-liable companies aiming at off-balance financing of environmental equipment, because it does not increase the company's loan capital. Often, investments in environmental equipment are not directly profitable, so the profit–invested capital ratio is low (or sometimes negative) for this type of investment. By using company-owned capital for this investment, the profit–invested company-owned capital ratio will be lower. So the application of off-balance financing for investment in environmental equipment may result in a comparatively high profit–invested company-owned capital ratio. The use of an operational lease is beneficial both for the lessor and the lessee, and promotes investments in environmental equipment. In

1995 almost 40% of investment in environmental equipment under the accelerated depreciation scheme was through operational leases. This amounted to €200 million.

Another important fiscal incentive is the tax deduction scheme for investments in energy-saving equipment and equipment run on sustainable energy sources. Like the accelerated depreciation scheme, this scheme makes use of the operational lease. This means that the lease of energy-saving or energy-sustainable equipment is an attractive option that is well used by entrepreneurs.

18.3 The origin of the GFS

The government had various objectives in introducing the GFS. In the Netherlands the basic quality of the environment is maintained through the use of a system of permits, and through the enforcement of environmental standards. A higher grade of protection of the environment is achieved by voluntary agreements or by incentives (e.g. the accelerated depreciation scheme and the energy investment tax deduction scheme). However, a more sustainable society needs more than the prevention of pollution or a reduction in the amount of energy used. New economic activities in fields such as organic agriculture and sustainable energy are needed, and there are too few of these activities because they are not yet profitable enough to be introduced on the desired scale. The Dutch government wanted to encourage these activities, but needed to compensate for the low profit levels achieved. Assuming that these activities should be self-supporting in future, there was a need to introduce an economic incentive to lower the costs of such projects over a certain crucial period.

Although the objective was clear, it was obvious that more instruments could be developed to achieve it. The GFS had some very important advantages, however:

- It provided a mechanism for private capital to be channelled into the green sector, many of whose projects require a high initial investment.

- The objective was to create economic activities that would be self-supporting. The private financial sector had the skills to ensure that new companies would be able to achieve this goal, and the GFS is an ideal mechanism to harness these skills.

- Green projects need a high financial input (e.g. 70% of the total invested capital). A subsidy could never meet this level, but the GFS could.

- The involvement of the general public was crucial in order to promote awareness of, and create support for, green economic activities.

- Considering the historical role of the financial sector in providing incentives, and its economic skills, it was essential to involve it more in green projects, and the GFS was a way of doing this. It was also felt that it would increase the environmental awareness of financial sector companies in general.

18.4 The workings of the GFS

Several processes are needed to keep the GFS going. Among the crucial ones are the founding of a GF, the designation of green projects, the arrangement of the loans, and the collection of the money by GFs.

18.4.1 Founding a Green Fund

A bank that intends to develop a GF is subject to the national regulations governing financial companies. The National Bank has been charged with the enforcement of these regulations, so commercial banks have to submit their proposals to this bank.

After the proposal for the fund has been accepted by the National Bank the fund has to be transformed into a GF. Green Fund status is assigned by the Tax Revenue Department, and the main requirement for such status is that at least 70% of the deposit must be invested in green projects. Occasionally the GF has to send reports to the National Bank and to the Tax Revenue Department. The tight regulation of the funds protects savers in the system by ensuring correct financial management of their investments.

18.4.2 Arrangement of loans and designation of projects

When an entrepreneur wants to invest in a new green project he or she contacts a GF. As all the major banks in the Netherlands own a GF, he or she may contact any local bank office. The GF checks the project's economic features (e.g. risks and profitability) and decides whether it is willing to lend money to the project owner. The GF submits the project to the government agency (Laser-Novem), which has to process the project within eight weeks. When the project meets all the criteria laid down, a so-called Green Certificate or Green Statement is issued to the project owner and to the GF. Now the project owner and the GF can arrange the loan. Project owners can change to another GF after obtaining a Green Statement, as they are not obliged to get the loan from the GF that submitted the project to the agency in the first place. The project owner can shop around at various GFs to arrange the most favourable loan. This contributes to a healthy competition among the GFs. When the GFS was introduced a major question was whether the project owner should be allowed to submit his or her project to the agency directly or not. In this author's opinion the system as now applied has some important advantages. Under the current system project owners first have to discuss the project with the GF's financial experts to check the economic feasibility and the other features of their projects. This prevents people from submitting projects that will not be able to generate enough money for redemption. Occasionally a project is altered or other project owners become involved as a result of the discussions between the GF and the entrepreneur. The involvement of bank experts undoubtedly contributes to the quality of the green projects submitted.

18.4.3 How Green Funds get their money

GFs obviously need money in the first place if they are to award green loans. One of the major problems the funds face is how to manage the timing of obtaining deposits and lending the money out again. GFs are also confronted with redemption of the loans and the obligation to have at least 70% of their deposits placed in green projects. In practice, the money is obtained by issues, the subscription for which is open for only a short period, so a considerable amount of money is generated quickly. The demand for loans is more gradual and spread out. All these factors make the management of a GF rather complicated, especially when the fund is still of a limited size. A better balance between incoming and outgoing funds has been achieved by introducing 'Green Banks' into the GFS.

18.4.4 Auditing in the GFS

The environmental aspects of GFS projects are checked by the Ministry of the Environment or its agencies during the processing of Green Certificates (see Section 18.5.3) and during the term of the green loan. The financial and economic aspects are also part of the assessment for a Green Certificate. During the term of the loan the GF is responsible for the quality of the administrative system of the project owner and the fund has to submit information on the project regularly to the Tax Revenue Department and to the National Bank.

18.5 The roles of the various stakeholders in the GFS

18.5.1 The public

The GFS is only successful because the various actors co-operate. The green saver is the one who provides the money. It was initially expected that no more than about €400 million would be invested in the scheme. It soon became evident that the public was willing to make much more money available, however, and the first GF issues were heavily over-subscribed. The general public pressured the banks into setting up GFs and promoting the GFS. A bank that does not participate in the system might lose clients.

The question is: Why do savers actually invest in the GFS? No research has as yet been done on this subject. In the past there were ethical funds in the Netherlands, but they had little economic output and the sums of money invested in them were small. Due to the tax incentive the output of the GFS is more or less competitive with other funds, but it is still far from excellent. In this author's opinion the GFS's success story is based on a vast group of savers that is willing to lend money for a normal economic return if they are convinced that the money is being used for 'good' projects that contribute to the welfare of society. This group cannot afford to accept a low return, but does accept an average one in the knowledge that the money is being used appropriately. This group is also attracted by the low risks attached to investments in the GFS. Moreover, the fact that the GFS has a good system of assessing green projects makes it more trustworthy.

Not only does the public invest money in the GFS, but individuals also borrow money from GFs, e.g. in the form of the Green Mortgage for sustainable housing. The Green

Mortgage system is so strongly supported by private home-owners that the banks in the Netherlands have been more or less obliged to participate in it.

18.5.2 Financial companies

The banks in the Netherlands play a major role in the GFS. First of all, for a bank the GFS is business just like any other business. You can make profits with a GF. Second, the banks use GFs for image-building and public relations purposes. However, the banks also play an important practical role. When the GFS was introduced the banks had clients willing to invest money, but there were few green projects available, so the GFs had to trace green projects and became active promoters of the system.

The banks are very important in the screening of projects. As they are the risk owners when a project fails, the banks perform the screening on the economic aspects and management capacities, among other factors. They are better placed to perform this type of screening than governmental agencies. During the lifetime of the project the bank is important in controlling the project. Overall, the skills of the financial sector are well used in the GFS and in this author's opinion the banks have a keystone position in the system.

Another positive result of the GFS was that the banks, needing skills to process the system, founded environmental departments or even departments for sustainable development. These departments are now developing new green products and promoting other green activities in the financial companies in general.

18.5.3 Government

The government was important initially in creating the GFS's tax facility. In the working system the role of the government is limited to awarding Green Certificates. Award of these certificates is centralised and part of a transparent process based on a published list of types of green project. It is considered desirable for the government to control the designation of green projects as it prevents endless discussions on what is green and what is not green.

The government is also heavily involved in the auditing of the system (see Section 18.4.4).

18.6 Types of project

The sustainability of a project depends on three aspects: environmental, economic and social. The GFS is applied to projects both in the Netherlands and abroad. The criteria for domestic projects cover only the economic and environmental merits of these projects. The projects eligible under the GFS are selected on general criteria. The major ones are:

- They offer a very high level of environmental benefits.

- They have a low level of economic output. Green projects with a high economic output are considered to be realisable without the GFS.

- They must be economically self-supporting; no 'bottomless pit' projects are considered.

- They employ applied technology or methods that are not yet in common use.

- Only new projects can qualify.

Types of project eligible for the scheme include:

- **Forestry and nature conservation** projects, incorporating new forests, landscape conservation, the creation of ecological migration zones connecting vulnerable biotopes, etc.

- **Agrification** projects, including those that use agricultural products as raw materials for new applications, e.g. biomass

- **Sustainable energy** projects, e.g. solar energy, wind energy, biomass

- **Sustainable housing**, including the Green Mortgage project described above, for sustainable housing. These houses have low energy and water use, are easily demolished and include a high level of recycled material.

- **Organic agriculture**

- **District heating**

As the GFS incorporated more and more activities, it became obvious that not all potential projects meeting the criteria could be enumerated in a list. The projects not mentioned on the list can be submitted to a governmental agency for a screening. The GFS can be applied to these projects if they meet the criteria.

There was a rapid rise in both the number of applications for a Green Certificate, and the amount of money invested in the GFS in the first few years after its inception. This rapid rise in the amount of money tied up in Green Certificates is shown in Table 18.3.

It should be mentioned that not all Green Certificates result in a loan that covers the total project costs. In most cases, part of the project is financed with company-owned

Year	Value (€ million)	Number of projects*	Average costs/project (€ thousand)
1995/1996	404	213	1,897
1997	990	396	2,502
1998	504	359	1,405
1999	676	439	1,547
Total	**2,574**	**1,407**	**1,831**

* One project may consist of, e.g., 20 windmills or 10 houses

Table 18.3 **The number of Green Certificates issued and the value of the projects**

capital. In addition, there is a time-lag between the delivery of the certificate and the starting point of the loan, as some projects have a construction period of several months or even years. The loans tend to amount to about 75% of the delivered statements.

The types of project for which Green Statements have been issued are listed in Table 18.4.

Type of project	€ million
Nature conservation, forestry	295
Organic agriculture	22
District heating grids	500
Green mortgage	197
Wind energy	265
Biomass	45
Low-energy greenhouses	145
Other projects*	898

* Other projects are mainly: nature conservation, sustainable energy, energy saving, recycling and mixed projects

Table 18.4 **Value of Green Certificates by type of project**

The GFS has a substantial environmental impact. GFS projects comprise more than 20,000 hectares of nature conservation areas, about 14,000 hectares of organic agriculture, 690 wind energy turbines, 40 district heating grids and 6,000 sustainable houses.

Despite the strength of the GFS in certain areas, the triggering effect of the system seems to be at a low level for pure nature conservation projects. These projects have a very weak economic base, so even the GFS can only bring a limited number of such projects to fruition. A stronger (or an additional) incentive will be needed to increase the number of such projects.

It is interesting to note that the scheme is effective in mixed projects. These are projects in which a commercial activity is realised under circumstances where nature protection is achieved. Relevant examples are eco-tourism, drinking water infiltration fields and marshes (see van Bellegem *et al.* 1977a).

Another fairly successful area of involvement for the GFS is organic agriculture (see van Bellegem *et al.* 1977b; van Bellegem 1998). While organic agriculture remains a small-scale activity, it is growing at about 25% a year.

Sustainable energy resources, e.g. wind energy and solar energy, require high investment with a limited return. The GFS has been particularly successful in the field of wind energy, as it has funded almost all wind turbines erected in the Netherlands. District heating projects, in which waste heat from power plants or combined cycle systems is transported to houses, are also important. Other energy projects include biomass conversion and heat pumps.

To promote sustainable housing under the GFS a standard method for ranking sustainable houses was developed. A house is screened and each measure (e.g. solar energy) is given a score. When the house reaches a score of 60 points a GFS Green Mortgage to the value of €34,000 may be awarded.

18.6.1 GFS projects abroad

The GFS was originally restricted to projects in the Netherlands, but in 1995 the scope of the incentive was widened to special projects abroad (see VROM 1997a, 1997b). The criteria used for assessing domestic projects are the starting point for the assessment of projects abroad. As mentioned above, criteria for projects in the Netherlands are restricted to economic and environmental aspects. Because the projects abroad are located in countries where circumstances are markedly different from those in the Netherlands, social and local criteria are also used in the assessment. Important criteria are, among others, the participation of the local (poor) population, absence of child labour, freedom of organisation, public health, and emancipation. One could say that under the 'Green Projects Abroad' regulations projects are screened not only on environmental aspects but on their general ethic merits.

The application of the GFS abroad is limited to certain regions:

- The Netherlands Antilles and Aruba (see VROM 1997b)

- Developing countries and other regions deemed to be of similar status. It concerns countries that are considered to lack sufficient resources to carry out the projects themselves. (A group of countries eligible for the scheme is mentioned in an addendum to the Decree on Green Projects Abroad; see VROM 1997a.)

- Countries in Central and Eastern Europe. In these countries the scheme is restricted to Joint Implementation Projects.[1]

The application of the GFS to projects abroad is more complicated both for governmental agencies and for GFs, partly because the economic and political risk level of projects abroad is higher than for domestic projects and it is far more difficult to assess the level of risk. This means that GFs have a cautious attitude to projects abroad. Nevertheless, a number of quite important projects have been certified under the scheme, in China, the Netherlands Antilles, Bolivia, Egypt, Ghana and Romania, among other places. Projects in Estonia, Indonesia, Costa Rica and Aruba are being processed. The projects invested in concern organic agriculture, wind energy, solar energy and nature conservation. The value of the projects amounts to about €20 million.

---

1 These are projects as referred to in Article 4 Paragraph 2 of the United Nations Framework Convention on Climate Change, as confirmed in the Kyoto Protocol to the United Nations Framework Convention on Climate Change.

18.7 The future of the GFS

The GFS is strengthened by the skills of its various stakeholders, and driven forward by the environmental awareness of these stakeholders. This awareness, plus the tax breaks it provides, makes the GFS a viable concept. In January 2001 the Dutch government changed the tax system so the taxation of income derived from capital is independent of the real value of the income. This change threatened to reduce the advantage of the GFS, but parliament insisted on introducing new regulations to reverse the undesired side-effects of the new tax system. As these new regulations have come into force, the future of the GFS is safe. The various partners (public and GFs) have reacted well to the changed system.

There is currently some debate in the Netherlands about whether the GFS could contribute to the reduction of greenhouse gas emissions by involving itself in the trade of carbon dioxide rights; it is anticipated that such rights will become ever more important in future. The redemption of green loans using tradable rights is a solution to be contemplated.

18.8 Conclusions

The GFS as introduced in the Netherlands has some major advantages:

- It promotes environmental awareness among both the general public and the banks.

- The willingness of the green investor to participate in GFs is much higher than in any similar system, and it has raised huge sums of money for green projects.

- Soft loans awarded under the GFS create better economic circumstances for green projects than under normal lending conditions.

- It strongly promotes investment in new green projects, e.g. sustainable housing, organic agriculture and sustainable energy.

- It has brought about successful co-operation between the financial sector and the government.

- The system has low administrative and processing costs.

The major disadvantages of the GFS are that it is limited to **soft loans**, and that it is restricted to **self-supporting projects**.

Part 4
ENVIRONMENTAL RISK AND BANKS' PRODUCTS

IN THIS SECTION THE RELATIONSHIP BETWEEN ENVIRONMENTAL PROBLEMS AND their associated financial risk is discussed.

First, Andrei Barannik (Chapter 19) provides insight into the extensions of management practice that consider environmental problems from the perspective of the providers of financial services (PFSs). It is argued that PFSs gain from new opportunities with respect to integrating environmental considerations into insurance products, dedicated green lending operations, debt-for-nature swaps and green merchant banking.

Frank Figge (Chapter 20) argues that there is a danger that environmental problems could lead to greater interdependency between risks. This is referred to as systematisation of economic risks. He claims that, in future, an effective instrument mix for risk management will have to rely less on diversification and more on reserve accumulation and good information instruments. It is pointed out that, if risk management is to be effective in the future, there must in any case be sufficient reserves available.

Robert Repetto and Duncan Austin (Chapter 21) present a new methodology with which to integrate environmental issues into financial risk and value analysis. The approach is demonstrated through an empirical case study of companies in the US pulp and paper industry. It is revealed that companies face quite different levels of exposure and associated financial risk from environmental issues. The methodology should assist financial analysts in gaining additional insights regarding companies' fundamental values and risks.

Dan Atkins and Charlotte Pedersen (Chapter 22) present some practical guidance for bankers in integrating environmental aspects into credit assessment procedures. In the so-called *Environmental Handbook*, the emphasis is on questionnaires in the form of checklists. The assessment is based on the answers compared against guidance notes to the question and the credit expert's own common sense.

Finally, Part 4 ends with a contribution from Andrea Coulson (Chapter 23). Her chapter presents the findings of a detailed case study of corporate environmental assessment by lending officers within Lloyds TSB conducted as part of the UK Economic and Social Research Council (ESRC) Global Environmental Change Programme. The study provides an insight into how and why corporate environmental performance considerations shape the lending process for the case in question.

PROVIDERS OF FINANCIAL SERVICES AND ENVIRONMENTAL RISK MANAGEMENT
Current experience*

Andrei D. Barannik
International EA Adviser, USA

Environmental problems are looming large in the assumptions, balance sheets and annual reports of providers of financial services (PFSs),[1] just as they challenged the assumptions and practices of natural resources-based companies and firms in other sectors of the economy a few decades ago.

Care and management of the environment belongs, in general, to everyone in society. PFSs that have amassed money and are inextricably linked by lending, investment and insurance to activities that degrade the environment should accept primary responsibility for ensuring that their borrowers and insured make environmentally and socially sustainable decisions. The buck obviously stops with PFSs.

---

* © Andrei D. Barannik, 1999–2000. All rights reserved. All findings, interpretations, and conclusions expressed in this chapter do not necessarily represent the views of any of the PFSs mentioned in it, or the countries in which they are registered or operate. Mention of a proprietary name does not constitute endorsement of the product and is given only for information.

1 Providers of financial services include banks, insurance companies, brokerage services, money managers, Export Credit Agencies (ECAs) mutual funds, etc. This broad definition of PFSs reflects recent growth in mobilisation of financial resources and services outside the traditional system of financial institutions as well as national and cross-border mergers and acquisitions. For example, M&As announced in USA in 2000 include: J.P Morgan and Chase Manhattan Corporation (US$36.5 billion), Associates First Capital Corporation and Citigroup, Inc. (US$30.7 billion), and US Bankcorp and Firstar Corporation (US$20.9 billion) (see www.mergerstat.com). What is more important and impressive is the amount of assets under the management of newly created entities. One should also take into consideration the important role professional associations, law firms and lobbyists play in shaping the policy agenda and practice of PFSs.

As PFSs discover that they are financially accountable for operations that adversely affect the environment—from the imposition of legal sanctions to market responses that reflect externalities—environmental management systems (EMS), including environmental assessment (EA) and environmental risk management (ERM) are put in place. Lending and insurance ERM approaches are driven increasingly by forward-looking strategic planning and ethical considerations.

Nevertheless, national and international rule-making remains the greatest determining factor in environment-related price movements and PFSs' response. Command-and-control methods are complemented by market-based instruments in the global market for environmental goods and services, which totals an estimated US$1 trillion a year.

Besides mainstreaming EMS, EA and ERM with the aim of ensuring overall management quality and operations sustainability, other opportunities are being explored by PFSs, including insurance products, dedicated green lending operations, debt-for-nature swaps and green merchant banking. By employing environmental considerations, PFSs gain market share, identify and influence growth in various sectors, and adjust and revalue their own portfolios.

The accounting profession is also investigating ways of adding pollution charges and clean-up costs to balance sheets, and is considering how current requirements for estimating liabilities might be applied to environmental obligations. These and other initiatives are helping to create increased levels of transparency and making it easier for PFSs to make operational decisions.

ERM is a new phenomenon in the life of PFSs. Its processes, systems and techniques continuously evolve and become more sophisticated. They are characterised by enlightened commitment and proactive efforts in the environmental area, rather than being driven exclusively by the PFSs' fear of potential exposures and defensive actions against environmental risks and liabilities.

It is worth noting that:

- PFSs have a 'natural' affinity with environmentalists as their business is about calculating risk, avoiding and limiting damages and losses, and maximising benefits; they also have a pragmatic self-interest in sustaining the environmental foundation of economic activity.

- PFSs' decisions are extremely influential in terms of the signals they are sending to the economy and governments, particularly as they can refuse to finance and service risks associated with certain sectors or types of operation; they can increase business costs by requiring higher premiums for environmentally risky activities and products, and, subsequently, can change the common view of what is risky.

- In their role as advisors to the firms and corporations they service, PFSs can influence and enhance approaches to environmental management and thus support environmentally and socially friendly economic development.

- PFSs are key players at national and international political and policy-making levels.

We would like to thank the many PFSs, especially NatWest Group, Barclays plc, UBS, Deutsche Bank, ING Group, HSBC Holdings plc, ABN AMRO, BankAmerica, the Yasuda Fire & Marine Insurance Company Ltd and Bayerische Landesbank, all of which have provided their publicly available environmental reports for use in this review.[2]

In this chapter we discuss environmental risk management only as it relates to the PFSs' core internal and external business. It was not our goal to review their practices aimed at efficient use of natural resources and compliance with environmental, health and safety (EHS) requirements in day-to-day operations.[3]

19.1 Types of environmental and associated risk [4]

The existence of environmental risks and uncertainties is as old as the world itself. These risks and uncertainties constitute an all-pervasive, inextricable, permanent and unavoidable part of life.[5] Humans are by nature risk-averse, though many are risk takers. If we cannot control risk, we usually want to avoid or minimise it. In many cases this also involves relating the riskiness and probability of adverse impacts and consequences of an event or activity to its potential benefit, i.e. willingly or unwillingly selecting the optimum risk–benefit ratio.

We believe that environmental risks fall under each of the following 'constraints' categories: **technical feasibility**, **economic and financial possibility**, **administrative operability** and **political viability**. Investigating whether the proposed operation will work in a technical sense and be acceptable to various stakeholders, whether the projected costs justify the benefits, and, more importantly, whether it may be imple-

2 Additional information is available at the following PFS websites: www.aig.com; www.hsbcgroup.com; www.abnamro.com; www.bankamerica.com; www.natwest.com; www.barclays.co.uk; www.ubs.com; www.yasuda.co.jp; www.btm.co.jp; www.citibank.com; www. midland.co.uk; www.gan-canada.com; www.socgen.com; www.nationsbank.com; www.commerzbank.com; www.blb.de; www.inggroup.com; www.co-operativebank.co.uk; www.credit-agricole.fr; www.abbeynational.plc.uk; www.deutsche-bank.de; www.allianz.de; www.calvertgroup.com; www.dreyfus.com; www.smithbarney.com; www.domini.com; www.eco-bank.com; www.greencentury.com; www.trilliuminvest.com; www.kemperinsurance.com.

3 This information is well described in the PFSs' annual environmental reports, available at the above corporate websites. For further discussion, see VfU 1997; German Federal Environmental Agency 1997.

4 The precise definition of an 'environmental risk' depends on one's perspective and on the professional expertise that one employs to analyse it. For the purpose of PFSs' activities, we can describe an environmental risk as a potential that a particular decision to act has to cause diverse, direct or indirect environmental outcomes, for which the probability of a loss (liability) or a profit can be calculated with certain precision (see Fig. 19.1). It can be avoided totally by not acting at all, as well as reduced to acceptable levels and mitigated by implementing various environmental due diligence and management techniques. An environmental risk becomes uncertain when its probability and cost cannot be predicted and calculated, thus leaving few, if any, institutions willing to finance, insure or reinsure it.

5 Risk is also a choice rather than a fate. The choice depends on how freely we can make it as well as on the quality and quantity of available information to support a particular decision.

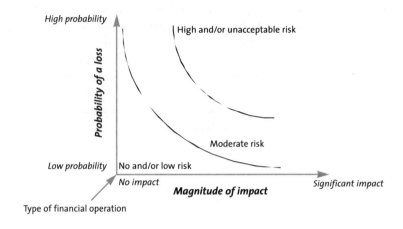

Figure 19.1 **Environmental risk as a function of its components**

mented within the existing administrative context and legal framework, nowadays frequently involves environmental dimensions.

Generally, PFSs worldwide face 'natural' and 'man-made' environmental risks; their activities also have both 'direct' and 'indirect' environmental impacts and consequences. Direct impacts are those related to PFSs' own efforts to ensure effective 'housekeeping' and efficient use of natural resources, particularly energy, water, paper, property, etc., in running their businesses.

But, in the opinion of many people, the greatest environmental effect of PFSs is the indirect impact of their main activities, such as lending money, which either stimulates or discourages the progress of economic sectors, products and services. Thus, it is obvious that the term 'environmental risks' goes well beyond references to the natural environment and straightforward interactions between companies and PFSs; this makes overall relationships very complicated.

The PFSs would dispute this statement, making it clear that they are not environmental regulators and do not have the authority or the ability to monitor individual spending decisions. Furthermore, PFSs widely accept the 'polluter pays principle'[6] and seek its consistent implementation and enforcement. We recognise that the truth lies in between, particularly as PFSs state that they would like to be 'good citizens'. The lending principles

6 To the best of our knowledge, the Athenian thinker Plato (427–347 BC) was the first to put into words what is now accepted as the 'polluter pays' principle, as well as approaches to environmental liabilities: 'If anyone deliberately spoils someone else's water supply . . . by poison or excavation or theft, the injured party should take his case to the City Wardens and submit his estimate of the damage in writing . . . Anyone convicted of fouling water by magic poisons should, in addition to his fine, purify the spring or reservoir the regulations of the Expounders prescribe as appropriate to the circumstances and the individuals involved' (see Cooper 1997). The 'polluter pays' principle was formulated anew by the OECD in the 1970s, primarily as an economic, rather than legal, principle, and has since then been applied to past, ongoing and accidental pollution (see OECD 1972, 1989a).

of some banks already stipulate clearly that they do not finance companies or projects that represent significant risk to the environment (see e.g. Deutsche Bank 1998).

At the same time, there are at least three broad and distinct groups of uncertainties in relation to the environmental dimensions of the economy at large, and the operations of the PFSs' customers in particular, that have emerged as a significant indirect or 'induced' concern pertaining to PFSs' own activities:

- Contamination remaining from past activities, or 'pollution stocks'

- Unacceptable levels of pollution from routine operations and activities, or 'pollution flows', as well as polluting accidents[7]

- Global or regional changes in the customary patterns of behaviour of environmental elements such as climate[8] and weather,[9] water, etc., due to human factors, that lead to increased frequency and severity of catastrophic 'natural'

---

7 Accidents, such as those that occurred at Seveso, Bhopal, Chernobyl or Niagara Falls/the 'Love Canal' (10 July 1976; 3 December 1984; 26 April 1986 and winter 1975/spring 1976 respectively) and those involving Sandoz, Exxon or Amoco (1 November 1986; 24 March 1989; 16 March 1978 respectively) often foster transformation and the tightening of international, national and corporate environmental rules and policies (see e.g. Seveso Directives 82/501/EEC and 96/82/EEC respectively, as well as the Convention on Assistance in the Case of a Nuclear Accident or Radiological Emergency, 26 September 1986, Vienna, in force 26 February 1987 and the Convention on Early Notification of a Nuclear Accident, 26 September 1986, Vienna, in force 27 October 1986; the Love Canal case led to the enactment of the US 'Superfund' legislation—the Comprehensive Environmental Responses, Compensation, and Liability Act of 1980 [PL96-510]: 10 December 1980). Corporate executives, managers and staff are becoming more aware of business `, particularly as legislation provides for both criminal and civil penalties for environmental violations, and court decisions set precedents for future prosecution. (On 13 November 1999, a lawsuit was filed in the US District Court for the Southern District of New York charging the Union Carbide Corporation and its former CEO Warren Anderson with violating international law and fundamental human rights of the victims and survivors of the 1984 Bhopal accident.) Often it is not the catastrophic environmental incidents, but small ones that shake the profitability of a small or medium-sized business (SME) or PFS.

8 The PFSs are also increasingly vulnerable to the consequences of climate changes in the property insurance/reinsurance sector. Climate change impacts, combined with natural disasters, result in more damage claims. For example, 'the giant El Niño of 1997–98 deranged weather patterns around the world, killed an estimated 2,100 people, and caused at least 33 billion dollars in property damage' (*National Geographic* 1999). There are also **opportunities**—particularly as they relate to the results of the Kyoto Climate Conference (December 1997),where industrialised nations committed themselves to a reduction in greenhouse emissions—for PFSs to facilitate and play an important financial intermediary role in joint implementation and trade in carbon dioxide emissions rights. Emission trading is already occurring for sulphur dioxide to mitigate acid rain. Various energy and commodity exchanges, and consulting companies such as PricewaterhouseCoopers and KPMG, are rushing into what some believe will be a global market that could eventually amount to US$1 trillion a year.

9 For example, extreme and adverse weather conditions persisting for long periods can have significant impacts on companies' revenues and the financial soundness of PFSs. Very recently some companies started trying to quantify these impacts and subsequently to write a weather option (weather derivative), which is a hedge against the weather-related risks a business may face. For example, AIG has developed Snow, Temperature or Rain Management (Storm product) to cover these weather-related risks, particularly as faced by energy companies.

environmental risks[10] (earthquakes,[11] typhoons, hurricanes, torrential rains, floods, forest fires, etc.)

In view of spreading pollution, over-use and depletion of various natural resources, we also suggest the singling out of an *environmental access risk* reflecting scarcity and lower quality of particular resources. This risk, in cases of resources restricted or untimely availability, and inadequate characteristics, results in companies paying higher prices for access to quality natural inputs, and may subsequently cause a 'monetary chain reaction'.

If the above issues are inadequately resolved and inadequately factored into decision-making, PFSs' customers may incur significant financial losses, particularly due to: criminal and civil liability claims; operations closure and time necessary for retrofitting to ensure compliance; rejection of or delay in obtaining licences and permits; refusal or withdrawal of permission to market a product; and an increased cost of capital.[12]

Subsequently, due to their customers' environment-related liabilities[13] and negligence, PFSs may have to face: (a) late payments or write-offs of loans and credits; (b) devaluation

10 Some experts place risks associated with natural disasters under *business* or *force majeure* risks. PFSs normally insist on being protected from losses caused by *force majeure*, and typically require repayment on an accelerated basis. In cases covered by insurance, lenders will require project sponsors to pledge the right to receive insurance payments as part of security for a loan. Because 'natural' environmental risks have become too great, many PFSs have begun imposing higher deductibles, premiums, restricting full-placement coverage, and, for example, are pressing for comprehensive and standardised building codes, and their proper enforcement. In accordance with World Bank estimates, in 1998 alone, natural disasters killed more than 50,000 people and destroyed $65 billion-worth of property and infrastructure. Some 95% of disaster-related deaths occurred in developing countries (*World Bank News Release* 2000/189/S; see also Frost 1999).

11 Because 'natural' environmental risks have become too great for insurers, many of them have begun imposing higher deductibles and restricting full-placement coverage. They are also taking related measures such as, for example, pressing for stronger, standardised building codes and proper enforcement. Prior to Hurricane Hugo in 1989, which cost insurers US$4.2 billion, no hurricane had resulted in claims over US$1 billion. Hurricane Andrew, which blasted South Florida in 1992, caused more than US$15.5 billion in insured losses. It is important to bear in mind that insured losses are not the same as overall damage.

12 In the event of a firm's bankruptcy, for example, a merchandise inventory violating quality (environmental, health and safety) standards, which has been assigned to the bank, may not only fail to bring earnings but might even incur additional expenses for the PFS, which will have to safely recycle or dispose of the inventory.

13 In general, 'pollution stock' environmental liabilities depend on: (a) defining types of pollution **on-site** and in the **area of influence**; (b) quantifying what and how much needs to be cleaned up; and (c) then actually calculating the cost of this clean-up. Environmental pollution that exists under the company on the site or in the area of influence can be defined as an **environmental damage**. This damage only becomes **liability** once standards have been established to define a permissible concentration of pollutants in various environmental media. Once the standards are established, it is possible to come up with a legal definition of 'clean'. Having defined the gap between the present physical condition on the site and in the area of influence and the 'clean' state, the most appropriate and cost-effective method for a clean-up can be chosen. Actually, it is the cost of the chosen and formally approved method of a clean-up that becomes a company's true environmental liability. Quite often, legislation sets liability caps in monetary terms for certain types of damage, or in time terms, in which an action can be brought. Banks also apply various standards to determine whether a property is sufficiently

of borrowing companies' securities;[14] (c) loss of market value in liquidation of collateral, (d) criminal liability through exercise of control; (e) significant legal defence expenses; (f) in some cases, personal professional liabilities and losses;(g) non-disclosure liability.[15] Some PFSs may also experience a risk, related to managing their customers' environmental failures, that they may lack the funds needed to meet their commitments when due.[16]

We would like to stress that environmental risks are not ordinary liability risks—they have a first-party as well as a third-party liability component. In addition to the legal liability component, they include physical components, extremely technically complex and protracted in space as well as in time, from the past through the present and to the future.

19.2 Environmental liability

There is still much confusion about interpreting the term 'environmental liability'.[17] In our opinion, it is clearly an umbrella definition that covers a number of major types of

'clean' to provide acceptable collateral for a loan. For example, see Fannie Mae's Announcement No. 91-20, dated 6 September 1991. This notice includes conditions that could cause Fannie Mae to refuse to purchase mortgage loans (see www.fanniemae.com). Damage is also often confused with a **loss**. While a damage refers to the **state** of an entity or a system after a particular action or inaction, a loss refers to the **effect** and **impact** of that action or inaction.

14   In 1999, shareholders of US Liquids Corporation filed a class action lawsuit against the company for misrepresenting and minimising its environmental liabilities. When this news broke out and it turned out that the company would be forced to pay a heavy fine and delay plant openings, US Liquids stock tanked, and eventually lost 50% of its value (as reported at www.foe.org).

15   In some countries banks are required to disclose knowledge of known environmental defects present in the communities where they lend. For example, if an individual bought a home in a common flooding area, and was not advised by the lender to buy flood insurance, the bank would be liable for non-disclosure of this 'defect' if a flood occurred. The lender is required to advise the purchase of insurance according to the nature of its relationship to the home buyer. See also Baran and Partan 1990.

16   In short, PFSs are concerned with the 'quality' of their clients and their portfolios, and therefore they periodically review and analyse them from various points of view. In this context, it is worth noting that PFSs also pose a risk to their customers (depositors and creditors) due to potential negative exposures and subsequently the ability to pay when due and on demand (in the case of insolvency). In other words, PFSs should ensure they themselves are transparent in their communications and that they maintain a good name in the marketplace. This is particularly important in view of recent mergers and acquisitions, as well as the continuing deregulation of the financial sector in some countries.

17   For the purposes of this chapter, we interpret an **environmental liability** as a legal obligation to make future expenditures due to past or ongoing activities that adversely affect the environment. Often, 'environmental liability' is used to refer to the potential for fines, penalties and jail terms for violation of environmental laws. A **potential environmental liability** is a potential legal obligation to make future expenditures due to ongoing or future activities that adversely affect the environment. The difference between these two general types of liability lies in the opportunity that an entity has to prevent liability from occurring by applying various

environmental liability and has important accounting and legal dimensions that are further complicated by timing, likelihood and the uncertainty characteristics of various liability categories.

Environmental liabilities arise from many international, national and local environmental laws and regulations enforced either by public agencies or through private citizens' suits. Another legal source of these liabilities is 'common law', which varies from country to country depending on that country's particular legal history and tradition.

A detailed list of environmental liabilities would be very long. Therefore, we distinguish the following broad categories: (a) compliance obligations; (b) remediation obligations; (c) obligations to pay civil and criminal fines and penalties; (d) obligations to compensate for personal injury, property damage and economic loss; (e) obligations to pay 'punitive damages' for negligent conduct; (f) obligations to pay for natural resources damages,[18] etc.

PFSs' concerns with the prospect of assuming liability for 'pollution stocks', 'pollution flows', 'pollution accidents' and a variety of related risks are complicated by uncertainties associated with:

- In Western democracies, the necessity to ensure compliance with a complex matrix of laws and regulations governing various aspects of interactions between sectors of the economy and the environment; their administration and enforcement falls under different national and international jurisdictions, and courts have a great deal of latitude.[19]

- In developing countries and those in transition, the fact that, in addition to the general problems described above, implementation is further aggravated by (a) lack of credibility, transparency and enforcement and (b) arbitrary interpretation of environmental legal framework

We also distinguish a corporate director/officer (CDO)'s potential 'personal environmental liability' (PEL) for criminal negligence or lack of reasonable care in exercising

mitigation and management techniques. Generally, liability is understood as an obligation to do or refrain from doing something, or to account for certain acts; it is also a penalty, debt or obligation incurred as a result of a violation of statutory or regulatory requirements or the common law. Among various elements required to establish liability—causality, **identifying the polluter**, proof and **measurement of harm**—an issue common to domestic and international law is the determination of the legal basis or degree of fault necessary to impose liability. In the international arena, these fundamental problems are further complicated by three issues: **jurisdiction, choice of law** and **execution of judgements**. One should clearly understand that environmental liability in the sense of responsibility for breaches of the law includes also **liability for harm resulting from an activity permitted under national and international law**.

18 This relatively new type of obligation is particularly common in the US and describes liability related to injury, destruction, loss, or loss of use of natural resources that do not constitute private property.

19 Some regard legal latitude as a sign of the strength of the system, for it provides the flexibility necessary to adjust to new situations without having to fundamentally remake the substantive law. Others argues that there are costs associated with 'generality', for it introduces a large element of uncertainty even into what are, at least on the face of it, routine environmental cases.

environmental due diligence (see Sørensen 1999; Campbell and Campbell 1993; Hodson *et al.* 1992: 34; Harig 1992: 42; Wick 1999). One may anticipate that the scope of a CDO's PEL may at least be argued on the basis of non-compliance, and the consequences of such non-compliance, with standards such as the ISO 14000 series or similar guidelines. Environmental protection will thus be further promoted through the personal liability of a CDO, which may include any person who holds managerial or operational control over the activities of a PFS.

Although CDOs may delegate some of their duties to lower management, the liability remains vested in their function. This highlights the urgency of creating an effective and transparent environmental dissemination and communication system in any PFS. PEL is a nightmare for any CDO who faces the challenge of balancing corporate interests with the potential for personal prosecution and penalty.

19.3 Risk evaluation criteria

In addition to the typology of environmental risks and liabilities related to the activities of PFSs' customers, as well as their own as outlined above, the following general criteria may be integrated into consistent risk assessment of a customer and its proposal.

19.3.1 *Character of environmental risks* [20]

Several factors could be used to determine the significance and acceptability to a PFS of environmental risks that may be associated with a customer's application. None of these should be regarded as more important than any other and the prime rationale for their use is to help in defining the environmental impacts: (a) probability of occurrence; (b) magnitude; (c) duration; (d) sensitivity and irreversibility; (e) social distribution of risks and benefits, i.e. whether the particular environmental impact is negative or positive, and whether it contributes to the equitable sharing of environmental risks and benefits; and (f) relevance to legal mandate, including the value or importance of an environmental attribute that may be exposed to an impact and which the law desires to protect.

19.3.2 *Character of a customer*

This includes, but is not limited to, variations in its: (a) capabilities, both managerial and technical; (b) value and capital, as well as its ability to generate and manage cash from and for environmental products and services; (c) commitment to meet environmental

---

20 We would like to stress that the significance and character of environmental risks and the precise configuration of their financing and insurance varies according to what stage of the project cycle they have reached. In the case of construction projects, for example, these would be: (a) identification and development; (b) approval, construction and start-up; (c) operation; and (d) decommissioning.

financial obligations, objectives and due diligence, innovation as well as commitment to share risks; (d) previous and current environmental performance; (e) quality of any proposed securities and collateral.

19.3.3 Character of environmental legal framework

The past and current status, implementation and enforcement of, and outlook for the future evolution of national and international environmental policies and standards that relate to operations of the PFSs' customer in a particular sector of the economy should be reviewed.

19.4 Risk evaluation approaches

PFSs are particularly interested in valuation, using sophisticated mathematical algorithms, of environmental risks that constitute business liabilities, i.e. 'private' or 'internal' future costs. They need to carry out this valuation in order to ensure the risks are budgeted for in a timely fashion and incorporated in corporate planning, decision-making and operations. They may not be particularly interested in addressing 'societal costs' or 'externalities' for which they are not financially liable or legally accountable. At the same time, ERM is primarily a practical activity concerned with the day-to-day operations and long-term health of a PFS.

In a constantly changing national and international legal framework the line between private and societal costs is rather vague and it is due diligence to consider the possible enactment or modification of environmental laws when deciding what constitutes a potential environmental risk and liability and putting a price tag on it.[21]

There are many ways in which one can try to attach monetary values to, and calculate the costs of, environmental risks and liabilities, such as (a) actuarial techniques; (b) professional judgement and valuation methods; (c) engineering cost estimates; (d) decision-making analysis techniques; (d) modelling; (e) scenario techniques, etc. Because no single financial analysis technique or descriptive tool suits all types of environmental risk and liability, and, because all techniques and tools have their strengths and weaknesses, such instruments are usually applied in combination and/or sequence for valuing specific environmental risks and liabilities that can arise from a certain activity or situation. The diversity of their features and orientations in these approaches makes them very difficult to classify.

Recently, in my opinion, some PFSs have also come to realise that the data you put in a model is as important, if not more important, than the model itself. It is clear that the

---

21 Very high legal and related costs can be incurred in handling claims resulting from environmental risks and liabilities due to non-compliance. Moreover, participation in an environment-related legal/court process consumes a lot of corporate management and staff time and also requires significant additional expenditure to preserve corporate image and reputation. These costs are extremely difficult to predict, estimate and factor in to the price of certain operations and products.

timely availability or collection of accurate and statistically significant environmental data is an increasingly critical issue for the PFS. PFS-wide environmental data management will soon become a strategic function.

In this respect, PFSs may soon start thinking about creating a common comprehensive environmental database to supply environmental risk practitioners with information and to share 'lessons learned' and 'best practice'. This potential system should take advantage of the Internet and provide confidential and public access to environmental risk-related information.

19.4.1 The standard ERM[22] process

ERM, which is different from traditional risk management because of the complexity of defining the full scope of environmental concerns, must be embedded in a PFS's EMS. One should note that there are no clear lines between ERM steps and tools. In many instances they overlap, could be broken into smaller components, and carry a dual role.[23] This has led to some confusion in defining an ERM and the respective roles and responsibilities of PFSs and their customers in it.

A broader-disciplined EA and due diligence process should be the responsibility of and be implemented by a designated PFS's corporate unit(s) and in-house specialists, its customers and contracted experts. ERM usually includes the following elements.

Identifying, by using appropriate tools and in a timely fashion, the exhaustive, accurate historic and projected environmental (plus occupational safety and health) risks to which the organisation is, or may be, exposed. Risk identification is conceptually straightforward, though very complex, because it serves several purposes at once and overlaps various jurisdictions. One should simply identify all environmental risks created by each product or business activity. Breaking down risk exposures into common categories helps a PFS to aggregate risk exposures across its business lines in the future.

Analysing and quantifying the identified environmental risks of each operation. Until an individual risk has been 'bisected', investigated and quantified as accurately as possible, it is difficult to communicate its nature and for the PFS to decide whether it is comfortable with the level of the risk. Quantification requires not only establishing

22 ERM is understood as a consistent and systematic process, implemented by responsible stakeholders, of managing an organisation's risk exposures to achieve its goals effectively and efficiently, and in a manner consistent with public interest, environmental dimensions, human health and safety, and the law.

23 Most ERM professionals initially approach an operation by using the methods and outlook of their discipline: environmentalists often see the problem first in terms of pollution and loss of natural habitats; health specialists will try to calculate finite carcinogenic and toxic risks to human health; economists see it in terms of costs and benefits; sociologists may first look at different impacts on groups of citizens; and attorneys will most certainly look at the legal aspects. The less time available, the more likely it is that some of the ERM steps will be collapsed or skipped. But complex environmental problems definitely demand integration of the evaluation of various dimensions of a particular operation in the ERM, as well as delegation of this task to a team of specialists with diverse skills. In-house environmental specialists should be assigned to handle the potential environmental concerns of each operation, and quality assurance should be factored in prior to its approval.

expected gains or losses associated with assuming the risk, but also distributing anticipated outcomes. PFSs should also have a capacity to aggregate environmental risk exposures across corporate lines, which is fundamental to overall corporate quality risk management.

Determining PFSs' environmental risk tolerance and control techniques, and how they will finance their environmental risk exposures. The feasibility of alternative risk management scenarios should also be evaluated. Alternatives should be analysed and compared, including 'worst-case scenarios' that reflect unfavourable changes in fundamental assumptions. Environmental science and engineering consulting companies are available to provide the necessary inputs. One should also decide on who is in the best position to manage each risk. For each risk exposure, a PFS must decide whether it wants to retain or transfer the risk. As risks tend not to disappear, they must be allocated, priced, mitigated and borne by the parties in accordance with contractual arrangements.

Negotiating a deal and **implementing** the chosen project's consolidated risk management plan; providing ongoing monitoring and supervision of environmental risks and processes through an internal control structure that is organised in the form of a logical, hierarchical pyramid. Key assumptions and models used to quantify environmental risks need to be reviewed regularly, as do the sources of risk exposure. Risk limits should also be reviewed and adjusted on a regular basis. Before these processes can be carried out, performance indicators must be decided on.

19.4.2 ERM tools

There are a number of strategies and management tools that have been adapted and developed by PFSs to transfer and control environmental risks and financial exposure associated with their core business.

Contractual provisions such as **indemnification**[24] (both private and government), representation and warranties that help to allocate responsibility for environmental problems and the risk of related costs, as well as protect against expensive surprises. Loan price and insurance premium rates may also be adjusted and increased to reflect the amount of potential environmental liability. Carefully prepared and worded contracts are an important environmental risk management tool for preventing financial losses. Their effectiveness depends on the ability of each party to enforce the terms of the contract against the other(s), particularly in jurisdictions where the contract is applicable.

Environmental insurance, usually sought on its own or in conjunction with general liability insurance, is one of the most important 'retroactive' tools of risk management. PFSs typically provide and seek coverage against unexpected losses due to environmental

24 A contractual indemnification provision (CIP) is designed to protect the indemnitee from third-party claims and/or other specified liabilities suffered by the indemnitee. CIPs are popular mechanisms for allocating environmental liabilities between a PFS and its customer, but they have some limitations: (a) an indemnity is only as good as the financial worth of the indemnitor; (b) the legal effect of a CIP for an environmental liability may be not very clear due to the nature of liability and choice of law; and (c) CIPs are very complex and difficult to design in such a way that they include all-encompassing indemnities.

damage that has not been identified and allocated during the pre-transaction environmental 'due diligence' process. At the same time an intention to seek insurance or reinsurance for environmental risks may change, and probably enhance, the valuation of a particular PFS's transaction or operation.[25]

Environmental risk communication (ERC), in my opinion, is an essential and integral part of the ERM process, both in crisis and non-crisis situations. It can be defined generally as a systematic and transparent exchange of information among interested parties about the nature, magnitude, significance and management of an environmental risk. The ERC is key to restoring public trust in industry as a credible source of information about environmental risks.

Guarantees are insurance policy contracts provided individually by PFSs[26] or in conjunction with those offered by a number of multinational and national financial institutions (MFIs), such as IBRD, MIGA,[27] OPIC, etc. MFIs help facilitate the flow of financing to developing nations and countries in transition, where demand for private money is high and where significant political and sovereign risks exist. In addition, proposed projects, particularly large infrastructural ones or those in resource-intensive sectors, may pose significant environmental risks. Though these types of guarantee regularly contain provisions obliging project sponsors to implement activities in an environmentally sustainable manner, they are not developed specifically for this purpose; neither do they explicitly protect either sponsor or financier against governmental decisions to enact, and sometimes retroactively apply, new environmental legislation or standards that may endanger the implementation of contractual obligations.

Environmental audit[28] entails a thorough, documented, periodic and objective investigation into the current environmental conditions of a specific customer and its proposal that is offered for the PFS's consideration, to determine the existence and extent of any past pollution, current environmental concerns, the quality of environmental manage-

---

25 Until very recently the environmental insurance market was dominated by three companies: AIG, Zurich Insurance Group and ECS (Reliance Reinsurance Group), which offered rather limited products. There has, however, been rapid growth not only in the number of companies that are active in environmental risk insurance and reinsurance but, more significantly, in the number of products and the coverage they offer. At the same time, existing insurance products are still rather narrow and limited in scope to meet the needs of 'giant' corporations with potentially significant environmental risks. See Banham 1999. Additional information is available at: www.aig.com; www.ecsinc.com; www.zurich.com; www.kemperenvironmental.com.

26 Though some PFSs (AIG, Zurich US Hiscox) provide political risk guarantees/insurance to banks and other investors, including products in favour of their customers, we are not aware of any commercial PFS that has specifically designed an 'environmental guarantee' programme or has clearly spelled out safeguard provisions against the 'volatility' of national environmental legal frameworks.

27 MIGA is offering an insurance product specifically designed to stimulate private insurers to offer political risk coverage for projects in the Institution's developing member countries. The participation of MIGA is generally perceived to be an additional risk reduction and mitigating factor.

28 There are different types of environmental audit, including compliance and/or liability audits, site audits, waste minimisation and pollution prevention audits, which may be implemented as a free-standing exercise or a sequence of activities, or be incorporated as an integral part of an EA.

ment and the status of compliance with regulatory requirements, including those for health and safety, as well as to identify ways and means of improving overall environmental performance.

Environmental assessment[29] (EA), in contrast to environmental audit—which captures a moment in time—systematically helps identify ways and means of evaluating and mitigating against future environmental consequences and risks (including health, safety and social), as well as enhancing benefits and ensuring the stability of earnings and growth, and ensuring the maximisation of profits through reducing waste and liabilities.

EA also helps weigh up environmental risks and benefits from the perspective of societal perceptions, which reflect the different demands of various stakeholders, including project sponsors, regulators, employees, pressure groups and the general public, and which may also change over time.

Because environmental audits and EAs are 'proactive' tools that may actively help change the situation on the ground, they are used primarily by those who seek PFSs' support, money or insurance. They are, however, increasingly utilised by, and contracted to, external consulting firms by the PFSs themselves.

It is important to emphasise that, while both environmental audits and EA reduce the risk, they do not eliminate it. Furthermore, they do not guarantee that there will be no environmental problems; nor do they pay for mitigation. What do offer protection and payment are EA-derived environmental management plan and environmental risk liability insurance policies and financing mechanisms.

A critical path of environmental risk (due diligence) management in PFSs begins at the operational level with formal or informal screening of the environmental risk of both a proposed operation and the applicant in accordance with internal checklists,[30] environmental risk handbooks and due diligence manuals that outline and interpret corporate environmental policies and procedures.[31]

---

29   EA covers a number of instruments and procedures designed for specific purposes, including environmental impact assessment (EIA), risk and hazard assessment, etc.

30   We argue that environmental risks, in a broad sense, occur not only in a few sensitive sectors of the economy, but that they come from all human activities. In our opinion, there is no such thing as an 'environmentally dubious' sector; rather there are companies with good or bad environmental management. Poor environmental performance should be a 'red flag' to a PFS, as this may be the first evidence that a high level of fines or other regulatory actions may be incurred, and that the company concerned may subsequently pose a serious environmental risk.

31   BankAmerica, for example, revised in July 1997 its Environmental Credit Policy to include reference to the then-draft 'World Bank Pollution Control and Abatement Guidelines' for the purpose of evaluating environmental performance in the projects it finances. It is worth noting that this happened long before the *Pollution Prevention and Abatement Handbook* was officially published and formally referred to by staff in terms of World Bank Operation Policy 4.01: Environmental Assessment, approved by the Board of Directors in late December 1998 (see BankAmerica Environmental Program, *1997 Progress Report*: 10). Others, such as Deutsche Bank and UBS, use the World Bank EA *Sourcebook* and other guidelines as a yardstick to judge the quality of customers' EAs and environmental performance.

Screening helps identify what important environmental data may be missing and what environmental risks may require further investigation, mitigation and allocation.[32] Legal screening of a proposed operation has become a routine and essential part of environmental screening to identify any past and current environmental liabilities as well as those that might be imposed in the future on account of changing environmental legislation and standards. Ideally, legislation should be one of the most important remedies to alleviate significant risks. In reality, non-compliance with regulations often exacerbates failures and inefficiencies.

ERM involves preventing losses from occurring (risk control) or paying for those losses that do occur (risk financing) by either retention or insurance. ERM/risk control techniques are generally similar to those employed by EA, including:

- Exposure **avoidance**,[33] which eliminates entirely any possibility of a loss because the proposed operation is simply not undertaken

- Loss **prevention**, which aims to reduce the frequency or likelihood of a particular loss

- Loss **reduction and minimisation**, which aims to reduce the probability, severity and magnitude of a particular loss

- **Segregation and spreading** of loss exposures, which involves arranging PFSs' activities and resources in such a way that no single event or sequence of events can cause simultaneous losses to all of them

- **Mitigation options** of specific environmental risks as determined by EA

- **Contractual transfer and assurance** of legal, financial and management responsibilities for the loss of a particularly risky environmental operation, or part of such an operation, to a customer and/or a separate entity

Without risk financing, risk control techniques are usually not sufficient, because some losses are almost certain to occur over time, and because of the many uncertainties inherent in environmental predictions.

Though we did not have a chance to review PFSs' specific contracts involving environmental risk management, due to their confidential nature, we feel confident in asserting that the recommendations of EIAs and ERM are reflected in legal documents and are worded in such terms that permit adequate supervision and 'punitive' actions by a PFS in cases of environmental non-compliance and/or non-performance.

Another important aspect of PFSs' environmental precautions that helps limit exposure to environmental risks and diverse liabilities is to avoid undue 'participation in

---

32 Some PFSs, such as the NatWest Group and Deutsche Bank, may ask their customers to prepare, where appropriate, an environmental impact assessment to complement their own overall credit risk assessments. Their decision to approve a transaction is determined by the quality of the EA.

33 Avoiding entanglements in managing the customer's business is the first essential condition to exclude the potential for environmental liabilities and risks.

managing' borrower's or insured's activities, as well as careful selection or fragmentation of customers' activities and processes to be supported, thus distancing the PFS from environmental problems. Depending on a country's legal traditions and practice, ongoing daily involvement in a project, even if it begins after an environmental violation or non-compliance, may confer responsibility because it suggests some knowledge or awareness of the failures.[34]

19.4.3 The role of environmental risk manager

The precise role of an 'environmental risk manager' and his/her functions, and prominence within any given PFS, is determined by the size of a firm, its philosophy and that of its leadership as well as by the capabilities that an ERM brings into the job.

Clearly, some ERMs have simpler traditional duties and confine themselves to a limited niche within an institution that is overwhelmed by economists and accountants. Others may be more proactive, both as leaders and team players, and may be heavily engaged in an integrated, cross-departmental management of and decision-making related to environmental risks, including their social, communal, reputational and international implications. Much depends on whether a PFS operates in a 'centralised' or 'decentralised' fashion and how line management and 'oversight' responsibilities are delegated.

An integrated ERM status requires a broad knowledge and understanding of various environmental and social disciplines, own company, its operations, policy and legal developments. Unequivocal support of the board and CEO, and adequate financial resources are all essential attributes of an effective and efficient ERM. It is also important that corporate management views ERM recommendations in an 'evolutionary' rather that 'static' form before making critical decisions.

One of the challenges of an ERM is to connect what seems 'disconnected' between expert judgements and perceptions of ordinary people and shareholders in relation to environmental risks. While experts tend to feel comfortable with a level of 'precaution = ERM', because they typically assess risks in quantitative terms, it may turn out to be inadequate for the majority of people who tend to care more about qualitative aspects and consequences of environmental risks.

---

34 For example, the US EPA Lender Liability Rule does not encourage institutions to control borrowers; rather, it supports proper loan management. The stated purpose of the US EPA Lender Liability Exemption is to define and specify the range of permissible activities a lender may carry out without exceeding the bounds of exemption. The four periods during which lenders can be involved in environmental inquiries and loan management without being regarded as 'participating in management' include: (a) before the loan transaction takes place, or at the inception of the loan; (b) during the tenure of the loan; (c) while undertaking a financial workout with a defaulting borrower; and (d) at foreclosure and when preparing the facility for sale or liquidation.

19.5 Trends

▪ National and global environmental risks do not disappear and relax; rather, new ones arise that constantly challenge PFSs' assumptions.

▪ Customers are demanding cleaner products, services and corporate behaviour.

▪ National and international environmental regulations are getting tougher and new economic instruments, such as taxes, charges and permits, are rewarding clean and well-managed companies and punishing non-performers.

▪ Banks and funds are willing to lend to, and invest in, environmentally and socially conscious companies[35] rather than paying for clean-up and litigation.

▪ Insurance companies are more amenable to covering clean companies; there is also a growing market for the 'transfer' of environmental liabilities.

▪ Competition among PFSs is increasing with respect to the scope of environmentally friendly products and services they offer.

▪ Employees prefer to work for environmentally and socially responsible companies.

▪ Environmental reporting is shifting from simply pronouncing environmental commitment to demonstrating good corporate governance, responsible environmental performance and accountability that embraces environmental, economic and social dimensions.

As we mentioned above, in the early 1990s a number of leading international PFSs articulated clearly their formal policy commitment to achieving best environmental practice throughout their business activities. This included an objective to continuously improve performance and ensure that it is consistent with current environmental knowledge, wherever practicable.[36] Having made a slow start and with relatively modest initial aims, PFSs have consciously accepted the responsibility of integrating environmental dimensions by creating designated corporate environmental units[37] and due diligence

35 A number of socially and environmentally responsible PFSs proclaimed that they would not deal with and support companies that are domestically or internationally involved in tobacco and alcohol production, environmental offences or animal testing, gambling and pornography, nuclear power, weapons manufacture, human rights violations and discrimination.

36 Over 150 PFSs have signed the UNEP 'Statement by Financial Institutions on the Environment and Sustainable Development', made in May 1992 and revised in May 1997; about 70 PFSs had signed the UNEP 'Statement of Environmental Commitment by the Insurance Industry' by 21 May 1997.

37 Many PFSs assigned corporate environmental responsibility to their COB, CEO or other senior managers, with environmental risk units also headed by senior officers at vice president level. In our opinion, however, the overall impact of environmental units on business practices is less than it could be. This is because it is obviously difficult for a few dozen environmental staff to ensure that environmental issues are incorporated into the daily practice of thousands of staff worldwide.

procedures into their day-to-day internal operations, in their community outreach and in the services and products they offer to customers.[38]

PFSs are now also seeking ways of ensuring environmental due diligence in procurement, as well as encouraging 'environmental friendliness' among their suppliers. Increasing numbers of PFSs inform both their shareholders and the general public of their environmental plans and achievements through their annual reports. To add credibility to their statements, some PFSs are inviting external consulting firms to conduct an environmental audit of their business and operations. The reputation of a PFS is becoming an important value that drives stakeholders' decisions on whether to buy corporate products and services.

PFSs have also rather quickly recognised that there is a 'risk of missed opportunities', particularly in view of the governmental commitment to support a 'green' way of life and the consumers' thirst for environmentally friendly financial services and products (see Brill *et al.* 1999). For example, ABN AMRO provides loans at attractive interest rates to support the Dutch government's policy of encouraging the use of energy-saving techniques and durable materials in residential construction.

A PFS's decision to support a customer's application depends on the customer's ability to repay on the agreed schedule and interest rate to cover the PFS's cost of capital and risks. PFSs are increasingly confronted with the question of how to calculate environmental risk tolerance and, more importantly, the premium of their services. An ability to make precise calculations improves PFSs' capabilities to (a) ensure high-quality customers and thus (b) better financial performance and, subsequently, (c) to offer competitive financial products through better adjusted 'environmental pricing'.[39]

38 A number of PFSs indicated that from 1997 they would begin setting up their environmental management systems based on the ISO 14000 series and voluntary participation in the European Eco-management and Audit Scheme (EMAS, regulation 1836/93/EEC, 29 June 1993). There are hints that EMAS will become mandatory in EU countries. A number of banks, including Deutsche Bank, ING and NatWest Group, drafted FEMAS (EMAS for the financial services sector) and in September 1997 submitted their recommendations for review at the European Commission.

39 Barclays Bank plc established, in conjunction with the European Investment Fund (EIF) and the European Investment Bank, the 'Environment Loan Facility' (ELF) to help businesses finance environmentally beneficial investments. In the ELF the usual interest rate is reduced by 0.5%–1%, and other incentives are available. ING Group has a similar arrangement with the EIF, offering environmental loans with 3–7 years' maturity at a discount to the market interest rate. Under its £50 million 'Environmental Lending Initiative' introduced in April 1997, NatWest Corporate Banking Service offers loans at a reduced rate for investment in projects to improve the environmental performance of businesses. The customer gets cheaper funds and NatWest Group's own risk is reduced. In June 1997 UBS launched its Eco-Performance Portfolio, which has committed itself to invest only in ecologically sound companies that seize environmental market opportunities. Eco-friendly assets constitute roughly 0.12% of the total assets under UBS management. On 1 January 1995 Postbank Groen, a member of the ING Group, began issuing loans for projects that have a green status in accordance with the Green Projects Scheme supported by the Dutch government. By the end of 1997 Postbank had arranged financing for projects totalling 770 million Dutch guilders. It also issued three subscription tranches of 'green' savings certificates.

19.6 Challenges ahead

PFSs should pre-empt both environmental and own-sector regulations by enlightened self-interest. They should offer prioritised and sound scientific justification for new legislation that allows flexibility in the ways and means of achieving environmental goals. Economic incentives and market-based approaches need to encourage PFSs' involvement in environmentally and socially sustainable development, particularly financing efficient redevelopment of idle and under-used properties that have an element of real or perceived contamination.

PFSs should reach out more proactively to other sectors of the economy, particularly SMEs (small and medium-sized enterprises) to foster their commitment to properly account for environmental dimensions and incorporate them into daily operations. It is also important to ensure that SMEs know where to find help, financial services and products to address their specific environmental concerns.

PFSs should incorporate environmental dimensions into consolidated risk management practice by establishing (a) country-by-country and (b) sector-by-sector commitment ceilings that reflect their 'general' and 'specific' environmental risks. Such ceilings should apply to all types of a PFS's services and products, managed by various 'departments', taken in aggregate and complemented by a rating system of a PFS's customers operating in a particular country or sector. In addition, an individual system of monitoring sensitive issues such as new environmental legislation and standards, punitive actions, accidents, etc., should be introduced as an early warning and problem identification service.

PFSs, particularly insurance companies, should pursue environmental opportunities more aggressively by offering a menu of diverse and transparent products with higher policy limits and broader coverage, for extended time-periods and for better prices.

To foster more proactive and enlightened management of environmental issues, and to ensure that such issues are brought to the forefront of the economic development agenda, PFSs may consider beefing up their own environmental capabilities by attracting additional environmental professionals and establishing long-term alliances with reputable environmental firms with diverse sectoral and country-specific expertise.

The capabilities and use of the Internet, offering extraordinarily broad access at minimal cost, should be significantly expanded, particularly as it allows institutions to pool together environmental and other 'brains' to manage a specific task, no matter where in the world they are located.

PFSs should continue to standardise their own reporting on environmental and social performance, and disclosure of information on environmental risks; they should also make it more transparent, coherent and focused.[40] PFSs' disclosure of environmental information should be comprehensive, systematic, material, timely and reliable, and it

---

40 Detailed and in-depth requirements developed by the US FDIC and SEC (www.fdic.gov and www.sec.gov) for assessing and pricing environmental risk and disclosure of information on environmental liabilities may serve as examples of good practice. The US FASB (www.fasb.org) has also developed guidance and standards for proper accounting for environmental contamination costs as well as disclosure and recording of environmental liabilities. Both FASB and SEC

should cover operations worldwide, not just in their home countries.[41] Again, the capabilities of the Internet should be used by PFSs to speed up the secure exchange of information, application and delivery of standardised products.

In addition, transparency of environmental information will enable users of that information to make an accurate assessment of a PFS's financial conditions and performance, its business activities and the risks related to those activities. This needs to be complemented by an independent verification system and by consistency in the use of environmental terminology.

Though widely acknowledged as being of increasing concern to the sector, environmental dimensions are firmly rooted only in the operations of a handful of 'big' PFSs.[42] More Western PFSs, particularly smaller ones, should start translating their understanding of sustainability into commitment and subsequently building EMSs; they should also look more favourably on environmental innovations in the sector.

PFSs should work with other disciplines and sectors to develop a corporate 'environmental risk rating' system, encompassing historic environmental and social performance in a similar manner to credit ratings.[43] The proposed 'environmental rating' will offer a 'one-stop shop' for obtaining a credible assessment of company's exposure to environmental liabilities as well as of its overall creditworthiness.

Rapid improvements in data processing and telecommunications have enabled PFSs to offer their services over ever-wider geographic areas. Most of the Western PFSs reviewed have extensive international exposures. This has two major implications for PFSs' operations in the international arena, both of which offer opportunities for growth and expansion of their services. First is the international and regional environmental rule-making that promotes strict and coherent requirements for public and private business

requirements insist on a full disclosure of environmental liabilities and a reserve commensurate with the exposure. In August 1999 the UK ONS for the first time included the Environmental Accounts as 'satellites' to the National Accounts (see www.ons.gov.uk).

41   Environmental information disclosure by PFSs should be fair and 'non-selective' in the sense that public disclosures of important environmental material information should be a **timely** and **comprehensive** exercise that is not limited to analysts, major shareholders or industry insiders.

42   The US alone has more than 8,700 commercial banks, plus 1,600 savings institutions, 10,000 credit unions, about 5,000 insurance companies and about 5,000 securities firms.

43   Eco-Rating International has developed approaches and tools for environmental rating that take the entire spectrum of a firm's activities into account and are based on a weighted aggregation of the phase-specific ratings, including environmental impacts, logistics, infrastructure, the eco-profile of products and services, legal compliance, management and 'soft' social and economic factors. Further information is available at www.eco-rating.com. Innovest Strategic Value Advisers developed the EcoValue 21 platform to identify the risks and opportunities associated with environment-related factors. This product helps assess corporate environmental and resources efficiency and present it in a meaningful format, particularly in terms of financial implications, to financiers and investors. Further information is available from www.innovestgroup.com. VISTA Information Solutions Inc. and Kinder, Lydenberg, Domini & Co. Inc. provide detailed environmental profiles and location-specific information as well as social screening of US corporations that is essential for PFS decision-making. Further information is available at www.vistainfor.com and www.kld.com.

environmental conduct and establishes a rigorous system for assigning liability, including financial, in the event of environmental damage.[44]

Second, in many cases the environmental legislation of a host country varies from and is less rigorous than that of the Western PFS's country of origin/registration. This situation is particularly worrisome in developing countries and those in transition, where national PFSs lack EMSs, do not apply environmental risk analysis and in many cases do not ensure compliance with national environmental legislation and standards. More importantly, these countries have inadequate commercial infrastructure, i.e. accounting, banking and insurance systems.

In this respect, the international PFS community, together with relevant MFIs, ECAs[45] and other interested parties, may explore ways and means to: (a) transfer their knowledge and help build environmental capabilities in the PFSs of developing nations and countries in transition; (b) to harmonise national standards and procedures, making them comparable with best international practice; (c) foster certainty about national liability rules and facilitate credible and transparent enforcement of environmental regulations; (d) ensure the flexibility of EMS/EA; and (e) improve the availability and credibility of data on past environmental practice and pollution.

PFSs should also explore opportunities to utilise political risk insurance or guarantees (PRIG) offered by a number of MFIs and to seek expansion of their coverage to protect against host governments' potential breach of environmental indemnification or immunity agreements as well as against the risk that governments may change environmental policies, regulations and standards in the course of project implementation.

44 For example, the Fifth Meeting of the Parties of the Basel Convention (the Convention on the Control of Transboundary Movements of Hazardous Wastes and their Disposal, adopted on 22 March 1989, in force 5 May 1992), adopted on 10 December 1999, a protocol on liability and compensation for damage resulting from transboundary movements of hazardous wastes and their disposal. The Protocol for the first time establishes a transparent system for assigning liability in incidents involving hazardous waste. The text of the Protocol and related information are available at www.basel.int/pub/Protocol.htm.

45 National public Export Credit Agencies, which provide loans and guarantees for projects with potentially significant environmental and social impacts and consequences, include US Ex–Im Bank and OPIC, Export Development Corporation (Canada), Hermes Kreditversicherungs AG (Germany), Exim Bank (Japan), SACE (Italy), Export Finance and Insurance (Australia), and The Swiss Export Risk Guarantee. Some of them still have to improve and strengthen compliance with own environmental and social safeguard policies and procedures.

ENVIRONMENT-INDUCED SYSTEMATISATION OF ECONOMIC RISKS

Frank Figge
University of Lüneburg, Germany/
Bank Pictet & Cie., Switzerland

Assessing companies' future prospects is one of the key tasks performed by banks. For example, they have to determine a company's value when rating its creditworthiness or deciding whether it offers a worthwhile investment. The financial assessment of a company's value concentrates on two main aspects: expected returns and expected risks.[1]

Environmental factors can impact on both these aspects (see e.g. Schaltegger and Figge 1997). This chapter concentrates on the impact that environmental aspects have on investment risks. These are generally referred to as **environment-induced economic risks**.

In practice it is often argued that greater environmental risks are generally a cause for concern. It is frequently asserted that a company's value is eroded by environment-induced risks. But such a generalised view of the problem fails to take into account the complexity of environmental risks. As this chapter shows, the most important factor is not so much the scale of risk or the probability of it occurring, but rather its composition. The main point to remember is that a change in the composition of environmental risks does not necessarily lead to an overall deterioration in loss experience. If, as a result of environmental problems, the interdependencies between the occurrence of individual risks increase without any change in the actual probability of occurrence, loss experience expectations may in fact improve.

A change in the composition of risks may mean that risk management instruments become less effective. This is exactly the threat posed by the economic risks induced by global environmental problems.

---

1   Here it is assumed that the company is valued on the basis of its potential earnings capacity.

Professional risk management is particularly important for businesses such as banks and insurers whose economic role is risk transformation. As far as business priorities go, effective risk management is one of the key success factors for these companies.

Both from a commercial and (macro)economic viewpoint, it is disconcerting to find environmental risks being discussed with very little differentiation of the individual issues involved.

20.1 Risks in investment decisions

Risks erode returns. This is something recognised by both decision-making theory and portfolio theory.[2] While the former provides guidelines on how to manage risks effectively in decision-making situations, portfolio theory allows conclusions to be drawn about the simultaneous handling of a large number of individual risks contained in a portfolio.[3] The main thing is to establish the relationship between the desired return and the expected risk.

A risk is always present if the actual yield turns out to be different (higher or lower) than the expected return.[4] When a stock fails to meet its price target as a result of environmental factors, this presents an environment-induced economic risk. The more the potential returns diverge and the less likely it is that the desired return will actually be achieved, the greater the risk. The risk is measured in statistical terms by a spread factor, usually known as the variance. The narrower the spread, the smaller the risk.

If the only difference between two investment alternatives, say share A and share B, is their associated risk, and if the riskier investment A promises a higher return, the difference between A and B (the one with a lower rate of return) is known as the **risk premium**.

Investors are obviously attracted to alternatives where the risks are the same but expected returns are higher. All other aspects are dominated by the investor's willingness to take risks. It is fair to assume that most players in the market, such as investors, are averse to risks, i.e. they try to avoid risks where possible. Put another way, they are only willing to take risks on board in return for a reasonable risk premium.

When discussing environment-induced economic risks, people often fail to fully examine their specific characteristics. This hypothesis is supported by the fact that an implicit assumption is generally made that it is possible to counteract the effects of environment-induced economic risks with existing risk management instruments, by simply adjusting the risk premiums, for example.

---

2 This assumes risk-averse investors, as usually found in practice.

3 For decision-making and portfolio theory, see e.g. Gäfgen 1974; Markowitz 1959.

4 If there is a chance that the return will be higher than expected, the risk can be described as an opportunity as well. For most people, however, the term 'risk' usually implies a result that is worse than expected. Strictly speaking, the risk could turn out to be positive or negative. In what follows, however, we always use the term 'risk' in the negative sense, as intuitively understood by most people.

There is, however, a strong case for arguing that the only way to respond to environment-induced economic risks—as opposed to other traditional risks—is to modify the instrument mix. If necessary, one has to resort to **other risk management instruments**. The ideal composition of this instrument mix depends on the situation-specific characteristics of the risks, not on their scale. This aspect is discussed below.

20.2 Risk characteristics

One of the most important factors in characterising environmental risks is the differentiation of risks according to the **decision period** and their **interdependencies**. The former differentiation is applied mainly in decision-making theory, while the latter is employed primarily in portfolio theory.

20.2.1 Differentiation by decision period

Relatively few decisions are made on the basis of comprehensive information. If there is insufficient information to reach a decision, this can present a risk. The risk can also be described as an uncertainty, or **pre-decision risk**. On the other hand, most investors are exposed to a general risk of failure, even if they are in possession of complete information when making their decisions. This risk is classed as a **post-decision risk**.[5] It is commonly assumed that only the probability of the post-decision risk can be accurately determined: for pre-decision risks, the best that one can do is make assumptions about probability.[6]

If there is reliable statistical information about the probability of a particular risk occurring, and if it is safe to assume that the probability is unlikely to change in future, this can be classified as a post-decision risk. 'Traditional' environmental incidents frequently have this sort of post-decision character—the wreck of the oil tanker *Exxon Valdez* in 1989 is a good example. Even though accidents involving tankers are fortunately very rare, insurance companies are able to estimate the probability of them occurring.

In contrast, new types of environmental risk for which no loss history exists often tend to demonstrate more of a pre-decision character (uncertainty). The use of high-risk innovative technologies frequently entails a pre-decision risk. The future importance of fuel cells and solar energy is a good example of this uncertainty. If the costs of solar energy fall dramatically, as predicted by some industry experts, they could turn out to be 'disruptive technologies' that sweep aside traditional forms of power generation and pose a threat to them.

5   For the differentiation of risk and uncertainty after a decision has been made, see Mag 1980: 479.
6   This classification can be attributed to Knight 1921.

20.2.2 *Differentiation by interdependencies*

Individual environmental risks are of only minor interest to investors prepared to take a number of different risks at the same time. As far as they are concerned, the following two questions are much more important:

- How high is the expected return and the predicted risk of the entire portfolio during each defined time-period?

- How high is the expected return at the end of the investment period and how great the risk of the actual return being higher or lower than expected?

The risk associated with a portfolio of stocks over a given period, such as a year, depends on the one hand on the volatility of the individual stocks and on the other on the interdependencies between risks. If two risks are interdependent, they are described as systematic, or unsystematic if they have no interdependency.

If, for example, two different stocks respond to the news of tougher environmental regulations by similar advances in share price, it shows that there may well be an interdependency. If all—or at least most—shares in a portfolio respond in the same way to such news, this will have an impact on the return achieved by the entire portfolio. In this case the individual risks associated with the stocks contribute to the overall risk of the portfolio and are of interest to investors. Here we can speak of a horizontal system-atology, i.e. a systematic relationship between the individual risks of a portfolio. In contrast, most environmental incidents are examples of risks that are not very system-atic in nature.

This distinction is important to the extent that the significance of unsystematic risks for the portfolio declines if there are more individual risks in the portfolio (see also Fig. 20.1). One way of putting this is that the unsystematic risk is eliminated through diversification.[7] The systematic risk, on the other hand, continues to apply even when a portfolio

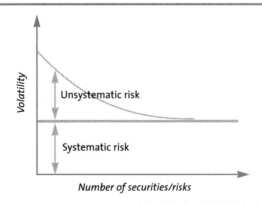

Figure 20.1 **Unsystematic/systematic risks in portfolios**

---

7 Diversification as a risk management instrument is examined in more detail later in this chapter.

is put together. Since the unsystematic risk can be eliminated through diversification, it is usually assumed that the risk is not compensated by the capital market.

The main focus of interest has traditionally been on how well stocks in the same portfolio perform in relation to each other over a given period. But there is another question that is of particular interest to investors, and subsequently to banks as well: how does share A or portfolio A perform in the second period if it has already lost, say, 5% of its value in the first period? In order to measure this aspect, we have to look at how the **shortfall risk** develops in relation to the observation period. The shortfall risk defines how likely it is that a minimum yield (e.g. 2% p.a.) will not be achieved. The general principle is: the longer the observation period, the lower the shortfall risk. This can be attributed to the fact that an exceptionally good performance during one period may be cancelled out by a particularly bad performance in the next. It is interesting to note that both theory and practice tend to overlook this relationship between performance over consecutive periods.[8] Here, too, a distinction can be made between systematic and unsystematic risks. For more effective differentiation, these risks are referred to as **vertically systematic**. The performance of a stock market over a given period can, for example, be partly explained by the economic cycle. It is fair to assume that these effects can to some extent be mitigated through diversification, i.e. by selecting a sufficiently long observation period (e.g. ten years). It is therefore difficult to eliminate the risk posed by the economic cycle over a one-year time-frame, but much easier for longer periods such as ten years.

This can lead to a 'double' systematisation process, which is illustrated in Figure 20.2.

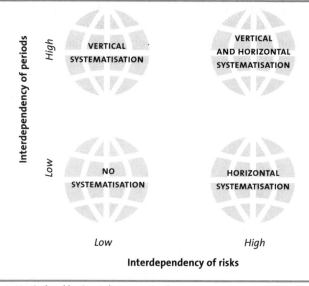

Figure 20.2 **Vertical and horizontal systematisation**

8 One reason for this could be that it is generally assumed that there are no interdependencies between the price performances of individual periods if considered over the longer term.

As far as environmental problems are concerned, all risks are both **vertically and horizontally systematic** if they impact on each individual period over a long time-frame, and also if their influence extends to many different sectors and regions. I would argue that this is certainly true for most global environmental problems.

In practice there are no purely systematic and unsystematic risks, or exclusively pre-decision and post-decision risks. A risk usually combines all these characteristics to varying degrees. As far as the use of risk management instruments is concerned, we are mainly interested in the extent to which a risk is systematic, and pre- or post-decision.

20.2.3 Development of a risk matrix

It makes sense to develop the differentiation process just described into a risk matrix, as shown in Figure 20.3, so as to facilitate the classification of risks on the basis of their characteristics.

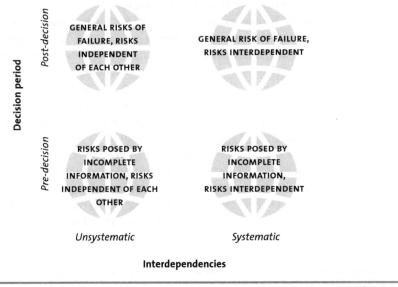

Figure 20.3 **Risk matrix**

20.3 Risk management instruments

Risk management is vital for the commercial success of banks and insurers, and they use a range of instruments for this purpose. Here we assume that the banks in question merely act as transformers of risk, i.e. they are unable to eliminate the risks as such. This would appear to be a realistic assumption on the whole, particularly as far as global environmental problems are concerned. Ultimately all the instruments available for risk management can be classified as one of three basic types:[9]

- Information

- Diversification

- Reserve accumulation

The role of **information instruments** is to reduce the uncertainty that exists prior to making a decision, by improving the quality of information available. This instrument is therefore suitable for dealing with pre-decision risks. Banks, for example, attempt to gain a competitive advantage over rivals through new and better information and through superior analysis of information. These activities are concentrated in the period before the decision is made, e.g. before granting a loan or purchasing stocks.[10] This is therefore a pre-decision instrument.

Diversification and reserve accumulation, on the other hand, are used to attenuate the consequences of the risks assumed, i.e. for risk mitigation.

The **diversification** instrument, as explained above, is based on the idea that the volatility of individual risks created by combining many risks in the same portfolio can be swapped for the virtual security of such a portfolio. Many investors are unable to put together their own portfolio, however, so they pay a premium to transfer their risk to another financial agent (bank, insurance company) that looks after diversification for them. One of the prerequisites for a risk to be eliminated through diversification is that the collective risks must all be unsystematic. A portfolio that contains only systematic risks is ultimately just as risky as the risks it is made up of.

In order to remove the unsystematic risk through diversification, there must be an adequate number of shares in a portfolio. The remaining horizontal systematic risk can in some circumstances be reduced by selecting a sufficiently long observation period. If this strategy is chosen, the investor takes a higher risk during each individual period in the expectation that the risks specific to each period will be balanced out over the entire observation period. The shortfall risk already mentioned declines as the observation period gets longer.

The instrument of **reserve accumulation** can in theory be used in all the situations just described. Reserves are the portion of assets set aside to cover possible losses. The reserves must be built up to a level that matches the risk they are supposed to cover. Opting for this instrument is a form of deliberate risk-taking. But if a large number of unsystematic risks are bundled together, diversification is achieved in any case, so there is no need for

---

9   For these instruments, see for example Mag 1980: 482, 491. One often hears of insurance on behalf of a third party, and self-insurance in this context. But the three instruments in question are ultimately used to insure risks. Our analysis therefore limits itself to the three instruments in question.

10   An information instrument can, of course, be used after a decision has been made, if there is an opportunity to 'think over' the decision. This is often the case when purchasing shares, for example. If an investor is faced with the decision whether to hold or sell a new security, this is of course a new decision. In this case, information instruments serve to reduce the pre-decision uncertainty.

reserves as an extra form of protection. They would be superfluous, and ultimately inefficient from an economic viewpoint. In such a situation an investor would not have any risk exposure at all—even though he or she had taken out several risky investments.

The instruments described can be positioned on our risk matrix as shown in Figure 20.4.

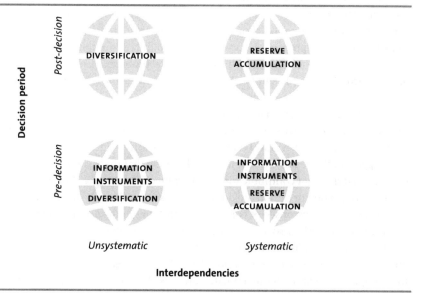

Figure 20.4 **Classification of risk management instruments**

20.4 Characteristics of environment-induced economic risks

20.4.1 Example: the greenhouse effect climate change

To find out how best to manage environment-induced economic risks, we first need to determine where to position the risks on our risk matrix. This task is made more difficult by the fact that one of the main features of pre-decision risks is that only a small amount of information is available about them. Economic risks caused by global environmental problems in particular show a high pre-decision element, since environmental and environment-related information is often not concerned with price (which makes it difficult to incorporate into financial decisions), is very fast-moving, and carries a big element of uncertainty.[11] Assessing the type, scale, probability and regional distribution of risks arising from environmental problems is often a difficult task. A number of divergent forecasts usually exist at the same time. Despite intensive research, for example, there are still no clear and undisputed forecasts about what losses we can expect when

11   Compare with features of environmental and environment-related information (Senn 1986: 71).

and where as a result of the greenhouse effect, nor is it possible to establish the probability of the various scenarios occurring.[12] This is of course attributable to the complexity of the underlying problems.

In conclusion it may be said that, as far as financial markets are concerned, the risks associated with the greenhouse effect or any other climatic environmental problem do not arise *in spite of* incomplete information but *because of* it. Anyone who argues that environment-induced economic risks are of no concern to financial markets because there is too little information about them fails to realise that they are actually important to financial markets precisely *because* we know too little about them.

The economic risk associated with environmental problems also has a **heavily systematic character**. This applies not only to the systematic relationship between individual risks, but also between individual periods.

Control measures taken in response to the greenhouse effect could, for example, result in environment-induced economic risks of a very systematic nature. One of the most likely control measures could be an energy tax or a levy on CO_2 emissions (see also Schaltegger and Figge 1997: 31-32). It is worth noting that there is not a single economy or sector that does not contribute directly or indirectly to the greenhouse effect through energy consumption or carbon dioxide (CO_2) emissions. The only difference is the extent to which the economy or sector concerned contributes to the greenhouse effect.

If the potential risks associated with environmental problems do become reality, this would undoubtedly affect both a wide section of the overall population and the national economy. This supports the assumption that risks have a heavily **systematic** character. If, for example, some of the more dramatic forecasts about the greenhouse effect turn out to be accurate, we have to realise that all coastal regions could be affected, storms will occur more frequently, and malaria will not only increase in the regions where it is already prevalent but will spread to new areas as well.

The financial risk associated with the greenhouse effect also has a systematic character as far as its time-frame is concerned. It is true that the existence of the greenhouse effect still has to be conclusively proven. But, if the greenhouse effect does turn out to be a genuine phenomenon, we can expect it to have consequences for many years to come. This is partly because it has a cumulative effect. It is widely assumed that its impact on our global climate depends on the CO_2 concentration in the atmosphere. Since the Industrial Revolution, the level of CO_2 concentration has already increased from 280 ppm (parts per million) to 360 ppm (see Rauber 1997). By the end of the next century the IPCC predicts that this concentration could climb to between 480 and 800 ppm. Even if we suddenly managed to halt all human-made carbon dioxide emissions, the CO_2 concentration in the atmosphere would only fall very slowly. There is a danger that the high levels of CO_2 will continue to have a detrimental effect on the environment for many years to come. In other words, we would see vertical systematisation. Extending the observation period would therefore only reduce the resulting risk slightly.

The more sweeping the consequences of an environmental problem, or the contribution to an environmental problem, the more systematic the risk. The depletion of the

12 An overview of unresolved research questions can be found in Volz *et al.* 1998.

ozone layer, acidification of the soil, excessive use of fertilisers and greater use of hormone-disrupting chemicals are other examples of environmental problems with a very systematic character.

To summarise, we can say there is strong evidence to show that **environment-induced economic risks** have a strong **systematic and pre-decision character**. This is especially true of economic risks caused by global environmental problems.

20.5 Instruments for managing environment-induced economic risks

If we accept the assumption made above that global environmental problems will (a) result in greater systematisation of environment-induced economic risks; and (b) increase the pre-decision proportion of risks, the positioning of the risk management instruments on our risk matrix shows that diversification leads to lower effectiveness. An effective instrument mix must therefore have a higher proportion of information instruments and reserve accumulation. It will become increasingly difficult to achieve a 'naïve' diversification of environment-induced risks, in other words to eliminate their threat by including a large number of them in a portfolio, or by extending the observation period.

20.5.1 Information instruments

These include any environmentally oriented measures that help provide a better understanding of the micro-economic or macro-economic consequences of global environmental problems. One example is climate research into the greenhouse effect. Most of these information instruments do, however, entail basic research, and their findings tend to be regarded as public goods. Public goods are unlikely to be financed by individuals seeking to forward their own interests. There is, therefore, a danger that insufficient information will become available. Without the knowledge provided by information instruments, however, investors have to rely on assumptions about the probability and scale of risks. This increases the risk associated with an investment even further and could lead to the imposition of higher risk premiums. These risk premiums would also have to be paid by companies that in reality—i.e. in a situation where the information base is superior—are less risky than assumed, as market players are unable to distinguish between good and bad risks because of inadequate information.[13] In other words, this would lead to a situation that would be detrimental to the economy, in which higher-risk companies would be cross-subsidised by lower-risk companies. This could stifle investors' willingness to take risks. The resulting cross-subsidy of high-risk options by lower-risk alternatives can prevent the optimum allocation of resources, which in turn usually has a detrimental effect on levels of prosperity.

13 A similar relationship has been described in the used car market by Akerlof (1970) and in environmental reporting by Schaltegger (1997).

20.5.2 *Reserve accumulation*

Obviously it is also important to have a sufficiently high level of reserves, i.e. enough to cover the maximum losses that can occur at any one time. If an investor takes on different types of systematic risk that have no systematic interrelationship, there is no need to set aside separate reserves for each type of risk: it is sufficient to set the reserves at a high enough level to cover the aggregate loss for all types of risk.

This multiple usage of reserves, a method also practised by insurance companies, for example, also has a number of important consequences in the event of a loss. If compensation paid on a loss is so high that it eats up a substantial part of the reserves, cover for other risks may have to be withdrawn. If, for example, the consequences of the greenhouse effect mean that reinsurers have to draw heavily on their reserves, a situation could arise in which other systematic risks, such as earthquakes, are no longer insurable in future.[14] But direct insurers also call on the resources of reinsurers to cover their conventional mass business.[15] The end result: reinsurers may be forced to scale down their business activity, while direct insurers may have to restrict the types of insurance offered.

The same situation applies to financial markets—and is obviously important as far as banks are concerned as well. After the Japanese stock market collapse in 1990, for example, there was repeated speculation that any further drop in the equity market could result in a situation where Japanese investors would be forced to pull out of investments outside Japan. In other words, the sharp decline in the Japanese stock market caused a steep fall in the level of reserves, which were no longer available for investment in other markets. If we translate this to the question of systematisation of environment-induced economic risks, this means that an investor whose reserves have been eroded due to the occurrence of a systematic environmental risk may have to pull out of investments in certain cases, even if these investments are not themselves affected by the environmental problem. This could trigger a chain reaction.

20.6 Conclusion

Global environmental problems can influence economic decisions. The debate both in expert circles and among the public at large has been biased towards possible loss of earnings and exacerbation of risk. However, an analysis using tools from decision-making and portfolio theory shows that the interdependency of risks is also of prime importance. There is the danger that global environmental problems could lead to greater inter-dependency between risks. This is referred to as systematisation of economic risks. This

---

14 Reinsurance is not usually necessary for unsystematic risks. One exception is insurance cover for nuclear power plants, for example. Such plants do not present a systematic risk, but one with high potential losses and a very low probability of occurrence.

15 For example through quota share reinsurance, where the direct insurer assumes a proportion of the risk agreed down in the treaty, or through excess of loss reinsurance, where the reinsurer covers any amount exceeding an agreed maximum loss

systematisation process should, however, not focus purely on the price performance of different stocks in relation to each other, but also on the performance of different shares of portfolios over consecutive periods. This 'double systematisation' of economic risks allows environment-induced economic risks to be clearly distinguished from traditional financial risks. Another factor to consider is that the consequences of environment-induced risks are extremely difficult to predict.

Greater systematisation of risks would, however, reduce the effectiveness of the instrument mix used up to now for risk management, since systematic risks, unlike unsystematic risks, can no longer be eliminated through diversification. In addition, it is not possible to refer to reliable statistical and empirical data when attempting to cover environment-induced economic risks.

In future an effective instrument mix will have to rely less on diversification and more on reserve accumulation and good information instruments. If risk management is to be effective in future, there must in any case be sufficient reserves available.

ESTIMATING THE FINANCIAL EFFECTS OF COMPANIES' ENVIRONMENTAL PERFORMANCE AND EXPOSURE[*]

Robert Repetto and Duncan Austin
World Resources Institute, USA

The financial performance of modern business is increasingly impacted by the costs and opportunities presented by environmental issues. Regulations, materials and energy prices, consumer demands, and the development of new markets may all be influenced by environmental concerns in ways that materially affect a company's earnings and balance sheet. Moreover, because the outcome of many environmental issues is uncertain, they present risks that companies need to manage. Yet firms and analysts find it difficult to translate the potential impacts and risks of environmental issues into the financial terms required for business planning and valuation. According to a recent survey, this difficulty is the main barrier keeping environmental issues apart from other business and financial concerns (UNEP 1999).

This chapter presents a new methodology that enables managers and analysts to evaluate impending environmental pressures in terms of their impact on the bottom line and on share price. The approach is conceptually similar to methods already used by managers and financial analysts to evaluate conventional business risks.

The methodology has many potential applications for financial analysts and business managers. It can be used to:

- Uncover hidden liabilities or risks in acquisitions and mergers

- Measure the true value of a project, facility or company

- Capture the value of investments that would reduce environmental exposures

[*] The material in this chapter is from 'Pure Profit: The Financial Implications of Environmental Performance' (Washington, DC: World Resources Institute, March 2000; available at www.wri.org).

▓ Measure the self-insurance value of environmental control programmes

▓ Benchmark a facility or a company against its competitors

To demonstrate and test the methodology, the World Resources Institute (WRI) has used it to evaluate the environmental risks facing leading US pulp and paper companies.[1]

21.1 The approach explained

The methodology, like financial analysis and asset markets, is forward-looking. It is transparent, consistent with the fundamentals of financial analysis, and applicable to an individual project, a firm, or to an entire industry. The steps in the methodology are: (a) identifying salient future environmental issues; (b) building scenarios around each; (c) assigning probabilities to scenarios; (d) assessing company exposures; (e) estimating financial impacts under each scenario; and (f) constructing overall measures of expected financial impact and risk. The methodology can be seen as iterative, since probabilities, exposures and likely financial impacts change over time. The underlying analysis is transparent and can readily be updated as new information emerges.

The following sections illustrate how this approach was applied in the US pulp and paper industry.

21.1.1 Building environmental scenarios for the US pulp and paper industry

In the pulp and paper industry, environmental developments will significantly affect future materials and energy costs, earnings, and balance sheets. This sector depends on forest harvests and recycled paper for its raw materials; it is one of the most energy-intensive of all industries; it emits a wide range of toxic and conventional pollutants to air, water and land; it is one of the largest contributors to the solid waste-stream; it is identified in the public mind with pollution and resource degradation; it is subject to an enormous range of environmental and natural resource regulation and litigation; and it must allocate significant fractions of investment and operating outlays to environmental control programmes. Scenarios can help identify these potential environmental value drivers, including new regulatory initiatives, new fiscal measures enacted for environmental purposes, potential future liabilities arising from past or current activities, and demand shifts arising from changing customer preferences or mandated product standards.

---

1   The companies included in this analysis are Boise Cascade, Bowater, Caraustar, Champion, Fort James, Georgia Pacific, International Paper, Mead, Potlatch, Smurfit Stone, Westvaco, Weyerhaeuser and Willamette. At the time of writing, figures for Weyerhaeuser do not reflect the recent take-over of Macmillan-Bloedel. Companies are not identified by name, nor are they ordered alphabetically in the figures that follow.

In constructing scenarios, the first step is to identify environmental and economic forces that are likely to have significant financial impacts on the pulp and paper industry. Significant environmental issues might emerge throughout the product life-cycle, from raw material availability to post-consumer waste. The industry association and its members from leading companies co-operated with the authors to identify and characterise potential future environmental pressures.[2] The US Environmental Protection Agency (EPA) and other government agencies, environmental advocacy groups and environmental scientists were also consulted, along with an extensive published literature.

The next step was to prioritise these issues according to their likely significance for future earnings and risks. Three key criteria were used:

1. **Magnitude of the potential impact on earnings stream**: potentially 'big ticket' items are obviously more critical to include in scenarios.

2. **Anticipated timing of an event or issue**. Other things equal, the further in the future the impact of an environmental issue is likely to be, the less its impact on shareholder value.

3. **Likelihood or probability of an event happening**. Though a nearly certain event might have significant financial implications, it may nonetheless be of lesser significance in a scenario-building exercise because those implications will probably already be reflected in financial valuations.

Table 21.1 provides a listing and brief description of the most significant environmental issues selected on the basis of these criteria. Scenarios were constructed for these issues by identifying plausible outcomes and their likelihoods, making use of expert knowledge in and about the industry. Outcomes were quantified in terms that can be translated into the elements of a financial analysis: impacts on prices, costs, revenues, expenditures, investment requirements, balance sheet liabilities and the like.[3]

21.1.2 Assessing firm-by-firm exposure to priority environmental issues

Even among the industry's large multi-plant firms, the scenarios would have substantially different financial implications. For some firms, should a particular scenario come to

2 We gratefully acknowledge the co-operation of the American Forest & Paper Association and member companies in engaging in a scenario-building session with us. They bear no responsibility for the material presented here, however.

3 One further issue that is potentially significant for the paper industry is that of climate change policies. Pulp and paper mills are energy-intensive and production costs are sensitive to energy price changes. Mills differ substantially in the degree to which they can meet their energy needs by burning their own organic wastes and in their external fuel sources, creating differences in exposure. Moreover, many paper companies own large timber tracts, on which significant additional amounts of carbon could be sequestered if incentives were provided. Unfortunately, publicly available data on individual companies' energy usage, energy self-sufficiency and fuel mixes was insufficient to carry out an adequate exposure assessment based on climate scenarios. The consequence of this omission for the subsequent analysis is to understate the environmental exposures and risks, positive and negative, that paper companies face.

Air quality regulations

Cluster rule air quality provisions ▶ MACT I, III for process emissions ▶ MACT II for combustion sources	Will require maximum available control technology for air toxics from pulping and bleaching lines, boilers, recovery furnaces, kilns, etc.
Long-range transport of smog precursors	Will require mills located in 22 eastern states to reduce nitrogen oxide emissions by 50%–75%
Ozone and PM2.5 standard	Will require substantial reductions in emissions of nitrogen and sulphur aerosols and fine particles

Water quality regulations

Compliance options under cluster rule	Provides longer compliance periods for mills that install technologies beyond compliance
Total maximum daily loads	May require effluent reductions beyond currently permitted levels to remediate impaired water bodies
Sediment remediation	Could require clean-up of polluted aquatic sediments causing water pollution downstream of mills
Endangered Species Act (ESA)	Could require effluent reductions to protect endangered aquatic species in specific locales

Environmental influences on fibre supply

Regulations on private lands	Stricter state and local forest regulations may limit harvests from private timberlands.
Actions under the ESA	A re-authorised ESA may limit harvests in specific regions, especially if extended to sub-species and vigorously enforced.

Table 21.1 **Significant impending environmental pressures on pulp and paper firms**

pass, the financial impact would be significant; for others, the impact would be insignificant or even opposite in direction. Companies have positioned themselves differently with respect to these environmental issues mainly through decisions taken in years past for broader business reasons. *Where* mills and forestlands are located, *what* products they turn out, and *what* technologies are embedded in the capital stock are historical factors that largely determine companies' exposure to impending environmental issues.

To assess exposures, firm-by-firm information was collected on the priority issues from publicly available sources, including annual reports, Securities and Exchange Commission (SEC) filings; news reports; pulp and paper industry directories; and EPA public data files on facility-by-facility environmental performance.[4] Geographical Information System (GIS) techniques were used to map the location of companies' mills and timberlands onto the regions of concern under impending environmental regulations, many of which have quite specific areas of applicability. Measures of environmental performance, such

---

4   For a full list of references, see WRI 2000.

as emissions rates and information on technologies in place, were also used. Aggregating mill data by company shed light on companies' potential overall liability.

21.1.3 Analysing scenario-specific financial impacts

To be useful to analysts, the financial implications of environmental issues must be conveyed in such a way that they can be incorporated into the valuation frameworks currently used to assess conventional business risks and opportunities. Fortunately, the disaggregated approach of mainstream valuation techniques facilitates the integration of environmental and conventional sources of value. Many of the prominent valuation techniques equate the value of a company to the sum of the discounted present values of all its cost and revenue streams. Hence, it is possible to estimate the incremental impact of specific cost and revenue changes on the company's value without estimating the value of the company as a whole.

For each company, the financial impacts of each scenario on revenues, production costs, investment spending and the value of owned assets were estimated individually for all years of the forecast period, then reduced to discounted present values using an estimate of the firm's weighted average cost of capital. These present values were then added to obtain a net financial impact for the scenario and the company in question. To relate these impacts to share values, these present value dollars were then expressed as a percentage of a company's current market valuation.

Several qualifications to the financial projections should be stated, beyond the fact that the information on which they are based becomes increasingly dated as time passes.[5] For most companies, self-reported data on the composition of production costs was scanty and so this composition had to be approximated from available public sources. Moreover, though the industry is highly cyclical, no attempt was made in the baseline projections to predict business cycle fluctuations over the period 1998–2010. Finally, though the industry is in the midst of a significant consolidation and restructuring phase, the baseline projections make no attempt to predict future mergers, acquisitions, divestitures, or consequences thereof.

21.2 Example: control of nitrogen oxide (NO$_x$) emissions

21.2.1 Scenarios

The EPA has promulgated regulations that will require 22 eastern states and the District of Columbia to reduce emissions of nitrogen oxides, a smog precursor partly responsible

---

5   The most recent information in this report dates from December 1998, when we began to write up the findings. Some data used in the analysis are considerably less recent. Consequently, readers are cautioned against relying on the results reported here as up-to-date forecasts of likely future developments. What we wish readers to take away is an understanding of the approach.

for the long-distance north-eastward drift of summertime air pollution in the eastern United States. The 22 states include many in the south-east and in the north where paper mills are located, but the impact of these regulations on the industry will be uneven: mills located in the north-west and far north-east are unaffected because they are too distant upwind or too far downwind. Final rules prescribe state-by-state overall limits on NO_x emissions. However, these rules have been challenged in court, leading downwind states to bring suit to force emissions reductions by midwestern power plants. The EPA has appealed the lower court ruling.

Though states are to develop their own implementation plans, EPA's budget is based on drastic cuts in emissions from electric utilities and large industrial furnaces, such as those used in the pulp and paper industry. According to the proposed rule, mills would have to lower summertime emissions by 50%–75%, mainly by retrofitting low-NO_x burners onto industrial boilers. However, EPA has also recommended that states jointly develop a cap-and-trade system similar to that being used in the sulphur emissions control programme. Emissions trading could lower total compliance costs substantially.

These regulations could evolve in ways that have significantly different cost implications for the pulp and paper industry. Cost implications were estimated from a region-wide study of implementation costs for the proposed regulations. Without a trading programme, typical pulp and paper mills would have to exercise virtually all of their NO_x control options in order to achieve the required emissions reductions, at relatively high marginal and average costs. With a trading programme, a typical mill could exercise only its relatively low-cost control options and make up the remaining reduction by purchasing NO_x permits on a region-wide market in which electric utilities and other energy-intensive industries would be important players. This suggests two broad scenarios.

- **Scenario A.** States fail to create a workable cap-and-trade programme and impose large percentage NO_x reduction requirements on pulp and paper mills in the designated states at average abatement costs of approximately $4,000 per ton.

- **Scenario B.** A region-wide cap-and-trade programme lowers compliance cost to about $2,300 per ton by allowing mills to substitute purchased permits for their most costly internal compliance options. Alternatively, a more moderate reduction rule is finally adopted.

In addition, sub-scenarios were constructed which assumed either that most of the aggregate industry costs of compliance would be passed forward to customers in the form of higher product prices, or that few of these costs would be passed forward. These sub-scenarios made use of estimates of demand price elasticities for paper products. The probability of offsetting price adjustments over the coming years depends in large part on the recovery of world demand for commodities and the absorption of excess capacity created by the Asian and Latin American economic crises. Should that happen, given the absence of excess or even normal profits in much of the US industry, price adjustments to industry-wide cost pressures become more likely.

In the first sub-scenario, demand price elasticity is estimated to be –0.8 and few environmental costs can be passed along. (These impacts are illustrated in the 'high-elasticity' scenarios in the figures that follow.) In the alternative sub-scenario, a lower demand price elasticity allows for a greater increase in the price of paper and, hence, a more favourable financial impact for companies.

Importantly, in both sub-scenarios, companies with relatively low compliance costs may experience *increases* in net operating incomes because revenues increase by larger percentages than do costs.[6] Thus, environmental issues create winners and losers among companies with different exposures.

21.2.2 Exposures

Many pulp and paper mills are located outside the 22-state region to which the proposed rule will apply and therefore will not be affected. At least one company (M) has all its facilities outside the compliance region, while another company (A) has all of its plants inside the region and will be significantly affected. The remaining companies have varying percentages of their productive capacity located within the compliance region. Consequently, this potentially costly regulation will have quite uneven impacts across companies in the industry.

Moreover, companies differ substantially in the volume of nitrogen oxide emissions they generate per ton of product turned out by mills inside the 22-state region. Company C's plants within the region apparently emit more than twice as much NO_x per ton of output than the industry average; those of D and I, half as much. This can be attributed to a variety of factors, including product mix, fuel source and mill technology. It implies that some companies may face a greater compliance burden than locational factors alone would suggest, and others may face less.

21.2.3 Financial impacts

Applying the cost estimates from the two main scenarios and the sub-scenarios to the exposure assessment leads to widely differing financial impacts among firms in all scenarios (see Figs. 21.1–21.4). In these scenarios, firms whose facilities are mostly or entirely located outside the 22-state region end up as net gainers from the rule, benefiting from industry-wide price increases but incurring minimal control costs.

21.3 Deriving overall financial results

This process was repeated for all of the high-priority environmental issues in Table 21.1, generating estimated scenario-specific financial impacts for all issues. One way in which

---

6 So, for example, a company facing relatively low compliance costs could have these costs more than offset by an increase in revenue from a rise in the market price of paper products, caused by an increase in the industry's overall cost of production. The degree to which this might occur depends on the extent to which the industry as a whole can pass on its higher production costs in the form of higher prices for its paper products.

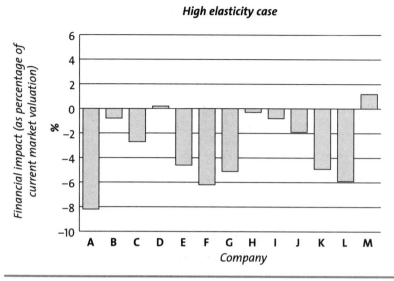

Figure 21.1 **NO$_x$ regulations (scenario A)**

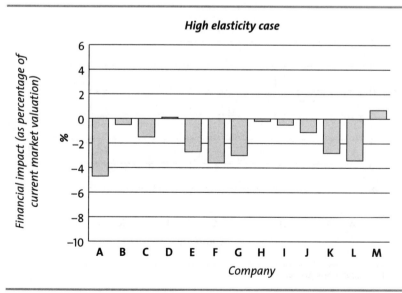

Figure 21.2 **NO$_x$ regulations (scenario B)**

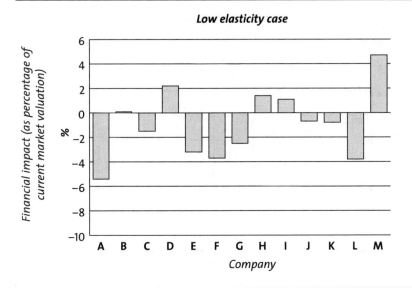

Figure 21.3 **NO$_x$ regulations (scenario A)**

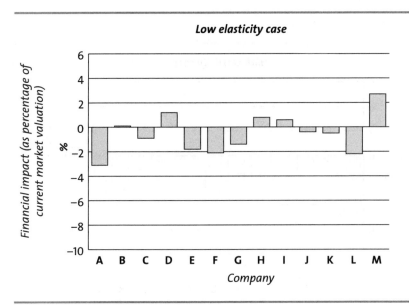

Figure 21.4 **NO$_x$ regulations (scenario B)**

the findings for individual issues could be combined is through macro-scenarios: one might ask, for example, 'What if a new Federal election led to heightened environmentalism across the board?' One would then choose among the individual issue scenarios in accordance with this overall perspective.

Another, perhaps more interesting, way is to combine the individual scenarios in an overall risk assessment. When industry and environmental experts participated in scenario development, they were asked to use their best judgements to assign probabilities to the occurrence of each scenario. We combined these judgemental probabilities into overall consensus probabilities.

Those consensus probabilities for individual scenarios were then used to construct a likelihood distribution across all scenarios. For example, using probabilities for individual scenarios, the joint probability of all the worst-case, most costly outcomes coming to pass was computed.[7] Then, the joint probability of all the best-case (from the companies' perspective), least costly outcomes coming to pass was computed and then all the intermediate cases were filled in.

When such probability distributions were constructed for each company from the information in the preceding sections of this report, substantial differences among companies became evident (see Figs. 21.5 and 21.6). Even though the underlying scenario and probability assumptions are the same for all companies, the probability distributions differ substantially with respect to the range of likely outcomes (variance) and with respect to the most likely outcome (mean). Distributions also vary in their degree of imbalance toward negative or positive outcomes (skewness). These differences are entirely due to differences among companies in their exposures to the underlying environmental issues.

Such differences are made even clearer when summary statistics for all the companies in the study are arrayed together, as in the summary chart below (Fig. 21.7). The most likely outcome for each company is represented by a dot, indicating the expected impact on its share value of impending environmental issues. A few companies can reasonably expect an insignificantly small positive or negative effect—less than 3% one way or the other. At the other extreme, three companies could, at this point expect a negative impact of greater than 10% of their total share value. The others face a most likely impact of between 4% and 8% of current share value.

The range of potential outcomes also varies greatly from one company to another. The variance of impacts, as a measure of financial risk arising from exposure to these environmental issues, is less than 1% of share value for three companies in the group. At the other extreme, it is greater than 9% of share value for two other companies. The former group is effectively hedged against environmental risk, in the sense that its future earnings will not be highly sensitive to the outcome of the issues it faces. The latter companies are greatly at risk: their earnings will depend heavily on the way these issues develop.

---

7   In this exercise, the probabilities associated with one issue were assumed to be independent of the probabilities associated with all other issues. Alternatively, it would be feasible to develop estimates of conditional probabilities for specific issues, contingent on the outcome of other issues.

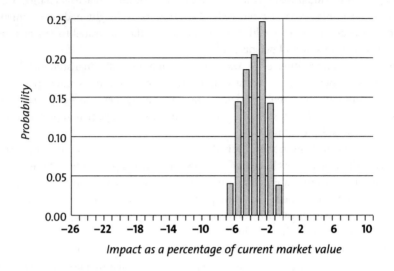

Figure 21.5 **Company C**

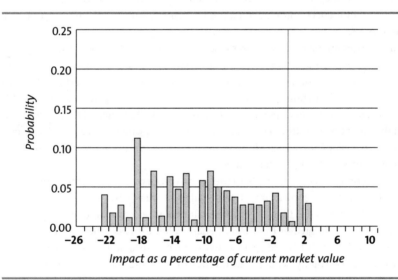

Figure 21.6 **Company K**

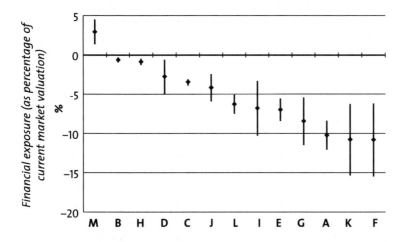

Figure 21.7 **Companies' aggregate financial exposure to pending environmental issues**

21.4 Are these exposures already incorporated into market valuations?

The question immediately arises whether these differences are already factored into the market valuations of individual companies. There is no way to answer that question definitively, since one cannot fully explain the differences among companies' market valuations. However, here are some potential clues to the answer.

First, obtaining the data on which analysis was built involved a great deal of digging in obscure, though public, data sources. In conversations with analysts, research firms providing environmental information to analysts, and with company representatives, we found that no comparable studies on these environmental issues had been carried out by others. Therefore, we cannot imagine how findings like these could previously have been conveyed to investors.

Second, the future environmental expenditures and contingencies reported by companies in their financial statements bear little relation to the magnitudes and exposures estimated in this report. In the US, despite relatively stringent securities laws and regulations, companies still differ in their reporting practices. Most do not report financial impacts that are still considered to be uncertain, as are all the scenarios underlying this analysis. Some companies only report on capital costs to be incurred to comply with environmental standards and regulations that have already been issued in final form and on remediation costs for which the company has already been implicated through EPA action. Even fewer companies report potential changes in operating costs or input prices that might arise from environmental pressures. A few companies discuss a potentially important impending environmental issue such as the Endangered Species Act in general terms without providing any quantitative estimates, or conclude that the issue is not expected to affect the company's operations significantly in the coming year but might do so in the future.

A typical statement from the financial report of one company in the study asserts that 'In the opinion of . . . management, environmental protection requirements are not likely to affect the company's competitive position since other domestic companies are subject to similar requirements.' In the light of the findings presented here, such statements are erroneous and potentially misleading to investors and financial analysts.

In view of this evidence, and from our discussions with Wall Street analysts, we are fairly confident that the current market valuations of companies in this sector do not incorporate these findings. The failure of analysts to have explored these issues themselves probably reflects a lack of familiarity with environmental issues in general; and a preconception that these issues will not have a significant impact on profits, and certainly not an impact that would be differential across firms. The high level of interest shown in our findings suggests that (at least some) Wall Street analysts see potential value in assessing environmental issues and in performing analyses similar to that described here.

21.5 Potential applications

Although environmental risks comprise only one consideration of many to be taken into account when investing in a company, financial analysts might use results from this approach as an additional factor in evaluating the potential returns and risks from an investment in a company's securities. Similarly, analysts involved in credit ratings might take into consideration the potential outcomes from such environmental exposures on a company's earnings, cash flow and balance sheets while forming an overall judgement of a company's financial risks. Investment bankers might incorporate this approach with greater specificity and detail in its due diligence investigations of a potential acquisition, merger or securities issue. Managers of screened portfolios might use this approach to determine which companies in a sector face the potentially most serious environmental problems. In all such applications, this approach can add value to the work of the banking industry when considering environmental issues that affect their clients.

Within industrial companies, environmental managers might use an approach such as this to quantify their environmental exposures and risks or to benchmark their companies (or facilities) against rivals. They might also use it to help identify which investments in environmental control would do most to reduce their outstanding environmental risks, allowing them to move beyond a compliance-based system toward a more forward-looking and strategic approach. Managers and chief financial officers might use a self-insurance model to estimate how much it would be worth annually to spend on control measures as a self-insurance quasi-premium in order to eliminate the likelihood of a loss due to environmental factors greater than a certain percentage of share value. For example, referring to Figure 21.5, suppose company C wished to eliminate all likelihood of negative environmentally related impacts greater than 5% of share value and could identify the control investments to do so, how much would it be reasonable to spend for that purpose? Taking the expected value of the impacts from this distribution and applying a conservative loading factor, it is easy to calculate that this company could reasonably spend $20 million per year over five years to eliminate this business risk.

In all these ways, the approach presented and illustrated in this study might become a useful tool with which to relate environmental exposure and performance to investor value and risk. It answers a question that many have asked but few, if any, have been able to answer satisfactorily. This approach is sufficiently broad to be applied to other sectors in which environmental factors can be value drivers. It is sufficiently general in that it can encompass not only the costs of meeting environmental standards but also the opportunities afforded by providing solutions to environmental problems.

21.6 Policy recommendations

Data availability limited the application of the methodology for this study. For example, lack of data on companies' energy sources and timber holdings precluded full evaluation of the impact of climate policy scenarios. Improving the flow of company-specific information on environmental issues would enable financial analysts and investors to evaluate environmental risks and opportunities more accurately. In the US, the EPA, the SEC and the companies themselves could all help in this regard.

Though theoretically in the public domain, much of EPA's data, especially on facility performance, is inconsistently formatted, difficult to retrieve and often incomplete and out of date. This study demonstrates how valuable such information could be if databases were accurate, timely, well maintained and readily accessible. The creation of the Sector Facility Index, which brings such information together in one publicly available data file, is a positive step. We recommend that EPA take further steps to provide accurate, timely and easily accessible information on company performance and facility exposure to environmental issues. Environmental agencies in other countries can also use such information strategically to create market incentives for better environmental performance.

Company reporting of environmental issues in annual reports and other filings fails to provide investors with sufficient information to make fully informed decisions. For example, more complete and consistent reporting of companies' timberland holdings, forestry practices and fibre sources would have permitted better analysis of potential impacts of land use regulations, the Endangered Species Act, and of carbon sequestration policies. Consistent industry-wide environmental reporting of the kind proposed by the Canadian Pulp & Paper Association under their 'EcoProfile' initiative would be potentially very useful to financial analysts. More broadly, the Global Reporting Initiative spearheaded by CERES (Coalition for Environmentally Responsible Economies) is aimed at improving and standardising companies' environmental reporting. We recommend that firms be more forthcoming on environmental exposure and performance, perhaps through the development of such a standardised reporting protocol.

Company reporting of environmental issues also falls far short of the full and adequate disclosure required for material issues, as set out in SEC rules and guidelines. Item 101 of SEC Regulation S-K requires specific disclosure of the material effects that compliance with federal, state and local environmental laws may have on the capital expenditures, earnings and competitive position of the company. Although there is room in the regulations for interpretation, implementation of these requirements leaves much to be desired. Of the companies reviewed here, there was inadequate reporting on pending environmental issues that this report suggests may be material. Consequently, we urge the SEC to devote more attention to the implementation of its current rules on disclosure. Securities regulatory bodies in other countries should also strengthen their rules on the reporting of material environmental issues.

THE ENVIRONMENT HANDBOOK
A Danish tool for including environmental aspects in credit evaluation

Dan Atkins
Deloitte & Touche Environmental Services, Australia

Charlotte Pedersen
Deloitte & Touche Environmental Services, Denmark

22.1 The reason for an environmental handbook for banks

Environmental issues need to be an integral part of credit assessment, in order to minimise the risk of loss through environmental disasters, etc., when granting credit facilities. However, it is not possible for banks to train their credit experts to be environmental experts as well. Small banks in particular therefore need standardised procedures and performance indicators that allow them to integrate environmental risk testing into their credit evaluation.

In 1997, Deloitte & Touche Environmental Services and the Danish Training Centre for Financial Institutions wrote a practical handbook to help credit experts integrate environmental aspects into credit assessment procedures. The *Environmental Handbook* (referred to in this chapter as the handbook) was developed as a result of a project financed by the Danish Environmental Protection Agency (DEPA) and the Danish Commerce and Companies Agency. The project also included training programmes to educate credit experts in the need to integrate these considerations into their evaluation procedures.

The handbook can be used to help the bank carry out an initial general investigation into a company in order to identify potential environmental risk. If any risks are found, the bank must perform further in-depth investigation by interviewing the client, demanding further documentation and consulting environmental experts.

22.2 **Structure of the handbook**

The handbook is a practical reference book for the credit expert. The emphasis is on questionnaires in the form of checklists, and one set of questionnaires is filled in for each customer. The purpose of the checklists is to gather information to form an environmental profile of the company, to be used in the credit assessment.

The handbook divides environmental issues into eight areas, each covering a vital aspect of business or important environmental issue:

1. Environmental management and organisation

2. Plant, machinery and approvals

3. Soil and groundwater

4. Market and customers

5. Products and product development

6. Raw materials and suppliers

7. Distribution and delivery systems

8. Other conditions

The relative importance of the eight areas may vary according to the type of business, and in some contexts there may be a close relationship between answers in two or more areas. The introduction to the various chapters describes the rationale behind each area.

The environmental assessment is made in steps, with the structure of the handbook matching the steps as shown in Figure 22.1.

Each of the eight areas listed above is divided into 2–6 subjects, and a number of questions are asked on each subject. The answers to each group of questions are assessed, and an overall mark awarded for each area. To facilitate subsequent assessment, questions should preferably be answered with 'yes' or 'no response'.

In each group of questions, questions 1 and 2 are the most important, and users of the handbook may choose to answer only these. If they do so, they will arrive at an environmental profile in a **standard version**. If an assessment based on the standard version reveals a need for further analysis, or if there is another reason to require a more thorough assessment, all questions on the checklist may be answered as a basis for the environmental profile, thereby providing an **extended version**. There are approximately five times more questions in the extended version.

Each checklist is preceded by guidance notes to simplify the process for the user.

The environmental profile that is drawn up according to the answers given by users is designed to be used as part of a general credit assessment in line with a SWOT (strengths–weaknesses–opportunities–threats) analysis, or something similar. In conjunction with the credit assessment, a meeting would normally be held between the person drawing up the profile and the company management, in the person of the managing director, financial director or technical director. This meeting should clarify most of the questions

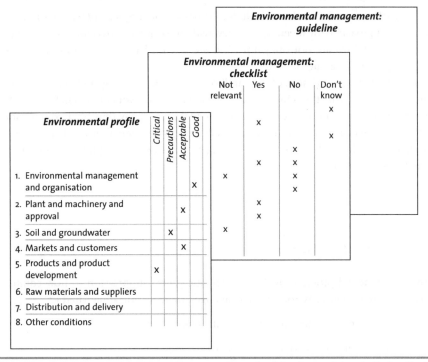

Figure 22.1 **Example of structure and steps in the handbook**

that arise in relation to the environmental profile. It may be necessary to contact the company again at a later stage to ask supplementary questions. It may also be advisable to submit the checklists to the relevant managers in advance to enable them to prepare answers to the questions prior to the meeting.

Once all the questions have been answered in the various areas (e.g. 3. Soil and ground-water), the relevant section of the environmental profile is filled in and inserted at the end of the questionnaire for each area. Finally, the responses can be transferred to the overall Environmental Profile assessment of the company, which creates the final picture.

There is no ready-made model for the actual assessment of a customer's environmental profile. The assessment is based on the answers given to the questions and the credit expert's own common sense. The environmental profile will allow the company to be assessed as **critical, precarious, acceptable** or **good**. If the company's environmental profile is considered acceptable or good, it means there are no environmental aspects that preclude the bank from granting credit facilities to the company. If, however, there are several conditions that are considered critical or precarious, more detailed analysis and possible changes to company procedures may be necessary before credit facilities can be granted. For example, approval-related matters may need to be sorted out with the environmental authorities.

For each area, the handbook includes proposals for supplementary questions, if a different approach to the meeting/interview with the company is required. These supplementary questions are not obligatory, but are intended to provide some ideas for a suitable direction of questioning.

The individual user (bank) of the handbook is also free to reorganise and/or rephrase the questions or write them into already-existing credit assessment material so that they match existing credit policies. The environmental profile may thus be used in connection with other assessment procedures. Once the environmental profile has been used several times, the credit expert may no longer need to read the guidance notes to the questions every time.

22.3 Uses of the handbook

An environmental profile provides a systematic general impression of how company management handles environmental challenges, thereby indicating whether:

- Environmental issues may increase the risk of loss.

- The security provided by the company is adequate.

- There is a need for further analysis.

The handbook is intended as a tool for credit assessment of small and medium-sized companies. This does not mean that it cannot be used for very large companies, but these will often be confronted with more complex environmental issues that require more extensive scrutiny and possibly assistance from consultants.

The handbook checklists and guidance notes do not provide a complete guide to assessing the reliability of management's answers. The guidance notes provide some help, but here, as in all other areas of credit assessment, individual account managers must base their assessment on their trust or confidence in the company, as well as on common sense and general experience.

Of course, an assessment may be supported by obtaining documentation (evidence) from the company. The handbook does not specify how much documentation is required, as this will vary from case to case. If a company has prepared green accounts or some other form of environmental statement, this will in many cases provide much useful information, such as the company's environmental policy, environmental impact or performance, approvals, etc. The handbook has some explanatory text about green accounts and environmental statements, and also provides some concrete examples.

In the case of an existing customer, the credit expert will often possess a substantial amount of information. For a new customer, however, more information will be required.

In addition, essential documentation may include copies of relevant approvals or notifications. In special cases, banks may have to ask the environmental authorities (such as county or municipality) for the company's case file in terms of the rules of disclosure of environmental information and/or the Danish Public Records Access Act.

The Danish handbook has been drawn up according to legislation and conditions in Denmark. If a company or a customer has activities abroad or is planning such activities, some areas of the environmental profile may have to be adapted to match these activities.

CORPORATE ENVIRONMENTAL ASSESSMENT BY A BANK LENDER
The reality

Andrea B. Coulson
University of Strathclyde, UK

Much has been written about emergent fears of lender liability for the environment during the 1990s. In particular, cases of potential lender liability under the strict liability regime of the US Comprehensive Environmental Response, Compensation and Liability Act (CERCLA) 1980, have been widely reported (Bryce 1992; Gray *et al.* 1993; Gleason 1994; Smith 1994; Vaughan 1994; Clark 1995). Today the US situation has been clarified, and the lender's position has been almost totally resolved by the CERCLA reform bills and the Asset, Conservation, Lender Liability and Deposit of Insurance Protection Act 1996 (Jewell and Waite 1997).

Research findings and bank commentaries have revealed that, in general, lenders appear to have become relatively confident that they have appropriate environmental due diligence procedures which will provide them with an adequate defence against direct and indirect environmental liability (Robbins and Bissett 1994; Coulson 1997; PricewaterhouseCoopers 1999). This confidence has recently led lenders to seek investment opportunities in 'sustainable companies' and develop 'green' products. One example of this trend is a series of green products offered to small and medium-sized enterprises under a European Investment Bank initiative (Coulson 1999).

Following claims of environmental responsibility the new fear among lenders appears to be one of risk to reputation through association with a polluter (Nicholson, Graham & Jones 1995; Coulson and Monks 1999). Communications issued by the banking community defend the banks on the basis that their environmental credit risk assessment procedures should not give the impression that lenders are acting, or indeed should act, as an environmental police force (BBA 1993, 1995; Hinterberger *et al.* 1998). This is supported by the view that they are not environmental experts but credit experts in the business of finance, not environmental protection.

In spite of increasing bank claims of environmental management, little research has been conducted to verify such claims other than surveys of signatories to the United Nations Environment Programme Statement by Financial Institutions on the Environment and Sustainable Development (UNEP 1992; EDR 1994; UNEP and Salomon Brothers Inc. 1995; Delphi and Ecologic 1997; Hill *et al.* 1997; PricewaterhouseCoopers 1999). To shed further light on this issue a detailed case study was conducted with the Lloyds TSB Group to examine the development and use of corporate environmental assessment techniques within its commercial and business lending function.

The Lloyds TSB Group (hereafter referred to as the Group) describes itself as a leading UK-based financial services group whose businesses provide a comprehensive range of banking and financial services in the UK and overseas. It is a customer-driven service business. Its credit function includes three main constituents: Corporate and Institutional Finance, Commercial Services, and Business Banking. The Group was created on 28 December 1995 by the merger of Lloyds Bank UK and TSB Group UK, and launched itself publicly as 'one Bank' in June 1999.

The study was conducted between October 1997 and October 1999 as part of the UK Economic and Social Research Council Global Environmental Change Programme. During the period of study Lloyds and TSB were in the process of operational merger and undergoing a period of pronounced institutional change. This provided an opportunity to witness new policy development and confirmation. Both banks had a history of environmental management that included lending operations.

The focus of the study was the Group's commercial and business banking credit services as opposed to 'big ticket' corporate and institutional finance. The case study was conducted in three stages, taking a top-down approach. The first stage of research involved an examination of the Group's public environmental commitment and internal environmental credit policies and procedural guidance. This provided the basis for a questionnaire survey of lending officers' views on environmental policy, procedural development and environmental risk assessment in stage two. The final stage of analysis encompassed a detailed examination of two hypothetical lending cases with officers drawn from branches based in the north-east of England, one of the Group's six designated UK regions.

Findings from each stage of the study will be reviewed in turn to build up a picture of corporate environmental assessment by Lloyds TSB lenders and the rationales used for assessment. The story begins with an outline of the evolution of Lloyds TSB's environmental commitment as publicly reported by the Group. This is followed by an account of lending reality and the contribution of internal policy development to corporate environmental assessment. The chapter ends with an overview of corporate environmental assessment in Lloyds TSB.

Research consideration of a Group-wide commitment to the environment and sustainable development is limited to its potential influence on environmental credit risk perceptions and management rationality. However, the potential influence of a wider commitment on employees' behaviour and environmental credit risk perception should not be ignored.

23.1 Lloyds TSB: environmental commitments

23.1.1 Public environmental policy

The TSB Group first formulated an internal environmental policy in 1990 covering all its products and procedures. In 1995 a specific clause was added on credit assessment. Lloyds developed a public environmental policy in 1992, building on an informal energy management policy established in the 1970s. Part of the policy was to 'include environmental considerations in lending, investment and other business decisions' (Lloyds Bank 1994).

When Lloyds and TSB underwent an operational merger, the first task was to integrate these two 'policies' and provide a clear public statement of commitment as a message to the Group's employees and other stakeholders. The task was the responsibility of a new team, drawn from former Lloyds and TSB employees and named Group Environment Risk (GER). Richard Cooper, formerly Head of Environmental Credit Risk with TSB, was chosen to head the team. GER was given day-to-day responsibility for environmental policy-making and operational management within the Group, including environmental credit risk assessment. Ultimate responsibility for environmental policy rests with the director of Group Risk Management who reports directly to the Group Chief Executive.

Richard Cooper was the key research contact and facilitated the study. As noted previously, the first stage of research involved an examination of the Group's public environmental commitment and internal environmental credit policies and procedural guidance. This was achieved through documentary review; a series of interviews/focus group meetings with GER members to examine their roles and rationale for the policy positions provided; and observations at environmental training workshops.

The first subject of analysis was the Group Environmental Policy. The policy was launched in 1997 following a period of lender consultation by GER. The policy recognises the Group's environmental commitment in response to its potential environmental impact. Lending activity is recognised as a key area where attention should be focused. As noted in Box 23.1, the policy sets out a programme of action accordingly.

23.1.2 Endorsing sustainable development

As a signatory to the United Nations Environment Programme (UNEP) Statement by Financial Institutions on the Environment and Sustainable Development, Lloyds TSB Group has made a specific commitment to sustainable development. Before 1997 Lloyds Bank UK held signatory status, and this status was transferred to the new Group on formation. As a sign of renewed commitment Richard Cooper publicly endorsed the statement's principles on behalf of Lloyds TSB Group in September 1999.

Cooper has taken an active part in promoting the environmental and sustainable development agendas, both within and on behalf of the banking community. He is a steering committee member of the UNEP Financial Institutions Initiative and chair of the British Bankers' Association, Environmental Issues Advisory Panel. The Lloyds TSB Group has also endorsed the ICC Business Charter for Sustainable Development.

OUR POTENTIAL IMPACT ON THE ENVIRONMENT STEMS FROM OFFICE-BASED operations and, to a large extent, this dictates where the bank can make progress in improving its environmental performance.

Key areas where we can focus attention are property management, purchasing and contracts and lending activities.

We will:

- Minimise the amount of waste we produce by raising staff awareness and encouraging the recycling of office waste, such as paper and plastics.

- Cut the amount of energy we consume by continuing to use energy-saving measures and by following recognised guidelines and codes of practice in our property management.

- Incorporate specific environmental requirements into contracts with principal suppliers.

- Wherever practicable, specify products from sustainable sources, products made from recycled materials or designed to be easy to re-use or recycle.

- *Continue to provide detailed guidelines to lending officials that will help them identify environmental risks in the UK and abroad.*

- Comply with all relevant environmental, health and safety regulations and legislation.

- Report publicly on our environmental management.

These commitments are backed by a programme of continuous assessment, checking our achievements against targets and seeking opportunities to raise awareness of environmental policy amongst our employees.

Responsibility for our environmental policy rests with our director of Group Risk Management who reports directly to the Group Chief Executive.

The policy will be reviewed on a regular basis and revised as appropriate.

Box 23.1 **Lloyds TSB Group Environmental Policy**

23.1.3 *Reporting on commitments*

The Lloyds TSB Group's first environmental report was issued in 1997. The reporting approach adopted was a practical one outlining key environmental management activities and corresponding objectives for 1998. In recent years an increasing number of European banks have published environmental reports, some of which are rather glossy and high-profile (Hill *et al.* 1997; PricewaterhouseCoopers 1999). At a time when risk to reputation has become a key issue for banks, Lloyds TSB, among others, has adopted a more conservative stance (Coulson and Monks 1999). The Lloyds TSB report, extracts from which are shown in Box 23.2, forms part of the Group's community brochure available on request to interested parties and displayed on their website.

The reporting has become an annual exercise in accountability. In 1998, the Group's second environmental report reviewed environmental performance against commitments and reported new objectives for 1999 (see Box 23.2). Inherent within the report is a reflection on Lloyds TSB's method of policy deployment including internal policy and procedural guidance. The Group's environmental reports have been independently verified by RPS Group plc. Their accuracy was further attested to by the case findings.

▇ Objective for 1998: *to complete the training of business lending officers and similar training and awareness-raising exercises for other Group lending companies.* Reported achievement 1998: over 120 environmental workshops were attended by 1,300 lending officers and a distance-learning workbook and video were produced for distribution to those not able to attend the workshop.

▇ Objective for 1998: *to continue to develop the* Environmental Risk Handbook *launched in 1997 to help our lending officers identify environmental risks and work with our customers to promote environmental good practice.* Reported achievement 1998: sectoral business issues in particular were addressed in more detail and an internal help-line established in 1997 provided advice on over 1,800 individual lending cases during 1998.

▇ Objective for 1999: *to promote awareness of environmental risks and environmental manage-ment among our small and medium-sized business customers.* This objective is still current and remains to be reported on. However, on the issue of customer dialogue, it is noted that as a part of a British Bankers' Association Initiative, Lloyds TSB have issued leaflets to their commercial and business customers explaining their environmental lending position and the value of environmental management.

Box 23.2 **Extracts from Lloyds TSB Group Environment Reports 1997 and 1998**

23.2 The lending reality

23.2.1 Internal policy and procedural guidance

The Lloyds TSB public policy and reported commitments form only one representation of policy and environmental management activities within the Group. Environmental credit risk assessment forms an integral part of the Group's internal credit risk policy and former procedural guidelines for Lloyds and TSB have been brought together to provide a procedural framework for environmental assessment.

The framework was introduced in 1997 following an initial period of consultation between GER and a sample of lending officers. Consultation with lending officers involved reviewing existing environmental credit risk assessment, or lack thereof, with lending officers of varying grades drawn from across the former Lloyds and TSB UK network and working on practical improvements. External environmental experts were drawn on for independent advice on current best practice.

The primary framework document is the *Environmental Risk Handbook*, the launch of which was documented in the 1997 environmental report. The handbook provides a step-by-step desktop guide to assessment. Richard Cooper notes that 'environmental risk assessment is an alien process for most lending officers. From experience, if it is too complicated or cumbersome, it will not be done. The process we introduced in Lloyds TSB is relatively simple and does not take too much time.' Procedural options and reference material provide flexibility so that the unique nature of lending proposals can be judged accordingly. Guidelines mirror fears displayed by the wider banking commu-nity that environmental credit risk is a function of direct and indirect risk of lender liability for the environment and should be managed accordingly (Barrett 1994).

As reported in 1998, a comprehensive training programme supported the launch of the handbook, with at least one person from every lending office receiving training. The research study involved reviewing the training materials and timetable, conducting interviews with trainers, and observation at a number of workshops across the UK. Training observations provided evidence that lending officers had received copies of the handbook and had begun to apply the 'new assessment' framework to lending cases. GER trainers clarified policy applications and procedural guidelines, and in turn received assurance that the framework offered a feasible proposal for integration in the existing lending process. Numerous accounts of environmental credit issues within the bank's lending portfolios were discussed. Examples noted by lending officers, and framework details, have been taken into account in the production of the final section of this chapter.

Training was later expanded to include the production of a distance learning workbook and a training video describing the risk assessment process and showing a practical case study. These were distributed to every branch, allowing all lenders to complete a branch-based training programme. Distribution and use of the workbook and video was verified during the course of the research study.

The GER team is viewed by the lenders as providing both lending *and* environmental expertise. Their role includes specialist consultation with the Group's established panel of environmental consultants. External environmental consultants play a key role in informing policy-makers and lenders about potential environmental risks. However, they are not viewed as credit experts and their advice is carefully considered by in-house experts to ensure translation into credit issues.

GER provides a help-line facility that offers close links with various external advisors should additional support be required. Internal Bank monitoring procedures show that in 1998, help-line specialists advised on more than 1,800 cases as well as answering hundreds of more general environmental queries. In addition, advice was provided on legal and technical updates through a regular newsletter.

Richard Cooper stresses that 'we do not expect our lenders to be environmental experts, but we do need them to understand how to operate the environmental risk assessment process'. The GER approach is therefore one of enabling lending officers to respond effectively to environmental risk and, ultimately, make sound credit decisions.

23.2.2 *Expertise in lending contingencies*

Putting Group and functional environmental policy into operation requires judgemental policy application within each lending situation. This can result in a narrower or wider interpretation of environmental credit risks, depending on the perceived risk inherent within each situation.

As found in many clearing banks, lending officers are given discretionary powers to make lending decisions based on Bank policy. Beyond discretionary limits, cases are referred for approval up the lending hierarchy (A.J. Berry *et al.* 1993; R.H. Berry *et al.* 1993). Referral thus provides one means of verifying policy applications. Another method is Group-wide internal audit. However, according to Vivienne Monks, a senior advisor in

GER, 'the assessment of environmental risk is a systematic approach, which allows suffi-cient flexibility for lenders to respond to the individual issues facing them at any one time'. An examination of policy implementation is not therefore purely an issue of establishing policy awareness, control verification and testing.

Stage two of the research was conducted during summer 1998 and involved a postal questionnaire survey of environmental risk assessment among Lloyds TSB lending officers. The objective of the survey was to gain an initial impression of the level of envi-ronmental consideration taking place within the lending process and of lending officers' views on the development of policy and procedural guidance regarding environmental risk assessment. To facilitate this, the questionnaire was designed after consultation with GER and a review of internal and external policy and procedural documentation. The questionnaire was piloted with lenders from two offices representing both commercial and business banking.

Questionnaires were issued to 2,000 lending officers across the Group. Circulation included all Group commercial banking offices in the UK and a sample of business banking offices. Care was taken to recognise the full extent of the newly formed Group.

Some 505 completed questionnaires were received. A satisfactory response rate of over 25% was achieved. Headline findings from the survey have been divided into three categories: environmental issues; environmental policy and procedural guidance; and environmental risk assessment. These are noted in Boxes 23.3–23.5.

■ 97% of respondents believe that all companies have a responsibility to consider environ-mental issues in their normal business activities.

■ 94% of respondents believe environmental risk assessments should form an integral part of the lending process.

Box 23.3 **Environmental issues**

■ 97% of respondents are aware of the Lloyds TSB Group environmental policy statement.

■ 98% of respondents are aware that the Bank has a Group *Environmental Risk Handbook*.

■ 89% of respondents had referred to the Group *Environmental Risk Handbook*.

Box 23.4 **Environmental policy and procedural guidance**

■ 87% of respondents conduct environmental risk assessment to support their lending decisions.

■ 81% of respondents believe the incorporation of environmental risk assessments within lending decisions is a generally accepted practice within the Bank.

Box 23.5 **Environmental risk assessment**

Survey findings showed that the majority of lending officers who responded do recognise the importance of environmental issues and are aware that the Group has an environmental policy statement and procedural guidance on environmental credit risk assessment. For 89% of respondents this awareness leads them to refer to guidance materials; almost as many (87%) conduct environmental risk assessments to support their lending decisions. Many respondents commented that environmental considerations should be an integral part of the lending process.

Lending officers responding to the survey appear to be including environmental considerations as an integral part of their lending decisions. Priority is given to new facilities, and in particular security considerations relating to those facilities. However, to put this into perspective, some lenders noted that environmental considerations were only one factor among many on business performance. Perceptions of environmental risk and the level of assessment subsequently conducted were found to vary considerably as a consequence of the nature of individual lending portfolios and risk exposure as a function of borrower size, industry and location. A number of lending officers noted that environmental risk assessment is conducted as a result of perceived environmental risk attached to individual lending circumstances as opposed to policy requirements. This is a point that was subject to further review in the final stage of the study.

A response rate of just over 25%, given the scope of the survey, provides some feeling of comfort that the results are representative of the lending population. Further assurance and clarification is provided when survey findings are considered alongside those obtained through observation of help-line procedures and views expressed at training workshops, pilot survey findings, and finally a review of hypothetical lending cases.

As noted above, the final stage of analysis involved a detailed examination of two hypothetical lending cases with officers based in the north-east of England. Case examinations were based on two lending cases that had taken place during the period prior to the survey. One involved finance to support a housing development on a potentially contaminated site and the other involved expansion of a metal plating works. In both cases lending officers had raised environmental concerns with the customer. Finance was provided when issues were satisfactorily resolved to the benefit of both parties. Full client file information, including financial statements, site profiles, valuation reports and environmental consultants reports, were provided in an anonymous form. (It should, however, be noted that to protect client confidentiality no direct observation of borrower/lender relations was possible.) Case reviews in particular required a practical illustration of the environmental risk assessment process, including an analysis of policy and procedural guidance.

The findings of the questionnaire survey provided confidence that case review as a method of investigation was feasible and would serve its purpose. The case reviews in turn helped to elaborate on survey findings and broaden, as well as deepen, the investigation. Of particular significance is the lender's understanding of 'policy' and its modelling, which the case reviews were able to provide.

23.2.3   Policy modelling

Many respondents to the survey questionnaire described an apparent deviation from specific environmental lending policy and procedural guidelines in the form of a partial or informal 'mental' assessment of environmental credit risk. Reliance on so-called mental models of assessment by experienced lenders has been revealed by a number of studies on general lending procedures. In some studies lenders have claimed that guidance tools are used only by new, inexperienced, lending officers (A.J. Berry *et al.* 1993; R.H. Berry *et al.* 1993).

On reviewing cases, lending officers identified and assessed by and large the same key environmental risks. Awareness of environmental risks and subsequent assessment procedures was referenced to personal lending experience of similar cases or a colleague's case rhetoric. Policy and procedural guidance documents were viewed as highlighting the environment as an issue for lenders and providing a skeletal framework for assessment which allowed lending officers scope to interpret results according to their lending experience. Policy deviations described earlier were explained according to the practice of flexing policy, as intended by GER, to evaluate unique case characteristics.

Lending officers with what could be classed as a high-risk portfolio, described in the following section, conducted environmental risk assessment as a matter of course. Such habitual assessment resulted in lenders drawing on 'mental' models of assessment created by adapting policy and procedural guidance to suit their portfolios, and then internalising the resultant procedures. Thus, mental assessment does not mean that policy was not being followed. Lending officers do not need to consult the environmental workbook for each lending case if they are familiar with procedures. Similarly, experienced officers do not need to consult their credit training manuals on every case. Lending officers with a low-risk portfolio, while familiar with the *Environmental Risk Handbook*, made direct reference to its content to guide their assessment process. Ultimately officers lending in each risk category shared a common framework of environmental risk assessment.

Just as new lending officers learn new procedures by following the guidelines, the introduction of environmental considerations in credit assessment has resulted in practical changes that require new procedures to be learned and an insight into environmental management to be gained. This is not to suggest that environmental credit risk assessment has been introduced in a top-down fashion. As noted previously by lending officers, environmental credit risk assessment is the result of risk perception and associated management rationality drawn from individual lending situations.

It has already been noted that guidance has evolved through consultation between GER policy-makers and a range of lending officers drawing on case experience. Policy was found to be further modelled as lending officers draw on their colleagues' experience during formal and informal training and case referral. Extensive reference to the GER help-line ensures that best practice proliferates throughout the lending hierarchy and its support services.

Many officers justified their method of environmental credit risk assessment by reference to 'the way we do things around here' and the company 'culture' as opposed to simply following laid-down Group policy. Procedural documentation may be seen as a way of coding procedures. However, acceptance of the framework is not free from conflict. As noted previously by Richard Cooper, 'if it is too complicated or cumbersome, it will not be done'. Within the Lloyds TSB lending hierarchy, new routines have been encouraged by those with senior lending authority, providing assurance that environmental risk assessment meets the practicalities of cost and timeliness.

23.2.4 *Environmental credit risk assessment*

The key features of environmental credit risk assessment described by lending officers during the hypothetical case reviews provided the basis for procedures detailed in this section. As stated above, the cases concerned finance to support a housing development on a potentially contaminated site and finance to support the expansion of a metal plating works. Full client file information, including financial statements, site profiles, valuation reports and environmental consultants reports, were provided by the bank in an anonymous form in order to preserve client confidentiality, as noted above.

The Lloyds TSB framework of environmental credit risk assessment revolves around three elements: **Land**, **Processes** and **Management**. Land use, past and present is examined, to protect the Bank from direct liability. Processes operated by the customer, and the management of those processes, are examined to protect the Bank from indirect and reputation risks.

Initial environmental risk perceptions are linked directly to the Standard Industrial Classification (SIC) codes and the sensitivity of the location in which the business operates: for example, whether the business is located next to a river or not. SIC codes are recorded for every business customer and information on location sensitivity is held on a database and recorded by postcode. By plotting SIC code and postcode on a simple matrix, the lender quickly makes an initial desktop assessment of the level of environmental risk associated with a particular business proposition. This simple assessment is followed up by a more informed series of questions which are incorporated into interviews with borrowers and, where feasible, site visits.

In considering land, the key question is whether the site is contaminated or not. If potential contamination exists the question becomes one of whether the potential contamination is likely to cause harm, taking into consideration the proposition at hand, exposure to local watercourses and the neighbouring property. Consideration of land quality also incorporates a consideration of the customer's operations in terms of potential pollutants. Lending officers seek to acquaint themselves with a customer's operations from input through to outputs and their disposal. Operations are examined in terms of current and foreseeable legislative requirements that the customer has to manage and respond to. Against this position the lender considers how well the customer manages the issues identified.

Lenders typically familiarise themselves with the business and its management through perceptions drawn during interviews, and, where possible, site visits. Client file information available for the hypothetical case reviews included site profiles, used to answer questions on land, and a brief history of the business and its most recent financial statements, used to assess operations and management. Lending officers found it difficult to follow other guidance notes on such judgemental issues. In a normal lending situation it is likely that the borrower would be an existing customer, with whom the lender was familiar, and have a track record. The cases under consideration were posed as 'new lends'.

Both cases under consideration were found to pose *potential* environmental credit risks. The proposed housing development was sited at a relatively sensitive location near a local watercourse. The risk potential attached to the proposal was seen to increase, as high-quality land is required for the siting and construction of domestic housing. A later discovery of pollution at the site could pose a risk to the reputation of the associated lender. On the other hand, the metal plating works occupied a relatively low-sensitivity location but the handling of hazardous chemicals in its cleaning and coating process posed a high risk.

Despite initial risk perceptions, lenders recognised that if the businesses were well managed *potential* risk should not be realised. Management should include consideration of contamination from past site use, which should already have been reviewed and any problems rectified by the potential borrower. After site profiles had been analysed, lenders requested that waste and water disposal licensing be validated and certification checks as appropriate. Valuation reports were provided on file and produced on request for review. The profile of the metal plating company illustrated excellent environmental housekeeping.

In the case of the housing development, the customers had commissioned a phase one environmental site survey prior to bank contact. The resulting survey report was subject to review to establish if a reputable firm had conducted appropriate procedures. A number of lending officers called on the specialist help of GER advisors at this point, to establish consultant credentials and specialist assessment procedures.

In summary, lending officers equated good environmental management with good all-round management and vice versa; they were also quick to note that environmental issues could have both a positive and a negative impact on financial performance. In both hypothetical cases posed lending officers agreed to provide finance, after close scrutiny of the borrower.

It is noted that the industrial heritage of the north-east of England ultimately influenced the lenders' environmental credit risk perceptions. However, it is felt that when considered within the wider context of the Lloyds TSB Group research study, the level of environmental awareness and lending approach discovered in the north-east is likely to be representative of the wider population of Bank lending officers. This said, the research study clearly influenced lending officers' environmental risk perception. Lenders were keen to know the 'real case outcomes' and reflected on their findings with similar examples drawn from live customer files. When lending teams chose to review the research cases together, lending officers operating low-risk portfolios as standard were enlightened by their colleagues' case experiences.

23.3 Conclusion

Case findings show that corporate environmental risk assessment is becoming a day-to-day reality for Lloyds TSB lending officers and their borrowers. It is stressed that lending officers should not be viewed as environmental experts but were found to be increasingly aware of best, and worst, corporate environmental practices. Officers guard against the risks of lender liability for the environment while pursuing lending opportunities with companies whose management seeks financial and environmental benefits through sustainable activities.

Given environmental uncertainties, what should be of interest to bank policy-makers is less the level of individual environmental assessment and more the method of consensus formation by which policy and procedures become routine. The Lloyds TSB example shows that sharing lending experiences and developing lending frameworks based on industry, customer and regional expertise can contribute significantly to improving levels of corporate environmental risk assessment.

Lending officers' perceptions of environmental risk can potentially influence the level of financial support available for economic development and environmental management. For Lloyds TSB borrowers this is becoming a reality. Companies seeking finance from the Bank can expect to be questioned on their environmental policy and management practices as an integral part of their lending evaluation. Such a stance poses no threat to borrowers who are aware of their environmental responsibilities and act accordingly.

Part 5
THE ROLE OF GOVERNMENT, NGOs AND MULTILATERAL BANKS

SUSTAINABLE BANKING EVOLVES IN AN INSTITUTIONAL CONTEXT WHERE DIFFERENT actors have their own roles. As well as the banks themselves, actors such as industrial companies, insurers, accountants and investments funds and raters have their own roles to play and stakes in the products and services banks offer. Also, between different countries there are large differences in traditions and legal frameworks that are strongly influenced by actors such as non-governmental organisations (NGOs) and governments and these can, to some extent, control banks' progress toward sustainability. Part 1 has focused on commercial banks, but multilateral banks can also shape the setting in which sustainable banking develops, as can governments and NGOs. In this section, authors from various backgrounds provide insight into the roles of governments, NGOs and multilateral banks.

The chapter by Andrei Barannik and Robert Goodland (Chapter 24) is the first attempt at an objective review of the evolution from 1970 until the present of the environmental and social policies and procedures of the World Bank, particularly those for environmental assessment (EA). These policies have evolved into guidelines that are used by large commercial banks in their project finance activities in developing countries. The policies have contributed to the development of risk assessment instruments within these large international commercial banks.

In their chapter (Chapter 25), Kate Kearins and Greg O'Malley discuss the role of (multilateral) financial institutions in sustainable development, illustrated by the Three Gorges Hydroelectric Power Scheme in China. It is explained why the Export–Import Bank of America refused export guarantees for this scheme. This has often been referred to as a landmark case.

Zsolt Pásztor and Dénes Bulkai focus in their chapter on a revolving Environmental Credit Scheme (ECS) to co-finance environmentally beneficial projects within the Republic of Hungary (Chapter 26). This scheme is created by a agreement between the Hungarian Ministry for Environment and Regional Policy, the European Bank for Reconstruction and Development (EBRD) and the European Commission. Within the ECS, environmental issues are critically reviewed. This scheme has now become well known and popular among Hungarian companies and has proved to be a successful tool with respect to incorporating environmental appraisal as part of credit appraisal, making firms familiar with the procedures of banks and raising the environmental performance of firms.

Marc Leistner (Chapter 27) discusses the role of the European Investment Fund. This EU scheme has been launched in order to facilitate environmentally friendly investments by small and medium-sized enterprises (SMEs) through favourable bank loans. The scope, size, process and procedures are the subject of this chapter.

Sabine Döbeli of the Zürcher Kantonalbank describes how an environmental investment fund was launched in co-operation with WWF Switzerland (Chapter 28). It is shown how special communication tools were implemented, partly to reduce WWF's risk of being criticised for labelling a fund. It is shown how additional communication tools permit a constant dialogue with different stakeholders and improve the quality of the fund.

The chapter by Mike Kelly and Ari Huhtala (Chapter 29) describes the activities of the United Nations Environment Programme (UNEP) regarding the financial services sector. Its initiative and its famous 'Statement by Financial Institutions on the Environment and Sustainable Development', now signed by some 170 banks, is discussed, as well as a case study of a UNEP programme to stimulate cleaner production (CP) in all sectors of the economy of developing nations and economies in transition (Guatemala, Nicaragua, Tanzania, Vietnam and Zimbabwe) by developing instruments and project initiatives to remove barriers towards CP within the financial services sector.

The chapter by Norbert Wohlgemuth (Chapter 30) presents a Global Environment Facility-funded project aimed at influencing investment decisions in favour of clean energy technologies (CETs) by providing advisory services to financial institutions. Loan officers in financial institutions have little practical experience in evaluating CETs. Often they do not always understand the full economic and environmental advantages of investments into CETs and view them as being too risky. The chapter discusses some cases to clarify the working of this CET project. The expected result of the project is that perception barriers, once removed, are unlikely to return and so the project will have contributed to a permanent change within the participating lending institutions towards sustainable banking.

Glenn Stuart Hodes (Chapter 31) considers the risks to the global environment and social equity posed by the conventional energy path. It is argued that building renewable energy markets and enterprises is critical, yet many impediments to appropriate and adequate financing in developing countries exist. The chapter describes these impediments and focuses on the role of multilateral banks, as well as the unique comparative advantage and limitations of financial intermediaries.

The chapter by Stephen Viederman (Chapter 32) discusses the way the financial sector is behaving towards sustainability at the present time and asks critical questions about whether the changes taking place are fundamental or that attitude and behaviour within the financial sector are still miles apart. For example: What is and can be the commitment of corporations and banking and financial institutions to satisfying needs rather than to creating greater wants, especially in a world of finite resources, inequitably distributed?

The chapters in this section clearly indicate how the further development of sustainable banking is shaped in an interplay between actors. Some banks find themselves among these actors as initiators—for example, offering an ethical policy based on a corporate mission—and, in other cases, as followers in the mainstream that is created by a legal setting. An example of this follow-up behaviour of banks is the growth of green funds in the Netherlands as a response to a tax credit scheme.

THE WORLD BANK'S ENVIRONMENTAL ASSESSMENT POLICIES
Review of institutional development*

Andrei D. Barannik
International EA Adviser, USA

Robert J.A. Goodland
The World Bank, USA

This chapter is the first attempt at a comprehensive and consistent review of the evolution of 'safeguard' policies and procedures within the World Bank Group's International Bank for Reconstruction and Development (IBRD) and International Development Association (IDA)[1]—particularly the policy as regards environmental assessment (EA),[2] which is currently an umbrella one that fosters compliance with all other policies.

While the term 'environment' is not mentioned specifically in the Articles of Agreement of IBRD and the IDA, both institutions have a mandate under their respective

---

1 The International Finance Corporation (IFC) and the Multilateral Investment Guarantee Agency (MIGA) of the World Bank Group (WBG) now have their own safeguards policies and procedures, which are consistent with those of the Bank but are tailored to suit their distinct operations and with modifications necessary to reflect different client base, project cycle and organisational structure. The EA policies and procedures of the IFC and MIGA, as well as relevant management systems within these two institutions, are not discussed in this chapter. The IBRD and IDA will hereinafter be referred to as the 'Bank', unless the context may require clear distinction between those two institutions.

2 EA is understood as a formal and systematic process of conflict resolution and risk management which, by consistently applying appropriate analytical tools, aims to predict environmental and social impacts and consequences of proposed human activities and alternatives, including their economic and financial evaluation, as well as to elaborate appropriate measures to avoid, prevent, minimise, mitigate or compensate for the identified adverse impacts and consequences and to enhance positive effects, and to facilitate projects' or programmes' selection,

Articles to 'ensure that the proceeds of any loan are used only for the purposes for which the loan was granted, with due attention to considerations of economy and efficiency'.[3] In supporting development and reconstruction in member countries, the Bank is the international organisation with the most resources devoted directly to environmental and social causes.

Over the years, the Bank has accumulated unique knowledge and experience in helping borrowers to resolve environmental and social problems arising from projects. It uses this diverse experience to 'distil and feed back' into the design and preparation of future projects, and to improve its policies, procedures and operations. Through this process the Bank has become one of the key players in international environmental protection. The Bank has also developed a sophisticated blend of systems and mechanisms to ensure compliance with the requirements of its Articles and policies. Quality monitoring and controls are designed to operate at all stages of the project cycle and related decision-making.

Over the last three decades the Bank has established the building blocks of what is now acknowledged to be a good environmental management system (EMS), with EA at its heart. Initially this evolution was rather haphazard but in recent years it has become more consistent, despite setbacks. We will review the history of the institutional development of the World Bank's EA along the following lines: (i) policies, procedures and requirements; and (ii) management, which includes systematic EA organisational structures and responsibilities, resources, operational controls and evaluation.

This review covers the following key periods: (i) 1970–84; (ii) 1984–89; (iii) 1989–93; (iv) 1993–98; (v) 1999–present.[4] These intervals were selected for convenience, as they covered periods of major policy and organisational change within the Bank. As we reviewed only broad EA institutional development rather than implementation of EA per se, we did not provide statistics on or analysis of the quality of project-specific EAs. Some data is available from Bank publications (World Bank 1990a, 1991, 1992a, 1993a, 1993b, 1994, 1995, 1996a, 1997a, 1998, 1999a) but in-depth and independent audit of the Bank's actual EA experience still challenges researchers.

planning, design and siting, and ultimately to improve decision-making. EA covers a wide range of risk management instruments, including environmental impact assessment, environmental audit, risk and hazard assessment, etc., which are employed by IBRD/IDA and their clients to ensure that their operations, projects, products and services are environmentally and socially sound and sustainable.

3   IBRD Articles of Agreement, Article III, Section 5(b), and IDA *Articles of Agreement*, Article V, Section 1(g) as amended effective 16 February 1989 (World Bank, 1st printing August 1991, 2nd printing April 1993).

4   This time-frame covers the tenure of five World Bank presidents: Robert S. McNamara (April 1968–June 1981), A.W. Clausen (July 1981–June 1986), Barber B. Conable (July 1986–August 1991), Lewis T. Preston (September 1991–May 1995), and James D. Wolfensohn (June 1995–).

24.1 1970-1984

24.1.1 Policy[5]

The first statement at the policy level was made by Robert McNamara[6] at United Nations Economic and Social Council in 1970. In this speech he articulated some of the fundamental principles of the Bank's EA:

> The problem facing . . . the World Bank is whether and how we can help the developing countries to avoid or mitigate some of the damage economic development can do to the environment, without at the same time slowing the pace of economic progress . . . It is equally clear that, in many cases, a small investment in prevention would be worth many times over what would have to be expended later to repair the damage . . . We want to work towards ·concepts that will enable us and other development financing agencies to consider the environmental factors of development projects in some kind of cost–benefit framework.[7]

President McNamara also mentioned that a unit had been established at the Bank in 1969 to predict the environmental consequences of development projects. He later indicated that guidelines encompassing the entire spectrum of development had also been drafted in 1970 to enable Bank staff to decide how to consider environmental factors in any given project.[8] Basically, these guidelines suggested that: (a) all projects be referred as early as possible in the *project cycle* to the Bank's environmental office; and (b) if the project warranted it, a *detailed assessment* should be undertaken to better understand the *nature, dimension, severity* and *timing* of the problems likely to arise from the proposed operation (see World Bank 1972; Baum 1979). McNamara clearly established the principle 'that in the issues of environmental damage, prevention is infinitely to be preferred to cure. Not only it is more effective, but it is clearly less expensive.'[9]

5 Adoption and evolution of the Bank's environmental (particularly EA) and social policies and procedures, in our opinion, were influenced and shaped to a great extent by relevant developments in its major shareholder countries, primarily the US, from the early 1970s to the 1980s. We feel that the US National Environmental Policy Act and US non-governmental organisations (NGOs) were instrumental in stimulating the Bank to pay attention to the environment. To further foster the Bank's commitment to EA, 'Several countries have . . . formally instructed their representatives on the Board of the World Bank to ensure that the environmental impacts of projects proposed for approval have been assessed and adequately taken into account' (WCED 1987: 338). From the mid-1980s until the present the Bank's European shareholder countries, as well as developing nations themselves and NGOs played significantly more proactive and important roles in influencing substantive aspects of the Bank's policies in regard to environmental and social matters.

6 Robert S. McNamara, the World Bank's fifth and longest-serving president, April 1968–June 1981.

7 Robert S. McNamara, Address to the United Nations Economic and Social Council, 13 November 1970, as cited in Tolba 1988.

8 Robert S. McNamara, Address to the United Nations Conference on the Human Environment (UNCHE), Stockholm, 8 June 1972, as cited in Tolba 1988.

  The World Bank endorsed a number of documents adopted during the UNCHE (5–16 June 1972), namely 'Declaration on the Human Environment', 'Declaration of Principles' and 'Recommendations for Action', and committed itself to institutionalising EA.

9 Robert S. McNamara. Address to the United Nations Conference on Human Environment, Stockholm, 8 June 1972.

In 1974 and 1980 the Bank declared its commitment, through the Cocoyoc and New York declarations[10] (UNEP 1981: 107-19) respectively, to develop, institute and use policies and instruments for *systematic* examination of all development activities, including policies, programmes and projects, to protect the environment and promote sustainable development. Though neither of the declarations has any legal standing, they do carry a significant moral obligation on behalf of the World Bank to promote the cause of sustainable development; in this respect, they may be used as a yardstick to critically review the Bank's actual achievements in EA.

It took the Bank almost 15 years[11] to translate these high-level environmental declarations into a clear and free-standing internal EA policy and staff instruction documents. Nevertheless, during these years some key elements and steps of EA process were injected into the Bank's project preparation through a number of environmental and social statements scattered in various Operational Manual Statements (OMSs) and Operational Policy Notes (OPNs).[12] Those elements of EA that were aimed at reducing the risks that might be associated with the preparation of Bank-supported operations are summarised below:

- Project ideas should aim to **conserve** and **preserve** natural resources and **safeguard** the environment, while recognising the fact that some decisions may have irreversible impacts, thus determining the quality of a project.

- The concept of a 'project cycle' was introduced. This requires the identification and screening of project ideas and **desirable geographic project areas**, which should be based on broad technical, **socioeconomic** and **environmental criteria**, particularly with regard to **level of risk**, and **attitudinal characteristics of the project area's population**.

- **Alternative project location, size** and **design standards** should be considered to reduce undesired effects, and excessive social or environmental costs.

10　The Cocoyoc Declaration was adopted at the UNEP/UNCTAD Symposium on 'Patterns of Resources Use, Environment and Development Strategies', Cocoyoc, Mexico, 8–12 October 1974. The New York 'Declaration of Environmental Policies and Procedures Relating to Economic Development' was adopted by nine international financial institutions and organisations, including the World Bank, on 1 February 1980 (see Burhenne 1996). These declarations were signed by the Bank during the presidency of Robert S. McNamara.

11　To the best of our knowledge, for almost 25 years after its establishment in 1946 the Bank had no formal or written policies at all. This is indirectly confirmed by the Bank's Vice President and General Counsel's statement in relation to the Bank's operations in the health sector: 'After several years of informal activity, the Bank adopted a formal health policy in 1974' (see Shihata 1988).

12　OMSs contained policy instructions, while OPNs, issued from time to time prior to the Bank's 1987 reorganisation, supplemented OMSs. See: OMS 1.19, August 1977; OMS 2.12, August 1978; OMS 2.13, April 1977; OMS 2.15, June 1981; OMS 2.20, March 1971 and January 1984; OMS 2.28, October 1977; OMS 2.32, April 1985; OMS 2.33, February 1980; OMS 2.34, February 1982; OMS 2.35, November 1983; OMS 3.02, December 1977; OMS 3.04, December 1977; OMS 3.18, April 1977; OMS 3.55, March 1977; OMS 3.72, September 1978; OMS 3.74, November 1977; OMS 3.80, June 1977; OPN 2.10, June 1980; OPN 5.03, April 1984; OPN 10.07, July 1984; OPN 11.01, March, 1985.

- The suggestion was introduced that, depending on the conclusions reached at the pre-feasibility stage, sociological, cultural and environmental studies should be conducted in a integrated manner during the preparation phase in order (a) to identify prerequisites for successful project implementation, operation and maintenance; (b) to identify any constraints and gaps (physical, environmental/ecological, financial, cultural or social) and means of mitigating or removing them; (c) to make a project compatible with international agreements.

- There should be a requirement that during project appraisal technical, environmental, health, sociological, management and organisational aspects must be subjected to cost–benefit and risk analysis by a Bank team that includes environmental and other professional staff; the project should incorporate environmental measures that are appropriate to the circumstances of the country to mitigate any adverse environmental consequences of a project; the project should be culturally acceptable and compatible with the behaviour and perceived needs of the intended beneficiaries.

- There should be proper planning of mitigation or corrective activities for **ecological hazards** and **risks** connected with the project, including preparation of a **resettlement plan.**

- The project's contractual documents should properly record the terms and conditions of the loan agreed between the parties, including covenants covering *inter alia* technical aspects of project execution. The borrower should be committed to carrying out the project with **due diligence** and **efficiency,** in conformity with appropriate specified standards and based on sound engineering principles.

- There should be a requirement for project monitoring and evaluation.

- The statement that the World Bank **will not finance certain types of projects,** including those involving encroachment on traditional territories or disputed areas, without adequate safeguards

24.1.2 *Management*

Despite McNamara's statement on the creation of an environmental unit in the World Bank, the dedicated post of permanent environmental advisor [13] was only created in 1970. In any event, the Bank became the first multilateral financial development institution to 'create a permanent in-house position addressing environmental issues' (El-Ashry 1993) and develop environmental guidelines for processing development projects.

---

13   Dr James A. Lee, a public health specialist by profession, was the first environmental official of the World Bank. He shaped to a great extent the Bank's initial approaches to and agenda on the environment (see Lee 1985).

In 1977 this environmental focal point grew to three staff, and to five by the mid-1980s. Known as the Office of Environmental Affairs (OEA), it was responsible for the 'promotion of environmental prudence in a professional staff of 3,500, for the review of US$11 billion in annual lending, and for an implementation portfolio of about US$100 billion' (Goodland 1992).

The Bank's recognition of the environmental dimension of development projects that it helped to finance grew slowly. It was hampered by an inadequate environmental commitment on the part of most of the staff, as well as by limited professional capabilities and a limited understanding of the interplay of the various aspects of a project, and ways and means to solve them. Project-specific environmental measures, if any, were limited to ameliorative activities (such as installing pollution abatement equipment or lining irrigation canals) or associated activities (such as environmental training) (see also examples in Ahmed 1995).

Though the OEA was responsible for reviewing and enhancing the environmental aspects and environmental quality of projects, including their adherence to Bank policy and conformity with environmental standards, as well as for providing training, advice and operational assistance on environmental matters, it actually had a rather limited impact in terms of improving projects' environmental and social dimensions. A significant number of borrowing countries lacked both environmental policies and capabilities, and so Bank staff and consultants carried out most project-related environmental and social work themselves.[14]

If requested to by the borrower, the OEA could help to prepare Terms of Reference (TORs) for environmental work, select consultants, oversee technical elements of consultants' work and review their findings and recommendations. Along with Bank project staff, the OEA was responsible for ensuring that the environmental measures agreed on with the borrower were incorporated into project design and execution.

The OEA had the authority to undertake, at its own discretion, a comprehensive environmental audit of completed projects. But to the best of our knowledge, until the late 1980s none of the Bank's institutions conducted an evaluation of the implementation of EA policies and procedures in any Bank-financed activities.

It is obvious that during this period the Bank had no clear-cut EA policy and procedures, very limited capabilities, including staff, financial and technical resources, and no organisational system, monitoring and evaluation, training, etc. to ensure the incorporation of environmental dimensions into project planning, design and implementation.

---

14 A Bank study reviewing loans and credits for the period 1 July 1971 to 20 June 1978 showed that, in 27% of all projects, the environmental problems identified were dealt by Bank staff and in less than 10% of projects, the environmental problems required special studies by consultants. See Shihata 1988: 62.

24.2 1984–1989

24.2.1 Policy

The Bank recognised that 'environmental spoilation is an international cancer' which respects no administrative or geographic boundaries and erodes hard-won economic gains of developing and developed countries alike. For this purpose, the Bank

> required, as part of project evaluation, that every project it finances be reviewed by a special environmental unit . . . and as a matter of policy [did not] finance a project that seriously compromises public health or safety; that causes severe or irreversible environmental deterioration; that displaces people without adequate provision for resettlement; or that has transnational environmental implications which are importantly negative (Clausen 1986).

President Clausen, the author of the above statement, went on to say that by the early 1980s the Bank's environmental experts had reviewed more than 2,000 projects and programmes in developing countries since 1970 and they were convinced that in almost all cases it had been less expensive to incorporate the environmental dimensions into project planning than to ignore them and pay the penalties at some time in the future.

Unfortunately such rosy declarations overshadowed the real shortcomings and failures of implementing the above fragmentary policy on environmental and social concerns; this forced the Bank to come up in 1984 with a clearer policy statement on the environmental aspects of its operations.[15]

The Bank acknowledged that its own experience between 1970 and the early 1980s clearly demonstrated that:

- Implementation of projects supported by the Bank in most economic sectors may cause **adverse and irreversible environmental impacts and risks** that can manifest themselves at **global, regional** and **local levels** and have **transboundary** implications.

- The resolution of environmental and social concerns requires **early, continuous and systematic** attention as well as **sound and integrated management**.

- **Preventative measures** give better protection from environmental damage at less cost than later remedial measures.

- Staff require **clear policy** and **procedural requirements** on handling environmental concerns in day-to-day operations, as well as a broader development framework.

---

15   OMS 2.36: Environmental Aspects of Bank Work, May 1984. We would like to highlight a rather characteristic provision at the bottom of all OMS and OPN statements referred to here, including OMS 2.36: '. . . It may be used only by personnel of the World Bank and IFC or others specifically authorised to use it. It may not be published, quoted or cited outside the World Bank and IFC.' This restriction was only lifted in the late 1980s.

OMS 2.36 clearly stated that: (a) the Bank[16] considers the environmental aspects of projects in terms of a longer time-frame (for example, 25–50 years and more[17]) than is relevant for most other aspects of cost–benefit analysis; (b) it is necessary to exercise prudence when assessing environmental effects and to regard each project as unique with respect to its total setting; (c) the Bank will have to tailor its approach to local circumstances, and respect the vast differences among its member countries; and (d) it is not the Bank's policy to adopt environmental standards, rather to periodically publish guidelines distilled from a wide range of national and international guidelines that set out the acceptable range to be followed in Bank operations. OMS 2.36 also proclaimed eight principles of the Bank's environmental work.

24.2.2 *Management*

Before its major reorganisation in 1987 spearheaded by President Conable, the Bank continued to address environmental concerns through a small Office of Environmental and Scientific Affairs (OESA). In practice, this was inadequate, largely because of the prevailing lending culture, the alarmingly small number of environmental staff, the lack of firm high-level environmental commitment and practical knowledge on the part of Bank staff, as well as poor accountability and minimal transparency of operations.

It became apparent that the Bank's response did not match the changing realities, either in the degree of effort devoted to environmental matters or in the approaches actually used. This, combined with a number of well-publicised cases such as the Carajas Iron Ore Project and the Northwest III Settlement Project ('Polonoroeste') in Brazil (El-Ashry 1992), in which Bank-financed projects had major negative environmental consequences, prompted the institution to rethink and adjust its policies towards environmental management and EA. In particular, the Bank's management decided to bring environmental concerns more systematically into the mainstream of its operations.

On 5 May 1987 Barber B. Conable, the seventh president of the Bank, announced in a speech to the World Resources Institute in Washington, DC, that, in addition to pledges made to the Development Committee in April 1987, and within the framework of general reorganisation proposals, the Bank would increase the number of its staff devoted to environmental work and would add a significant new dimension to its work in this area.

Regional Environmental Divisions (REDs) were established in July 1987 in all four Regional Vice Presidencies (RVPs) and a central Environment Department (ENV),[18]

16 This Statement covered IBRD, IDA and IFC work as well as sub-projects financed by Development Finance Companies. All references to the World Bank included the IFC.

17 To the best of our knowledge, none of the EAs completed for Bank-financed projects during the whole period under review in this chapter have attempted to analyse and predict environmental impacts and consequences for such a long perspective. Nor was there any attempt to conduct *ex post evaluation* of projects prepared prior to the 1984 Statement. No EAs have ever expanded their analysis to the decommissioning phase of projects' life-spans. Current Bank EA policy also does not require EA for policies and legislation, thus omitting a strategic dimension of development. These are key areas where the Bank provides advice and attaches conditionalities to its loans.

18 Kenneth Piddington was appointed the first director of the Environment Department almost a year after it had been created.

consisting of three divisions, was established in the newly created Senior Vice Presidency for Policy, Planning and Research.[19] ENV was tasked to help to set the direction of Bank environmental and social policy, planning and research work, and to take the lead in developing strategies to integrate environmental considerations into the Bank's overall lending and policy activities. ENV, particularly its Environmental Assessments and Programmes Division (ENVAP),[20] facilitated the transfer of experience from one region to another and monitored the EA process to help ensure the consistent application of policy and guidelines in different geographical regions. REDs, located in regional technical departments, were intended to 'function as watchdogs over Bank-supported projects and as scouts and advocates for potential resources-management operations' (World Bank 1988a).

In a few years the Bank's environmental community grew to about 55 high-level staff and more than 20 consultants in the Environment Department and REDs. However, there were no more than six professionally trained ecologists, and many environmental positions were filled by economists reassigned from other Bank units with no particular training in the environmental field.

More importantly, the total annual financial resources allocated by the Bank to support environmental work—less than US$10 million, complemented by about US$2 million of bilateral grants (World Bank 1990b)—continued to prove totally inadequate, particularly in comparison with the Bank's overall budget—more than US$950 million, including over US$500 million for operations, and a net profit of around US$1 billion.

24.3 1989–1993[21]

24.3.1 Policy

Following the 1987 reorganisation the new Operational Directives (ODs) began replacing previous OMSs, OPNs and other ad hoc instructions to the staff, outlining in a more coherent and streamlined manner the Bank's policies and procedures. ODs were also made available to interested parties outside the Bank (World Bank 1989). This was an impressive step forward, because for almost 20 years borrowers had been required to comply with the Bank's environmental and social policies, yet these had not been available to them in their original form.

---

19 W. David Hopper, Senior Vice President and member of President's Council. Later this vice presidency was renamed 'Senior Vice Presidency for Policy, Research and External Affairs' under Wilfried P. Thalwitz. Before the 1993 reorganisation, the Environment Department was located in the Vice Presidency for Sector and Operations Policy (SOPVP) under Visvanathan Rajagopalan.

20 Jane Pratt and Maritta R. v. Bieberstein Koch-Weser were the first chiefs of the ENVAP. In April 1999 Ms Koch-Weser assumed the post of Director-General of the IUCN, Gland, Switzerland.

21 During this period the following environment- and social-related ODs, incorporating guidance contained in earlier OMSs and OPNs, have been adopted: OD 2.00, March 1989; OD 2.10, September 1990; OD 2.11, November 1992; OD 4.03, July 1992; OD 4.15, December 1991; OD 4.20, September 1991; OD 4.30, June 1990; OD 4.76, December 1992; OD 7.50, 30 April 1990; OD 7.60, April 1989; OD 8.00, April 1990; OD 8.40, June 1992; OD 8.41, June 1992; OD 8.50, November 1989; OD 9.00, June 1991; OD 9.01, May 1992; OD 13.05, March 1989; OD 14.70, August 1989.

The first environment-related statement to be issued was OD 4.00, Annex B: Environmental Policy for Dam and Reservoir Projects,[22] which codified the best practice prevailing in carrying out such projects. It elaborated on four major principles and areas:

- The requirement for **environmental reconnaissance** by independent, recognised experts or firms, selected by the borrower and approved by the Bank, to identify timeously (a) environmental effects; (b) the scope of further EA; (c) the ability of the borrower to undertake an EA; and (d) the need for an environmental panel

- The requirement for the borrower to engage under normal circumstances an **advisory panel** of independent, internationally recognised environmental specialists for projects involving large dams or having major implications

- The requirement that bidding documents and contracts include **environmental clauses**

- The requirement that an environmental unit be established within the borrower's project implementing agency for large dams and other projects with significant environmental implications

OD 4.00, Annex A: Environmental Assessment[23] was developed to standardise and formalise an EA process[24] that had already been taking place on projects with major environmental impacts. It codified EA policies and procedures, which now became either mandatory or optional[25] (depending on the project) for Bank staff and member countries.

22 Issued on 28 April 1989.
23 OD 4.00, Annex A was issued on 31 October 1989 and subsequently revised and reissued on 15 September 1991. OMS 2.36 remained an umbrella Bank environmental policy and was supposed to be replaced in due course by OD 4.00. (OD 4.00 was never issued, though a number of drafts of OP 4.00 were circulated and discussed internally in the Bank in 1994.) All references to the Bank in this Statement included only IBRD and IDA. IFC started developing similar procedures for environmental review, which were supposed to reflect the special circumstances of its work. MIGA committed itself to co-operate with the Bank as far as possible, to ensure that the objectives of the 1989 Statement are met in its operations.
24 Significant pressure was put on the Bank to introduce a formal and mandatory requirement for EA. James A. Baker, then the US Secretary of State, stated: 'What [the United States] wants the World Bank . . . to do is make environmental analysis, systematically and routinely, a central part of every loan proposal. We want the Bank to draw on the expertise of trained environmental analysts . . . who know developing countries and can assess just what impacts any new project or policy will have on the ecology of those countries. It should then incorporate that analysis into its lending decisions and assistance from the very beginning of the lending process' (see Robinson 1992).
25 For a legal interpretation of 'mandatory' and 'optional' nature of the Bank's EA and social policies and procedures, see Shihata 1994a. In this book, Shihata made an interesting statement: 'While not all the standards provided in the ODs are binding (it depends on the wording of each standard), those stated in binding terms create *a duty for the staff* to exert their best efforts to achieve them' (1994a: 45). This interpretation by the Bank's General Counsel is rather confusing, particularly considering that (a) OMS 2.36, para 8, clearly states that the Bank's approach is not to adopt standards, but rather to suggest acceptable ranges to be followed in Bank operations, and (b) Shihata himself stated that they are simply 'general instructions from

It has been stressed that both the member country and the Bank must exercise judgement in using this OD, to ensure consistency with national environmental laws, policies and procedures. As far as possible capital and recurrent costs, and the benefits of proposed alternatives, mitigation and monitoring measures, should be quantified. To address cumulative environmental impacts of a number of activities in a reasonably localised area and design of sector investment programmes, a notion of regional and sectoral EAs was developed in 1989.[26]

An **environmental screening** system for projects was also introduced in 1989. Depending on the nature, magnitude and sensitivity of environmental impacts, a project could be classified into four EA categories. A category A project requires EA because it may have diverse and significant environmental impacts, while in the case of a category B project environmental analysis may be sufficient as such a project usually has well-defined and limited environmental impacts. This classification system was supported by a checklist of potential issues for an EA as well as illustrative screening lists, based on prior Bank staff experience.

The 1989 EA statement also included other important policy instructions, stressing that:

- The borrower should ensure **co-ordination among government agencies** by convening inter-agency meetings at least twice: after the decision to prepare an EA has been taken, and when the EA report is completed and submitted for final government review.[27]

- The final EA report should normally be available to the Bank prior to appraisal.

the management to staff issued for their guidance'. This leaves room for arbitrary interpretations of ODs by Bank staff. Shihata later acknowledged this vagueness, suggesting that 'Obviously, it is to the benefit of all that this issue be settled for future projects by the conversion of the remaining OMSs, OPNs and ODs to the new operational documents the nature and role of which are much clearer to the Bank *staff'* (1994a: 46). Finally, the same Bank's General Counsel, in another context distantly related to the environmental theme, indicated that 'the World Bank Group could not issue binding rules to govern the conduct of member States in this or other fields.' See 'Introductory Note' by Ibrahim F.I. Shihata, Vice President and General Counsel, World Bank, Secretary-General ICSID, 25 September 1992 in World Bank 1992b: 5. Additionally, Shihata stated that Bank 'guidelines . . . clearly are not intended to . . . assume for the Bank a legislative role which it does not have. The guidelines are meant to present a general framework which complements, but cannot substitute for, the broad array of international instruments.'

26 Many of the above requirements were in line with those described in the OECD 'Development Co-operation in the 1990s: Policy Statement by DAC Aid Ministers and Heads of Aid Agencies', adopted by DAC Member Countries, the World Bank, the IMF and the UNDP on 4–5 December 1989 (paras 19–21). This Statement proclaimed that: 'For environmentally sensitive projects and programmes as well as structural adjustment, environmental impact assessments are an indispensable management tool . . . Environmental concerns must be fully taken into account also at individual project level. Projects with significant environmental impacts . . . should be subject to environmental impact assessment . . . Donors should also encourage developing countries to submit their own projects and programmes to an environmental impact assessment. Local environmental NGOs should be actively involved in this process.' See OECD 1989b.

27 This requirement was changed in the September 1991 and October 1991 EA statements to a statement that the second inter-agency meeting should be convened once the draft EA report had been completed. Reference to the final government review was dropped.

▦ The implementation of the final EA report requires strengthening of borrower capacity for carrying out, analysing, and incorporating the recommendations of EAs; Bank country departments (CDs) should therefore discuss with borrowers how to achieve smooth and efficient implementation of this Annex.

▦ Progress and problems in EA implementation needed to be carefully monitored.

▦ This directive may subsequently be modified based on the lessons learned.

The revised EA policy (OD 4.00, Annex A, dated 15 September 1991) elaborated on the previous ones and contained additional instructions, particularly:

▦ Clearly defining the Bank's internal EA process, organisational responsibilities and documentation and reducing the number of EA categories from four to three

▦ Expanding the application of the directive to cover GEF[28] projects or GEF components of Bank projects

▦ Requiring the borrower to make the EA report **publicly available** to ensure **meaningful consultations** with affected groups and local non-governmental organisations (NGOs)

▦ Requiring the Bank to formally **request borrower's permission to release the EA report** to the Board of Executive Directors

▦ Requiring preparation of an environmental mitigation or management plan

▦ Requiring the Bank to prepare, update and make publicly available an **environmental data sheet** (EDS) for all projects in the IBRD/IDA lending programme

▦ Requiring the IFC and MIGA to ensure compliance with all relevant Bank environmental policies, adapted to the extent possible to their special needs

To provide further technical guidance to Bank staff and borrowers on the implementation of EA requirements, the Bank developed a three-volume *Environmental Assessment Sourcebook*. The first volume of this manual, dealing with EA policies, procedures and cross-sectoral issues was published as the World Bank Technical Paper No. 139 in July 1991.[29] Specific advice was provided on social issues, economic analysis, strengthening

---

28 The Global Environment Facility was launched as a pilot programme in 1991 to assist developing countries and those with economies in transition, in pursuit of global benefits in the four areas of biodiversity, climate change, international waters and ozone layer depletion. The World Bank, the United Nations Development Programme (UNDP) and the United Nations Environmental Programme (UNEP) are the GEF implementing agencies. Mohamed T. El-Ashry, the second director of the Environment Department and *ex officio* Chief Environmental Advisor to the President of the World Bank Group, was appointed the first GEF CEO and Chairman.

29 Another two volumes of the *EA Sourcebook*, namely Technical Papers No. 140 and No. 154, were published in August and October 1991 respectively. They address critical environmental issues in key sectors, including agriculture, transportation, urban infrastructure and industry. Guidance to the staff was previously provided in World Bank 1988b, 1988c, 1988d, 1990c.

local environmental management capabilities and institutions, financial intermediary loans, community involvement and the role of NGOs.

On 3 October 1991 the Bank issued OD 4.01: Environmental Assessment,[30] which incorporated the guidelines contained in OD 4.00, Annex A, as well as other instructions, particularly on disclosure of information.[31] OD 4.01 was almost identical to the September 1991 statement. In view of its importance, the EA statement, both in its original and revised forms, was discussed in draft by the Bank's Executive Directors at a board seminar. In the view of Ibrahim Shihata, the Bank's former Senior Vice President and General Counsel, 'this was an unusual step, as ODs and their annexes represent management's instructions to staff and as such fall within the prerogative of Bank management in the implementation of policies determined by the Board' (Shihata 1994b).

In our opinion, in accordance with the IBRD Articles of Agreement[32] and particularly in view of the Bank's previous failures to properly help the borrower to manage environmental issues, Executive Directors had both a legitimate responsibility and authority and a moral obligation to review this fundamental issue of environmental policy and conduct on the part of the Bank. Furthermore, OMS 2.36 was still in force and as such it provided guidance for the interpretation of the Bank's environmental (including EA) policies and procedures, as well as requiring their internal consistency.

30 In 1993 and 1996, OD 4.01 was updated in a minor way to reflect on policy and organisational changes that had taken place in the Bank in previous years.

31 'Transparency' (i.e. disclosure of information) of the Bank's operations, particularly in the environmental field, was for a long time an issue in the US Congress, especially as it related to congressional approval of the Bank's appropriations. In our opinion, one particular act of the US Congress triggered the Bank's rapid strengthening of disclosure policy and requirements as provided in both OD 4.00, Annex A (15 September 1991) and OD 4.01 (3 October 1991). Under the International Financial Institutions Act as amended by the 1989 International Development and Finance Act (so-called *Pelosi Amendment*, after Representative Nancy Pelosi, D-Calif.) (22 USC$ 262 m-7, Section 1307[d], as added by Section 521 of Public Law 101-240 on 19 December 1989), the US Executive Director in the World Bank has been required since December 1991 'not to vote in favor of any action proposed to be taken . . . which would have a significant effect on the human environment' unless an environmental impact assessment had been made available to the Bank and to affected groups and local non-governmental organisations 'at least 120 days before the date of the vote'. Subsequent US appropriations legislation (Section 532 of the *Foreign Operations, Export Financing, and Related Programs Appropriations Act 1993* [Public Law 102-391] of 6 October 1992) expanded the requirement for timely availability of draft and final environmental assessment reports 'to the public in borrowing and donor countries'. Ibrahim F.I. Shihata, then Vice President and General Counsel at the World Bank, wrote to Messrs Sandstrom and El-Ashry in his memo dated 7 July 1992 that 'The procedure is likely to increase outside *intrusion* in the Bank's handling of assessments . . . [and] may require Bank comments explaining possible conflicts with Bank policies.' In late 1999, the US House of Representatives clearly stated that 'The World Bank repeatedly exhibits a failure to comply with these environmental and social policies' (see 'Ecosystem and Indigenous Peoples Protection Act' [HR 2969], Sec. 2. Findings: Sense of the Congress [a] [6], 29 September 1999). The proposed Bill is intended 'to prevent United States funds from being used for environmentally destructive projects or projects involving involuntary resettlement funded by any institutions of the World Bank Group'.

32 See IBRD Articles of Agreement, as amended effective 16 February 1989, Section 2 (a) (b) (f), Section 4 (a) (I), Section 5 (b).

In terms of OD 4.01, the Bank/task manager (BTM) assists and monitors the EA process. This EA statement reconfirmed these functions and gave the BTM powers that went beyond the merely advisory, enabling the BTM to significantly influence implementation of the EA process by the borrower:

- The BTM has the sole responsibility to screen a project, classify and reclassify it into one of the three EA categories (*without seeking the borrower's agreement!*), to review the EA report, appraise the project and incorporate any environmental recommendations into the Staff Appraisal Report and loan agreement as he/she deems necessary based on the EA report and relevant national capabilities (RED provides clearance for the BTM decisions in relation to: EA category, draft EA report [essentially 'yes' or 'no' to go ahead with project appraisal] and to proceed to project negotiations).

- The BTM also has the responsibility of preparing an EDS and a Project Information Document (PID) and releasing both documents to the public through the Monthly Operational Summary of Bank and IDA-proposed Projects (MOS) and the Project Information Centre (PIC).

- The BTM has the power to provide concurrence with almost all of the borrower's decisions.

- The BTM is required to: (a) formally provide the borrower with the 'Outline of a Project-Specific EA Report' (but the BTM is not required to provide the borrower with a copy of OD 4.01); (b) inform the borrower of the need to have the EA report submitted to the Bank in English, French or Spanish and an Executive Summary in English; and (c) request the borrower in writing to give advance permission to release the EA report to the Executive Directors and to the public—if the borrower refuses, the Bank does not proceed with further work unless Bank senior management (or Executive Directors) decide otherwise for objective reasons unrelated to the environmental soundness of the project.

- The BTM advises the borrower on the scope of EA, TOR for EA, EA procedures, and the schedule, and assists the borrower, at its request, with arranging financial resources (either grant or from the Project Preparation Facility [PPF]) for preparation of EA; this is one of the most critical responsibilities of the BTM as most of the borrowers do not have sufficient funds (or do not want to spend them) to initiate a comprehensive EA in a timely fashion.

OD 4.01 reconfirmed the borrower's responsibility for preparation of the EA in compliance both with Bank policies and procedures and with national legislation and standards. This EA statement stressed in particular that the borrower should:

- Develop and agree with the Bank on TOR for EA, EA procedures (that are consistent with national environmental laws, policies and procedures), schedule, outline and consultants, as well as ensure that the EA is prepared by consultants not affiliated with the project's sponsoring agency.

- Ensure public consultations (at least twice for category A projects), inter-agency co-ordination and public availability of relevant environmental information, particularly the draft TOR and draft EA reports.

- Ensure, during EA preparation, analysis of alternatives and their economic evaluation, preparation of an EMP, and submission of EA report to the Bank prior to the departure of the appraisal mission, and subsequently ensure compliance with agreed environmental deliverables during project implementation.

During preparation and appraisal of projects the Bank has to assure itself that any measures agreed on with the borrower will in fact be carried out by the borrower during the project's implementation and after its completion. Typically, such measures are incorporated into the project's design and implementation plan. The main EA findings and recommendations are also reflected in the Bank's Staff Appraisal Report (SAR), which has no legally binding power in relation to borrowers' commitments. Translation of EA recommendations into legally binding obligations is a critical step in terms of the effectiveness of a project's final design and implementation.

The Bank uses a number of legal techniques and instruments to ensure that the environmental actions are implemented:

- The Loan (for IBRD) and/or Development Credit (for IDA) Agreement,[33] which normally contain, *inter alia*, a description of the terms and purposes for which the loan was granted, provisions for the use of the proceeds of the loan and, in this context, borrowers' obligations and commitment with respect to carrying out the project with due diligence and efficiency and in conformity with specified standards.

- **Covenants** written in a Loan or Credit Agreement setting out borrowers' environmental and other technical obligations clearly and specifically; covenants can also be built on specific conditions linked to loan or credit negotiations, board approval, effectiveness and disbursement.

- In order to amplify environmental objectives and particular activities derived from the EA that are to be undertaken by the borrower, Loan or Credit Agreements usually contain implementation programmes or plans as incorporated as 'schedules' in the legal documents.

- As appropriate, covenants in the legal documents do not by themselves ensure compliance, both the General Agreements and Loan or Credit Agreements contain provisions giving the Bank power to suspend, or threaten to suspend, disbursements (as well as to suspend, cancel or accelerate the loan) if the

---

33   Both types of Agreement incorporate by reference the IBRD *General Conditions Applicable to Loan and Guarantee Agreements* or IDA *General Conditions Applicable to Development Credit Agreements* as well as *Guidelines on Procurement . . . and Use of Consultants* as revised and amended on the date of signing of a Loan or Credit Agreement.

borrower defaults in carrying out agreed-upon actions. In the case of certain types of contract, the Bank also has the right to prior review and approval.

● The procurement-related documentation of projects, including (a) Loan or Credit Agreements; (b) schedules; (c) supplemental letters and references; (d) Procurement Guidelines,[34] and bidding documents subsequently prepared based on the requirements on the above, must provide carefully drafted specifications of the required performance of the product, service and works in accordance and consistent with internationally recognised health, safety and environmental standards as well as those for packaging, labelling, transportation, handling, storage, use and disposal.

The Bank does not rely solely on legal instruments to ensure adequate implementation and compliance. Each project financed by the Bank is subject to supervision, which is carried out by its own staff. Preparation of an Implementation Completion Report (ICR), elaborating the details related to the execution and initial operation of the project[35] and its costs and benefits, is also a requirements of all loans and credits.

On the policy level, the Bank participated in the United Nations Conference on Environment and Development (UNCED), which took place in Rio de Janeiro, Brazil, from 3–14 June 1992. UNCED adopted the 'Rio Declaration on Environment and Development', which specifically stressed the importance of public participation, access to information and environmental impact assessment in planning and decision-making for development activities.[36]

In his address to UNCED, the Bank's eighth President Lewis T. Preston summarised his institution's thinking on the environmental and social aspects of the development agenda:

> If the benefits of a project are offset by negative effects on health and the quality of life, this is not development . . . We are also improving our policies and, even more important, their implementation . . . Bank-supported projects now include environmental assessments. Consultation with the local people affected by development projects is a priority. We are working together with *all* partners in the effort to achieve sustainable development.[37]

34 Documents referred to in (a), (b), (c), (d) are binding on the parties to the Loan or Credit Agreement and together with applicable Bank ODs and other policy Statements must be followed in the administration of procurement in Bank-financed projects. The Loan or Credit Agreement between the Bank and the borrower takes precedence over any conflicting legislation of the borrowing country (see OD 11.01: Country Procurement Assessment Reports, dated 30 January 1992, para 6). They also take precedence over other Bank documents issued to interpret, explain, illustrate and elaborate on procedures acceptable to the Bank.

35 Before the Bank's ICR mission, the borrower prepares or updates the plan for the operational phase of the project, including performance indicators to monitor operations and development impact; the borrower sends this plan to the Bank.

36 'Rio Declaration on Environment and Development', adopted by UNCED in Rio de Janeiro, 13 June 1992. See Principles 10 and 17 respectively.

37 'Reducing Poverty and Protecting the Environment: A Call for Action'. An Address by Lewis T. Preston, President, World Bank Group, to the United Nations Conference on Environment and Development, Rio de Janeiro, 4 June 1992.

During this period the Bank initiated discussions on a broad range of EA-related policy and management issues and experience with other multilateral financial institutions (MFIs), such as the EBRD, ADB, EIB, NIB, IADB and AfDB, with which it continued to co-finance projects (see World Bank 1993c). This initiative was intended to: (a) foster EA 'cross-fertilisation' and coherence among institutions; (b) reduce borrowers' confusion with regard to different EA requirements; (c) to improve their capability to prepare quality EAs; (d) to review approaches to project EA; and (e) to stimulate more proactive use of social assessments and public consultations in EAs.

24.3.2 *Management*

During this period both ENV and REDs sought to strengthen their capabilities, both in terms of numbers and in terms of professional credibility, to ensure implementation of the Bank's fourfold environmental agenda, particularly with regard to the way in which potential adverse environmental impacts from Bank-financed projects are addressed. An informal EA Steering Committee (EASC), consisting of representatives from REDs, Technical Departments, IFC[38] and ENV, was established in 1990 to ensure consistency in the implementation of, and compliance with, EA and social policies and procedures as well as to disseminate knowledge and best practice. ENVs, particularly the Senior EA Advisor and Environmental Assessments and Programmes Division (ENVAP), supported EASC work on policy, technical and administrative matters. The Environmental Law Unit of the Legal Department provided legal advice and guidance.

Each RED appointed one senior environmental staff as a Regional EA Co-ordinator (REAC) to facilitate the EA process in country departments and to ensure consistency in EA screening and review decisions, as well as to spearhead training, synthesise experience and disseminate lessons learned. REDs organised staff and assignments on the premise of borrower responsibility for EA preparation. REACs chaired weekly project EA review meetings and provided preliminary concurrence with environmental and social decisions taken by Bank project task managers, to be confirmed later in writing by a RED chief.

RED staff worked as environmental specialists on Bank project teams. To avoid a potential conflict of interest, RED staff assigned to a particular project team as environmental specialists were excluded from providing 'clearances' on environmental aspects of the project during its processing by the Bank.

To enhance control and quality of operations, the Bank employs a graduated system of **comments**, **clearances** and **approvals** implemented through project 'peer reviewers' and other corporate managers of various levels. REDs, procurement advisors, loan and legal departments[39] have the power to formally 'clear' relevant documents and thus to

38 IFC, which was responsible for environmental and social oversight of MIGA's operations, represented this Institution on the EASC. Maritta Koch-Weser and Colin Rees chaired *ex officio* the EASC during 1990–98. From 1996 onwards the EASC meetings became rare and its influence declined significantly.

39 An Environmental Law Unit (LEGEN) was established in the Legal Department during this period. Peter H. Sand, a well-known and respected international environmental lawyer, was appointed the first LEGEN chief. A few years later he was replaced by David Freestone, another prominent scholar of environmental law.

authorise processing of a project from one step in the project cycle to another. In cases of disagreement between 'clearance' and 'operational' units responsible for project processing, and depending on the nature and scope of this disagreement, the decision is delegated to RVP and/or ESDVP or managing directors and, in exceptional cases, Executive Directors.

On 16 October 1992 President Preston announced[40] structural changes to improve the Bank's ability to implement existing policies more effectively, reflect its priorities more accurately and to implement the recommendations of the Task Force Report on Portfolio Management (World Bank 1992c). The Bank's agenda was now dominated by three themes, each of which supported the fundamental goal of poverty reduction: (1) Human Resources Development; (2) Private Sector Development; and (3) Environmentally Sustainable Development. The Vice Presidency for Environmentally Sustainable Development (ESDVP) was established, incorporating ENV. The ESDVP intended to achieve 'critical mass and economies of scale', ensure that the Bank had clearly identified technical authority in its areas of operation, and provide effective policy guidance and support to sector operations in CDs.

When OD 4.00, Annex A was issued in 1989, the Bank's management committed the institution to carefully monitor progress and problems in implementation of a new EA OD. It also promised to prepare a review of experience for the board's consideration in the 1991 financial year (FY).[41] This review was prepared by the ENV in collaboration with REDs, under the guidance of the EASC, and submitted to the board on 25 February 1993 (World Bank 1993b).

While the first EA Review confirmed that EA had become a valuable tool for identifying and resolving project-related environmental and social problems as well as for 'enlightening' the Bank's and borrowers' planning, design and decision-making processes, a number of fundamental deficiencies constrained the full utilisation of EA in Bank-financed operations:

- Most Bank staff were not familiar with EA procedures and an appropriate skill mix, adequate financial resources and training were not readily available to support the implementation of EA processes and systems in the Bank.

- The Bank's EA requirements differed from those mandated by borrowers' legislation and many borrowers had limited EA institutional capabilities; furthermore, borrowers' knowledge of the Bank's EA policy and procedures was deficient.

- EA was usually initiated too late in the project cycle and its key elements and steps were not fully implemented.

- EA was frequently used to justify project decisions that had already been taken rather than to help select a project's options and make it environmentally and socially sustainable.

40 See memo 'To All Staff' from Bank president Lewis T. Preston, 16 October 1992, and pamphlet 'Strengthening the Bank's Thematic and Sectoral Capabilities', 13 November 1992.
41 See: Operational Directive 4.00, Annex A: Environmental Assessment, Manual Transmittal Memorandum, 31 October 1989, para 6.

▓ Bank staff were deeply involved in EA preparation, sometimes taking over borrowers' responsibilities.

▓ The cost of EAs accounted for about 5%–10% of total project preparation costs, reflecting the variety of investments.[42]

24.4 1993–1998

24.4.1 Policy

In January 1993 the Bank introduced a new system of Operational Manual Statements, which began replacing the previous system of ODs that had been in place for less than five years. Three categories of document were introduced: Operational Policies (OPs), Bank Procedures (BPs) and Good Practices (GPs). OPs and BPs once again attempted to clearly set out policy and procedural requirements that are mandatory for implementation by the Bank's staff and its borrowers. GP statements are advisory in nature.

The Bank planned to incorporate, consolidate or convert all old statements into the new format in the course of 18–24 months, i.e. by the end of 1995. Unfortunately, this did not happen—in fact the conversion was incomplete as of early 2000—though Robert Watson, then Director of the Environment Department, publicly stated that 'all World Bank safeguard policies are finalised', and (even more misleadingly) 'harmonised with those of IFC' (World Bank 1998b: 9).

After the new system of OPs/BPs had been introduced, it was still felt by the Bank's staff that (a) there were too many rules to follow; (b) the rules were too complex; and (c) clear guidance on interpreting the practical implications of Bank policies and procedures was often lacking. More importantly, it became evident that the Bank had made many firm commitments to external audiences on the policy level, particularly in relation to the environment, that could not be broken. Any abrogation or softening of its environmental commitment would be viewed as a breach of faith with significant negative consequences for the institution's reputation. It was also obvious that the Bank's credibility on sensitive issues, particularly in relation to EA, could only be re-established if the Bank was seen to be more actively ensuring that agreed rules were consistently being followed and were not being changed.

---

42 It is worth noting that, being a leading global financial institution, the Bank was never able to disclose precise figures related to the costs of a project-specific EA preparation, claiming that it was difficult to separate EA from other project preparation costs. This might have contributed to inadequate EA accounting for the following reasons: (a) the deep involvement of the Bank's own environmental and social staff in EA; (b) the mixture and varying amounts of project preparation advances and grant resources allocated; and (c) borrowers' own expenditures. Implementation of EA recommendations, including monitoring, mitigation and institutional strengthening, accounted for higher figures than EA preparation itself. But again, there is limited solid data to make an enlightened judgement, particularly as the Bank's accounting and supervision ends with project's disbursement. After that, borrowers provide no data on expenditures, cost-effectiveness and savings associated with implementation of EA recommendations during the life of the project.

During this period a number of environment- and social-related OPs/BPs were issued; they incorporated certain policy changes and procedural provisions that reflected on organisational transformations in the Bank.[43] The Bank also made two other crucial and interrelated decisions: (1) to issue a free-standing procedure on **disclosure of information** (BP 17.50, September 1993) and (2) to create the **Inspection Panel** (IP). As both decisions are closely linked to the EA process, we describe them briefly below.

The Bank and its shareholders recognise that sharing of information is essential for effective and sustainable development as it stimulates debate, broadens understanding of issues and facilitates co-ordination among the many parties involved as well as strengthening public support for efforts to improve people's lives. Under the revised policy the Bank significantly expanded the range of documents that it released, including environmental documents, and improved public access[44] to such documents.

Two distinct but interwoven concerns, expressed both internally and externally, led to the creation of the three-person Inspection Panel: one of these was the suggestion that the management of the Bank's portfolio of loans required significant improvement, and the other was the perception that the Bank was not highly accountable for its performance (see World Bank 1992c, 1993d, 1993e; Shihata 1994a).

The purpose of the Inspection Panel is to provide 'people directly and adversely affected by a Bank-financed project with an independent forum through which they can request the Bank to act in accordance with its own policies and procedures'.[45] It aims to: (a) protect the rights and interests of those parties that may be unintentionally undermined by Bank actions or omissions; and (b) improve the very process of development, i.e. environmentally and socially sustainable development, which is at the centre of the Bank's mandate as interpreted at present. Detailed steps are laid out and explained in the Panel's operating procedures.

The review of the Panel's first two years of operation confirmed that it was having the effects intended by the board. At the same time, the experience showed the Bank's 'operational deficiencies in project monitoring, enforcement of loan/credit covenants, and observance of policies and procedures'.[46] The Panel also indicated that the 'plethora

43 These included: BP 3.11, January 1994 and January 1995; BP 2.20, January 1997; OP/BP/GP 4.02, October 1994; OP/BP/GP 4.04, September 1995; OP 4.07, July 1993; OP 4.09, July 1996 and December 1998; OP 4.20, April 1994; OP/GP 4.36, March 1993; OP/BP 4.37, September 1996; OP/BP/GP 7.50, October 1994; OP/BP/GP 7.60, October/November 1994; OP/BP 8.10, May 1994; OP/BP 8.30, July 1998; OP/BP/GP 8.40, October 1994; OP/BP/GP 8.41, February 1994 (*retired in July 1999*); OP/BP/GP 8.50, August 1995; OP/BP 10.00, June 1994; OP/BP 10.04, September 1994; OP/BP 10.21, November 1993; OP/BP/GP 13.55, April 1994 (*revised in July 1999*); OP/BP 14.25, July 1998; OP/BP 14.40, February 1997; BP 17.50, September 1993; BP 17.55, February 1997; BP 17.60, February 1998.

44 For this purpose, a Public Information Centre (PIC) was established and opened for business on 3 January 1994 at the World Bank Headquarters in Washington, DC. The requests to the PIC may be submitted through the Internet, the Bank's European and Tokyo offices and all Bank field offices.

45 'The Inspection Panel. Operating Procedures', IBRD, August 1994. The board clarified on 17 October 1996 its own Resolution (IBRD Resolution No. 93-10, IDA Resolution No. 93-6 of September 1993) establishing the Panel, and subsequently approved additional Changes and Clarifications on 20 April 1999 after reviewing the report of the Working Group on the Second Review of the Inspection Panel.

46 'The Inspection Panel. Report. August 1, 1994 to July 1, 1996', IBRD, 1996, page 5.

and detail' of Bank policies and procedures makes their full application at times unrealistic. The board stressed (in 1996 Clarifications) that the Bank's management should try harder to make the IP known in borrowing countries.

At the time of writing, 12 formal requests had been received since the Panel began operations in 1994, and most of them were based on the argument that the Bank did not comply with its own environmental and social policies. The IP's investigation of the proposed Arun III Hydroelectric Project in Nepal, for example, led to President Wolfensohn's decision to withdraw the IDA's support for this project.

The Bank recognised that, notwithstanding the risks inherent in lending for development, the failure rate of its portfolio was too high and harming its reputation as an institution. To address this alarming situation, in July 1996 it introduced institution-wide guidelines for streamlined business processes.[47] These guidelines focused on two fronts: (a) improving quality at entry,[48] i.e. of new operations and products, through simpler design, better analysis, development of performance indicators and sharper focus on participatory approaches; and (b) improving the implementation of existing projects through more proactive and problem-solving management.

All projects were subject to two mandatory reviews at the director level—these reviews are taking place at the **concept** (immediately after identification) and **decision** (prior to appraisal/negotiations) stages. All projects may be further reviewed either by the Regional or Bank-wide Operations Committees (ROC and OC). In terms of the new guidelines, the EA clearance function of REDs (for EDS/PID and appraisal/negotiations) was reconfirmed. It was also recommended that at least two project peer reviewers should come from outside the managing division, and preferably from outside the CD concerned. The peer review system had largely been abandoned by 1998.

The Bank board also approved and made mandatory after 1 August 1997 a new, simplified approach to project documents for investment operations. When project identification begins, the BTM records information in the Project Concept Document (PCD), which serves, together with PID, as the documentation for Project Concept Review (PCR) and subsequently evolves into a form-based Project Appraisal Document (PAD). A new format of the Memorandum of the President (MOP) was also introduced.

In the above guidelines, the Bank confirmed that it was compiling an internal 'Watchlist of Environmentally and Socially Sensitive Projects' (see also World Bank 1997b: xxiii, footnote 6), proposed by RVPs and CVPs and issued by MDs, that involve major policy issues or unusual risks. Together with the 'Projects at Risk' list compiled by the Bank's Quality Assurance Group (QAG),[49] which included both **actual** and **potential**

---

47 See 'Guidelines on Simplification of Business Processes', 27 June 1996 under the joint cover memorandum from Caio Koch-Weser and Gautam S. Kaji, World Bank Managing Directors (MDs) for Operations.

48 As required under OP 10.00: Investment Lending: Identification to Board Presentation, June 1994.

49 The QAG, established in 1996, is expected to monitor periodic samples of the quality of the Bank portfolio, and conduct quality assessments of projects around the time of approval and during supervision. It promotes excellence in Bank performance by enhancing learning from experience, and increasing accountability for the results; it also provides credible feedback to staff and managers on the quality of their work. It is also anticipated that the QAG's work will enhance in-house accountability related to the quality of environmental supervision.

problem projects, this list effectively started building a 'Project Alert System'[50] to help anticipate and identify risks early on and factor them into project preparation and decision-making by focusing managerial attention on them.

Finally, after almost five years of work, on 20 October 1998 the Board of Executive Directors approved OP/BP/GP 4.01: Environmental Assessment. The final text of the EA statement dated 30 December 1998 and published on the Internet in January 1999 included clarification on certain matters by the Bank's management.[51]

OP/BP/GP 4.01 codified policy and organisational developments that had occurred in relation to the Bank's operation, particularly concerning the role of EA in projects in member countries. The new document recognised the vast diversity in project and country conditions, national legislation and institutional capabilities, obligations under relevant international environmental treaties and agreements, and included:

- Adoption of OP/BP 4.01 as an **umbrella statement**

- Explicit application of EA policy and procedures to all types of Bank operations (loans, credits and guarantees) and a variety of supported projects, except structural adjustment loans (SALs)[52] and debt and debt service operations

- Application of OP/BP 4.01 to all project components regardless of the source of financing and sponsorship (public or private)

- EA evaluates a project's potential **environmental risks**[53] and impacts in its **area**

50 This system is to some extent similar to those maintained by the US Agency for International Development (USAID). Since 1986 USAID has actively monitored environmental aspects of projects financed by multilateral development banks (see for example a 'List of Projects with Possible Environmental Issues', transmitted to Congress by US Agency for International Development, 1987, as included in Public Law 99-591). Inclusion on the USAID list indicates that the project could have serious environmental impacts. These lists may be found on the USAID home page on the Internet.

51 See a presentation by Andrei Barannik, 'The World Bank Policies and Procedures for Environmental Assessment', January 1999. It includes Annex A, 'Comparison of Operational Directive 4.01: Environmental Assessment and Operational Policies/Bank Procedures/Good Practices 4.01: Environmental Assessment', January 1999.

52 SALs accounted for about 60% of total Bank lending by 1999. The justification for excluding SALs from EA policy was made on the grounds that there were no environmental and social impacts from this type of operation. If there were impacts, they would be minor, and in any event they would be too complicated to isolate and assess. In the view of Robert Goodland, 'this was curious, as most SALs are similar: they impose fiscal austerity, cutting consumption and budgets, increasing taxes, raising interest rates, causing devaluation, and accelerating the drawdown of natural capital. Removal of subsidies raised prices, especially those affecting the poor, causing bread riots, kerosene riots and so on for decades' (see Goodland 2000).

53 In view of the continuing decline in environmental quality of project preparation and implementation, it is telling that the Bank explicitly reintroduced the notion of *environmental risk*. In our opinion, the Bank refers here to projects' potential negative environmental consequences, as well as to the risk of failure that could undermine the credibility of environmental advice and reputation of the Bank itself. The risk of failure is even more important as the Bank is always deeply involved in all of the projects' preparation and implementation phases, providing advice and 'concurrence'. The Bank stated that in evaluation it considers the sources, magnitude and effects of the risks associated with the project. The Bank also evaluates projects' *cross-border* and *global externalities*, i.e. effects on neighbouring countries and the entire world (see OP 10.04: Economic Evaluation of Investment Operations, April 1994).

of influence, examines project alternatives[54] and includes the process of mitigating and managing adverse significant[55] environmental impacts throughout project implementation in a cost-effective fashion.

▣ Description of EA as a process that results in an EA report and the introduction of a range of EA instruments (and their **definitions**) to satisfy the Bank's EA requirements, including **environmental impact assessment** (EIA), **environmental audit,**[56] **hazard** or **risk assessment**

▣ Reference to the *Pollution Prevention and Abatement Handbook* describing environmental protection measures and emission levels that are normally acceptable to the Bank and a requirement to the borrower to provide full and detailed justification for the levels and approaches chosen for the particular project or site

▣ Introduction of the fourth EA screening category to reflect on potential for adverse environmental impacts when a project involves investment of Bank funds through a financial intermediary

▣ A requirement for a field visit by the Bank environmental specialist for category A projects is introduced.

▣ The EMP becomes a mandatory component of a category A EA report, and borrowers' project implementation plans should incorporate EA findings and recommendations, including any EMP; the loan conditions include an obligation to carry out the EMP and include any specific measures recommended.

▣ Procurement arrangements should be consistent with environmental requirements set out in the project's legal documents; environment-related covenants of the loan agreement should be included in the monitoring system.

54 Consideration of alternatives is regarded by the Bank as one of the most important features of proper project analysis throughout the project's cycle. It includes consideration and comparison of feasible options in terms of project site, technology, mutually exclusive designs, operation and starting date and sequence of components, as well as the 'without project' scenario in terms of potential environmental impacts and capital and recurrent costs.

55 Several criteria could be used to determine the significance of an impact. None of the criteria that we suggest below should be considered as inherently more important that any other; the prime rationale for their use is to help in framing the overall assessment: (a) **probability of occurrence,** (b) **magnitude,** (c) **duration,** (d) **reversibility,** (e) **relevance to legal mandate,** and (f) **social distribution of risks and benefits.** It should be considered whether the impact of the above criteria, whether *adverse* or *beneficial*, contributes or mitigates against the equitable sharing of environmental risks and benefits. To further refine the significance of the impact, it is important to take account of priorities held by governments, organisations and local people *directly* or *indirectly* associated with the project.

56 The term 'environmental auditing', unofficially coined in the United States in the mid-1970s, grew mainly from corporate fear of prosecution, fines and even imprisonment for violation of a vast set of federal and state environmental regulations. In contrast to the US, environmental auditing in Europe reflected a social shift caused largely by environmental pollution and disasters (Seveso, Basel, etc.).

▦ ENV carries out project audits to help ensure compliance with Bank's EA policy and conducts periodic reviews of Bank's EA experience.

24.4.2 *Management*

General organisational arrangements that were put in place within the Bank from 1987 to 1992 to manage environmental (including EA) and social concerns continued to function to a certain extent during the period under review. Together with REDs, the ENV was estimated to have more than 100 staff in 1992 working full-time on the environment. This number was estimated to have increased to almost 300 Bank-wide by the end of 1997. Not many of the staff were professionally trained environmentalists and few had practical EA managerial experience. The number of experienced environmental staff within the Bank began to fall sharply in early 1998.

When President Preston came on board, he had concerns that not all was well with the results on Bank-financed projects and with its processes and procedures affecting lending, supervision and implementation. It became clear that lending priorities had been driven by the Bank's own concerns rather than by those of borrowers and their realities. More importantly, much of the actual responsibility for project identification and preparation rested with the Bank rather than the borrower, in contrast with the desired theoretical position.[57] The pervasive emphasis on loan approval ('the Bank's approval culture')[58] was not matched by equal emphasis on proper implementation planning, assessment of major risks for project performance, and adequate supervision. From 1981 to 1991 the proportion of projects judged satisfactory according to the OED's evaluation ratings had fallen from 85% to 63% (World Bank 1993d: 3).

To address the situation, the Bank's management prepared a report entitled 'Portfolio Management: Next Steps—A Programme of Action', approved by the board on 9 July 1993, which set out what action needed to be taken to improve the development impact of the programmes and projects which the Bank helps to finance. Many of initiatives outlined in the above statement persisted and received new impetus during the tenure of President Wolfensohn. After about four months in office he reconfirmed previous agendas for institutional change and outlined his vision of the Bank's future evolution, making the following declarations:

> Without environmental protection, development can be neither lasting nor equitable. My commitment to the task is unequivocal.

> We will accept nothing less than absolute standards of excellence. We must be prepared to be held accountable.[59]

---

57 President Preston's cover memorandum to Jean-Pierre Landau, Chairman, The Board Joint Audit Committee (JAC), 2 October 1992.

58 Another aspect of this culture is that it does not welcome honest appraisal of environmental and social risks ('risk is bad news') associated with Bank-financed projects, thus losing an opportunity to solve problems in a timely and comprehensive fashion.

59 See 'New Directions and New Partnerships,. Address by James D. Wolfensohn, President, World Bank Group, to the Board of Governors, Washington, DC, 10 October 1995.

Following the board's mandate, and in keeping with its promise to conduct occasional EA reviews, the Bank prepared a second report on its EA experience in the course of 1996. It was complemented by an independent evaluation of the effectiveness of EAs and Bank-supported National Environmental Action Plans prepared by the OED (see World Bank 1996b, 1996c). In the opinion of Robert Picciotto, the Director-General, OED, EA leads to 'greater attention paid to environmental issues in Bank projects and has generally been complied with. However, the EA has yet to live up to its potential to influence project design.'[60]

Noting that more than 1,000 projects had been screened for their potential environmental impacts between October 1989 and June 1995 (this figure included 99 approved category A and 415 category B projects), the Bank claimed that EA had become 'firmly rooted' in its normal business activity. Not only this, but the quality of EAs had improved as well. Increased EA experience, guidance[61] and training contributed to this progress. Co-ordination between IBRD, IFC and MIGA on EA and social issues was strengthened. At the same time, certain problems persisted and new ones emerged:

- Because the Bank was having to deal with an increasing number of ever more complex projects, its professional capacity to advise on the preparation of EAs, and to efficiently supervise the implementation of the EAs' recommendations, was deteriorating. The particular challenge was to maintain a strong EA review capacity separate from operational functions.

- Environmental awareness remained low and training of the Bank staff in EA had almost ceased—only 64 staff out of almost 8,800 had received EA training in just under three years; no division chiefs, directors or vice presidents had found time to participate in even a half-day session.

- Environmental scoping, systematic analysis of alternatives, quantification of cumulative and/or induced impacts, economic evaluation, public consultations, integration of EA recommendations into project design and legal documents remained the weakest points in EA work of borrowers assisted by the Bank's staff.

- The EA requirements, planning and decision-making cycles of the Bank and its borrowers varied and were inadequately synchronised; EA work also had to accommodate new realities by more fully utilising strategic, regional and sectoral EAs and alternative instruments and mechanisms for environmental analysis and quality assurance.

---

60 Memorandum from the Director-General, Operations Evaluation, to the Executive Directors and the President, 28 June 1996.

61 The Bank's EA *Sourcebook* and subsequent *Updates* became real 'bestsellers' and were widely disseminated and used by other multilateral and private-sector financial institutions, organisations and consultants. At the same time it is obvious that the EA *Sourcebook* required major updates to match the international 'state of the art' in EA, as well as to make it more user-friendly.

In order to halt the continuing skills erosion, fragmentation of technical expertise and limited transfer of knowledge, on 16 September 1996 the Bank launched the 'networks' initiative, with the major goals of achieving a higher level of excellence and creating a mechanism to improve the quality of products and services for clients.

All Bank environmental staff were clustered into an Environmentally and Socially Sustainable Network (ESSD), comprising Environment, Social and Rural Sector Families and a small Global Water Unit. The top managers from each RVP and CVP comprised the ESSD Council. Each 'family' was in turn chaired by the Sector Boards built on sector leaders from each region and the centre. The ESSD Council was supported by the ENV. Unfortunately, neither the Bank's environmental strategy nor the ESSD's *modus operandi* was clearly stated.

In mid-1998, the three remaining divisions of the ENV had been abolished and centrally based staff clustered around existing environmental themes and remaining functions. During two years of Bank-wide transformation, the ENV was scaled down from above 110 staff to fewer than 50 regular and support staff and externally funded consultants. In 1999 the decline continued and the director left his post. It was stated that the EA function would be delegated to the yet-to-be-created Safeguard Policies Compliance Unit (SPCU) or an amorphous Environmental Assessment Oversight and Compliance Monitoring (EAOCM) body. It was intended that the EAOCM would receive support from designated regional EA co-ordinators. The 'old EA team' was reduced to two high-level staff and no budget.

The responsibility for EA and other safeguard policy and procedural compliance rests with the six regional vice presidents[62] and project task managers/team leaders (TM/TL). This arrangement provides room for a conflict of interest, particularly in view of the fact that RVP and country departments decide on budget allocations, including those for environment and social project work. The TM/TL solely and arbitrarily decides the selection of a project's environmental and social specialists, who are now competing against each other for assignments.

To complement the Bank's environmental work with clients and set a good example of corporate environmental due diligence, the General Services Department (GSD) took a number of initiatives at Bank Headquarters to accelerate the 'greening' of the World Bank Group. These included: energy conservation measures, environmental guidelines for food services and for rental properties, promoting the management of paper and recycling rubbish. The Bank Staff Association conducted a limited environmental audit of the Bank.

President Wolfensohn suggested that the following should be institutionalised: (a) 'the Bank's Group greening process', including that in the Resident Missions; (b) 'independent environmental audit of the World Bank Group'; and (c) ENV co-ordination of the preparation of an annual report on greening priorities and on progress made'.[63] He went

---

62 This arrangement is different from that of IFC, which has chosen to centralise the environmental and social project processing clearance under one roof, namely the Environmental and Social Review Unit.

63 'Greening the Bank Group', a memo to the staff from James. D. Wolfensohn, President, World Bank, 12 September 1996.

on to suggest that environmental standards for procurement merited further study and could be used to draw up long-term strategies for changing the Bank's practices.

ENV readily agreed to (a) 'develop a coherent World Bank Group corporate environmental strategy' and (b) 'demonstrate the effectiveness of the SPCU.[64] The Bank committed itself [65] *inter alia* to:

- Ensure consistent compliance with the safeguard policies across the six regions and strengthen review, advisory, and monitoring activities

- Conduct random audits of the safeguard aspects of representative projects at the Project Concept Document, Project Appraisal Document and supervision stages in accordance with a to-be-developed 'selection for audit criteria'

- Ensure a prompt response by regional staff in case of non-compliance with a safeguard policy within a to-be-developed framework intended to facilitate greater accountability, including the possibility of sanctions, for staff and managers responsible for non-compliance identified through the audit process

24.5 1999–present

24.5.1 Policy

During this period there were no major policy or procedural developments in relation to environmental and social aspects of Bank operations, though both the Bank and its partner organisations came to a growing recognition that environmental considerations must be systematically included in country assistance strategy and policy lending. Incorporation of EA at policy level is particularly important in view of the fact that in FY 1999, for example, over 50% of Bank lending was for either structural adjustment or programmatic investment lending (a new instrument)—areas that are not subject to EA. In this respect, it became clear that a 'new methodology is needed, focusing on (a) how the objectives of safeguard policies can be applied in a "beyond-project" context; and (b) compliance criteria for programmatic approaches' (see World Bank 1999a: 63).

The Bank has indicated that the emphasis is shifting from preventing harm to incorporating environmental and social values into everyday operations of the major sectors in which it invests. This task is complicated by the globalisation in terms of communication and information, and the increasingly free flow of capital, goods and people. To meet this challenge senior management has confirmed its commitment to develop a new environment strategy for the Bank.

---

64 Robert T. Watson (Director, Environment Department, 1998), 'Progress and Challenges in Mainstreaming the Environment', in World Bank 1998b: 7.
65 See Colin Rees, 'Safeguard Update', in World Bank 1998b: 60.

24.5.2 *Management*

The Quality Assurance and Compliance Unit (QACU) was established in the ESSD to strengthen EA and social-related capabilities and improve the quality of Bank-wide project and policy work. Though fewer than 16 seasoned social and environmental specialists from various parts of the Bank have been 'mapped' in the QACU, in practice two separate units exist in the ENV—(a) the Quality Assurance and Compliance Unit (QACU) and (b) the Environmental Management, Assessment and Quality Programme Team (EMAQPT), with only one senior social professional and two environmental professionals (World Bank 1999b; ESSD 1999).

24.6 Findings

As we have shown above, the emergence and evolution of the World Bank's EMS, with EA at its heart, is still an unfinished business. Though the Bank became the first multilateral development financial institution to adopt EA and related policies and create an internal organisational system to implement them,[66] EA institutional development turned out to be a rather painful exercise, entailing:

- **Recognition** of the potential for adverse environmental and social impacts and consequences from Bank-supported development projects

- The emergence of corporate **awareness** and **commitment** to try to address these environmental risks

- The **formulation** of environmental and social *policies and principles*

- The **translation of commitments, policies and principles** into directives, procedures and guidelines to ensure a **disciplined EA process**

- The **creation** of an internal **organisational structure and capacity** to manage and implement the EA process as well as to **ensure self-monitoring and quality control**

- The **dissemination** and **training** of both own staff and borrowers in the application of EA policies and procedures as well as **supporting development and strengthening of EA processes and systems in member countries**

66 Besides other multilateral development banks, such as EBRD, ADB, IADB, AfDB, EIB, etc., which have learned from IBRD EA experience, many commercial banks are extensively using World Bank EA and related guidelines and handbooks in their operations (e.g. 'Extract from the UBS Environmental Report 1998–99', UBS Environmental Risk Management Services, Zurich, 1999: 9). It is worth noting that in addition to UBS, other financial institutions such as HSBC Holdings plc, Barclays plc, NatWest Group, ING Group, ABN AMRO, BankAmerica Corporation and Deutsche Bank adopted environmental policies and procedures in the early 1990s, as well as offering environmental products and services far more diverse and sophisticated than those of the World Bank.

- The creation of mechanisms and procedures **internally** and **externally** in the course of preparing and implementing Bank-financed development projects

- The **evaluation** of projects' environmental and social performance[67] and subsequent **revision** of EA policies depending on changing circumstances and lessons learned

- **The gradual incorporation of environmental dimensions into the full range of own day-to-day operations,** particularly as this relates to **announcing targets in resources savings, waste minimisation,** preference **for 'green' products** and **community goodwill**

Evolution of the World Bank's EA policies and management was determined by a complex system of corporate rules, formal and informal concepts, cultural habits, values and behaviours, not to mention personalities. In addition, it was significantly influenced by initiatives on the part of its stakeholders, and pressures by civil society which expressed preferences for and/or dissatisfaction with the Bank's environmental performance. Sometimes, rapid institutional change on the surface went hand in hand with a frozen set of informal rules and corporate 'cultural' traditions below the surface, yielding little or no behavioural or quality improvement.

Apparently, there is no 'cast-in-stone' approach to ensure the success of an institutional environmental management system (EMS), with EA at its heart. The approach needs to fit the corporate circumstances in which the EMS and EA are being implemented. However, certain general principles help to ensure its success, i.e. achievement of the tasks its has been designed for:

- **Clarity of goals and objectives.** These should be carefully and accurately selected as they determine the whole thrust and scope of EA policy and requirements. All management and organisational arrangements will have to be in line with the policy.

- **Level of the policy.** All EA policy provisions should be custom-tailored and accurately related to the organisational structures with which they are concerned and should be implemented by. It is not that easy to make a corporate environmental policy commitment—it is even more difficult to sustain this will to implement environmental safeguards for a long time and support them with necessary resources.

- **Realism.** EA requirements should relate directly to the diverse nature of corporate operations and products, and take into account the level of decentralisation of institutional capabilities and decision-making.

---

67 It is important to describe exactly what a 'successful project' is. In its simplest terms, we suggest that the success of a project can be thought of as incorporating the following four facets: (a) comes in on schedule—**time criterion**; (b) comes in on budget—**monetary criterion**; (c) achieves all goals and objectives, including environmental and social, set for it—**sustainability and effectiveness criterion**; and (d) is accepted and used by the clients for whom the project is intended—**satisfaction criterion**. It seems reasonable that any *ex post* evaluation of project implementation should include these four indicators.

- **Flexibility**. Because external EA institutional frameworks tend to evolve and change over time, all corporate EMS arrangements should be rather flexible to accommodate 'externalities'.

- **Co-ordination**. Since integration and co-ordination of efforts is critical for an effective EA process, the EMS should be developed with the idea of designing optimum arrangements for ensuring policy direction and co-ordination between various corporate structures during implementation.

- **Definition of responsibility**. It is critical that EA internal and external responsibilities are clearly and unambiguously defined to reduce to a minimum the risk of misunderstandings, duplications and omissions, as well as to help in co-ordinating efforts and ensuring compliance, transparency and accountability.

- **Leadership in implementation**. It is often difficult to mobilise necessary corporate capabilities to full effect. In this respect the leadership of individuals such as the CEO or COB is a very important consideration. Champions of the EA must be entrusted with senior 'transboundary' corporate authority and responsibility.

- **Ease of use**. The EMS should be formulated in such a way that it is easy to use and understand; the EA should be kept as clear and concise as possible.

- **Viability and check points**. The EMS should include arrangements and steps for preserving an 'institutional memory' and periodically checking that the EA lives up to its promise, is kept up to date and fully viable for its intended purposes. Routine public disclosure of environmental and social performance adds a new dimension for measuring the soundness of corporate business and will foster greater competition towards sustainability. Finally, any EA should be well documented,[68] i.e. *written*—or it will not be remembered and disseminated. In this respect, the importance of **mentoring** Bank staff and clients should not be neglected in the design of a corporate EMS.

24.7 Next steps

Obviously, the World Bank should 'walk the talk', i.e. stick to and elaborate on the commitments it has advertised continuously for the past 30 years. These will have to include:

68 The EAPM documentation directory, both in printed and electronic form, usually includes: (a) EA policies and requirements; (b) EA manuals, checklists, work operational instructions and training materials; (c) a library of EA references and legislation; (d) standardised corporate EA forms, records and internal communications; (e) copies of projects' EA and other types of analysis and investigation; (f) any media reports on specific project, etc. The EAPM documentation should be integrated into corporate online systems, and be tailored to meet corporate and individual needs.

- Adoption of a unified World Bank Group (WBG) **Environmental Policy** (EP); the EP should be discussed with *all* member counties and stakeholders; furthermore the EP should be a foundation for elaboration of WBG **Environmental Strategies** (both sector and regional) and **Action Plans** (ES and AP)— perhaps broken down into four-year periods to coincide with the President's term in office; these will help to ensure transparency and accountability of the WBG.

- Elaboration of WBG EP, ES and AP that is consistent with the ISO 14000 and ISO 9000 series; they should cover *inter alia* WBG own environmental (e.g. energy conservation/waste minimisation, etc.), health, safety 'housekeeping' and performance as well as relationships with contractors (certain environmental requirements to products and services/no child or forced labour, etc.).

- Subsequent revision of EA Policy and Procedures to unambiguously determine what is mandatory and what is voluntary; this will have to ensure compliance with applicable legislation and requirements of a borrower as well as any international agreements it may be a party to.

- Expanding EA policies to *all* types of WBG-supported activities and extending EA to a project decommissioning phase

- Subjecting its own policies and initiatives to rigorous scrutiny of EA and *cost–benefit analysis*

- Averting the collapse of the World Bank's EA institutional framework

- Creating an WBG EA Revolving Concessionary Fund (EARCF) to support EA preparation by borrowers; financing for EARCF should come from WBG's own profits rather than donor grant money, to which conditions are routinely attached.

- Conducting a WBG-wide environmental audit to determine areas for improvement both in EA management and 'environmental housekeeping'; this environmental audit should be commissioned in accordance with terms of reference approved by the Board of Executive Directors and conducted by an international team of experts; the audit team should include professionals from various countries and disciplines rather just from the 'big five' consulting firms, which regularly audited the WBG and advised on its institutional transformation.

24.8 Postscript

Since this chapter was penned in mid-1999, the World Bank Group continued broad institutional change under the leadership of president Wolfensohn. This transformation has caused intensive international debate, including in civil society, and unfortunate confrontation (in Washington, DC, and Prague) which has been well covered by the global media.

For the Bank's own interpretation of its environmental institutional development, including in EA, we refer the reader to the following publications:

- *Fuel for Thought: An Environmental Strategy for the Energy Sector* (Washington, DC: World Bank, 2000)

- *Toward Environmental Strategy for the World Bank Group: A Progress Report and Discussion Draft* (Washington, DC: Environment Department, World Bank, April 2000)

- *The World Bank and the Global Environment* (Washington, DC: Environment Department, World Bank, May 2000)

- *Environment Matters at the World Bank. Annual Review: Toward Environmentally and Socially Sustainable Development* (Washington, DC: Environment Department, World Bank Group, Summer 2000)

We believe that an objective review of these publications will allow an intelligent reader to make an independent and enlightened judgement on the vector and speed of environmental reforms pursued by the World Bank.

INTERNATIONAL FINANCIAL INSTITUTIONS AND THE THREE GORGES HYDROELECTRIC POWER SCHEME

Kate Kearins and Greg O'Malley
University of Waikato, New Zealand

Sustainable development (SD) provides a significant challenge for the international financial services sector, as the activities of this sector impact strongly on economic systems, and hence play a part in both national and individual prosperity, and ultimately in determining the wellbeing of future generations. The social and environmental implications of the activities of the international financial services sector in funding developing nations' basic infrastructure and growth, in particular, are becoming increasingly apparent, with some charging financial institutions with these responsibilities, or risking loss of reputation and potential ruin at home (Monroe 1999). At the most fundamental level, the challenge to the international financial services sector is about how to chart and navigate a path towards the global achievement of SD, in the context of economic integration, while maintaining equity and diversity. Clearly, this challenge is immense, and is likely to be extremely long-lived.

We define the more immediate SD challenge for the international financial services sector as providing for economic growth unaccompanied by environmental degradation or social upheaval. Economic growth, particularly in developing countries, is heavily dependent on trade and foreign investment, with environmental provisions increasingly becoming part of bilateral and multilateral trade agreements. Inadequate environmental, health and safety regimes within developing countries can therefore be construed as potential barriers to global trade and investment, unless developers (and ultimately their financial backers) can provide guarantees that high standards of environmental, health and safety practice can be maintained or, indeed, even enhanced.

Already, financial services leaders are increasing the integration of environmental issues into core banking activities, often driven by environmental due diligence, lender liability, and the possibilities of being faced with both foreclosure and later site remediation responsibilities. A 1992 United Nations Environment Programme (UNEP)-sponsored position paper on banking and the environment addressed these concerns, emphasising the links between lending and investing and sustainable development (UNEP 1999: 5).[1]

The UNEP Financial Institutions Initiative 1998 Survey identified environmental policies and procedures covering corporate credit, project finance, investment banking and insurance. Environmental risk was identified as being most appropriately incorporated into credit decisions. The most significant obstacles cited to advancing integration of this risk into credit and investment analysis was the translation of environmental impacts into financial implications, and the perceived lack of materiality of environmental issues to bottom-line performance (UNEP 1999: 12).

With financial institutions being challenged to integrate environmental considerations into their decision-making processes at all levels (WRI 1997: 2-3), involvement in economic development projects in developing countries provides an obvious testing ground. A major element of financial investments, the financing of developing countries' infrastructure, has tended to shift from commercial lending toward foreign direct investment and portfolio investment. Fulfilling developing nations' energy and power needs requires significant international investment in both technology and trade, with considerable, though often difficult to quantify, environmental and social implications arising from such investments. The situation regarding electricity projects in China provides a compelling example of the SD challenge faced by international financial institutions.

25.1 Financing electricity projects in China

China's investment landscape changed rapidly during the 1990s as large parts of its economy transformed from a planned to a market economy. Foreign direct investment has dominated foreign capital flows into China since 1992, comprising three-quarters of foreign capital flows in the years 1993–96 (WRI 1997: 2-3). The investment requirements of the electricity sector in China for the period 1996–2010 are estimated at US$270 billion (Razavi 1996: 28-30). This amount equates to an average rate of US$18 billion per year over the 15-year period through to 2010, from a base of US$12 billion in 1995.

Until 1980, the electricity industry in China had been fully funded and controlled by the central government. Funding for capital investment projects was allocated according to national plans. Institutional electricity reforms in China over the last ten years have allowed for innovative funding options, drawing on the resources of emerging markets, private finance and private investment. More recent power projects have pulled from a

---

1   Over 150 banks have endorsed the UNEP Financial Institutions Initiative on the Environment (see pages 397-400).

wider pool of funds, for both equity and debt-financing, complementing structural changes in a more deregulated global electricity sector that provides greater opportunities for private ownership. We have witnessed the floating of public power plant assets in international stock markets, the issuing of corporate bonds, the establishment of power development funds, and the channelling of various types of foreign investment. The investment requirements and the sources of finance for power sector requirements in China over the period 1985–95 have been estimated in Table 25.1.

Investment requirements	1985	1990	1995
Transmission/distribution	555	833	1,947
Generation	1,913	4,724	10,115
Nuclear	(1,127)	(3,167)	(7,384)
Hydro power	(751)	(1,111)	(2,141)
Thermal power	(35)	(446)	(590)
Total investments	**2,468**	**5,557**	**12,062**
Sources of finance (%)			
Government support	40.2	10.9	5.6
Internal cash	16.5	25.3	29.6
Borrowing	36.9	50.8	46.8
Domestic	(27.3)	(25.4)	(21.3)
Foreign	(9.6)	(25.4)	(25.5)
Foreign investment	6.4	13.0	18.0
Total	**100%**	**100%**	**100%**

Table 25.1 **Investment requirements and sources of financing power sector requirements in China 1985–95 (US$ million)**

Source: Taken from Razavi 1996

One massive electricity project requiring innovative funding options drawing on the resources of emerging financial markets is the Three Gorges Hydroelectric Power Scheme. An icon of China's modernising ambition (Hajari 1999), the Three Gorges Dam Project has proven to be something of a test case for operationalising the SD concept within the international financial services sector, arousing the interest of environmental and human rights groups across the globe. The prospect of similar mega-dams being proposed in China and in other emerging economies means that international financiers' policies on the Three Gorges Project can be seen as setting precedents. Such precedents can either aid or hamper efforts to promote sounder environmental policies within the international financial services sector, and, by implication, in the worldwide energy and power sectors.

25.1.1 *The Three Gorges Hydroelectric Power Scheme*

The Three Gorges Hydroelectric Power Scheme currently under construction on China's Yangtze River is expected to cost more than virtually any other single construction project in history. Financial costs pale, however, in comparison to the ecological costs of submerging around 23,800 hectares of land and the social and human costs of resettling well over a million people. More than 1,700 towns and villages will be flooded, and 300,000 farmers are having to relocate onto mostly poorer soils. The project is said to pose significant ecological dangers, technical challenges and human rights issues, and to lead to the loss of important archaeological sites and cultural artefacts (Probe International 1998).

The large size of the project and its financial and technical dimensions alone constitute a need for international involvement. Involving the diversion of China's longest river and the construction of a 600 km-long lake, the Three Gorges Dam Project is predicted to be capable of pumping out 18,200 megawatts of electricity, significantly more than any other hydro power station in the world (*Inside China Today* 1999).[2] As well as powering China's industrialisation, the project is designed to open the river above the gorges for shipping. Whether it is the best means of allowing China to hold back from burning its vast coal reserves, and whether it will provide for the much-vaunted and much-needed flood protection downstream, are more matters of conjecture (Pearce 1997). Project civil works officially began in December 1994 with an estimated completion date between 2009 and 2013 (China Embassy 1997). Estimated costs from China, as late as 1996, ran to US$28 billion (Razavi 1996), while international estimates predict costs up to US$75 billion (Kojima *et al.* 1997).

The China Yangtze Three Gorges Project Development Corporation is responsible for overseeing the entire project, and has opened some stages of construction to bids from international companies. The Chinese government approved importing key technologies, materials and spare parts required to build the 26 680,000-kilowatt turbo-generators and the 50,000-volt high-tension transmission lines. Joint ventures for the dam have not been ruled out, as core parts and equipment are expensive, and high levels of technical expertise are vital to the project's success.

The funding of the Three Gorges Dam Project has been clouded with controversy, however. After completing a four-year study of the project's feasibility in 1995, the World Bank concluded that the project design was not an economically viable proposition, and refused financing (Aslam 1997: 2). Likewise, a number of private international financial service institutions have been reluctant to become involved.

Export credit agencies remain an important source of foreign financing. These government agencies, which provide financing and insurance to companies bidding on

---

2 The Brazil–Paraguay Itaipu Dam, which can generate 12,600 megawatts, is billed as the current world champion (*Inside China Today* 1999).

foreign projects, do not routinely carry the sustainable development mandate, and thus tend to have fewer environmental or human rights constraints on their operations. Because export–import banks and investment agencies traditionally lack strict environmental and social guidelines, and appear to have few, if any, requirements for transparency in their operations, there is the potential for them to incur considerable risk in becoming involved in unsustainable projects (Knight 1998). The example of the US export credit agency, in operationalising its congressional mandate to establish environmental review procedures, provides a platform for potentially more sustainable financing.

25.2 The Export–Import Bank of the United States

The Export–Import Bank of the United States (Ex–Im Bank) was founded in 1934, and established under its present law in 1945, to assist in the financing and facilitation of US exports. Ex–Im Bank provides guarantees of working capital loans for US exporters, guarantees the repayment of loans, or makes loans to foreign purchasers of US goods and services, and provides credit insurance against non-payment by foreign buyers for political or commercial risk.

As the official export credit agency of the United States, Ex–Im Bank has a clear mission to help create and sustain American jobs through exports. Ex–Im Bank does not compete directly with private-sector lenders. For the fiscal year ending 1997, Ex–Im Bank authorised US$12.2 billion in financing to support US exports; annually, Ex–Im Bank claims to support over 200,000 jobs directly, and more than one million indirectly.[3] In conjunction with US strategy for continuing export growth, Ex–Im Bank focuses on exports to developing countries by aggressively countering trade subsidies of other governments, stimulating small-business transactions, promoting the export of environmentally beneficial goods and services, and expanding project finance capabilities.

It was the potential involvement of Ex–Im Bank in the Three Gorges Dam Project, and other projects like it, that prompted the US Congress to require Ex–Im Bank in 1992 to consider the environmental impact of all projects requesting its support. The Ex–Im Bank Charter also authorises the Bank's board of directors 'to grant or withhold financing support after taking into account the beneficial and adverse effects of proposed transactions'.[4] Following implementation of interim procedures, Ex–Im Bank's environmental procedures and guidelines were duly issued on 1 February 1995, and have since been revised twice.

Ex–Im Bank staff members spent many months considering the Three Gorges Dam Project, consulting other governmental agencies including the National Security Council, holding a series of open meetings with exporters, non-governmental organisations and Chinese officials, and meeting with numerous members of Congress and Congressional staff (Ex–Im Bank 1996a). On 30 May 1996, The Ex–Im Bank board concluded, in

---

3 Ex–Im Bank website (www.exim.gov), 1999.
4 *Ibid.*

line with its congressional charter, that Ex–Im Bank could not issue a letter of interest for the Three Gorges Project at that time. The official reason was that 'the information received, though voluminous, fails to establish the project's consistency with the Bank's environmental guidelines' (Ex–Im Bank 1996b). Major issues of concern included:

- The maintenance of adequate water quality in the project's reservoir

- The protection of ecological resources, and preservation of endangered species potentially affected by the project

- The environmental and socioeconomic impacts associated with the proposed resettlement of up to 1.3 million people to be displaced by the reservoir

- The protection of cultural resources affected by the project

It is noteworthy that Ex–Im Bank (1999b) reported that no serious concerns had been raised in its consideration of the Three Gorges Dam Project with respect to the credit-worthiness of the project, or its technical feasibility. Environmental and social concerns were paramount in the decision, as reported.[5]

Though lauded by environmentalists (Probe International 1998), Ex–Im Bank's decision not to provide financing for US equipment suppliers vying for Three Gorges Project contracts was criticised by the affected American corporations. Had the Chinese government approved bids by American firms, they concluded, the ensuing US$1 billion of exports to the project would have generated over 19,000 American jobs and assured entry into the booming Chinese market for US companies (Kojima *et al.* 1997: 4).

Supporters of the Ex–Im Bank decision argued that the United States had a moral obligation to stand up for the environment, and for human and social rights. They also argued that the withholding of economic benefits is the quickest and, sometimes, the only way to attract the attention of unco-operative foreign governments—even in cases such as the Three Gorges Dam Project where the outcome might appear futile, with dam construction having already begun (Kojima *et al.* 1997: 4).

However, other export credit agencies in Canada, France, Germany, Japan and Switzerland, apparently unconstrained by environmental policies, have not only expressed interest in, but are participating in Three Gorges Dam Project procurement contracts. Some agreed to loan guarantees in 1996 with the provision that all details remain secret. Environmentalists have criticised this approach as 'typical of an organisation suffering from a lack of accountability and transparency' (*World Rivers Review* 1996).

---

5   Environmental concerns were foremost in the records of the Special Meeting of the Board of Directors in which the requests for letters of interest made by US suppliers Caterpillar and Rotec were considered, and both environmental and social concerns elaborated in the subsequent press briefing on the special board meeting later that same day.

25.3 Analysis of the Ex–Im Bank decision

25.3.1 Rethinking risk assessment

Ex–Im Bank operates within a dominant US economy where the Superfund legacy has resulted in a greater awareness of environmental and social problems, and where there is perhaps greater luxury to turn down business on these grounds. There are signs in the US, too, of an acceptance by banks that, under certain circumstances, they can be held responsible through the legal system for the environmental mistakes of their borrowers. Within this socio-political, legal and economic climate, it is not surprising that Ex–Im Bank was required not only to consider environmental and social aspects of projects, but also to be more transparent in its decision-making processes.

Ex–Im Bank's decision runs contrary to many of its competitor export credit agencies and many other financial institutions regarding participation in the Three Gorges Dam Project. Traditionally, much financial investment has been conducted with little consideration of eco-sustainability (Thompson 1998: 129), consistent with a generalised lack of full-cost accounting (Gray *et al.* 1993). Given that environmental issues are receiving greater attention and are likely to become increasingly integrated with core business activities (Houldin 1993), a broader challenge appears for the financial services sector, the activities of which, it could be argued, are responsible, directly and indirectly, for most industrial impacts on the earth's ecosystems. The Ex–Im Bank example shows that not only is strong policy required but also mechanisms to operationalise policy through what appears to be a reformulation of risk management priorities to include the ecological and social challenges inherent in sustainability. In order to adopt the SD concept within a risk management frame, banking enterprises need to go beyond the rhetoric of policy proclamations and the like, and consider both the broader ramifications and long-term future of investment projects beyond payback periods and short-term financial benefit. Raising environmental performance levels of sponsored investment projects may be seen to minimise long-term financial risk.

We conclude that, in its refusal to participate in the Three Gorges Dam Project, Ex–Im Bank's decision reflects both a broader conception of risk, and a somewhat novel prioritising of the various elements of risk assessment. In our model of decision-making from a sustainable development perspective, we portray risk assessment as represented by six sub-categories (see Fig. 25.1). Traditional financial sector risk management, we suggest, has given greater weighting to the first four sub-categories of risk: financial risk, legal/political risk, technical risk, and economic risk. Under an SD framework, this unanimity principle currently underlying financial decision-making rules is considered both unacceptable and empirically invalid (Robinson 1996: 187).

Elevation in importance of the remaining two elements of risk assessment—environmental and social risk—together with a focus on economic risk, we suggest, is the paradigm shift required for financial services institutions to achieve SD. The overall risk profile can be viewed within an iterative decision-making model that highlights the key elements of economic, environmental and social sustainability, and, we would add, transparency. Addressing risk in this way requires a proactive and participatory approach

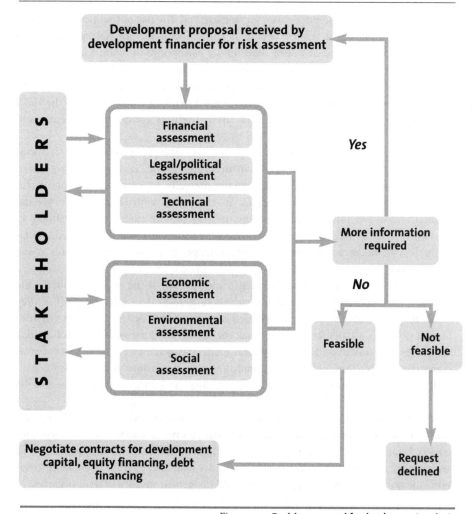

Figure 25.1 **Decision proposal for development projects**

involving a greater number of stakeholders, an approach that identifies, analyses, evaluates and manages risk with an SD focus.

25.4 The role of stakeholders

Lynch (1994: 14-18) suggests that, within what he terms the *global bank*, stakeholders of the future will exercise much greater power and influence and choice in financial transactions. Given the growing concern by stakeholders about the effects of economic growth on natural resources and the environment, financial institutions funding such growth are likely to come under even greater scrutiny. The use of traditional modes of financial risk assessment is problematic as such models do not routinely take into account attitudes or intrinsic values. Stakeholder perceptions of moral correctness, and the intrinsic value of natural resources such as water and minerals, for example, do not generally feature high in the assessment of investments. Operating within an SD frame calls for financial rules and behaviour to be adjusted to reflect much more fully the views of stakeholders from both domestic and affected remote communities, present and future.

Heightened stakeholder awareness of environmental issues presents both opportunities and liabilities for financial service institutions. On the one hand, a greater green consciousness opens opportunities for environmentally responsible investments (for example, in environmental technologies, in companies with strong environmental records, and in green investment funds themselves). On the other hand, investment in an activity perceived as not environmentally beneficial may result in damaged reputations, loss of business, and financial disadvantage, along with potential for costly remediation.

At the UNEP 1998 conference, banking leaders spoke of the required shift in the financial services industry sector as a paradigm shift towards a triple bottom line.[6] Key stated themes by speakers at the UNEP 1998 conference included the need for environmental policy as a basis for improved risk management, along with more robust risk assessment practices in credit decisions, and greater transparency. Such transparency was seen to be possible through the incorporation of new dimensions of corporate accountability emerging in terms of corporate governance, and social reporting, as well as sustainability reporting.

SD risk assessment within the financial services sector should seek to efficiently and equitably satisfy present and future economic, environmental and social needs. A greater sense of such satisfaction can be achieved by embracing both the participatory and anticipatory approaches to risk assessment, under which an attempt is made to determine the true cost of environmental and social impacts in advance of their occurrence.

25.5 The precautionary approach to environmental risk

For further guidance in pursuing the SD challenge, the financial services sector can look to the *precautionary principle*. In essence, the precautionary principle requires action to prevent serious and irreversible damage before harm can be scientifically demonstrated or economically assessed (Rogers *et al.* 1997: 343). The precautionary principle has

---

6   The notion of the triple bottom line, as propounded by Elkington (1997), is inherent in the SD concept, but appears, on the surface at least, to be a more attainable agenda for action within the financial services sector than, say, the notion of full-cost accounting which would necessitate radical change at a far more fundamental level and on a far broader scale.

emerged in response to the need for an effective method for dealing with risks and uncertainties in implementing sustainable development.

Emphasis on the preventative and precautionary approaches to decision-making denotes a shift towards attempts to manage risks that involve the environment and communities. Managing risk means finding ways to avoid, reduce, mitigate, or simply learning to live with risks. How this is done often depends on the acceptability of the risk. Some risks are considered unacceptable, with some societies being prepared to pay a high cost to avoid such risks. Other risks may be more acceptable.[7] Two main factors affecting stakeholders' willingness to accept risk are the degree to which they believe they are personally involved in the decision to accept the risk, and the extent to which the risk is incurred voluntarily. In either case, stakeholders need to be aware of the risks they are likely to face.

Scientific uncertainties and methodological limitations in quantitative risk assessment strike at the core of environmental decision-making and financial risk management strategies. Knowledge of traditional financial risk is often presented as 'correct' answers to factual questions. But, in a report to the US Congress, Schierow (1994: 2-10) notes that, for environmental hazards (and for most social and ecological effects), there exists little data, and methods used to capture this data are controversial, at best.

Sustainability reporting can be seen as an attempt to embrace the precautionary principle. In communicating issues of concern and the work being done to address such issues, and, where possible, citing indicators of progress, there is greater potential for meaningful stakeholder participation. The negative consequences of environmental and social risk uncertainty within the financial services sector can be further ameliorated by increased use of peer review, monitoring and post hoc assessment.

25.6 In the wake of the Ex–Im Bank decision

Many international environmental lobby groups have become involved in discussions and action around the Three Gorges Dam Project, often citing the Ex–Im Bank decision not to issue letters of interest for the project as a landmark decision (Probe International 1998). In the wake of the Ex–Im Bank decision and the divergent decisions of other similar agencies, lobby groups have called for worldwide agreement on common environmental standards for foreign investments and exports. Lobby group campaigns have targeted other sources of project finance. As a result, major financial services institutions such as Merrill Lynch, Morgan Stanley Dean Witter and Salomon Smith Barney are being exposed to criticism, based on association with environmentally sensitive investments.

---

7 Given that evaluation of risk is very subjective, financial institutions face an even greater dilemma in operating outside their countries of origin as to what standards they should apply. The solution lies in the participative approach embodied in sustainability efforts which underscores the importance of understanding the perspectives of multiple stakeholders, those in affected local communities, as well as others, internationally.

These more recent campaigns strike at the very heart of financial organisations: their shareholders. Shareholders' perceptions of the projects being financed by the institutions in whom they invest are affected by how problems are framed or presented. Traditional financial risk assessment elements of financial, technical, economic and political/legal risk are based on expert knowledge, and focus on direct and indirect consequences, with high levels of uncertainty. It is this uncertainty that environmental lobby groups are using as a leverage tool. Use of expert knowledge as the basis for presenting risk raises problems as, ironically, environmental risk and hazards for which stakeholder ignorance/conflict seems to upset experts most (e.g. ecological effects, flooding and earthquakes) are often those for which expert knowledge is most uncertain.

Environmental lobby groups are focusing on the *reputation risk* elements of the environmental and social risk assessment stages. For example, in May 1999, four US environmental groups, the International Rivers Network, Friends of the Earth, the Sierra Club and Environmental Defence, publicly challenged a host of financial services industry institutions to 'comply with their environmental rhetoric and to establish sound polices to stop foreign capital flows to the Three Gorges Project' (International Rivers Network 1999).

Both public and private institutions were targeted, including letters to Salomon Smith Barney, Merrill Lynch & Co., Inc., Goldman, Sachs & Co., The Nature Conservancy, the United Nations Environment Programme and the World Bank. The letters and associated media releases pledged that, until investment banks adopted polices that precluded them from providing direct or indirect support for projects such as the Three Gorges Dam Project, activist groups were committed to enlisting the support of these companies' clients and shareholders to ensure that their concerns were addressed.

Such efforts on the part of activists have already yielded results. In April 1999, the demands of shareholders concerned with potential association with the Three Gorges Dam Project resulted in Morgan Stanley Dean Witter management agreeing to develop social and environmental guidelines for their lending, investment and underwriting practices. Earlier in 1997, BankAmerica had already responded to activists' concerns by drafting a policy specific to the Three Gorges Dam Project. This action followed both the World Bank's refusal for funding and the Ex–Im Bank decision not to participate.

The potential for media exposure, customer boycotts and public protest has resulted in a small but increasing number of banks adopting mitigating strategies to limit their exposure to reputation risk. Policies and internal procedures to assess and manage risk are, however, just one focus of attention. On a more positive note, financing environmentally beneficial projects and technologies from wind energy projects through to water purification systems can serve to boost reputations. Moreover, there has been an increase in the number and status of investment funds offering individual and institutional investors the opportunity to invest in companies that have been selected not only for financial performance, but also for their performance according to environmental and social indicators.

There is some evidence to suggest, then, that financial services institutions are rethinking the traditional risk management approach which has been described as reactive and defensive (Brkic 1999). The adoption of innovative, proactive strategies to capture new markets, and the refusal to participate in environmentally suspect ones, is fundamental to addressing the economic, environmental and social elements of SD.

25.7 Conclusion

The Three Gorges Dam Project highlights a fundamental dilemma in operationalising the SD concept that is likely to remain for years to come: how to balance the economic and commercial interests of development with environmental and social responsibilities. It is a problem for China and other developing nations, but equally it is a problem for the rest of the world where international financial institutions' involvement is a prerequisite for the completion of development projects.

Banking enterprises seeking to work within the SD framework cannot do so in isolation. The minimisation of potentially negative impacts of foreign investment requires both host and sponsor countries to strengthen social and environmental policies and programmes. Indeed, while all financial service institutions operate within governmentally regulated frameworks to a greater or lesser degree, it may well be that government export credit agencies hold the key to operationalising government policy in regard to SD globally.

The lead of Ex–Im Bank and the success of environmental lobby groups in the wake of the Ex–Im Bank decision not to participate in the Three Gorges Dam Project, we contend, introduces into the public arena an example of both environmental and social responsibility in credit decisions. That Ex–Im's decision was based primarily on environmental and social factors, and deliberately de-emphasised creditworthiness, suggests a rethinking of the risk assessment priorities within the decision process for development projects.

Financial institutions, we contend, have an important role to play in SD by both integrating and giving greater weight to environmental and social considerations in their core investment and lending business. Rather than anthropocentric, utility-based decisions being made, greater weighting of ecocentric considerations based on the precautionary principle with a long-term focus is signalled as the way ahead. As financial service institutions' greatest environmental impact is in their lending, robust environmental and social assessment practices are required to improve risk management.

The role of environmental lobby groups and other stakeholder representatives in shaping this new moral dimension of financial institutions should not be underestimated. We conclude with a sector challenge for the financial services industry for more transparency in international trade financing. If the use of risk assessment is used to justify only 'development', and ignores the environmental and social components of SD, then the financial services sector will not be achieving its role in helping to build a sustainable world.

THE HUNGARIAN ENVIRONMENTAL CREDIT LINE

Zsolt Pásztor

Deloitte & Touche,
Hungary

Dénes Bulkai

European Bank for Reconstruction
and Development

The Hungarian Ministry for Environment and Regional Policy (the Ministry), the European Bank for Reconstruction and Development (EBRD) and the European Commission (EC) have together agreed to create a revolving Environmental Credit Line (ECL) to co-fund certain projects that generate environmental benefits. By 'revolving credit' it is meant that the proceeds of loan repayment may be re-lent to other suitable projects. The main reason for establishing the ECL was to foster environmentally sound development (one of the major goals of the EBRD, as outlined below) as part of the overall drive to improve the environmental state of Central and Eastern European countries.

26.1 The EBRD

The EBRD was established in 1991 to foster the transition towards market-oriented economies in the 26 countries of Central and Eastern Europe (CEE) and the former Soviet Union. This was to be achieved by promoting private entrepreneurial activities in particular. The EBRD is the largest single foreign direct investor in its region. For every euro invested by EBRD, a further € 2.6, on average, is mobilised from other sources.

The EBRD is directed by its mandate to 'promote, in the full range of its activities, environmentally sound and sustainable development, and the bank is strongly committed to this mandate'. One specific step taken by the EBRD to address this mandate is to ensure that all of its investment and technical co-operation activities undergo environmental appraisal as part of the overall financial, economic, legal and technical due diligence that is carried out. Using the OECD's definition of environmental and health and safety expenditure, nearly 20% of the EBRD's total annual commitments, which are currently over €2 billion, are devoted to environmental improvements.

26.2 Central and Eastern European overview

The decades of central planning in CEE countries and in the former Soviet Union, and the peculiar priorities and methods it embodied, left a legacy of marked environmental degradation that is taking a great deal of time, resources, effort and commitment to overcome. Although under socialism environmental policies and management were characterised by stringent environmental standards and high non-compliance penalties, the implementation, monitoring and enforcement of this system was generally feeble. As a result, it has been estimated that well over €100 billion is still needed to transform the environmental infrastructure of the ten EU accession countries of Central and Eastern Europe, including investments in water supply, sewerage systems, waste-water treatment, municipal solid waste services and heating networks. This requires companies to consider environmental issues carefully when investing in these countries, because of possible environmental liabilities and environmental costs.

26.3 Creation of the Environmental Credit Line

26.3.1 Background

The EBRD has recognised that environment-related investments in CEE countries cannot be funded by governments alone. The private sector, particularly those multinational enterprises that invest in the transitional countries, has a crucial role to play in disseminating best practice, by financing investments in energy efficiency and pollution control, and by helping to 'jump-start' the manufacture of environment-related products.

As a result the EBRD has initiated several programmes to promote the financing of proactive environmental and energy efficiency investments through its financial intermediaries. One of these programmes is the ECL, for which Hungary was chosen as a recipient country. The key reasons for its selection were the advanced implementation of EU regulations and directives there, the country's recent strong economic performance, and the attention given to environmental issues there.

Following the selection, the Hungarian Ministry for Environment and Regional Policy, the EBRD and the EC agreed to create a revolving credit agreement.

The financial intermediary, Budapest Bank (BB), was selected by a tendering process. The Revolving Credit Agreement between EBRD and BB was signed in December 1996, for up to €10 million, available in instalments. The Phare capital grant amounts to €5 million.

In accordance with EBRD's mandate, all projects requiring credit must undergo environmental appraisal. To provide BB with environmental advisory expertise, two consulting companies were selected by a tendering process. Coopers & Lybrand was retained to identify projects with satisfactory environmental benefits. It assisted BB in the early stage of the credit line. In addition Deloitte & Touche, in association with Tractebel Engineering, was engaged as environmental manager (EM) to conduct environmental appraisals on the proposed projects. The consulting firm was selected because its Hungarian practice has extensive experience related to the ECL. It has conducted numerous environmental due diligence surveys, related mainly to the privatisation of Hungarian and CEE companies. It also developed an *Environmental Handbook* (Deloitte & Touche 1998) for a major Hungarian commercial bank, incorporating environmental appraisal with credit appraisal.

Under the credit line EBRD provides a loan and Phare provides grants to BB. BB combines these sources of funding with its own funds to make sub-loans. The EBRD funds and BB's own funds, provided at commercial interest rates, are blended with the interest-free Phare funds at a blending ratio of 2.5 (EBRD + BB) to 1 (Phare). This reduces the overall cost of borrowing by some 30% compared to full market rates, and this benefit is passed on to the project recipients.

The credit line became fully operational in early 1998. By the end of September 1999, 30 projects had been appraised. Of the €17.5 million available under the first tranche, €13.2 million has been committed, or offers made.

The details of the operation, including sub-loan approval and environmental appraisal, as well as the appraised and selected projects, are discussed below.

26.3.2 Budapest Bank

Budapest Bank is the seventh-largest bank in Hungary in terms of total assets, and sixth in terms of equity. BB's 1997 year-end IAS audited accounts show consolidated total assets of US$1.3 billion and shareholders' equity of US$146 million. Traditionally BB's main business has been corporate banking—a market characterised by some 150 large corporations and some 80,000 SMEs. BB's market share in this sector is estimated at between 4% and 5%, depending on maturity, currency and the type of customer. With competition in the larger corporate sector becoming more intense, due to liberalisation and the entry of foreign banks into the Hungarian domestic market, BB's strategy has been to build up market share in the mid-corporate segment and to develop its retail banking business.

26.3.3 Goals and conditions of the ECL

The objective of the ECL is to offer preferential loans to private-sector companies for environmental protection investments to help achieve compliance with the Hungarian environmental regulations and EU environmental standards, and to further improve the environmental performance of Hungarian companies. The loans can be used for founding, making, maintaining and extending industrial and other productive investments.

The main benefits arising from the credit line include:

- An increase in investments in the environmental protection sector

- Investment by the private sector in environmental protection

- An increase in the capabilities of privately owned banks and companies to assess the environmental benefits of investments

A detailed description of environmental protection aims and conditions is given in the eligibility criteria of the credit line. The eligibility criteria include the types of project to be supported by the credit line, as well as evaluation measures, specific conditions, priorities and certain definitions (such as the definition of the environmental protection industry). Given that the eligibility criteria are lengthy and complicated, they will not be presented in detail in this chapter. Instead, general conditions of utilisation, along with a few key criteria, will be examined.

One important criterion of eligibility is that borrowers under the credit line must be private companies or, in the case of companies legally owned or controlled by the public sector, must be run on a commercial basis, operating in a competitive market environment and implementing a programme for achieving private ownership and control.

In accordance with the aims of the programme, loans can be given for the following:

- Investment projects planned by solvent companies that directly serve the cause of environmental protection

- Projects that reduce costs or enhance capacities by reducing the emission of pollutants

- Environmental protection investments which, though they do not generate business profit, will help the investors comply with future environmental protection standards

- Investments and developments aimed at preventing environmental pollution; a reduction in the environmental load; encouraging environmentally friendly consumer behaviour and promotion of the application of environmentally friendly materials; and facilitating the recollection and utilisation of wastes generated from various products

- The recycling, processing and collection of waste-generating products

Priority is given to projects that:

- Are connected with Hungary's National Environmental Protection Programme, or other governmental programmes

- Are associated with solving environmental problems in contiguous regions

- Carry out environmental developments with the co-operation of several participants

- Serve the establishment of the environmental protection industry

Industrial manufacturing investments and developments (extensions and modernisation) can be supported if:

- They apply the BAT (best available technology) principle.

- Their products comply with the requirements of 'clean production', namely that the company manufactures environmentally friendly products throughout its lifetime.

- They use 'clean technology'.

26.4 Operation of the credit line

26.4.1 Sub-loan approval procedures

Sub-loans granted amount to between € 200,000 and € 1.8 million per project, with the maximum amount awarded to a single beneficiary being € 3 million. Although there is no restriction on the size of the project or borrower, given these borrowing limits and BB's sector presence, the facility was conceived with medium-sized enterprises in mind.

BB may receive applications for sub-loans from any source, including those from a portfolio of projects developed through Phare programmes in the environmental sector, arising from marketing campaigns organised by BB or proposed by the Ministry, but not from the environmental manager (EM). When BB receives a sub-loan application, it forwards it to the EM, who reviews it on technical grounds. In the early stage of ECL operation Coopers & Lybrand assisted BB by conducting the pre-screening of the projects.

The EM either approves or rejects the sub-loan within 20 working days of receipt of the application; the EM has to furnish a justification of its decision. After obtaining the EM's written approval of a sub-loan, BB undertakes the financial assessment of the application and bears sole responsibility for granting or refusing a sub-loan.

26.4.2 Environmental appraisals

Environmental appraisal is a process that covers the whole life of a project, from submission of the project application to the winding up of the project and repayment of the loan.

Due to the nature and objectives of the ECL, as well as the mandate of EBRD, different kinds of environmental investigations are performed by the EM. These investigations involve:

- Eligibility criteria assessment
- An environmental benefit assessment
- An environmental audit
- Monitoring

The environmental appraisal process has been designed for ECL operations based on (a) EBRD's environmental procedures; (b) the evaluation procedure of the Hungarian Central Environmental Protection Fund; and (c) the *Environmental Handbook* developed by Deloitte & Touche Hungary for financial institutions.

The role of the EM is to carry out these investigations. Budapest Bank's role is to review the results of environmental appraisal and to ensure that the EM's findings are taken into account in operation financing and implementation.

26.4.2.1 Eligibility criteria assessment

All projects submitted are reviewed to filter and reject at an early stage any project that cannot be supported by the credit line. Projects that fail to comply with the relevant general and/or actual environmental protection and health provisions (e.g. technology using CFCs) cannot be approved at the technical evaluation stage.

The EM also determines whether an environmental impact assessment (EIA) should be conducted and whether the environmental licence (if any) has been granted. If required, the EIA is not conducted by the EM.

26.4.2.2 Environmental benefit assessment

The purpose of environmental benefit assessment is to gauge the environmental advantages and disadvantages of the proposed project.

In certain projects environmental advantages can be easily quantified; examples include the installation of an air filter or a waste-water treatment plant. In other cases, environmental advantages are difficult to quantify. Such cases might include emission reduction projects, the construction of a hazardous waste storage facility at a given company to reduce harmful impacts, or supporting the establishment of environmental protection industry.

Based on the net balance of advantages and disadvantages, the project may be approved or rejected.

26.4.2.3 Environmental audit

Environmental audits are typically required by the EBRD before loans are granted. One aim of the credit line is to encourage this practice among Hungarian banks and companies.

Based on the findings of an environmental audit, environmental enhancement measures or an environmental action plan could be prescribed for the company. Early incorporation of environmental enhancement measures into the operational design is likely to improve the overall efficiency of an enterprise and thus increase its medium- to long-term profitability. It may also help to establish baseline conditions for agreeing on responsibility for environmental damage, or the valuation of immovable assets that the bank may consider taking as security.

The EM has developed a four-phase approach protocol for environmental audits: (1) identification of environmental issues based on a questionnaire and a short site visit; (2) analysis of existing environmental liabilities based on more detailed data gathering; (3) a detailed site investigation including drillings; and (4) review of action plan based on the audit's findings.

The audit protocol used for the assessment of the ECL projects is based on this approach and on the EBRD's environmental audit protocol.

26.4.2.4 Monitoring

Monitoring is an important aspect of the environmental appraisal process. Environmental monitoring, in accordance with the aims of the credit line and other environmental investigations, serves two distinct purposes.

The first—related to environmental benefit assessment—is to undertake reviews of financed projects in order to verify that the promised environmental benefits have been realised, and to ensure that the applicable environmental regulations and standards have been respected, both during installation and operation. The second—related to environmental auditing—is to undertake a review of the environmental performance of the company. It keeps track of the ongoing environmental impact associated with operations and the effectiveness of mitigation measures used as a 'feedback' mechanism.

Monitoring includes the completion of a follow-up questionnaire as well as site inspections. Monitoring might be undertaken, with the agreement of BB, on a routine or occasional basis. The findings of environmental monitoring are an integral part of the credit monitoring report. From the results of environmental monitoring, BB might, if necessary, change loan conditions, ask for immediate repayment, or amend environmental covenants.

26.5 Appraised projects

By the end of September 1999 some 90 inquiries had been received. Sixty-five applications were then submitted to BB, and 30 were forwarded to the EM for environmental appraisal. Of these, 25 were approved, while the environmental appraisal of five projects is in process. Fifteen of the 25 approved projects were contracted or committed. Some applications were rejected by BB on account of high environmental risks or insufficient financial performance, and some were withdrawn by the applicants themselves. Generally, the reason for withdrawal was that the investment had been postponed, or in a few cases financing had been obtained from other sources.

As a result of the involvement of Coopers & Lybrand in the early stage of the credit line, and discussions between BB and the EM, no projects were rejected on the grounds of non-compliance with eligibility criteria or insufficient environmental benefits.

In cases where the environmental eligibility of a project is not evident, the EM initiates a discussion with EBRD and the Ministry to get their opinions.

A variety of appraised projects is listed below.

- Construction of a residue processing plant

- Construction of a cooling tower, a damage prevention unit and connection of the sewerage system to the public sewer

- Production capacity expansion of mixing and band units

- Purchase of new environmentally friendly buses

- Construction of a collection and recycling plant for plastic waste

- Reconstruction of the bell/furnace park of a tempering plant

- Establishment of hazardous waste landfill

- Converter hall dust extraction and precipitation

- Introduction of freon-free technology in the production of refrigerators

▧ Construction of a sewage cleaning plant

▧ Reduction of the salt content of the waste-water and recycling of the salt produced

▧ Construction of modern gas production equipment

▧ Modernisation and expansion of manufacturing capacity to produce air purity protection systems

The successful applications fall into the environmental categories and industrial sectors shown in Table 26.1. Despite the fact that many projects addressed only one area (e.g. air protection, waste management, etc.), most of them have multiple benefits, such as the protection of air purity, quantity and quality of water supplies and reduction of harmful impacts of wastes.

Environmental categories	Industrial sectors
Air pollution: 66%	Public transport: 22%
Water pollution: 17%	Chemical industry: 28%
Solid waste: 17%	Food processing: 22%
	Oil industry: 7%
	Machinery: 7%

Table 26.1 **Breakdown of successful applications**

26.6 Case studies

A few case studies are presented here to give an overview of the nature of the projects. Case studies were selected in such a way as to show the variety of

▧ **Topics** (air emissions, waste-water, waste management, etc.)

▧ **Technological solutions** (end-of-pipe technology, cleaner production, new technology, technological modifications)

▧ **Sizes of the companies** involved (small, medium, large)

▧ **Incentives** for the investment (reduction of environmental load, increasing competitiveness, the founding of an environment protection industry, etc.)

▧ Aspects of **environmental performance and liability**

▧ Results of the **overall appraisal** (project approval, rejection)

Case studies are presented without naming the applicant. Each case study concentrates on the issues that were of key importance in the final decision-making process, i.e. in the approval or rejection of the project. Based on the assessments performed to date, the most important conclusions drawn are as follows:

- For companies with multiple sites, it is necessary to take all sites into account, and concentrate on those where contamination and non-compliance can be expected. Often environmental risk and liability is identified at a site different from the investment site.

- It is worth consulting an environmental specialist at an early stage of the credit application, or meeting with the prospective borrower in doubtful cases. It may save time and avoid surprises in later phases.

- The level of environmental investigation might depend on (and have to be carried out in accordance with) the size of the loan, the area of company's operation, financial performance, history, and general environmental performance.

- Evidence of an existing environmental audit report, a realistic environmental action plan, an environmental policy, and a sound environmental strategy all shorten the time spent on the environmental assessment and build confidence in the company, even if it has environmental liabilities. These suggest that the company is able to manage and solve its environmental problems without 'big surprises', thereby reducing environmental risks.

26.6.1 Case 1

Gas production company: installation of a modern gas production facility

The main activity of the company is the production of a variety of gases. At present gases are produced in old facilities. The company intends to install a new, modern air separation facility. This is in accordance with an agreement it reached with a major client.

The most important environmental benefit of the new facility will be the reduction in emissions of air pollutants owing to lower energy consumption. The new technology will lead to a saving of some 62,686 MWh/year, which amounts to 0.2% of Hungary's total energy production. In this case it is difficult to quantify the air emission reduction but it is partly proportional to the reduction in consumption.

The company has no environmental liabilities for historical contamination. Its current environmental performance is good, and the company strives continually to improve it. Furthermore, the company has implemented the ISO 14001 standard and operates according to that standard. A strong environmental commitment, a viable environmental strategy, proven efforts in environmental issues, as well as strong financial performance all contributed to the positive result of environmental and financial appraisal.

26.6.2 Case 2

Plastic waste processing company: collection and recycling plant

The company was created in 1997. Its task is to receive, select and prepare plastic waste materials for further processing. The bulk of the prepared waste is then forwarded to another company and recycled.

The key factor motivating the implementation of the project was that Hungary's production of plastic waste amounts to 150,000–200,000 tons annually. However, only a fraction of that quantity is recycled at present; most plastic waste is simply incinerated or deposited at landfill sites.

The aim of the project is to build a plastic waste collection and recycling facility with a capacity of 4,200 tons a year.

The environmental benefit appraisal revealed that the company would be able to collect and recycle 4,200 tons of polluted and mixed plastic waste per year (2.1%–2.8% of the Hungarian total). Of this amount, 4,000 tons of re-usable material (re-granulates, base material for further processing) can be produced.

The plant is to be built in an unpolluted area. As there is no polluting activity, no environmental problems have been identified. The company has a reliable environmental and business plan. As no financial or environmental problems have been identified, the project has been approved.

26.6.3 Case 3

Waste-processing plant: construction of iron-containing waste processing plant

The company concerned in this application was established in 1998 to install and operate a waste processing plant.

The following estimated quantities of material have amassed at disposal sites and in containers at Hungarian smelters and steelworks: 8 million tons of slag derived from smelting; approximately 250,000 tons of slurry containing iron; and some 25,000 tons of waste from demolished furnaces. At present a major portion of iron-containing waste is also taken to disposal sites. The disposal site for this hazardous waste does not have the prescribed technical protection, so it is deemed to be a potential source of environmental pollution.

The purpose of the project is to build a waste-processing plant with a capacity of 160,000 tons, that would allow the recycling of ferrous wastes that are difficult to deal with, polluted, and semi-liquid or fine-grained in consistency.

The environmental benefit appraisal revealed that the plant would allow recently generated ferrous wastes to be utilised, as well as permit the emptying and closure of old factory waste-storage facilities. This would reduce the harmful impact of hazardous wastes. Furthermore, with the material produced the company could replace scrap iron in steel-making and iron ore in the manufacture of pig iron. The process does not produce industrial waste-water. The flue gas is cleaned with electrofilters and no hazardous waste is created during the process.

A negative environmental effect of the project would be the emission of air pollutants, amounting to 300,000 m³/hr of flue gas, and 27 kg/hr of dust. However, the expected result of the project will generate an environmental benefit that significantly offsets the emissions, by converting a major amount of hazardous pollution-causing waste into usable raw material.

Although the project would have produced a number of environmental benefits, the company was asked to conduct further investigations and clarify a number of issues arising from (a) an unexpected decision by the environmental inspectorate regarding the issue of the environmental permit; and (b) the incompleteness of the company's business plan.

26.7 Conclusions

One and half years of experience has proved that the creation of the ECL was worthwhile. The ECL is becoming better known and more popular among Hungarian companies and has proved to be a useful and important tool for environmental improvement. This is confirmed by the fact that, to date, more than 30 project applications have been appraised by the EM.

The ECL has very important advantages in several areas:

- It supports private-sector projects that enable beneficiaries to increase competitiveness and reach compliance with Hungarian and EU environmental standards.

- It assists government policy aimed at improving the environment through a private-sector financing instrument.

- It facilitates institutional and banking development by providing a financing instrument tailored to medium-sized companies.

- It helps to incorporate environmental assessments as part of loan appraisal procedures in banks. It is interesting to note that other commercial banks have also started to apply environmental appraisal for a certain group of credits, though admittedly not to a very deep level.

- It has enabled BB and a number of other companies to become familiar with environmental appraisal procedures.

Experience has shown that the ECL is a good way for banks to attract the attention of, and to establish contact with, existing and potential clients. Companies that have a strong environmental performance, an environmental strategy, a viable action plan to achieve the strategy, an environmental management system, or published corporate environmental reports, are more attractive to the banks. By recognising such companies' commitment to environmental issues, banks encourage them to better their environmental performance and contribute in this way to sustainable development. At the same time, the banks reduce their risks of granting bad loans.

The importance of environmental issues and risks is also demonstrated by the fact that the Federation of European Accountants is pressing for an increase in companies' disclosure of environmental costs, liabilities and other issues in their financial statements. The new international accounting standards being drafted by the International Accounting Standards Committee also require the inclusion of such items.

A similar ECL could play an important role and might achieve the same effect in other CEE counties, as well as in economically less developed EU countries. The commercial interest rates in the transition countries are very high, particularly for companies fighting to survive. Rates below the commercial level can play the role of catalyst in environmentally desirable projects.

Such a credit line also has an advantage compared to non-refundable aid. While non-refundable aid can solve only one problem, with a lower interest rate credit several problems can be solved with the same amount of aid. This makes the utilisation of the aid more efficient. However, for the ECL to operate efficiently, relatively advanced environmental regulations and a sound banking system are required, as well as strong environmental enforcement.

THE GROWTH AND ENVIRONMENT SCHEME

The EU, the financial sector and small and medium-sized enterprises as partners in promoting sustainability

Marc Leistner

European Investment Fund, Luxembourg

The growth and environment scheme is designed to facilitate environmentally friendly investments by SMEs (small or medium-sized enterprises) with up to 100 employees in the European Union. SMEs constitute by far the majority of enterprises active in the European Union, so, while on an individual basis larger corporations may potentially be significantly more polluting than individual SMEs, the potential of environmental pollution by SMEs is enormous when viewed on an aggregate basis. However, SMEs often do not have the financial means or the same degree of access to financing as larger corporations when faced with the need to invest, and so legislation requiring environment-related investment may well be a significant burden. It was with this predicament in mind that the Growth and Environment (G&E) Scheme was initiated by the European Parliament in 1995. Apart from the immediate material benefit enjoyed by SMEs and banks, a primary aim of the scheme is to promote environmental awareness among the parties involved.

Under the G&E Scheme, SMEs benefit from preferential financing terms, i.e. terms that are more favourable than those that the bank would normally charge a borrower of the same risk category in similar conditions, for environmentally friendly investments. Such preferential terms may take the form of a lower interest rate, improved access to financing or a waiver of charges such as commitment or cancellation fees. These benefits are granted to the relevant SMEs by the financing bank, on the basis of a contract between the bank and the European Investment Fund (EIF),[1] who manages the scheme. According to this contract (framework guarantee agreement), the EIF provides a free-of-charge guarantee to the financing bank or intermediary for up to 50% of each loan extended to SMEs under the scheme. The benefit granted to the SME by the bank is therefore a 'transfer' of the benefit that the intermediary itself enjoys on account of the guarantee. The scheme is sponsored by the European Commission and guarantee premiums for the guarantees extended to banks by the EIF are accordingly paid by the budget of the European Union.

27.1 Scope of the scheme

The scheme is currently being operated as a pilot project of the European Union. Before its parameters were finalised in 1995, several banks from different member states of the European Union were consulted and invited to comment on the proposed project. At a later stage, following an internal review by the EIF in spring 1998, the scheme was revised in agreement with the European Commission in order to benefit from experience gathered by all parties concerned in the first period of the scheme's implementation without, however, changing the basic parameters.

The European Commission has made an amount of €25.0 million available for the scheme.[2] Apart from covering guarantee premiums, these funds are also available for paying a part of the marketing costs of participating banks and the EIF in relation to the scheme. The operation of the scheme is restricted to the European Union and investments must take place within its territory.

The network of banks participating in the scheme currently consists of 25 institutions[3] and covers all 15 member states of the European Union. Typically, banks administer the scheme only within one country, their home market, because of the established contact with SME clients. Participating banks have been selected to participate in the scheme on

---

1　The EIF was established in 1994 following a decision of the Heads of State and Government of the European Union at their summit in Edinburgh in December 1992. It is a financial institution of the European Union that supports the integration of the European economy by promoting medium- and long-term investment in two fields essential to the development of the European economy: TENs (i.e. Trans-European Networks [infrastructure projects in the areas of energy, telecommunications and transport]) and SMEs.

2　From budgetary allocations in the years 1995–97.

3　The participating institutions are the following (in alphabetical order by country then bank): Bank Austria, Raiffeisen Zentralbank (Austria); Générale de Banque, KBC Bank (Belgium); Merkur (Denmark); Finnvera (Finland); Banque Populaire du Haut-Rhin, Caisse Nationale de Crédit Agricole, Crédit Lyonnais (France); Deutsche Ausgleichsbank, Kreditanstalt für Wiederaufbau (Germany); Alpha Credit Bank, Ionian & Popular Bank (Greece); Allied Irish Banks (Ireland); Banca Monte dei Paschi di Siena, Banca Popolare di Verona, Finlombarda/Cariplo/Mediocredito Lombardo (Italy); Banque Générale du Luxembourg (Luxembourg); ING Bank, Rabobank (Netherlands); Banco Comercial Português (Portugal); Banco Bilbao Vizcaya, Caja de Ahorros y Monte de Piedad de Madrid (Spain); FöreningsSparbanken (Sweden); Barclays Bank (UK). An updated list of intermediaries, including contact names and telephone numbers, is maintained on the EIF's website, www.eif.org.

the basis of their application following a Call for Expression of Interest.[4] Great significance is attached to the level of commitment to environmental activities set out in the bank's application. However, past activity in the environmental field is not a precondition for acceptance into the G&E Scheme, although this would be a supporting factor. It is equally possible that the bank expresses in a credible way its commitment to use the scheme to launch its activity in this area. The resources an intermediary intends to allocate to the implementation of the scheme is an important indication in this regard.

27.2 Operation of the scheme

The scheme is operated on the basis of virtually full delegation by the EIF to the intermediaries. Subject to certain parameters, it is entirely the intermediary's responsibility to select the SMEs that can benefit from the scheme and the EIF is not involved in individual credit decisions. SMEs wishing to enjoy support under the scheme should therefore contact the respective intermediaries.[5] The framework guarantee agreement between the EIF and the intermediary specifies the total maximum loan volume of the credit portfolio covered by the EIF under the scheme and the intermediary reports to the EIF once every calendar quarter on the loans that have been included in its G&E portfolio.

The framework guarantee agreement between the EIF and the intermediary is a standard contract which may, however, require limited adjustments to allow for the specific structure of individual intermediaries (e.g. decentralised as opposed to centralised structure). Furthermore, the contract is in all cases governed by the law of the intermediary's country and this too may make some limited contractual changes necessary.

The EIF has the status of a Multilateral Development Bank under the European Union's solvency ratio directive. This means that financial institutions benefiting from an EIF guarantee under the scheme are allowed to allocate capital to the part of the loan covered by the EIF guarantee at the rate of 20% instead of 100%. This is, of course, a substantial advantage in addition to the lower risk and provisioning costs associated with the EIF guarantee.

It should be noted that the guarantee premium received by the EIF from the European Commission for assuming a part of the bank's risk is determined upfront and that any risk exceeding that covered by the premium is borne by the EIF on its own balance sheet. The EIF, therefore, needs to ensure best practice by intermediaries and accordingly undertakes a detailed due diligence of each potential intermediary's credit policy, including any

---

4   The initial call was published in the *Official Journal of the European Union* on 12 July 95 (OJ 95/C 177/08); it was followed by a second call distributed to the banking associations of the 15 member states of the European Union in 1997 and it is envisaged that further restricted calls in some countries of the European Union may take place in the future in order to extend the network as appropriate, subject to availability of funds.

5   See footnote 3.

credit scoring system used, before the intermediary is finally selected. Banks apply their normal credit policy in the operation of the scheme.

Apart from the criterion of environmental eligibility, the main parameters of the scheme are the following: loans must be to SMEs with not more than 100 employees, with special preference being given to SMEs with not more than 50 employees.[6] Individual loan amounts can be for up to €1 million. The maturity of individual loans may be from three up to ten years, with individual guarantee cover by the EIF being restricted to a maximum of seven years. Only newly signed investment loans qualify. Investments must be new for the borrower, must be implemented in a member state of the European Union and must be directly related to the borrower's business activities and objectives.

The EIF guarantee is a residual loss guarantee: when a loan defaults, the EIF pays 50% of the loss that remains after any recoveries from collateral have taken place. Default and recovery procedures are also largely delegated to the participating institution.

27.3 Environmental eligibility

Being aimed at environmentally friendly investments, environmental eligibility is, of course, the crucial criterion under the Growth and Environment Scheme. It is required that investments must produce significant environmental benefits. Environmental benefits may be the main purpose of the investment: for example, when a company specifically makes an investment in order to comply with particular environmental legislation. However, it is also possible under the scheme to support investments made for other reasons: for example, investments undertaken due to relocation or to replace worn-out machinery, subject to the objective test (significant environmental benefits) being met. The only exception is for enterprises in the eco-industry: such enterprises may benefit from the scheme for any investment as long as the investment contributes to the development or production of environmentally beneficial goods or services (which will almost always be the case).

For the purposes of the scheme, the eco-industry is defined as an industry whose economic activity consists of the supply of goods or services for environmental purposes. This would include businesses specialising in air pollution control, contaminated land and water remediation, environmental consultancy services, waste-water treatment, etc. There is no limit as to the particular form of specialisation, as long as the relevant businesses fall within the general scope of the above definition of eco-industry.

No comprehensive list exists of the investments that actually produce significant environmental benefits. Not only would it be impossible to capture all the possible investments that could potentially qualify for support under the scheme, but banks and their clients are positively encouraged to identify and assess the potential opportunities

---

6   The guarantee agreement generally specifies that not more than 30% of the total loan volume in the portfolio should be for SMEs with more than 50 employees. SMEs must have net fixed assets not exceeding €75 million and must comply with the independence criterion, i.e. not more than one-third of the SME's capital may be held by a non-SME.

for benefiting from the scheme themselves, rather than relying on a standard list. This approach is intended to enhance loan officers' and their clients' awareness of environmentally relevant issues and thus realise the general aims of the scheme in a more effective and lasting way.

The EIF does, however, make information available to intermediaries that is designed to assist them in identifying projects eligible under the scheme. A dual approach is used: one looking at investments in the context of the environmental issues involved and the other applying a sectoral focus. In line with the former, the EIF provides background materials on environmental themes such as water pollution, waste generation and management, climate change, etc. The factors that impact on the problems under discussion are traced and the areas in which the activity of SMEs may be relevant are analysed. Under the sectoral approach, the EIF offers intermediaries a description of the environmental implications of selected industry sectors. When the scheme was conceived, the automotive, dry-cleaning, electroplating, foundry and printing sectors were identified as being particularly relevant for support under the scheme. However, in principle, investments in any sector are eligible for support.

The EIF also provides intermediaries with concrete examples of investments that have already been financed under the scheme or that could potentially be financed, as this greatly facilitates the identification of eligible investments. It is always emphasised that these examples are indicative only. The following examples are categorised by **environmental theme**: a smoke system with air cleaning devices (air pollution); engines with reduced levels of CO_2 emissions (climate change); wind power-generating equipment (energy saving); installation for the reduced use of non-renewable resources by a paper manufacturing company (nature protection and biodiversity); factory relocation from a residential area to an industrial area (noise pollution); solar cells for hotels (sustainable tourism).

By **sector**, the following examples—which stem from investments actually made under the scheme—are relevant: a painting machine for the use of water-soluble paint (automotive sector); a new storage hall with a floor that is water- and acid-proof (construction); a chemical waste infiltration prevention system (dry-cleaning); an air filter system installation (electroplating); energy-saving scanning and reproduction system (printing); a steel floor for a ship transporting chemicals, replacing a wooden floor that absorbed chemicals and needed regular replacement and disposal as special waste (transport).

Under the requirements of the scheme, borrowers have to fill in a one-page form ('Statement of Environmental Characteristics') briefly describing the investment and the benefit it has for the environment, while also stating whether the investment is induced by legal requirements, whether it will benefit from other public financing and whether an external environmental expert has been consulted. While consultation with an environmental expert is viewed positively, the related costs to the SME have to be taken into account and may be a discouraging factor especially for smaller loans; it is therefore not a standard requirement.

The financing bank has an important supporting role to play in relation to the evaluation of environmental eligibility. The ability of the bank to perform this function is one of the factors carefully assessed by the EIF before a framework guarantee agreement is signed. Where banks have an environmental desk, i.e. a department dedicated to environmental assessment, the evaluation of environmental eligibility is usually performed here, at least for larger loans; where none exists, the EIF encourages banks to centralise the final evaluation of environmental eligibility by allocating this function to a small group of loan officers to allow them to acquire the necessary know-how over time. In some cases, banks make use of external environmental consultants to assist them in evaluating environmental eligibility.

In spite of these combined efforts of borrower and bank to ensure that the criterion of environmental eligibility is fulfilled, there may, of course, be cases where the EIF or the European Commission take the view that this criterion has not been met. In order to avoid any uncertainty relating to the validity of the guarantee in such cases, the EIF and the European Commission have, however, undertaken not to question the validity of the guarantee, unless information relating to environmental eligibility was intentionally false. On the other hand, the EIF and the Commission reserve the right to notify intermediaries if they consider a particular investment as not being environmentally eligible and to exclude the inclusion of loans for that type of investment in the portfolio for the future.

27.4 What has been achieved so far

By the end of June 1999, some 1,400 SMEs had benefited from the Growth and Environment Scheme for total investments of €525 million. Loan amounts averaged €265,000 and the respective SMEs had an average of 19 employees.

It is more difficult to measure the progress of the scheme in promoting environmental awareness, but it may be stated with certainty that such progress is not restricted to cases that have actually led to concrete investments.

As indicated above, the scheme is operated on the basis that loan officers and clients have an essential role to play in identifying and evaluating environmental eligibility. For SMEs, this entails having to look at their own activities from an environmental perspective in order to determine whether they might qualify for support under the scheme or not. It may even extend further: an SME wanting to invest in a particular machine may be prompted to inquire from the manufacturer what environmental benefits the equipment actually has and may decide to buy an alternative if the machine does not meet the required standards.

Banks, likewise, have to scrutinise their clients' activities from an environmental point of view in order to be able to approach their clients effectively with regard to the Scheme. Although many banks already analyse environmental risks associated with the extension of credit to certain sectors or activities, it would seem that this is often for 'negative' reasons, i.e. to avoid risk. The Growth and Environment Scheme encourages a positive view: namely, to spot opportunities in the area of the environment—opportunities both for the bank and its clients, that are also in the interest of sustainability.

The banks who have, so far, been most successful in implementing the Scheme are those that have identified themselves with the scheme's environmental cause and have also used it to build or extend their own environmental image. In the first instance, this requires a commitment from management, but it also involves active internal and external marketing, internal training, awareness campaigns and possibly the changing of internal procedures. Indeed, intermediaries have been active in numerous ways to promote the scheme—for example, by organising workshops for their clients and training staff—and this has greatly contributed to enhancing environmental awareness.

27.5 Conclusion

The Growth and Environment Scheme is an example of a successful partnership between European institutions and bank intermediaries to implement public goals in a commercially attractive way. By choosing the guarantee instrument, the European Commission has significantly leveraged the amount allocated to the scheme, thereby achieving maximum support for a large number of SMEs to make environmentally friendly investments throughout the European Union. More than that, the scheme helps to promote environmental awareness among SMEs and banks in numerous ways and encourages the view that responsible, environmentally friendly investments can be rewarding.

AN ENVIRONMENTAL FUND WITH THE WWF LABEL
The importance of appropriate communication tools

Sabine Döbeli
Zürcher Kantonalbank, Switzerland

In November 1998 Swissca[1] launched an environmental fund in co-operation with World Wide Fund for Nature (WWF) Switzerland. 'Swissca Green Invest' invests its funds in the shares of international companies and has the ambitious target of tracking the MSCI World Index as a benchmark, although the fund's investment possibilities are limited by several exclusion and positive criteria. Green Invest was the first eco-efficiency fund in the Swiss market to be launched in close co-operation with a non-governmental organisation (NGO). The WWF exerted a strong influence on the evaluation criteria of the investment fund and endorsed the fund with the logo of the 'Living Planet Campaign'.[2]

The WWF can look back on a long tradition of promoting sustainable consumption. It has done so by regularly informing on the effects of consumer habits as well as by offering a wide range of ethical and environmentally compatible consumer products via joint-venture companies. Consumers can make a contribution through environmental awareness when purchasing, but also by considering environmental and ethical criteria when investing their money (Odermatt 1998). By labelling Green Invest with the Living Planet Campaign logo, WWF wants to encourage ethical consumers to influence the environmental commitment and responsibility of companies. Ethical investments are seen as one tool to make companies improve their environmental performance and give greater weight to ethical criteria in everyday business. As far as Green Invest is concerned,

1 Swissca is a joint venture of the Swiss Cantonal Banks and is a major provider of investment funds in Switzerland.
2 The Living Planet Campaign is a major WWF campaign which aims to conserve the representative treasures of nature, to save endangered species and to change patterns of resource consumption by co-operating with companies (WWF 1997).

pressure results mainly from the environmental research process, which is carried out by the environmental research team of Zürcher Kantonalbank (ZKB).

Although the research process guarantees that the environmental leaders will be found, people may not immediately recognise and accept the evaluated companies as being 'green'. Large multinational companies are often considered to be the major environmental polluters, and the improvements achieved are hardly recognised or are considered to be mere drops in the ocean. Moreover, the inclusion of a company in a green investment fund is often misinterpreted as a green label for the company concerned, which is not the purpose of the inclusion. Endorsing an environmental fund therefore included a certain reputational risk for WWF. Hence it was vital to guarantee a careful evaluation process as well as precise communication with investors.

28.1 Environmental research process for Swissca Green Invest

The WWF is known for its strong environmental commitment and high credibility. The environmental research process must do justice to these high standards and cover all sensitive areas. The process is based on four elements: exclusion criteria; financial analysis; environmental analysis; and social check (see Fig. 28.1). The purpose of the evaluation process is to identify the environmental leaders in each industry.

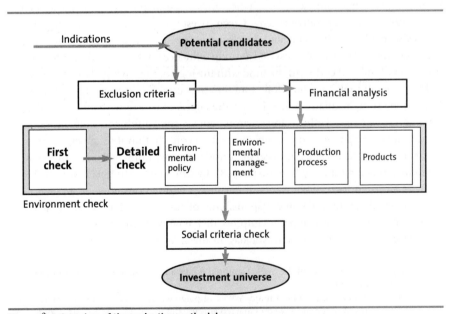

Figure 28.1 **Overview of the evaluation methodology**

28.1.1 Exclusion criteria

The exclusion criteria were defined in co-operation with the WWF and cover industries contributing heavily to the most severe environmental problems and risks worldwide. The co-operation with a pressure group required a fairly stringent exclusion of environmentally sensitive industries. The criteria were defined in a very specific manner reflecting the actual risk situation, rather than in general terms.

For example, genetic engineering was not excluded as a whole, but genetic engineering with the target of releasing manipulated organisms into the environment was excluded.

Concerning the problem of climate change, the extraction and sale of fossil fuels leads to exclusion from the fund. Furthermore, car producers and airlines are excluded, unless they implement drastic measures to reduce the average fuel consumption of their fleet.

In order to address biodiversity, exclusion criteria were defined for non-sustainable forestry and fishing. Endorsements by the Forest Stewardship Council (FSC) and the Marine Stewardship Council (MSC), both of which are promoted by the WWF, are serving as a guideline for sustainable production in these industries.

To avoid controversy over the inclusion or otherwise of a given company, the exclusion criteria were published in full in the fund brochure and were further explained in a more detailed manual for investment advisors.

28.1.2 Environmental performance analysis

As a second step the companies' environmental performance was evaluated according to the criteria defined in four major fields: environmental policy (EP), environmental management (EM), production process (PP) and product stewardship (PS). In each field indicators were defined—approximately 60 in total—to evaluate the environmental performance of each company. Table 28.1 shows some of the major indicators in each field.

Environmental policy	Environmental guidelines and their quality; environmental report and its quality; stakeholder contacts; standards required of suppliers; environmental awards and sponsoring
Environmental management	Implementation and responsibilities; audit systems; risk management; legal compliance; environmental staff; training of employees
Production process	Controlling and quantitative targets for all important inputs and outputs; measures to lower environmental impact; performance indicators
Product stewardship	Life-cycle analysis; environmental strategies in R&D; recycling and remanufacturing concepts

Table 28.1 **Major indicators in the four fields of the environmental performance analysis**

The most important sources of information are corporate environmental reports (CERs). Other sources—for instance, the databanks of environmental research centres, specialist journals or NGO web pages—are also used to collect as much information as possible before addressing the companies with questionnaires. NGO web pages are the final tool to gather the necessary information serving as a basis for a fair rating.

When all the required information is available, an environmental performance rating is carried out. ZKB has developed a tool for quantitatively rating the environmental performance of companies. The tool is based on the following elements: the environmental indicators for each of the above-named fields, a weighting factor for each indicator, a defined maximum performance for each indicator, and a maximum score. The weighting factors vary according to the main environmental impacts of different industries. Producers of electrical appliances, for example, face a higher weight in product stewardship than steel producers, because the main environmental impact of the former results from the use of the products whereas for the latter it results from the production process. The weighting factors were defined by the environmental research team and were discussed with the Advisory Council.

Comparing the company's performance for each indicator with the defined maximum performance enabled a score to be calculated for each indicator. The weighted scores are aggregated to a rating for each field and finally to a total rating for environmental performance. The final rating is expressed as a percentage of the maximum environmental performance. ZKB's Environmental Performance Rating has been attached as an example (see Fig. 28.2). In addition to the quantitative rating, qualitative information is summarised in a 'strengths-and-weaknesses' profile of the environmental performance of a company. On the basis of the rating and the qualitative summary the best-performing companies are selected for the investment universe of the Green Invest fund.

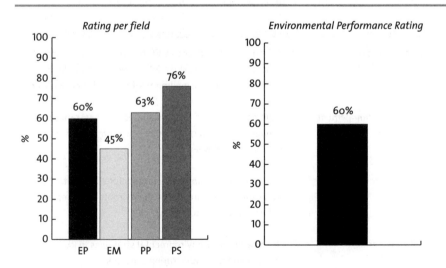

EP = environmental policy; EM = environmental management; PP = production process; PS = product stewardship

Figure 28.2 **Environmental Performance Rating of Zürcher Kantonalbank**

28.1.3 Social criteria check

There has been a shift in ethical investment from simple exclusion criteria—as often used in US pension funds—or the exclusive use of environmental criteria (as implemented by the first European environmental funds) to a wider focus with the triple bottom line of social, environmental and economical sustainability. Against this backdrop it was essential for WWF to include social criteria in the evaluation process as well. Since the data available to determine social criteria is still rather poor and little social information is currently published, a more qualitative approach was chosen for the social criteria check.

In the evaluation process various databases and specific publications are screened specifically for six main aspects (forced child labour, violation of human rights, high level of work accidents, disregard of labour laws and safety regulations, disregard of aboriginal rights, massive job cuts without redundancy measures) to gain information on non-compliance. If major non-compliance is found, a company is excluded from the investment universe. Additionally the environmental research team is currently developing a questionnaire for social screening to address social issues in as comprehensive a way as with environmental issues.

28.2 Communication tools

Co-operating with Swissca in the launch of the new investment fund has given the WWF a platform to communicate its aims and policies not only to the general public but also to new and relevant stakeholders in the world of business and finance. At the same time, however, endorsing a fund exposes the WWF to a certain risk of public criticism in the event that one of the companies in the fund causes an environmental accident or is publicly criticised. To prevent such criticism the WWF has demanded precise and inter-active communication tools, designed to maintain a constant dialogue with the stake-holders. In addition, an advisory board was set up to control the research process as well as to provide a forum for discussion about a continual improvement of the research process.

Table 28.2 gives an overview of the available tools and their relevance for the different stakeholder groups. The characteristics of the different tools are discussed below.

28.2.1 Brochures and other information material

The WWF insisted on having the underlying concept communicated in a transparent, authentic and dialogue-oriented way. The eco-leader concept was therefore described in detail, including the publication of many of the criteria and of the evaluation system. The exclusion criteria were fully disclosed.

In order not to flood customers with information, two different publications were produced: one containing primarily qualitative information in the form of a regular sales

	To customers	From companies	Advisory Council
Brochures/material/ information on the Internet	Information in detailed brochures as well as additional material for investment advisors. Internet page with latest information on the fund.		
Feedback link	Interactive link on the Internet for comments or questions		
Environmental reports/ questionnaires		Environmental reports as the main source of information Two questionnaires, the second one being more detailed, for additional information	
Watchlist	Watchlist on the Internet	Information about inclusion in Watchlist Letter with specific questions concerning Watchlist	Discussion about inclusion in Watchlist
Meetings with Advisory Council			Quarterly meetings with Advisory Council to discuss current problems

Table 28.2 **Communication tools and their relevance for the different stakeholder groups**

brochure, the other focusing on quantitative details, addressing mainly investment advisors but, if necessary, also customers.

Despite concerns that a full disclosure of the exclusion criteria might lead to pressure from the excluded industries, there have been no major problems. The use of an existing label for sustainable forestry (Forest Stewardship Council [FSC]) resulted in protests from another association promoting a different label. Following discussions, a compromise was reached through more neutral wording.

The publication of full details of the underlying criteria, and of the inclusion process as a whole, contributed to a clear profile in the Swiss market and resulted in favourable press.

The latest information on the fund performance, as well as a list of the companies in which the fund is invested, are published on the Internet.[3]

3   Website: www.swissca.ch, and then choose Anlagefonds; Aktienfonds; Green Invest.

28.2.2 Feedback link on the Internet

An interactive feedback link was installed on the Internet page, giving customers the opportunity to address the fund management and the research team with questions and comments on the fund and the companies included.

Customer feedback falls into two categories: suggestions for companies to be considered, and comments on companies already included in the fund. So far suggestions have hardly ever resulted in the inclusion of a new company, because most of the companies named had already been screened. On several occasions comments on an included company resulted in further research, especially when the customer had brought up a critical issue. In one case a customer's comment resulted the company being put on the Watchlist (see below) because it brought critical information to the attention of the fund.

At first it was feared that it would be too time-consuming to answer all questions. However, it has been found that the feedback link does not generate very much additional work. At the same time the knowledge of customers and other interested people has opened up new doors. All in all, the link is advantageous for everyone involved.

28.2.3 Environmental reports and questionnaires

Corporate environmental reports (CERs) are the most important source of information. However, the amount of information that can be gathered from CERs depends heavily on their quality, and varies accordingly. Therefore it is still necessary to obtain further information through questionnaires.

ZKB uses two different questionnaires to obtain the required information. The first one covers key issues only, and asks for background information. A company is further evaluated only if the first check reveals potential. A more detailed questionnaire is used in the second check. So far the questions regarding social issues have been comparatively few, but the research team is developing a special social questionnaire.

In addition to helping gather information, the bank questionnaires are also aimed at persuading companies to publish more environmental and social information.

Customers and critics sometimes express doubt whether an environmental fund can have any effect on the environment. There is one area, however, where it definitely can have an effect: when banks and research bodies ask companies to complete questionnaires on environmental and even social performance, this motivates companies to publish the requested information in a consistent form. As environmental funds expand and attain a larger market share, the pressure resulting from banks demanding standardised environmental information continues to grow. The initiatives named below show that environmental and social issues are becoming increasingly important in the corporate world.

At present the most powerful initiative is probably the Global Reporting Initiative (GRI), which was launched by the Coalition for Environmentally Responsive Economies (CERES) and several partners (*Business and the Environment* 1999a). The purpose of the GRI is to set up guidelines for a sustainability reporting system that cover all needs of different stakeholders. Industry associations such as the World Business Council for Sustainable

Development and UNEP are also represented in the Steering Committee. Some 21 companies indicated that they were interested in testing the set of guidelines published in a draft version in spring 1999.

It is hardly surprising that companies are also interested in best-practice guidelines on environmental reporting, given that environmental reporting award schemes increasingly offer the possibility to make one's mark with an outstanding environmental report. Several countries now belong to the European Environmental Reporting Award Scheme (*Business and the Environment* 1999b). Under the scheme chaired by the Association of Chartered Certified Accountants (ACCA), winners of national reporting award schemes are included in a European award scheme.

Switzerland saw its first awards for environmental reporting in a scheme launched by the Association for Corporate Environmental Issues (ÖBU) in summer 1999 (Hildesheimer and Döbeli 1999). The winners of the 'Multinationals' category typically achieved a good rating in ZKB's evaluation as well.

Other examples illustrate that it is only a matter of time before social reporting catches up with environmental reporting: British Telecom—a pioneer in environmental reporting—recently launched its first social report. Other multinationals have already followed suit (*CSR Magazine* 1999). Multinationals are also coming under increasing pressure to implement codes of conduct, including social and human rights criteria for their trade activities with developing countries.[4] As soon as codes of conduct are implemented, reporting on these issues will gain significance.

The wave of environmental reporting and rating has spread to eastern economies as well. In India, the Centre for Science and the Environment launched a 'Green Rating Project' to assess industry's environmental performance (Agarwal 1999). The project is based on voluntary environmental reporting. Its principal target is to generate public pressure on the companies to improve their environmental performance. In Japan, too, environmental rating institutes are being established in order to provide information for eco-efficiency funds.[5]

When multinationals finally adopt consistent triple-bottom-line reporting, banks and research institutes will be able to stop sending them questionnaires.

28.2.4 Watchlist

When lending its Living Planet Campaign[6] label to the Green Invest fund, the WWF was justifiably concerned that one of the companies included in the fund might suddenly find itself involved in a major environmental accident or facing a serious environmental problem. Hence a Watchlist was developed in co-operation with the Advisory Council

---

4 The European Parliament has published a resolution on the creation of a European Code of Conduct for European Multinational Enterprises Operating Abroad (European Parliament 1999), and considers it vital to encourage companies to adopt social standards.

5 Meeting with Mr T. Mizuguchi, Takasaki City University of Economics, Japan, and Mr K. Kokubu, Kobe University, School of Business Administration, Kobe, in August 1999.

6 See footnote 2 on page 379.

(see below) in order to deal with sudden bad publicity or a major change in the structure of a company (e.g. merger).

When news on a company necessitates an urgent review of its environmental rating, the company is put on the Watchlist. At the same time the company will be told about the concerns, and more information on the problem will be required. Such information can be provided either in writing or in a discussion between the research team and the company's environmental manager. Once additional information has been obtained, the company's rating will be adjusted and any further action will be determined in co-operation with the Advisory Board. Customers may retrieve Watchlist information from the Internet.

An inclusion in the Watchlist is based purely on environmental or social information. If a company has a poor financial performance it is solely the portfolio manager's responsibility to react to this fact and sell the shares. The bank's environmental research department monitors various media and reacts immediately to news concerning a company included in the investment universe.

Up to this point the Watchlist has proved to be a most adequate tool, giving the research team greater scope to clarify a situation without immediately having to exclude a company from the fund. By informing a company that it has been placed on the Watchlist, the environmental research department can make it very clear that a specific issue is seen as a major problem. Customers will find the research more credible if they see that expressing their concern about a certain company in the fund has led to further investigations .

Initially Swissca feared that companies might protest about being put on a Watchlist. So far, however, no company has ever reacted negatively; all companies concerned have been co-operative and provided the desired information. In some cases the pressure has even caused a company to develop new policies or better communication tools.

In general, companies seem to be increasingly interested in maintaining an open dialogue with stakeholders on critical topics. For instance, Nike introduced the new function of a 'Vice President of Corporate Responsibility'[7] specifically to deal with corporate responsibility issues and stakeholder dialogue. In its environmental report Novo Nordisk has made room for an extensive and critical stakeholder discussion.[8]

28.2.5 Regular meetings with the Advisory Council

An Advisory Council consisting of environmental, social and business experts was set up to assist the environmental research team. The WWF is represented on the Advisory Council by one expert. The Council's principal duty is to help improve the evaluation methodology and to advise the research unit on the inclusion of companies in the investment universe. The research team and Advisory Council meet on a quarterly basis. For these meetings the research team prepares papers, for instance, on individual companies or on concepts for the research process.

7 ZKB Questionnaire of February 1999
8 www.novo.dk/environm/ebr98/index.html

The discussion about individual companies—only the controversial ones are discussed in the meetings—helps to determine the chances and risks of including a company in the fund. The debate is equally helpful when it comes to defining measures to be taken once a company has been put on the Watchlist. Moreover, the discussion contributes to an increasingly precise definition of the exclusion criteria. The following examples illustrate the importance of this forum for gaining a more consistent profile.

A bank included in the fund was attacked by an NGO for taking part in the financing of a controversial dam project. Financing a dam project is not in itself an exclusion criterion for Swissca Green Invest, but it is considered problematic if a bank is involved in a very controversial project. The Advisory Council came to the following conclusions: the bank is not one of the lead managers of the project and is advancing only a very small amount. The research team was asked to find out more about the bank's policy regarding project finance. It turned out that the bank was in fact in the process of developing a consistent environmental policy for project finance, and as a result it has not been excluded from the fund.

One specialised chemicals company has a very comprehensive environmental management system and a good environmental performance. A small part of revenue is generated through pesticides, none of which belongs to the 'Dirty Dozen'[9] pesticides list. Should the company be included in the fund's investment universe? The Advisory Council decided 'yes' because the company had developed many new solutions for formerly very toxic products and because emissions had been reduced significantly.[10]

Thus the meetings with the Advisory Council are an important instrument helping the Environmental Research Team decide on difficult questions and improve the research process.

28.3 Conclusions

Co-operating with the WWF, and endorsement by the Living Planet Campaign label, had a strong influence on the definition of the evaluation criteria for Swissca Green Invest. Having endorsed the fund, the WWF justly demanded the exclusion of many industries that have contributed heavily to the most severe environmental problems and risks globally. In addition the WWF emphasised the importance of a very careful evaluation of environmental leaders. A balance had to be found between using strict criteria and limiting the number of restrictions placed on the fund manager. The WWF's influence has led to a product with a distinct environmental profile that met with a lively response in the market and in the press.

9 The 'Dirty Dozen' list is published by the Pesticide Action Network (PAN) and includes 18 highly toxic chemicals. PAN demands a ban of these highly toxic pesticides. Producing a pesticide that belongs to the Dirty Dozen is an exclusion criteria for Swissca Green Invest.

10 We include data provided by environmental pressure groups such as PAN and information about industry-specific awards (e.g. US Presidential Green Chemistry Challenge Award) in our evaluation process. Such information helps us to decide whether a company's performance in environmental product stewardship is above average.

ZKB's environmental research team has found that active environmental research pushes companies to publish environmental data and improve their environmental performance. Among other things, the demand for environmental and social data has resulted in several initiatives for a more consistent triple-bottom-line reporting. And, considering that 'what gets measured gets done',[11] the pressure results not only in better reporting but also in an improved environmental or social performance. Periodical benchmark surveys such as Business in the Environment (BiE)'s third annual survey of corporate environmental commitment in the UK reveal progress in environmental performance: the 1999 index indicates a year-on-year increase in each of the ten parameters of environmental management assessed (*Business and the Environment* 1999c). Such results reflect a process of continual improvement in different industries that can be further encouraged by environmental and social research and rating.

The WWF always stressed the importance of an open dialogue with all stakeholders involved. In addition to normal communication tools such as brochures (for customers) and questionnaires (for companies), some new tools were implemented for Swissca Green Invest. The interactive Internet link, the Watchlist and the regular meetings with the Advisory Council are core elements for an active dialogue with the stakeholders. These tools have been used regularly and contribute to the high credibility of the fund. They also turned out to be an ideal means of spreading WWF's principles as well as reducing its risk of being criticised for including certain companies in the fund.

Maintaining a continual dialogue is a great effort for the research unit. However, experience gained in the past has shown that it pays to offer additional communication tools. The research unit gained additional information and was often forced to further scrutinise a certain company. This improved the research quality and also contributed to a clearer profile of the fund. Furthermore, the above-average growth of the fund in its first[12] year gives an indication that extensive communication tools increase a product's attractiveness to investors.

All in all, the co-operation with WWF has been an important step for Swissca and for ZKB's environmental research department. It improved the environmental profile of Swissca Green Invest, through the endorsement on the one hand, and the process of defining strict criteria that match WWF's policy on the other hand. It also encouraged Swissca and the research team to maintain a dialogue with companies and investors, leading to a constant improvement of the research process and the fund itself.

---

11 A comment by Rudy van der Meer, member of the Environmental Board of Management of Akzo Nobel in their latest environmental report. He referred to the improved environmental performance of Akzo Nobel in the fields where targets had been set.

12 The continental European funds listed in *Öko Invest* (*Öko Invest* 1999, 2000) had an average volume increase of 22.6% in 1999, whereas Swissca Green Invest gained 425% volume in the same period. Some of the increase can be related to performance but at least 85 million Swiss francs (320%) resulted from new funds.

THE ROLE OF THE UNITED NATIONS ENVIRONMENT PROGRAMME AND THE FINANCIAL SERVICES SECTOR

Mike Kelly
United Nations Environment
Programme, Geneva*

Ari Huhtala
United Nations Environment
Programme, France

Since its creation in 1972, the United Nations Environment Programme (UNEP) has had a mandate to encourage economic growth compatible with the protection of the environment. But this element of UNEP's role was considerably enhanced by the Earth Summit of world leaders who met in Rio de Janeiro, Brazil, in 1992 and placed great emphasis on promoting development that did not compromise the quality of life of future generations. It was then that the UNEP Financial Institutions Initiative on the Environment was founded when the 'Statement by Financial Institutions on the Environment and Sustainable Development' was signed by some 30 banks. Now almost 170 financial institutions with a market capitalisation in excess of US$2 trillion and more than half a million employees are signatories. A list of signatories is given in Annexe 2 on page 398.

29.1 The motivation behind the initiative

UNEP was convinced that bankers and investors had a valuable contribution to make in protecting the environment while maintaining the health and profitability of their businesses. In 1991 the then Executive Director, Dr Mostafa Tolba, approached a small number of international financial institutions as part of the preparations for the Earth Summit in Rio. He wanted to find out whether they shared his view that the finance sector could play a role in sustainable development. The banks approached had already demonstrated publicly in a variety of different ways that they were aware of environ-

---

* Mike Kelly is now with KPMG.

mental issues. This awareness had generally taken the form of commentary within their financial statements; at that time no bank had published an environment report, although some of their largest customers were beginning to produce separate environment reports. The banks responded to Tolba's call, working with UNEP to draw up a statement of environmental commitment for the sector.

It was clear that protecting the environment could not be achieved by governments alone. The private sector had a particular perspective on environmental issues and its expertise was needed if a radical shift was to be achieved in public attitudes about the compatibility of an ecological outlook and ordinary commercial and industrial life. Bankers and investors have crucial links with commercial activity, including activity that degrades the natural environment.

The idea was extended to insurance and reinsurance companies with the launch of the Insurance Industry Initiative on the Environment at the end of 1995. The insurers, while sharing many of the characteristics and concerns of the banks, had traditionally been managed in a different fashion and grouped themselves as a separate industry. UNEP and the small group of insurers and reinsurers who were trying to involve the insurance industry in this initiative recognised this and took the strategic decision to produce a separate statement to better engage the industry. To date more than 85 insurers and reinsurers have signed the Insurance Industry Statement.

The Statement by Financial Institutions, initially launched as the Banking Statement, was revised in 1997. This was undertaken by a group of signatories in association with UNEP and presented to all signatories on the occasion of the third global round-table conference on the subject, held by UNEP in New York. The revision did not dilute any of the original commitments or aspirations. It did, however, update the language used to describe the industry and to reflect the changes in the make-up of banks since the first drafting in late 1991.

Major banks and insurance groups from around the world have put their name to the statements. A major cornerstone of both is a commitment to sustainable development and support for the precautionary approach to environmental management which attempts to anticipate and prevent environmental degradation. The signatories also undertake to promote public awareness and communication.

29.2 The objectives of the UNEP initiatives

The primary objective is to generate a dialogue between commercial banks, venture capitalists, insurance and reinsurance companies, multilateral development agencies and asset managers, those involved in economic development and managing risks, and environmentalists. A secondary objective is to foster private-sector investment in environmentally sound technologies and services.

In order to fulfil its primary objective, UNEP has convened meetings of bankers, insurers and other interested groups in all regions of the world. These have ranged from the very first meeting in Geneva in September 1994, attended by some 50 bankers, to the third international round-table in New York, which attracted some 350 participants. The agenda for these meetings has changed very little in the intervening years. There is still a very great concern about the impact of environmental risk on clients' financial performance and the knock-on effect that this might have on the banks' own results. But there is also an increasing awareness of the opportunities created by greater environmental awareness. Financial institutions are big businesses in their own right and taking an eco-efficient approach to their own operations is sometimes their first real exposure to environmental issues. This improved environmental performance generally brings with it an improved financial performance and a willingness to consider this area more proactively. In our experience the awareness-raising is best done at a regional or national level rather than at a global level. It is also important to get practitioners talking to their peers about it. Some years ago the phrase 'environmental sense makes business sense' was first used; since then it has been a key theme in convening meetings around this subject.

The common theme in all of these gatherings has been that it is industry practitioners who are addressing these subjects, and that they are addressing them from the perspective of being inside their business looking out rather than an outsider looking in. The persuasive arguments employed by a banker talking to his peers are very different to those that would be employed by a different constituency and have a different set of results.

Initially UNEP's role was an educational and information-giving role in partnership with a few banks. Now it is very much as a catalyst as the sector has started to educate itself on the importance of addressing these issues for the long term, as key survival issues for the sector. UNEP acts as a guide in this unique partnership and facilitates change among informed banks. It has a clear leadership role as the environmental voice of the United Nations, and it is one that is increasingly listened to by the private sector. For example, in fulfilment of its secondary objective UNEP has, as part of its assessment of the level of implementation of the Statement, collected examples of innovative products and services that have been created by signatories and promulgated such information among the industry. At the time of the last review in 1999 almost 60% of signatories had introduced specific products or services with an environmental as well as financial dimension. By far the most common was a discounted loan facility for an environmental improvement or a 'green' savings product, but products and services also included environmental consultancy, biodegradable credit cards and a 'green' refuse disposal business. Signatories have also become involved in other areas of UNEP's work, and with other UN agencies either as participants or advisors in a number of work programmes. In 1998 a number of signatories acted as peer reviewers of a training manual, *Accounting and Financial Reporting for Environmental Liabilities and Costs*, which was then used to train national standard-setters, regulators and others involved in this area of the financial services industry. A direct result of this programme, which is still in operation, is that a major bank which hosted one of the workshops has introduced a rating system using this information and is planning two sector-specific seminars. Other institutions have also used the material to inform their own internal risk training programmes.

This is the background to the latest phase of UNEP's work with the financial services sector and may well serve as a model for its future work with the sector. This involves a wide range of financial institutions and other interested parties in addressing one of the most critical issues in the current financial services sector and environment debate: the promotion of environmentally sound technologies through the supply of innovative products and services leading to the promotion of environmentally superior technology. It is a virtuous circle, bringing with it environmental and financial benefits for all involved local communities, suppliers, customers and of course the environment, as well as for the more traditional parties of owner, worker and financier.

29.3 UNEP's involvement in cleaner production: a case description

A concrete example of a UNEP technical co-operation project that promotes 'win–win' technology options is the project 'Strategies and Mechanisms for Promoting Cleaner Production (CP) Investments in Developing Countries', which was launched by UNEP in 1998 and has been funded by the government of Norway. The project aims to demonstrate how investments in CP can be stimulated by helping financial institutions to understand its benefits, and by training national experts to develop creditworthy CP investments proposals. Demonstration activities are being organised in Guatemala, Nicaragua, Tanzania, Vietnam and Zimbabwe. UNIDO/UNEP National Cleaner Production Centres (NCPCs) support the initiative in all these countries.

29.3.1 Constraints to CP investments

Investments in CP can have attractive economics due to the reduction of costs for input materials, energy and water, and expenditures on waste treatment and disposal, as well as increases in production and better output quality. Their payback period may, however, be longer than is customary in a typical ROI (return on investment) for a new investment. Small and medium-sized industries have a particularly hard time making CP investments for a variety of reasons, ranging from the cost of capital to the absence of appropriate funding mechanisms. Furthermore, CP is less likely to be economically attractive in countries with few and lax environmental regulations, under-priced or free natural resources and no green consumer movement. Table 29.1 summarises the major problems of funding CP investments from the perspective of the financial sector.

Even where the management of a company is willing to invest in CP, the implementation of such projects can be hindered by a lack of financial resources. The appraisal of a loan application from a commercial bank depends not only on the way financial costs and benefits are identified and quantified but also on the existing relationship between the bank and the company and on the firm's overall creditworthiness.

29.3.2 Possible solutions

The following considerations may help banks to orient their lending towards CP: management competence (CP as an integral part of 'total quality management'), cash

Problems to be addressed	Underlying causes
1. Inability of financial institutions and industrial authorities to assess the technical and financial merits of CP investment proposals	► Impact of CP on profitability of investments and creditworthiness of of borrowers not understood by credit providers ► Inability of credit providers to assess the CP content of investment proposals
2. Lack of credit schemes customised to CP investments	► Limited development stage of banking system, reflected in focus on traditional collateral value (land and buildings), short repayment periods and provision of working capital only ► High interest rates, (largely) caused by macro-economic and financial instability
3. Inability of institutions to develop creditworthy CP investment proposals	► Lack of CP assessments undertaken not directed to result in creditworthy investment proposals (including business plans)
4. High cost of implementation of CP	► Limited local availability of CP-adapted technology and devices and engineering and installation services ► Perceptions regarding high technology risks associated with CP investments
5. Lack of enabling environment for CP	► Lack of conducive policy environment for CP ► Lack of demand for CP from industrial community

Table 29.1 **Major problems in funding cleaner production (CP) investments**

flow (CP reducing costs of environmental compliance), and long-term competitiveness. In most financial institutions by far the greatest level of attention is paid to past costs, including regulatory costs. It is not common for future potential costs to receive the same level of assessment in a loan application as past financial costs. Yet the weight of regulation is getting heavier, not just in developed countries but in developing countries and those countries with economies in transition. This does mean that a true assessment of risk must factor in the future costs of operation as well as the past performance.

In terms of equity financing, companies must comply with stock exchange reporting standards if they are to generate capital through the issue of shares. As environmental awareness increases, shareholders may take ecological aspects into account when deciding on their investment behaviour. This has led to the emergence of green investment funds and other measures; for instance, the Swiss bank UBS AG offers the possibility to invest in 'ecological leaders' or 'innovators' with a significant window for CP opportunities. Another alternative source of financing is leasing that can be geared towards facilitating the financing of CP investments.

The success of environmental funds depends on the extent to which they manage to attract capital. Such funds can encompass various financial structures, including restricted accounts, lines of credit, revolving loans and guaranty funds with special emphasis on

CP. For instance, in 1997 the Nordic Environment Financing Corporation (NEFCO) launched a revolving facility for CP investments in Lithuania and north-west Russia. Development assistance presents a specific form of special-purpose funds that are often provided through financial intermediaries in developing countries. An example of such a facility is a credit line for CP financing in China.

29.3.3 UNEP's project

The expected results of the project at the country level are:

- More effective interaction between financial and manufacturing sectors

- Improved ability of public and private financial institutions to assess investment proposals and provide preferential treatment to CP

- Improved ability of CP assessors to develop creditworthy CP investment proposals and mediate in obtaining funding for their implementation

- An increase in CP investment in participating countries, particularly in selected priority sectors[1]

At the global level, the project aims at developing new instruments and project initiatives (including credit lines, trust funds, policy changes, training, etc.) to foster additional CP. The project is supported by national co-ordinators and advisory boards. An international Advisory Board provides overall guidance and ensures that there is no overlap of activities between countries or regions. It will use the accumulated experience gained with UNEP's Cleaner Production Programme and the UNEP Financial Institutions Initiative which promotes the integration of environmental considerations into the financial sector's operations and services.

Project implementation started in spring 1999 with a major study of past investment practices. It became clear at an early stage that there is a wealth of knowledge outside the selected countries and these resources are also being tapped. Parallel activities are currently identifying the existing tools used by investors, appraisers and project developers to integrate CP into project assessment. The same expert group is also developing what could be the elements of an ideal assessment tool. It is hoped to bring this to the market in the form of trial project assessments in the first half of 2001. The project is scheduled to be completed in 2002 and is working in close co-operation with partner agencies such as UNIDO, ICC, IFC, the World Bank, OECD, selected bilateral programmes and commercial banks, and UNDP.

---

1 Three to four sub-sectors have been selected in each demonstration country, representing most important industries. In Tanzania, for example, food processing, textiles, tanneries and small-scale mining have been chosen. This will provide an opportunity to formulate draft benchmarks to for use by authorities and financial institutions at the country level.

29.3 **Conclusion**

Since its beginnings in the early 1990s the Financial Institutions Initiative has grown from an initiative addressing one aspect of the financial services sector, the private sector, and within that just commercial banks, through to a broad-based initiative addressing the whole range of financial institutions in the marketplace today. This has been due in part to the growth of understanding, among both financial service providers and UNEP, and in part to the growth in private-sector financial investment. Capital investments in developing countries multiplied during the 1990s. International financing institutions such as the World Bank and regional development banks played an important role in this development, but the most spectacular growth took place in private-sector investments. This flow has mostly been for investments similar to those undertaken during the industrialisation period of OECD countries. Such investments, while necessary, often lead to increased pollution loads and use of energy and natural resources. The awareness of this potentially double cost, first to industrialise and second to upgrade to cleaner production processes, has been a strong motivator in driving this programme forward.

Globalisation also presents a major challenge to developing countries in their attempts to promote economically viable domestic and international investments, and to financial institutions that are looking for new and emerging markets. Ecological considerations often relate to environmental impact assessments (EIAs) and/or emission standards only, without any linkage between social, environmental and economic performance. The challenge is to achieve sustained income growth for these economies by raising investment rates, strengthening technological capacities and skills, and improving the competitiveness of products and services in world markets; distributing the benefits of growth equitably by creating more and better employment opportunities and protecting and conserving the physical environment for future generations. That is why the CP Investments project and the CP Programme generally is so critically important for developed and developing countries alike. Although the CP project is working in only five countries at the moment, the results will have an impact on a large number of economies. Already the number of countries actively engaged has more than doubled, with further inquires from most regions of the globe. It is clear that there is great interest and an eagerness to find out more. It is also clear that there is a lot to be done and very few institutions working in this area. The challenge will be to use the multiplier effect of the demonstration projects to best advantage so that the legacy of this project is not a series of reports but rather a series of manufacturing businesses demonstrating that sustainable development works. The reports will be important in pointing the way for others to follow these pioneers of industry.

UNEP will face a number of challenges in making this vision a reality. No one underestimates the difficulties facing world economies, and the changing shape of the financial services sector adds to the problems. UNEP has to change the way it addresses the market in response to such changes and has to do this with very limited resources. While it is unlikely that any new Statements will be created to face the sector, there have been changes in the way engagement is addressed. Broader consultation, and the participation of a variety of stakeholders, national governments, NGOs and academics helps to bring these issues to the top of the agenda. This is how UNEP will continue to work: raising difficult issues in an atmosphere of dialogue and openness and continuing to push the agenda so that complacency is never an option.

◢ Annexe 1

UNEP Statement by Financial Institutions
on the Environment and Sustainable Development
(as revised May 1997)

We members of the financial services industry recognize that sustainable development depends upon a positive interaction between economic and social development, and environmental protection, to balance the interests of this and future generations. We further recognize that sustainable development is the collective responsibility of government, business, and individuals. We are committed to working cooperatively with these sectors within the framework of market mechanisms toward common environmental goals.

1. Commitment to Sustainable Development

1.1 We regard sustainable development as a fundamental aspect of sound business management.

1.2 We believe that sustainable development can best be achieved by allowing markets to work within an appropriate framework of cost-efficient regulations and economic instruments. Governments in all countries have a leadership role in establishing and enforcing long-term common environmental priorities and values.

1.3 We regard the financial services sector as an important contributor towards sustainable development, in association with other economic sectors.

1.4 We recognize that sustainable development is a corporate commitment and an integral part of our pursuit of good corporate citizenship.

2. Environmental Management and Financial Institutions

2.1 We support the precautionary approach to environmental management, which strives to anticipate and prevent potential environmental degradation.

2.2 We are committed to complying with local, national, and international environmental regulations applicable to our operations and business services. We will work towards integrating environmental considerations into our operations, asset management, and other business decisions, in all markets.

2.3 We recognize that identifying and quantifying environmental risks should be part of the normal process of risk assessment and management, both in domestic and international operations. With regard to our customers, we regard compliance with applicable environmental regulations and the use of sound environmental practices as important factors in demonstrating effective corporate management.

2.4 We will endeavor to pursue the best practice in environmental management, including energy efficiency, recycling and waste reduction. We will seek to form business relations with partners, suppliers, and subcontractors who follow similarly high environmental standards.

2.5 We intend to update our practices periodically to incorporate relevant developments in environmental management. We encourage the industry to undertake research in these and related areas.

2.6 We recognize the need to conduct internal environmental reviews on a periodic basis, and to measure our activities against our environmental goals.

2.7 We encourage the financial services sector to develop products and services which will promote environmental protection.

3. Public Awareness and Communication

3.1 We recommend that financial institutions develop and publish a statement of their environmental policy and periodically report on the steps they have taken to promote integration of environmental considerations into their operations.

3.2 We will share information with customers, as appropriate, so that they may strengthen their own capacity to reduce environmental risk and promote sustainable development.

3.3 We will foster openness and dialogue relating to environmental matters with relevant audiences, including shareholders, employees, customers, governments, and the public.

3.4 We ask the United Nations Environment Programme (UNEP) to assist the industry to further the principles and goals of this Statement by providing, within its capacity, relevant information relating to sustainable development.

3.5 We will encourage other financial institutions to support this Statement. We are committed to share with them our experiences and knowledge in order to extend best practices.

3.6 We will work with UNEP periodically to review the success in implementing this Statement and will revise it as appropriate.

We, the undersigned, endorse the principles set forth in the above statement and will endeavor to ensure that our policies and business actions promote the consideration of the environment and sustainable development.

◢ Annexe 2

Signatories to the UNEP Statement by Financial Institutions on the Environment and Sustainable Development
(as revised May 1997)

1. Abbey National plc, UK
2. Algemene Spaarbank voor Nederland, Netherlands
3. Arab Bank, plc, Jordan
4. Balkanbank Ltd, Bulgaria
5. Banca Catalana SA, Spain
6. Banca Internacional D'Andorra–Banca Mora, Andorra
7. Banca Monte dei Paschi di Siena SpA, Italy
8. Banco BHIF, Chile
9. Banco Bilbao Vizcaya SA, Spain
10. Banco Bilbao Vizcaya (Portugal) SA, Portugal
11. Banco Continental, Peru
12. Banco del Comercio SA, Spain
13. Banco do Estado de São Paulo SA, Brazil
14. Banco Frances, Argentina
15. Banco Ganadero, Colombia
16. Banco Nacional de Angola, Angola
17. Banco Nacional de Desenvolvimento Economic e Social, Brazil
18. Banco Português do Atlantico SA, Portugal
19. Banco Provincial, Venezuela
20. Banesto, Banco Español de Credito, Spain
21. Bank Austria, Austria
22. Bank Depozytowo-Kredytowy SA, Poland
23. Bank für Tirol und Vorarlberg Aktiengesellschaft, Austria
24. Bank Gdanski SA, Poland
25. Bankhaus Bauer AG, Germany
26. Bankhaus Carl Spängler & Co. Aktiengesellschaft, Austria
27. Bankhaus C.L. Seeliger, Germany
28. Bankhaus Max Flessa & Co., Germany
29. Bankhaus Neelmeyer AG, Germany
30. Bank Ochrony Srodowiska, Poland
31. Bank of Baroda, India

32. Bank of Cyprus, Cyprus
33. Bank of Handlowy W. Warszawie SA, Poland
34. Bank of Ireland Group, Ireland
35. Bank of Montreal, Canada
36. Bank of Philippine Islands, Philippines
37. Bank Polska Kasa Opieki SA, Poland
38. Bank Przemystowo-Handlowy SA, Poland
39. Bank Rozwoju Eksportu SA, Poland
40. Bank Sarasin & Cie., Switzerland
41. Bank Slakski SA, Poland
42. Bank Zachodni SA, Poland
43. Bankverein Werther AG, Germany
44. Banky Fampandrosoana ny Varotra, Madagascar
45. Banque Populaire du Haut-Rhin, France
46. Barclays Group plc, UK
47. Basellandschaftliche Kantonalbank, Switzerland
48. Bayersiche Handelsbank AG, Germany
49. Bayerische Hypo- und Vereinsbank AG, Germany*
50. Bayerische Landesbank Girozentrale, Germany
51. BBV Brasil, Brazil
52. BBV Privanza Banco SA, Spain
53. BBV Probursa, Mexico
54. BBV Puerto Rico, Puerto Rico
55. Beneficial Bank AG, Germany
56. Bezirkssparkasse Heidelberg, Germany
57. BfG Bank AG, Germany
58. B. Metzler seel. Sohn & Co. KgaA, Germany
59. Budapest Bank RT, Hungary
60. Canadian Imperial Bank of Commerce, Canada
61. Central Hispano, Spain
62. Commercial Bank of Greece, Greece
63. Commerzbank AG, Germany
64. Community Capital Bank, USA
65. Conrad Hinrich Donner Bank AG, Germany
66. The Co-operative Bank, Manchester, UK
67. Corporación Andina de Fomento, Venezuela
68. Crédit Andorrá, Andorra
69. Crédit Local de France, France
70. Credit Suisse Group, Switzerland
71. Credito Italiano, Italy
72. Creditanstalt-Bankverein, Austria
73. DEG—German Investment and Development Company
74. Degussa Bank GmbH, Germany
75. Delbrück & Co., Privatbankiers, Germany
76. Den Danske Bank, A/S, Denmark
77. Den Norske Bank ASA, Norway
78. Deutsche Ausgleichsbank, Germany
79. Deutsche Bank AG, Germany
80. Deutsche Bank Saar, Germany
81. Deutsche Pfandbrief- und Hypothekenbank AG, Germany
82. Deutsche Postbank AG, Germany

83. Development Bank of the Philippines, Philippines
84. DG Bank, Germany
85. Dresdner Bank AG, Germany
86. EBI Capital Group LLP, USA
87. Ecobanken, Sweden
88. Econatsbank, Russian Federation
89. EPS Finance Ltd, Switzerland
90. Eurohypo AG, Europäische Hypothekenbank der Deutschen Bank, Germany
91. Export Bank of Africa Ltd, Kenya
92. Export Development Corporation, Canada
93. Finanzia, Banca de Credito SA, Spain
94. FMO, Netherlands
95. Friends Provident Life Office, UK
96. Friends Ivory & Sime Trust Company, USA
97. Fürstlich Castellische Bank, Credit-Casse, Germany
98. Hamburgische Landesbank Girozentrale, Germany
99. Hesse Newman Bank (BNL Group), Germany
100. HKB Hypotheken- und Kommunalkredit Bank, Germany
101. HSBC Holdings plc, UK
102. Investitionsbank des Landes Brandenburg, Germany
103. Istituto Nazionale di Credito Agrario SpA, Italy
104. JAK—Jord, Arbete, Kapital, Sweden
105. Kansallis-Osake-Pankki, Finland
106. Kenya Commercial Bank Group, Kenya
107. Kreditanstalt für Wiederaufbau, Germany
108. Kreditna banka Maribor d.d., Slovenia
109. Kreissparkasse Düsseldorf, Germany
110. Kreissparkasse Göppingen, Germany
111. Land Bank of the Philippines, Philippines
112. Landesbank Baden-Württemberg**
113. Landesbank Schleswig-Holstein Girozentrale, Germany
114. Landsbanki Islands, Iceland
115. LBS Badische Landesbausparkasse, Germany
116. Lloyds TSB Bank, UK
117. Luzerner Kantonalbank, Switzerland
118. Merck Finck & Co., Germany
119. M.M. Warburg & Co., Germany
120. National Bank of Kuwait SAK, Kuwait
121. National Fund for Environmental Management and Water Protection, Poland
122. National Savings and Commercial Bank Ltd, Hungary
123. NatWest Group, UK
124. Österreichische Investitionskredit Aktiengesellschaft, Austria
125. Österreichische Kommunalkredit Aktiengesellschaft, Austria
126. Polski Bank Inwestycyjny SA, Poland
127. Pomorski Bank Kredytowy SA, Poland
128. Powszechna Kasa Oszczednosci—Bank Panstwowy, Poland

---

* *Bayerische Hypotheken- und Wechselbank, Germany/Bayerische Vereinsbank AG, Germany (merged 1998)*
** *Südwestdeutsche Landesbank Girozentrale, Germany/Landesgirokasse Bank, Germany and Landeskreditbank (merged 1998)*

129. Powszechny Bank Gospodarczy SA w todzi, Poland
130. Powszechny Bank Kredytowy SA, Poland
131. Quelle Bank AG, Germany
132. Rabobank, Netherlands
133. Raiffeisen Zentralbank Austria AG, Austria
134. Republic National Bank, USA
135. Romanian Commercial Bank SA, Romania
136. Royal Bank of Canada, Canada
137. Royal Bank of Scotland plc, UK
138. Salomon Inc., USA
139. Sal. Oppenheim jr. & Cie, Germany
140. SchmidtBank KGaA, Germany
141. Schröder Münchmeyer Hengst AG, Germany
142. Schwäbische Bank AG, Germany
143. Scotia Bank (The Bank of Nova Scotia), Canada
144. Service Bank GmbH & Co. KG, Germany
145. Skandinaviska Enskilda Banken, Sweden
146. Sparkasse Leichlingen, Germany
147. Sparkasse Staufen, Germany
148. Stadtsparkasse Hannover, Germany
149. Stadtsparkasse München, Germany
150. Stadtsparkasse Wuppertal, Germany
151. Sustainable Asset Management, Switzerland
152. Svenska Handelsbanken, Sweden
153. Swedbank AB, Sweden[†]
154. Thai Investment and Securities Co. Ltd, Thailand
155. Toronto-Dominion Bank, Canada
156. Triodos Bank, Netherlands
157. Uganda Commercial Bank, Uganda
158. UBS AG, Switzerland[‡]
159. Unibank, Denmark
160. UmweltBank AG, Germany
161. Vereins- und Westbank AG, Germany
162. Volksbank Siegen–Netphen eG, Germany
163. Westpac Banking Corporation, Australia
164. Woolwich plc, UK
165. Zürcher Kantonalbank, Switzerland

Associate Members
1. Coopers & Lybrand, UK

[†] *Föreningsbanken, Sweden/Sparbanken Sverige AB, Sweden (merged 1997)*
[‡] *Union Bank of Switzerland/Swiss Bank Corporation (merged 1998)*

DIRECTING INVESTMENT TO CLEANER ENERGY TECHNOLOGIES
The role of financial institutions

Norbert Wohlgemuth
UNEP Collaborating Centre on Energy and Environment, Denmark

Too much investment is still being directed towards outdated energy technologies, even where commercially available energy efficient and renewable technologies are technically feasible and financially attractive. Clean energy technologies (CETs) have to overcome a series of financial and non-financial barriers before they can penetrate the market. The financial sector plays a crucial role in overcoming the financial barriers. Loan officers in financial institutions have little practical experience in evaluating applications that have a cleaner energy technology (CET) (i.e. either energy efficiency [EE] or renewable energy technology [RET]) component.[1] They do not always understand the full economic and environmental advantages of investments in CETs and sometimes view them as being too risky on the basis of outdated or incorrect information on their technical and financial performance. Because banks fail to support CET projects, these technologies are penetrating the market at rates slower than is socially desirable. Global environmental benefits, including a reduction of greenhouse gas emissions as imposed by the United Nations Framework Convention on Climate Change (UNFCCC), also go unrealised because of a lack of knowledge and skills on the part of investment officers in lending institutions.

---

1 RETs use non-depleting sources of energy, such as the sun or wind, and so are generally more environmentally benign than conventional (fossil fuel-based) energy technologies. RETs can provide either electricity or heat; examples include biomass boilers, hydropower generators, solar thermal and wind power plants, and photovoltaic systems. RETs are supply-side technologies in that they supply energy. Those that generate electricity can either be used **on-grid**, thereby offsetting energy produced from conventional sources, or **off-grid**, to provide power in remote locations. EE technologies are generally used to reduce consumption by end-users, and so are called demand-side technologies. They bring about environmental benefits by reducing the demand for energy. Examples include high-efficiency motors and lighting, district heating and heat/electricity co-generation systems, heat pumps and building insulation.

The chapter presents a list of barriers that CETs have to overcome and details the experience of a Global Environment Facility-funded project aimed at influencing investment decisions in favour of CETs in developing and transition economies by providing advisory services to financial institutions. By working directly with banks and their clients, the project overcomes informational barriers in the financing of CETs. Through carefully targeted appraisals of alternative technologies the project increases loan officers' familiarity with investments in CETs. Knowledge and perception barriers, once removed, are unlikely to return. This permanent change in the institutional capacities developed through the project can be expected to favour replication by the participating lending institutions.

30.1 Why promote CETs?

The use of cleaner energy technologies contributes to all dimensions of sustainable development. Therefore, one of the challenges for energy, developmental and environmental policy is to ensure that environmentally sound technologies have a fair opportunity to compete with other resources required for the provision of energy services.

Developing bigger markets for CETs is beneficial as each additional CET system deployed displaces greenhouse gas emissions from conventional, i.e. fossil, energy technologies. Supporters of CETs fear that these options may be an inadvertent casualty in the transition towards a more competitive energy industry due to market failure (Energy Information Administration 1998; Olson 1998; Pollitt 1997; World Energy Council 1998). CETs have many advantages in terms of the public interest and enhanced economic efficiency (IEA 1998a, 1998b; GEF 1998). Among these are increased local employment and income; enhanced local tax revenues; a more diversified resource base, which minimises fuel supply and price risks; provision of infrastructure and economic flexibility by modular and small technologies; creation of more choice for consumers; contribution to overall system reliability; and the potential to eliminate pollution. Socioeconomic benefits include: diversifying and securing energy supply, thereby promoting price stability; providing job opportunities in rural areas, thereby slowing urbanisation; promoting the decentralisation of energy markets by providing small, modular, rapidly deployable schemes; and reducing developing economies' dependence on fuel imports. Another major benefit is that they assist in the electrification of rural communities in developing countries.

At the Third Conference of the Parties (COP-3) to the UNFCCC in Kyoto in December 1997, legally binding reduction targets on emissions of greenhouse gases were adopted for industrialised countries. The Kyoto Protocol to the Climate Convention (UNFCCC 1997) also provides a range of mechanisms that should help developed countries to meet their emission reduction commitments at least cost. While the Kyoto Protocol has not yet proposed any binding emissions limitation commitments for developing nations, instruments such as the Clean Development Mechanism (CDM) and the possibilities of emissions trading[2] (ET) are likely to provide economic incentives for significant emissions abatement in developing countries. The altered competitive dynamics should also prove favourable for CETs.[3] With respect to the Kyoto Mechanisms, traditional investment criteria for projects to be funded under the Mechanisms are not the only criteria; the CDM, for example, is supposed to contribute to sustainability.[4] Therefore, since CETs do contribute to this goal, there is a 'match' between CETs and the CDM which could contribute to a mutual enhancement.

30.2 Barriers to CETs, and instruments to overcome them

CETs have to overcome a series of barriers before they can penetrate the market. In the initial stages of development, technical barriers predominate. In order for a technology to become cost-effective, market barriers such as inconsistent pricing structures typically have to be overcome. Then there are institutional, political and legislative barriers that hinder the market penetration of technologies, including problems arising from a lack of awareness of, and experience with, new technologies and lack of a suitable institutional and regulatory structure. Finally, there are social and environmental barriers, resulting mainly from a lack of experience with planning regulations, which hinder the public acceptance of a technology. It is clear that a strategy that aims to increase market penetration should address the full spectrum of barriers (OECD 1997b).

The largest barrier to greater CET use is cost, despite the cost reductions achieved in recent years. But other obstacles include subsidies and other support for conventional fuels. Lack of full-cost pricing when determining the cost of competing energy supplies also hinders the development of CETs, because the cost of environmental impacts is usually not included in energy prices. Furthermore, the development of competitive

---

2   To date attention has focused mainly on ET, both because of the extent of emission reductions that may be met abroad and because of the uncertainty surrounding the concrete design of ET. The arguments in favour of ET are convincing from an economic viewpoint: like a carbon tax, ET has been shown to lead to emission reductions where (marginal) costs of abatement are least. ET is thus a suitable mechanism to exploit efficiency gains in terms of cost reduction. However, following Kyoto there was some concern that emission reduction targets had been set too low for these efficiency gains to come about.

3   With respect to EE/RETs, Article 2 of the Kyoto Protocol states that 'Each Party included in Annex I . . . in order to promote sustainable development, shall: (a) Implement and/or further elaborate policies and measures in accordance with its national circumstances, such as: (i) Enhancement of energy efficiency in relevant sectors of the national economy . . . (iv) Research on, and promotion, development and increased use of, new and renewable forms of energy, of carbon dioxide sequestration technologies and of advanced and innovative environmentally sound technologies.'

4   'The purpose of the clean development mechanism shall be to assist Parties not included in Annex I in achieving sustainable development and in contributing to the ultimate objective of the Convention, and to assist Parties included in Annex I in achieving compliance with their quantified emission limitation and reduction commitments under Article 3' (UNFCCC 1997: Article 12, p. 13).

markets has not yet reached such a stage as to provide a market value for the extra diversification and security of supply brought by the introduction of renewable energy (World Energy Council 1998). High discount rates and competition on short-term electricity prices, as seen in electricity markets undergoing a change in regulatory frameworks, may disadvantage projects with high capital costs but low running costs, unless governments set up schemes designed to replace and substitute for estimated deficiencies of the marketplace. In addition to cost-related barriers, non-cost barriers can also inhibit the greater use of CETs. This is particularly the case with the imperfect flow of information and the lack of integrated planning procedures and guidelines.

In short, there are numerous causes for imperfections in energy markets which constitute a hindrance for the socially optimal penetration of CETs:

- **Insufficient public information and awareness**. Users are not sufficiently informed of the technical possibilities, benefits and cost of CETs.

- **Financial willingness and feasibility**. The user may not have the willingness to pay or the ability to afford the additional investment on CETs equipment. An additional difficulty is that conventional credit does not fit well with the specific conditions for investment in CETs. Renewable energy systems are capital-intensive and require larger upfront investments and longer repayment periods than other energy technologies. Investors may therefore prefer to invest in sources with shorter payback periods, thus lowering their long-term risk exposure, even if those sources are more expensive on a long-term life-cycle basis (Thompson 1997).

- **Chicken and egg situation**. Most renewables still have some way to go before they are competitive with fossil technologies, especially for power generation purposes. This will demand intense further R&D efforts. Therefore, many CETs are in a classic chicken and egg situation at present: financiers and manufacturers are reluctant to invest the capital needed to reduce costs when demand is low and uncertain, but demand stays low because potential economies of scale cannot be realised at low levels of production.

- **Relatively small size of CET projects**. Technological constraints usually limit the project size. As a result, projects often have low gross returns, even while the rate of return may be well within market standards of what is considered an attractive investment.

- **Transaction costs** of smaller projects are disproportionately high compared with conventional projects. Pre-investment costs (including financing, legal and engineering fees, consultants) have a proportionately higher impact on the total costs of CET projects. Public agencies can make grants to cover the costs associated with establishing collaborative arrangements which, if successful, can be converted into an equity or royalty stake. The resulting financial return can then be redeployed as grants for successive projects.[5]

---

5   The Rockefeller Foundation has an ambitious programme of this kind aimed at stimulating private-sector investment in renewable energy and energy efficiency enterprises across the

■ **The 'free rider' or 'public goods' issue.** Individual consumers might be unwilling to pay for CETs because the benefits from reduced emissions are shared equally by everyone, regardless of who pays.

■ Setting up a solar electricity system for a single home can still cost between US$500 and $1,000: a large sum to spend in one lump. The problem is that rural customers often cannot get affordable credit. That makes it difficult for them to pay the high start-up costs of improving their energy supplies. One solution may be to establish a local member-supported bank to make small loans (such as the Grameen Bank in Bangladesh, which lends mainly to women and poor people). Another is to promote companies that lease basic equipment to consumers, communities, and local energy suppliers (World Bank 1996e). Evidence suggests that people will spend a significant proportion of their incomes on better energy, which improves their quality of life or enables them to become more productive. In Bangladesh even the poorest people are connecting to the grid when the service is available. In rural China, many people without easy access to cooking fuels are investing in efficient stoves and tree planting.

There are many instruments available to promote CETs (Pearce *et al.* 1997). On the international level, the Kyoto Mechanisms could result in additional investment in CETs, and, on the domestic level, policy mechanisms to improve the competitiveness of CETs include: energy labelling; energy efficiency standards; energy conservation centres; voluntary programmes; energy pricing and taxation; energy service companies; and demand-side management. Financial measures include (Gutermuth 1998; Piscitello and Bogach 1997): power purchase agreements; investment incentives; production incentives; renewables set-asides; externality adders;[6] environmental taxation; research, development and demonstration grants; government-assisted business development, green marketing; and other mechanisms such as wheeling and electricity banking. On both levels, international and domestic, the financial sector is of key importance. Most of these governmental policies to encourage renewable energy are moving in the following directions (Piscitello and Bogach 1997):

---

developing world. CET projects typically range from US$500,000 to $10 million. This also means that they are often unable to tap the international financial markets or other sources of private capital such as that available from the IFC, the arm of the World Bank that is the largest source of direct private-sector financing in the developing world. Except in sub-Saharan Africa, the IFC does not usually consider projects smaller than $20 million (Schmidheiny and Zorraquín 1996).

6   As traditional energy planning has largely ignored the environmental externalities of energy production, this has favoured technologies with high environmental impacts and discriminated against more environmentally benign technologies. Some regulators have attempted to address this issue by increasing the hypothetical cost of conventional power plants through an environmental externality charge ('adder') in the planning stage. Such adders can improve the likelihood of a CET-based plants being built by increasing the apparent cost of conventional technologies.

◼ Incentives are clearly intended to be temporary measures.

◼ Performance-based incentives are being used to encourage efficient projects.

◼ Competition is being explicitly or informally integrated into the implementation of financial incentives, to promote reduced technology and project development costs.

◼ The size of financial incentives is being targeted to match incremental life-cycle financial costs.

◼ Incentives are being developed with consideration of the potential for changing market conditions.

30.3 The 'RET/EE Investment Advisory Service'

The project 'Redirecting Commercial Investment Decisions to Cleaner Technologies: A Technology Transfer Clearinghouse' (volume: US$930,000; duration: 18 months; geographical scope: global) provides advisory services to financing parties evaluating specific RET and EE investments. The services focus on the incremental risk issues related to commercialisation of the technologies. The ongoing project will have the following results: additional lending directed at energy-efficient and renewable energy technologies; upgrading of skills in loan officers in developing-country financial institutions; and reduced emission of greenhouse gases.

Assumptions to achieve results include that partner banks will join in the project to achieve mutual goals; financial intermediaries in developing countries will be persuaded to identify suitable investment projects; and borrowers will avail themselves of the alternative appraisal services.

30.3.1 Purpose and objective

The purpose is to assist financial institutions and other investors to evaluate financing requests for RET and EE projects operating in developing and transition economies. Using Global Environment Facility[7] (GEF) funds, UNEP as the initiator of this project pays for and helps implement selected advisory services either to (a) compare new RET/EE options with traditional energy production technologies; or (b) evaluate RET/EE investments that are stand-alone. The services are not meant to cover all aspects of project evaluation, but rather to focus on the incremental risk issues related to these new technologies that abate greenhouse gases when used in lieu of traditional energy supply options.

---

7 The GEF is a pool of funds provided by developed countries to finance environmental projects in developing countries.

The project objective is to help bank loan officers and other financiers in the due diligence process for RET and EE investment requests, making it more likely that these kinds of project go forward. Initially, UNEP offers targeted advisory services that will resolve, on a case-by-case basis, issues unique to the financing of non-conventional energy technologies. The long-term goals are to help financial institutions develop the capability to appraise CET projects on their own, and reduce emission of greenhouse gases.

30.3.2 Activities

Using a need-based, targeted approach, the project provides customised advisory and project appraisal services to loan officers and their clients on projects where a GHG abatement potential exists but where informational barriers prevent it from going forward. Baseline appraisals will be the responsibility of the private-sector borrowers participating in the project. In selecting candidate investment projects for alternative appraisals, each proposal will be judged individually to determine that there is sufficient incremental global benefit.

30.3.3 Why focus on the finance sector?

Wiser and Pickle (1998) find that one of the key reasons why RET policies are not more effective is that project development and financing processes are frequently ignored or misunderstood when renewable energy policies are designed and implemented. Many CETs are no longer considered experimental: they have been proven to work well in commercial settings throughout the world. In many countries public policies and government regulations are starting to change market conditions, making it easier for non-conventional technologies to compete. Even though many CET investments are 'bankable', the financial community overall has been slow to provide financing for projects.

Financial institutions and other sources of private-sector funding follow a well-defined process when evaluating loan and investment proposals, generally referred to as **due diligence**. This consists of verifying the technical, financial and legal aspects of a project being considered, evaluating the creditworthiness of the borrower, and assessing the different risks involved. When a proposal involves a new technology or business activity, the risk assessment is more difficult because there is little practical experience with these technologies or activities. In the case of CET investments, cautious financial institutions often overestimate the risks and decide against extending loans or providing other forms of financial support for otherwise sound projects. In the end, projects that might really be good investments and yield a global environmental benefit fail to go forward because of a misperception of the risks involved.

Often the issues in question are not directly related to technology or financial risk, but rather concern secondary issues that are well understood with conventional investment projects. Examples include the potential market for a RET manufacturing operation, the stability of a shifting regulatory environment for an independent power producer, and the legal aspects surrounding new EE business activities such as performance contracting. Although financiers do not oppose investments in green technologies, most insist on following their standard project evaluation process before agreeing to provide support.

30.3.4 Examples

There follow three hypothetical examples of how the Investment Advisory Service works.[8]

30.3.4.1 Example 1: district heating ESCO

An organisation operating in Central and Eastern Europe specialises in evaluating and upgrading district heating (DH) systems for local municipalities. Using metering techniques, it benchmarks and improves system performance, and determines which equipment upgrades will provide the highest returns on investment. Based on this expertise, the organisation seeks to create an energy service company (ESCO) that makes upgrades to DH systems in return for a contractual share of the cost savings. It has approached a financial institution to back a portfolio of projects.

Although the financial institution is satisfied that the technical improvements realisable by the ESCO can lead to significant financial savings, there are two areas where lack of supporting information leads to problems with the standard due diligence process. The financial institution is concerned that: (a) it will be difficult to establish baselines for the energy performance contracts and therefore the exact savings will be difficult to determine; and (b) the customer default risk may be unacceptably high. If these two issues can be resolved positively, the financial institution has agreed to back the project.

For this example, the financial institution could prepare a Terms of Reference and use the Investment Advisory Service to hire:

- An industrial energy-use specialist, to evaluate how effectively one can set baselines for DH system energy consumption and therefore the ESCO's ability to negotiate firm performance contracts

- An analyst working for an in-country partner bank, to value the receivables of the business activity if they are used as a security for the investment

UNEP would hypothetically provide up to $50,000 to support these advisory services for a period of three to four months, after which an investment decision would be taken.

30.3.4.2 Example 2: wind energy independent power producer

A developer has proposed the creation of a sole-purpose company that would build and operate a wind power project in country X. A feasibility study has found that the wind resource is viable at the prospective site and that the public electricity supplier is willing to negotiate a long-term power purchase agreement (PPA). Assuming a reasonable kWh

---

8 The examples are meant only to clarify how the Investment Advisory Service can be used by financial institutions to evaluate a potential investment in a renewable energy or energy efficiency project. The examples are not based on specific projects and should therefore not be viewed as endorsements of particular business activities.

rate is negotiated, the project financials are attractive. A financial institution has been approached to take an equity stake in the company.

Although the financial institution believes the project could be a sound investment, there are two areas where assistance is required to enable them to take a decision. As it is a new type of investment for the financial institution, the operating and maintenance costs of the new technology are difficult to forecast in their financial model. In addition, since this will be the first wind energy PPA to be negotiated in country X, the financial institution expects it to be a complicated process and therefore wants it completed prior to their making a commitment. If these two remaining issues can be resolved positively, the financial institution will back the project.

In this situation, the financial institution could write the Terms of Reference and with UNEP assistance choose and hire:

- An independent consultant specialised in the operation of wind farms, to forecast the proposed plant's operating and maintenance costs and to provide statistics on turbine failure rates

- A legal advisor based in country X who understands the electric utility legislation, to provide expert opinion on the related contract and regulatory issues, and to assist the project promoters in negotiating the PPA

Since aspects of the proposed work are not incremental in nature, UNEP might cost-share the effort 60–40.

30.3.4.3 Example 3: agricultural waste biogas plant

A joint venture has been created between a large South American pig farm and a waste treatment company to build and operate a biogas digester. This digester will manage the waste disposal from several farms in the region and will generate additional revenues from the sale of the methane gas produced. This business activity is directly related to a soon-to-be-enacted environmental directive on agricultural waste disposal. The partners in the project have approached a development bank for loan financing.

Although the development bank is satisfied with the basic financials of the project, it is unsure that the environmental issues have been sufficiently resolved for the investment to go forward. Specifically, it is unclear how much farmers will be willing to pay to dispose of their waste and whether the residuals from the plant will require further processing prior to final disposal.

For this project, a Terms of Reference could be prepared jointly by UNEP and the development bank specifying:

- That consultations would be organised in-country between the development bank, joint-venture partners and ministry officials to discuss how rigorously the directive would be applied and therefore the value of a disposal service to farmers

- That UNEP would evaluate, in conjunction with ministry officials, the toxicity of the residues from such a plant, whether uses for them could be found, or whether further processing would be required prior to final disposal

For this work, UNEP might provide $25,000 in funding and $25,000 in direct technical assistance.

30.4 Conclusions

CETs are generally more expensive than conventional technology. If subsidies were not given to fossil fuels and if there were policies to internalise the social cost of conventional technologies, many CETs would already be fully cost-competitive. Despite their acknowledged benefits, the economic future for CETs remains uncertain and there are barriers that must be overcome. There is a need to level the playing field by withdrawing subsidies to conventional fossil fuels and by including externalities in energy prices. Governments can also apply legislation, market measures and temporary incentives to encourage investment by the private and financial sectors. Measures that have proved successful should be replicated, where appropriate, in other countries. In order to provide tomorrow's technologies, substantial long-term research and development is needed to decrease costs and environmental impact and to increase the reliability and maintainability of CETs.

The key financing issue in developing countries is the availability of capital to CET developers and rural end-users, while the key issues in developed countries involve the cost of money, the ease of obtaining low-cost funds, and institutional complexities that hinder financing and market growth. Several innovative financing mechanisms for CET developers and end-users have been devised and tested by the international organisations, governments and NGOs to promote CETs, especially in developing countries. One of these measures is the RET/EE Investment Advisory Service.

Actual project proposals under this Facility (evaluated during 1999) include, for example, a wind park in Ghana, rehabilitation of district heating systems in Romania and coffee production waste recovery and its energetic utilisation in Costa Rica. The most critical aspect when evaluating these proposals has been the identification of 'additionality': i.e. the scope of additional activities required for the assessment of renewable energy/energy-efficient projects.

The industrialised countries of the North have most of the technologies and the financial resources for utilising CETs, while many developing countries have great potential for CETs. Therefore, technology transfer to developing countries is needed, and the Kyoto Mechanisms could play an important role in this regard. However, only proven state-of-the-art technologies should be transferred to developing countries and not technologies with only minor impact on climate change mitigation. Factors that can make investments in CETs an attractive option include:

- In the short run, by the Kyoto time-frame 2008–12, RETs are in many cases likely to be competitive because of their relative short lead times for implementation.

- Due to the requirement of the CDM to contribute to sustainable development, there is a greater likelihood that RETs will be included in a portfolio of feasible CDM projects.

UNEP's Financial Institutions Initiative (UNEP 1999) has been instrumental in drawing to the attention of the financial services industry environmental concerns.[9] By signing the Statement by Financial Institutions on the Environment and Sustainable Development, bank leaders commit their organisations to incorporate environmental considerations into internal and external business activities. This management commitment makes its way 'down' to bank loan officers in the form of new issues that they must consider in the due diligence process; it does not, however, provide the information or tools required to do so. Where CET investments are concerned, the RET/EE Investment Advisory Service helps financial institutions follow through with their commitments. The combined top-down/bottom-up approach is an effective way to help financial institutions in promoting investment in CETs, thereby contributing to sustainable banking.

9   UNEP's efforts on energy are organised into four parallel and inter-linked sub-programmes. They emphasise: making decision-makers in governments and the private sector aware of the potential of energy-efficient technologies and the policies and practices available to promote their wider adoption throughout society, as well as giving them skills to put that knowledge to work; promoting understanding of the role that renewable energy sources can play in providing energy services with low environmental impacts, and building capacity to recognise and remove barriers to their more widespread use; making policy-makers and energy planners aware of the environmental impacts associated with energy production and use, and promoting the incorporation of good environmental management practices into energy planning and policy; and enhancing awareness on climate change mitigation and adaptation policies, strategies and technologies to reduce the emission of greenhouse gases. The project also contributes directly to the realisation of UNEP's sub-programme on Environment, Trade and Economics.

SUSTAINABLE FINANCE FOR SUSTAINABLE ENERGY
The role of financial intermediaries

Glenn Stuart Hodes
Princeton University, USA

A sea change in development assistance is required to avert the grave consequences to the environment, social equity and global security that are assured by perpetuating the conventional energy development path of the past century. This chapter reviews the main implementation barriers faced by developing-country entrepreneurs attempting to advance renewable energy and energy efficiency projects, focusing in particular on gaps in development finance and development assistance. While several academic studies and policy analyses have addressed the political, technical or market-specific barriers to developing renewable energy and energy efficiency projects, relatively few have examined perhaps the most salient obstacle: adequate and appropriate financing for such initiatives. I would like to state the case for the unique role that **financial intermediaries** can play in accelerating commercialisation of renewable energy enterprises, in the hope of demonstrating the potential impact and benefit of expanding intermediary activities in developing countries.

I define 'financial intermediaries' rather narrowly, and use this term for lack of a better alternative. Intermediaries provide capital and specialised services to project developers on flexible, concessionary terms, acting as a liaison between entrepreneurs, commercial investors, donors and development banks. Financial intermediaries operate at investment levels that are smaller than commercial financial channels, yet larger than typical micro-credit programmes. Whereas private project finance tends to be 'passive', an intermediary takes on a greater role in management oversight and technical assistance, involving itself at the earliest stages of an investment.

Financial intermediaries are poised to play a pivotal role in expanding rural electrification and distributed electricity services by bridging existing financial and implementation gaps. It is unlikely that private-sector actors will ever fully incorporate environmental externalities or social development goals into their energy financing decisions. Not unlike private lending institutions, multilateral financial organisations such as the World Bank, the International Finance Corporation and the Inter-American Development Bank, devote only a small fraction of their energy lending to renewable or efficiency projects. Such projects' relatively small scale, high transaction costs and inherently greater risks limit more extensive financing by such actors. On the other hand, traditional overseas development assistance (ODA), or bilateral aid, is stabilising or even diminishing; moreover, its record of effectiveness in achieving impact has been poor. Consequently, a great number of exciting ideas and technological innovations from 'social entre-preneurs' in the energy field fail to get off the ground, as such entrepreneurs lack even the small amounts of money and enterprise development assistance required to foster self-sustaining initiatives. Intermediaries can link good ideas with small-scale loans, equity investments and other financial services, thereby strengthening the capacity of private enterprises to meet social objectives.

This chapter begins by considering the risks to the global environment and social equity posed by the conventional energy path. I argue that building renewable energy markets and enterprises is critical, yet many impediments to appropriate and adequate financing in developing countries exist. I outline several reasons why traditional project finance terms tend to favour thermal power projects versus renewable energy or efficiency projects. I then describe limitations on development assistance to the energy sector and concessional lending by multilateral development banks, as well as the unique compara-tive advantages and limitations of financial intermediaries.

31.1 Financial barriers to the commercialisation of renewable energy

The conventional energy paradigm has 'run out of gas'. The premise that the least-cost expansion of output from fossil fuels is either desirable or just unavoidable simply cannot be sustained in the light of emerging scientific evidence and the past experiences of rapidly developing countries. A confluence of interests among multinational oil corpo-rations, the coal industry, petroleum-producing states and the leaders of rapidly indus-trialising countries seeking unlimited growth at any price has perpetuated this myth. Developed and developing nations alike continue to rely on the burning of fossil fuels and the exploitation of natural resources with minimal regard to the consequences of resource depletion and environmental degradation (see Raskin and Margolis 1998). The effects are exacerbating local air pollution, acid rain and the already irreversible damage to the global climate. The consequences of this local and transnational environmental pollution and volatile climatic impacts associated with global warming could seriously disrupt natural ecosystems, induce serious long-term health risks and threaten the natural course of economic productivity and growth in many societies. Moreover, fossil fuels are not inexhaustible, and will become increasingly costly to extract and refine as their supply continues to diminish over the next century. One study conducted by the Stockholm Environmental Institute predicts that at projected 'business-as-usual' scenarios of development, currently estimated proven reserves of oil may be depleted as early as 2025 (Raskin and Margolis 1998: 376).

Meanwhile, one-third of the entire world's population still lacks access to electricity, despite the fact that electrification catalyses both agricultural and industrial productivity, can help stem the tide of rural–urban migration and may promote social cohesion and political stability in areas plagued by chronic poverty (see Borg 1990). Unless legislation requires or facilitates subsidisation of rural customers or the provision of power to low-income areas, privatised utilities are not likely to reduce their profits by extending service to such areas. Current energy use in developing countries is also highly inefficient and detrimental to social and human development. Millions of people—women and children in particular—spend hours each day collecting subsistence energy at a great opportunity cost to productive income generation or education.[1] The World Bank estimates that, even if the developing countries' demand for primary energy were to grow at a rate 2% lower than the historical trend line, demand in 2010 will still be more than two and a half times greater than at 1990 levels.[2] How that energy is produced is of enormous consequence, since developing countries will collectively overtake the US and Europe as the largest sources of greenhouse gas emissions within a few decades. This explosive growth in energy services greatly increases threats to human health and safety in its direct impacts on indoor and outdoor air quality, water purity and land use.

31.1.1 *Current trends in development assistance for energy*

In spite of these projections, and evidence of deepening socioeconomic inequity between the developed and the developing world, traditional overseas bilateral assistance from OECD countries earmarked for energy projects is declining (Borg 1990: 45). Specialised multilateral organisations, such as the Global Environment Facility, do not have enough resources or the expertise to shape the energy investment choices of developing countries.

Technological interventions that lack a sound implementation strategy are doomed to failure. Among many factors, a successful implementation strategy should consider: a country's development priorities; how a particular project would build on the capacity of local institutions and leadership; end-user affordability and willingness to pay; the cultural appropriateness of a given technology; responses to unpredictability in energy supply and demand; and mechanisms for community participation and review. Some donors are trying to bridge existing implementation gaps by implementing renewable energy demonstration projects with a more explicit focus on community participation and training, and developing a local repair and maintenance infrastructure alongside the technology transfer component. While these are positive directions, they fail to bring

1   Comments by Susan McDade, Energy and Atmosphere Programme, United Nations Development Programme, quoted in *Solar and Renewable Energy Outlook* 24.10 (1 October 1998).
2   On this assumption, energy demand in 2030 is predicted to be four and half times greater than 1990 levels (see Princeton University 1999).

about the commercial viability of technological innovations and enterprises, which also requires building indigenous infrastructure for distribution and maintenance of services, and providing appropriate finance mechanisms. The priority in development assistance for energy should be to establish an enabling environment for financially self-sustaining renewable energy and efficiency enterprises. Effective technology transfer or 'leapfrogging' cannot occur without the support of private industry and private capital flows. Foreign direct investment far surpasses multilateral loans and bilateral donor aid—especially in the power sector.[3] Fortunately, one-quarter of all global development capital is consumed by the power sector (Hawken *et al.* 1999: 251). However many impediments to directing such capital to renewable energy and energy efficiency projects still exist. The following section outlines these impediments.

31.1.2 *Market conditions for renewable energy in developing countries*

A large potential market for renewable energy ventures exists. Many citizens in developing areas spend enormous sums of money per unit of energy for lighting in the form of inferior-grade candles, paraffin lanterns or dry-cell batteries. Renewable energy projects in developing countries are most competitive in off-grid applications, because the marginal costs of expanding transmission lines from centralised power grids are often higher than the costs of stand-alone renewable electricity systems. In some cases, even renewable technologies located on power grids can be cost-competitive, by generating power closer to consumers and reducing transmission and distribution costs (see Greene and Duke 1999). Nevertheless, the bulk of energy capacity deficits in developing countries are not being met through renewable energy or efficiency projects.[4] Market development has been constrained by a variety of factors, not least of which is inadequate financing options and under-developed capital markets.

31.1.3 *Barriers to implementation*

Some of the most significant barriers to implementing renewable energy and efficiency projects are constraints on financing. Renewable energy entrepreneurs face an uphill battle in their efforts to translate good ideas into viable or 'bankable' projects. Most private banks will not do business with a project developer lacking an extensive track record and highly liquid assets. In some countries, credit decisions by local or state-

---

3 It is estimated that the explosive growth in electricity expansion in developing countries will generate over \$1.7 trillion in potential investments in generating capacity along by 2020 (IEA 2000: 25).

4 Using a back-of-the-envelope calculation, relying on dry-cell batteries for lighting can cost as much as US\$60 per kWh, compared to about 3 cents per kWh for natural gas combined cycle power generation in the US. Based on this scale, current energy technology in some developing areas is 5,000 times less cost-efficient than the baseline standard in the developed world. From these numbers alone it is easy to see that the potential market for alternative energy technologies is massive.

owned banks are determined to a greater extent by patronage, corruption and clan politics than by financial fundamentals (*Impact* 1999: 25). Moreover, the structure and elements of financing for such ventures *vis-à-vis* traditional fossil fuel power plants is quite different. Table 31.1 juxtaposes key input variables in a project finance calculus to illustrate the many ways in which thermal power projects are more favourably assessed when standard cost–benefit analyses are employed.

Project finance variable	Thermal power ventures	Renewable energy and energy efficiency projects
Risk	Concentration of assets; fuel supply and variable costs	High resource and technology risks
Recovery of capital costs	Short or long time-horizon	Long time-horizon
Siting	Extended to power grid infrastructure	Frequently off-grid or stand-alone systems
Technology	Demonstrated/familiar	Experimental/evolving
Scale	Generally large	Generally small-scale or requiring aggregation to be more viable
Residual value	Turbines and generating equipment	Little to none
Collateral	Often based on PPAs	None
Enterprise track record	Established	Limited
Returns to scale	Large	Small
Creditworthiness	Proven, self-financed or syndicated	Questionable
Efficiency	Poor yet consistent	Variable/intermittent
Capital cost–capacity ratio	Low	High
Transaction costs–pay-off ratio	Low	High
Terms of power purchase agreements	Standard/favourable	Unfavourable/nascent
Government support/ policy environment	Receptive yet corruption-prone	Erratic or nascent

Table 31.1   **Comparison of key variables in an energy project finance calculus**

31.1.3.1 Deregulation and renewable energy enterprises

The privatisation trend sweeping energy markets around the world has had an indirect impact on renewable energy project financing, since many of these projects are being undertaken by independent power producers (IPPs). Not backed by sovereign guarantees or a power purchase agreement (PPA), independent developers finance projects on the basis of expected returns and the rate at which they can recover an investment.[5] Typically, IPP projects are characterised by higher costs of capital. Without the security of long-term contracts, IPPs are under pressure to obtain more equity, less debt, and debt with a shorter maturity, as higher interest rates are demanded in view of the greater risks involved (Wiser *et al.* 1997). This acts as an incentive to minimise the ratio of required capital to energy generation capacity. This ratio tends to be higher for most renewable energy projects than for thermal power projects. Thus, even though lower operating costs (primarily because of lower fuel and operational costs) render renewable energy ventures cost competitive on a **life-cycle** basis, higher upfront capital costs and lower capacity factors make them less attractive to private developers than thermal power plants. On top of that, infrastructure investments in developing countries also face higher discount rates because inflation is more difficult to control, which favours projects whose positive cash flow is front-loaded.

Many IPP renewable energy projects must sell their power into spot electricity markets rather than under a guaranteed PPA. In developing countries spot markets are uniquely risky, not least because of uncertain end-user affordability. According to one private investor, 'the biggest risk is not project risk, but country or market risk'.[6] Compared to renewable project ventures, managers of fossil fuel plants can exercise greater control not only over their average energy output, but also over the **timing** of their sale of power. Since the ability to generate power during peak periods earns a premium in spot markets, renewable energy enterprises may again find themselves at a disadvantage.

31.1.4 PPAs, government policies and renewable energy enterprises

Some renewable energy ventures are being financed on the basis of a PPA with a federal or regional government body. The terms of a PPA are critical to determining the type of power venture to be financed. Renewable energy projects tend to be more viable in countries that have specifically geared the terms of PPAs to account for inherent differences in technologies and technological risk, such as India, Indonesia and the Philippines. In most of the developing world, however, the terms and payment schedules of PPAs are still more favourable to thermal power projects. Lenders and lawyers are more accustomed to designing PPAs to mitigate risks associated with fossil fuel power plants,[7] rather than the unique risks of renewable energy ventures.

More generally, the position of most developing country governments towards efficiency and renewable energy projects has been either ambivalent or unpredictable. The march toward rapid modernisation and industrialisation encourages any venture

---

5 Private independent power producers engage in the building of electrical generation facilities for industrial, commercial and residential applications using finance from global capital markets. IPPs are thought to handle fuel supply arrangements, demand management and construction of facilities better than government-owned utilities.

6 Remarks by Keith Henry, CEO of National Power, UK, quoted in Dansie 1998: 8.

7 For example, most PPAs index purchase price to fuel costs so as to control for adverse supply shocks.

designed to expand power at lowest near-term cost, regardless of environmental implications. Public bodies that can address market distortions in order to level the playing
field for renewable energy enterprises, such as public utilities commissions, do not exist
in many developing countries. Moreover, some countries provide large subsidies for fossil
fuels while maintaining import duties on equipment used to generate renewable power.
This has been more or less the norm in developing countries, with examples as diverse
as Indonesia, Uganda and Turkmenistan, where such duties can be an important source
of government revenue. Taking market expansion of photovoltaic (PV) technology in
Africa as an example, a World Bank study estimated that restrictive VAT and import duties
on PV components in Kenya effectively added 40% to the capital investment costs of solar
home systems, rendering market penetration exceedingly difficult (Cabraal *et al.* 1998).
Similar barriers were faced by a NREL/DOE Village Power prototype project in Uganda,
where import duties on PV panel components amounted to as much as 30% of the cost.[8]
In contrast, both Botswana and Zambia recently removed sales taxes and import duties
on PV systems, and both countries are working towards the removal of subsidies on
paraffin and other commonly used fossil fuels. While many governments have the power
to leverage reforms in the commercial banking sector to give renewable ventures increased
access to capital (e.g. establishing concessional rates, limits on foreign exchange, indigenous equipment requirements and even basic loan conditions), many have failed to
exercise it.

Other key input variables in a project finance calculation also tend to favour thermal
investments:

- **Construction times and cost.** Construction times for renewable energy ventures can be both longer and more unpredictable than single-cycle natural gas
generation plants, which may deter investment. Hydroelectric projects in
particular can have very long lead times. Since construction costs, such as site
establishment and building access roads, are similar for small projects (e.g.
micro-hydro) as for large ones, construction cost as a percentage of total costs
can be considerably greater for renewable energy projects than for thermal ones
(Foley 1991).

- **Period of operation/resource risks.** Energy generated from wind, solar and
biomass sources can be affected by seasonal and weather variations—volatility
that can reduce the bottom line. Traditional investors are reluctant to assume
these kinds of 'uncontrollable' resource risks, although insurance to cover price
volatility for weather variations is an option. While comprehensive hydro-
logical data tends to be more readily available than data on wind patterns—
facilitating statistical projections of reliability—water flow in general tends to
be more unpredictable than wind speed. While there is significant technological promise in PV panels, based on the trajectory of solar energy's 'experience
curve', the intermittent nature of solar energy and the primitiveness of energy

---

8   Dr Marie-Louise Caravatti, Office of Energy Efficiency and Renewable Energy, US Department
of Energy. Interview by author, 20 April 2000.

storage technologies mean that few small-scale PV projects are truly attractive to serious private investors.

- **Transaction costs.** Because renewable energy projects are more site-specific and dependent on the predictability of weather patterns, the costs of bid preparations, statistical projections of future weather patterns, market feasibility studies and environmental impact assessments may be higher than for thermal projects. The stages of due diligence and associated costs that an investor incurs for any given deal (i.e. evaluating proposals, conducting market research, managing environmental and legal risks, packaging financial services, contracting with a utility, account monitoring and evaluation) are fairly similar regardless of the generation capacity. Renewable energy projects are often smaller in terms of ultimate electricity output; therefore, diseconomies of scale associated with these transaction and portfolio management costs can represent a major barrier to obtaining adequate finance.

- **Despatchability and transmission costs.** Renewable energy projects may also face higher costs for transmission to a centralised grid. For instance, if transmission access charges are based on peak capacity generation, then solar and wind power projects are likely to face higher costs, due to the intermittent nature of supply. Rural renewable energy projects may also face higher transmission costs if tariffs are calculated according to distance from the grid.

- **Political and currency risk.** In some countries, the availability of political risk insurance to protect an investment against government overthrow, war or seizure of assets can make or break an investment deal. Large-scale thermal power ventures often benefit from political risk insurance provided by co-investors such as the Overseas Private Investment Corporation (OPIC) and the International Finance Corporation (IFC). The provision of such insurance for renewable projects, on the other hand, is not well established.

- **Lack of profitable models.** Large private power companies are best positioned to secure reasonable debt financing and assume the unique risks for renewable energy projects. However, the unfamiliarity of the technology to most strategic energy investors and the lack of successful models have been major barriers to their participation.

- **Prestige.** Investors and governments have been conditioned to view large-scale thermal power projects as 'prestigious' or symbolic of development status. Smaller renewable energy projects do not yet have this cachet.

- **End-user affordability.** Spot power markets in developing countries have heightened sensitivities to end-user affordability. While renewable energy projects can distinguish themselves as environmentally friendly, the average consumer is more concerned with attractive payment options, low rates, reliability and constant tariffs. Insufficient information on the environmental and social impacts of fossil fuels, coupled with low household budgets, leaves little room for renewable energy ventures that cannot provide electricity on a cost-competitive basis. But, as in developed countries, environmental considerations are not factored into end-user costs.

31.2 Surveying the landscape of development assistance

As the previous section illustrates, reducing the incremental financing costs and risks associated with renewable energy ventures is critical to commercialising actors in this emerging industry. The unique construction, resource and technology risks associated with renewable energy ventures would seem to demand 'deep-pocket' investors who can tolerate longer periods of financial exposure. But as the corresponding returns are currently not high or fast enough for such traditional investors to give renewable energy ventures more serious attention, it is clear that some projects will necessitate a financial 'push' from government or development assistance entities in order to close this gap.

Yet is the existing architecture of development assistance adequate to meet this challenge? Despite an increasing consensus among donors that renewable energy projects should receive greater support and financial assistance, fundamental weaknesses in the structure, processes and programmes of development assistance have curtailed more rapid and dramatic advances. As of 1993, only 5% of the US$4.5 billion in development assistance earmarked for energy had been extended to a renewable project (Kozloff and Shobowale 1994: vii). This section outlines some of the shortcomings in development assistance and illustrates some of the financial cracks in the development assistance architecture.

31.2.1 Philanthropy

Philanthropic activities in support of renewable energy have been as unpredictable as government policies. Foundation initiatives generally do not have untarnished reputations for achieving the level of 'sustainability' that they themselves tend to demand from individual project managers. Indeed, it is not inconceivable that many of the donors that have championed renewable energy and rural electrification[9] may divert their lending activities to other 'priority areas' in the future. This may result, ironically, from two opposing interpretations of the outlook for the near term. On the one hand, foundations may perceive their assistance as making too insignificant a mark, believing that energy and development challenges are so endemic to low-income countries that they can only be supported at the inter-governmental level. On the other hand, there is the danger that, after having assisted in the development of prototype projects in a few developing

---

9 Some of the major foundations that have supported renewable energy include the Rockefeller Foundation, Rockefeller Brothers Fund, Joyce Mertz Gilmore Foundation, W. Alton Jones Foundation, MacArthur Foundation and the Heinz Endowments.

countries, the donor community will have deemed its role as being to all intents and purposes 'non-essential'.

Institutional guidelines and politics may also constrain foundations from supporting energy and development initiatives. Many foundation officers are reluctant to support initiatives and sector strategies that they, their organisation or the foundation community have not themselves conceived. Even more fundamentally, foundation guidelines prohibiting assistance to private ventures can limit participation in otherwise attractive renewable energy initiatives, which often fall into blurry quasi-private or public/private categories. Finally, the San Francisco-based Energy Foundation, which is the only major foundation devoted exclusively to energy-specific programming, maintains a largely domestic scope in its operations.

31.2.2 *Overseas development assistance*

Bilateral development agencies have not made dramatic advances in this area, despite having disbursed hundreds of millions of dollars' worth of aid monies for renewable energy. In past decades, much of the foreign aid for renewable energy has neglected commercial sustainability, with predictable consequences. Many donor-supported renewable energy projects failed to generate sufficient interest from either local governments or traditional investors, lacked adequate infrastructure for maintenance and repair, or fell victim to implementation deadlock or follow-up neglect.[10] Most donors have now learned the hard way that disseminating highly subsidised equipment without due regard to developing a market infrastructure for continuing services on a commercial basis has little hope of success (Foley 1991: 7). However, bilateral aid continues to focus on technology transfer (the hardware), rather than the human capacity constraints and managerial skills necessary to sustain markets to support and expand these technologies (the software).

Furthermore, many bilateral development assistance agencies, such as USAID (United States), GTZ (Germany) and DANIDA (Denmark), continue to require that the recipient countries purchase equipment or other products and services from the donor country. Ethical and economic factors often receive a lower priority than export promotion. While technology may be transferred, the development of indigenous enterprises or jobs cannot be assured. For example, a new programme of the US Department of Energy and the Export–Import Bank is providing small and medium-sized renewable energy and efficiency projects in China with a small line of credit to promote sustainable energy development. However, the loans must be used to acquire goods and services from US companies seeking entry into China's burgeoning power market, thereby limiting the development of the country's upstream suppliers (Loveless 1997: 1).

---

10 Kozloff and Shobowale 1994: 20. For example, a review of the energy lending in the 1980s conducted by the Deutsche Gesellschaft für Technische Zusammenarbeit (GTZ) led to the conclusion that technical assistance outweighed financial assistance almost five to one, despite the fact that purely technical solutions almost always fail without a commercial infrastructure, adequate access to capital and regional planning.

Another shortcoming is that donors often compete with each other to support the same (and least risky) projects. Such competition increases the opportunity cost of not supporting more deserving projects or entrepreneurs, and can lead to 'tunnel vision' by aid agencies. Worse, in the absence of inter-agency policy dialogue or country-based co-ordination of development strategies, donor activities have in the past unintentionally squeezed out local enterprises struggling to commercialise renewable technologies. Donor-financed projects can flood renewable energy technologies that are fully subsidised into the same market in which upstart renewable energy enterprises are struggling to compete and mature on purely commercial terms.[11]

31.2.3 Multilateral development banks

The World Bank's mandate, mode of operations and lending criteria act as factors that render its financing of renewable energy problematic. By mandate, the World Bank must limit its role in energy and development to government-backed projects. Its 'stake' in a particular project is generally large; indeed, few investment entities meeting developing-country power needs operate at the same level as the World Bank, which was created over 50 years ago to address insufficient commercial finance for infrastructure and public goods, such as toll roads. Historically, the World Bank has supported large public infrastructure projects, such as thermal power plants and very large hydroelectric dams, where the scope and risks were so large that the Bank's participation was deemed essential to proceed.

From the World Bank's perspective, the scale of most renewable energy projects is generally much smaller than appropriate for its typical mode of operations. The transaction costs associated with identifying or following through on a small-scale renewable project are likely to be as high, if not higher, than for a traditional power project. Regardless of the disproportionate risks and pay-off structures, the small scale, output, and cash flows of most renewable energy projects relative to their transaction costs seriously reduces their attractiveness. Moreover, management incentives faced by World Bank personnel, such as performance evaluation criteria that encourage 'getting money out the door fast', also favour larger-scale conventional power projects. The Wappenhans Report, a famous internal critique of World Bank lending, noted that innovation is not rewarded at the Bank, because the types of project that tend to be approved are those likely to have been done before or which have had a large degree of pre-screening. The ground-breaking nature of renewable energy projects and the lack of independent resources for detailed feasibility studies thus work against obtaining World Bank funding. For all of these reasons, activists and non-governmental organisations that have challenged the Work Bank to make dramatic changes in its energy portfolio should be realistic in their expectations. Nonetheless, a small pipeline of renewable energy projects within the World Bank Group is beginning to emerge, albeit slowly.

The private-sector lending arm of the World Bank Group, the International Finance Corporation (IFC), also generally requires a significant stake in its projects (around

11   Johanna Hjerthén, Programme Associate, E&Co, 22 April 1999.

20%–25%). The IFC expects project developers to have sound credit and to have done extensive project preparation. These standards may not be realistic for most small- and medium-sized renewable energy enterprises in developing economies. And, ironically, enterprises with impeccable financial credentials may prefer private finance to the assistance of the IFC, due to the organisation's stringent reporting and monitoring requirements. Given its private-sector orientation, the IFC has a tendency to finance 'sure things', such as breweries, telecom ventures, cement factories or large-scale thermal power plants. Excluding its actions as a co-manager of the inter-agency Global Environment Facility (GEF), the IFC currently has only one geothermal project, one biomass project and five small- and medium-sized hydroelectric power projects on its balance sheet.[12] While the IFC has specialised financing programmes that are particularly well suited for small and medium-sized enterprises, such as the Africa Project Development Facility and the Mekong Project Development Facility, they have not yet supported a renewable energy venture. On the other hand, the IFC has taken a leadership role in managing some important new funds available for smaller-scale renewable ventures, namely the Renewable Energy and Energy Efficiency Fund (REEF), the PV Market Transformation Initiative (PVMTI), and the Solar Development Corporation. It has also provided capital to Energia Globa International, which has developed several hydroelectric and wind power projects in Latin America. The success of these very encouraging initiatives needs to be carefully assessed in the years to come.

Regional development banks (e.g. the Inter-American Development Bank, Asian Development Bank) face similar constraints as those of the World Bank. The incentive to lend out the greatest amount of money for the smallest transaction costs, which is particularly disadvantageous to renewable energy projects, may simply be magnified for regional development banks due to their relatively smaller budgets.[13]

31.3 Financial intermediaries: advantages, case studies and future prospects

Financial intermediaries have emerged as new and critical stakeholders in the field of renewable energy finance. Such intermediaries provide capital and specialised services on generally more flexible and favourable terms than strictly commercial entities. They operate at smaller investment levels than most traditional financiers or multilateral development banks, yet larger than typical micro-credit programmes. Support ranges from as little as US$5,000 to a few million dollars in some cases. Intermediaries also tend to take on greater management oversight, entrepreneurial development and technical assistance responsibilities than private investors, especially in the earliest stages of a venture. One financial intermediary distinguishes itself by supporting projects passed

---

12 Kamal Dorabawila, Investment Officer, IFC, communication of 29 January 2000.
13 Deborah L. Bleviss, Inter-American Development Bank, 23 April 1999.

over by donors or traditional investors at critical and more riskier junctures in their lifetime.

31.3.1 *Comparative advantages of financial intermediaries*

What are the comparative advantages of financial intermediaries in promoting the development of renewable energy and energy efficiency projects relative to other funding sources?

- **Flexible capital**. Because most renewable energy entrepreneurs are insufficiently capitalised and have limited track records, access to flexible capital to get past the 'pilot' stage is an extremely important and difficult hurdle. Unlike multilateral investment banks and private investors, financial intermediaries' investment guidelines (i.e. type of project supported, size of investment) are less stringent. They may provide only a modest amount of debt or equity—just enough for projects to leverage later-stage funding. The importance of flexible capital cannot be overstated. Renewable energy enterprises have little incentive or capacity to address important issues such as reliability of service, maintenance and repair, efficiency, and effective marketing and diffusion techniques on the basis of grant aid. More generally, incentives to achieve a certain level of performance without the exchange of risk and return are weakened. Since intermediaries expect their loans and equity investments to be repaid promptly, and to generate a modest return on equity, their interventions—especially at the earliest stages of a project—can help prepare entrepreneurs for the realistic demands of private investors in the future.

- **Entrepreneurial services and technical assistance**. In addition to providing capital, intermediaries often provide project developers with entrepreneurial development services and technical assistance. The former includes assisting entrepreneurs with acquiring basic business and entrepreneurial skills (e.g. developing detailed business plans, instituting more sophisticated or internationally recognised accounting practices), marketing their investment ideas, and negotiating with private financiers and international development agencies for partnership support. Since many of the best renewable energy project ideas are generated by technical experts, the business and marketing skills development that may come with the participation of a financial intermediary can make all the difference in translating such ideas into bankable projects. Technical assistance commonly includes support for financial analyses, feasibility studies and impact assessments—whether of a business, engineering or environmental nature—that are generally not supported by commercial institutions.

- **Sector-specific experience**. Intermediaries have a definite advantage over most private sources of financing in their level of knowledge specific to renewable energy, which can significantly reduce transaction costs. Many private energy companies have been reluctant to invest in alternative energy, partly because they lack the resources necessary to distinguish between the relative merits of the wide array of new technologies in the field. Ideally, intermediaries provide the right balance between good business instincts and an in-depth understanding of the technological merits of various projects.

■ **Donor liaison and project packaging.** Intermediary services may also include assisting developing-country entrepreneurs to identify not only current, but also later-stage, funding. Existing linkages between these entrepreneurs and development agencies are relatively weak. By serving as a liaison between these groups, intermediaries can improve the chances that viable projects receive adequate funding consideration at all stages. Their unique positioning between policy-makers, donors and 'the field' allows for connecting entrepreneurs that have 'graduated' from intermediary support to larger donors. From the perspective of commercial entities and multilateral development banks (including the GEF), projects that have already received early-stage funding from an intermediary may be considered as 'vetted', and therefore less risky. Any financial analysis conducted by the intermediary also reduces the costs to later-stage investors. In this sense, an intermediary's role may be viewed as packaging a project for less experienced or patient renewable energy investors. From the perspective of the entrepreneur, assistance in deal 'packaging' for other investors may be as great a customer requirement as the capital itself.

31.3.1.1 Case study: E&Co

E&Co is a financial intermediary based in Bloomfield, New Jersey, with a network of global offices and representatives. Its activities spun off from the Rockefeller Foundation's Global Environment Programme, and it became an independent entity in 1994. E&Co has active investments in 51 enterprises in 24 countries. About half of these are in Latin America and the Caribbean, a third in Asia, and a quarter in Africa. The organisation has provided debt and equity instruments to emerging enterprises for renewable energy technologies such as geothermal, photovoltaic, wind, biomass/biogas, hydroelectric and solar thermal power. It has also capitalised revolving loan funds to facilitate sales and leases of solar home systems and has supported various energy efficiency projects as well as urban transportation innovations.

E&Co's mission is to promote developing-country energy enterprises that create economically self-sustaining energy projects, use environmentally superior technologies and produce a more equal distribution of energy, especially to the poor. In its role as a financial intermediary, E&Co works to bridge the gap between local enterprises and sources of capital, at project stages when access to traditional capital is most difficult. The organisation also may provide various entrepreneurial development services, including project preparation assistance and proposal writing. Thus, E&Co offers flexible support that can give a 'push' to projects in between the pre-investment/enterprise development stage and large-scale project finance or active implementation.

31.3.2 *Weaknesses and constraints of financial intermediaries*

While financial intermediaries offer a set of distinct, attractive advantages as actors in development assistance, they should not be viewed as a panacea for the myriad obstacles and barriers to meeting the developing world's growing energy needs in an environmentally sustainable way. As relatively experimental organisations in a constantly evolving field, it is not surprising that financial intermediaries are constrained by their own set of institutional weakness and challenges, which are outlined below.

- **Inability to demonstrate quick results**. A sound track record must form the basis of any argument that intermediaries in fact have a unique comparative advantage in catalysing renewable energy projects. However, since intermediary services geared toward renewable energy is a relatively novel concept, and their involvement is often at the earliest stage of a project's life, it often takes many years before a comprehensive assessment of the economic, social and environmental impacts of an intermediary's involvement can be determined. Moreover, since intermediaries support inherently riskier projects than do larger development banks, the success rate for any given portfolio is likely to be quite low, at least for the foreseeable future.

- **The need for subsidisation**. While intermediaries operate on business principles, they themselves are not purely commercial. Since the transaction costs per project are relatively high, and many early-stage projects are bound to fail, over the long term intermediaries require a degree of subsidisation before they can become financially self-sustaining operations. Intermediaries receive grant money from foundations or government funds as seed money, and may administer specialised 'soft' loan funds on behalf of other development banks. However, the more that intermediary assistance is perceived as 'charitable', the greater the probability of borrower default and that commercial funding will avoid the renewable energy sector.

- **Poor policy leverage**. Unlike the World Bank or other large private-sector investors, financial intermediaries lack the clout and specific instruments of conditionality that can, at times, lever important policy reforms on the part of developing-country governments. Because financial intermediaries support relatively small-scale projects not directly sanctioned by the government, they have a limited ability to effectively lobby politicians and bureaucrats on issues influencing the market environment for renewable energy technologies, such as deregulation, tariff equalisation or other fiscal incentives.

- **'Crowding out' Southern initiatives**. Financial intermediaries need to be careful to avoid displacing activities that would otherwise be undertaken by Southern-initiated or managed organisations. In the medium-term view, financial intermediaries that are indigenous to the South should take the lead in penetrating their own markets, because of their better knowledge of local conditions and the potential to generate more sustainable local capital markets and job creation activities.

◾ **Leanness**. Additional support for intermediaries also hinges on their ability to demonstrate their organisational 'leanness'. This means maximising the ratio of funds loaned to those set aside for management and overheads. However, the high transaction costs associated with the type of lending that financial intermediaries specialise in are directly related to high management and operational costs.

◾ **Attracting the 'right' people**. In order for financial intermediaries to grow, there must be a suitable human resource pool at both the intermediary and the enterprise level in order to expand this social entrepreneurial work. An ideal intermediary staff member would possess a rare combination of energy sector-specific expertise, business and project finance skills and experience, a sophisticated understanding of technology and technological innovation, as well as sensitivity to development and environmental issues. That is a tall order, especially in a sector that offers compensation packages generally much less generous than those in the private sector. For the foreseeable future, labour supply constraints may be a serious obstacle to significantly expanding the work of intermediaries.[14] Of course, this problem pales in comparison to the capacity restraints facing developing countries in terms of implementing and following through with good projects. As a veteran of the field notes, 'constraints on human capacity will always be the weakest link in the chain'.[15]

31.3.2.1 Case study: India Renewable Energy Development Agency (IREDA)

IREDA was founded in 1987 with the help of the Indian Ministry of Non-Conventional Energy Sources and the Asian Development Bank to provide small loans and entrepreneurial development skills to Indian developers of micro-hydro projects, residential solar PV systems, biomass fuels and wind farms. Since then it has served as the leading financial lending arm of the Ministry. In addition to government support, IREDA receives funding from other donors, including the Dutch government and the Asian Development Bank; it also raises internal revenues on local capital markets through the issuing of bonds.

In 1994, the World Bank extended a US$55 million line of credit to IREDA to leverage additional financing. A critical element of the loan was the creation of appropriate marketing and financing mechanisms ideally suited to the unique requirements of renewable energy technologies (*International Solar Energy Intelligence Report* 1994: 1). For example, IREDA has initiated a credit system for low-income households to purchase PV systems for applications such as small household appliances, residential lighting, water pumping and community health clinics. Recently, IREDA was extended a DM 120 million

---

14 Foundations are poised to play a critical role in this classic 'train-the-trainers' model. Donors should consider providing capacity-building, training and human resource development to intermediaries themselves, so as to foster a cadre of financiers-cum-social entrepreneurs. However, the social entrepreneurs of the future will need to break down boundaries between the public and private sector, rendering foundation support difficult.

15 Phil LaRocco, LaRocco & Associates, 22 April 1999.

credit line from the German development bank Kreditanstalt für Wiederaufbau (KfW) to carry out these activities on a greater scale (*Asia Pulse* 1999).

IREDA bills itself as a 'Public Financial Institution' and has demonstrated a record of generating a profit on its investments since its first year of existence. It supports up to 85% of project finance requirements and up to 90% of equipment financing, with interest rates that compare favourably to traditional commercial institutions. IREDA extends a three-year moratorium on debt repayment to its borrowers.

Important lessons can be learned from some of IREDA's shortcomings in how intermediaries should structure their operations:

- **Intermediaries should lend at interest rates that approach the commercial rate, but not at rates that vastly exceed their actual operating costs**. Lending at rates marginally below commercial rates can act as a positive stimulus for catalysing greater commercialisation of renewable energy projects. Critics charge that IREDA has provided loans at inflated rates given its real overhead and the degree of risk assumed. Despite the fact that the bulk of IREDA's capitalisation was subsidised by a World Bank loan at the extremely low rate of 2.5%, the average rate of loans leveraged by IREDA was 8%–9%. The terms of the recent cash infusion by KfW were even more favourable, at only 1.5% with a 40-year repayment period.

- **Intermediaries should refrain from financing projects in which the technologies have already being given a favourable 'push' by fiscal or other policy incentives**. A significant portion of IREDA's portfolio was in the area of wind power. However, wind power projects in India were *already* subject to favourable tax incentives and 100% depreciation in the first year of investment. In this respect, IREDA's financing served as a 'double' subsidy; its involvement did little to incrementally mitigate risks or advance commercialisation of new enterprises for renewable energy as a whole.

- **By their very nature, intermediaries should be willing to bear a greater degree of risk than commercial institutions**. In at least one instance, IREDA offered a loan to a solar PV company in India on the condition of a 100% guarantee on the debt (i.e. collateral of a dollar-for-dollar bank deposit). Such demands are unreasonable for developing-country entrepreneurs who lack sufficient credit, and contradict an intermediary's *raison d'être*, which is to assume greater risk than commercial entities and multilateral development banks so as to increase the number of 'prototype' projects that get off the ground.

- **Given the size and scale of projects, paperwork should be minimised**. IREDA has developed a reputation for being excessively 'bureaucratic', which can dissuade project developers from seeking assistance. Streamlined and more individually tailored services are part of the comparative advantage of financial intermediaries *vis-à-vis* larger development banks or aid agencies.

31.4 Conclusion

The alternative development model presented by financial intermediaries does not, in itself, provide a magical solution to the numerous implementation barriers that stand between current realities and greater commercialisation of renewable energy enterprises. Rather, the complexities associated with building and maintaining new markets for innovative energy technologies require that partnerships and links binding developing country entrepreneurs, donors, investors, governments and consumers interlock in more mutually reinforcing ways. In their role as go-betweens, financial intermediaries can not only help to spur innovation, but also to ensure that viable projects do not fall through cracks in the development assistance architecture. Opportunities currently emerging to securitise greenhouse gas emission reduction credits from renewable energy and energy efficiency projects as an asset or future income stream may also serve to increase interest by traditional investors in such projects, and create new niches and services for existing financial intermediaries.[16] In sum, the comparative advantages of financial intermediaries provide a strong rationale for considerably expanding their activities—and integrating their unique roles in more significant ways—within the larger architecture of energy development assistance.

A more detailed study of the past experiences and lessons learned by the forerunners in providing such intermediary services, such as E&Co, Winrock International, Environmental Enterprises Assistance Fund (EEAF), Energy Investment Fund, Impax Capital Corporation and IREDA, should be undertaken to determine the most appropriate timing, scale and scope of their interventions.[17] Meanwhile, multilateral development banks, foundations and bilateral aid agencies would do well to carefully weigh the costs and benefits of leveraging their own funds through intermediaries that may be able to better manage the risks and enterprise development needs associated with renewable energy ventures.[18] Institutions that profess an interest in embracing renewable energy have considerable room to utilise existing financial intermediaries to a greater extent, or to establish entirely new operations based in the South.

As for the intermediaries themselves, it goes without saying that they are best placed to identify worthy projects and build human capacity the closer they are to the field. The next major step faced by intermediaries is to expand their presence on a regional level through the establishment of additional locally staffed, autonomous field offices. In

16   I refer specifically to the development of rules and markets for climate change mitigation projects under the Kyoto Protocol flexible mechanisms of Joint Implementation and the Clean Development Mechanism.

17   EEAF and Impax Capital Corporation have made a number of small- to medium-scale investments in renewable energy, energy efficiency and pollution abatement projects. While they can still be regarded as financial intermediaries, they operate under a more commercial approach than some of their colleagues, expecting higher rates of return on their financial services.

18   At a time when multilateral development banks (MDBs) are facing greater criticism and scrutiny by non-governmental organisations for their shortcomings in environmentally responsible practices, there is a real risk that such a strategy may not be seen to be in their institutional interest. The more MDBs 'outsource' large pieces of their energy lending activities to intermediaries, the less 'green ink' appears on their balance sheets and annual reports.

addition, financial intermediaries need to fully exploit the comparative advantage of their organisational nimbleness to package even larger and more creative partnerships between smaller renewable energy enterprises and large private power companies, multinational oil conglomerates and more mainstream commercial investors looking to invest in our common future.

CAN FINANCIAL INSTITUTIONS CONTRIBUTE TO SUSTAINABILITY?

Stephen Viederman
Former President, Jessie Smith Noyes Foundation

Issues of 'sustainable banking' raise a number of questions for which answers are not yet available. But as the playwright Eugene Ionesco observed: 'It is not the answer that enlightens but the question.' This chapter is presented to stimulate debate on issues that do not seem to have received much attention until now.

If we read and believe global surveys about public attitudes towards the environment, and many other 'sustainability' issues of expressed public concern such as community, poverty and the like, we would have to conclude that the myriad conferences and publications on these issues are a waste of time. Everyone insists that they are deeply concerned. For example, I have never met anyone in finance or banking who does not profess to being an environmentalist, as a person, a parent, a grandparent, as a citizen and, more often than not, as a financial contributor to and member of one or more environmental organisations. Some years ago a managing partner of Lehman Brothers, who had profited personally and professionally from some recent tax breaks for the wealthy, admitted that, after working hours, in his capacity as a private citizen, he felt some pangs of concern about the impacts of these tax breaks on society.[1] Like this man, we all seem capable of leaving our concerns at home when we go off to work, however. Vocation and avocation seem to be separated. The issue here is not one of some people being 'good' (us, by definition) and some being 'evil' (those who do not share our passion, by definition). As the theologian and activist Rabbi Abraham Heschel suggested: 'The opposite of good is not evil, it is indifference.' Indifference here is doing 'business as usual'.

---

1   *New York Times*, 1 December 1996: A1.

32.1 Reducing the dissonance between what we value and how we behave

Much of the information provided to bankers and financiers, on the environment and other aspects of 'sustainability', is produced by people and institutions that have a cause, and who see it as part of their job to enlist others in that cause. For example, UNEP, the *environment* programme of the UN, tries to persuade the financial and banking industry to become more environmentally aware. The data they and other environmentalists produce, the articles published, the speeches made are supply-driven. There is a hope that there will be a demand, but not enough attention has been focused on **how to create** the demand. The 'special interests' know, or think they know, the behaviours they want from financial recalcitrants. They have a vision. But they spend less time, if any at all, on the processes by which change will occur—the processes by which those in the business, banking and finance community will begin to demand and produce for themselves information on issues. In 1996 Stefan Schmidheiny and his colleagues at the World Business Council for Sustainable Development published the book *Financing Change* (Schmidheiny and Zorraquín 1996). However, the book that may be of greater importance is yet to be written: *Changing Finance*. We need transformation, not simply reformation, if the issues of sustainability and banking and finance are to be truly linked. The constraint is that 'banking' and 'finance' do not seem to want to listen to, or perhaps do not trust, the interest groups, since they come from a different culture.

What are the processes of change—among others, psychological, cultural, institutional, intellectual and economic—that will lead to a demand for sustainability information from the mainstream banking and financial community? And how will that information be utilised to change institutional arrangements and individual behaviour? What are the institutions that can produce the information that will be 'trusted' by the world of banking and finance, if information providers are suspected of having a special interest? Who are the key actors in the banking and financial community to focus attention on as producers and users of sustainability information? What incentives are available, or need to be created, so that banking and financial institutions can lead their employees towards a more holistic view of the impacts of their investments?

We must begin with the realisation that the term 'sustainability' is itself problematic. More often than not, 'sustainability' is shorthand for 'environmental sustainability'. But therein lies a problem that everyone concerned with banking and finance must address, namely: the environment cannot be sustained in a vacuum. As the UN Conference on Environment and Development in 1992 reminded us, to save the environment we must also deal with issues of development, and this requires that we address questions of poverty, of equity, and of justice, of power, directly. But read corporate 'sustainability' reports and try to find serious attention—any attention—to community or equity. It isn't there. Eco-efficiency is there, and is important, as a necessary component of environmental sustainability. But efficiency in the marketplace is not a sufficient condition for truly sustainable development. In fact, equity and justice are preconditions of efficiency in the larger social context. Since Rabbi Heschel reminded us that words create worlds, we must begin to use the language of sustainability more precisely.

32.2 What does 'sustainability' really mean, and how does it impact on banking and finance?

If we agree that sustainability is broader than the environment, we must then address the role of corporations and the banking and financial world in sustainable development. Alicia Barcena, former director of the Earth Council, suggests that 'sustainability' encompasses the five 'E's: ethics, equity, environment, economy and empowerment. A number of questions arise from this:

- What is, and can be, the commitment of corporations and the banking and financial world to community? Can they truly be stakeholders in communities, just as communities are stakeholders in corporations? Can they commit themselves to restoring a community shattered by downsizing or plant closures, in the same way that many have made a commitment to restoring ecosystems they might destroy, assuming that is possible?

- What is, and can be, the commitment of corporations and banking and financial institutions to democracy? Will they commit themselves to listening to and sharing with communities? What is the role of money in politics?

- What is, and can be, the commitment of corporations and banking and financial institutions to future generations, when they do not have the attention span to look forward to the next quarter (if not the next day) as opposed to the next century?

- What is, and can be, the commitment of corporations and banking and financial institutions to satisfying needs rather than to creating greater wants, especially in a world of finite resources, inequitably distributed (see Viederman 1997, 1998)?

We often speak of 'profit and responsibility in the 21st century'. The original meaning of 'profit' comes from the Latin word *proficiere*, to 'advance' or 'be advantageous'. Responsibility comes from the Latin *respondere*, 'promise in return', carrying with it a moral and ethical obligation. Neither definition limits us to a narrow concern for financial reward, which is necessary but not sufficient. This is especially important when we reflect on the unintended consequences to society that often arise from the quest for financial profit. Dee Hock, founder, president and CEO emeritus of VISA, has observed:

> Institutions that operate so as to capitalise all gain in the interests of the few, while socialising all loss to the detriment of the many, are ethically, socially and operationally unsound. Yet that is precisely what far too many corporations demand and far too many societies tolerate. It must change.

If we consider the broader canvas of sustainability, we must then be concerned with the consequences of our behaviours in the financial world, beyond the financial bottom line. This leaves us with two final questions:

1. What are the components of 'profitability'? Can we assess profitability and responsibility without assessing the social costs borne by the society at large which are incurred in achieving financial profit? Are cash values all that count?

Fiduciary responsibility is usually defined as making the maximum profit at a reasonable level of risk. In the US, for foundations and non-profit organisations this means being a 'prudent man'. This is a legal concept going back to the 1830s when the responsible investor believed that waste had a place to go, when tobacco was not believed to be harmful to one's health and when corporations were still chartered by the state for the public good. Times have changed, and the truly 'prudent person' of the 21st century cannot exercise his or her fiduciary responsibility in a vacuum. Fiduciary responsibility must be subsumed under the broader tent of social responsibility.

2. To whom are we responsible, and in what ways? What behaviours must we change to become truly responsible?

It has been suggested that the obscure takes a while to see, the obvious, longer. The philosopher Schopenhauer believed that all truth passes through three stages: first it is ridiculed; second it is violently opposed; third, it is accepted as self-evident. We have arrived at, or are close to, stage three, in our beliefs that the sustainability and finance must be linked. Now it is up to us to be certain that our behaviour is consistent within these beliefs, while striving to get others to join us.

BIBLIOGRAPHY

ACBE (Advisory Committee on Business and the Environment) (1997) *Environmental Reporting and the Financial Sector: An Approach to Good Practice* (London: ACBE).

ADC (Andean Development Corporation) (1998) *Annual Report* (Caracas: ADC).

Agarwal, A. (1999) 'Enter the Green Rating Project', *Down to Earth*, 31 July 1999: 20-23.

Ahmed, K. (1995) 'Industry and the Environment: Patterns in World Bank Lending', in *IEN Staff Report: Restricted Distribution, Industry and Energy Department* (Washington, DC: World Bank).

Akerlof, G. (1970) 'The Market for "Lemons": Quality Uncertainty and the Market Mechanism', *Quarterly Journal of Economics* 84: 488-500.

Albert, M. (1991) *Capitalisme contra Capitalisme* (Paris: Éditions du Seuil).

Alexander, G.J., and R.A. Buchholz (1978) 'Corporate Social Responsibility and Stock Market Performance', *Academy of Management Journal* 21.3: 479-86.

Armbruster, C. (1998) untitled piece in *Green Investment: Market Transparency and Consumer Information. Workshop Summary* (Proceedings of the International Workshop, Berlin, 7 October 1998; Berlin: Ecologic): 30-37.

Arrowsmith, S.L., J. Linaretti and D. Wallace, Jr (2000) *Regulating Public Procurement: National and International Perspectives* (The Hague/London/Boston, MA: Kluwer International).

Asia Pulse (1999) 'Germany's KfW to fund Indian renewable energy projects', *Asia Pulse*, 19 March 1999.

Aslam, A. (1997) 'Advertising campaign targets Three Gorges Dam bonds', *World News Inter Press Service* (Washington, DC; www.oneworld.org/ips2/nov/china_dam.html, 17 November 1997).

Ayres, R,U., P. Fluckiger and K. Hockets (1995) *Achieving Eco-efficiency in Business* (Report of the World Business Council for Sustainable Development; Second Antwerp Eco-efficiency Workshop, Antwerp, March 1995).

Azzone, G., and U. Bertelè (1992) 'L'ambiente sta diventando una variabile strategica' ('The environment is becoming a strategic factor'), *L'Impresa*, June 1992.

Azzone, G., and R. Manzini (1994) 'Measuring Strategic Environmental Performance', *Business Strategy and the Environment* 3.1 (Spring 1994): 1-4.

Banham, R. (1999) 'A Cautionary tale about Du Pont's Pompton Lake, NJ, environmental nightmare that all risk managers should heed', *Treasury and Risk Management Magazine*, January/February 1999.

BankAmerica (1997) *Environmental Program: 1997 Progress Report* (San Francisco: BankAmerica; www.bankofamerica.com).

Baran, M.S., and D.G. Partan (eds.) (1990) *Corporate Disclosure of Environmental Risks: US and European Law* (USA: Butterworth Legal Publishers).

Barrett, J. (1994) 'Weighing Up the Risks', *Certified Accountant*, October 1994: 42-44.

Barrett, J.A. (ed.) (1998) *Environmental Issues in Insolvency Proceedings* (The Hague/London/Boston, MA: Kluwer International).

Baum, W.C. (1979) *The Project Cycle* (Washington, DC: World Bank).

BBA (British Bankers' Association) (1993) *Position Statement: Banks and the Environment* (London: BBA).

BBA (British Bankers' Association) (1995) *The Environment Bill: Lender Liability.* (London: BBA).

BBS (Bangladesh Bureau of Statistics) (1998) *Statistical Yearbook 1997* (Dhaka, Bangladesh: BBS).

BCAS (Bangladesh Centre for Advanced Studies) (1998) *Final Report on Wind Energy Study Project* (Dhaka, Bangladesh: BCAS).

BCSIR (Bangladesh Council of Scientific and Industrial Research) (1998) *Evaluation Report on Biogas Extension Project* (Dhaka, Bangladesh: BCSIR).

Becker, C. (1998) *Wertorientiertes Umwelt-Management* (Bamberg, Germany: Difo).

Bellah, R. (1991) *The Good Society* (New York: Knopf).

Bello, W., S. Cunningham and N. Chandravithun (1998) *A Siamese Tragedy: Development and Disintegration in Modern Thailand* (Bangkok: White Lotus Company).

Belsom, T. (1998) 'Information Required by Fund Managers', in *Final Report of the Workshop 'Sustainable Development: Challenge for the Financial Sector'*, organised by the European Commission, DG XI, Brussels, 30 October 1998; Luxembourg: European Commission.

Bennett, M., and P. James (1998) 'Views of Financial Stakeholders on Environmental Accounting and Performance Measurement in Business: Report on a Consultation Project', Proceedings of *Continuity, Credibility and Comparability: Key Challenges for Corporate Environmental Performance Measurement and Communication*, Invitational Expert Seminar, Eze, France, 13–16 June 1998, International Institute for Industrial Environmental Economics, Lund University, Sweden.

Berry, A.J., S. Faulkner, M. Hughes and R. Jarvis (1993) 'Financial Information, the Banker and the Small Business', *British Accounting Review* 25: 131-50.

Berry, R.H., R.E. Crum and A. Waring (1993) *Corporate Performance Evaluation in Bank Lending Decisions* (Research Studies; London: Chartered Institute of Management Accountants).

Bertolini, F., and G. Troilo (1994) *Green Management: L'ecologia come vantaggio competitivo per l'impresa (Green Management: Ecology as Competitive Advantage for the Enterprise)* (Milan: EGEA).

BIFU (Banking Insurance and Finance Union) (1998) *Dialling the Future?* (Special Report; London: BIFU).

Bloom, G.F., and M.S.S. Morton (1991) 'Hazardous waste is every manager's problem', *Sloan Management Review*, Summer 1991: 75-83.

Borg, M. (1990) *Financial and Economic Analysis of Rural Electrification in Developing Countries* (Stockholm: Stockholm Environmental Institute/SIDA).

Boyer, M., and J.-J. Laffont (1994) *Environmental Risks and Bank Liability* (Scientific Series N 94s-22; Montreal: CIRANO; ftp://ftp.cirano.umontreal.ca/pub/publication/94s-22.pdf.zip).

Bragdon, J.H., and J. Marlin (1972) 'Is pollution profitable?', *Risk Management* 19.4: 9-18.

Brill, H., J.A. Brill and C. Feigenbaum (1999) *Investing with your Values: Making Money and Making a Difference* (Princeton, NJ: Bloomberg Press).

Brkic, T. (1999) 'Trends, Key Drivers and the Role of Banks', *Banking and Sustainable Development* (IISnet; http://iisdl.iisd.ca/business/aboutbanking.html).

Brophy, M. (1996) 'Environmental Policies', in R. Welford (ed.), *Corporate Environmental Management* (London: Earthscan): 92-103.

Brophy, M., and R. Starkey (1996) 'Environmental Reporting', in R. Welford (ed.), *Corporate Environmental Management* (London: Earthscan): 177-98.

Brown, L., and E. Ayers (eds.) (1998) *The World Watch Reader: On Global Environmental Issues* (New York/London: W.W. Norton, 1998 edn).

Brumwell, M. (ed.) (1999) *Cross-Border Transaction and Environmental Law* (London: Butterworth).

Bryce, A. (1992) 'Environmental Liability: Practical Issues for Lenders', *Journal of International Banking Law* 7.4 (April 1992): 131-37.

Bundesumweltministerium/Verein für Umweltmanagement in Banken, Sparkassen und Versicherungen (eds.) (1997) *Umwelt und Finanzdienstleistungen* (Munich: Beck).

Burhenne, W.E. (ed.) (1996) *International Environmental Soft Law: Collection of Relevant Instruments* (selected and compiled by Marlene Jahnke; The Hague: International Council of Environmental Law/Martinus Nijhoff Publishers/Kluwer Law International).

Business and the Environment (1999a) 'Launch of GRI guidelines intensifies debate on sustainability reporting', *Business and the Environment* 10.4 (April 1999): 2-6.

Business and the Environment (1999b) 'European environmental reporting awards scheme expands', *Business and the Environment* 10.4 (April 1999): 6-7.

Business and the Environment (1999c) 'BiE Index shows increase in UK corporate environmental engagement', *Business and the Environment* 10.8 (August 1999): 6.

Butz, C., and A. Plattner (1999) *Nachhaltige Aktienanlagen: Eine Analyse der Rendite in Abhängigkeit von Umwelt- und Sozialkriterien* (Sarasin Studie; Basel: Sarasin).

Cabraal, A., M. Cosgrove-Davies and L. Schaeffer (1998) *Reducing Barriers to PV Market Development* (Washington, DC: World Bank, Asia Alternative Energy Programme).

Campbell, D., and C. Campbell (eds.) (1993) *International Liability of Corporate Directors* (London: Lloyd's of London Press).

Casserley, D., and G. Gibbs (1999) *Banking in Asia: The End of Entitlement* (Singapore: John Wiley [Asia]).

CEPAA (Council on Economic Priorities Accreditation Agencies) (1997) *Guidance Document for Social Accountability 8000* (London: CEPAA).

Chen, K.M., and R.W. Metcalf (1980) 'The Relationship between Pollution Control Records and Financial Indicators Revisited', *Accounting Review* 55: 168-77.

China Embassy (1997) 'Chronology of the Three Gorges Project' (China Embassy official website; www.China-embassy.org, 5 November 1997).

Clark, C. (1995) 'Banks weigh the price of liability', *Financial Times*, 26 June 1995.

Clausen, A.W. (1986) 'Sustainable Development: The Global Imperative. Fairfield Osborn Memorial Lecture in Environmental Science', Washington, DC, 12 November 1981, in World Bank, *The Development Challenge of the Eighties. A.W. Clausen at the World Bank: Major Policy Addresses 1981–1986.* (Washington, DC: World Bank).

Cohen, M.A., A.A. Fenn, S. Konar and J. Naimon (1997) *Environmental and Financial Performance: Are they related?* (Working paper; Nashville, TN: Vanderbilt University).

Co-operative Bank (1997) *Strength in Numbers: Our Partnership Approach. A First Report* (Manchester, UK: The Co-operative Bank).

Co-operative Bank (1998) *The Partnership Report 1997* (Manchester, UK: The Co-operative Bank).

Co-operative Bank (1999) *The Partnership Report 1998* (Manchester, UK: The Co-operative Bank).

Cooper, J.M. (ed.) (1997) *Plato: Complete Works* (Indianapolis, IN/Cambridge, MA: Hackett Publishing Company).

Coppola, G., and D. Corsini (1996) 'Demoni o banchieri per l'ecosviluppo?' ('Devils or Bakers for Eco-Development?'), *L'Impresa Ambiente*, May 1996: 7-14.

Coulson, A.B. (1997) *Corporate Environmental Performance Considerations within Bank Lending Processes: The Social Construction of Risk Perception* (PhD thesis; Durham, UK: University of Durham Business School).

Coulson, A.B. (1999) *Capital Market Risk* (Workshop report of the Economic and Social Research Council Financial Sector Environment Forum, No. 3; Glasgow: University of Strathclyde).

Coulson, A.B., and V. Monks (1999) 'Corporate Environmental Performance Considerations within Bank Lending Decisions', *Eco-management and Auditing* 6: 1-10.

CSG (Credit Suisse Group) (1998) *Environmental Report 1997/98* (Zurich: CSG; www.csg.ch).

CSR Magazine (1999) 'Social Reporting: Is this the way forward?', *CSR Magazine* 2.3 (September 1999): 3-6.

Dal Maso, D. (1998) 'Finanza facile per l'impresa ecoefficiente' ('Easy Finance for the Eco-Efficient Company'), *L'Impresa Ambiente*, April 1998: 32-43.

Dal Maso, D. (1998) 'Perché le banche dovrebbero (pre)occuparsi dell'ambiente' ('Why banks should worry about the environment'), *Equilibri*, January 1998: 139-49.

Dansie, J. (1998) 'More Equity, More Entrepreneurs, Less Bureaucracy', *Petroleum Times Energy Report* 18.15 (7 August 1998).

Deloitte & Touche (1998) *Environmental Handbook for Financial Institutions* (Budapest: Deloitte & Touche).

Delphi International Ltd and Ecologic (1997) *The Role of the Financial Institutions in Achieving Sustainable Development* (Report to the European Commission; London: Delphi International; Berlin: Ecologic GmbH, November 1997).

Deml, M. (1994) *Grünes Geld: Jahrbuch für ethisch-ökologische Geldanlagen 1995/6.* (Vienna: Service-Fachverlag, 2nd edn).

Deml, M., and J. Baumgarten (1998) *Grünes Geld: Jahrbuch für ethisch-ökologische Geldanlagen 1998/99* (Ritterhude: Waldthausen Verlag).

De Moor, J.W., and A. Knörzer (1995) *Eco-Efficiency: A Way to Assess a Company's Sustainability* (special report; Basel: Bank Sarasin & Co., July 1995).

Descano, K. (1998) 'Introduction', in UNEP *Financial Institutions Initiative. Fourth Roundtable Meeting on Finance and the Environment: Profitability and Responsibility in the 21st Century* (Geneva: UNEP).

Deutsche Bank (1998) *Promoting Initiative: Deutsche Bank's Commitment to the Environment* (Frankfurt-am-Main: Deutsche Bank, 2nd edn): 13.

Devries, J. (1997) *Verbraucher und Verantwortung: Ausgewählte Ergebnisse einer empirischen Untersuchung* (imug-Arbeitspapier 6/97; Hannover: imug).

Diltz, J.D. (1995) 'Does social screening affect portfolio performance?', *Journal of Investing*, Spring 1995: 64.

DJSGI (Dow Jones Sustainability Group Index) (1999) *Guide to the Dow Jones Sustainability Group Indexes* (Version 1.0; Zurich: DJSGI, September 1999).

DoE (UK Department of the Environment) (1996) *Indicators of Sustainable Development for the United Kingdom* (London: HMSO).

EBRD (European Bank for Reconstruction and Development) (1995) *Environmental Risk Management for Financial Institutions: A Handbook* (London: EBRD).

EBRD (European Bank for Reconstruction and Development) (1996) *Environmental Procedures* (London: EBRD).

EBRD (European Bank for Reconstruction and Development) (1998) *Alternative Sources of Finance* (London: EBRD).

Ecologic (1998) *Green Investment: Market Transparency and Consumer Information. Workshop Summary* (Proceedings of the International Workshop, Berlin, 7 October 1998; Berlin: Ecologic).

EDR (Environmental Data Resources) (1994) *Second Annual Financial Institution Environmental Survey* (Conducted by Dun and Bradstreet Information Services and Environmental Data Resources, Inc.; Southport, CT: EDR).

EIRIS (Ethical Investment Research Service) (1989) *The Financial Performance of Ethical Investments* (London: EIRIS).

EIRIS (Ethical Investment Research Service) (1998) *Money and Ethics* (London: EIRIS).

El-Ashry, Mohamed T. (1992) 'Environmental Assessment and the World Bank', speech at World Bank/IAIA Congress, *Industrial and Third World Environmental Assessment: The Urgent Transition to Sustainability*, 19 August 1992.

El-Ashry, Mohamed T. (1993) 'Development Assistance Institutions and Sustainable Development', *The Washington Quarterly*, Spring 1993: 83-96.

Ellery, M. (1999) *Renewable Energy Program in Bangladesh* (ISTP Discussion Paper; Perth, Australia: Murdoch University).

Elkington, J. (1997) *Cannibals with Forks: The Triple Bottom Line of 21st Century Business* (Oxford, UK: Capstone Publishing).

Energy Information Administration (1998) *The Changing Structure of the Electric Power Industry: Selected Issues* (DOE/EIA-0562[98]; Washington, DC: Energy Information Administration).

EPA (US Environmental Protection Agency) (1989) *Pollution Prevention Benefits Manual: Phase II* (Washington, DC: EPA).

ESSD (Environmentally and Socially Sustainable Development Network) (1999) *Environmentally and Socially Sustainable Development Network Directory* (Washington, DC: ESSD, November 1999).

ETI (Ethical Trading Initiative) (1998) *Purpose, Programme, Membership Information* (London: ETI).

Eurodad (1998) *Taking Stock of Debt* (Brussels: Eurodad).

European Commission DG XI (1997) *The Role of Financial Institutions in Achieving Sustainable Development* (Brussels: EU).

European Commission DG XI (1998) *Report of the Workshop 'Sustainable Development: Challenge for the Financial Sector'* (Brussels: EU).

European Parliament (1999) 'Resolution on the Creation of a European Code of Conduct for European MNCs Operating Abroad', www.multinationals.law.eur.nl/documents/cmp/coc99.html.

Ex-Im Bank (Export-Import Bank of the United States) (1996a) 'Frequently Asked Questions about the Three Gorges Dam Project' (Washington, DC; www.exim.gov/3gorges.html, revised 5 June 1996).

Ex-Im Bank (Export-Import Bank of the United States) (1996b) 'Transcript of Press Briefing on Board Meeting: Three Gorges Dam in China' (Washington, DC; www.exim.gov/t3gorges.html, 30 May 1996).

Figge, F. (1997) 'Systematisierung ökonomischer Risiken durch globale Umweltprobleme', *Zeitschrift für angewandte Umweltforschung* 10.2: 256-66.

Figge, F. (1998) 'Wasser: Grenze des asiatischen Wachstums', in *Sustainable Investment Outlook* (Basel: Sarasin, July 1998).

Finanztest (1991) 'Marsch in die Grünanlagen', *Finanztest*, March 1991: 12-27.

Flavin, C., and M. O'Meara (1998) 'Solar Power Market Boom', *World Watch* 11.5 (September/October 1998): 23-27.

Flavin, C., and S. Dunn (1997) *Rising Sun, Gathering Winds: Policies to Stabilize the Climate and Strengthen Economies* (World Watch Paper 138; Washington, DC: World Watch Institute).

Foley, G. (1991) *Energy Assistance Revisited: A Discussion Paper* (Stockholm: Stockholm Environmental Institute/SIDA): 19.

Forestieri, G. (1998) 'L'impresa e il rischio ambientale: sfide e opportunità per il sistema bancario italiano' ('The Enterprise and Environmental Risk: Challenges and Opportunities for the Italian Bank System'), *Economia e Management*, January 1998: 16-26.

Forsyth, T. (1998) 'Technology Transfer and the Climate Change Debate', *Environment* 40.9: 16-20, 39-43.

Frost, K.A. (ed.) (1999) *The Financing of Catastrophe Risk* (Chicago: The University of Chicago Press).

Gäfgen, G. (1974) *Theorie der wirtschaftlichen Entscheidung* (Tübingen: J.C.B. Mohr, 3rd edn).

Ganzi, J.T., and J. Tanner (1997) *Global Survey on Environmental Policies and Practices of the Financial Services Industry: The Private Sector* (Washington, DC: Environment and Finance Enterprise).

GEF (Global Environment Facility) (1998) *The Outlook for Renewable Energy Technologies* (GEF Working Paper, 14; Washington, DC: GEF).

Genero, G. (1998) 'Via libera al credito per gli investimenti ambientali' ('Credits for Environmental Investments'), *L'Impresa Ambiente*, April 1998: 48-50.

German Federal Environmental Agency (1997) *A Guide to Corporate Environmental Indicators* (Bonn: German Federal Environmental Ministry; Berlin: German Federal Environmental Agency).

Gibson, C.H. (1995) *Financial Statement Analysis: Using Financial Accounting Information* (Cincinnati: South-western Publishing Co., 6th edn).

Gilardoni, A., and A. Marangoni (1996) 'Rischi e opportunità per finanza e ambiente' ('Risks and Opportunities for Finance and the Environment'), *L'Impresa Ambiente*, May 1996: 15-23.

Gleason, S.M. (1994) 'Banks need Environmental Risk Programme more than ever', *Texas Banking* 83.7 (July 1994): 3.

Goldemberg, J. (1998) 'Leapfrog Energy Technologies', *Energy Policy* 26.10: 729-41.

Goodland, R.J.A. (1992) 'Environmental Priorities for Financing Institutions', *Environmental Conservation* 19.1: 10.

Goodland, R.J.A. (2000) *Social and Environmental Assessment to Promote Sustainability: An Informal View from he World Bank* (Environmental Management Series, 74; Washington, DC: ESSD, World Bank, January 2000).

Goodland, R., and J. Anhang (eds.) (2000) 'IAIA Presidents' Visions for Impact Assessment: Where will impact assessment be in 10 years and how do we get there?', *International Association for Impact Assessment*, IAIA, Hong Kong, June 2000.

Grameen Bank (1998) *Annual Report 1997* (Dhaka, Bangladesh: Grameen Bank).

Grameen Shakti (1999) *Status Report* (Dhaka, Bangladesh: Grameen Shakti).

Granger, B., M. Lynch, L. Haidar, U. Reifner and J. Evers (1997) *The Social Responsibility of Credit Institutions in the EU* (Hamburg: Institut für Finanzdienstleistungen eV).

Graves, B.S,. and S.A. Waddock (1997) 'Quality of Management and Quality of Stakeholder Relations: Are they synonymous?', *Business and Society* 36.3 (September 1997): 250-79.

Gray, R.H., J. Bebbington and D. Walters (1993) *Accounting for the Environment: The Greening of Accounting Part II* (Association of Chartered Certified Accountants; London: Paul Chapman Publishing).

Gray, R., D. Owen and C. Adams (1996) *Accounting and Accountability: Changes and Challenges in Corporate Social and Environmental Reporting* (London: Prentice-Hall).

Green Futures (1998) 'Money Changers', *Green Futures*, January/February 1998: 28-29.

Greene, N., and R. Duke (1999) *Regulatory Policy toward Off-Grid Technologies in LDCs* (Washington, DC: Natural Resources Defense Council).

GRI (Global Reporting Initiative) (1999) *Sustainability Reporting Guidelines: Exposure Draft for Public Comment and Pilot Testing* (www.globalreporting.org/GuidelinesOverview.htm, March 1999).

Griffin, J.J., and J.F. Mahon (1997) 'The Corporate Social Performance and Corporate Financial Performance Debate', *Business and Society* 36.1 (March 1997): 62-66.

Gutermuth, P.-G. (1998) 'Financial Measures by the State for the Enhanced Deployment of Renewable Energies', *Solar Energy* 64.1-3: 67-78.

HABITAT (United Nations Centre for Human Settlements) (1996) 'Finance for Housing, Infrastructure and Services', in D. Satterthwaite (ed.), *An Urbanizing World: Global Report on Human Settlements* (Oxford, UK: Oxford University Press).

Hajari, N. (1999) 'Some Cracks in the Façade', *Time Magazine* 153.24 (www.time.com/time/magazine/articles/intl/0,3266,27581,00.html, 21 June 1999).

Hamel, G., and C.K. Prahalad (1994) *Competing for the Future* (Boston, MA: Harvard Business School Press).

Hamilton, S., J. Hoje and M. Stateman (1993) 'Doing Well While Doing Good? The Investment Performance of Socially Responsible Mutual Funds', *Financial Analysts' Journal*, November/December 1993: 5-31.

Harig, L.A. (1992) 'Ignorance is Not Bliss: Responsible Corporate Officers Convicted of Environmental Crimes and the Federal Sentencing Guidelines', *Duke Law Journal* 145.

Hart, S.L., and G. Ahuja (1996) 'Does it pay to be green?', *Business Strategy and the Environment* 5: 30-37.

Harte, G., L. Lewis and D. Owen (1991) 'Ethical Investment and the Corporate Reporting Function', *Critical Perspectives on Accounting* 2: 227-53.

Hawken, P., A. Lovins and L.H. Lovins (1999) *Natural Capitalism: Creating New Industrial Revolution* (Boston, MA/New York/London: Little, Brown & Co.).

Held, D., A. McGrew, D. Goldblatt and J. Perraton (1999) *Global Transformations: Politics, Economics and Culture* (Stanford, CA: Stanford University Press).

Hersel, P. (1998) 'The London Debt Agreement of 1953 on German External Debt: Lessons for the HIPC Initiative', in Eurodad, *Taking Stock of Debt* (Brussels: Eurodad).

Hildesheimer, G., and S. Döbeli (1999) 'Bewertungsmethode für Umweltberichte', *Umwelt Focus*, June 1999: 26-29.

Hill, J., D. Fedrigo and I. Marshall (1997) *Banking on the Future: A Survey of Implementation of the UNEP Statement by Banks on the Environment and Sustainable Development* (London: Green Alliance).

Hinterberger, F., D. Bannasch, K. Schlegelmilch, H. Stiller, T. Orbach and A. Mundl (1998) *Greening the Financial Sector* (Berlin: Carl Duisberg).

Hodson, K.A., *et al.* (1992) 'The Prosecution of Corporations and Corporate Officers for Environmental Crimes: Limiting One's Exposure for Environmental Criminal Liability', *Arizona Law Review* 553.

Hollingsworth, J.R., and R. Boyer (eds.) (1997) *Contemporary Capitalism* (Cambridge, UK: Cambridge University Press).

Houldin, M. (1993) 'Part A: An Introduction to the Issues', in R. Gray with J. Bebbington and D. Walters (1993) *Accounting for the Environment* (London: Paul Chapman): 3-8.

Hyde, S. (1998) untitled piece in *Green Investment: Market Transparency and Consumer Information. Workshop Summary* (Proceedings of the International Workshop, Berlin, 7 October 1998; Berlin: Ecologic): 22-28.

IEA (International Energy Agency) (1998a) *Benign Energy? The Environmental Implications of Renewables* (Paris: IEA).

IEA (International Energy Agency) (1998b) *Energy Efficiency Initiative. Volume 1. Energy Policy Analysis* (Paris: IEA).

IEA (International Energy Agency) (2000) *World Energy Outlook 2000* (Paris: Organisation for Economic Co-operation and Development): 25.

Immergluck, D. (1998) *The Community Reinvestment Act and Community Development Financial Institutions: Qualified Investments, Community Development Lending, and Lessons from the New CRA Performance Evaluations* (Chicago: Woodstock Institute, September 1998).

Impact (1999) 'Building Business: The Mekong Model', *Impact* 3.1 (Winter 1999, www.ifc.org/publications/pubs/impwt99/impwt99.html).

ING Bank (1997) *Environmental Annual Report 1997* (Amsterdam: ING Bank).

ING Group (1998) *Environmental Annual Report 1998* (Amsterdam: ING; www.ing.com).

Inside China Today (1999) 'Key Facts about China's Three Gorges Dam', *Inside China Today* website (www.insidechina.com/special/damkey.php3, 15 July 1999).

International Herald Tribune (1999) 'Businesses discover that going green is financially friendly', *International Herald Tribune*, 22 September 1999: 24.

International Rivers Network (1999) 'Major environmental groups escalate pressure to halt Three Gorges Dam financing', *International Rivers Network Press Release* (www.irn.org.programs/threeg/, 6 May 1999).

International Solar Energy Intelligence Report (1994) 'World Bank backs $55 million for Indian energy projects', *International Solar Energy Intelligence Report*, 25 July 1994.

ISO (International Organization for Standardization) (1996a) *ISO 14001 Environmental Management Systems: Specification with Guidance for Use* (Geneva: ISO).

ISO (International Organization for Standardization) (1996b) *Environmental Management: Environmental Performance Evaluation* (ISO/TC 207/SC 4, ISO /CD 14031; Geneva: ISO, December 1996).

Jasch, C. (1996) 'Environmental Performance Evaluation: The Links between Financial and Environmental Management', *IIIEE Communications* 97.3: 203-13.

Jasch, C., M. Burzler and R. Rauberger (1997) *Environmental Management and Auditing for the Banking Sector* (Schriftenreihe des BMUJF: Band 9/1997; Vienna: Ministry of the Environment).

Jeucken, M.H.A. (1998) *Duurzaam bankieren: Een visie op bankieren en duurzame ontwikkeling* (Utrecht: Rabobank).

Jewell, T., and A. Waite (1997) *Environmental Law in Property Transactions* (London: Butterworths).

Johnson, S.D. (1995) *An Analysis of the Relationship between Corporate Environmental and Economic Performance at the Level of the Firm* (doctoral dissertation; Irvine, CA: University of California).

Kahlenborn, W. (1998) 'The International Workshop "Green Investment: Market Transparency and Consumer Information"*: Introductory Paper', in *Green Investment: Market Transparency and Consumer Information. Workshop Summary* (Proceedings of the International Workshop, Berlin, 7 October 1998; Berlin: Ecologic): 3-6.

Kahlenborn, W., and R. Andreas Kraemer (1997) 'Ökolabel für Ökofonds? Das Angebot von Umweltfonds ist viel zu unübersichtlich', *Politische Ökologie* 53: 71.

Kahlenborn, W., S. Oberthür, A. Carius, N. Sharma-Höfelein, H. Jörgens and A. March (1998) *Sustainability in Germany and Europe: Report to the Heinrich Böll Foundation* (Berlin: Centre for International and European Environmental Research).

Kaplan, R., and D. Norton (1996) 'Using the Balanced Scorecard as a Strategic Management System', *Harvard Business Review*, January/February 1996: 75-85.

Kempson, E., A. Bryson and K. Rowlingson (1994) *Hard Times: How Poor Families Make Ends Meet* (London: Policy Studies Institute).

Kinder, P., S. Lydenberg and A. Domini (1991) *The Social Investment Almanac: A Comprehensive Guide to Socially Responsible Investing* (New York: Henry Holt).

Klassen, R.D., and C.P. McLaughlin (1996) 'The Impact of Environmental Management on Firm Performance', *Management Science* 42.8 (August 1996): 119-24.

Knight, D. (1998) 'Environment–Finance: NGOs seek global environmental standards', World News Inter Press Service (Washington, DC, 24 April 1998).

Knight, F. (1921) *Risk, Uncertainty and Profit* (Boston: Houghton Mifflin)

Knörzer, A. (1995) *Ökologische Aspekte im Investment Research* (Bern: Haupt).

Kojima, Y., K. Murai, H. Pang, and E. Vitale (1997) 'The United States, China and the Three Gorges Dam: Toward a Sounder Foreign Environmental Policy' (Princeton University, NJ; www.wws. princeton.edu/~ipia/8.html).

Kommunalkredit AG (1996) 'Environmental Statement 1996', www.kommunalkredit.at.

Kommunalkredit AG (1997) 'Environmental Statement 1997', www.kommunalkredit.at.

Korten, D. (1996) 'Civic Engagement in Creating Future Cities', *Environment and Urbanization* 8.1: 35-49.

Kozloff, K., and O. Shobowale (1994) *Rethinking Development Assistance for Renewable Electricity* (Washington, DC: World Resources Institute).

KPMG (1997) *Environmental Reporting* (Copenhagen: KPMG).

KPMG (1998) *Hyvä ympäristöraportoinnin käytäntö Suomessa: Benchmarking-tutkimus 1997* (Helsinki: KPMG).

KPMG (1999) *Onderzoek milieuverslaglegging van Financiële instellingen* (The Hague: KPMG).

KPMG and WIMM (Institute for Environmental Management of University of Amsterdam) (1999) *KPMG International Survey of Environmental Reporting 1999* (The Hague: KPMG).

Kummer, K. (1995) *International Management of Hazardous Waste: The Basel Convention and Related Legal Rules* (London: Clarendon Press).

Larsson, M.-L. (1999) *The Law of Environmental Damage: Liability and Reparation* (The Hague/London/Boston, MA: Kluwer International).

Latin America Weekly Report (1994) 'Debt-for-Nature Swaps', *Latin America Weekly Report* WR-94-18 (19 May 1994): 211.

Lee, J.A. (1985) *The Environment, Public Health and Human Ecology: Considerations for Economic Development* (Baltimore, MD: Johns Hopkins University Press).

Lee, N., and C. George (eds.) (2000) *Environmental Assessment in Developing and Transitional Countries* (Chichester, UK: John Wiley).

Lewis, A., P. Webley and A. Furnham (1995) *The New Economic Mind: The Social Psychology of Economic Behaviour* (New York: Harvester Wheatsheaf).

Lewis, A., and J. Cullis (1990) 'Ethical Investment: Preferences and Morality', *The Journal of Behavioral Economics* 19.4: 395-411.

Lewis, A., and C. Mackenzie (2000) 'Morals, Money, Ethical Investing and Economic Psychology', *Human Relations* 53.2: 179-91.

Lloyds Bank (1994) *Lloyds Bank Environmental Policy* (London: Lloyds Bank).

Lloyds TSB Group (1997) *Environmental Report* (Birmingham, UK: Lloyds TSB).

Lloyds TSB Group (1998) *Environmental Report* (Birmingham, UK: Lloyds TSB).

Louche, C. (1998) *Environmental and Financial Business Performance in Europe* (EAEME thesis; Rotterdam: European Association for Environmental Management Education, September 1998).

Loveless, B. (1997) 'Ex–Im to finance China energy projects', *Inside Energy*, 2 June 1997.

Luther, R.G., and J. Matako (1994) 'The Performance of Ethical Unit Trusts: Choosing an Appropriate Benchmark', *British Accounting Review* 26: 77-89.

Lynch, J. (1994) *Banking and Finance: Managing the Moral Dimension* (Cambridge: Gresham Books).

MacIntyre, A.C. (1981) *After Virtue: A Study of Moral Theory* (London: Duckworth).

Mag, W. (1980) 'Risiko und Ungewißheit', in *Handwörterbuch der Wirtschaftswissenschaften:* 6 (Stuttgart: Fischer).

Mansley, M., D. Owen, W. Kahlenborn and R. Andreas Kraemer (1997) *The Role of Financial Institutions in Achieving Sustainable Development* (report commissioned by European Union DG XI; Brussels: Delphi International Ltd/Ecologic GmbH).

Markowitz, H. (1959) *Portfolio Selection: Efficient Diversification of Investments* (New York: John Wiley).

Mätäsaho R., M. Niskala and J. Tuomala (1998) *Ympäristölaskenta johdon apuvälineenä* (Porvoo, Finland: Werner Söderstörm Oyj).

Mathews, R. (1987) 'Social Responsibility Accounting Disclosures and Information Content for Shareholders: A Comment', *British Accounting Review* 19.2: 161-67.

Mayo, E., T. Fisher, P. Conaty, J. Doling and A. Mullineux (1998) *Small is Bankable: Community Reinvestment in the UK* (York, UK: Joseph Rowntree Foundation, November 1998).

McIntosh, M., D. Leipziger, K. Jones and G. Coleman (1998) *Corporate Citizenship: Successful Strategies for Responsible Companies* (London: Financial Times Professional).

Monroe, A. (1999) 'The Looming EcoWar: Environmentalists' new tactics threaten to take a toll on Wall Street financing', *Investment Dealers' Digest* 20–25 (24 May 1999).

Näsi, J. (1995) 'What is stakeholder thinking? A Snapshot of a Social Theory of the Firm', in J. Näsi (ed.), *Understanding Stakeholder Thinking* (Jyväskylä, Finland: LSR-Publications).

National Geographic (1999) 'El Niño/La Niña', *National Geographic* 195.3 (March 1999): 72-95.

NatWest Group (1998) *Environment Report 1997/98* (London: NatWest; www.natwest.com).

NCBS (National Centre for Business and Sustainability) (1996) *The Co-operative Bank: An Environmental Review and Ecological Action Plan* (Salford, UK: NCBE).

NCBS (National Centre for Business and Sustainability) (1999) *The Co-operative Bank's Service Delivery Channels: Developing Ecological and Social Performance Indicators* (Report to the Co-operative Bank, March 1999; Salford, UK: NCBS).

NCC (National Consumer Council) (1997) *In the Bank's Bad Books: How the Banking Code of Practice Works for Customers in Hardship* (London: NCC).

NEF (New Economics Foundation) (1997) *Financial Exclusion in London* (London: NEF).

Newman, P., and J. Kenworthy (1999) *Sustainability and Cities* (Washington, DC: Island Press).

Newman, P., M. Salequzzaman and B. Corry (1999) 'Tidal Power Prospects: Western Australia and Bangladesh', paper presented at SOLAR '99 ANZSE (Australia and New Zealand Solar Energy Society) Conference, Melbourne, Australia.

Newson, M., and C. Deegan (1996) *ABCD: Environmental Performance Evaluation and Reporting for Private and Public Organisations* (report and recommendations; Sydney: UNSW Press).

Nicholson, Graham & Jones (1995) *Bank Liable for Environmental Clean-up* ('Banknotes: Property'; London: Nicholson, Graham & Jones, August 1995): 1.

Niskala, M., and R. Mätäsaho (1996) *Ympäristölaskentatoimi* (Porvoo, Finland: Werner Söderstörm Oyj).

NPI (National Provident Institution) (1995) *Report on Socially Responsible Investment Funds in Continental Europe* (London: NPI).

Odermatt, M. (1998) 'Via den Finanzmarkt Einfluß auf Unternehmen nehmen', WWF speech for press conference, unpublished.

OECD (Organisation for Economic Co-operation and Development) (1972) *Recommendation on Guiding Principles Concerning International Economic Aspects of Environmental Policies* (C[72] 128; Paris: OECD).

OECD (Organisation for Economic Co-operation and Development) (1984) *Recommendation of the Council of November 14, 1984 on Implementation of the Polluter-Pays Principle* (C[74]223; Paris: OECD).

OECD (Organisation for Economic Co-operation and Development) (1989a) *Council Recommendation of July 7, 1989 on Application of the Polluter-Pays Principle to Accidental Pollution* (C[89]88 [Final], 28 LLM 1320; Paris: OECD).

OECD (Organisation for Economic Co-operation and Development) (1989b) *Development Co-opera-tion in the 90s: Efforts and Policies of the Members of the Development Assistance Committee* (Paris: OECD).

OECD (Organisation for Economic Co-operation and Development) (1997a) *Microfinance for the Poor?* (Paris: OECD).

OECD (Organisation for Economic Co-operation and Development) (1997b) *Penetration of Renew-able Energy in the Electricity Sector. Annex I. Expert Group on the United Nations Framework Conven-tion on Climate Change* (Working Paper 15 ENV/EPOC[98]7; Paris: OECD).

OeNB (Österreichische Nationalbank) (1999) 'Draft Environmental Statement 1999', www.oenb.co.at.

Öko Invest (1999): 'Entwicklung deutschsprachiger Umweltfonds', *Öko Invest* 8.2 (January 1999): 4.

Öko Invest (2000): 'Entwicklung deutschsprachiger Umweltfonds', *Öko Invest* 9.2 (January 2000): 7.

Olson, W.P. (1998) *From Monopoly to Markets: Milestones along the Road* (Occasional Paper 25; Columbus, OH: The National Regulatory Research Institute, August 1998).

Ordinance on the inclusion of additional sectors to the EMAS-Regulation, 11 October 1996, Federal law bulletin no. 350, Austria.

Orgland, M. (1990) *Environmental Investment Funds: An Assessment of their Chances of Success in Different Industrial Countries* (St Gallen, Switzerland: Hochschule St Gallen).

Parker, T. (1996) 'Environmental Indicators in Energy Production: Case Study at Lund Energy', *IIIEE Communications* 97.3: 191-202.

Pava, M.L., and J. Krausz (1996) 'The Association between Corporate Social Responsibility and Financial Performance: The Paradox of Social Cost', *Journal of Business Ethics* 15: 321-57.

Pearce, F. (1997) 'The Biggest Dam in the World', in L. Owen and T. Unwin, *Environmental Management Readings and Case Studies* (Oxford, UK: Blackwell): 349-54.

Pearce, D., E. Ozdemirogluand and S. Dobson (1997) 'Replicating Innovative National Financing Mechanisms for Sustainable Development', in J. Holst, P. Koudal and J. Vincent (eds.), *Finance for Sustainable Development: The Road Ahead* (New York: United Nations): 405-30.

PIRC (Pensions Investment Resources Consultancy Ltd) (1998) *Environmental and Social Reporting: A Survey of Current Practice at FTSE 350 Companies* (PIRC Seminar; London: PIRC, 26 February 1998).

Piscitello, E.S., and V.S. Bogach (1997) *Financial Incentives for Renewable Energy Development* (World Bank Discussion Paper, 391; Washington, DC: World Bank).

Pollitt, M. (1997) 'The Impact of Liberalization on the Performance of the Electricity Supply Industry: An International Survey', *The Journal of Energy Literature* 3.2 (December 1997): 3-31.

Porter, M.C. (1980) *Competitive Strategy: Techniques for Analysing Industries and Competitors* (New York: Free Press).

Preston, E.L., and P. Douglas O'Bannon (1997) 'The Corporate Social–Financial Performance Relation-ship', *Business and Society* 36.4 (December 1997): 419-29.

PricewaterhouseCoopers (1999) *UNEP Financial Institutions Initiative 1998 Survey* (Geneva: United Nations Environment Programme).

Princeton University (1999) *Strategies for Promoting Innovative Energy Technologies in the Electric Power Sector: Final Report of the Graduate Policy Workshop* (Princeton, NJ: Woodrow Wilson School, Princeton University): 30.

Probe International (1998) 'Three Gorges Dam Campaign', Probe International website, www.nextcity.com/ProbeInternational/ThreeGorges/index.html.

Rabobank International (1998) *Sustainability: Choices and Challenges for Future Development* (Utrecht: Rabobank International).

Raffer, K. (1998) 'The Necessity of International Chapter 9 Insolvency Procedures', in Eurodad, *Taking Stock of Debt* (Brussels: Eurodad).

Raskin, P.D., and R.M. Margolis (1998) 'Global Energy, Sustainability, and the Conventional Development Paradigm', *Energy Sources* 20: 363-83.

Rauber, P. (1997) 'Heat Wave: Heat', *Sierra* 82.5 (September/October 1997): 36.

Razavi, H. (1996) 'Innovative Approaches to Financing Environment Sustainable Energy: Energy Development in Northeast Asia' (www.glocom.ac.jp/eco/esena/resource/razavi/Razavi.html).

RLB (Raiffeisen Landesbank Wien Niederösterreich) (1997) 'Environmental Statement 1997', www.rlbnoew.at.

Robbins, L., and D.M. Bissett (1994) 'The Role of Environmental Risk Management in the Credit Process', *Journal of Commercial Lending*, June 1994: 18.

Robèrt, K.-H., H. Daly, P. Hawken and J. Holmberg (1997) 'A Compass for Sustainable Develop-ment', *International Journal of Sustainable Development and World Ecology* 4: 79-92.

Róbert, R., P. Varga and Zs. Horváth (1998) *Management of Environmental Clean-up Works* (Baja, Hungary: Eötvös József College Baja).

Robinson, C. (1996) 'Can we reconcile finance with nature?', *International Review of Financial Analysis* 5.3: 185-95.

Robinson, N.A. (1992) 'International Trends in Environmental Impact Assessment', *Environmental Affairs* 19: 591-92.

Rogers, M.F., J.A. Sinden and T. De Lacy (1997) 'The Precautionary Principle for Environmental Management: A Defensive-Expenditure Application', *Journal of Environmental Management* 51.4: 343-60.

Rossignol, P. (1997) *Reporting on Environmental Performance in the context of EMAS: A Conceptual Framework for Analysis* (EAEME project; Rotterdam: European Association for Environmental Management Education).

Sandoval, R. (1995) 'How green are green funds? Fiscal and Philosophical Ups and Downs of Environmental Investing', *The Amicus Journal*, Spring 1995.

Schaltegger, S. (1997) 'Information Costs, Quality of Information and Stakeholder Involvement: The Necessity of International Standards of Ecological Accounting', *Journal of Eco-management and Auditing* 4: 87-97.

Schaltegger, S., and R. Burritt (2000) *Contemporary Environmental Accounting: Issues, Concepts and Practice* (Sheffield, UK: Greenleaf Publishing).

Schaltegger, S., and F. Figge (1997) *Environmental Shareholder Value* (Study No. 54; Basel: WWZ/Bank Sarasin, 12th edn, 1999).

Schaltegger, S., and F. Figge (1999) 'Öko-Investment: Spagat zwischen Shareholder Value und Sustainable Development?', *UmweltWirtschaftsForum* 3: 4-8.

Schaltegger, S., and F. Figge (2000) 'Finanzmärkte: Zukünftige Treiber des betrieblichen Umweltmanagements?', in K. Fichter and U. Schneidewind (eds.), *Neue Spielregeln für den Unternehmenserfolg* (Berlin: Springer Verlag).

Schierenbeck, H., and E. Seidel (eds.) (1992) *Banken und Ökologie* (Wiesbaden, Germany: Gabler).

Schierow, L. (1994) 'The Role of Risk Analysis and Risk Management in Environmental Protection', *CRS Issue Brief* (www.fas.org/spp/civil/crs/94-036.html updated version, 13 December 1996).

Schmidheiny, S., and F.J.L. Zorraquín with the World Business Council for Sustainable Development (1996) *Financing Change: The Financial Community, Eco-efficiency, and Sustainable Development* (Cambridge, MA: The MIT Press).

Schwarze, J. (1997) *Umweltorientierung als strategischer Erfolgsfaktor von Universalbanken* (Cologne: Difo).

Schweizerische Bankiervereinigung (1997) *Umweltmanagement in Banken* (Basel: SBA).

Sen, A. (1997) *Inequality, Unemployment and Contemporary Europe* (Development Economics Research Programme No 7; London: STICERD, London School of Economics).

Senn, J.F. (1986) *Ökologieorientierte Unternehmensführung* (Frankfurt: Lang).

Sennett, R. (1974) *The Fall of Public Man* (Cambridge, UK: Cambridge University Press).

SEU (Social Exclusion Unit) (1998) *Bringing Britain Together: A National Strategy for Neighbourhood Renewal* (London: The Cabinet Office).

Shihata, I.F.I. (1988) 'The World Bank and Human Rights: An Analysis of the Legal Issues and the Record of Achievements', *Denver Journal of International Law and Policy* 17.1: 54.

Shihata, I.F.I. (1994a) *The World Bank Inspection Panel* (Oxford, UK: Oxford University Press).

Shihata, I.F.I. (1994b) 'The Role of the World Bank: Legal Instruments for Achieving Environmental Objectives', paper submitted to the *Conference on International Environment Law*, Oslo, 31 August–1 September 1994: 6.

Shrivastava, P. and S. Hart (1994) 'Greening Organisations: 2000', *International Journal of Public Administration* 17.3–4: 607-36.

SME Milieuadviseurs (1995) *Succesvol milieubeleid in de zakelijke dienstverlening: Kansen voor banken en verzekeraars* (Utrecht: SME).

Smith, D.R. (1994) *Environmental Risk: Credit Approaches and Opportunities, an Interim Report* (prepared for the UNEP Roundtable on Commercial Banks and the Environment, 26–27 September, Geneva).

Smyth, J., and D. Cassan (1999) *Guide to UK Company Giving* (London: Directory of Social Change).

Snyder, J.V., and C.H. Collins (1993) *The Performance Impact of an Environmental Screen* (Boston, MA: Winslow Management Company).

Social Investment Forum (1998) 'Fund Performance', www.socialinvest.org.

Sørensen, A. (ed.) (1999) *Directors' Liability in Case of Insolvency* (The Hague/London/Boston: Kluwer Law International).

Sornarajan, M. (1994) *The International Law on Foreign Investment* (Cambridge, UK: Cambridge University Press).

Spencer-Cooke, A. (1999) 'The Color of Money', *Tomorrow* 4.9 (July/August 1999): 26-27.

SustainAbility/UNEP (United Nations Environment Programme) (1997) *Engaging Stakeholders: The 1997 Benchmark Survey* (London: SustainAbility/UNEP).

Teubner, K. (1994) 'The Invisible Cupola: From Causal to Collective Attribution in Ecological Liability', in G. Teubner, L. Farmer and D. Murphy (eds.), *Environmental Law and Ecological Responsibility* (New York: John Wiley).

Thompson, P.B. (1997) 'Evaluating Energy Efficiency Investments: Accounting for Risk in the Discounting Process', *Energy Policy* 25.12: 989-96.

Thompson, P. (1998) 'Assessing the Environmental Risk Exposure of UK Banks', *International Journal of Bank Marketing* 16.3: 129-39.

Tomorrow (1993) 'Banking on the Planet', *Tomorrow*, July 1993: 32-34.

Tolba, M.K. (ed.) (1988) *Evolving Environmental Perceptions: From Stockholm to Nairobi* (UNEP/Butterworths): 14.

Töpfer, K. (1998) 'Preface', in UNEP *Financial Institutions Initiative. Fourth Roundtable Meeting on Finance and the Environment: Profitability and Responsibility in the 21st Century* (Geneva: UNEP).

Triodos Bank (1998) *Added Value Investment Fund* (Zeist, Netherlands: Triodos Bank, July 1998).

Triodos Bank (1999) *Triodos Newsletter* (Zeist, Netherlands: Triodos Bank, August 1999).

UBS (Union Bank of Switzerland) (1999) *Environmental Report 1998/99* (Zurich: UBS; www.ubs.com/e/umweltbericht).

UKSIF (UK Social Investment Forum) (1998) *Report* (London: UKSIF).

Ullman, A.A. (1985) 'Data in Search of a Theory: A Critical Examination of the Relationships among Social Performance, Social Disclosure and Economic Performance of US Firms', *Academy of Management Review* 10.3: 540-57.

UNCTAD (United Nations Conference on Trade and Development)/UNDP (United Nations Development Programme) (1994) *The Interlinkages between Trade and Environment in Thailand: Final Report* (Bangkok: UNDP).

UNEP (United Nations Environment Programme) (1981) *In Defence of the Earth: The Basic Texts on the Environment. Founex, Stockholm, Cocoyoc* (Executive Series No. 1; Nairobi: UNEP).

UNEP (United Nations Environment Programme) (1992) *Banking and the Environment: A Statement by Banks on the Environment and Sustainable Development* (Geneva: UNEP).

UNEP (United Nations Environment Programme) (1995) *UNEP Global Survey: Environmental Policies and Practices of the Financial Services Sector* (Geneva: UNEP Environment and Economics).

UNEP (United Nations Environment Programme) (1997) *Finance for Sustainable Development: The Road Ahead* (New York: UNEP).

UNEP (United Nations Environment Programme) (1998a) *Financial Services and the Environment: Questions and Answers* (Geneva: UNEP).

UNEP (United Nations Environment Programme) (1998b) 'UNEP Financial Institutions Initiative 4th International Roundtable Meeting on Finance and Environment, www.unep.ch/eteu/finserv/Report98.html, 17–18 September 1998.

UNEP (United Nations Environment Programme) (1999) *Financial Institutions Initiative 1998 Survey* (Paris: UNEP, January 1999; www.unep.ch/etu/fi/publica.htm).

UNEP (United Nations Environment Programme) Insurance Industry Initiative for the Environment (1995) *Insurance Industry Initiative for the Environment* (Geneva: UNEP)

UNEP IE (United Nations Environment Programme: Industry and Environment Programme) (1995) *Rapports des entreprises sur l'environnement* (UNEP IE Technical Report, 24; Paris: UNEP).

UNEP (United Nations Environment Programme) and Salomon Brothers Inc. (1995) *Banks Foresee Growing Opportunities and Importance of Environment in First Global Survey* (Geneva: UNEP).

UNFCCC (United Nations Framework Convention on Climate Change) (1997) *The Kyoto Protocol to the Convention on Climate Change* (UNEP/IUC/98/2; Bonn: UNFCCC; available at www.unfccc.int/resource/convkp.html).

US State Department (1999) 'Country Commercial Guides Fiscal Year 1999', www.state.gov/www/about_state/business/com_guides/1999/eastasia/thailand99.html.

Van Bellegem, T.M., A. Beijerman and A. Eijs (1977a) *Green Investment Funds* (OECD, ENV/EPOC/GEE/BIO[98]11; Paris: Pim Project).

Van Bellegem, T.M., A. Beijerman, A. Eijs, M. Boxtel, C. Graveland and H. Wieringa (1977b) *Green Investment Funds: Organic Farming* (ENV/EPOC/GEE/BIO[98]10; Paris: OECD).

Van Bellegem, T.M. (1998) 'Green Investment Funds in The Netherlands', paper presented at the *Tenth Session of the Global Biodiversity Forum*, Bratislava, Slovakia.

Van der Meulen, J. (1997) *The Paradox of Social Cost: A Portfolio Approach* (Rotterdam: Erasmus University).

Van der Woerd, K.F., and P. Vellinga (1997) *Eco-rentabiliteit* (Amsterdam: Free University of Amsterdam).

Vaughan, S. (1994) *Environmental Risk and Commercial Banks: Discussion Paper* (Prepared for the UNEP Roundtable on Commercial Banks and the Environment, 26–27 September 1994, Geneva).

Viederman, S. (1997) 'Can business be sustainable?', paper prepared for the NYU *Journalism Seminar on Business and the Environment*, 29 November 1997 (available from Jessie Smith Noyes Foundation).

Viederman, S. (1998) 'Multinational Corporations and Sustainable Development', *Business and the Environment* 9.5 (May 1998): 5-6.

VfU (Verein für Umweltmanagement in Banken, Sparkassen und Versicherungen) (1997) *Environmental Reporting of Financial Service Providers: A Guide to Content, Structure and Performance Ratios of Environmental Reports for Banks and Savings Banks* (Berlin: VfU).

VfU (Verein fur Umweltmanagement in Banken, Sparkassen und Versicherungen) (1998) *Time to Act: Environmental Management in Financial Institutions* (Berlin: VfU; www.vfu.de).

Volz, R., M. Nauser, C. Schiess and M. Küttel (1998) 'Auswirkungen von Klimaänderungen: Fragen an die Forschung', in *Umwelt-Materialien* 93 (Bern: Buwal).

VROM (Ministerie van Volkshiusvesting, Ruimtelijke Ordening en Miieubeheer [Ministry of Housing, Spatial Planning and the Environment, Netherlands]) (1989) *National Environmental Policy Plan* (The Hague: VROM).

VROM (Ministerie van Volkshiusvesting, Ruimtelijke Ordening en Miieubeheer [Ministry of Housing, Spatial Planning and the Environment, Netherlands]) (1990) *National Environmental Policy Plan Plus* (The Hague: VROM).

VROM (Ministerie van Volkshiusvesting, Ruimtelijke Ordening en Miieubeheer [Ministry of Housing, Spatial Planning and the Environment, Netherlands]) (1996) *Accelerated Depreciation on Environmental Investments in the Netherlands* (The Hague: Ministry of Housing).

VROM (Ministerie van Volkshiusvesting, Ruimtelijke Ordening en Miieubeheer [Ministry of Housing, Spatial Planning and the Environment, Netherlands]) (1997a) *Green Investment Funds: Green Projects Abroad* (The Hague: Ministry of Housing).

VROM (Ministerie van Volkshiusvesting, Ruimtelijke Ordening en Miieubeheer [Ministry of Housing, Spatial Planning and the Environment, Netherlands]) (1997b) *Green Investment Funds: Green Projects Netherlands Antilles and Aruba* (The Hague: Ministry of Housing).

VROM (Ministerie van Volkshiusvesting, Ruimtelijke Ordening en Miieubeheer [Ministry of Housing, Spatial Planning and the Environment, Netherlands]) (1998) *Policy Document on Environment and Economy* (The Hague: VROM).

VROM (Ministerie van Volkshiusvesting, Ruimtelijke Ordening en Miieubeheer [Ministry of Housing, Spatial Planning and the Environment, Netherlands]) (1999) *Milieuberaad Banken en Overheden: Verslag van de werkconferentiue Banken en Milieu op 20 april 1999, Hilversum* (The Hague: VROM).

VROM (Ministerie van Volkshiusvesting, Ruimtelijke Ordening en Miieubeheer [Ministry of Housing, Spatial Planning and the Environment, Netherlands]) (2000) *Regeling Groenprojecten* (Dutch language; The Hague: Ministry of Housing, rev. edn).

Waddock, A.S., and B.S. Graves (1997) 'The Corporate Social Performance–Financial Performance Link', *Strategic Management Journal* 18.4: 303-19.

WBCSD (World Business Council for Sustainable Development) (1997a) *Environmental Performance and Shareholder Value* (Geneva: WBCSD).

WBCSD (World Business Council for Sustainable Development) (1997b) *Signals of Change* (Geneva: WBCSD).

WBCSD (World Business Council for Sustainable Development) (2000a) *Measuring Eco-efficiency: A Guide to Reporting Company Performance* (Geneva: WBCSD).

WBCSD (World Business Council for Sustainable Development) (2000b) *Eco-efficiency: Creating More Value with Less Impact* (Geneva: WBCSD).

WCED (World Commission on Environment and Development) (1987) *Our Common Future* ('The Brundtland Report'; Oxford: Oxford University Press).

White, M. (1991) *Does it pay to be green? Corporate Environmental Responsibility and Shareholder Value* (working paper; Charlottesville, VA: University of Virginia).

Wick, W.D. (1999) 'President in Prison: Corporate Officer Convicted under the Clean Water Act', *The Los Angeles and San Francisco Daily Journal*, 8 January 1999.

Wiser, R.H. (1997) 'Renewable Energy Finance and Project Ownership: The Impact of Alternative Development Structures on the Cost of Wind Power', *Energy Policy* 25.1: 15-27.

Wiser, R.H., and S.J. Pickle (1998) 'Financing Investments in Renewable Energy: The Impacts of Policy Design', *Renewable and Sustainable Energy Reviews* 2: 361-86.

Wiser, R.H., S. Pickle and C. Goldman (1997) 'Renewable Energy and Restructuring: Policy Solutions for the Financing Dilemma', *The Electricity Journal* 10.10 (December 1997): 65-75.

Woelfel, C.J. (1994) *Financial Statement Analysis: The Investor's Self-Study Guide to Interpreting and Analysing Financial Statements* (Chicago: Probus Publishing, rev. edn).

Wohlgemuth, N., and J. Painuly (1999) 'Promoting Private Sector Financing of Commercial Investments in Renewable Energy Technologies', paper presented at the *Fifth Expert Group Meeting on Financial Issues of Agenda 21*, Nairobi, Kenya, 1-4 December 1999.

World Bank (1972) 'World Bank: Environmental, Health and Ecological Considerations', in World Bank, *Economic Projects* (Washington, DC: World Bank).

World Bank (1988a) *The World Bank Annual Report 1987* (Washington, DC: World Bank).

World Bank (1988b) *Environmental Guidelines* (reproduction of various Bank environmental industrial waste control guidelines published in April–August 1983; Washington, DC: World Bank Environment Department, August 1988).

World Bank (1988c) *Occupational Health and Safety Guidelines* (Washington, DC: World Bank, September 1988).

World Bank (1988d) *Techniques of Assessing Industrial Hazards: A Manual* (Technical Paper No. 55; Washington, DC: World Bank).

World Bank (1989) *World Bank Support for the Environment: A Progress Report* (Development Committee pamphlet No. 22.39; Washington, DC: World Bank).

World Bank (1990a) *The World Bank and the Environment: First Annual Report. Annex II: Expenditures by Bank Environmental Units in Fiscal 1990* (Washington, DC: World Bank).

World Bank (1990b) *The World Bank and the Environment: First Annual Report. Fiscal 1990* (Washington, DC: World Bank).

World Bank (1990c) *Environmental Considerations for Port and Harbor Developments* (Technical Paper no. 126; Washington, DC: World Bank).

World Bank (1991) *The World Bank and the Environment: A Progress Report* (Washington, DC: World Bank).

World Bank (1992a) *The World Bank and the Environment: Fiscal 1992* (Washington, DC: World Bank).

World Bank (1992b) *Legal Framework for the Treatment of Foreign Investment. II. Guidelines. Report to the Development Committee and Guidelines on the Treatment of Foreign Direct Investment* (Washington, DC: World Bank Group).

World Bank (1992c) *Effective Implementation: Key to Development Impact* ('The Wapenhans Report'; Washington, DC: Portfolio Management Task Force, World Bank 22 September 1992).

World Bank (1993a) *The World Bank and the Environment: Fiscal 1993* (Washington, DC: World Bank).

World Bank (1993b) *Annual Review of Environmental Assessment 1992* (restricted distribution, SecM93-212; Washington, DC: World Bank Environment Department).

World Bank (1993c) *Proceedings from the First Annual Environmental Technical Workshop of Multilateral Financial Institutions* (Washington, DC: Land, Water and Natural Habitats Division, Environment Department, World Bank, September 1993).

World Bank (1993d) *Getting Results: The World Bank's Agenda for Improving Development Effectiveness* (Washington, DC: World Bank, July 1993).

World Bank (1993e) *Portfolio Management: Next Steps. A Program of Action* (Washington, DC: World Bank, 22 July 1993).

World Bank (1994) *Making Development Sustainable: The World Bank Group and the Environment. Fiscal 1994* (Washington, DC: World Bank).

World Bank (1995) *Mainstreaming the Environment: The World Bank Group and the Environment since the Rio Summit. Fiscal 1995* (Washington, DC: World Bank).

World Bank (1996a) *Annual Review: Environment Matters at the World Bank* (Washington, DC: World Bank).

World Bank (1996b) *The Impact of Environmental Assessment: The World Bank's Experience. Second Environmental Assessment Review* (Land, Water, and Natural Habitats Division, Environment Department, World Bank, November 1996).

World Bank (1996c) *Effectiveness of Environmental Assessments and National Environmental Action Plans: A Process Study* (Report No. 15835; Washington, DC: Operations Evaluation Department, World Bank, 28 June 1996).

World Bank (1996d) *Sustainable Banking with the Poor: A Worldwide Inventory of Microfinance Institutions* (Washington, DC: World Bank).

World Bank (1996e) 'Rural Energy and Development: Improving Energy Supplies for Two Billion People' (Development in Practice Series; available at www.worldbank.org/html/fpd/energy/ ruralenergy.htm).

World Bank (1997a) *Annual Review: Environment Matters at the World Bank* (Washington, DC: World Bank).

World Bank (1997b) *The Impact of Environmental Assessment: A Review of World Bank Experience* (World Bank Technical Paper No. 363; Washington, DC: Environment Department, World Bank, September 1997).

World Bank (1998a) *Bangladesh: From Counting the Poor to Making the Poor Count'* (based on 95/96 Household Expenditure Survey; Washington, DC: World Bank).

World Bank (1998b) *Annual Review: Environment Matters at the World Bank* (Washington, DC: World Bank).

World Bank (1999a) *Annual Review: Environment Matters at the World Bank* (Washington, DC: World Bank).

World Bank (1999b) *World Bank Group Directory: September 1999* (Washington, DC: Information Solutions Group, World Bank, September 1999).

World Bank (1999c) *World Development Report 1999/2000* (Washington, DC: World Bank).

World Development Movement (1995) *Gunrunners' Gold* (London: World Development Movement May 1995).

World Energy Council (1998) *The Benefits and Deficiencies of Energy Sector Liberalisation* (London: World Energy Council).

World News Inter Press Service (1997) 'Banned voices speak on Three Gorges Dam', World News Inter Press Service (Washington, DC; http://members.aol.com/cmwwrc/marmamnews/ 97121202.html, 12 December 1997).

World Rivers Review (1996) 'German Export–Import Bank to lend for Three Gorges', *World Rivers Review* 11.5 (December 1996).

WRI (World Resources Institute) (1997) 'International Financial Flows and the Environment: The Effect of Financial Globalisation on the Prospects for Sustainable Development in China', www.wri.org/ iffe/zouji.html.

WRI (World Resources Institute) (2000) *Pure Profit: The Financial Implications of Environmental Performance* (Washington, DC: World Resources Institute, March 2000; available at www.wri.org).

WWF (World Wide Fund for Nature) (1997) *The Living Planet Campaign: Countdown to the Year 2000* (Gland, Switzerland: WWF International).

ABBREVIATIONS

ABB	Asea Brown Boveri
ACBE	Advisory Committee for Business in the Environment (UK)
ACCA	Association of Chartered Certified Accountants (UK)
ADB	Asian Development Bank
ADC	Andean Development Corporation
AEX	Amsterdam Stock Exchange
AfDB	African Development Bank
AIB	Allied Irish Banks
AP	Action Plan (World Bank)
ASN	Algemene Spaarbank voor Nederland
ATM	automated teller machine
BAT	best available technology
BB	Budapest Bank
BBA	British Bankers' Association
BBS	Bangladesh Bureau of Statistics
BCAS	Bangladesh Centre for Advanced Studies
BCH	Banco Central Hispanoamericano
BCP	Banco Comercial Português
BCS	Business Customer Services (Co-operative Bank)
BCSIR	Bangladesh Council of Scientific and Industrial Research
BIFU	Banking Insurance and Finance Union (UK)
BLB	Bayerische Landesbank
BMR	Bangkok Metropolitan Region
BMS	Bristol Myers Squibb
BP	Bank Procedure (World Bank)
BTM	Bank/task manager (World Bank)
CD	country department (World Bank)
CDM	Clean Development Mechanism
CDO	corporate director/officer
CEE	Central and Eastern Europe
CEO	chief executive officer
CEPAA	Council on Economic Priorities Accreditation Agencies
CER	corporate environmental report
CERCLA	Comprehensive Environmental Response, Compensation, and Liability Act of 1980 (USA)
CERES	Coalition for Environmentally Responsible Economies
CET	clean energy technology

CFC	chlorofluorocarbon
CHF	Swiss franc
CIP	contractual indemnification provision
CO_2	carbon dioxide
COB	chairman of the board
COP-3	Third Conference of the Parties to the UNFCCC
CP	cleaner production
CRA	Community Reinvestment Act (USA)
CSG	Credit Suisse Group
CVP	Country Vice Presidency (World Bank)
DAC	Development Assistance Committee
DAX	Deutscher Aktienindex
DC	direct current
DEPA	Danish Environmental Protection Agency
DG	Deutsche Genossenschaftsbank
DH	district heating
DJGI	Dow Jones Group Index
DJSGI	Dow Jones Sustainability Group Index
DM	deutsche mark
DNS	debt-for-nature swap
DoE	Department of the Environment (UK)
DRB	debt review body
EA	environmental assessment
EAEME	European Association for Environmental Management Education
EAOCM	Environmental Assessment Oversight and Compliance Monitoring (World Bank)
EARCF	Environmental Assessment Revolving Concessionary Fund (World Bank)
EASC	Environmental Assessment Steering Committee (World Bank)
EBRD	European Bank for Reconstruction and Development
EC	European Commission
ECA	Export Credit Agency
ECL	Environmental Credit Line
ECRA	Ethical Consumer Research Association (UK)
ECS	Environmental Credit Scheme
EDR	Environmental Data Resources (USA)
EDS	environmental data sheet
EE	energy efficiency
EEAF	Environmental Enterprises Assistance Fund
EEEI	European Eco-Efficiency Initiative
EHS	environmental, health and safety
EIB	European Investment Bank
EIF	European Investment Fund
EIRIS	Ethical Investment Research Service (UK)
ELF	Environment Loan Facility
EM	environmental manager
EMAQPT	Environmental Management, Assessment and Quality Programme Team (World Bank)
EMAS	Eco-management and Audit Scheme
EMC	Environmental Management Consultants
EMS	environmental management system
ENV	Environment Department (World Bank)
ENVAP	Environmental Assessments and Programmes Division (World Bank)
EP	Environmental Policy (World Bank)
EPA	Environmental Protection Agency (USA)
EPE	European Partners for the Environment
EPI	environmental performance indicator

ERC	environmental risk communication
ERM	environmental risk management
ERMS	Environmental Risk Management Services
ES	Environmental Strategy (World Bank)
ESA	Endangered Species Act (USA)
ESCO	energy service company
ESDVP	Environmentally Sustainable Development (World Bank)
ESRC	Economic and Social Research Council (UK)
ESSD	Environmentally and Socially Sustainable Network (World Bank)
ET	Emissions Trading
ETH	Eidgenössische Technische Hochschule (Switzerland)
ETI	Ethical Trading Initiative (UK)
EU	European Union
FAPAS	Fondo para la Protección de los Animales Salvajes (Fund for the Protection of Wild Animals, Spain)
FASB	Financial Accounting Standards Board (USA)
FDIC	Federal Deposit Insurance Corporation (USA)
FEMAS	EMAS for the financial services sector
FNV	Federatie Nederlandse Vakbeweging
FSC	Financial Service Centre (Co-operative Bank)
FSC	Forest Stewardship Council
FY	financial year
G&E	Growth and Environment
GB	Grameen Bank
GDP	gross domestic product
GEF	Global Environment Facility
GER	Group Environment Risk (Lloyds TSB)
GF	Green Fund (Netherlands)
GFS	Green Fund System (Netherlands)
GHG	greenhouse gas
GIS	Geographical Information System
GP	Good Practice (World Bank)
GRI	Global Reporting Initiative
GSD	General Services Department (World Bank)
GTZ	Gesellschaft für Technische Zusammenarbeit (Germany)
HIPC	Heavily Indebted Poor Country
HSBC	Hong Kong and Shanghai Banking Corp. Ltd
IADB	Inter-American Development Bank
IAS	International Accounting Standard (of the International Accounting Standards Committee)
IBRD	International Bank for Reconstruction and Development
ICC	International Chamber of Commerce
ICEP	Independent Committee of Eminent Persons
ICR	Implementation Completion Report (World Bank)
ICSID	International Centre for Settlement of Investment Disputes
ICT	information and communication technologies
IDA	International Development Association
IEA	International Energy Agency
IET	International Emissions Trading
IFC	International Finance Corporation
IIEC	International Institute of Energy Conservation
ILO	International Labour Organisation
IMF	International Monetary Fund
IMU	Institut für Management und Umwelt (Institute for Management and Environment, Austria)

INAISE	International Association of Investors in the Social Economy
INPL	Institut National Polytechnique de Lorraine
IÖW	Institut für Ökologische Wirtschaftsforschung (Institute for Environmental Management and Economics, Austria)
IP	Inspection Panel (World Bank)
IPCC	Intergovernmental Panel on Climate Change
IPO	Initial Public Offerings (UBS)
IPP	independent power producers
IPPC	Integrated Pollution Prevention and Control
IPTS	Institute of Prospective Technological Studies (Spain)
IREDA	India Renewable Energy Development Agency
IRRC	Investor Responsibility Research Center (USA)
ISO	International Organization for Standardization
ISTP	Institute for Sustainability and Technology Policy, Murdoch University, Australia
IT	information technology
IUCN	International Union for the Conservation of Nature (The World Conservation Union)
IVR	Interactive Voice Response (Co-operative Bank)
JAC	Joint Audit Committee (World Bank)
JI	Joint Implementation
JOP	Joint Venture Programme
KfW	Kreditanstalt für Wiederaufbau (Germany)
KLD	Kinder, Lydenberg and Domini
LAMB	Lloyds and Midland Boycott
LBB	Landesbank Berlin
LEGEN	Environmental Law Unit (World Bank)
LG	Landesgirokasse
LLB	Liechtensteinische Landesbank
M&A	mergers and acquisitions
MACT	maximum achievable control technology
MD	managing director
MDB	multilateral development bank
MFI	multinational financial institution
MIGA	Multilateral Investment Guarantee Agency, World Bank Group
MOP	Memorandum of the President (World Bank)
MOS	Monthly Operational Summary (World Bank)
MSC	Marine Stewardship Council
MSCI	Morgan Stanley Capital International
NAX	Natur–Aktien–Index
NCBE	National Centre for Business and Ecology (UK)
NCBS	National Centre for Business and Sustainability (UK)
NCC	National Consumer Council (UK)
NCPC	National Cleaner Production Centre
NEF	New Economics Foundation (UK)
NEFCO	Nordic Environment Financing Corporation
NEPP	National Environmental Policy Plan, Netherlands
NEPP+	National Environmental Policy Plan Plus, Netherlands
NGO	non-governmental organisation
NIB	Nedcor Investment Bank
NLG	Dutch guilder
NO_x	nitrogen oxide
ÖBU	Schweizerische Vereinigung für Ökologisch bewußte Unternehmungsführung (Swiss Association for Environmentally Responsible Management)
OC	Operations Committee (World Bank)
OD	Operational Directive (World Bank)

ODA	overseas development assistance
OEA	Office of Environmental Affairs (World Bank)
OECD	Organisation for Economic Co-operation and Development
OeNB	Österreichische Nationalbank
OESA	Office of Environmental and Scientific Affairs (World Bank)
OMS	Operational Manual Statements (World Bank)
ONS	Office for National Statistics (UK)
OP	Operational Policy (World Bank)
OPIC	Overseas Private Investment Corporation
OPN	Operational Policy Note (World Bank)
PAD	Project Appraisal Document (World Bank)
PAN	Pesticide Action Network
PC	personal computer
PCD	Project Concept Document (World Bank)
PCR	Project Concept Review (World Bank)
PCS	Personal Customer Services (Co-operative Bank)
PEL	personal environmental liability
PERI	Public Environmental Reporting Initiative
PFS	provider of financial services
PIC	Project Information Centre (World Bank)
PIC	Public Information Centre (World Bank)
PID	Project Information Document (World Bank)
PIRC	Pensions Investment Resources Consultancy (UK)
POCL	Post Office Counters Limited (UK)
PPA	power purchase agreement
PPF	Project Preparation Facility (World Bank)
ppm	parts per million
PR	public relations
PREST	Policy Research in Engineering Science and Technology, University of Manchester, UK
PRIG	political risk insurance or guarantee
PSK	Postsparkasse (Post Office Savings Bank, Austria)
PV	photovoltaic
PVC	polyvinyl chloride
PVMTI	Photovoltaic Market Transformation Initiative
QACU	Quality Assurance and Compliance Unit (World Bank)
QAG	Quality Assurance Group (World Bank)
R&D	research and development
REAC	Regional Environmental Assessment Co-ordinator (World Bank)
RED	Regional Environmental Division (World Bank)
REEF	Renewable Energy and Energy Efficiency Fund
RET	renewable energy technology
RG	Rabobank Group
RLB	Raiffeisen Landesbank
ROA	return on assets
ROC	Regional Operations Committee (World Bank)
ROE	return on equity
ROI	return on investment
RVP	Regional Vice Presidency (World Bank)
S&P	Standard & Poor's Corp.
SAL	structural adjustment loan
SAPARD	Special Accession Programme for Agriculture and Rural Development
SAR	Staff Appraisal Report (World Bank)
SC	systems condition (TNS)
Sch	Austrian schilling
SD	sustainable development

SEC	Securities and Exchange Commission (USA)
SEI	Stockholm Environment Institute
SEU	Social Exclusion Unit (UK)
SHS	solar home system
SIC	Standard Industrial Classification
SME	small or medium-sized enterprise
SOPVP	Vice Presidency for Sector and Operations Policy (World Bank)
SPCU	Safeguard Policies Compliance Unit (World Bank)
SPI	Swiss Performance Index
SRI	socially responsible investment
SSI	Sarasin Sustainable Investment
SVNE	Social Venture Network Europe
SWOT	strengths–weaknesses–opportunities–threats
TEN	Trans-European Network
TL	team leader (World Bank)
TM	task manager (World Bank)
TNS	The Natural Step
TOR	Terms of Reference
TV	television
UBS	Union Bank of Switzerland
UCI	Unicredito Italiano
UEM	Urban Environmental Management programme (Thailand)
UKSIF	UK Social Investment Forum
UN	United Nations
UNCED	United Nations Conference on Environment and Development
UNCHE	United Nations Conference on the Human Environment
UNCTAD	United Nations Conference on Trade and Development
UNDP	United Nations Development Programme
UNEP	United Nations Environment Programme
UNFCCC	United Nations Framework Convention on Climate Change
UNIDO	United Nations International Development Organisation
USAID	United States Agency for International Development
VAT	value-added tax
VfU	Verein für Umweltmanagement in Banken, Sparkassen und Versicherungen (Association for Environmental Management in Banks, Savings Banks and Insurance Companies, Germany)
VROM	Ministerie van Volkshiusvesting, Ruimtelijke Ordening en Miieubeheer (Ministry of Housing, Spatial Planning and the Environment, Netherlands)
WBCSD	World Business Council for Sustainable Development
WBG	World Bank Group
WCED	World Commission on Environment and Development
WDR	Warburg Dillon Read
WICE	World Industry Council for the Environment
WIMM	Wetenschappelijk Instituut voor Milieu-Management (Scientific Institute for Environmental Management, University of Amsterdam)
WRI	World Resources Institute
WWF	World Wide Fund for Nature
WWZ	Wirtschaftswissenschaftliches Zentrum (Centre of Economics and Management, University of Basel)
ZKB	Zürcher Kantonalbank

AUTHOR BIOGRAPHIES

Dan Atkins is a Client Director with Deloitte's Australian Environmental Services Group. He has recently returned to Melbourne after spending the last three years working in Copenhagen, Denmark. During this time, Dan participated in establishing Deloitte's Global Environmental Services Group, which is now represented in over 20 countries. Dan's experience embraces the financial implications of environmental aspects. This understanding has led to engagements at major multi-nationals—including Novo Nordisk, Norsk Hydro and UBS—around Corporate Sustainability Reporting, Eco-Efficiency Indicators, Climate Change Strategies and assisting financial institutions integrate sustainability considerations into investment evaluation procedures. Dan participated in the World Business Council for Sustainable Development pilot testing of eco-efficiency indicators and was involved in the UNEP Insurance and Financial Institutions Initiative.
daatkins@deloitte.com.au

Duncan Austin is an Associate in the World Resources Institute's Economics Programme
Duncan@wri.org

Andrei D. Barannik has been an international environmental assessment and business development advisor to global companies and organisations since November 1997. From 1992–97 he was an Environmental Assessment Specialist in the Environment Department of the World Bank, and a member of its EA Steering Committee. He has also been Press Secretary and Director of the Press Center at the Soviet Ministry of Environment from 1988–92, and between 1979 and 1988 team leader at the 'think-tank' of the Soviet Committee on Hydrometeorology and Environmental Monitoring. Between 1982 and 1984 he completed postgraduate studies in the history of European green and grass-roots movements at the Moscow Institute of International Workers' Movement, having graduated with an MA from the Geography Department of the Moscow State Pedagogical University in 1979.
marinac@erols.com   abarannik@usa.com

Judit Barta is the research manager of GKI Economic Research Co., Budapest, an independent private organisation dealing with economic surveys, forecasting and economic analysis. She is an economist with a doctorate in macroeconomics, and has worked on environmental issues relating to energy and natural resources, and the financial problems of a transitional economy, publishing several research papers and scientific articles. She has also prepared various studies for the clients of GKI, such as the Hungarian Banking Association, Hungarian ministries and internationally owned major Hungarian companies. Recently, she has been working on a project investigating monetary and financial conditions relating to Hungary's accession to the EU.
jbarta@gki.hu

Jan Jaap Bouma is Assistant Professor at the Erasmus University in Rotterdam, Netherlands. He is an economist and took his doctor's degree at the Erasmus University in 1995 on a dissertation on environmental management in the Dutch Royal Airforce and industrial corporations. His research field includes environmental management accounting and financing environmental management within the business sector and public agencies.
bouma@mil.fsw.eur.nl

Dénes Bulkai has been Principal Environmental Advisor, Environmental Appraisal Group, European Bank for Reconstruction and Development (EBRD) since 1992, involved in environmental appraisal and monitoring of some of the Bank's large industrial projects, especially those related to metallurgical and chemical process industries. He developed Environmental Guidelines for Energy Service Companies, a special area of interest being energy-efficiency projects. From 1990–92 he was technical director of American Appraisal (pre-privatisation appraisal of more than a hundred industrial, commercial and utility companies). From 1986–90 he was establisher and technical director of the Hungarian Energy Efficiency Office (energy and environment conservation projects, publicity campaigns, auditing demonstrations, training programmes, R&D sponsoring). Prior to that, he was with the Hungarian Aluminium Corporation in research and technology development, at which time he was the author and co-author of several UNIDO and UNEP studies on the bauxite/aluminium industry.

Andrea Coulson is lecturer in Accounting at Strathclyde University, Glasgow. Her teaching portfolio includes accounting for sustainability, risk, and accounting research methodologies. She is also a consultant to the United Nations Conference on Trade and Development (UNCTAD) on Accounting for Environmental Costs and Liabilities. Her UNCTAD role has included delivery of workshops in Africa, Asia, Central Europe and South America. Andrea has been engaged in research with the financial sector for eight years. Her starting point was a doctorate focusing on Corporate Environmental Performance Considerations within Bank Lending Processes; this was followed by an ESRC (Economic and Social Research Council) research fellowship award to examine environmental assessment issues with Lloyds TSB Group. She currently chairs a Financial Sector Environment Forum, is working on the UNEP Insurance Industry Initiative's first Survey of Implementation and is conducting a review of bank securities for the Scottish Executive.
A.B.Coulson@strath.ac.uk

Davide Dal Maso holds a BA in law, a European Master in environmental management (EAEME), and is a qualified environmental auditor. He specialises in environmental management research, and, at Avanzi, a Milan-based environmental think-tank, he is responsible for research into sustainable development and financial institutions, with a focus on environmentally and socially responsible products and services. In addition, he has worked as an environmental consultant with an agency specialising in the implementation of environmental management systems for SMEs. He has also worked for the research centre Fondazione Eni Enrico Mattei in Milan. He has undertaken and managed training and education projects for companies, local authorities, training centres and NGOs. He is the author of a number of papers on these issues and a book (with Matteo Bartolomeo) on financial institutions and sustainable development.
dalmaso@avanzi.org

Sabine Döbeli is Head of Environmental Research of Zürcher Kantonalbank, Switzerland. After graduating in Environmental Sciences from the Eidgenössische Technische Hochschule (ETH) in Zürich, she worked for an environmental consultant. Since 1995 she has been employed by Zürcher Kantonalbank, where she has been responsible for building up the Environmental Research Unit. Its principal research subjects currently include environmental and social ratings of multinationals and of bond issuers.
sabine.doebeli@zkb.ch

Vilma Éri is the Executive Director of the Center for Environmental Studies, Budapest, an independent non-profit organisation, dealing with public policy research and education related to environmental policy and sustainable development, and providing advocacy on these issues. She is an economist with a doctorate in macroeconomics and has worked on energy, agricultural and environmental policy analyses, and published several research papers on these issues. She has also prepared various studies for the Hungarian ministries of environment, agriculture and industry. Recently, she worked on projects investigating business contribution to sustainable development, the potential for energy use of biomass, as well as on adapting the European Union's Eco-management and Audit Scheme for local governments of Central and Eastern Europe.
v_eri@ktk-ces.hu

Dr **Frank Figge** is assistant professor at the chair of Corporate Environmental Management and Economics at the University of Lüneburg, Germany, and Sustainability Consultant of Pictet & Cie., a Geneva-based Private Bank. He studied economics at the University of Fribourg, Switzerland, and received a PhD from the University of Basel for his thesis on 'Environmental Rating of Companies'. He worked at the same time for the Sustainability Research Department of a Swiss Private Bank in Basel. His main interest, both in his research and his consulting activities, is sustainable finance, and has published extensively in this field. A distinctive focus of many of his publications is the causal link between environmental, social and economic performance of companies.
figge@sustainablevalue.com

After receiving a PhD in business administration at the University of St Gallen, Switzerland, **Alois Flatz** worked as a permanent advisor to the Austrian Minister of Environment, Martin Bartenstein. During his PhD Alois worked for a well-known business consultant. Alois joined SAM Sustainability Group in Zurich in 1996 and is responsible for Sustainability Research.
alois@sam-group.com

Robert J.A. Goodland has been Environmental Advisor at the World Bank since 1978, where he drafted most of the Bank's environmental policies, created the EA Unit and the Latin America Environment Division. Prior to joining the Bank, Mr Goodland was a freelance consultant in environmental assessment on major infrastructure projects in Brazil, Central America, Malaysia, Indonesia, Bangladesh and elsewhere. He has published 20 books on environment and development and was elected President of the International Environmental Impact Association and Chair of the Ecological Society of America.

James Giuseppi joined the NPI Global Care Team as a researcher in September 1998 and, prior to that, worked at Mitsui & Co. UK Ltd as a trader for consumer durables in Russia and the Former Soviet Union. When AMP bought NPI, James moved with the Global Care Team to join Henderson Global Investors in September 1999. Recent activities include being part of the Project Forge Consultative Committee on Environmental Management Systems for Financial Services and ACBE (Advisory Committee for Business in the Environment) looking at 'Internalising the Sustainability Agenda in Business'. He is also responsible for developing the Henderson SRI web presence. James has an honours degree in Russian and Soviet studies.

Glenn Stuart Hodes is a graduate student in Development, Energy and Environmental Policy at the Woodrow Wilson School of Princeton University, USA, focusing on environmental economics and finance as they relate to sustainable energy and climate change. Mr Hodes is currently co-managing an energy efficiency audit for the city of Johannesburg and climate change-related projects in South Africa for the International Institute of Energy Conservation (IIEC). He has worked for, or consulted to, USAID/Central Asia Region, E&Co, the Minerals and Energy Policy Centre, the Stockholm Environment Institute (SEI) and the Carnegie Endowment for International Peace. He has also been a Summer Associate with GE Capital/Structured Finance Group. Mr Hodes is the author of *Designing*

a Next-Generation National Climate Policy: Strategies for Sweden in an International Context (forth-coming SEI report), and Senior Editor of *Greenhouse Gas Abatement: A Project Developer's Manual* (USAID/Central Asia, 2000).
gshodes@princeton.edu

Dr **Heinrich Hugenschmidt** is Director of UBS Warburg in London. In his PhD thesis, he focused on the influence of environmental issues on industry competition and has been with UBS e-services at UBS Warburg since January 2000. Before that, he headed UBS Environmental Risk Management Services for four years.
heinrich.hugenschmidt@ubs.com

Ari Huhtala (MSc Econ) has a background in development co-operation with the Finnish govern-ment and for 16 years with the United Nations Industrial Development Organisation (UNIDO), last as the Country Director in Bangkok in charge of, among other things, managing technical co-opera-tion projects and promoting ecologically sustainable industrial investments in Thailand, Cambodia, Lao PDR and Myanmar. In February 1999 he took up his present assignment as a Senior Programme Officer at the Production and Consumption Unit of the Division of Technology, Industry and Economics of UNEP in Paris in charge of the management of project 'Strategies and Mechanisms for Promoting Cleaner Production Investments in Developing Countries'.
ari.huhtala@unep.fr

Josef Janssen is an economist specialising in the Kyoto Mechanisms. He has carried out various consulting projects in this field, e.g. with UBS, an Italian investment bank, and the World Bank. In 1998, he was economic advisor to the Italian Ministry of Environment on Kyoto Mechanisms and member of the Italian delegation at international climate policy negotiations. His PhD focuses on JI/CDM investment funds and commercial insurance related to the Kyoto Mechanisms.
Josef.Janssen@unisg.ch

Christine Jasch runs the Vienna Institute for Environmental Management and Economics and also works as an independent tax advisor and certified public accountant in Vienna. She was accredited as lead verifier under the EMAS Regulation in December 1995, also covering the banking sector. She is also member of the scientific board of the Ecofund Ökovision of the German Ökobank at Frankfurt.
info@ioew.at

Marcel Jeucken is a research economist at Rabobank Group. He holds a degree in economics with a specialisation in environmental economics. At Rabobank he researches the (European) banking sector in general and sustainable banking in particular. He has contributed a number of articles and is author of *Duurzaam Bankieren* (to be translated into English in the near future). He is currently working on a PhD project on the role of the financial sector regarding tradable CO_2 emission permits.
m.h.a.jeucken@rn.rabobank.nl

Dipl. Ing. **Walter Kahlenborn,** MA, studied business engineering at the Technische Universität, Berlin, and philosophy and modern history at the Freie Universität, Berlin. Additionally, he spent one year in the graduate business programme at the Tulane University in New Orleans and one year at the Università di Bologna. From 1994–95 he took part in a project conducted at the Science Centre, Berlin. In 1996, he joined Ecologic; his work focuses on the integration of environmental concerns into different sectoral policies, e.g. financial services and tourism. Walter Kahlenborn is the author of a number of reports and articles specifically dedicated to green investment as well as a number of books on environmental policy.
kahlenborn@ecologic.de

Dr **Kate Kearins** is Director of the Environment and Management Programme, and Senior Lecturer in Strategic Management at the University of Waikato, Hamilton, New Zealand. Her research interests include business history and rhetoric, sustainability strategies and the greening of organisational culture.
knk@mngt.waikato.ac.nz

Mike Kelly has a background in commercial risk management within the financial services sector. For the last 18 months he has been the Senior Programme Officer at the Economics and Trade Unit of the Division of Technology, Industry and Economics of UNEP in Geneva responsible for the Financial Institutions Initiative. He has recently returned to the United Kingdom to take up the position of UK Environment Manager with KPMG.
michael.kelly@kpmg.co.uk

Yann Kermode holds a Master's degree in environmental management from the European Association for Environmental Management Education (EAEME). He has been working in Zurich for UBS Environmental Risk Management Services since 1997. His main area of responsibility covers environmental risk management and controlling for the Investment Banking Division, UBS Warburg.
yann.kermode@ubs.com

Leon Klinkers holds a degree in biology, political sciences and business administration. He has published several international articles and books on environmental issues, recently co-editing *Sustainable Measures: Evaluation and Reporting of Environmental and Social Performance* with Martin Bennett and Peter James (Greenleaf Publishing 1999). He currently works for Deloitte & Touche at the Corporate Real Estate Management Group (CREM) and teaches sustainable development at the Fontys University in Eindhoven.
LKlinkers@deloitte.nl

Andreas Knörzer is First Vice President and Head of Sarasin Sustainable Investment (SSI), Switzerland. He has been with Bank Sarasin for 12 years in various research functions, the most recent being Head of Investment Research. He graduated from the University of Applied Science, School of Economics, Berne, and holds a diploma from the Swiss Banking School. He has 13 years' experience as a financial analyst and seven years as fund manager. He is founder and manager of Sarasin's sustainable investment fund, 'OekoSar Portfolio', the first eco-efficiency fund worldwide, and also of 'ValueSar Equity'. As a specialist in sustainable investment research, he has published various studies and articles and speaks regularly on the subject. He is also member of the Environmental Working Group of the Swiss Bankers' Association and member of of the board of ÖBU, the Swiss Association for Environmentally Responsible Management.
andreas.knoerzer@sarasin.ch

Marc Leistner is a Product Manager at the European Investment Fund (EIF) and Programme Manager for the Growth and Environment Scheme.
m.leistner@eif.org

Céline Louche is a PhD student at the Erasmus Centre for Sustainable Development and Management, Erasmus University, Rotterdam. Her research, begun in 1999, deals with ethical investment as a change agent towards sustainable development. The research focuses on the social process of ethical investment, analysing the way it might influence corporate behaviour regarding social and environmental issues. She has also worked since 1998 at the Triodos Bank in the Netherlands as a researcher for ethical investment. She previously completed a European master in environmental management (European Association for Environmental Management Education) as well as a master in Management Sciences (Strategy, Human Resources) at the Institut d'Administration des Entreprises in Aix en Provence, France.
louchec@fsw.eur.nl

Beatriz Mayer has studied architecture in Argentina and has a master's degree in urban environmental management. She is a research associate in the Urban Environmental Management (UEM) Programme, Thailand, and works closely with Willi Zimmermann
beatrizmayer@hotmail.com

During the time of the study described in this volume, **Philip Monaghan** was the National Centre for Business and Sustainability (NCBS)'s Project Manager for social responsibility. His work involved assisting organisations with issues of business ethics and social accounting. Prior to joining the NCBS, Philip worked as an economist in the field of economic development consultancy, most notably in Scotland and Northern Ireland. A main area of work was on EU programmes which sought to build local and regional capacity to address social marginalisation and economic deprivation. Primarily this involved interacting with organisations in the 'Social Economy'—the so-called third sector—such as charities, community enterprises and co-operatives. Before this he worked with several ethical and environmental organisations, including the Ethical Consumer Research Association (ECRA), a workers' co-operative which produces the *Ethical Consumer* magazine, and the Scottish Wildlife Trust, a nature conservation charity. Philip is now Sustainability Consultant at WSP Environmental Ltd.
philip.monaghan@wspgroup.com

Michel Negenman has been General Manager of ASN Bank, Netherlands, since 1992. ASN has a €1 billion savings liability and €500 million participation in investment funds. Previously, from 1986, he was treasurer and member of the board of the Federatie Nederlandse Vakbeweging (FNV), the confederation of Dutch trade unions. From 1977–86 he was responsible for social welfare policies at FNV.
michel.negenman@asnbank.nl

Professor **Peter Newman** completed his honours and PhD in chemistry at the University of Western Australia, and postgraduate and doctoral degrees at Delft University in the Netherlands and Stanford University in California. He is the Director of the Institute for Sustainability and Technology Policy (ISTP) at Murdoch University in Perth, Australia. The ISTP is an interdisciplinary institute which examines global and local issues concerning sustainability. Peter worked as a consultant to the Organisation for Economic Co-operation and Development (OECD) and the World Bank in urban policy issues. His work on an international scale has mostly been on a comparison of global cities. He has written a number of academic and popular publications and his books include *Sustainability and Cities: Overcoming Automobile Dependence* (Island Press; which was launched in 1999 in the White House) and *Winning Back the Cities* and *Case Studies in Environmental Hope* (TPT Technical Publications, 1988). He also works on appropriate technology and renewable energy in developing countries such as Indonesia and Bangladesh. Peter is a Visiting Professor at the University of Pennsylvania, USA.
newman@central.murdoch.au

Greg O'Malley is a partner of Environmental Management Consultants (EMC) with 20 years' experience in Environmental and Health and Safety Risk Management within the chemical and energy industries. He is currently completing postgraduate study in Environment and Management at the University of Waikato, Hamilton, New Zealand.
grego.emc@xtra.co.nz

Zsolt Pásztor is a Manager at Deloitte & Touche Hungary in the Environmental Advisory Services department. His main areas of interests are environmental risk management, environmental reporting and sustainable strategy. He has extensive experience in conducting risk management for banks and manages the environmental appraisals for a Hungarian credit line created for environmental investments. He led the development of an *Environmental Handbook*, which incorporates

environmental issues into the credit rating for a Hungarian commercial bank. He has conducted several surveys on sustainability-related issues, actively taking part in the organisation of forums in the Central and Eastern European region covering sustainable development issues. He graduated from the University of Veszprém in 1991 as a chemical engineer; he received his PhD from INPL Nancy, France, in 1995. Before joining Deloitte & Touche he worked for a French waste management company for a year and a half. As a guest lecturer he has been invited to several universities to speak on environmental issues.
zpasztor@deloitteCE.com

Charlotte Pedersen is a manager at Deloitte & Touche in Denmark, where she has worked for six years. She has an MSc in political science. Charlotte has worked with the Deloitte & Touche Environmental Services in Denmark for the first five years of her employment at Deloitte. Here, she primarily collected, evaluated and communicated experiences about environmental management, as well as being involved in implementing environmental management systems (EMAS, ISO 14001 and ISO 14031) in private and public companies. For the last year, Charlotte's professionel focus has developed towards knowledge management and intellectual capital reporting. She is now placed in the research and development department in Deloitte Denmark, where she is taking part in developing a service-line regarding these new areas.
cpedersen@deloitte.dk

Born in 1971, **Paola Perin** took her degree in Economics in April 1996 at the Bocconi University, Milan. Five months later she began her job in Credito Italiano in a local branch. In 1998 she started working in UniCredito's Corporate Marketing Department, addressing, among other things, environmental issues. Paola has been involved in 'Project Environment' for two years, involved with products and services for the environmental certification of corporate customers, the Memorandum of Understanding with the Italian Ministry of Environment and other strategic relationships with associations, corporations, etc., aiming to promote environmental awareness and goals in Italian industry. In recent months she has been working on the implementation and development of 'Greenlab'—UniCredito's Internet gateway on environment and safety.
perinp@gruppocredit.it

Dr **Robert Repetto** is Senior Fellow, and former Vice President, of the World Resources Institute.
BobR@wri.org

Dr **Stefan Schaltegger** was appointed a full Professor of Management and Business Economics at the University of Lüneburg, Germany, in 1999. Between 1996 and 1998 he was an Assistant Professor of Economics at the Centre of Economics and Management (WWZ) at the University of Basel, Switzerland, where in 1998 he became an Associate Professor of Business Administration. His research areas include corporate environmental accounting and environmental information management, sustainable finance, sustainable entrepreneurship, stakeholder management, environmental and spatial economics and the integration of environmental management and economics. Stefan is a member of a number of international editorial boards and committees associated with business and environment interrelationships and has presented papers and lectured widely throughout Europe. He also spent one year as Visiting Research Fellow at the University of Washington, Seattle, USA.
schaltegger@uni-lueneburg.de

Inge Schumacher studied ecology and business administration at the University of Lüneburg and the University of Avignon. She joined the Swiss Bank Corporation's Environmental Co-ordination Unit in 1995, working on the incorporation of environmental criteria into financial analysis. Since 1996 she has been working in the Environmental Performance Analysis group at UBS.
ingeborg.schumacher@ubs.com

Lena Serck-Hanssen graduated in environmental sciences with a focus on life-cycle assessment and eco-efficiency at the Swiss Federal Institute of Technology (ETH) in Zurich. She gained working experience in risk management with the Swiss Re Insurance Group, Zurich, and in life-cycle assessment with Amstein & Walthert, Zurich, an environmental engineering and consulting firm. Within the research team, Lena covers sustainability pioneer companies in the food and agricultural sector.
lena@sam-group.com

Firoze Ahmed Siddiqui is pursuing a PhD in Technology Policy and Management (with a scholarship from the Bangladesh government) at the Institute for Sustainability and Technology Policy (ISTP) of Murdoch University in Perth, Australia. He graduated in mechanical engineering from Patrice Lumumba University, Moscow, and completed his Master's in 1979. He began his professional career as a research engineer in a multidisciplinary R&D organisation: Bangladesh Council of Scientific and Industrial Research (BCSIR). Over the past 20 years he has worked in various R&D projects in Bangladesh and has wide experience of development issues in the third world. He has been published in a number of national and international journals; specific areas of interest are technology innovation (especially renewable energy) and local uptake (e.g. microcredit, community development initiatives, etc.).
firoze@central.murdoch.edu.au

A leading advocate for business and sustainable development, **Björn Stigson** has been President of the World Business Council for Sustainable Development (WBCSD) since its inception in January 1995. He began his career in financial analysis and joined ABB Fläkt as President and CEO in 1982. From 1991 to 1993, he was appointed Executive Vice President and a member of ABB Asea Brown Boveri's Executive Management Group. From 1993 to 1994 he ran his own management consultancy. Mr Stigson serves on the board of several international companies, and is an advisor on sustainability issues to a number of inter-governmental agencies and to the Chinese government.
info@wbcsd.org

Penny Street is a Project Manager at the NCBS (National Centre for Business and Sustainability, UK). In addition to working with The Co-operative Bank on its Service Channel study, she is involved in a range of projects including: the development of an environmental learning package for SMEs; work with the PVC Co-ordination Group (a group of PVC manufacturers and retailers) to identify ways of bringing about environmental improvements in the PVC industry; and the use of The Natural Step (a sustainability tool) across a range of activities and departments in the Kelda Group. Prior to joining NCBS, Penny spent six years at PREST (Policy Research in Engineering Science and Technology) at the University of Manchester, UK, where she pursued her interests in environmental policy and management, diffusion of cleaner technologies, and in the evaluation of government-funded research programmes. During this period, she also spent six months at IPTS (the Institute of Prospective Technological Studies) in Spain, where she was involved in a project to identify possible priorities for a future European Environmental Action Programme.
P.Street@thencbs.co.uk

Kaisa Tarna works as an advisor within KPMG Environmental Services (Finland). She has professional experience in the fields of environmental strategy, environmental reporting and performance measurement and social accountability.
kaisa.tarna@kpmg.fi

Erica Tucker-Bassin's previous work experience includes communication and knowledge management project work for Zurich Financial Services Group, as well as communication and environmental project work for the Swiss Organisation for Facilitating Investments/KPMG. She also helped to establish and secure funding for the Environmental Management and Law Association in Budapest, Hungary. Erica received a master's degree in international economics from the University of Maastricht, Netherlands. She also holds a bachelor's degree in urban and regional studies from the College of Architecture, Art and Planning at Cornell University, USA. Erica is responsible for research client services and communication. She is also an analyst for the entertainment, recreational products and textile industries.
erica@sam-group.com

Theo van Bellegem is based in the Department of Economics and Technology, Ministry of Housing, Spatial Planning and the Environment, the Netherlands. He is educated in microbiology, biochemistry and law. He previously worked in environmental technology and is currently involved in the greening of the Dutch tax system. He has developed incentive systems and mechanisms to speed up the development of environmental technology and environmental investment, e.g. accelerated depreciations, green funds and tax deduction systems.
Theo.vanbellegem@minvrom.nl

Stephen Viederman is a lecturer, author and adviser to corporations and non-governmental organisations on issues of corporate social responsibility, sustainability and mission-related investing. In 2000 Steve retired from the Presidency of the Jessie Smith Noyes Foundation, which focused on community organising at the intersection of economic and environmental justice. He has lectured at universities and conferences in the US, Europe and Asia. His articles have appeared in a wide variety of journals including *GeneWatch, Pensions and Investments,* and the forthcoming *Encyclopedia on Life Support Systems.* A native New Yorker, he studied history at Columbia University.
stevev@noyes.org

Norbert Wohlgemuth is assistant professor at the Department of Economics, University of Klagenfurt, Austria. Current research focuses on renewable energy supply options, institutional changes in the electricity supply industry and their implications on sustainable development objectives, and the design of the Kyoto Mechanisms. Norbert holds a Master's degree in business administration and computer science and a PhD in economics from the University of Vienna. Before joining the university, he was with the International Energy Agency, member of a group preparing the Agency's *World Energy Outlook* publication, editions 1993–96. From 1998 to early 2000 he was on leave to the UNEP Collaborating Centre on Energy and Environment, Risø National Laboratory, Roskilde, Denmark.
norbert.wohlgemuth@uni-klu.ac.at

Willi Zimmermann is currently Associate Professor in the Urban Environmental Management (UEM) Programme, Thailand. His interests cover the areas of public-sector management, the implementation of environmental policy, and the role of the state, regions and cities in the context of globalisation.
wzimmerm@ait.ac.th

INDEX